Footprint Namibia

Lizzie Williams

4th edition

*"Africa smells of nothing but dust,
and that dust lingers with sweetness in the nose
and like powder on the skin."*

Joanna Greenfield, *Hyena (1996)*

1 Kaokoland
An untamed wilderness of vast empty plains, ancient home of the Himba people

2 Skeleton Coast National Park
A harsh strip of coastline pounded by the unforgiving Atlantic.

3 Damaraland
Rock art, petrified trees, unusual and dramatic stony scenery and maybe a desert elephant

4 Cape Cross Seal Colony
Hundreds of thousands of seals in what is surely one of the smelliest places on earth; a compelling sight, nonetheless.

5 Swakopmund
Characterful and attractive seaside town surrounded by desert and ocean

6 Adventure activities
Skydive over the massive dunes near Swakopmund, or explore them by sandboard, quad-bike or dune buggy

7 Namib-Naukluft Park
The world's largest sand dunes gleam in vibrant reds and oranges at sunrise and sunset

8 Duwisib Castle
A man-made fortress with a fascinating history, in the middle of the desert

Namibia Highlights

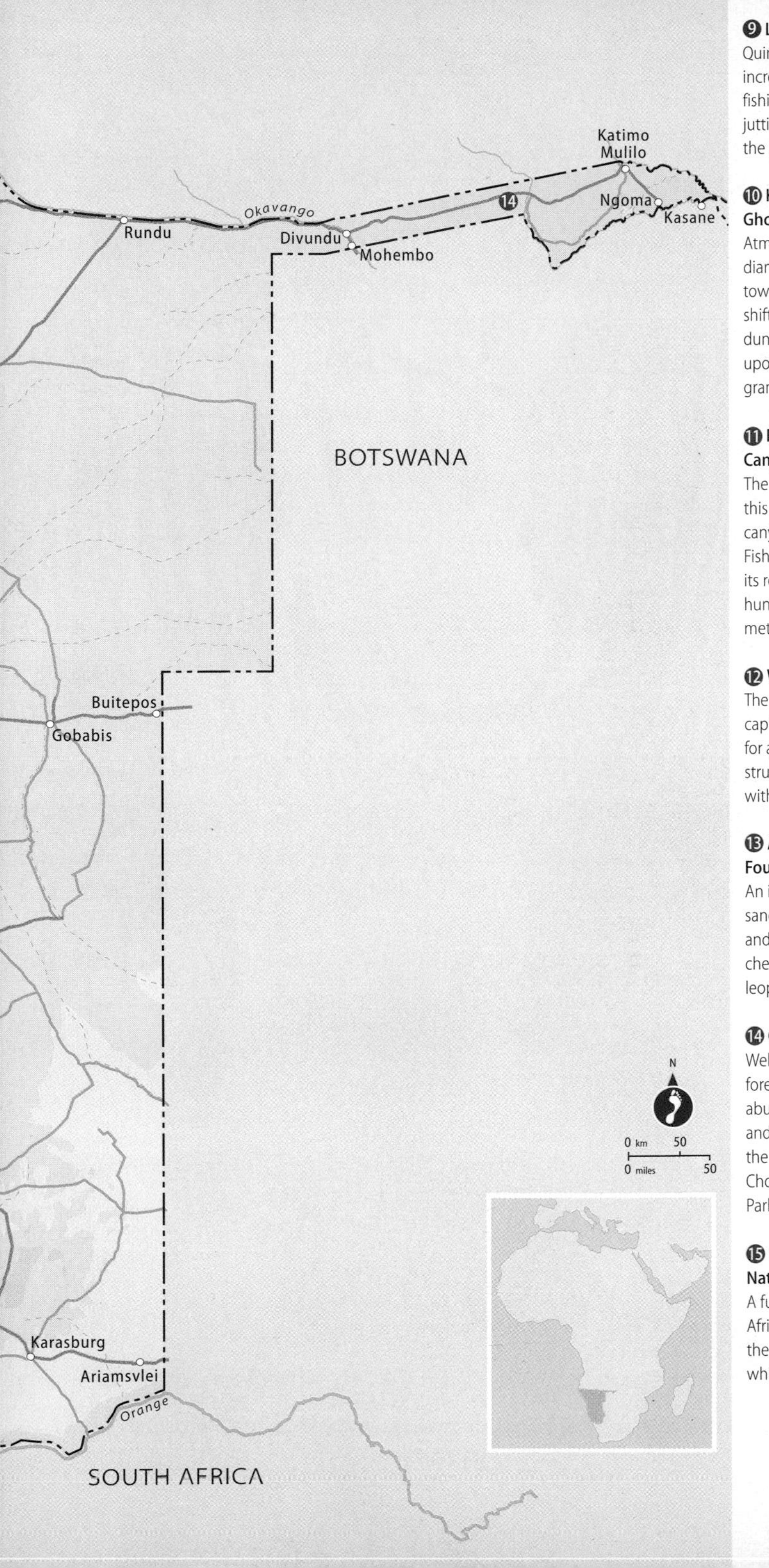

9 Lüderitz
Quirky and incredibly windy fishing port jutting out into the Atlantic

10 Kolmanskop Ghost Town
Atmospheric old diamond-mining town where shifting sand dunes encroach upon once-grand houses

11 Fish River Canyon
The sun melts over this dramatic canyon where the Fish River weaves its rocky course hundreds of metres below

12 Windhoek
The relaxed, colonial capital city, ideal for a German apple strudel or eisbein with sauerkraut

13 AfriCat Foundation
An important sanctuary for sick and abandoned cheetahs and leopards

14 Caprivi Strip
Well watered and forested, with abundant game, and just a hop over the border to the Chobe National Park in Botswana

15 Etosha National Park
A full range of African animals at the shimmering white Etosha Pan

The Himba

Married Himba women wear a small soft-skinned headpiece on top of their braided hair and an additional heavy ornament around their necks that includes a conch shell that hangs in the front and a metal-studded leather plate that hangs down the back.

A foot in the door

Exposed to the mercy of the elements, Namibia's landscapes are not what you expect to find in Africa. Deserts, tortured rock, open plains and a bleak and eerie coastline that for much of the year is bathed in thick fog. The country is dominated by the brooding Namib Desert, where the world's highest sand dunes march determinedly towards the sea in a dune field 300 km wide. The Skeleton Coast, Fish River Canyon, Damaraland, Kaokoland and the diamond-producing Sperrgebiet, too, are vast expanses of silent, unspoilt wilderness. But, despite these hostile environments, Namibia is home to a wealth of African animals and birds – easily seen at Etosha's magical waterholes or at one of the many game farms. This is the last place on earth that black rhino roam free, it's the only home of the desert elephant, and 25% of the world's cheetah stalk the arid plains.

The cities in Namibia are clean and modern, with a fully developed infrastructure. Windhoek is as sleek as any European city and the quirky seaside town of Swakopmund, with its pastel-coloured turrets, comes as a delightful surprise on the barren coast. Quite by contrast to these urban centres are communities in the far-reaching north, where life hasn't changed for hundreds of years. The traditions of the magnificent Himba and the Bushmen of the Kalahari survive in these unyielding landscapes.

Namibia is the first country in the world to include protection of the environment and wildlife in its constitution, and a large proportion of the country is protected in parks and reserves. It has realized the importance of tourism so travelling here is safe and hassle-free. It's also a destination that's about adventure; whether you drive, hike or bike, the opportunities to enjoy the wild beauty of this empty, ancient land are almost limitless.

1

2

4

5

7

8

10

11

3

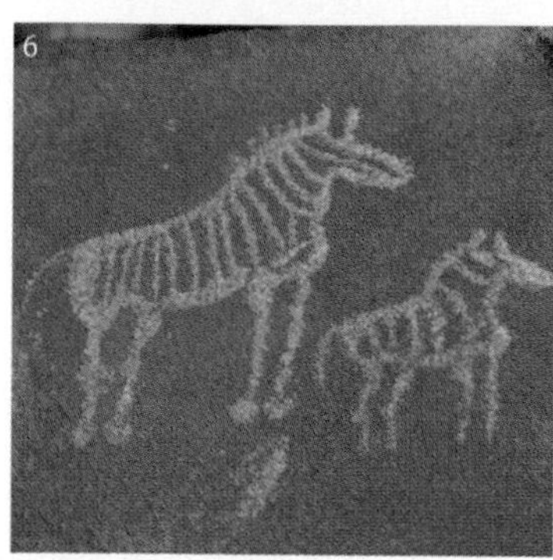
6

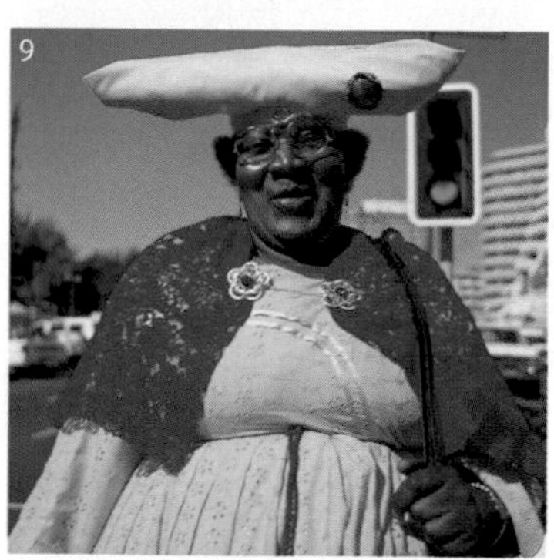
9

12

1 *Quiver trees are so-called because the San and Nama peoples used to hollow out the light, tough-skinned branches to use as quivers for their arrows.* *▸▸ See page 313.*

2 *The 85-km hike through the vast Fish River Canyon is a magical experience, but only for the fit and experienced.* *▸▸ See page 333.*

3 *Conquer the towering dunes of the Namib Desert at 80 kph on a Swakopmund sandboard.* *▸▸ See page 247.*

4 *The Himba occupy land that is so harsh and unyielding that it has rarely been coveted by colonialists or commercial farmers. But today their traditional way of life is under threat.* *▸▸ See page 193.*

5 *At the Epupa Falls, the Kunene River divides into a multitude of channels, creating hundreds of small vegetated islands.* *▸▸ See page 201.*

6 *Experts believe that the engravings at Twyfelfontein featured in ceremonies intended to imbue the hunters with the power to catch game.* *▸▸ See page 185.*

7 *Because of its olde-worlde charm and relaxed atmosphere, Swakopmund is Namibia's premier holiday resort.* *▸▸ See page 218.*

8 *Damaraland is home to some of Namibia's most dramatic natural features, as well as desert elephants and the world's last free-roaming black rhinos.* *▸▸ See page 180.*

9 *The Herero women's 'traditional' dress is a remnant of the influence of 19th-century German missionaries.* *▸▸ See page 364.*

10 *One of the lonely shipwrecks that litter Namibia's barren Skeleton Coast.* *▸▸ See page 258.*

11 *It's worth splashing out on a flight over the dunes from Swakopmund or a balloon ride from Sesriem.* *▸▸ See page 285.*

12 *The former diamond boom town of Kolmanskop is now a ghost town crumbling in the desert.* *▸▸ See page 322.*

If it wasnae for the weavers what would we do…
The extraordinary weaver birds use intricate stitching techniques to build the globular nests seen hanging in trees or off telephone poles throughout Namibia.

Contemporary Namibia

Namibia is one of the most sparsely populated countries in the world with only 1.8 million people occupying over 800,000 sq km. It is a land divided between old and new. While many still dwell in traditional homesteads, hunting and herding their livestock, the towns and cities have modern amenities and excellent infrastructure. Namibia is better off than many other countries in the region, particularly because of its diamond wealth, though the distribution of this wealth is not always fair. Namibia's government is forward thinking and efficient, health and education standards are far higher than in neighbouring countries, and there have been some very successful conservation projects in recent years.

Cultural blend

The Herero and the Owambo, no longer just poorly paid migrant labourers, represent the backbone of modern Namibia. Their cousins, the Himba, still wear traditional clothing in the remote and wild Kaokoveld; they are the last nomadic, herding peoples in southern Africa. The oldest inhabitants of Namibia are the Bushmen, or San. Today, Botswana and Namibia are the last refuge of these ancient and fragile tribes, struggling to keep a sense of identity in the modern world.

Wide open spaces

Around 60% of Namibia is semi-desert. To the east is the red sand of the Kalahari Desert; to the west lies the 80 million-year-old Namib, with its endless, seemingly lifeless sand dunes, its barren coastline and its uniquely adapted plants and animals that survive on the life-nourishing fog that rolls inland off the cold Atlantic Ocean. Fish River Canyon in the south is Africa's second largest canyon, a 300-million-year-old gash in the earth forcing the river to wind tortuously through the towering sandstone rocks. To the north are the stony, parched plains of Damaraland and Kaokoland that harbour free-roaming rhino and elephant and some unusual rock formations. Also in this region is the fabulous Etosha National Park where a network of waterholes gives life to a staggering number of animals.

Adventure sports

Throughout Namibia, there are plenty of opportunities for serious hiking, from the mountainous Naukluft Trail to the sandy, ephemeral Ugab River. If the sky is your thing, try ballooning, gliding or skydiving, followed by quad-biking or sandboarding down a giant dune. On water there are leisurely canoe trips on the Zambezi and Orange rivers and whitewater rafting on the Kunene River. The cool Benguela Current creates a perfect breeding ground for big game fish and Namibia is popular for angling and deep-sea fishing. The Caprivi Strip is one of the world's top birdwatching spots, as well as being home to hippo, elephant and crocodile.

Contents

Essentials

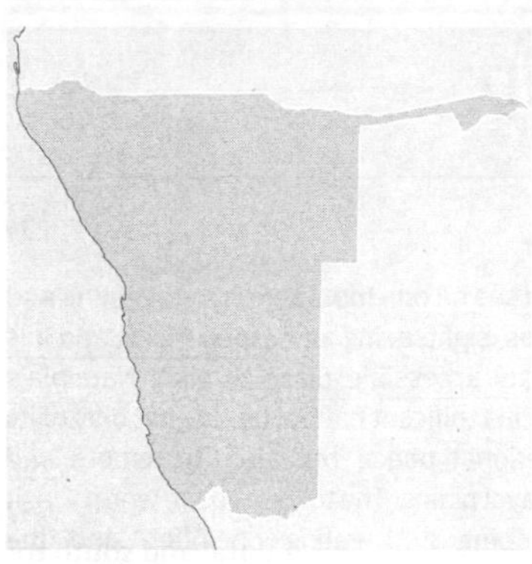

Footprint features

Planning your trip

Where to go

Namibia has more to offer than you could ever see on one trip. There is a staggering and ever-expanding array of destinations, activities, sightseeing and experiences, and it is becoming an increasingly accessible place to visit. Namibia's greatest attraction is the magnificent natural beauty not only of its game reserves and national parks, but also its remote and beautiful deserts and gravel plains. The towns too are worth a visit for the excellent shopping and eating on offer, and the opportunity to learn about some of Namibia's colonial history on display in the museums and reflected in the architecture. Adventure junkies will be well rewarded with the numerous adrenalin activities on offer such as quad-biking through the dunes or sand boarding. Preparation for your trip should include careful research into which of the great range of activities and destinations you find most appealing. Your itinerary will also depend on whether you are more interested in a general cultural visit or a more wildlife-oriented trip, in which case you may prefer to skip places such as Swakopmund or Lüderitz, and focus more on Etosha, Sossusvlei, the Naukluft Mountains and a private game lodge. Beware of setting yourself too ambitious an agenda as distances are significant and there is little in the way of public transport. Rather than cram in too much, try to arrange stops of two to four days in each location or region to fully appreciate what there is on offer; you can always return some time in the future. How you travel around Namibia has some influence on where you go. The best option for budget travellers is to either take a camping tour to the major highlights, or self-drive staying in the cheaper accommodation options and/or camping. For those with more cash to splash, flying between destinations affords the opportunity to really get away from it all at the remote luxury lodges and allows extra time to fit more in during your visit.

Seeing Namibia from the air is a very special experience; even those on a budget should consider a short sightseeing flight from Swakopmund.

Two weeks

The absolute minimum time to spend in Namibia is two weeks. Windhoek, the usual point of arrival, is an attractive city to wander around and easily warrants a day at the beginning or end of your trip. From Windhoek there are essentially two circuits to choose from whether on a self-drive or organized holiday, but you would be hard pushed to fit both in over two weeks. The first heads due north through Okahandja, Otjiwarango and the triangle towns to the east of the Etosha National Park. There are a number of distractions along this route and Etosha itself warrants at least three nights staying at the park's rest camps. Leaving the park in the southwest at Okaukuejo, the route goes through Damaraland where at least a couple of days are needed to explore the extraordinary scenery. Once on the coast, you can follow the coast road through part of the Skeleton Coast National Park or the West Coast Recreation Area and stop off to see the seals at Cape Cross. How long you stay in Swakopmund rather depends on what you want to do as there are a number of activities, but at least two days is recommended to enjoy the atmosphere of this quirky seaside town.

The second route from Windhoek heads south and east into the vast Namib Desert protected by the Namib-Naukluft Park. At least two days is recommended to explore the region around Sesriem and Sossusvlei and most certainly to enter the park at sawn to watch a sunrise melt over the giant dunes. From here you can head south and visit the coast at Lüderitz, stopping to see the Duwisib Castle and the desert horses near Aus. Another two days are needed at Lüderitz, although it can be visited on a long day trip from Aus, to explore the ghost mine town of Kolmonskop and perhaps take a boat trip out to see seals and penguins. Further south, at least one night is recommended at Hobas Rest Camp at the top of Fish River Canyon to watch the sunset, and another night at Ai-Ais Hot Springs at the bottom of the canyon. If you intend to tackle the 85-km Fish River Canyon Hike, then an extra five days are needed.

Four weeks and more

If you are confident about driving, a complete tour of the country will require a month or more with a car. Hiring a car will involve a considerable initial outlay but will provide flexibility and access to out of the way places which will be key to your appreciation of the country. What's more, you can save money on accommodation by camping in some of the picturesque sites. Depending on how much driving you are prepared to do, the options are to combine the two routes described above in the north or south of the country. After exploring the north, it is easy enough to go from Swakopmund straight to the Namib-Naukluft Park and continue south from there. Those with more time and the penchant to get right off the beaten track can travel to the extreme north of Namibia where you'll experience the thirstlands of Kaokoland and possibly meet the Himba. If you are driving through Namibia en route to Zimbabwe, Botswana or Zambia you will have the chance to sample a bit of all the country, including the Kavango and Caprivi regions in the extreme northeast along the Caprivi Strip, where there are game-filled forests and rivers unlike the arid deserts and plains of the rest of the country. Finally, there are a number of excellent guest farms in Namibia providing interesting wildlife encounters and horse riding or farm tours; a stay at one of these makes for a relaxing couple of days at the end of your holiday. All of the above destinations are accessible by car and most tour companies operate fully comprehensive tours but you will need several weeks to fit everything in. Flying cuts the travelling times down considerably, though the lodges and camps that have airstrips are usually in the luxury bracket, so fly-in safaris in Namibia can be expensive. There is, however, the option to combine fly-in safaris to the more out-of-the-way destinations such as the Skeleton Coast and the Caprivi Strip with an overland organized or self-drive tour to destinations such as Etosha, Swakopmund and the Namib-Naukluft Park.

Namibia is regionally located very close to many of southern Africa's highlights, and many visitors combine a trip to Namibia with excursions to Botswana, Zambia, Zimbabwe and South Africa. It can easily be combined with a self-drive trip to South Africa and most car hire companies allow you take a car over the border. Cape Town is two days' drive (or an overnight bus journey) from Windhoek, and Johannesburg (also linked by bus) can be reached in two to three days, via Botswana. In the northeast, Katimo Mulilo is just a couple of hours' drive away from Livingstone in Zambia and Victoria Falls in Zimbabwe, both springboard towns to see the mighty Victoria Falls and enjoy all the adventures on offer there. Also along the Caprivi Strip from the Ngoma Gate border, Kasane in Botswana can be reached in little more than an hour, gateway to the wonderful Chobe National Park famous for its large population of elephants. Further west from the Mohembo border, Maun can be reached in a day for excursions into the watery wilderness of Botswana's Okavango Delta.

When to go

> *Much of the countryside is totally unrecognizable after the rains, when the landscape is green and full of unusual flowering plants.*

Namibia can be visited all year round as the climate is continually warm and dry. The average temperature in winter (May to September) is 18-25° C, though the summer months (December to March) can be brutal with the average temperature of 35° C often creeping into the 40°s; this may not be the best time to visit for those who struggle with the heat. Temperatures along the coast are cooled by the cold Benguela Current and are comfortable all year round. With 300 days of sunshine per year, Namibia is definitely a sunny country, and the central, southern and coastal areas constitute some of the most arid landscapes south of the Sahara. As with all desert regions, days are hot while nights are generally cool. In winter months, particularly July, nights get very cold and there are frosts, so be prepared for some extreme weather. As well as hats, sunblock and sunglasses, you'll need to have a warm fleece handy for when the sun starts to fade. Most of the rain falls between February and March, but there's so little it shouldn't hamper any visit to the country. The average annual rainfall varies from 50 mm along the coast to 350 mm in the central interior and 700 mm in the Caprivi Strip. The only thing likely to happen is that the normally dry riverbeds that criss-cross the dirt roads fill with water; after the occasional heavy bout of rain, many roads in rural areas can be closed to saloon cars for several days. Also the game in Etosha is more dispersed because the animals do not have to rely on the waterholes, so this is not the best time for wildlife watching. However, birdwatching is best after the rains when there are numerous flooded depressions which attract migrant species.

Swakopmund only gets an average of 50 mm of rain a year. The town does not even have any drains or infrastructure to deal with rainwater, so if it does rain heavily, it floods.

There is no bad time to visit Namibia, but depending upon what you wish to see and do there are certain months which are better than others. Despite being cold, July and August are fairly busy months for tourism as they coincide with the European (and especially German) school holidays. December and January are by far the busiest months for tourism, as they coincide with the South African long summer holiday when Namibia becomes the virtual playground for outdoorsy type South Africans. Be sure to book your car hire and accommodation well in advance and remember that accommodation in the larger parks is restricted to a certain number of nights because of their popularity during these periods.

Hiking should not be attempted during the hot summer months; in fact the Fish River Canyon trail is closed between 15 September and 15 April, because of temperatures in excess of 45°C.

There are a number of colourful festivals that are worth enjoying while you are in Namibia. While none of them is significant enough to base your entire trip around, should you be in the area at the time, they do provide an interesting insight into the heritage of the different ethnic groups of this cosmopolitan country (see page 51)

For information on activities, safaris and what you can do and where to go in terms of responsible tourism, see pages 33 and 53.

Tour operators

If you plan to book an organized tour from your own country, the best bet is to locate a travel agent with a link to a tour company in Namibia, as they will probably be able to get you the best deals. Alternatively, you could contact a Namibia specialist travel agency in Europe – such as **Expert Africa** (formerly **Sunvil Africa**, see below). Within Namibia there is a bewildering array of tour operators offering safaris in Namibia and southern Africa, by plane, by 4WD and on foot, from fly-in safaris to the Skeleton Coast and Okavango Delta, to hiking tours of Damaraland and canoe safaris down the Kunene River. The tour operators can organize all arrangements within Namibia including flights to get there. There is no reason why you cannot deal with them directly and they may often be cheaper and better informed than travel agents in your home country. Many companies offer guided trips for small groups to the more remote parts of the country. Most of their websites offer information in English and German. *Tour operators in Namibia are listed under Windhoek, page 99, and Swakopmund, page 249.*

United Kingdom

Aardvark Safaris, T01980-849160, www.aardvarksafaris.com.
Abercrombie & Kent, T0800-5547016, www.abercrombiekent.com.
Acacia Adventure Holidays, T020-77064700, www.acacia-africa.com.
Africa Exclusive, T01604-628979, www.africaexclusive.com.
Africa Travel Centre, 21 Leigh St, London WC1H 9EW, T0845-4501520, www.africatravel.co.uk.
Africa Travel Resource, T01306-880770, www.africatravelresource.com.
African Odyssey, T01242-224482, www.africanodyssey.co.uk.
Audley Travel Ltd, T01869-276250, www.audleytravelcom.
Expert Africa (formerly Sunvil Africa), 7 and 8 Upper Square, Old Isleworth, Middlesex, TW7 7BJ, T020-82329777, www.expertafrica.com.
Footprint Adventures, T01522-804929, www.footprint-adventures.co.uk.
Global Village, T0870-999484, www.globalvillage-travel.com.
Rainbow Tours, T020-72261004, www.rainbowtours.co.uk.
Safari Consultants, T01787-228494, www.safari-consultants.co.uk.
Safari Drive, Windy Hollow, Sheepdrove, Lambourn, Berkshire RH17 7XA, T01488-71140, www.safaridrive.com.
Sherpa Expeditions, T020-85772717, www.sherpa-walking-holidays.co.uk.
Somak, T0208-4233000, www.somak.co.uk.
Steppes Africa, T01285-650011, www.steppesafrica.co.uk.

Rest of Europe

Iwanowski's Individuelles Reisen GmbH, T021-3326030, www.afrika.de.
Jambo Tours, T029-3579191, www.jambotours.de.

North America

Adventure Centre, T0800-2288747, www.adventure-centre.com.
Africa Adventure Company, T0800-8829453, T954-4918877, www.africa-adventure.com.

Namibia's tourism industry

Since independence in 1990, tourism has become a significant foreign exchange earner and employment provider for Namibia, which currently receives in the region of 800,000 visitors a year. The Namibia Tourism Board (NTB) is one of the world's most efficient tourism organizations and it goes to great lengths to govern and promote the tourist industry in and out of the country. There are several overseas offices (see page 17) and the NTB attends every worldwide tourism trade fair and event. All car hire companies and tour operators must be registered and be members of the relevant associations such as the Car Rental Association of Namibia (CARAN) or the Association of Namibian Travel Agents (ANTA). Every tour guide working in Namibia has to be registered with the Tour and Safari Association of Namibia (TASA) and any foreign guide working in the country requires a work permit. Other organizations include the Hospitality Association of Namibia (HAN) which represents the wider hospitality industry and promotes high standards for accommodation facilities by issuing annual awards in various categories, referred to under accommodation options listed in this book as HAN awards. Other tourism bodies are the Namibian Community Based Tourism Association (NACOBTA, see box, page 41), the Namibian Academy for Tourism and Hospitality (NATH), which provides training in the hospitality industry, the Namibian Professional Hunters Association (NAPHA), and the Bed and Breakfast Association of Namibia (B&BA). Finally, all of these associations come under the umbrella of the Federation of Namibian Tourism Associations (FENATA), a non-profit organization that was established in 1992 to govern the tourism industry and act as a voice between the private sector, the NTB and the Ministry for the Environment and Tourism (MET). From 2004 it has been a requirement for every hotel, lodge, guest farm, campsite and backpackers' hostel to be graded and registered by NTB tourism inspectors to ensure minimum standards. If they don't meet the standards, establishments are not permitted to operate. A Tourism Levy from accommodation establishments (2% of the bed and breakfast rate) was also introduced in 2004; the money raised goes towards promoting Namibia throughout the rest of the world on behalf of all the registered members. Some establishments and tour operators have complained that the new rules and regulations are excessive and over-controlling, but the NTB explains that their purpose is to improve the quality and standards of the services offered.

Distant Horizons, T0800-3331240, T562-9838828, www.distant-horizons.com.
Legendary Adventure Co, T303-4131182, www.legendaryadventure.com.

Australia and New Zealand

Classic Safari Company, T1300-130218, www.classicsafaricompany.com.au.
Peregrine Travel, T303-96638611, www.peregrine.net.au.

South Africa

Pulse Africa, T011-3252290, www.pulseafrica.com.
Thompson's Tours, T011-770770, www.thompsons.co.za.
Wild Frontiers, T011-7022035, www.wildfrontiers.com.

Finding out more

A good way of finding out more information for your trip is to contact the **Namibia Tourism Board** (NTB) office either in Namibia (Ground Floor, Sanlam Centre, Independence Avenue, Windhoek, T061-2906000, info@namibiatourism.com.na), or through one of its worldwide offices (see box), or to consult its website, www.namibiatourism.com.na. The NTB produces an extensive array of publications each year listing tour operators and accommodation options and the information available is staggering. Go into any of the southern African tourist offices and you will need a wheelbarrow to take away all the brochures and leaflets produced on Namibia! Among other publications the NTB produces are *Welcome to Namibia – Official Visitors' Guide*, which offers information about visiting the parks and contains extensive accommodation listings, and the very good Namibia Map, which shows all the minor road numbers and tourist highlights and is essential if you are on a self-drive holiday. Get in touch before you leave home and will send them to you. They are published in English and German. ▸▸ *Local tourist offices are listed in the directory section of individual towns.*

Tourist offices overseas

Germany 42-44 Schillerstrasse, 60313 Frankfurt, T69-1337360, info@namibia-tourism.com.
Italy Via Adolfo Rava 106, 00142 Rome, T06-45230032, namibiatourism@airconsult.it.
France 20 Av Recteur Poincaré, 75016 Paris, T/F140-508863, isalomone@noos.fr.
South Africa **Cape Town**, Ground Floor, Pinnacle Building (beneath the Cape Town Tourist Office), Burg St, Cape Town, T+27(0)21-4223298, namibia@saol.com. Also here is the desk for **Namibia Wildlife**

Resorts, T+27(0)21-4223761, ct.bookings@nwr.com.na. If starting a trip to Namibia from Cape Town this is the perfect place to get ideas and make reservations for parks accommodation. **Johannesburg,** 1 Orchard Lane, Rivonia, T+27(0)11-7854626, namibia@lloydorr.com.

UK 6 Chandos St, London, WIG 9LU, T020-7636 2924/28, www.namibiatourism.co.uk.

Useful websites

There are literally hundreds of websites about travel in Namibia, both in English and German and a number of other languages.

www.africaonline.com Comprehensive site covering news, sport and travel all over Africa.

Www.africanwildliferesources.org Research tool and resource centre promoting sustainable wildlife practices.

www.economist.com.na Business news and economic outlook.

www.fco.gov.uk UK's Foreign Office site, for the 'official' advice on latest political situations.

www.go2africa.com Full accommodation and safari booking service for Africa, with useful practical information.

www.grnnet.gov.na Namibian government site, for up to date visa requirements.

www.met.gov.na Website of the Ministry of Environment and Toursim, with environmental policies and park information.

www.namibian.com.na The country's independent newspaper online, with useful classifieds.

www.namibianews.com Also comprehensive latest news and sport.

www.namibiatourism.com.na Official site of the Namibia Tourist Board, indispensable.

www.namibweb.com Multilingual, hugely informative online travel agent and information source, but not very stylish or easy to navigate.

www.nwr.com.na Website of Namibia Wildlife Resorts which manage accommodation in the national parks; now offers online bookings.

www.overlandafrica.com A variety of overland tours offered throughout Africa.

www.travelafricamag.com For subscriptions to Travel Africa Magazine.

Language

Namibia has an ethnically diverse population. It includes the Bantu-speaking Ovambo, Kavango and Herero, the Damara, the San (Bushmen) and whites of South African, German and British descent. There are more than 11 indigenous languages, with the most common being Oshiwambo. About 50% or one million people in Namibia speak it. Although English is the official language, Afrikaans is still the lingua franca in the central and southern parts of the country. In the north, the majority of people are Oshiwambo speakers with English as second choice. Afrikaans is spoken in the Kavango while English is most common in the Caprivi Strip. Visitors who speak German will find that many white-owned businesses in the tourist industry are owned and run by German-speaking people, and Namibia is very popular with German tourists.

For some simple opening phrases in each of the common languages, see page 382.

Lekker is an Afrikaans word for 'very good' or 'things are going well'.

Specialist travel

Disabled travellers

Wheelchairs are very difficult to accommodate on public transport, but as this is practically non-existent anyway, Namibia is best visited on an organized tour or in a rented vehicle. Almost all of the tour operators in Namibia will cater for disabled travellers and **Air Namibia** makes adequate provision for wheelchair-bound customers both on board and on the ground at the airports. Many of the more modern hotels have specially adapted rooms for disabled people and it is worth asking about these even in the smaller or more remote establishments when enquiring about accommodation. Safaris should not pose too much of a problem either, given that most of the time is spent in the vehicle; wheelchair-bound travellers may want to consider a camping or tented safari which provides easy access to a tent at ground level. On the down side, however, most buildings in Namibia are unlikely to be disabled friendly, and many roads, even in towns, are gravel and very few outside Windhoek have pavements, reducing mobility for wheelchairs.

Gay and lesbian travellers

The climate is not particularly welcoming for lesbian and gay visitors. This has been especially evident during the last few years that Nujoma was president from around 1998 to 2002. During this period he made random comments denouncing homosexuality. These have included a 2001 statement: "The Republic of Namibia does not allow homosexuality or lesbianism here. Police are ordered to arrest you, deport you and imprison you". Also notable were the president's comments on the new laws in the Netherlands, permitting same-sex couples to marry. Nujoma expressed his disgust at the first weddings of gay and lesbian couples, executed by the Amsterdam mayor in person, saying: "It is the devil at work". The EU condemned Nujoma for his comments, and in response to his 2001 comments said: "Official statements against minorities, inter alia against homosexuals, as well as declarations of xenophobic nature, are unacceptable and indicate worrying signs of increasing intolerance." There is in fact no such law against homosexuality in Namibia but it is considered illegal and can be prosecuted under indecent sexual acts laws. Conversely, there is a law against discrimination. However, in more recent years, tolerance towards the gay community in Namibia seems to have improved. There is a gay rights support group, the **Rainbow Project**, with over 1000 members, which in 2005 held a successful Gay Pride march in Windhoek that coincided with a Gay Awareness week of events. However, given the attitude of the government during recent years, it is wise for gay visitors to be discrete. By doing so you should encounter no problems. For more information visit www.mask.org.za, a website dedicated to gay and lesbian affairs in Africa.

Student travellers

Namibia is a nation of young people and in this respect is a good place for students to travel. Similarly, there are many volunteers (VSO, Peace Corps, Operation Raleigh, etc) working in the country, so you are likely to find good company when you travel. While the cost of camping or staying in backpackers' hostels is not prohibitive on a student budget, the cost of car hire is and there is little public transport outside the main centres. Therefore, whilst being rewarding, it is not the cheapest of countries to travel in for budget travellers. There are generally no discounts for students in Namibia and student rates advertised for museums and parks will usually only apply to local residents.

Travelling with children

In the main towns with supermarkets, you will find plentiful supplies of all you need to feed and look after your little ones. Hygiene throughout the country is of a good standard; stomach upsets are rare and the tap water everywhere is safe to drink. However, be sure to cover your children against the intense sun's rays, and be aware of the potential dangers of wild animals, snakes and insects in the bush. Most of the accommodation options welcome families with young children; many have either specific family rooms or adjoining rooms

Namibia is a popular family holiday destination; in December and January, during school holidays, accommodation in Swakopmund and Etosha is packed with South African families .

 suitable for families, and there are plenty of family chalets or bungalows, especially in the parks. These are always worth asking about when booking accommodation. Children get significant discounts for accommodation and entry fees. In fact Namibia Wildlife Resorts only charges adults park entry fees and under 16s go free. Namibia has a great appeal to children: animals and safaris are very exciting for them (and their parents), especially when they catch their first glimpse of an elephant or lion. However, small children may get bored driving around a hot game park or national park all day if there is no animal activity. If you travel in a group, think about the long hours inside the vehicle sharing little room with other people. Noisy and bickering children can annoy your travel mates and scare the animals away. Many travel agencies organize family safaris that are especially designed for couples travelling with children, and there is also the option of self-drive which is ideal for families.

Inform the airline in advance that you are travelling with a baby or toddler and check out the facilities when booking as these vary with each aircraft. Check out www.babygoes2.com.

Women travellers

Namibia does not have a high record of sexual crime and tourists are unlikely to be targeted. It is a relatively safe country for women to travel in, but always keep vigilant, especially for petty theft, and follow the usual common sense rules about not travelling alone after dark and avoiding quiet places. As in any country, there are risks associated with single women travellers, however, these are no greater in Namibia than elsewhere. In fact, given the lack of big cities and the low population density perhaps the risks are lower. Women travellers at some point, may meet with some unreconstructed male chauvinism or unwanted attention from men, but this can usually be dealt with if you are assertive and you are unlikely to encounter anything more serious.

Working in Namibia

There are no opportunities for travellers to obtain casual paid employment in Namibia and it is illegal for a foreigner to work without an official work permit. Most foreign workers in Namibia are employed through embassies, development or volunteer agencies or through foreign companies. For the most part these people will have been recruited in their countries of origin. A number of NGOs and voluntary organizations can arrange placements for volunteers, usually for periods ranging from six months to two years, visit www.volunteerafrica.org.

Before you travel

Visas and immigration

All visitors must be in possession of a passport which is valid for a minimum of six months from their date of entry. At present, visitors from Angola, Australia, Austria, Belgium, Botswana, Brazil, Canada, Cuba, France, Germany, Iceland, Ireland, Italy, Japan, Kenya, Lesotho, Luxembourg, Netherlands, New Zealand, Malawi, Malaysia, Moçambique, Netherlands, Russia, Scandinavian countries, Singapore, Spain, South Africa, Switzerland, Tanzania, United Kingdom, United States of America, Zambia and Zimbabwe do not require a visa and can stay in the country for a period of 90 days with a permit issued on arrival at the point of entry. Extensions have to be applied for from the **Ministry of Home Affairs**, Independence Avenue, Windhoek, T061-2929111. Tourist visas for those countries that do need a visa can also be obtained from Namibian embassies overseas. Work and study visas must be applied for from your home country and granted before you depart. Alternatively, if you are going to Namibia via South Africa, visas can be obtained at the **Namibia Tourism Board** office in Cape Town (see page 17), or the **Namibia High Commission** in Johannesburg, Ground Floor, Grosvenor Corner, 195 Jan Smuts Avenue (Corner 7th Avenue), Rosebank, T+27 (0)11-327-1006/9. Photographs are not required, processing time is one to two working days and the present cost is R138 (US$20). For more information visit the website for the Ministry of Foreign Affairs, www.mfa.gov.na.

For detailed health advice and information, see page 61.

Namibian embassies and consulates

Angola Rwa Dos Cocqueiros No 37, Luanda, T2395483.
Austria Strozzigasse 10-14, Vienna, T0431-402937.
Belgium ave de Tervuren 454, 1150 Brussels, T2-7711410, F7719689.
Botswana, Debswana House, Gaborone, T3902181, nhc.gabs@info.bw.
European Union, ave de Tavuren 454, Brussels, Belgium, T02-7711410.
France 80 ave Foch/ 17 Square de l'Ave Foch, Paris, T044-173265.
Germany Germany, Wichmannstrasse 5, Berlin, T030-2540950.
South Africa Grosvenor Corner, 195 Jan Smuts Av (Corner 7th Av), Rosebank, Johannesburg, T011-327-1006/9.
Sweden Luntmakargatan 86-88, 11122, PO Box 26042, S 100 31, Stockholm, T6127788, F6126655.
United Kingdom 6 Chandos St, London, W1G 9LU, T020-7636 6244, F7637 5694.
USA 1605 New Hampshire Av, NW, Washington DC 20009, T01-202-9860540, F9860443.
Zambia 30B Mutende Rd, Lusaka, T01-263858.
Zimbabwe 31A Lincoln Rd, Avondale, Harare, T04-885841.

Customs

Duty free There are no restrictions for South African travellers. For overseas visitors duty-free allowances are: 400 cigarettes or 50 cigars or 250 g of tobacco, 50 ml of perfume and 250 ml of toilet water, two litres of wine and one litre of spirits, gifts up to the value of N$50,000 (US$7,825) are allowed to be imported duty free. All hunting rifles must be declared on arrival; permits are issued by customs when entering the country, other firearms are not permitted.

If you are buying expensive items like diamonds; be sure to claim the 15% tax back as the refund can be quite considerable.

There is a small duty-free shop at Hosea Kutako airport for outbound travellers, but the choice is limited. Remember to use up your currency (Namibian dollars are not transferable once overseas) and buy any souvenirs before you reach the airport. Failing that, **Air Namibia** has a limited stock of goods for sale in the air. In 2000 Namibia introduced a VAT of 15% for accommodation and goods (included in the price). As in South Africa, visitors may now reclaim the VAT back on purchases bought in Namibia exceeding the value of N$250 (US$39) at the VAT reclaim desks at the Hosea Kutako International Airport or at the border posts at Ariamsvlei and Noordoewer. Refunds are given by cheque in South African rand, which can be paid into home bank accounts. Goods need to be shown to the refund officer as proof of purchase with VAT receipts, so be sure to ask for these when you buy something, and at the airport this needs to be done before you check in your luggage. Refunds only apply to items taken out of the country and not on services rendered such as accommodation or goods consumed or used within the country. For example, if you are buying clothes, keep the shop tags on them to prove that you haven't worn or 'used' that item in Namibia and you'll get the tax back. For more information contact the Ministry of Finance, T061-230773.

Export restrictions The **CITES Convention** made illegal the trade in products derived from endangered species, such as elephant ivory, sea turtle products and the skins of wild cats. Restrictions have been imposed on the trade in reptile skins, coral, and certain plants and wild birds. The restricted animal products that tourists are most likely to encounter in Namibia are ivory, *biltong* made from protected species such as elephant or endangered antelope, and wallets, shoes and handbags made from kudu, crocodile or snake skins. While these products may be freely available for the domestic market, you should always consider the environmental and social impact before purchasing any such item.

Within the country, be aware that you are not permitted to transfer any animal products as you travel from the Far North, Caprivi or northwest regions across the Red Line (veterinary fence) to the south. This includes souvenir animal horns and skins and fresh meat, ostensibly to prevent the spread of disease, without prior clearance from a vet.

Vaccinations

Neither smallpox nor cholera vaccination certificates are required by visitors to Namibia, but those travelling from other African countries to the north of Namibia do require yellow fever certificates. Vaccinations against infectious hepatitis, polio, tetanus and typhoid are recommended – see Health section, page 61 for further details and seek advice from your doctor or travel clinic about six weeks before departure.

What to take

Checklist

Everybody has their own list. Obviously what you take depends on where you are intending to go and how you plan to travel. Backpackers will want to travel light as lugging a heavy pack around in the heat is not much of a holiday. Laundry services are readily available (and clothes dry in minutes), so there is no need for many clothes. If you have arranged to hire a car from the airport, you can be more generous with what you carry such as books and camping gear. Virtually anything you require is available in Namibia, but be aware that outside Windhoek the choice reduces dramatically – and outside the larger towns it dwindles to essentials only. Dust will get into everything you take, so particularly sensitive equipment such as computers and digital cameras should be looked after carefully or left behind.

Send yourself an email with details of such things as traveller's cheques, passport, driving licence, credit cards and travel insurance numbers. Someone at home should also have access to important details.

Essentials Air tickets; camera; camera film (though film and batteries are available in all Namibia's major towns, if you don't have a digital); cash; credit cards; driver's licence; passport including visa; photocopies of main documents (keep separate) and traveller's cheques. Apart from these everybody has their own list. Apart from these everybody has their own list, though binoculars, money belt, Swiss army knife or Leatherman, torch and water bottle are all useful items to take. All toiletries are available to buy in Namibia and cost no more than they do back home, though it may be a good idea to bring favourite brands or specialist items such as contact lens cleaner or sun protection cream; eye drops are essential on the dusty roads.

Clothing Dress in Namibia tends to be casual and most people on holiday wear shorts, sandals and a T-shirt. Night-time temperatures in winter can get very low and deserts are very cold at night. If you are camping, a fleece jacket or a thick sweater are essential. By the coast, the wind can really blow; bring a windproof top of some kind. By day, sunstroke and sunburn can be a serious problem and a wide-brimmed hat, long-sleeved cotton shirts, high SPF sunscreen and sunglasses are vital. It is a good idea to bring two basic sets of clothes, one set of sturdy cotton outdoor clothes and one set of evening wear, appropriate for the surroundings you expect to find yourself in.

Always take half the clothes you think you'll need and twice the amount of money.

Footwear should be as well ventilated as possible for the hot weather; sandals or canvas trainers are recommended. European-style, leather walking boots are too heavy except perhaps for the Fish River Canyon or the Waterberg Plateau hikes, when a good pair of comfortable, sturdy boots are essential. Lightweight hiking boots (no need for fabulous waterproofing in this climate) are popular. In Windhoek and Swakopmund you can buy a good range of local handmade leather desert boots. While these are usually very comfortable, check that they are properly stitched and remember they will need time to break in.

Camping equipment If you are camping in Namibia the choice is either to bring equipment from home (though this adds considerably to weight allowances on airlines), or hire or buy equipment once in Namibia. The car hire companies and camping shops that rent out or sell camping equipment are listed under Windhoek (pages 98 and 102); it is best to contact them in advance and pre-arrange the hire of equipment or check that the camping gear you want is in stock. Camping equipment (particularly tents and sleeping bags) is limited and imported items are fairly expensive, so you may want to consider at least bringing these along. You will need a minimum of a tent with built-in mosquito net; sleeping bag; mattress – Thermarest are the best; portable gas stove and lamp (though nearly all campsites have *braai* – barbeque – grates and you can buy firewood if you are confident about cooking over an open fire); cool bag/box (or opt for a hire car with a fridge); cooking and eating equipment; airtight containers to keep food in; and a plastic jerry can for water and additional ones for fuel if you are going way off the beaten track.

Some of the car hire companies offer 4WD cars with rooftop tents and every piece of equipment you will need for a camping holiday from a fork or frying pan to a table or chemical toilet.

Insurance

Before departure, it is vital to take out comprehensive travel insurance. There is a wide variety of policies to choose from, so shop around. At the very least, the policy should cover medical expenses, including repatriation to your home country in the event of a medical emergency. Make sure the policy covers any activities you may be considering, trekking or skydiving for example. There is no substitute for suitable precautions against petty crime, but if you do have something stolen whilst in Namibia, report the incident to the nearest police station and ensure you get a police report and case number. You will need these to make any claim from your insurance company.

Take a photocopy with you of the relevant sections of your policy outlining procedures to follow when things go wrong.

It is always best to dig out all the receipts for personal effects like jewellery and cameras. Take photocopies of these items and note down all serial numbers.

In the event of a medical emergency in Namibia **International SOS Namibia,** T061-230505, emergency number through MTC's cellular network T112, www.internationalsos.com, are likely to be the medical company that comes to your assistance. This was established in Namibia in 2001 and offers 24-hour countrywide emergency medical rescue specifically for tourists, with permanent bases in Windhoek, Swakopmund, Walvis Bay, Tsumeb, Otjiwarongo, Kombat and Rosh

Pinah. They are the only doctor-based paramedical emergency evacuation provider in Namibia with 18 dedicated response vehicles and ambulances throughout Namibia and a number of air ambulances that can reach every corner of the country. When arranging medical insurance it is a good idea to ask if your insurer will cover you for the use of this service. Medical facilities in Namibia are on par with Europe, but most of the facilities are in Windhoek. This means that because of the remote distances, air evacuation in the event of an emergency is much more common than in other countries and the service here is very developed. Unfortunately, the majority of accidents involving tourists are road accidents on the gravel roads by drivers unaccustomed to driving 4WDs on untarred roads. » *See also Driving, page 39.*

Money

The Namibian dollar is pegged one to one with the South African rand and both currencies can be used in Namibia interchangeably. However, outside Namibia the local currency is not convertible and you cannot use it in South Africa or anywhere else, so remember to change any surplus Namibian dollars back into your own currency before your departure. This is a straightforward transaction which can be completed at any bank so long as you have a coupon proving your original purchase of Namibian dollars. Alternatively change it into rand which can be converted back into your own currency once back at home.

Currency

In 1993 Namibia issued its first set of bank notes, prior to which the South African rand had been legal tender (which it still is). At first, only three notes were issued: N$10, N$50 and N$100. In 1996 the N$20 note and N$200 note were introduced to complete the series. The famous Nama chief, Hendrik Witbooi, features on all the notes. There are few forged Namibian notes in circulation and no black market for currency. Whilst the prices listed in this book are mostly in US dollars, unlike other African countries US dollars cash cannot be spent in Namibia and is of no use here at all except for changing at a bank into Namibian dollars.

Whilst both South African rand and Namibian dollars can be used in Namibia, Namibian dollars are not transferable outside Namibia and cannot be used in South Africa.

Notes N$10, N$20, N$50, N$100 and N$200. **Coins** 5c, 10c, 50c, N$1 and N$5. As South African rand is still legal tender you will certainly come across notes and coins, particularly in national parks and in the south where you encounter a higher frequency of South African visitors. If your return flight is via Johannesburg, you might want to stash some rand away for a meal, drink, duty free or souvenirs on the way home (the choice is poor at Hosea Kutako).

Banks

The following are the main branches of the high-street banks, each of which offers foreign exchange services: **Bank of Windhoek**, T061-2991122, www.bankwindhoek.com.na; **First National Bank**, T061-2997087, www.fnbnamibia.com.na; **Nedbank**, T061-2952222, www.nedbanknamibia.com; **Standard Bank**, T061-2949111, www.standardbank.com.na. Banks are open weekdays 0900-1530 and Saturdays 0830-1030. Some small branches may close for an hour over lunch. All branches should be able to sell you foreign currency (ie South African rand or US dollar) should you need the cash for continuing your travels in southern Africa or elsewhere after Namibia. You will need to prove your foreign national status and source of funds outside Namibia (eg ATM receipt) if not withdrawing directly with a credit card. Interestingly, **First National Bank** has a single branch network across South Africa and

Namibia, while all the others are separate legal entities. This makes access to funds easier for South Africans if they bank with First National back home.

Credit and debit cards

Credit and debit cards are widely accepted all over the country; there are ATMs at just about every bank and the larger hotels, shops and restaurants accept them. However, most campsites or smaller guesthouses may not have facilities. It is a convenient way to cover large transactions and purchase Namibian dollars/South African rand, allows you to book accommodation in advance (particularly useful in national parks), or to leave a deposit for a hire car or mobile phone without having to hand over cash. In most shops (although not petrol stations), Visa, MasterCard/Eurocard, American Express and Diners Club are accepted, although some shops charge extra for Amex due to the high service cost to them. Once approval is granted, staff in shops in Namibia and South Africa hardly look at your signature or check it against your card so be sure to cancel lost/stolen cards quickly. All the major banks are connected to the Cirrus and Plus global cash systems, meaning that, as long as you have your card and PIN, you can use ATMs as easily as at home. Withdrawing cash from an ATM offers the most competitive (wholesale) exchange rate, though your bank at home will charge approximately 1-2% per transaction for an ATM withdrawal in a foreign country. The amount you can withdraw seems to vary between systems and cards, but you should be able to take out up to N$1000 (just under US$150) per day. The chip and pin system has not yet been introduced in southern Africa, but it is expected in time.

Credit cards are not accepted at petrol stations but are very useful for car hire and accommodation.

Useful websites
www.visa.com.
www.americanexpress.com.
www.mastercard.com.
For up-to-the-minute exchange rates, go to **www.xe.com**.

Lost or stolen cards
American Express, T061-2952017.
Diners Club, T061-2942141.
MasterCard, contact the Standard Bank, T061-2949111.
Visa Card, contact the First National Bank of Namibia, T061-2997087.

Traveller's cheques

One advantage of traveller's cheques is that if you lose them there is a relatively efficient system of replacement which should not cost the customer anything. For this reason, make sure you keep a full record of their numbers and value, separate from the cheques themselves, and/or send yourself a detailed email (to a web-based service). One drawback with traveller's cheques is that only the banks in Windhoek are likely to be able to issue replacement cheques. See the instructions provided with your traveller's cheques for specific telephone numbers.

A major disadvantage of traveller's cheques is the time it takes to cash them and the commission charged by the bank. Different branches of the same bank tend to raise their commission as the distance from major banking centres increases. Bank commission ranges between 0.2% and 0.5%. The most widely recognized cheques are American Express, Citicorp, Thomas Cook (they have a local partner, Rennies, 193 Independence Avenue, Windhoek, T061-229667, and at the Arrivals Hall, Terminal 2, Hosea Kutako International airport, T062 540013, www.rennies.co.za) and Visa. US dollar, Eurocheques and sterling traveller's cheques can be exchanged at banks throughout the country. Whilst these can only be cashed, by contrast South African traveller's cheques can be spent, as they of course match prices rand to Namibian dollars. If you are arriving in Namibia from South Africa, you may want to consider purchasing traveller's cheques in rand. These can be used at many hotels and the parks' rest camps to pay for accommodation.

Cost of travelling

Prices in Namibia used to be especially cheap by European standards and offered excellent value for money for the tourist spending US dollars, pounds sterling or euros. Not the case these days. Over the last three to four years the South African rand and consequently the Namibian dollar has gone from strength to strength against these other currencies and exchange rates are about half of what they were four years ago. In Namibia this has coincided with a sharp increase in accommodation rates, mainly due to the introduction of accommodation grading in 2004 (where the less expensive accommodation options were forced to close or refurbish if standards were not good enough), and the mushrooming of new lodges, guest farms and hotels aimed at the top end of the market. There is now limited budget accommodation in the country, although there is always the option to camp. It seems clear that Namibia's tourism policy is aimed at providing luxurious accommodation in stunning settings for a limited number of people. This is not a bad thing for a country that is home to so many fantastic wilderness areas; the high cost, low impact theory of tourism is ideally suited to a country like Namibia.

If you are travelling independently and propose to hire a car, you will need to budget US$80-150 per day, depending on season, type of vehicle and equipment included – a considerable outlay, but for a family of four or group of friends, the cost per person is obviously spread out. The cost of fuel is similar to that in the US, about two thirds of what Europeans are used to, but distances travelled can be considerable so be prepared for a hefty fuel bill too.

Accommodation will represent your other principal daily expense. In first-rate luxury lodges, tented camps or guest farms expect to pay in excess of US$150 per night for a double, rising to US$500 per night per person in the most exclusive establishments. For this you will get impeccable service, cuisine and decor in fantastic locations. If staying in simple B&Bs and hotels, budget US$50-60 per couple per night. By camping, you can bring this down to US$9, on average, per person per night.

Food and drink is still good value in southern Africa and an evening meal with wine in a reasonable restaurant will cost under US$30 for two people, and you can be pretty assured of good food and large portions. Costs can be brought down by self-catering either at campsites or in self-catering accommodation. Food in supermarkets is considerably cheaper than, say, in Europe, especially meat, and wine is inexpensive as it comes straight from South Africa. There are also some reasonably cheap locally brewed beers available in Namibia's (very many) bottle stores.

Getting there

Air

International flights from Europe arrive at **Hosea Kutako International Airport**, 42 km east of Windhoek on the road to Gobabis. The majority of charter, private and **Air Namibia** internal and regional services fly from **Windhoek – Eros Airport**, 5 km south of the city, T061-2955500.

Namibia has 11 international airports with customs and immigration facilities, though not all offer scheduled services, and another 200 registered airstrips.

From Europe

Air Namibia flies direct from London (Gatwick) to Windhoek, 10½ hours, and Frankfurt to Windhoek, nine hours; London to Windhoek, three flights a week (Tuesday, Thursday and Saturday); Windhoek to London, three flights a week (Tuesday, Thursday and Saturday); Franfurt to Windhoek, four flights a week (Monday, Tuesday, Thursday and Saturday); Windhoek to Frankfurt, four flights a week (Sunday, Tuesday, Wednesday and Friday). Expect to pay in the region of US$750-1200 for a return economy ticket on both these routes. The main problem is seat availability, particularly in July and August; book as far ahead as you can, and turn up three hours before take off (both on the way out and coming home) to ensure you get on. » *See page 72 for the Air Namibia timetable.*

LTU, a German charter company, flies on Tuesdays and Fridays between Düsseldorf via Münich to Windhoek from May to October. It also flies between Canada and the US to Germany. **Angola Airlines/TAG** has a weekly service between Windhoek and Paris, via Luanda, that departs Paris on Tuesday and Windhoek on Wednesday. By far the most frequent service to Namibia is via South Africa, using either **South African Airways** (SAA) or your national carrier from Europe to Johannesburg or Cape Town, and adding the final hop to Windhoek with a local airline such as **Air Namibia** or **South African Express** (a regional subsidiary of SAA). **SAA** has at least one or two flights per day between Johannesburg and most of the major European cities. **British Airways** has two overnight flights from London to Johannesburg every day, with later connections to Windhoek. It also has a daily overnight flight from London to Cape Town, but no connection on to Windhoek so you would have to use another carrier. **Lufthansa** flies between Frankfurt and Windhoek twice daily, 13½ hours, via Johannesburg.

! Jetlag is not usually an issue as there is only a minimal time difference between Europe and Namibia and all flights are overnight.

From North America

SAA flies daily from Atlanta via Fort Lauderdale. Once in South Africa there are regular connections from Johannesburg or Cape Town to Windhoek. Alternatively, fly from North America to London, Frankfurt or Düsseldorf in Germany to connect to the flights mentioned above.

From Australia and New Zealand

Unless your travel agent can offer a particularly good alternative, the best route to Namibia is via Johannesburg or Cape Town in South Africa and then make your own arrangements for an onward flight to Windhoek.

Between them **Qantas** and **SAA**, on a code share agreement, fly between Auckland, Sydney, Melbourne and Perth, and Johannesburg and there are several flights a week. Other options from Australasia to Johannesburg include **Singapore Airlines** which code share with **Air New Zealand**, and flights link Wellington with Johannesburg via Sydney and Singapore.

From Dubai

Johannesburg is served by **Emirates** daily from Dubai and **Emirates** flies to Dubai from just about everywhere else in the world.

From southern Africa

South African Airways and **British Airways** fly daily between Windhoek and Johannesburg. **SAA Express** has two flights a day between Cape Town and Windhoek, one flight a day (except Saturday) from Cape Town to Walvis Bay, two flights a day (Monday to Friday) between Johannesburg and Windhoek, and one flight a day (except Saturday) from Johannesburg to Walvis Bay. **Air Namibia** operates two daily flights (one on Saturday) between Cape Town and Windhoek, as well as two flights a day to Johannesburg. It also has flights between Windhoek and Maun in Botswana three times a week (Wednesday, Friday and Sunday), between Windhoek and Victoria Falls in Zimbabwe three times a week (Wednesday, Friday and Sunday), and between Windhoek and Luanda in Angola twice a week (Friday and Sunday). » *See page 72 for the Air Namibia timetable.*

Airlines

Air Namibia, T061-2996333 (Namibia), www.airnamibia.com.na.
Air New Zealand, T0800-737000 (NZ), www.airnz.co.nz.
Angola Airlines/TAAG (UK representative), T01293-618617, www.transvalair.com/taagair.
British Airways, T0870-8509850 (UK), www.britishairways.com.
Emirates, T0870-2432222 (UK), www.emirates.com.
LTU, Windhoek, T+49-2119418 (Germany), www.ltu.com.
Lufthansa, T0180-5838426 (Germany), www.lufthansa.com.
Qantas, T2-96913636 (Australia), www.qantas.com.au.
Singapore Airlines, T065-62238888, (Singapore), www.singaporeair.com.
SAA Express, T11-9785577 (South Africa), www.saexpress.co.za.
South African Airways, T011-9361111 (South Africa), www.flysaa.com.

Discount flight agents

UK and Ireland

Bridge the World, T0870-4432399, www.bridgetheworld.com.
Flight Centre, T0870-4990040, www.flightcentre.co.uk.
Flightbookers, T0870-0107000, www.ebookers.com.
STA Travel, T0870-1600599, www.statravel.co.uk.
Trailfinders, T020-79383939, www.trailfinders.co.uk.
Travelbag, T0870-9001351, www.travelbag.co.uk.

North America

Air Brokers International, T01-800883-3273, www.airbrokers.com.
STA Travel, T1800-7814040, www.statravel.com.
Travel Cuts, T1866-2469762 (Canada), www.travelcuts.com.
Worldtek, T1800-2421723, www.worldtek.com.

Australia and New Zealand

Flight Centre, T133-133, www.flightcentre.com.au.
Skylinks, T02-9234277, www.skylink.com.au.
STA Travel, T1-300733035 (Australia), T09-3099723 (New Zealand), www.statravel.com.au.
Travel.com.au, T02-9246000, www.travel.com.au.

Rail

Namibia's railway company, **Transnamib Starline Passenger Services,** runs a service between Upington in South Africa to Windhoek twice a week. However, as Namibia's trains are primarily used for freight, it is slow going with a lot of stops. Despite this the passenger compartments are comfortable with airline-like seats, videos are shown and there are vending machines for drinks and snacks. The service departs Upington on Thursday and Sunday at 0500 and arrives in Windhoek the following morning at 0700. In the other direction the train departs Windhoek on Wednesday and Saturday at 1940 and arrives in Upington the following day at 2130 with a lengthy stop at Keetmanshoop en route. (Note that the **Intercape Mainliner** bus takes 10 hours to do the same route as opposed to around 24 hours on the train.) **Transnamib Starline Passenger Services,** central reservations T061-2982032, www.transnamib.com.na. The office at Windhoek Train Station is open daily 0600-2000. » *For the Transnamib timetable, see page 68.*

Road

If you are taking your own car into Namibia you will need to show documentary proof of ownership such as the registration document or Carnet de Passages issued by a body in your own country (such as the **Automobile Association**), and a letter of authorization to drive from the owner if the car is not registered in the driver's name. If

Intercape Mainliner coach

Intercape Mainliner, one of the major South African coach companies, runs a service linking Windhoek with Cape Town, Pretoria and Johannesburg (via Upington). The Cape Town service continues to Livingstone in Zambia and there is also a daily service between Windhoek and Swakopmund on the coast. If you want to spend a few days in Cape Town before entering Namibia then the coach journey up the west coast offers fine views, although it is a long day. The coaches are extremely comfortable with reclining seats and air conditioning, videos are shown and snacks and drinks are available. Note that it is illegal to carry or drink alcohol on public buses.

The departure points for **Intercape** are: **Cape Town**, Station Tourist Centre; **Johannesburg**, Park City Transit Centre; **Pretoria**, Station 1928 Building; **Windhoek**, corner of Michael Scott St and Peter Muller St; **Swakopmund**, bus station on Hendrik Witbooi Street; **Victoria Falls**, Livingstone, CR Holings bus stop.

Intercape, Windhoek, T061-227847, South Africa, T021-3804400, www.intercape.co.za, book online. See page 70 for the **Intercape Mainliner** timetable and check the website for up to date fares. Expect to pay in the region of US$55 for a one-way trip between Cape Town and Windhoek.

driving a hire car in from South Africa, you need a letter of permission from the car rental agency and a ZA sticker (available in South Africa from any AA shop) which has to be stuck on the car whilst in Namibia. Cross border charges apply to all vehicles and are N$/R110 (US$17) for a vehicle and N$/R70 (US$11) for a trailer. You also need to purchase third party insurance for Namibia at the border which currently costs about N$/R15 (US$2.20) per month. Be sure to have the correct amount of cash for these fees as there is not always change. ▸▸ *For border opening times, see page 31. For information on driving conditions and truck safaris, see pages 38-42.*

From Angola

The principal road crossing is between Oshikango and Santa Clara. Although Angola has been off-limits for decades because of the civil war there, since the ceasefire between the Angolan Government and Unita in 2002 things have been relatively peaceful and Angola is most certainly making moves into the African tourism market. It now has its own tourism website, www.angola.org, exhibits at the world's trade tourism fairs, and in November 2005 Luanda was host to a conference of the Africa Travel Association (ATA). Many overlanders have successfully gone into Angola, mostly adventurous South African 4WD owners, and reports so far seem very positive. It is, however, a very new place to visit so get expert up-to-date advice before crossing into Angola. A good resource is the South African magazine *Getaway*, www.getaway toafrica.com, which has some useful articles about people who have gone to Angola, and if you trawl the internet you will find a number of South African tour companies offering guided tours into Angola starting from Johannesburg or Windhoek.

From Botswana

The main border crossings between Botswana and Namibia are at Buitepos to the east of Gobabis (the nearest crossing to Windhoek), and Ngoma Bridge at the extreme east of the Caprivi Strip. Both of these border posts are in remote country but the newly completed tarred Trans-Kalahari Highway between Botswana's capital Gaborone and Windhoek, and the newly tarred Trans-Caprivi Highway in the north, mean that both routes are easily navigable in an ordinary car. **Note** If driving between Namibia and Gaborone, fill up with fuel at either Buitepos or Jwaneng in Botswana, as there is no other fuel between these two towns except at Kang, 350 km from Jwaneng and 400 km from Buitepos.

From South Africa

The two main border posts between Namibia and South Africa are at Noordoewer, to the south of Keetmanshoop and the Fish River Canyon en route to Cape Town, and Ariamsvlei to the east of Karasburg on the road to Upington in South Africa. If coming from Cape Town the N7 goes all the way up to the border with Namibia at Voolsdrif/Noordoewer, a distance of 714 km. After crossing the border, the road becomes the B1 to Grunau and then Keetmanshoop. Note that the last shops on the South African side are at Springbok, though there are simple shops and petrol stations in Noordoewer on the Namibian side of the border. From Johannesburg the best way to get to Namibia is via Botswana. The N4 goes from Johannesburg and Pretoria via Zeerust and enters Botswana at Pioneer Gate. Then the road crosses Botswana via Lobatse as the newly tarred Trans-Kalahari Highway. You can enter Namibia at the Buitepos border post which is 120 km east of Gobabis on the road to Windhoek. The journey from Johannesburg to the Namibian border is roughly 1070 km and fuel stations are infrequent so fill up when you see one. The longest stretch between petrol stations on this route is 350 km.

From Zambia

There is one border post, Wanella, at the extreme northeast of the Caprivi Strip, which involves a bridge crossing over the Zambezi River. The Sesheke Bridge opened in 2004 completing the 2100-km Trans-Caprivi Highway that now links the port of Walvis Bay with Zambia's capital city, Lusaka. The Trans-Caprivi Highway was built by the Walvis Bay Corridor Group which was established in 1998 to coordinate international trade with the **Southern African Development Community** (SADC) through the port at Walvis Bay. In addition to trade, the bridge has already boosted tourism as it offers excellent access to all the sights in the region. From the Zambian side of the bridge it is less than an hour's drive to Livingstone.

From Zimbabwe

Although Namibia does not share a border with Zimbabwe, it is close and easily accessible enough to be included here, and many visitors combine a trip to northern Namibia with a visit to the Victoria Falls. You need to cross at the Ngoma Bridge border at the extreme east of the Caprivi Strip into Botswana. From here the road runs 64 km along the very top of Botswana's Chobe National Park to Kasane and the border with Zimbabwe. If you are only transiting though Chobe, you do not have to pay park fees, but keep your speed down as there are often elephant on this road. Once in Zimbabwe, it is only 70 km from Kasane to the town of Victoria Falls. If coming from Victoria Falls or Kasane to Namibia via Ngoma Bridge, it is best to leave Victoria Falls no later than 1530 and Kasane no later than 1630 to reach Ngoma Bridge by 1800 when the border shuts.

Sea

RMS St Helena is a cargo-passenger liner with a range of cabins from budget multi-share cabins to superior two-berth cabins, which sleep up to 128 people. The boat is the British-registered Royal Mail Ship that goes from Cape Town in South Africa, up the coast of Namibia via Lüderitz and Walvis Bay and then on to the island of St Helena, 1800 km northwest of Walvis Bay. The ship takes two days to reach Lüderitz, US$650-180; three days to Walvis Bay, US$1050-290; and two weeks to St Helena,

Border opening times

With Angola
Oshikango 0800-1800
Ruacana 0800-1800
Rundu 0800-1800
Omahenene 0800-1800

With Botswana
Buitepos 0700-2400
Impalila Island 0700-1700
Mohembo 0600-1800
Ngoma Bridge 0700-2400

With South Africa
Hohlweg 0800-1630
Rietfontein 0800-1630
Ariamsvlei 24 hours
Noordoewer 24 hours
Oranjemund 0600-2200 (permit holders only)
Velloorsdrif 24 hours

With Zambia
Wenella 0600-1800

US$2000-500. Rates are full board, except for drinks. The service also obviously runs in reverse and there are several departures each year. As the ship carries cargo, it can also transport 4WD vehicles and many South Africans with their own vehicles have used this service as an alternative and novel way of getting from Cape Town to Namibia. **Andrew Weir Shipping** operates the ship on behalf of the **St Helena** line, 17th Floor, 1 Thibault Square, Cape Town, T+27 (0)21-4251165; Shop 4, Baystar Mall, Sam Nujoma Avenue, Walvis Bay, T064-220495, www.rms.st.helena.com.

Touching down

Airport information

Hosea Kutako International Airport is 42 km east of Windhoek on the road to Gobabis, enquiries T062-540315-6. For those anxious about arriving in chaotic third world capital cities, have no fear. Hosea Kutako is calm, clean and free from thieves and hawkers, which is an appropriate introduction to the country. As a rough guide, a Boeing 747 empties (including baggage collection) in about 30 minutes and, should you be fortunate enough to be met, your welcoming committee can wave to you as you make your way towards immigration, through the glass 'fish bowl' walls of Nelson's café. The airport was completely refurbished in 2001 and facilities include two bureaux de change, several car rental desks, mobile phone rental desk, public telephones, large recently renovated parking area, and a petrol station.

If you are not picking up a car at the airport, pretty much any car hire company you have booked (which you should have done in advance, if you are planning to drive yourself) will be able to collect you or bring your car to the airport. On leaving the terminal you will be approached by taxi drivers offering their services. They are legitimate and reliable; expect to pay N$250-300/US$40-48 to central Windhoek, but fix the price in advance. There is no public bus or rail service but there are efficient shuttle services which charge about N$150/US$23 per person depending on how may people there are (eg **Elena Travel Services,** T061-244443, or **Marenko Shuttle,** T061-226331). They wait until they have two or more passengers and transport you to your chosen downtown destination as quickly as a taxi. Journey time to downtown Windhoek is about 30 minutes. You will pass through a police checkpoint; no need for alarm, they are only on the lookout for shabby vehicles and drunk, unbelted or unlicenced drivers. Enjoy your first glimpse of the straight roads and the camelthorn trees, and keep an eye out for kudu, warthogs, meercats, baboons, foxes and squashed snakes.

Touching down

Business hours **Banks:** Monday-Friday 0800-1530, Saturday, 0800-1000. **Businesses:** Monday-Friday 0800-1730, Saturday 0800-1300. **Government offices:** Monday-Friday 0830-1630 (most shut for lunch 1300-1400); **Post offices:** Monday-Friday 0830-1600, Saturday 0800-1200. **Shops and supermarkets:** Monday-Friday 0800-1800, Saturday 0800-1300.

Official time **Winter:** GMT + one hour (6 April-6 September); **Summer:** GMT + two hours (7 September-5 April). The Caprivi Strip stays on the same time as Botswana, South Africa and Zimbabwe.

Voltage 220/240 volts AC at 50 Hz, using three-point, round-pin (one 10 mm and two 8 mm prongs), 15-amp plugs. Check supermarkets and hardware stores in Windhoek for adaptors. Hotels usually have two round-pin sockets for razors and hairdryers, but take a battery razor in case.

Weights and measures The metric system is used.

Tourist information

In general, Namibia is fairly well provided with tourist information. Most towns have dedicated staff and offices and the staff at most of the accommodation options are more than helpful. Where you have a choice between a private information centre and the government one, the private one will tend to have more helpful and knowledgeable staff simply because they may want to try and sell you a tour, etc. If you are arriving in Windhoek there are a number of establishments in the city offering information (see page 78). These include the **Namibia Tourist Board,** which produces a number of publications including an excellent map showing all the minor road numbers in the country (essential if you are driving), and the **Namibia Wildlife Resorts,** which offers information about the parks and takes reservations for parks accommodation. Ideally, you should have arranged this well in advance, but head here for last-minute bookings. Of the many free publications available to tourists to Namibia, firstly take the (complementary) in-flight magazine for **Air Namibia** from the plane, *Flamingo* (www.flamingo.com.na), which has good Namibia travel articles and facts for visitors. Also look out for the free bi-monthly magazine *Travel News* (www.travelnews.com.na), which covers all aspects of travel in Namibia with some interesting ideas, as well as a tourist news update (new lodges, closures, HAN award winners, etc). ▸▸ *For tourist offices overseas, see page 17; local tourist offices are listed in the directory section of individual towns.*

Local customs and laws

Codes of conduct

Be sensitive to the numerous customs relating to behaviour when visiting tribespeople in their rural environment. These are identified in the relevant chapters. In 'normal' urban environments, there are no obvious differences from Europe/North America in dress, behaviour or customs. In conversation, especially in more rural areas, it is customary to engage in a few pleasantries before asking for help or a service. A handshake is almost always welcome (man to man); you will quickly master the three-grip handshake. Before asking whatever it is you want of a person in the street or a shopkeeper, take a moment to ask how they are, etc. While this may seem unnecessary, it greatly improves the likelihood and accuracy of the response.

Always ask before photographing local people.

If you are travelling from so-called 'liberal' countries, be prepared for the occasional uncomfortable conversation with bigoted males – the white immigrants from South Africa and Germany tend to be staunch conservatives, with old-fashioned lifestyles and opinions.

Dress

Dress in Namibia tends to be casual and most people on holiday wear shorts, sandals and a T-shirt. If you intend to do any game-viewing, wear green, muted browns and khaki colours as these are less likely to attract mosquitoes at dawn and dusk. In some of the more upmarket lodges, restaurants and bars you are expected to wear more formal clothes in the evenings, when trainers, sandals, jeans and shorts are not appreciated.

Prohibitions

Marijuana is fairly prevalent around Namibia, but remains firmly illegal, as are all narcotics. Drink-driving is a problem in Namibia, especially in the rural farming regions; although illegal, the laws are routinely ignored by locals.

Do be aware of the restrictions on access into the restricted Diamond Areas. The authorities take a dim view of trespassers, even if it is strictly a mistake, and there are very heavy fines imposed if you are caught. Note that because of the very hot summers, access to the Fish River Canyon is prohibited from September to April each year.

Tipping

Waiters, hotel porters, stewards, chambermaids and tour guides expect 10-15%. It is common practice to tip petrol pump attendants, depending on their service – up to N$5/US$0.80 for a fill up, oil and water check and comprehensive windscreen clean. When leaving tips make sure they go where you intend, there is no guarantee that kitty money gets to everyone. Photographing local people such as the Himba should be followed by a tip of some kind, which should always be negotiated first. If you are on a tour, your tour guide will arrange this.

Responsible tourism

Much has been written about the adverse impacts of tourism on the environment and local communities, especially in areas 'off the beaten track', where local people may not be used to Western conventions or lifestyles and where natural environments are sensitive. Namibia is a beautiful, dramatic and wild country but also a living, working landscape and a fragile and vulnerable place. By observing the simple guidelines outlined in the box on page 34 and behaving responsibly you can help to minimize your impact and protect the natural and cultural heritage of this wonderful country. Of course tourism can have a beneficial impact and this is something to which every traveller can contribute. Many national parks and game reserves are partly funded by entry fees paid by people who want to see the animals and plants. Similarly, tourists can promote protection of valuable archaeological sites and museums through their interest and entry fees. Also, some of the tour operators, guest farms and lodges fund conservation and community projects though fees taken from tourists, and tourism is the biggest formal employer in the country. However, where visitor pressure is high and/or poorly regulated, damage can occur. In Namibia access to certain areas of pristine wilderness is restricted by controls over the number of visitors, which in many cases is dictated by price. Having a high-price/low-impact policy over these wilderness regions means that, although only very wealthy visitors can enjoy them, their environment is protected from damage or overuse.

Namibia is the first country in the world to incorporate the protection of the environment into its constitution.

How big is your footprint?

The point of a holiday is, of course, to have a good time, but if it's relatively guilt-free as well, that's even better. Perfect eco-tourism would ensure a good living for local inhabitants, while not detracting from their traditional lifestyles, encroaching on their customs or spoiling their environment. Perfect ecotourism probably doesn't exist, but everyone can play their part. Here are a few points worth bearing in mind:

- Think about where your money goes, and be fair and realistic about how cheaply you travel. Try and put money into local people's hands; drink local beer or fruit juice rather than imported brands and stay in locally owned accommodation wherever possible.
- Haggle with humour and not aggressively. Remember that you are likely to be much wealthier than the person you're buying from.
- Think about what happens to your rubbish. Take biodegradable products and a water bottle filter. Be sensitive to limited resources like water, fuel and electricity.
- Help preserve local wildlife and habitats by respecting rules and regulations, such as sticking to footpaths and not buying products made from endangered plants or animals.
- Don't treat people as part of the landscape; they may not want their picture taken. Ask first and respect their wishes.
- Learn the local language and be mindful of local customs and norms. It can enhance your travel experience and you'll earn respect and be more readily welcomed by local people.
- And finally, use your guidebook as a starting point, not the only source of information. Talk to local people, then discover your own adventure.

Namibia also has a diverse range of peoples and for many visitors meeting and interacting with the colourful and intriguing cultural groups such as the Himba or Bushmen is a highlight of their trip. But interaction at all times must remain sensitive, sympathetic and polite and, if at all possible, conducted in such a way that both the tourist and the local people benefit. Don't just rock up to a Himba village and start taking photographs – how would you like it if someone knocked on your front door at home just to take a photo of you because you look different? Instead, visit the people through a guide; take an interest in learning about their lifestyles and share information about your own; don't push Western values or ideals; and above all respect their beliefs and behaviour. The **Namibia Community Based Tourism Association (NACTOBA,** see box, page 41) is doing much to support tourism initiatives amongst the local people and to ensure that some of the tourism revenue generated in the country gets back to basic levels. By earning from tourism, the poorer people who rely on the land for their livelihoods are more likely to protect their environments for the benefit of tourism and these projects are well worth supporting.

Finally, it is also important to respect local conditions. Namibia has a very limited supply of water and it is very important not to waste water. Always take a shower instead of a bath, don't let the tap run while brushing your teeth, and only wash your vehicles at official car washes (in the towns) as you are not permitted to wash cars anywhere else.

Safety

Generally speaking, Namibia is a safe country in which to travel, with low crime rates and a well-trained police force, although there are of course some exceptions. It is important to stress that although Namibia borders South Africa, crime and personal safety conditions are not the same and there is nothing in Namibia to compare with South Africa's urban danger.

Cities

As with all larger towns and cities in the world, care should be taken with valuables such as wallets and expensive jewellery when walking in the streets. Obvious rules like putting money safely away before leaving the bank and not leaving purses or wallets on tables in outdoor restaurants/cafés apply in Namibia as much as anywhere else. Pickpockets operate in the busy shopping areas of Windhoek by day. Recently, there have been isolated incidents where tourists have been mugged or cars broken into in Windhoek and Swakopmund. Travellers should therefore exercise caution, particularly at night and at weekends, when the central shopping districts of all towns generally become deserted and a lone traveller might be unlucky. Overall, common sense precautions will be sufficient to ensure that your holiday is not spoiled by any unpleasant incidents.

Beware of pickpockets on Independence Avenue, Windhoek.

Townships

All central and southern Namibian towns have townships, the largest being Khomasdal and Katutura in Windhoek. While by no means out of bounds to tourists, it would not be wise to wander into a township by yourself. On the other hand, if you know a local or have friends living and working in Namibia who know their way around, a trip to a township market or nightclub can be an interesting and rewarding experience. If you do have the chance to spend some time in a township, it will undoubtedly give you a different picture of the way a very large number of urban Namibians live (see page 84).

Getting around

Namibia is an enormous country and there are some vast distances through remote terrain to cover between sights. It does, however, have an excellent road network and, because of these remote locations, a very well-developed air service with almost 300 airstrips around the country. The public transport system, on the other hand, is very limited and, compared to other African countries whose roads are pumping with buses and shared vehicles, Namibia has only a few lonely buses travelling along the main arteries. For the visitor, the choices of exploring Namibia are on a tour, by expensive air safari, or to self-drive. Those on a budget could try hitching but they will wait for a very long time for a ride by the side of a stinking hot road. Travel details including car hire can be found under individual towns' transport sections.

Air

Be sure to get a window seat to fully enjoy the landscape.

Internal flights

Internal flights are the quickest way to get around the country. Namibia has almost 300 airstrips and most destinations are within two hours' flying time of each other. **Air Namibia** serves all the regional centres and has regular services between Windhoek and Lüderitz, Mpacha, Ondangwa, Oranjemund, Swakopmund and Walvis Bay, and between Walvis Bay and Lüderitz and Swakopmund. All internal flights arrive/depart from Windhoek's Eros Airport, which is next to the Safari Court Hotel complex, a 10-minute drive south from the city centre. Prices for flights change regularly but expect to pay in the region of around US$150 for a one-way flight between Windhoek and Lüderitz for example. » *See page 72 for the Air Namibia timetable.*

Charter flights

There are a number of small companies offering short sightseeing flights over the dunes, down to the Fish River Canyon, along the Skeleton Coast, out to the Kalahari for a 'Bushman experience', or to Opuwo for a visit to the Himba. Most of the charter planes in Namibia are Cessna 210s, which can carry a pilot and five passengers. The advantages of these planes is that the wings are above the windows, allowing for better sightseeing, they are fast over long distances and hardy enough to land on dirt runways. In the past, flights only attracted the top end of the tourism market, but today seeing the Namibian landscapes from the air is an inarguable highlight, and short sightseeing flights can work out as a reasonable expense for a group of four or

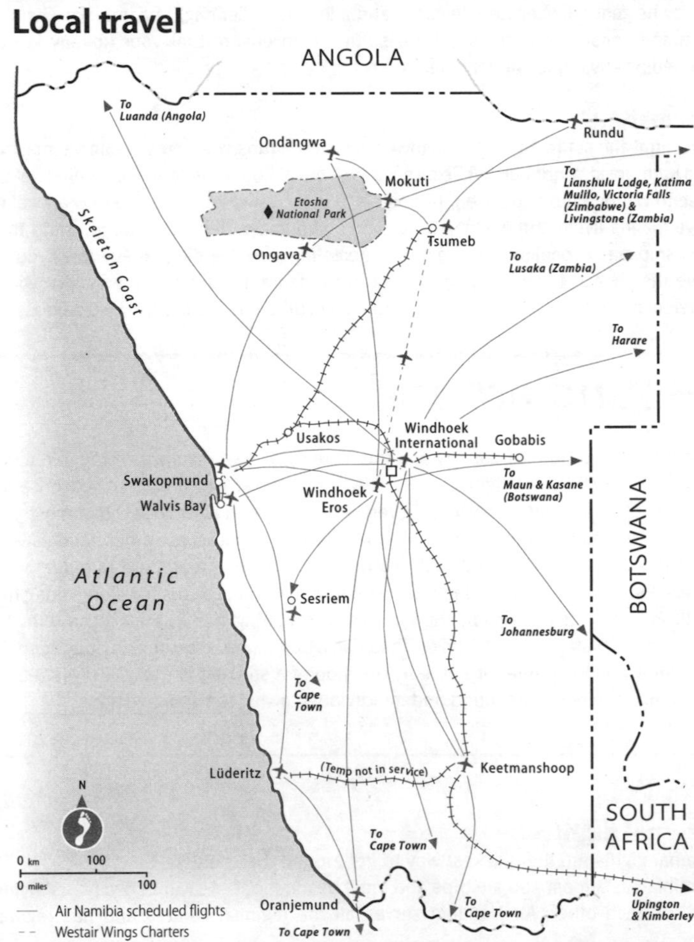

five people. For an example of costs, a one-hour flight, say over Sesriem and the coast, can work out at about US$150 per person if there are five people in the plane, but over US$360 per person if there are only two passengers. If there are only two of you the companies will endeavour to find other people to fill the plane. If you have more cash to splash, charter operators and tour companies can organize multi-day fly-in safaris to the remote regions, game parks and private guest farms and lodges with landing strips. Fly-in safaris offer a more expensive alternative to long road trips, especially for those visitors who are not accustomed to local road conditions. One of the many typical fly-in safaris on offer would be Windhoek-Sossusvlei-Swakopmund-Opuwo-Caprivi-Windhoek. A tour like this can be completed in only eight days or so, with most of the time spent on the ground exploring the sights and familiarizing yourself with the environment, rather than on the road. These can be combined with longer trips to Victoria Falls or Botswana. The tour operators will tailor a trip to your interests, and advise what is possible and what is over-ambitious. Prices for multi-day safaris from four days start at about US$4000 per person including flights and accommodation. The main charter companies are based in Windhoek, with a few others in Swakopmund. » *See also tour operators listed under Windhoek, page 99.*

Charter companies

Atlantic Aviation, T064-404749, www.flyinnamibia.com.
Bush Pilots, T061-248316, www.iwwn.com/bushpilots.
Comav, T061-227512, www.comav.com.na.
Desert Air, T061-228101, www.desertair.com.na.
Namibia Commercial Aviation, T061-223562, cjs@iway.na.
NatureFriend Safaris, T061-234739, www.naturefriendsafaris.com.
Pleasure Flights and Safaris, T064-404500, www.pleasureflights.com.na.
Sefofane Air Charters, T061-255735, www.sefofane.com.
Sunbird Safaris, T061-272090, www.sunbirdtours-namibia.com.
Westair Wings Charters, T061-221091, www.westwing.com.na.
Wings over Africa, Windhoek, T061-255001, Swakopmund, T064-403720, www.flyinafrica.com.

Rail

Few tourists use the Namibian railway service (**Transnamib**) because it is slow and serves few centres of interest to the overseas visitor. Once you have completed one journey by train you are likely to choose a bus for your next leg. The passenger trains that do run, however, are very cheap and have comfortable airline-style seats in air-conditioned carriages. Videos are shown and there are vending machines for snacks and drinks. Most services depart in the early evening and arrive at their destination the following morning. Trains stop everywhere along the way (thus their slow progress) and, given their main use is freight haulage, there can be a good deal of noise and shunting, often in the small hours of the morning. **Transnamib Starline Passenger Services** ⓘ *central reservations T061-2982032, www.transnamib.com.na. The office at Windhoek Train Station is open daily 0600-2000.* » *For Transnamib's timetable, see page 68.*

Luxury trains

Transnamib runs two luxury services from Windhoek. The **Desert Express** runs to Swakopmund and back twice a week. In fact it won the HAN award for excellence in 2004. Facilities on board the train include accommodation in 24 air-conditioned en suite sleeper compartments that are converted to lounges during the day, an elegant lounge carriage, and a dining car which serves three-course dinners. The experience doesn't come cheap at around US$250 (depending on season) per person, sharing, one way. Another service, the **Northern Desert Express**, runs to Etosha and there are several departures throughout the year. It leaves Windhoek in the morning, with a long afternoon stop (and wine-tasting tour) at Omaruru, then overnight on the train to Tsumeb; transfer by bus to Namutoni, afternoon game drives, overnight at Namutoni, morning game drive, lunch and back to Tsumeb to catch the return train to Windhoek. The round trip costs from US$400 per person, sharing, and depending on season. Reports have all been positive. The train is also equipped to take cars, so if you are on a self-drive trip, you can still enjoy the train and take your car with you! But this must be arranged in advance. For further details, see Windhoek travel section, page 104. **Desert Express Reservations** ⓘ *Windhoek Train Station, Bahnhof St, T061-2982600, www.desertexpress.com.na, Mon-Fri 0800-1700.*

Road

Bus

Namibia's long-distance buses are marginally more comfortable, somewhat more expensive and much quicker than the trains, but are still very limited in terms of destinations offered. **Intercape Mainliner**, T061-227847, www.intercape.co.za, is a South African company that runs luxury buses between Windhoek, Livingstone in Zambia and South Africa, stopping at any town of reasonable size en route. It also runs a service between Windhoek and Walvis Bay. For the budget traveller, this service is only of value for long journeys. Coaches are air conditioned, have toilets, some show videos and the crew will serve tea and biscuits. » *See timetable on page 70 and the box on page 29 for more details.*

Namibia has 5450 km of tarred road and 37,000 km of gravel road.

Car

Car hire More and more visitors are choosing to drive themselves around the country. This provides maximum flexibility and is often the only way to cram your itinerary into the time available without resorting to specialist travel agents and flights. There is a good choice of car hire companies, particularly in Windhoek (see page 102), and it is worth comparing the rates of a few before committing yourself. The best rates will be fixed if you make a firm booking several months in advance. If you leave car hire until you arrive in Namibia you may find it difficult to get a car and the rates will be high. Shop around on the internet for a car hire company that you like, offers good service, and is clear about what is and is not included in the price. Try to get a car that is no more than about two years old. Also get a full list of all equipment that is included in the price for you to check off when you pick up the car in Namibia. A 2WD car will cost in the region of US$50-70 per day depending on season and length of hire; a 4WD (necessary if travelling to remote areas) will cost US$90-160 depending on the season and whether a roof tent and camping equipment is included.

We cannot over-emphasize the dangers of driving at night.

Drivers must be at least 23 years of age (some companies stipulate 25) and need to have an international driver's licence, passport and credit card to hire a car in Namibia. For drivers accustomed to European roads, the traffic is virtually non-existent, but the roads are not without their dangers. It is not by chance that credit card deposits for damage and collision run into the thousands of Namibian dollars. Third-party insurance is included in the hire price but drivers are advised to take out extra insurance for 100% collision damage and loss waiver. The dangers of unexpected people/animals, poor roads and bad driving are considerable. » *See On the road, below, for further details.*

When collecting your vehicle, as well as checking it for bumps and scratches it is worth taking 10 minutes to familiarize yourself with it. Check the spare tyre (two are preferable) and how to use it. Is there a puncture repair kit and a pump? Do you know how to use them? What sort of fuel does it take? Do you have sufficient clearance for the terrain you are planning to cross? You don't want to be discovering a problem for the first time in an emergency, in the middle of nowhere.

Buying your own car If you plan to stay in the country for a while, buying your own car may be a sensible option. With the dry climate, most cars will be free from rust but, with the great distances to be travelled and rough gravel roads, even young cars may be a little tired and scratched. Windhoek (or, better still, Johannesburg or Cape Town) is the best place to buy or sell. In Windhoek, dealerships are concentrated around the John Meinert Street and Independence Avenue junction. Check the local press for private sales. Be sure to discuss the possibility of selling back to your dealer. Alternatively, if you are going to be spending several weeks or months in southern Africa consider buying a car on a buy-back scheme. There are companies that will sell you a car and sign a contract to buy it back at an agreed price once you have finished with it. Work out the costs, though, and compare them to long-term car hire. Sometimes the price difference is minimal and with the buy-back scheme you don't get the back up of a car hire company in the case of an emergency. The following websites are useful: www.drivesouthafrica.co.za, www.drivesouthernafrica.com, www.resqrentacar.co.za.

Hitch-hiking

Hitching is not generally recommended, simply because the distances in Namibia are vast, there are few people, and consequently few vehicles, and hitch-hikers may have some very long waits in the hot sun at the side of the road. It is a risky method of travelling, particularly if you are alone, in a hurry or inexperienced. If you do decide to give it a try, it is a good idea to walk or take a taxi to the edge of town (perhaps the last petrol station on the main road) and start hitching from there. As a general rule, a sign stating your destination is a good idea, as is standing at a junction or fuel station in full view, so that your hosts can give you a once over from close range before committing and have time to brake safely. Whatever the case, be sure to take some food and plenty of liquids with you.

The major problem facing hitch-hikers is the lack of traffic rather than security or the willingness of Namibians to give lifts.

Motorbike

Probably the only European bikers you will see will be bearded, tanned, trans-Africa adventurers, but for the tourist with a motorbike licence and experience at handling gravel roads it is possible to go on a guided motorbike tour of Namibia. **Gravel Travel Motorbike Adventures,** T+49-(0)5822-1717, www.gravel-travel.de, is a German operator offering guided safaris on its desert-modified Yamaha XT600Es. Another company that arranges motocycle tours in South Africa and Namibia is **Ayres Adventures Motorcycle Tours,** T+27 (0)83-3778855, www.ronayres.com. If you fancy a burn on a Harley, try 333 Airport Shuttle in Walvis Bay who have two Harleys to rent out, T064-206686, www.333.com.na. They are a stylish way to explore the coast, but they don't come cheap at US$200 a day and a whopping US$1500 deposit.

Driving

Driving is on the left side of the road and speed limits are 60-80 kph in built up areas, 80-90 kph on gravel roads, and 120 kph on tar roads. By law, you must wear a seat belt in the front seats at all times and have your driving licence and passport available for inspection. The police are very strict on drink-driving and checkpoints and speed traps with on-the-spot fines are employed. The distances to be travelled are massive, and must be done during daylight hours, so plan your overnight stops carefully. Away from the tarred highways, Namibia has an excellent network of gravel roads through some beautiful scenery, but if you intend to drive through some of the more remote regions, it is worth coming here prepared. In 2003 a German couple in their sixties hired a car from Cape Town and drove to Namibia where they broke down on a remote northwestern road. They were only found after a week. Tragically the husband had died and the wife was found delirious from thirst, hunger and the heat. If driving way off the beaten track go in a group of at least two vehicles and remember that mobile phone coverage is limited in very remote spots. When looking at a map of Namibia, remember all roads off the main highways are gravel, and although well maintained regularly by the big yellow graders seen all over the country, driving on gravel takes a bit of skill and care. This surface can be very slippery, especially if driving at speed, and there have been some serious accidents involving tourists in the past. When a car goes too fast on gravel, slight bends in the road cause the vehicle to slide, and over correction by the driver can cause an accident or roll. Also many of the gravel roads have quite a high camber so exercise caution when overtaking or passing an oncoming vehicle and watch that the car does not slide down to the edge of the road. In dusty conditions it is a good idea to put on your headlights so other road users can see you more easily. Although mostly tarred, the 'salt' roads along the coast can also be slippery, especially in the dense fog. Their foundation is gypsum from the desert which is soaked with brine, turning it into a surface as hard and smooth as tar. Also watch out for animals on the road, as kudu, springbok and warthog often graze along the side of the road and can leap into the road without warning. A 4WD is preferred, though most of Namibia's roads are passable in a normal saloon car, except in the wet when the dried up riverbeds that cross the roads fill with water. Southern Africans are great outdoors types and 4WD driving is a hugely popular pastime, but this is something few overseas visitors may have tried. Good 4WD companies are not going to look too favourably on hiring out their cars to complete novices. Consider doing a course in 4WD driving in your home country, or at least watch a video or buy a book, which greatly enhances confidence in driving around remote regions. A good basic mechanical knowledge is also useful in the event that you break down in the middle of nowhere.

Automobile Association of Namibia, T061-224201, available 24 hours, corner of Independence Avenue and Fidel Castro Street, Windhoek.

Be sure you have enough fuel to cover the distance you are planning to travel; there are often no petrol stations between main towns. Also, petrol stations do not accept credit cards, so you will have to budget sufficient cash for fuel as part of your day-to-day needs. On the whole, petrol stations are clean and efficient, often with a takeaway attached to them. An attendant will fill up your car while you fill up on provisions; a small tip is expected for efficient service (which includes cleaning windscreens).

Safaris

For the budget traveller, the best way to see the principal tourist attractions – albeit with a crowd and at a pace that may not be optimal – may be with one of the safari companies that operate from Windhoek and Swakopmund. See under tour companies in the relative sections, or choose an operator once there after discussion in the tourist offices and with other travellers in the backpacker hostels. Compare prices and itineraries carefully as you may spend the great majority of your time squeezed into a minibus. *See also Sport and activities, page 57.*

Some of the lodges in the Namib-Naukluft Region offer shuttle services from Windhoek; worth asking about if you don't want to drive.

Shared taxi

In the absence of a public transport network, entrepreneurs have stepped in with vehicles of greater or lesser safety, size and comfort. They are almost without exception serving the non-white market and run from town centre to town centre rather than to the tourist spots. Given this limitation, you are advised to make the

NACOBTA

The **Namibia Community Based Tourism Association** is a non-profit membership organization that supports local communities in their efforts to develop tourism enterprises and thereby gain income and employment. In their own words, they are "taking indigenous people and their environment seriously and adapting to local circumstances without feeling isolated or lost". NACOBTA was established in 1995. The central body not only provides source funding for new ventures, but takes care of marketing and lobbying for each enterprise, and provides training in guiding and tourism, business advice and reservations and admin systems. Essentially, the central body aims to free the local communities to concentrate on providing local, people-focused services. The NACOBTA projects are, to a greater or lesser degree, managing to direct some of the income generated from foreign tourists travelling to Namibia to the local community. Without them, most tourists would have no direct contact with non-whites, as virtually all lodges are owned and managed by whites. While this is a result of individual energy and expertise, it also highlights the division of wealth (land and capital) and opportunity (education and training) that exist in the country over a decade after independence. NACOBTA is one institution attempting to rebalance this situation.

A separate, but equally important, point is that without local communities benefiting from tourism, it will be very difficult to encourage them to 'preserve' their wildlife, let alone the trees and habitat that support it. NACOBTA is, quite literally, turning poachers into gamekeepers. There are three main groups of enterprises: Activites, Arts and Crafts and Accommodation. NACOBTA has currently got 30 members and the website is very comprehensive, listing each project in detail and offering online reservations. Further information: Weber Street, Windhoek, T061-221918, www.nacobta.com.na.

Karas Region (South)
Bruckaros Campsite, Warmbad Museum.

Kunene Region (Northwest)
Aba-Huab Campsite, Elephant Song Campsite, Hoadi Campsite, Kaoka Information Centre and Guides, Kunene Village Rest Camp, Okarohombo Campsite, Petrified Forest Guides, Purros Campsite, Purros Traditional Village, Twyfelfontein Guides.

Erongo Region (Northwest)
Brandberg Mountain Guides, Daureb Crafts (Uis), Hata/Angu Tours (Swakopmund), Mondesa Tours (Swakopmund), Spitzkoppe Restcamp, Ugab Wilderness Camping, Uis Information Centre.

Khomas Region (Windhoek)
Katatura Face-to-Face tours, Penduka Craft Cooperative.

North Central Region
Hippo Pools Campsite, Nakambale Museum and Restcamp, Tsandi Royal Homestead.

Otjozondjupa Region (Tsumkwe, the North)
Nyae Nyae Conservancy, Omatako Village Rest Camp.

Caprivi Region (Northeast)
Bumhill Campsite, Caprivi Arts Centre, Kubunyana Campsite, N//goabaca Campsite, Mashi Craft Centre, Nambwa Campsite, Salambala Campsite.

Hardap region
Daweb Cultural Group (Maltahohe), Garies Lodge.

most of their services and then hitch-hike the final stages, remembering of course that you may be in a remote spot and might have to wait a while for your lift. Whatever happens, start your day early; we would certainly not recommend getting into any stranger's vehicle after dark.

The price demanded for a journey will vary according to the quality of the vehicle, the distance travelled and, occasionally, how much of a 'ride' they think you can be taken for, but average about US$5 per 100 km. Check out what your fellow travellers are paying and agree to pay exactly that amount, on arrival.

Trucks

Overland truck safaris are a popular way of exploring southern and East Africa by road. They demand a little more fortitude and adventurous spirit from the traveller, but the compensation is usually the camaraderie and life-long friendships that result from what is invariably a real adventure, going to places the more luxurious travellers will never visit. The standard three-week overland route most commercial trucks take through southern Africa (in either direction) is from Cape Town up to Swakopmund via the Fish River Canyon and Sesriem for the Namib-Naukluft Park. The first weekend is usually spent in Swakopmund to enjoy the activities before heading north to the Etosha National Park via Damaraland, then into Botswana to visit the Okavango Delta and Chobe National Park and finishing in either Victoria Falls in Zimbabwe or Livingstone in Zambia to enjoy the activities around the Victoria Falls. This three-week trip can be combined with another three weeks to or from Nairobi via Zambia, Malawi, Tanzania and Zanzibar, and finishing in Kenya. Again the circuit continues with a two-week route into Uganda to see the mountain gorillas via some of the Kenyan national parks. There are several overland companies and there are departures along the circuit almost weekly from Cape Town, Livingstone/Victoria Falls and Nairobi throughout the year.

Overland truck safari operators

In the UK

Dragoman, T01728-861133, www.dragoman.co.uk.
Encounter, T01728-861133, www.encounter.co.uk.
Exodus Travels, T020-87723822, www.exodus.co.uk.
Explore, T0125-239448, www.explore.co.uk.
Kumuka Expeditions,T020-79378855, www.kumuka.com.
Oasis Overland, T01963-363400, www.oasisoverland.co.uk.
Phoenix Expeditions, T 01509-881341, www.phoenix-expeditions.co.uk.

In South Africa

Africa Travel Co, T021-5568590, www.africatravelco.com.
Wildlife Adventures, T021-7020643, www.wildlifeadventures.co.za.

Maps

The best map and travel guide store in the UK is **Stanfords** ⓘ *12-14 Longacre, Covent Garden, London WC2 9LP, T020-78361321, www.stanfords.co.uk*, with branches in Manchester and Bristol. **The Map Studio** ⓘ *T0860-105050, www.mapstudio.co.za*, produces a wide range of maps covering much of Africa. The **Namibia Tourist Board** produces a very good road map highlighting all the minor roads and road numbers. This is available from all their offices and very usefully it can also be found online in downloadable PDF format from the **Namibia Wildlife Resorts** website, www.nwr.com.na.

Sleeping

Until a few years ago, accommodation in most Namibian towns was a choice between a characterless hotel and a municipal campsite. Only visitors with their own transport made their way to the few isolated guest lodges and game farms. However, in the past five to 10 years, the standard and range of accommodation has improved enormously. Many hotels have been refurbished and a number of new top-end options have appeared. There is a wide variety of accommodation on offer from top-of-the-range game lodges and tented camps that charge US$150-1000 per couple per day, to mid-range safari lodges and coastal guesthouses with self-contained air-conditioned double rooms for around US$50-100, to dorm beds or camping for around US$10 a day. From 2004 it has been a requirement for every hotel, lodge, guest farm, campsite and backpackers hostel to be graded and registered by tourism inspectors to ensure minimum standards and to ensure that the establishment deserves the right to be registered with Namibia Tourist Board and promoted to tourists. If they don't meet the standards, establishments are not permitted to operate. Because of these moves, the quality of the tourism establishments in Namibia in every price bracket is very good, though not especially cheap. If the establishment does not match the stringent grades, it will not be registered and therefore cannot operate. (See also box on page 41). Reservations, especially in the parks, should be made well in advance if possible, particularly around the southern African school holidays, the longest of which is in December and January. Generally accommodation booked through a European agent will be more expensive than if you contact the hotel or lodge directly. Almost all of Namibia's hoteliers have embraced the age of the internet, and an ever-increasing number can take a reservation by email or through their websites. Very usefully, **Namibia Wildlife Resorts** who manage the accommodation in the parks, now offers an online booking service.

Backpacker hostels

Apart from camping, these hostels provide the cheapest accommodation in Namibia. Budget up to US$8 for a dorm bed and US$35 plus for a double room. Most are well-run communal houses. There is usually a well-equipped kitchen (with utensils, stove, fridge, cupboards, etc), a range of rooms including a dormitory, bar, lounge with library and TV, and often at least a notice board for travellers if not someone who can arrange budget safari tours and car hire, book local restaurants and advise on entertainment. For independent travellers, these places are the best source of information, companionship, parties and advice. The down side is that, far away from home, you may be tempted to remain within the isolated 'comfort' of a hostel; do not succumb, you came to Africa for more than this!

Bed and breakfast

Once confined to Windhoek, the B&B concept has really begun to take off in the past two or three years. Most operate along conventional lines, providing a full cooked breakfast, while others will have small kitchens where you can make your own. As with all B&Bs you will be staying in someone's home, which can be a good way to meet local (white) people and gain some insight into their lives and sentiments. As they represent an ill-defined category, in most sections of this book B&Bs are not separately identified; for further details, take a look at the **B&B Association of Namibia**'s website, www.bed-breakfast-namibia.com, for details.

Hotel price codes explained

L	US$300 and over	C	US$25-49
AL	US$150-299	D	US$10-24
A	US$100-149	E	under US$10
B	US$50-99		

Unless otherwise stated, prices refer to the cost of a double room, not including service charge or meals. In the case of dormitory beds and camping, the price, usually in the D-E range, is per person. In 2004 the Namibia Tourism Board introduced a Tourism Levy calculated at 2% of the bed and breakfast rate and included in the accommodation rates.

Camping and caravan parks

For visitors on a limited budget who wish to see as much of the country as possible, staying in campsites and using the money saved towards hiring a car is probably the best option. Camping is not a neglected end of the market as a good number of domestic and South African tourists spend their annual family holidays in caravans or large tents. In the most popular game reserves, even the tent and caravan pitches get booked up to a year in advance, so if you are in Namibia during the school holidays (see page 52 for dates) don't automatically assume there will be space at a campsite.

Be sure to stock up with provisions in the supermarkets and bottle stores of the major cities.

The popularity of camping has meant that there are good facilities at many parks, and most game farms have their own private campsites. Even the most basic site will have a clean washblock, many with electric points, lighting and hot water. For a small extra fee you can use electricity points at your site, particularly useful for caravans. Many will also have self-catering rooms, of varying quality and facilities, ranging from a single room with a couple of beds to chalets with several rooms and fully equipped kitchens.

Camping equipment can be bought in Windhoek and Swakopmund; look for **Cymot**, in particular, although supermarkets often stock useful supplies. Some items are rather dated and can seem heavy and cumbersome when compared to the latest hi-tech products from the USA and Europe. We would recommend you bring at least your own tent and sleeping bag (see also page 23). A bit of advance reading about the areas you plan to visit will help in deciding what else to bring. The cooking side of camping can be the most awkward for overseas visitors; however, many of the car hire companies hire out vehicles with everything you need including bulky items such as tables, chairs and cool boxes to small items such as cooking utensils and towels. If cost is no concern you can hire one with a built-in refrigerator, water tank, solar-heated portable shower, roof tents, long-range fuel tanks and all the smaller items necessary for a successful and safe journey into the bush. To save time do not leave the hire of a vehicle and camping equipment until you arrive in Namibia, you could easily have to wait for several days at the busiest time of year. Arranging everything in advance will enable you to head straight off from the airport, not wasting a minute in town. » *For details of camping shops to hire or buy equipment, and car rental companies, see pages 98 and 102.*

Somewhat surprisingly, the **Namibia Wildlife Resorts'** sites do not necessarily work out that cheap as visitors pay for entry for themselves (US$13 per person) and their vehicles (US$1.50) and then pay for the site (US$20-45) on top. These sites, each with a parking place, fireplace and usually a tap, take up to six or eight persons per site, so if there is a group the cost per person

Full details are included under the separate entries for the parks and reserves; prices are given in the box on page 46.

works out reasonably cheap, but if there are only two people it is expensive. Most of these campsites are adequate with clean ablution blocks with plenty of hot water, and some have communal kitchen facilities with sinks for washing up and sometimes a hot plate or stove. They do, however, get crowded in high season and there is very much the feeling of everyone being on top of each other. At some, such as those in Etosha, there is the presence of wildlife, despite the fact that the campsites are fenced. Smaller mammals such as jackals, mongooses and honey badgers regularly make their way through the fences on night-time raids of the rubbish bins and there have been many an occasion when a saucepan or shoe has been scurried away! Expect to pay US$8-15 per person in private campsites depending on location and facilities; as with the NWR campsites, the charges may be for a 'site' that can take several people and not per person, which works out expensive for two people.

Game farms and guest farms

Before independence, most visitors to Namibia originated from South Africa and visiting a working farm or game ranch was confined to those who knew the owner in some way or another. Over the past decade, well over 100 guest farms have sprung up all over the country. Some were farmers noting a gap in the market, and who now offer riding, hiking, good country food and relaxation in a tranquil, rural setting. Other farmers and entrepreneurs jumped on the bandwagon, looking simply to make easy money from passing tourists. Still others, hard hit by drought, looked at it as a lifeline for survival. There is now a fantastic range of excellent guest and game farms which offer a superb opportunity to experience the bush first hand, with guides who know their land and everything that lives on it intimately.

A number of game farms offer licensed trophy hunting, but as hunting is such a contentious issue, we have refrained from listing them in this book.

If you are coming from Europe, it is easy to be misled by the word 'farm'. In fact, most Namibian farms are vast tracts of land, typically as large as 10,000 ha (10 km x 10 km) used predominantly for livestock farming. The basic difference between a guest farm and a game farm is that the former will usually be a working commercial farm offering visitors the chance to experience it at first hand. There may be hiking or horse-riding trails, there will usually be a swimming pool, and often the opportunity for a tour around the farm. Although most guest farms will usually have some game such as springbok, gemsbok and warthogs, the 'game drives' offered will tend to be scenic, rather than wild, experiences.

A game farm or ranch on the other hand will usually have been especially stocked with wild game such as elephant, rhino, the carnivorous cats and the antelope on which they feed. Here the emphasis will be on game-viewing drives and possibly guided hikes in the bush, offering a first-hand view of the bush, the 'spoor' (footprints and droppings) and the animals themselves. A stay at a good game ranch does not come cheap but is well worth the expense for the unique experience it offers visitors.

There are over 100 farms in Namibia that accept guests. Aim to spend at least two nights on a working game or guest farm to enjoy the hospitality and experience.

Most guest farms cater for a limited number of visitors and provide an intimate, personable service. Generally your hosts will be very friendly, and will be happy to discuss any and everything about Namibia with you; on the other hand it is worth noting that a small number of farms are predominantly German speaking and not really geared for the non-German-speaking visitor. If you fall in the latter category you may prefer to avoid such places; calling in advance is the best way to ensure all is in order.

Guesthouses

These tend to be a cross between a hotel and a B&B and are generally found in Windhoek, Swakopmund and the towns of the central and southern regions. Guesthouses generally offer en suite twin rooms, sometimes with phone and TV, and

Accommodation prices for national parks and resorts

Admission fees
(NAM residents less 50%, and less 25% on accommodation).
General Adults US$13; adults (Southern Africa) US$9.50; children free; cars US$1.50. Central reservations and online bookings: T061-236975, www.nwr.com.na.

Ai-Ais Hot Springs
Luxury flat (2 bed) US$87
Flat (4 bed) US$84
Hut (4 bed) US$76
Camping per site US$24

Duwisib Castle
Camping per site US$19

Daan Viljoen
Luxury suite (4 bed with breakfast) US$119
Bungalow (2 bed) US$56
Camping per site US$19

Etosha National Park
Okaukuejo
Luxury suite (4 bed) US$178
Luxury bungalow (4 bed) US$110
Bungalow (4 bed) US$78
Bungalow (3 bed) US$49
Bungalow (2 bed) US$62
Standard room (2 bed) US$62
Camping per site US$36.50

Halali
Luxury suite (4 bed) US$156
Luxury bungalow (4 bed) US$90
Economy bungalow (4 bed) US$79
Standard room (2 bed) US$69
Camping per site US$37.50

Namutoni
Luxury suite (4 bed) US$168
Luxury flat (4 bed) US$107
Standard chalet (4 bed) US$94
Standard flat (4 bed) US$86
Standard room (2 bed) US$78
Economy room (2 bed) US$51
Camping US$38

Gross Barmen Hot Springs
Luxury suite (4 bed) US$138
Standard bungalow (5 bed) US$92
Standard bungalow (2 bed) US$52
Camping per site US$19

Hardap Dam Recreational Resort
Luxury suite (4 bed) US$127
Luxury bungalow (5 bed) US$75
Standard bungalow (5 bed) US$65
Economy bungalow (2 bed) US$52
Economy dormitory (12 bed, must be taken as one unit) US$86
Camping per night US$21

Hobas and Fish River Canyon
Camping per site US$27

with a small swimming pool. A hearty cooked breakfast is often included in the price which will range from US$40-90 per double room.

Guesthouses do not usually have bars or restaurants, although there may be a small fridge in your room and it may also be possible to arrange an evening meal by calling ahead. Smaller than your average hotel, guesthouses tend to offer a more personal service which some people enjoy; while others prefer the relative anonymity of a hotel where they can come and go unnoticed.

Hotels and lodges

Every medium-sized town has at least one small hotel, often providing the only comfortable bar and restaurant in town. Many of these hotels are family run and have been so since they were built. Under these circumstances the owners are not always that susceptible to any form of criticism about the way things operate. As more visitors from overseas stay in Namibia so many of the small hotels are improving their facilities and image.

Khorixas Lodge
(including breakfast in rooms)
Luxury double US$122
Semi-luxury double US$100
Standard double US$93
Camping US$8 per person

Lüderitz (Shark Island)
Light house (5 bed) US$125
Standard bungalow US$65
Camping per site US$19

Mamili National Park
No accommodation

Namib-Naukluft Park
Sossusvlei/Sesriem
Camping US$38

Naukluft
Camping US$19

Namib Desert Park
Camping US$17.50

Popa Falls Rest Camp
Standard hut (4 bed) US$68
Economy hut (4 bed) US$62
Camping US$5 per person

Reho Spa Recreational Resort
Luxury bungalow (3 bed) US$68
Economy bungalow (6 bed) US$60
Economy bungalow (5 bed) US$48
Economy bungalow (4 bed) US$41
Camping per site US$16

Skeleton Coast Park
North of Ugab River
(permit holders only)

Terrace Bay
(all include three meals per day)
Luxury suite (8 bed) US$473
Bungalows (2 bed) US$181
Economy bungalow (2 bed) US$129

Torra Bay
Camping US$21

West Coast Recreational Area
Mile 14, Mile 72, Mile 108 and
Jakkalsputz
Camping US$21

Von Bach Recreational Resort
Economy hut (2 bed) US$25
Camping US$19

Waterberg Plateau Park
Luxury suite (5 bed, DSTV, phone) US$136
Luxury bungalow (5 bed) US$88
Standard bungalow (3 bed) US$78
Standard room (2 bed) US$73
Camping US$19

Most small country hotels fall into the two-star category, offering basic, clean rooms, a restaurant serving three meals a day and a bar. Prices will generally range from US$40-90 per double room and usually include a full cooked breakfast. For such places it is not usually necessary to book in advance, although during school holidays it is possible that places en route to Etosha and in Swakopmund will get crowded. The more upmarket hotels in the cities and towns provide good service and international standards, though the very large ones can feel a bit anonymous. Most have several public areas, restaurants and bars, maybe a gym, swimming pool and underground car park, and usually conference facilities. For these you can expect to pay in the region of US$90-150 per double room. Under the new grading system introduced by the **Namibia Tourism Board**, a **hotel** must have at least 20 en suite guest rooms, whilst a **hotel pension** must have at least 10 but not more than 20 en suite guest rooms. To be called a **lodge** or **resort**, the establishment has to be located in a rural area or within a natural environment and must have at least five guest rooms, a dining room or restaurant, and provide recreational activities. Consequently a lot of places have had to change their names to fit in with the new criteria.

National parks accommodation

ⓘ *NWR Reservations Office, Windhoek: Independence Av near the clock tower, T061-236975-8, pro@nwr.com.na, open for information Mon-Fri 0800-1700; for reservations 0800-1500; Cape Town: Ground Floor, Pinnacle Building, (beneath the Cape Town Tourist Office), Burg St, T+27 (0)21-4223761, ct.bookings@nwr.com.na, Alternatively you can book online at www.nwr.com.na.*

Namibia Wildlife Resorts (NWR) is responsible for management of all the services at the Ministry of Environment and Tourism's 20 declared game reserves and parks. These range from the totally untouched Mamili National Park to the fully developed Gross Barmen Hot Springs Resort, complete with accommodation, restaurant and conference facilities. Most of the parks and resorts have some form of accommodation, which can be booked up to 18 months in advance. The accommodation is a mix of self-catering bungalows with two to six beds, well-serviced campsites and simple camps with overnight huts. Payment must be made in full if the accommodation is to be taken up less than 25 days from the date of the reservation. Visitors from overseas can organize their accommodation by phone, email or online through the website, and pay in advance with a credit card. This is worth considering, particularly for Etosha National Park, if you are going to be in Namibia during school holidays. Note that there are cancellation charges. Written reservations can be made up to 18 months in advance and phone reservations 11 months in advance. Entry fees into the parks are paid separately at the entrance gates on arrival.

During school holidays bookings are limited to three nights per rest camp in Etosha National Park, the Namib Naukluft Park and Terrace Bay.

On the whole, the accommodation is clean and in good working order, although some are in need of minor repair and almost everywhere could be made significantly more attractive with a coat of paint or an overhaul using local, natural materials. Overall, they represent reasonable value and in most cases the camps are located in beautiful positions. Chalets and cottages start at US$40-50 for a one bed unit to US$150 for a four bed unit.

Eating

Food

The staple diet for most black Namibians is a stiff maize porridge known as *pap*, served with a stew. Pap tends to be rather bland, but the accompanying stews can be quite tasty. Carnivores heading to Namibia should lick their lips as meat is plentiful, excellent and very cheap (by European standards). By contrast vegetarians should consider bringing supplements! Everywhere, German and Afrikaans influence prevails and you will soon realize why so many of them have that distinctive 'thick-set' physique. Supermarkets and butchers sell a wide range of sausages, kebabs, ribs and choice cuts (the *sosaties* are delicious), often prepared in the traditional way, and self-caterers are spoilt for choice in the variety of prepared meats. Restaurants tend to serve large, good-value, if fairly simple meals, with menus revolving around steak, chicken and schnitzel, plus good, fresh seafood (and shellfish, in season) by the coast. Meals in guest farms, lodges and houses are always plentiful and usually excellent. Even the breakfasts are meat based, with the usually fry up of eggs, sausage and bacon, but also savoury mince and *boerewors* (a fat spicy beef sausage). As just about everything is grown organically in this land (imported fertilizers being beyond the budget of most farmers) and levels of hygiene and standards of preparation are good, we advise being adventurous with dishes you may be unfamiliar with, particularly the local game specialities. Also try *biltong*, a heavily salted and sun-dried meat that is very moreish. By contrast to the mountains of meat, fresh produce can be hard to find in smaller towns, so vegetarians should stock up when they can; even in restaurants, the choice is

Restaurant price codes explained

ΨΨΨ	Expensive	over US$10
ΨΨ	Mid-range	US$5-10
Ψ	Cheap	under US$5

The price includes at least one main course with either a soft drink or a beer.

limited. For example a supermarket in a northern town may only get a delivery of fresh fruit and vegetables (usually imported from South Africa) once a week, so if you happen to visit on delivery day there will be a good selection but hardly anything will be left at the end of the week.

The braai

One of the first local terms you are likely to learn will be *braai*, which quite simply means barbecue. The *braai* is incredibly popular, part of the Namibian way of life, and every campsite, picnic spot and lay-by has a *braai* pit. Given the excellent range of meat available, learning how to cook good food on a *braai* is an art that needs to be mastered quickly and is part of the fun of eating in Namibia. Once you have established a core of heat using firelighters and wood or charcoal (charcoal is more eco-friendly and less smoky but wood makes for a wonderful fire), wrap up potatoes, sweet potatoes, squash, butternut, etc, in heavy-duty foil and cook them in the coals for an hour or so. Set beside a good piece of meat, with a sauce and a cold beer, and you will be living the Namibian dream.

A common indication of the ideal heat of a braai *to cook on is to hold your hand over the braai grill and count to ten. If you have to pull your hand back before ten it's too hot, any later than ten than it's too cold.*

An extension of the *braai* is the *potjie* (pronounced 'poy-kee'), literally a cast-iron pot with legs that sits on top of coals. This is the traditional cooking vessel of many African people and is wonderfully simple to use. Just brown your meat and throw in any vegetables and leftover meat, together with fruits, dried fruit, stock, chutneys and herbs and leave the pot to simmer away on the coals. Once prepared, apart from occasionally replenishing the coals, the dish requires no attention whatsoever. Allow to cook slowly so that all the flavours blend. A chicken *potjie* might take up to two hours to cook, lamb two to three, and oxtail perhaps six hours to reach its best. Most Namibian bookstores will have sections devoted to *braai* and *potjiekos* (*kos* is food in Afrikaans).

Drink

Namibia's tap water is treated and safe to drink, though does have rather a metallic taste due to the treatments used. Bottled water is widely available as are a number of good brands of soft drinks and juices, many are part of the Ceres or Liquifruit range imported from the fruit-growing regions of South Africa. The lager in Namibia is excellent, as you would expect given the German heritage. The prize-winning **Windhoek Lager** is made with mineral water and is very tasty. Other locally brewed beer is **Tafel**, and South African **Castle** lager and **Black Label** are also common. Germany's famous **Beck's** beer has been brewed under licence in Namibia since 2000. A 330 ml bottle will cost you no more than US$1.70 from a bottle store and not much more in most bars. Wine is plentiful and cheap given that it is all imported from South Africa, and some of the bottle stores and restaurants even in the rural areas offer a selection of wine that would rival a wine shop in Cape Town. The Afrikaans influence means that low-grade brandy is available everywhere (ask for a **Klipdrift** and coke – 'klippies and coke' – in a bar and see how you go).

You will have no problem finding a drank-winkel *(Afrikaans for bottle store) in every town.*

Namibian braai recipes

Butternut soup
1 small butternut cut in 1-inch squares
1 tsp ginger, ground (crushed if fresh)
1 tsp salt
1 tsp curry powder
1 cup cream or milk
Cover butternut with water and boil, together with all ingredients except cream, until soft. Mash. Return to the heat for a couple of minutes, add cream and allowing to heat through.

Chicken potjie (serves 2)
500g chicken
oil
1 onion, chopped
1 clove garlic, crushed
carrots, diced
sweet potatoes, cubed
celery
dried peaches
1 cup white wine, ½ cup water
seasoning
Fry chicken with oil, onion and garlic until brown. Add (in order) layers of carrots, sweet potato, celery, peaches and seasoning, pour in wine and stock, cover and leave to simmer gently for one hour. Do not stir, the layering is important. Serve with rice. This dish has long been the local method of using up whatever leftovers and produce that is available, so be bold and perfect (even name!) your own *potjie*, using your choice of meat and whatever vegetables you have to hand: chillies, mushrooms, tomatoes, squash, parsley, leeks, apple, dried fruit, etc.

Stuffed potatoes
Wrap clean potatoes in foil (shiny side in) cook deep in the coals of the fire for one hour, remove, unwrap, scoop out some flesh and refill with your favourite filling. (such as tuna and mayonnaise, mixed with a shredded carrot, onion, curry powder, paprika and lemon juice; ham cubes and cottage cheese, with black pepper; home-made sour cream (lemon juice and long-life cream) mixed with tinned oysters or mussels and black pepper; fish (preferably smoked) mixed with cocktail sauce and lemon juice.

Ratatouille (serves 2)
1 onion, chopped
1 green pepper, chopped
1 clove garlic, crushed
oil
½ small carrot, diced
1 tin chopped tomatoes
1 courgette, sliced
salt and seasoning
Fry onion, pepper and garlic until soft, add the rest and simmer until tender (you may have to add a little water).

Quick braai sauce/marinade
½ cup ketchup
1/4 cup Worcester Sauce
1 tbsp chutney
1 tsp mustard powder
½ cup vinegar
1 tbsp oil
1 clove garlic, crushed
1 tbsp sugar
½ cup cream
Mix all ingredients together and simmer for five minutes; use as a marinade for any meat dish.

Cowboy dampers
250g self-raising flour
1 tsp baking powder
pinch salt
little water
30 g margarine
Work all ingredients into a sticky dough. Whittle a stick (multi-pronged if you want) to get a clean end. Wrap a fingerful around the end of the stick and bake over the fire. Serve with jam as a simple 'dessert'; or with savouries (see potato fillings, above) as a starter.

Bottle stores are open Monday to Saturday 0900-1800. You are unable to buy drink from shops in the evening or on a Sunday when it is illegal to sell alcohol. All booze is available at the bottle stores, whilst supermarkets are only permitted to stock wine. At the end of each month you will see queues of Namibians withdrawing their wages and going straight to the bottle store. Alcohol abuse is a serious problem in the country. Drink-driving is also a major problem, so take extra care over the last weekend of the month.

Entertainment

Bars and clubs

Although Windhoek and Swakopmund have a few bars worth exploring and a couple of nightclubs, on the whole, Namibia is not the place to come to for nightlife. Outside of Windhoek and Swakopmund, it is restricted to a few hotel bars which only really get going at weekends and on the major holidays. On these evenings you'll mingle with beer-bellied farmers in their trademark khaki shorts and shirts and *vellies* (leather boots) speaking in English, Afrikaans and some in German.

You will be surprised at how quiet towns become at night; the locals mostly favour TV and early nights.

Cinema

Only Windhoek and Swakopmund have large, comfortable cinemas which show international releases. The main cinema in Windhoek, **Ster-Kinekor** (five screens), is located in the Maerua Park complex; the cinema in Swakopmund is the **Atlanta** (three screens). Admission is around US$5 per person. There are smaller cinemas (**Paradiso**) in Ondangwa and Oshakati as well.

Performing arts

The larger towns often have shows, jazz and local dance performances. They rarely publish a schedule more than a month in advance and usually restrict performances to weekends. Ask at local tourist information centres or consult the town's monthly magazines for details. Latest details of theatre, movies, music and art are posted in the newspapers. In Windhoek, there are regular performances at the **National Theatre of Namibia** (NTN) on Robert Mugabe Avenue, involving the Windhoek Symphony Orchestra and African music groups, as well as ballet and plays. Additional events are hosted by the **Franco-Namibian Cultural Centre** at the College for the Arts in Fidel Castro Street, as well as at the **Warehouse** in the Old Breweries Building on Tal Street. Many of these events are performed by students at the College of Arts, the Performing Arts Department of the University of Namibia and the Nedbank Theatre School.

Festivals and events

Public holidays

1 Jan New Year's Day.
21 Mar Independence Day.
Mar-Apr Good Fri and Easter Mon.
1 May Labour Day.
4 May Cassinga Day.
20 May Ascension Day.
25 May Africa Day.
26 Aug Heroes' Day.
7 Oct Goodwill Day.
10 Dec International Human Rights Day.
25 Dec Christmas Day.
26 Dec Boxing Day/Family Day.

Festivals

Apr-May Windhoek Carnival (last week of Apr and first week of May); Rundu Barge Carnival.
Jun Holiday and Travel Expo, Küska Carnival in Swakopmund.

Aug **Maherero Day**, Okahandja, on the weekend closest to 26 Aug. Thousands of Herero people gather in traditional dress for a memorial service to their chiefs. This is a spectacular and fun occasion and worth visitiong if you are going to be in Namibia around this time. Tours are often arranged from Windhoek.
Oct **Oktoberfest**, usually held at the Swakopmund Football Club on the second week of Oct.
Nov **Enjando Street Festival**.

School holidays

Mid-Dec to mid-Jan; mid-Apr to early May; early Aug to early Sep.
www.natron.net has precise dates for Namibian school holidays and **www.routes.co.za** has dates for South African school holidays.

While seemingly trivial, the dates of Namibian and South African school holidays can have a significant bearing on your visit. Not only are prices often higher, but most of the popular destinations become fully booked. In Swakopmund over Christmas there simply won't be anywhere to stay if you have not made an advance reservation. This also applies to national parks accommodation in late Aug, in particular the 3 camps in Etosha National Park.

Shopping

African **art and crafts** are of widely varying quality and can be surprisingly expensive in Namibia, given that many are imported from African countries further north. Sculptures, baskets, ceramics and other souvenirs start as curios sold at roadside stalls but as the quality and craftsmanship improves these products are reclassified as art with prices to match. Animal products made from ivory and reptile skins are on sale in Namibia but if you take them back home you could well fall foul of CITES regulations. There are a number of excellent craft and curio shops in Windhoek, but don't expect any bargains when looking at the quality products.

Further details of shops and craft centres can be found under individual towns.

Items unique to Namibia include the exceptional **wool** of Namibia's hardy, desert-reared karakul sheep which is woven into **clothing** and **carpets,** often with attractive local and animal designs. These items are also named under their trade name of **Swakara** (South West African Karakul). There are furriers in Windhoek and Swakopmund, and weavers in Dordabis and Karabib.

Other locally produced goods are **leather shoes.** Every farmer, tour guide and hiker in the country will wear his vellies – short boots made from kudu or gemsbok leather which are durable and comfortable. The best place to buy these is at the **Africa Leather Creations** shop in Swakopmund which replaces the former Swakopmund Tannery.

Namibia is of course a good place to buy **diamonds** at a good price. Each diamond retailer is a member of the **Jewellery Association of Namibia,** a programme sponsored by the Diamond Trading Company and the Diamond Board of Namibia. Diamonds have been mined in Namibia for almost a century but they have only been polished here since 1999. The polished product is marketed under the banner **Namibian Manufactured Fine Diamond.** There are a number of good jewellers in Windhoek and Swakopmund, and designs are very contemporary. When purchasing a diamond remember the four Cs; cut, colour, clarity and carat. Only buy diamonds from a licensed dealer, as it is illegal to buy uncut or not polished diamonds in Namibia.

There are four main regional **handicraft** centres in the country, produce from all of which can be found at reasonable prices in Windhoek in the **Namibia Craft Centre** next to the Warehouse Theatre, Tal Street. In the south, **Gibeon** is a centre for embroidery, producing attractive black-backed cotton embroidery work. The

Bushmen of remote east Bushmanland produce colourful and intricate beadwork. Baskets, woodcarving and simple pots are produced in the Kavango and Caprivi regions, with the greater abundance of palms, wood and clay (go to the **Caprivi Arts Centre** in Katima Mulilo for the country's best selection). In the northwest, centred on Opuwo and Epupa, the Himba have learned to adapt their traditional costumes and jewellery into attractive and intricate designs, using leather, metal, plastic and wood. Shop opening hours are usually Monday to Friday 0830-1700 and Saturday 0830-1300. » *For information about VAT refunds, see page 21.*

Sport and activities

Namibia has good opportunities to get active and there is a variety of adventure activities on offer. Around Swakopmund there are a number of ways to explore the dune fields on land and by air, there are some challenging hikes in the south of the country, and the coast offers boat trips to see seals and penguins. » *Details about local operators are given in the Activities and tours sections of each chapter.*

Namibia has 26 parks and reserves which cover approximately 15% of the country.

Ballooning

With virtually year-round clear blue skies and warm sunshine, Namibia is an ideal place to go ballooning. A one-hour trip over the desert at Sossusvlei is a favourite with many people, and there are a number of guest farms which also offer balloon safaris. The only drawback is the expense – a one-hour trip costs around US$400 per person, champagne breakfast included. » *See page 285 for a description of a balloon trip over Sossusvlei or visit www.namibsky.com.*

Birdwatching

With a wide range of habitats from coastal wetlands or savannahs to riverine forest, Namibia is home to over 630 species of bird. Of these, 14 species are near endemic including the white-tailed shrike, Carp's black tit, Hartlaub's francolin and Ruppell's korhaan. Birdwatchers should head for the parks and reserves along the Caprivi Strip, which has the highest concentration of birds in the whole country, and also to the wetlands of Walvis Bay and Sandwich Harbour, which are some of the most important coastal wetlands in Africa. Here, pelicans and flamingos are common and this is the breeding ground of the endangered Damara tern, while the nearby dunes are home to the Gray's lark and the dune lark. These last three species are endemic to Namibia. Visit www.africanbirdclub.org for more regional information. This organization rates the Caprivi Strip in its top 10 birding sites in Africa.

Boat cruises

There are a number of tour operators along the coast at Walvis Bay, Swakopmund and Lüderitz offering cruises on the ocean to spot dolphins, seals and penguins. See under the relevant chapters for details. The cool Atlantic is home to two species of dolphin, the heavyside dolphin, which favours the inshore bays, and the bottlenose dolphin, which is sighted usually between August and March. Sea kayaking is also available on the Walvis Bay Lagoon which is ideal for birdwatching and getting close to seals and dolphins.

Canoeing and whitewater rafting

Whether it's a casual 30-minute paddle on the Zambezi or a fully fledged expedition down the Kunene or Orange rivers, a canoe trip on one of Namibia's perennial rivers is great fun. For wildlife enthusiasts, gliding down the river in a canoe is an excellent way of getting a close look at birds and game without frightening them away. A number of organizations (see below) offer the chance to shoot the rapids along the Kunene and Orange rivers. Prices are reasonable, with a four- or five-day trip starting at around US$300 all inclusive.

Whilst most of the Kunene flows gently, at Ondorusso and Enyandi the river loses height rapidly and produces some Grade 2-4 rapids.

All operators of Orange River canoe safaris are headquartered in Cape Town: **Felix Unite**, T+27 (0)21-4255181, www.felixunite.com, the original and best, also offers a fabulous Kunene trip, taking in the highlights of northern Namibia on the way (five days on the river). The competition is led by **River Rafters**, T+27 (0)21-9759727, www.riverrafters.co.za, but take a look also at www.rafting.co.za, and www.wildthing.co.za. The **Kunene River Lodge**, www.kuneneriverlodge.com (see page 213) also offers half-day rafting trips down the Ondorusso Gorge and longer five-day trips from Hippo Falls to Epupa Falls.

Diving and caving

Scuba-diving is run through the **Namibian Underwater Federation** (NUF), T061-238320, theo@schoemans.com.na, which recommends that all divers are experienced, as sea temperatures are low (9-17°C). The best region for ocean diving is along the coast between Lüderitz and Spencer Bay where conditions are best between December and May with visibility ranging from 3-10 m. There is some fascinating diving available in Lake Otjikoto, near the eastern gate to Etosha, where a retreating German army dumped much of its weaponry in 1915. The lake bed has been declared a national monument. Some of the items have been landed and are shown in the Tsumeb Museum, but there is a great deal still underwater. Additionally, the Dragon's Breath on Haruchas Farm (between Grootfontein and Tsumeb) is thought to be the world's largest underwater lake. Groups must organize their own gear, transport and permission and, needless to say, should be highly experienced.

There are over 100 caves in Namibia, though only a few have been explored. For more information visit **National Museum of Namibia** website, www.natmus.cul.na.

Flying

There are numerous charter companies and air taxi operators that will happily take paying guests on scenic flights over the dunes and mountains, along the coast to the inaccessible wrecks and adapted wildlife that live there. Details of some are given on page 35, but a local pilot can usually be arranged through any upmarket lodge or hotel. Most pilots train in South Africa, and there are no formal facilities for overseas visitors to learn the trade within Namibia; rather, you will be enjoying the services of a local pilot and his machine. **Pitts Special**, T081-2482545, pits@mweb.com.na, has two aerobatic planes with open cock pits, one based in Swakopmund and one in Windhoek, and it offers short rides in the single seat behind the pilot which includes loops, rolls and spins – very exciting.

Game fishing

Extremely popular with Namibians, fishing trips can be organized either from Walvis Bay, Henties Bay or Swakopmund. The cold, clean waters of the South Atlantic provide rich feeding grounds for a wide range of species (refer to the Swakopmund section, pages 246 and 249, for specific fishing excursions and tour operators). Be aware that there are hundreds of regulations restricting location, season, methods, species and catch sizes, with significant penalties imposed on those who contravene them. Information is available from the local tourist and MET offices. The best time of the year for angling on the coast is from November to March, whilst the angling season on the Zambezi, Linyati and Okavango rivers is August to December and most fisherman go to these rivers on the hunt for tiger fish.

Hiking in the bush

As experienced walkers will know, good preparation is the key to a successful and enjoyable hike. It is also important to remember that, however short or easy a walk may appear to be, walking in the bush is not like going for a stroll in the park – a few basic steps should be followed. Below is a short checklist of equipment and guidelines to hiking in the bush:

Day hikes Good walking boots or shoes; sunhat; minimum of two litres of water per person; first aid kit; penknife; trail snacks (peanuts, *biltong*, dried fruit); binoculars, camera and birdbook/gamebook; toilet paper; matches to burn paper.

Additional overnight gear
Sleeping bag; fleece or equivalent top (even in summer); torch; lightweight camping stove (it is not always permitted to collect firewood); matches/lighter/fire-lighters; dehydrated food (pasta, instant soups etc).

Tips
- Don't leave litter or throw away cigarette butts.
- Leave everything as you find it; don't pick plants or remove fossils or rocks.
- Stick to marked trails especially in the bush – it's easy to lose your way.
- Camp away from waterholes so as not to frighten game away.
- Never feed the animals.
- Remember, in the southern hemisphere the sun goes via the north not the south.

Gliding

Namibia is reputed to be one of the best places in the world for gliding due to near perfect atmospheric conditions. Near Mariental is the **Bitterwasser Flying Centre and Lodge**, T063-265300, www.bitterwasser.com, which caters expertly for proficient gliders (and can arrange transport of equipment from Europe). During the season (November to February), you will be lucky to find accommodation on site. You may be able to occupy the passenger seat for a fee (although you'll need a strong stomach). Peak season is December to January, longer if the rains are late. At this time, the centre fills up with European enthusiasts. Numerous '1000-km triangles' are flown, and soaring altitudes are 2000-4500 m.

Golf

Golf may not be an adventure sport in many people's eyes, but played in the searing heat, off the desert sand, with endless dunes in the background, it must be one of the more unusual rounds to play, so it gets our vote. The two best-known courses are at the **Windhoek Country Club**, T061-2055911, www.legacyhotels.com, and, near Swakopmund, the **Rossmund Golf Course**, T/F064-405644, rossmund@iafrica.com.na, originally built for use by mineworkers but now open to visitors. The course is one of five registered all-grass desert golf courses in the world. These are the only two grassed 18-hole courses in the country; both are challenging, clubs can be hired, there are club houses with bar and restaurant. Other courses (many in poor condition) are detailed in the relevant sections.

Hiking

For those visitors interested in experiencing the bush at first hand, there are excellent bush hikes in Namibia, whatever your experience and level of fitness. For the uninitiated, walking in the bush is an excellent way of getting a close look at Namibia's diverse flora and fauna, and whether you walk for an hour or a day, you are sure to see something new and interesting. Most parks and many guest farms have well-marked trails suitable for inexperienced walkers. For a more in-depth experience, enquire locally about guides, who can fill in the detail on plants, birds and game in what might be a new and unfamiliar environment. Visit **Namibia Wildlife Resorts**, www.nwr.com.na, for information about hikes in the national parks.

For the experienced hiker there is the challenge of the Fish River Canyon (see page 331), Ugab River (see page 257) and Naukluft hiking trails (see page 282), all of which require high levels of fitness and a willingness to carry everything necessary with you on your back. At an intermediate level there are fantastic hikes in the Naukluft Mountain Park (see page 284), at the Waterberg Plateau Park (see page 125) and in the south near Aus for the Namib Feral Horse Hiking Trail (see pages 317 and 315). Finally, for those people not wishing to get too serious, there are rewarding but manageable hikes at Daan Viljoen Game Park near Windhoek (see page 106) and easy trails around the base camp at Waterberg Plateau. » *For further details, see under individual hikes in the relevant chapters.*

Horse riding and camel safaris

Reitsafaris Namibia, T061-250764 www.natron.net/reitsafaris, offers the 400-km Namib Desert Ride which they have completed over 50 times in the past 10 years, despite it being ranked as one of the toughest horse trails in the world. The route runs from the Khomas Hochland across the gravel plains of the Namib-Naukluft Park, ending on the beach in Swakopmund 12 days later. **Reitsafaris** also has 25 camels and offers a number of camel trails lasting between one and five days, where you can either hike alongside the camel or ride on top. Visit www.cameltrails.iway.na. For the less experienced **Okakambe Trails**, T064-402799, www.okakambe.iway.na, just outside of Swakopmund, offers two-hour sunset and moonlight rides into the desert for beginners as well as experienced riders, and can also arrange multi-day rides. **Desert Homestead and Horse Trails**, near Sesriem, T063-293243, www.deserthomestead-namibia.com, offers sunrise rides which include a full breakfast and sunset rides into the desert with gin and tonics. There are also plenty of horse-riding opportunities on the many privately owned guest farms, where an experienced hand will guide you as part of a multi-day safari or a simple scenic/game ride. We have tried to highlight the farms that offer this in the text, but even if you are just passing through it is worth asking at any farm should you be interested in a ride.

Microlighting

Microlighting, whether as an experienced pilot or first timer, is available for the brave and provides a fantastic opportunity to see game and nature from a new perspective. **Adventure in Namibia**, T061-244443, www.namibweb.com/micro, offers 30-minute flights over Damaraland with the possibility of seeing desert elephant from the air.

Off-road driving

In a country that offers varied and challenging terrain, stunning landscapes, uncharted expanses, remote wilderness campsites, isolated rural communities and plentiful game, it comes as no surprise that off-road driving is one of Namibia's most popular pastimes. There are many 4WD trails on the guest farms, and several companies have recently been granted concessions to take guided 4WD trails through the dunes between Lüderitz and Walvis Bay, an area of the Sperrgebiet, access to which was formerly forbidden. As well as the 4WD tours arranged by nearly all of the car hire companies, we recommend **Uri Adventures**, T061-231246, www.uriadventures.com, for an opportunity to take specialized, Namibian-made, 2WD, off-road vehicles (known as 'Uris' which means jump in the Nama language) along riverbeds, rocky ground and stretches of dune desert, in multiple-day tours. Its most popular routes travel from Windhoek to Swakopmund, taking three to four days across the mountains and desert. However, it has itineraries of up to 14 days, taking in the main sites and covering considerable ground.

Paragliding

Namibia has some of the clearest conditions and best thermals in the world. The dune belt between Swakopmund and Walvis Bay is a favourite spot, especially the dunes overlooking Long Beach (Langstrand). The southwesterly winds here offer an ideal 'lift' and once in the air there are spectacular views of the ocean and dune field. The **Namibia Paragliding School** offers introduction courses that take half a day and include at least two flights, a basic pilot course and a tandem flight. Contact Alexander van der Stauch, T064-403473, abstauch@iway.na, or go through one of the booking offices in Swakopmund. This excursion costs in the region of US$100.

Quad-biking

A number of lodges and guest farms offer quad-biking and usually no previous motor biking experience is needed. The most popular of Namibia's quad-bike trails is in the dune field outside of Swakopmund (see Swakopmund for details of operators). There are two types of bike you can choose from. For those who are a little unsure of their biking prowess there are 160 cc semi-automatic bikes. Those who wish to go hell for leather and have some idea of what they are doing can ride the 200 cc manual quad-bikes. Helmets, goggles and gloves are provided. Tours are multi-guiding with slow and fast groups in the same tour, catering for both the adrenalin seeker and the complete novice. The route follows the crests of the dunes and there are some very steep ascents and descents. The full ride takes about two hours and covers 35 km. Expect to pay in the region of US$70-80 for a two-hour ride.

Safaris

Game viewing There are a number of conservation and wildlife watching areas in Namibia, some owned by the government, and some in the private sector such as local farmers and local communities. Namibia's national parks and game reserves are managed by the **Ministry of Environment and Tourism (MET)** and are run by **Namibia Wildlife Resorts**. The majority of game viewing in Namibia's national parks is undertaken independently. With the exception of Etosha in peak season, the reserves are uncrowded and have an extensive network of gravel roads which are laid out to provide access to waterholes, hides and the various different ecosystems within a park. ▸▸ *See under individual national parks and reserves for further details.*

As visitors are left to their own devices to such a great extent it is a good idea to buy some of the wildlife identification books which are available in bookshops and camp shops. Best viewing is early in the morning and late in the afternoon. The midday heat is usually too intense for the animals, who rest up in thickets for most of the day. The best season for viewing is winter (July-October) when the lack of surface water forces animals to congregate around rivers and waterholes. The height and thickness of vegetation is much less at this time of year, making it easier to spot wildlife. The disadvantage of winter viewing is the relatively weak condition of the animals and harshness of the landscape. Summer weather, from November to January, when rain is expected, is the best time of year for the animals. They will be in good condition after feeding on the new shoots and you might be lucky enough to see breeding displays. In late February and March there is a chance of seeing new offspring in green and lush surroundings, but the thicker vegetation and the wider availability of water mean that the wildlife is more evenly spread throughout the park and therefore more difficult to spot.

Driving around endlessly searching for animals is not the best way to spot many of these creatures. While speed limits are often 40 kph, the optimum speed for game viewing by car is

Don't forget your binoculars and spare film or memory card.

around 15 kph. Drives can be broken up by stops at waterholes, picnic sites and hides. Time spent around a waterhole gives you an opportunity to listen to the sounds of the bush and experience the rhythms of nature as game moves to and from the water.

Namibia's game reserves are well organized; following the few park rules will ensure an enjoyable stay. Most parks are only open to visitors during daylight hours, the camp leaflets will give you the details of seasonal changes, so it is important to plan your game-viewing drive so that you can start at first light and return before the camp gates shut just before dark.

National parks & reserves

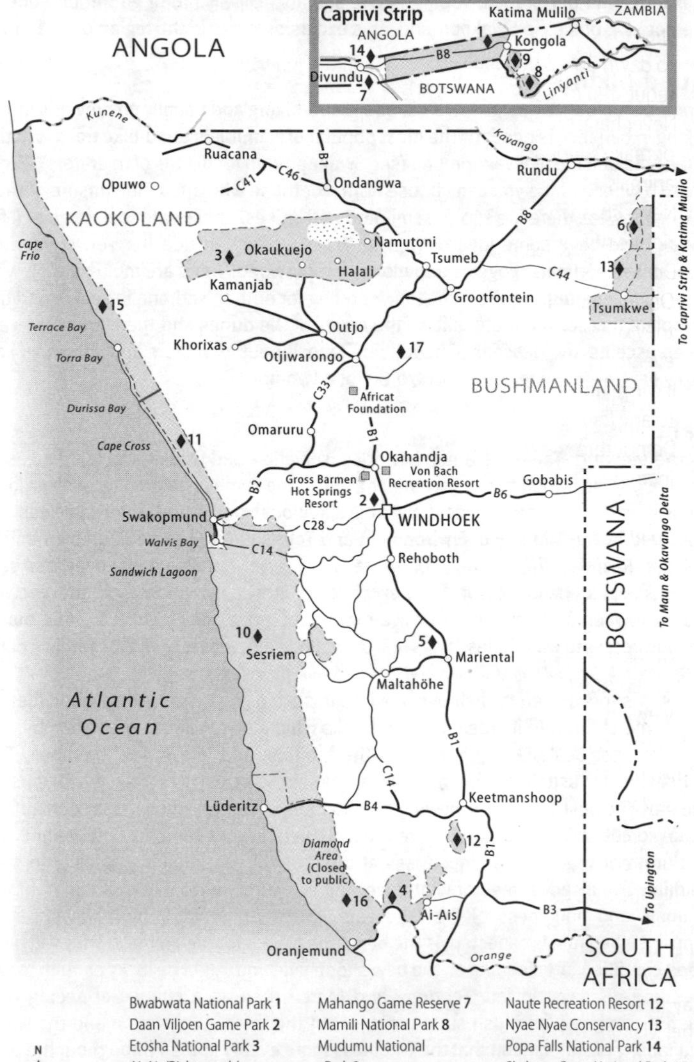

Bwabwata National Park **1**
Daan Viljoen Game Park **2**
Etosha National Park **3**
Ai-Ais/Richtersveld Transfrontier Park **4**
Hardap Dam Recreation Resort & Game Park **5**
Khaudum Game Park **6**
Mahango Game Reserve **7**
Mamili National Park **8**
Mudumu National Park **9**
Namib-Naukluft National Park **10**
National West Coast Recreation Area **11**
Naute Recreation Resort **12**
Nyae Nyae Conservancy **13**
Popa Falls National Park **14**
Skeleton Coast National Park **15**
Sperrgebiet National Park **16**
Waterberg Plateau Park **17**

Game-viewing rules and regulations

- Keep on the well-marked roads and track; off-road driving is harmful because smoke, oil and destruction of the grass layer cause soil erosion.
- Do not drive through closed roads or park areas. It is mandatory to enter and exit the parks through the authorized gates.
- For your own safety, stay in your vehicle at all times. Your vehicle serves as a blind or hide, since animals will not usually identify it with humans. In all the parks that are visited by car, it is forbidden to leave the vehicle except in designated places, such as picnic sites or walking trails.
- Stick to the parks' opening hours; it is usually forbidden to drive from dusk to dawn unless you are granted a special authorization. At night you are requested to stay at your lodge or campsite.
- Never harass the animals. Make as little noise as possible; do not flash lights or make sudden movements to scare them away; never try and attract the animals' attention by calling out or whistling.
- Never chase the animals and always give way to them, they always have right of way.
- Do not feed the animals; the food you provide might make them ill. Once animals such as elephants learn that food is available from humans they can become aggressive and dangerous when looking for more and will eventually have to be shot.
- If camping at night in the parks, ensure that the animals cannot gain access to any food you are carrying.
- Do not throw any litter, used matches and cigarette butts; this not only increases fire risk in the dry season, but also some animals will eat whatever they find.
- Do not disturb other visitors. They have the same right as you to enjoy nature. If you discover a stopped vehicle and you want to check what they are looking at, never hinder their sight nor stop within their photographic field. If there is no room for another car, wait patiently for your turn, the others will finally leave and the animals will still be there. If there is a group of vehicles, most drivers will take it in turns to occupy the prime viewing spot.
- Always turn the engine off when you are watching game up close.
- Do not speed; the speed limit is usually 40 kph. Speeding damages road surfaces, increases noise and raises the risk of running over animals.
- Wild animals are dangerous; despite their beauty their reactions are unpredictable. Don't expose yourself to unnecessary risks; excessive confidence can lead to severe accidents.

If your car breaks down while you are in the park, do not leave it in search of help. Stay inside the vehicle until a park ranger comes to your rescue. Chances are that other visitors will be using the same roads as you and you will be able to pass a message on to the park authorities through them. If the worst happens and night falls before you are rescued, remember that the park keeps a record of all the cars that have entered each day. If your car has not returned before dark, the park rangers will know you are missing and send out a search party. While game viewing in some of the

Park entrance and daily usage fees

Park	Fee per day		
Etosha National Park, Namib-Naukluft Park (Sesriem entrance), Waterberg Plateau Park, Ai-Ais Transfrontier Park, Skeleton Coast Park.	Adults	(Namibian residents)	US$ 4.50
		(SADC)	US$ 9
		(foreign)	US$12
	Children under 16		Free
	Vehicle (10 seats or less)		US$ 1.50
	(11-25 seats)		US$ 6
	(26-50 seats)		US$45
	(51 seats or more)		US$75
All other parks where usage fees are charged	Adults	(Namibian residents)	US$ 1.50
		(SADC)	US$ 4.50
		(foreign)	US$ 6
	Children under 16		Free
	Vehicles		As above

larger parks, remember that the weather can be hot and dusty. It is a good idea to take water bottles and fruit juice with you, as well as snacks in case of emergency.

Travelling on gravel roads means that the car and passengers inside will be covered in dust before the end of the trip. The only sure way of avoiding this is to travel with the windows rolled up and the air-conditioning unit on full. Expect dust to get into everything that is not locked in air-tight containers. Wear comfortable old clothes, preferably in dull greens or khakis.

Invaluable for game viewing is a good pair of binoculars. The wildlife is not always conveniently close to the car and binoculars will help you pick out animals and features at a range that leaves your subjects undisturbed. It is a good idea to buy your binoculars before you reach Namibia as they are imported here and will be more expensive. When you are buying a pair of binoculars don't just consider the strength of magnification, much of the best game viewing is done when light levels are low so a large aperture letting in more light can be as useful as high magnification. Consider also weight; a compact pair is much more comfortable on game walks.

Game reserve accommodation Once you have reserved your accommodation in a game reserve (see page 48), you will be able to move in anytime after midday until the camp gates shut at nightfall. The camps in Etosha have a shop, restaurant and bar, but overall visitors will find them fairly basic. Shops typically sell a range of relevant books as well as maps, leaflets and food. At the camp office, you must register and can enquire about available game walks and drives. Most accommodation is self-catering, so you may well find that there is no restaurant – be sure to check ahead and plan accordingly. The camp shops usually sell some pots and pans, utensils and food but the range tends to be limited. In most reserves (including Etosha and all of Sossusvlei to the 2WD car park by the dunes), road conditions between camps are good; well-maintained gravel roads are navigable by saloon car, a 4WD is not necessary.

Safari companies If you don't want to self-drive or are short of time there are numerous safari companies operating out of Windhoek (see Windhoek tour operators, page 99) which can arrange accommodation and game-viewing trips as part of a wider tour. The cost of tours varies: there are good budget camping options as well as more expensive luxury safaris. In fact, given Namibia's limited public transport and the need for a car while game viewing, these companies often offer the cheapest access to game reserves.

Sandboarding

The Namib Desert is famous for its giant dunes and there's no better way to conquer these towering beauties than to zoom down them head first on a traditional Swakopmund sandboard, or carve up the dune with style and skill on a snowboard adapted for sand. The beauty about sandboarding is the sand is not abrasive, and as it's obviously not cold, you can board in shorts and T-shirts. The worst that can happen is that you walk away covered in sand. For the lie down option you're supplied with a large flat piece of waxed hardboard, safety hat, elbow guards and gloves before heading off to climb a dune. The idea is to lie on the board, push off from the top and speed head first down the sandy surface. Speeds easily reach 80 kph and some of the dunes are very steep, though first you'll do a few training rides on the lower dunes. No experience is necessary; it's exhilarating and lots of fun. Stand-up boarding requires more skill. It is exactly the same as snowboarding, but on sand, using standard snowboarding equipment to surf your way down the dunes. If you've got snowboarding experience then this is an opportunity to try out those turns, free-style jumps and big spray curves. All trips include lunch and a few drinks and cost in the region of US$40. One operator offering sandboarding trips is **Alter Action**, Swakopmund T064-402737, www.alter-action.com.

The dunes are constantly shifting and can move 10 m in a week; sandboard tracks soon disappear.

Skydiving

Swakopmund Skydiving Club runs extremely popular tandem free-fall jumps for novices. Jumps take place daily, normally after the fog has lifted in the morning. After a brief safety chat, you board a small plane for a 35-minute scenic flight over Swakopmund and the surrounding coast and desert as you prepare yourself for your jump. This involves being strapped between the thighs of your tandem jump master and shuffling to the door of the plane. At 12,000 ft you both tumble into the sky for a mind-blowing 30-second free-fall at around 220 kph – a totally exhilarating experience. Then the parachute opens and you float to the ground for a 10-minute ride enjoying the breathtaking desert scenery. The jump costs US$250-270 and if you are in Swakopmund for a week or more, you can go on a static-line course. **Ground Rush Adventures**, T081-1245167, www.namibweb.com/sky, organizes jumps.

Health

Before you go

Ideally, you should see your GP/Practice nurse or travel clinic at least six weeks before your departure for general advice on travel risks, malaria and recommended vaccinations. Your local pharmacist can also be a good source of readily accessible advice. Make sure you have travel insurance, get a dental check (especially if you are going to be away for more than a month), know your own blood group and if you suffer from a long-term condition such as diabetes or epilepsy make sure someone knows or that you have a Medic Alert bracelet/necklace with this information on it.

Vaccinations and malaria precautions

First of all confirm that your primary courses and boosters are up to date (usually hepatitis A, typhoid, poliomyelitis and tetanus). Vaccines commonly recommended for travel in Namibia are diphtheria, hepatitis B, rabies, tuberculosis and meningococcal meningitis. A yellow fever certificate is only required if entering from an infected area (for people over one year of age) or if travelling from other African countries to the north of Namibia. The final decision on vaccinations should be based on your consultation with the GP or travel clinic. Also, advice can change so check again for future visits.

Malaria precautions are essential in the northern third of the country from November to June and along the Kavango and Kunene rivers throughout the year. Check with your doctor or nurse about suitable antimalarial tablets. If travelling to remote areas, a course of emergency 'standby' treatment should be carried.

A-Z of health risks

Altitude sickness

Acute mountain sickness can strike from about 3000 m upwards and in general is more likely to affect those who ascend rapidly (for example by plane) and those who over-exert themselves. Acute mountain sickness takes a few hours or days to come on and presents with heachache, lassitude, dizziness, loss of appetite, nausea and vomiting. Insomnia is common and often associated with a suffocating feeling when lying down in bed. You may notice that your breathing tends to wax and wane at night and your face is puffy in the mornings – this is all part of the syndrome. If the symptoms are mild, the treatment is rest and painkillers (preferably not aspirin-based) for the headaches. Should the symptoms be severe and prolonged it is best to descend to a lower altitude immediately and reascend, if necessary, slowly and in stages. The symptoms disappear very quickly – even after a few hundred metres of descent.

The best way of preventing acute mountain sickness is a relatively slow ascent. When trekking to high altitude, some time spent walking at medium altitude, getting fit and acclimatizing is beneficial. When flying to places over 3000 m a few hours' rest and the avoidance of alcohol, cigarettes and heavy food will go a long way towards preventing acute mountain sickness.

Bites and stings

This is a very rare event indeed for travellers, but if you are unlucky (or careless) enough to be bitten by a venomous snake, spider, scorpion or sea creature, try to identify the culprit, without putting yourself in further danger (do not try to catch a live snake).

Snake bites in particular are very frightening, but in fact rarely poisonous – even venomous snakes can bite without injecting venom. Victims should be taken to a hospital or a doctor without delay. Snake bite antivenom is not usually carried by travellers as in inexperienced hands their use can do more harm than good. Reassure and comfort the victim frequently. Immobilize the limb with a bandage or a splint and get the patient to lie still. Do not slash the bite area or try to suck out the poison because this sort of heroism does more harm than good. If you know how to use a tourniquet in these circumstances, you will not need this advice. If you are not experienced, do not apply a tourniquet.

Certain tropical fish inject venom into bathers' feet when trodden on, which can be exceptionally painful. Wear plastic shoes if such creatures are reported. The pain can be relieved by immersing the foot in hot water (as hot as you can bear) for as long as the pain persists.

Dengue fever

This is a viral disease spread by mosquitoes that tend to bite during the day. The symptoms are fever and often intense joint pains, also some people develop a rash. Symptoms last about a week but it can take a few weeks to recover fully. Dengue can be difficult to distinguish from malaria as both diseases tend to occur in the same countries. There are no effective vaccines or antiviral drugs though, fortunately, travellers rarely develop the more severe forms of the disease (these can prove fatal). Rest, plenty of fluids and paracetamol (not aspirin) is the recommended treatment.

Diarrhoea and intestinal upset

Diarrhoea can refer to either loose stools or an increased frequency of bowel movement, both of which can be a nuisance. Symptoms should be relatively short-lived but if they persist beyond two weeks specialist medical attention should be sought. Also seek medical help if there is blood in the stools and/or fever.

Adults can use an antidiarrhoeal medication such as loperamide to control the symptoms but only for up to 24 hours. In addition, keep well hydrated by drinking plenty of fluids and eat bland foods. Oral rehydration sachets taken after each loose stool are a useful way to keep well hydrated. They should always be used when treating children and the elderly.

Bacterial travellers' diarrhoea is the most common form. **Ciproxin** (**Ciprofloxacin**) is a useful antibiotic and can be obtained by private prescription in the UK. You need to take one 500 mg tablet when the diarrhoea starts. If there are no signs of improvement after 24 hours the diarrhoea is likely to be viral and not bacterial. If it is due to other organisms such as those causing giardia or amoebic dysentery, different antibiotics will be required.

The standard advice to prevent problems is to be careful with water and ice for drinking. Ask yourself where the water came from. If you have any doubts then boil it or filter and treat it. There are many filter/treatment devices now available on the market. Food can also transmit disease. Be wary of salads (what were they washed in, who handled them), re-heated foods or food that has been left out in the sun having been cooked earlier in the day. There is a simple adage that says wash it, peel it, boil it or forget it. Also be wary of unpasteurized dairy products as these can transmit a range of diseases.

Hepatitis

Hepatitis means inflammation of the liver. Viral causes of the disease can be acquired anywhere in the world. The most obvious symptom is a yellowing of your skin or the whites of your eyes. However, prior to this all that you may notice is itching and tiredness. Pre-travel hepatitis A vaccine is the best bet. Hepatitis B (for which there is also a vaccine) is spread through blood and unprotected sexual intercourse; both of these can be avoided.

Malaria

Malaria can cause death within 24 hours. It can start as something just resembling an attack of flu. You may feel tired, lethargic, headachy, feverish; or, more seriously, develop fits, followed by coma and then death. Have a low index of suspicion because it is very easy to write off vague symptoms, which may actually be malaria. If you have a temperature, go to a doctor as soon as you can and ask for a malaria test. On your return home if you suffer any of these symptoms, get tested as soon as possible, even if any previous test proved negative, the test could save your life.

Remember ABCD: ***Awareness*** *(of whether malaria is present in the area you are travelling in),* ***Bite avoidance, Chemoprohylaxis, Diagnosis.***

Treatment is with drugs and may be oral or into a vein depending on the seriousness of the infection.

To prevent mosquito bites wear clothes that cover arms and legs, use effective insect repellents in areas with known risks of insect-spread disease and use a mosquito net treated with an insecticide. Repellents containing 30-50% DEET (Di-ethyltoluamide) are recommended when visiting malaria endemic areas; lemon eucalyptus (Mosiguard) is a reasonable alternative. The key advice is to guard against contracting malaria by taking the correct anti-malarials (see above) and finishing the recommended course.

Remember that it is risky to buy medicinal tablets and in particular antimalarials in some developing countries because they may be sub-standard or the danger of a trade in counterfeit drugs. If you are popular target for insect bites or develop lumps quite soon after being bitten use antihistamine tablets and apply a cream such as hydrocortisone.

Rabies

Remember that rabies is endemic throughout certain parts of the world so be aware of the dangers of the bite from any animal. Rabies vaccination before travel can be considered, but if bitten always seek urgent medical attention whether or not previously vaccinated, after cleaning the wound and treating with an iodine base disinfectant or alcohol.

Sun

Take heed of advice regarding protection against sun. Overexposure can lead to sunburn and, in the longer term, skin cancers and premature skin aging. The best advice is simply to avoid exposure to the sun by covering exposed skin, wearing a hat and staying out of the sun if possible, particularly between late morning and early afternoon. Apply a higher-factor sunscreen (greater than SPF15) to the skin and also make sure it screens against UVB. A further danger in hot climates is heat exhaustion or more seriously heat stroke. This can be avoided by good hydration, which means drinking water past the point of simply quenching thirst. Also when first exposed to tropical heat take time to acclimatize by avoiding strenuous activity in the middle of the day. If you cannot avoid heavy exercise in the tropics it is also a good idea to increase salt intake.

Underwater health

If you go diving make sure that you are fit do so. The **British Sub-Aqua Club (BSAC)** ⓘ *Telford's Quay, South Pier Road, Ellesmere Port, Cheshire CH65 4FL, UK, T01513-506200, www.bsac.com*, can put you in touch with doctors who do medical examinations. Check that any dive company you use knows what it is doing, has appropriate certification from **BSAC** or **Professional Association of Diving Instructors (PADI)** ⓘ *Unit 7, St Philips Central, Albert Rd, St Philips, Bristol, BS2 OTD, T0117-3007234, www.padi.com*, and that the equipment is well maintained.

Water

There are a number of ways of purifying water. Dirty water should first be strained through a filter bag and then boiled or treated. Bring water to a rolling boil for several minutes. There are sterilizing methods that can be used and products generally contain chlorine (eg Puritabs) or iodine (eg Pota Aqua) compounds. There are a number of water sterilizers now on the market available in personal and expedition size. Make sure you take the spare parts or spare chemicals with you and do not believe everything the manufacturers say.

Other diseases and risks

There are a range of other insect-borne diseases that are quite rare in travellers, but worth finding out about if going to particular destinations. Examples are sleeping sickness, river blindness and leishmaniasis. Fresh water can also be a source of diseases such as bilharzia and leptospirosis and it is worth finding out whether these are a danger before bathing in lakes and streams. Unprotected sex always carries a risk and extra care is required when visiting some parts of the world.

Further information

Websites

Foreign and Commonwealth Office (FCO) (UK), www.fco.gov.uk
The National Travel Health Network and Centre (NaTHNaC) www.nathnac.org/
World Health Organisation, www.who.int
Fit for Travel (UK), www.fitfortravel.scot.nhs.uk. This site from Scotland provides a quick A-Z of vaccine and travel health advice requirements for each country.

Books

Dawood R, editor. *Travellers' health*. 3rd Ed. Oxford: Oxford University Press, 2002.
Warrell David and Sarah Anderson, editors. *Expedition Medicine*. The Royal Geographic Society, ISBN 1 86197 040-4.

Keeping in touch

Communications

Internet

Internet cafés and email facilities are plentiful in the major towns, and range from the upmarket hotels and cybercafés with fast connections to small shops and business centres that may just have a single computer. The cost of access has fallen considerably over the last few years and is available from about US$1 per hour, although the use of more modern equipment is likely to cost US$1 per 15 minutes.

Post

Post offices are open Monday to Friday 0830-1600 and Saturday 0800-1200. For poste restante services, encourage your friends and family to make sure mail is labelled clearly, with the surname first and underlined to speed the process of discovery. Internal mail can be very slow – up to three weeks. Expect letters to take a minimum of 10 days to get to Europe by airmail and larger items sent via surface mail to take up to three months. The post office will allow international calls on a meter and sends faxes overseas. All the main courier companies are represented in Namibia including **DHL**, T061-223161, www.dhl.com, and **Fedex**, T061-264777, www.fedex.com.

Telephone

Namibia has an efficient telephone system which was originally installed by the South Africans. Most numbers are on digital exchanges and have a three-digit area code (06x) followed by a six-digit number. If you are in the same town or region it is not necessary to phone the three-digit code. Other numbers are dialled by calling the local exchange, where an operator answers and puts you through manually. Beware of making calls from hotel phones; as anywhere, they can be very expensive. Public phones boxes are all over the country, sometimes in very remote settlements. Note that phone calls between Namibia, Botswana and South Africa are on a slightly cheaper regional rate than normal international call rates.

Namibia's country code is 264.

 Telecards Telecards are sold for N$10, N$20 and N$50, divided into 20 cent units. They are obtainable at post offices, dealers and teleshops. These are normally the type that you insert into the phone, although there are cards with a PIN that you dial. Local calls are good value.

Directory enquiries International: T1025. International calls are expensive. There is one price band no matter what time of day you make the call. **Local:** T1188.

Mobile phones Namibia's **Mobile Telecommunications Company** (MTC), www.mtc.com.na, provides a reliable but limited-range GSM system for mobile phones. A cell phone can be very useful, both for booking ahead and keeping in touch with your loved ones. Overseas visitors are able to use their phones in the country provided they have arranged roaming with their service providers at home. Not only are outgoing calls (both local and interantional) expensive, beware of high charges for receiving calls under these arrangements. A better value alternative is to buy a Namibian SIM card which, along with pay-as-you-go top-up cards, are available from phone shops. You can hire mobile phones through **Get Smart Mobile**, gsmrent@ iafrica.com.na, which has a desk at Hosea Kutako Airport, T062-540101, and in the Mutual Platz shopping centre (next to Edgars) in Windhoek, T061-245227. You will need a credit card as deposit, but rental and domestic calls are good value and incoming calls and voicemail are free. Telephone numbers can be pre-booked, so that you can tell everyone at home your number before you travel. Mobile phone coverage countrywide is improving all the time but be aware that you will not get coverage in the more remote regions that are often a long way from the nearest phone mast.

Bring your own mobile phone; you can hire SIM cards cheaply for local calls.

Media

Newspapers

If it's local scandal, crime and debate that you're after, head straight for the newspaper stand. *The Namibian* is the country's only English-language, independent daily, with some international news; you can get a year's subscription sent to Europe, or perhaps better value to check www.namibian.com.na from time to time. Others are the *Observer* on Saturday and *Tempo* (multilingual) on Sunday; *Republikain* (daily, Afrikaans); *Mail* and *Guardian* (weekly South African and international news). For tourists, *Travel News Namibia*, bi-monthly, provides relevant updates. You can subscribe through www.holidaytravel.com.na. German visitors will enjoy the monthly *Tourismus* publication.

Radio

The government encourages free speech and there are lively oral debates and phone-ins on the radio each day. As well as the **Namibian Broadcasting Corporation** (NBC), available almost everywhere throughout the country, and broadcast in English, there are five commercial radio stations in Windhoek. **Radio 99** and **Radio Energy** are recommended. Don't expect much reception (other than NBC) out of urban centres.

Short Wave Radio If you are not familiar with short wave radio read the notes in the manual about reception; a simple attachment can greatly enhance the quality of your signal. Digital tuning makes finding weak frequencies considerably easier. Signal strength varies throughout the day, with lower frequencies generally better at night. For programme listings visit www.bbc.co.uk.

British Broadcasting Corporation (BBC) These bands cover the whole region from Namibia to Moçambique, as well as different times of the day. **90m band**: 3255 kHz; **49m band**: 6005 kHz, 6190 kHz; **25m band**: 11860 kHz, 11940 kHz; **19m band**: 15400 kHz; **16m band**: 17885 kHz; **13m band**: 21470 kHz, 21660 kHz.

Voice of America (VoA) **25m band**: 11920 kHz; **22m band**: 13680 kHz; **19m band**: 15580 kHz; **16m band**: 17895 kHz; **13m band**: 21485 kHz.

Television

The state broadcaster, **NBC**, broadcasts one television channel in English. Many hotels will have satellite TV. This is usually **DSTV** (Digital Satellite Television), South African satellite TV, with over 40 channels of film, music, sport and light entertainment. The most popular are the sports channels, especially **Supersport**, which provides extensive coverage of European football.

Transnamib Train Services

Windhoek-Tsumeb-Windhoek (outward and return: Mon, Wed and Fri)	Arrival time	Departure time
Windhoek		1815
Okahandja	2040	2155
Karibib	2325	2325
Kranzberg	2355	0015
Omaruru	0140	0210
Otjiwarongo	0500	0630
Otavi	0850	0920
Tsumeb	1045	1140
Otavi	1300	1325
Otjiwarongo	1620	1815
Omaruru	2100	2200
Kranzberg	2355	0015
Karibib	0110	0340
Okahandja	0340	0400
Windhoek	0540	

Windhoek-Gobabis-Windhoek (outward: Sun, Tue, Thu; return: Mon, Wed, Fri)	Arrival time	Departure time
Windhoek		2150
Omitara	0210	0215
Witvlei	0400	0400
Gobabis	0525	2050
Witvlei	2220	2220
Omitara	2400	0001
Windhoek	0425	

Tsumeb-Walvis Bay-Tsumeb (outward and return: Mon, Wed and Fri)	Arrival time	Departure time
Tsumeb		1140
Otavi	1300	1325
Otjiwarongo	1620	1715
Omaruru	2000	2040
Kranzberg	2210	2230
Usakos	2255	2255
Arandis	0055	0055
Swakopmund	0210	0235
Kuiseb	0350	0350
Walvis Bay	0400	1615
Kuiseb	1635	1635
Swakopmund	1750	1800
Arandis	1940	1940
Usakos	2155	2155
Kranzberg	2220	2230
Omaruru	0005	0020
Otjiwarongo	0315	0630
Otavi	0850	0920
Tsumeb	1045	

Windhoek-Walvis Bay-Windhoek (outward and return: daily except Sat)	Arrival time	Departure time
Windhoek		1955
Okahandja	2155	2205
Karibib	0040	0040
Kranzberg	0105	0130
Usakos	0150	0150
Arandis	0345	0345
Swakopmund	0520	0530
Kuiseb	0650	0650
Walvis Bay	0715	1900
Kuiseb	1920	1920
Swakopmund	2035	2045
Arandis	2230	2230
Usakos	0045	0045
Kranzberg	0105	0135
Karibib	0220	0220
Okahandja	0500	0510
Windhoek	0700	

Upington-Windhoek-Upington (Windhoek-Keetmanshoop-Windhoek: daily except Sat; Keetmanshoop-Upington-Keetmanshoop: Sun and Thu only)	Arrival time	Departure time
Upington		0500
Ariamsvlei	0855	0855
Karasburg	1120	1120
Grünau	1225	1225
Keetmanshoop	1630	1850
Tses	2035	2040
Asab	2135	2140
Gibeon	2220	2225
Mariental	2335	0020
Kalkrand	0230	0230
Rehoboth	0425	0425
Windhoek	0700	1940
Rehoboth	2210	2210
Kalkrand	2400	2400
Mariental	0200	0220
Gibeon	0325	0330
Asab	0410	0415
Tses	0505	0510
Keetmanshoop	0700	0850
Grünau	1310	1310
Karasburg	1430	1430
Ariamsvlei	1825	1825
Upington	2130	

Intercape Mainliner Coach Services

Cape Town-Windhoek-Cape Town (South Africa Time) (outward: Tue, Thu, Fri, Sun; return: Mon, Wed, Fri, Sun)	Arrival time	Departure time
Cape Town station		1000
Namibian border (near Noord Oewer)	1859	1900
Grünau	2140	2145
Keetmanshoop	2400	0001
Mariental	0215	0230
Rehoboth	0410	0415
Windhoek	0600	1600
Rehoboth	1755	1800
Mariental	2000	2015
Keetmanshoop	2235	2245
Grünau	0025	0030
Namibia border (near Noord Oewer)	0155	0200
Cape Town	1330	

Windhoek-Upington-Windhoek (South African Time)	Arrival time	Departure time
Windhoek		1600
Rehoboth	1755	1800
Mariental	2010	1800
Keetmanshoop	2240	2245
Grünau	0025	0030
Karasburg	0055	0100
Namibian border (near Ariamsvlei)	0225	0230
Upington	0630	1745
Namibian border (near Ariamsvlei)	1925	1930
Karasburg	2040	2045
Grünau	2140	2145
Keetmanshoop	2400	0001
Mariental	0225	0230
Rehoboth	0410	0415
Windhoek	0600	

Windhoek-Walvis Bay-Windhoek (outward: Mon, Wed, Fri, Sat; return: Mon, Wed, Fri, Sun)	Arrival time	Departure time
Windhoek		0500
Okahandja	0655	0700
Karibib	0800	0805
Usakos	0830	0845
Swakopmund	1025	1030
Walvis Bay	1050	1115
Swakopmund	1155	1200
Usakos	1330	1345
Karibib	1400	1405
Okahandja	1510	1515
Windhoek	1645	

Windhoek-Victoria Falls-Windhoek (outward: Mon, Wed, Fri; return: Wed, Fri, Sun)	Arrival Time	Departure time
Windhoek		1615
Okahandja	1755	1800
Otjiwarongo	2025	2030
Otavi	2140	2145
Tsumeb	2225	2230
Grootfontein	2300	2330
Rundu	0225	0230
Kongola	0640	0645
Livingstone	1255	1300
Victoria Falls (Zambia)	1400	1000
Livingstone	1125	1130
Kongola	1425	1430
Rundu	1540	1545
Grootfontein	1755	1800
Tsumeb	2010	2015
Otavi	0055	0100
Otjiwarongo	0225	0230
Okahandja	0425	0430
Windhoek	0545	

Air Namibia

	Days	Departure time	Arrival time
Windhoek-London	Tue, Thu, Sat	1840	0455
London-Windhoek	Sun, Wed, Fri	2130	0745
Windhoek-Frankfurt	Sun, Wed, Fri	1900	0555
	Tue	1040	2135
Frankfurt-Windhoek	Mon, Tue, Thu, Sat	2245	0745
Windhoek-Johannesburg	Sun-Fri	0930; 1745	1215; 2030
	Sat	1515	1800
Johannesburg-Windhoek	Sun-Fri	0745; 1615	0845; 1715
	Sat	0745	0845
Windhoek-Cape Town	Sun-Fri	0945;1740	1245; 2040
	Sat	0945	1245
Cape Town-Windhoek	Sun-Fri	0800;1600	0900; 1700
Windhoek-Victoria Falls	Sun, Wed, Fri	1000	1400
Victoria Falls-Windhoek	Sun, Wed, Fri	1430	1630
Cape Town-Oranjemund	Sun-Fri	0900	0950
Oranjemund-Cape Town	Sun-Fri	1600	1850
Oranjemund-Lüderitz	Sun-Fri	1020	1110
Lüderitz-Oranjemund	Sun-Fri	1440	1530
Lüderitz-Walvis Bay	Sun-Fri	1130	1300
Walvis Bay-Lüderitz	Sun-Fri	1250	1420
Lüderitz-Windhoek (Eros Airport)	Sun-Fri	1130	1410
Windhoek (Eros Airport)-Lüderitz	Sun-Fri	1130	1420
Walvis Bay-Oranjemund	Sun-Fri	1250	1530
Oranjemund-Walvis Bay	Sun-Fri	1020	1300
Windhoek (Eros Airport)-Walvis Bay	Sun-Fri	1130	1220
Walvis Bay-Windhoek (Eros Airport)	Sun-Fri	1320	1410
Windhoek (Eros Airport)-Swakopmund	Sun-Fri	1500	1600
Swakopmund-Windhoek (Eros Airport)	Sun-Fri	1630	1730
Windhoek (Eros Airport)-Ondangwa	Sun-Fri	0700; 1500	0830; 1630
	Sat	0700	0830
Ondangwa-Windhoek (Eros Airport)	Mon-Fri	0900; 1700	1030; 1830
	Sat	0900	1030
Windhoek (Eros Airport)-Katima Mulilo	Sun-Fri	0700	0940
Katima Mulilo-Windhoek (Eros Airport)	Sun-Fri	1600	1840
Windhoek (Eros Airport)-Oranjemund	Tue, Thu	0830; 1130	1010;1530
	Sun, Mon, Wed, Fri	1130	1530
Oranjemund-Windhoek (Eros Airport)	Tue, Thu	1020; 1400	1410; 1545
Walvis Bay-Cape Town	Sun-Fri	1250	1850
Cape Town-Walvis Bay	Sun-Fri	0900	1300
Lüderitz-Cape Town	Sun-Fri	1440	1850
Cape Town-Lüderitz	Sun-Fri	0900	1110

Flights also from Windhoek to Maun (Botswana) and Luanda (Angola)

African Wildlife

Introduction

A large proportion of people who visit Africa do so to see its spectacular wildlife. This colour section is a quick photographic guide to some of the more spectacular mammals found in east and southern Africa (it covers the countries shown on the map here). From the 'Big Nine', once thought by hunters to be the ultimate 'trophies' on safari and now most prized of all by those who shoot with their cameras, to the more everyday warthog, and from the wildebeest to the tiny Kirk's Dikdik antelope, which stands at a mere 40 cm at the shoulder, here we give you pictures and information about habitat, habits and characteristic appearance to help you when you are on safari. It is by no means a comprehensive survey and some of the animals listed may not be found throughout the whole region (where this is the case, we have listed the areas where they occur). For further information about the mammals, birds, marine life and other wildlife of the country, see the Land and environment section of the Background chapter.

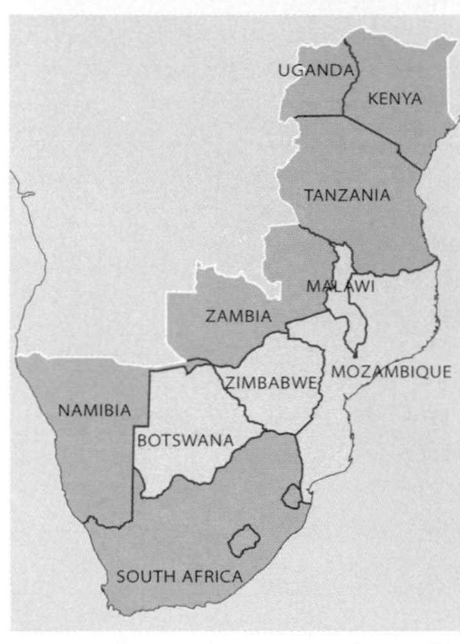

The Big Nine

■ **Hippopotamus** *Hippopotamus amphibius* (below). Prefers shallow water, grazes on land over a wide area at night, so can be found quite a distance from water, and has a strong sense of territory, which it protects aggressively. Lives in large family groups known as "schools".

■ **Black Rhinoceros** *Diceros bicornis* (bottom left). Long, hooked upper lip distinguishes it from White Rhino rather than colour. Prefers dry bush and thorn scrub habitat and in the past was found in mountain uplands. Males usually solitary. Females seen in small groups with their calves (very rarely more than four), sometimes with two generations. Mother always walks in front of offspring, unlike the White Rhino, where the mother walks behind, guiding calf with her horn. Their distribution has been massively reduced by poaching and work continues to save both the Black and the White Rhino from extinction. You might be lucky and see the Black Rhino in: Etosha NP, Namibia; Ngorongoro Crater, Tanzania; Masai Mara, Kenya; Kruger, Shamwari and Pilansberg NPs and private reserves like Mala Mala and Londolozi, South Africa.

■ **White Rhinoceros** *Diceros simus* (bottom right). Square muzzle and bulkier than the Black Rhino, they are grazers rather than browsers, hence the different lip. Found in open grassland, they are more sociable and can be seen in groups of five or more. More common in Southern Africa due to a successful breeding program in Hluhluwe/Umfolozi NP, South Africa.

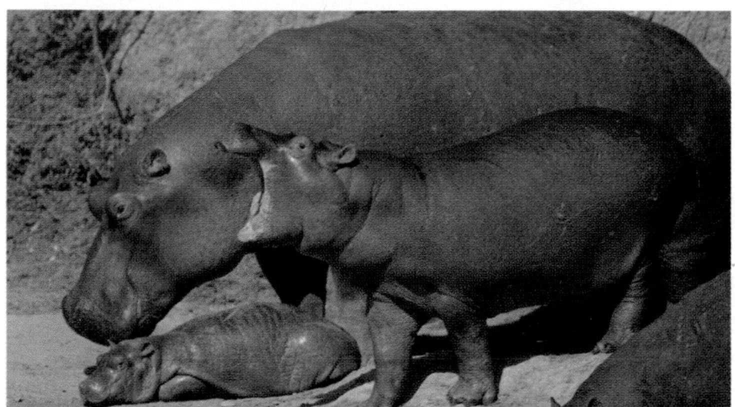

Reticulated Giraffe *Giraffa reticulata* (right). Reddish brown coat and a network of distinct, pale, narrow lines. Found from the Tana River, Kenya, north and east into Somalia and Ethiopia. Giraffes found in East Africa have darker coloured legs and their spots are dark and of an irregular shape with a jagged outline. In southern Africa the patches tend to be much larger and have well defined outlines, although giraffes found in the desert margins of Namibia are very pale in colour and less tall – probably due to a poor diet lacking in minerals.

Leopard *Panthera pardus* (below). Found in varied habitats ranging from forest to open savanna. They are generally nocturnal, hunting at night or before the sun comes up to avoid the heat. You may see them resting during the day in the lower branches of trees, see picture page ii.

Common Zebra (Burchell's) *Equus burchelli* (right). Generally has broad stripes (some with lighter shadow stripes next to the dark ones) which cross the top of the hind leg in unbroken lines. The true species is probably extinct but there are many varying subspecies found in different locations across Africa, including: Grant's (found in East Africa) Selous (Malawi, Zimbabwe and Mozambique) and Chapman's (Etosha NP, Namibia, east across Southern Africa to Kruger NP).

■ **Common/Masai Giraffe** *Giraffa camelopardis* (left). Yellowish-buff with patchwork of brownish marks and jagged edges, usually two different horns, sometimes three. Found throughout Africa in several differing subspecies.

■ **Cheetah** *Acinonyx jubatus* (below). Often seen in family groups walking across plains or resting in the shade. The black 'tear' mark is usually obvious through binoculars. Can reach speeds of 90 km per hour over short distances. Found in open, semi-arid savanna, never in forested country. Endangered in some parts of Africa, Namibia is believed to have the largest free-roaming population on the continent. More commonly seen than the leopard, they are not as widespread as the **lion** *Panthera leo* (see picture on front page of this section).

■ **Grevy's Zebra** *Equus grevyi* (left). Larger than the Burchell's Zebra, with bigger and broader ears and noticably narrower white stripes that meet in star above hind leg. Lives in small herds. Generally found north of the equator. A further zebra species, the **Mountain Zebra** *Equus zebra zebra*, is found in the Western Cape region of South Africa on hills and stony mountains. It is smaller than the two shown here and has a short mane and broad stripes.

Lion *Panthera leo* (page i). The largest (adult males can weigh up to 450 pounds) of the big cats in Africa and also the most common, lions are found on open savanna all over the continent. They are often not at all disturbed by the presence of humans and so it is possible to get quite close to them. They are sociable animals living in prides or permanent family groups of up to around 30 animals and are the only felid to do so. The females do most of the hunting (usually ungulates like zebra and antelopes).

Buffalo *Syncerus caffer* (below). Were considered by hunters to be the most dangerous of the big game and the most difficult to track and, therefore, the biggest trophy. Generally found on open plains but also at home in dense forest, they are fairly common in most African national parks but, like the elephant, they need a large area to roam in, so they are not usually found in the smaller parks.

Elephant *Loxodonta africana* (bottom and page xvi). Commonly seen, even on short safaris, throughout east and southern Africa, elephants have suffered from the activities of war and from ivory poachers. It is no longer possible to see herds of 500 or more animals but in southern Africa there are problems of over population and culling programmes have been introduced.

Larger antelope

■ **Gemsbok** *Oryx gazella* 122cm (below). Unmistakable, with black line down spine and black stripe between coloured body and white underparts. Horns (both sexes) straight, long and look v-shaped (seen face-on). Only found in Southern Africa, in arid, semi-desert country, though the very similar **Beisa Oryx** *Oryx beisa* occurs in East Africa. ■ **Nyala** *Tragelaphus angasi* 110cm (bottom left). Slender frame, shaggy, dark brown coat with mauve tinge (males). Horns (male only) single open curve. The female is a different chestnut colour. They like dense bush and are usually found close to water. Gather in herds of up to 30 but smaller groups more likely. Found across Zimbabwe and Malawi. ■ **Common** *Kobus ellipsiprymnus* and **Defassa** *Kobus defassa* **Waterbuck** 122-137cm (bottom right). Very similar with shaggy coats and white marking on buttocks. On the common variety, this is a clear half ring on rump and round tails; on Defassa, the ring is a filled in solid white area. Both species occur in small herds in grassy areas, often near water. Common in east and southern Africa.

■ **Greater Kudu** *Tragelaphus strepsiceros* 140-153cm (right). Colour varies from greyish to fawn with several vertical white stripes down the sides of the body. Horns long and spreading, with two or three twists (male only). Distinctive thick fringe of hair running from the chin down the neck. Found in fairly thick bush, sometimes in quite dry areas. Usually live in family groups of up to six, but occasionally larger herds of up to about 30. The **Lesser Kudu** *Strepsiceros imberis* 99-102 cm, looks similar but lacks the throat fringe and has two conspicuous white patches on the underside of the neck. Unlike the Greater Kudu, it is not found south of Tanzania.

■ **Topi** *Damaliscus korrigum* 122-127cm (below). Very rich dark rufous, with dark patches on the tops of the legs and more ordinary looking, lyre-shaped horns.

■ **Sable Antelope** *Hippotragus niger* 140-145cm (right) and **Roan Antelope** *Hippotragus equinus* 127-137cm. Both similar shape, with ringed horns curving backwards (both sexes), longer in the Sable. Female Sables are reddish brown and can be mistaken for the Roan. Males are very dark with a white underbelly. The Roan has distinct tufts of hair at the tips of its long ears. Found in east and southern Africa (although the Sable is not found naturally in east Africa, there is a small herd in the Shimba Hills Game Reserve). Sable prefers wooded areas and the Roan is generally only seen near water. Both species live in herds.

Hartebeest. In the Hartebeest the horns arise from a boney protuberance on the top of the head and curve outwards and backwards. There are 3 sub-species: **Coke's Hartebeest** *Alcephalus buselaphus* 122cm, also called the **Kongoni** in Kenya, is a drab pale brown with a paler rump; **Lichtenstein's Hartebeest** *Alcephalus lichtensteinii* 127-132cm, is also fawn in general colouration, with a rufous wash over the back and dark marks on the front of the legs and often a dark patch near shoulder; the **Red Hartebeest** *Alcephalus caama* (left), is another subspecies that occurs only throughout Southern Africa, although not in Kruger NP. All are found in herds, sometimes they mix with other plain dwellers such as zebra.

Brindled or **Blue Wildebeest** or **Gnu** *Connochaetes taurinus* (above) 132cm is found only in southern Africa; the **White bearded Wildebeest** *Connochaetes taurinus albojubatus* is found in central Tanzania and Kenya and distinguished by the white 'beard' under the neck. Both often seen grazing with Zebra.

Eland *Taurotragus oryx* 175-183cm (left). The largest of the antelope, it has a noticeable dewlap and shortish spiral horns (both sexes). Greyish to fawn, sometimes with rufous tinge and narrow white stripes down side of body. Occurs in groups of up to 30 in both east and southern Africa in grassy habitats.

Smaller antelope

■ **Bushbuck** *Tragelaphus scriptus* 76-92cm (top). Shaggy coat with variable pattern of white spots and stripes on the side and back and two white, crescent-shaped marks on front of neck. Short horns (male only) slightly spiral. High rump gives characteristic crouch. White underside of tail is noticeable when running. Occurs in thick bush, especially near water. Either seen in pairs or singly in east and southern Africa.

■ **Thomson's Gazelle** *Gazella thomsonii*, 64-69cm (above) and **Grant's Gazelle** *Gazella granti* 81-99cm. Superficially similar, Grant's, the larger of the two, has slightly longer horns (carried by both sexes in both species). Colour of both varies from bright to sandy rufous. Thomson's Gazelle can usually be distinguished by the broad black band along the side between the upperparts and abdomen, but some forms of Grant's also have this dark lateral stripe. Look for the white area on the buttocks which extends above the tail on to the rump in Grant's, but does not extend above the tail in Thomson's. Thomson's occur commonly on plains of Kenya and Tanzania in large herds. Grant's Gazelle occur on rather dry grass plains, in various forms, from Ethiopia and Somalia to Tanzania. Not found in southern Africa.

Kirk's Dikdik *Rhynchotragus kirkii* 36-41cm (top left). So small it cannot be mistaken, it is greyish brown, often washed with rufous. Legs are thin and stick-like. Slightly elongated snout and a conspicuous tuft of hair on the top of the head. Straight, small horns (male only). Found in bush country, singly or in pairs. East Africa only.

Steenbok *Raphicerus campestris* 58cm (top right). An even, rufous brown colour with clean white underside and white ring around eye. Small dark patch at the tip of the nose and long broad ears. The horns (male only) are slightly longer than the ears: they are sharp, have a smooth surface and curve slightly forward. Generally seen alone, prefers open plains, often found in more arid regions. A slight creature which usually runs off very quickly on being spotted. Common resident throughout southern Africa, Tanzania and parts of southern Kenya.

Bohor Reedbuck *Redunca redunca* 71-76cm (bottom left). Horns (males only) sharply hooked forwards at the tip, distinguishing them from the Oribi (see next page). It is reddish fawn with white underparts and has a short bushy tail. They usually live in pairs or otherwise in small family groups. Found in east and southern Africa. Often seen with Oribi, in bushed grassland and always near water.

Klipspringer *Oreotragus oreotragus* 56cm (bottom right). Brownish-yellow with grey speckles and white chin and underparts with a short tail. Has distinctive, blunt hoof tips and short horns (male only). Likes dry, stony hills and mountains. Only found in southern Africa.

Common (Grimm's) Duiker *Sylvicapra grimmia* 58cm (below). Grey fawn colour with darker rump and pale colour on the underside. Its dark muzzle and prominent ears are divided by straight, upright, narrow pointed horns. This particular species is the only duiker found in open grasslands. Usually the duiker is associated with a forested environment. It's common throughout southern and eastern Africa, but difficult to see because it is shy and will quickly disappear into the bush.

Oribi *Ourebia ourebi* 61cm (bottom left). Slender and delicate looking with a longish neck and a sandy to brownish fawn coat. It has oval-shaped ears and short, straight horns with a few rings at their base (male only). Like the Reedbuck (see previous page) it has a patch of bare skin just below each ear. They live in small groups or as a pair and are never far from water. Found in east and southern Africa.

Suni *Nesotragus moschatus* 37cm (bottom right). Dark chestnut to grey fawn in colour with slight speckles along the back, its head and neck are slightly paler and the throat is white. It has a distinct bushy tail with a white tip. Its longish horns (male only) are thick, ribbed and slope backwards. This is one of the smallest antelope, lives alone and prefers dense bush cover and reed beds in east and southern Africa.

Springbuck *Antidorcas marsupialis* or **Springbok**, 76-84cm (below). The upper part of the body is fawn, and this is separated from the white underparts by a dark brown lateral stripe. It is distinguished by a dark stripe which runs between the base of the horns and the mouth, passing through the eye. This is the only type of gazelle found south of the Zambezi River and you will not see this animal futher north. You no longer see the giant herds the animal was famous for, but you will see them along the roadside as you drive between Cape Town and Bloemfontein in South Africa. They get their name from their habit of leaping stiff-legged and high into the air.

Impala *Aepyceros melampus* 92-107cm (bottom). One of the largest of the smaller antelope, the Impala is a bright rufous colour on its back and has a white abdomen, a white 'eyebrow' and chin and white hair inside its ears. From behind, the white rump with black stripes on each side is characteristic and makes it easy to identify. It has long lyre-shaped horns (male only). Above the heels of the hind legs is a tuft of thick black bristles (unique to Impala) which are easy to see when the animal runs. There's also a black mark on the side of abdomen, just in front of the back leg. Found in herds of 15 to 20 in both east and southern Africa, it likes open grassland or sometimes the cover of partially wooded areas and is usually close to water.

Other mammals

There are many other fascinating mammals worth keeping an eye out for. This is a selection of some of the more interesting, or particularly common, ones.

■ **African Wild Dog** or **Hunting Dog** *Lycacon pictus* (right). Easy to identify since they have all the features of a large mongrel dog: a large head and slender body. Their coat is a mixed pattern of dark shapes and white and yellow patches and no two dogs are quite alike. They are very rarely seen and are seriously threatened with extinction (there may be as few as 6,000 left). Found in east and southern Africa on the open plains around dead animals, they are not in fact scavengers but effective pack hunters.

■ **Brown Hyena** *Hyaena brunnea* (above). High shoulders and low back give the hyena its characteristic appearance. The spotted variety, larger and brownish with dark spots, has a large head and rounded ears. The brown hyena, slightly smaller, has pointed ears and a shaggy coat, and is more noctural. The spotted hyena is only found in east Africa and the brown hyena is only found in southern Africa. Although sometimes shy animals they have been know to wander around campsites stealing food from humans.

■ **Spotted Hyena** *Crocuta crocuta* 69-91cm (middle right).

■ **Warthog** *Phacochoerus aethiopicus* (left). The warthog is almost hairless and grey with a very large head, tusks and wart-like growths on its face. It frequently occurs in family parties and when startled will run away at speed with its tail held straight up in the air. They are often seen near water caking themselves in thick mud which helps to keep them both cool and free of ticks and flies. They are found in both east and southern Africa.

■ **Chacma Baboon** *Papio ursinus* (opposite page bottom). An adult male baboon is slender and weighs about 40 kg. Their general colour is a brownish grey, with lighter undersides. Usually seen in trees, but rocks can also provide sufficient protection, they occur in large family troops and have a reputation for being aggressive where they have become used to man's presence. Found in east and southern Africa.

■ **Gorilla** *Gorilla gorilla* (left) are not animals you will see casually in passing – you have to go and look for them. They are sociable animals living in large family groups and have a vegetarian diet. Gorillas are the largest and most powerful of the apes. Adult males reach an average height of 150-170 cm and weigh from 135 to 230 kg. They occur only in the forests in the west of the region in Uganda, Rwanda and DR Congo.

Windhoek & Central Namibia

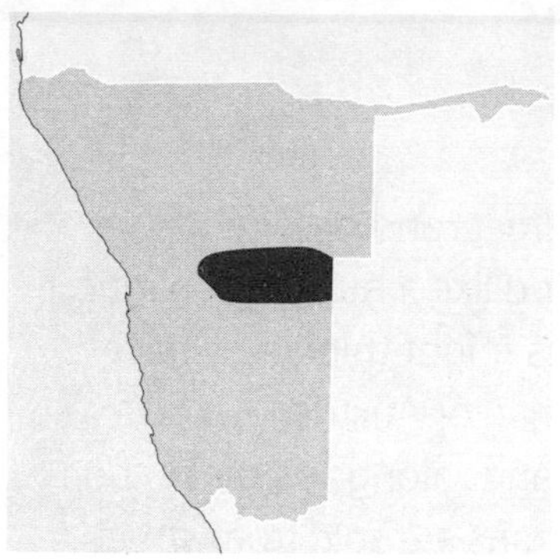

Footprint features

Introduction

With its neatly laid out grid of streets and orderly atmosphere, Windhoek is nothing like a bustling, chaotic African city and first-time visitors might think they have arrived in a medium-sized Bavarian or Austrian town. German colonial architecture stands alongside gleaming high-rise office blocks; African crafts are sold from street stalls next to the trendy shopping malls and cafés serve up traditional African food as well as German *Eisbien* and *Sauerkraut*.

The city's interesting museums and historical buildings warrant at least a day of exploration, and there's good shopping and eating on offer too. Windhoek is home to the country's international airport and the smaller Eros Airport that is the central base for all regional flights and, as a central strategic point to get to all points of Namibia, visitors may find themselves passing through on more than one occasion.

Away from the city the countryside opens up in all directions over vast camelthorn savannahs, and within only an hour's journey of the city you can visit several worthwhile guest farms. Also close to Windhoek is the Daan Viljoen Game Park, which is well stocked with plains game and attracts a good number of birds, and the Gross Barmen Resort, famous for its thermal springs. The regional towns such as Gobabis, Rehoboth and Okahandja don't warrant too much time, but they have a few worthy distractions if passing through and offer good facilities for those heading out to more remote regions.

★ Don't miss...

1 **Namibia Crafts Centre** Shop for crafts and curios; many of the crafts are made by artists from the local communities, page 85.

2 **State Museum** Explore Namibia's colonial past and its liberation struggle in the Alte Feste overlooking the city, page 87.

3 **Heinitzburg Castle** Have a sundowner on the terrace as the mountains of the Khomas Hochland turn purple, orange and gold, page 88.

4 **La Marmite or Restaurant Africa** Enjoy an authentic African meal at either of these Windhoek restaurants; both serve up dishes from all over the continent, page 94.

5 **Daan Viljoen Game Park** Experience the bush and see how close you can get to the antelopes and baboons, page 105.

6 **Harnas Wildlife Foundation** Visit this important rehabilitation centre for game and get up close to a huge variety of African animals, page 117.

Windhoek

→ *Phone code: 061. Colour map 1, C5. Pop: 240,000. Alt: 1,646 m.*

Windhoek, Namibia's capital city, is located at an altitude of 1646 m in the country's central highlands, with the Auas Mountains to the southeast, the Eros Mountains to the northeast and the hills of the Khomas Hochland rolling away to the west. Lying more or less in the geographical centre of the country, the city and surrounding suburbs are spread out over a series of picturesque valleys which lie at the crossroads of all Namibia's major road and rail routes. Although relatively small for a capital city by international standards, and despite talk about decentralization, Windhoek remains the political, judicial, economic and cultural centre of the country.

» *For Sleeping, Eating and other listings, see pages 90-104.*

Ins and outs

Getting there

There are two airports serving Windhoek, which can confuse first-time visitors. However, all the international flights arrive at **Hosea Kutako Airport** 45 km out of town. The taxi fare into the city is comparatively high (in the region of US$40 to hotels in the centre of town). A cheaper option is to catch one of the many minibus shuttles which charge in the region of US$20 per person. These drop off at any hotel or guesthouse in town. You will find both the minibuses and taxis directly outside the arrivals hall. Going back to the airport from the city by shuttle, either take the drivers' cell phone number on the way in and call to arrange a pick up, or go to the Tourist Information Office on the corner of Independence Avenue and Fidel Castro Street. There is a small car park outside the office where the shuttle drivers wait with their vehicles.

Internal and some regional flights use the smaller **Eros Airport** in the suburbs, 3 km south of the town centre, next to the **Safari Court Hotel** There is no public transport and you have to telephone for a taxi to come and collect you. If you are travelling with very little luggage you could walk the 400 m to the **Safari Court Hotel** complex, and then either ask the hotel reception to call for a taxi, or use their complementary town centre transfer service, a minibus which runs every 10-15 minutes to the Tourist Information Office on Independence Avenue. Once there, you will always find waiting taxis. **Intercape coaches** for Swakopmund and South Africa also arrive and depart from the car park in front of the Tourist Information Office (see page 70 for timetable). **Windhoek train station** is situated close to the town centre at the northern end of Mandume Ndemufayo Street. All passenger services depart from here, so too does the luxury **Desert Express** train. » *For further information, see Transport, page 101.*

When departing change any remaining Namibian dollars at the airport, you cannot exchange the currency once you have cleared exit formalities.

Getting around

The most obvious feature of the city centre is its size – or lack of it. The central district consists of **Independence Avenue** running from south to north, and a series of well-ordered streets laid out on a grid around it. It is easy to walk around. The main shops, banks, post office, tourism offices and larger hotels are all found along Independence Avenue, so it doesn't take long for the visitor to feel comfortable getting around. **Zoo Park**, with its lawns and palm trees, lies on Independence Avenue right at the heart of the city, and offers a green and shady place used for some Windhoekers to relax at lunchtimes. **Post Street Mall**, the main shopping area, is close by with its department stores and traditional arts and crafts street market; at the far end lies the main **Werne Hill Shopping Mall**.

As long as you are up to walking around the city there isn't really any need to sign up for an organized tour of Windhoek. Most of the tour companies (see page 99) offer one-day game-viewing and sundowner tours to guest farms around Windhoek and if you're really pressed for time you might well want to consider opting for one of these. If you're in the country on business for a few days, then a day in the bush with a knowledgeable guide followed by a sundowner and optional *braai* makes for a good break and is well worth it.

Best time to visit

Windhoek is situated in a semi-desert region. Rainfall occurs mostly during the summer months of January to March with an average annual rainfall of 370 mm. In recent years, however, there have been excessive rains and flooding in Windhoek. Days are mostly warm and sunny, though it gets quite hot during the summer months between December and February, when temperatures reach 34°C. By contrast, even during this period and because of the surrounding hills, nights can be cool, so bring adequate clothing to wrap up at night. The winter months of June to August are

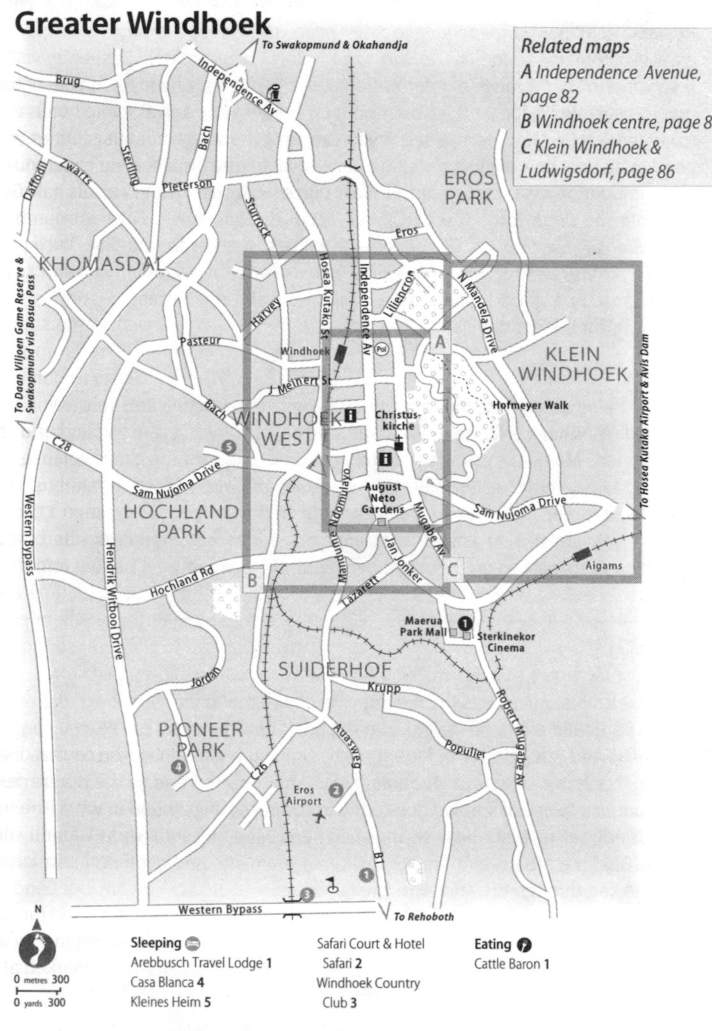

generally dry, mild and sunny, though nights are cold. Minimum temperatures then are between 5°C and 18°C.

Tourist information

The Windhoek head office of the **Namibia Tourism Board** (NTB) ⓘ *corner of Werner List St and Fidel Castro St, T061-2906000, www.namibiantourism.com.na*, has various brochures and publications, including a very good map that shows all the minor road numbers (essential if you're driving). There are two **Windhoek Tourist Information Offices** ⓘ *Post Street Mall, T061-2902092, maj@windhoekcc.org.na, Mon-Fri 0730-1630; and corner of Fidel Castro St and Independence Av, T061-2902596, tourism@iafrica.com.na, Mon-Fri 0700-1900, Sat-Sun 0900-1300.* Both offices are run by the **Windhoek Council** ⓘ *www.windhoekcc.org.na*, and have information for all over Namibia. **Namibia Community Based Tourism Association** (NACOBTA) ⓘ *3 Weber St, T061-255977, www.nacobta.com.na*, is the head office and reservations contact for tourism initiatives throughout the country that involve the local people (see box, page 41). This office is not a drop-in facility so they would infinitely prefer reservations by phone or through the website. **Namibia Wildlife Resorts** (NWR) ⓘ *Independence Av near the clock tower, T061-2857200, www.nwr.com.na, Mon-Fri 0800-1700 (for information), 0800-1500 (for reservations)*, has a range of information about the parks, and if you haven't already made reservations for park accommodation before your arrival (which you should have done) then head here to see if you can get last-minute bookings. Alternatively you can book online. If you are visiting Cape Town before Namibia you can make park accommodation reservations at the **NWR office** ⓘ *Ground Floor, Pinnacle Building, (beneath the Cape Town Tourist Office), Burg St, Cape Town, T+27 (0)21-4223761, ct.bookings@nwr.com.na*. Of the private offices, the **Cardboard Box Travel Shop** ⓘ *Kaiserkrone Centre, Post St Mall, T061-256580, www.namibian.org, Mon-Fri 0800-1700*, is a good friendly drop-in shop for all travel arrangements and tours especially for budget travellers.

Safety

Despite being a sleek and modern city with good infrastructure and services, don't be deluded. Windhoek is far from crime free, and obvious tourists are usually the ones to be targeted. Muggings and bag snatchings do occur, so be vigilant when walking around the city centre, especially at the weekend and when the shops start to close in the late afternoon and there are fewer people on the streets; always take a taxi after dark. If you are driving ensure that your place of accommodation has off-street parking as cars parked on the street overnight will invariably get broken into.

History

Windhoek's history reflects the movements of different peoples through the country, and in particular offers an insight into the past hundred years of colonial conquest, apartheid and struggle for independence. Originally Windhoek was known by the Khoikhoi or Nama people as *Ai-gams* (steam or fire-water) and by the Herero people as *Otjomuise* (place of smoke) due to the hot water springs found in what is now the Klein Windhoek district. These springs had been used for centuries as watering holes by the Bushmen (San) and Khoikhoi (Nama), nomadic and semi-nomadic peoples who trekked through the area with their animals.

24 hours in the city

Start the day with a hearty breakfast at one of Windhoek's central cafés around Independence Avenue. Try **Squares Bistro** or **Brix Bistro** for fresh juice, trendy coffees, fat omelettes and German sausage. Head out for a few hours on the walking tour of the city centre, to take in the quirky colonial architecture nestled amongst the more modern office blocks and shopping malls, and to look at the unusual display of meteorites on Post St. On the way, drop in at the Alte Feste Museum to learn about Namibia's colonial history as well as its fight for independence, and the Owela Museum for information about Namibia's indigenous cultural history. Be sure to combine some shopping on your walk; well worth a stop is the Bushmen Art and Africa Museum shop on Independence Avenue and the Namibia Crafts centre on Tal Street. Whilst browsing the excellent selection of crafts and curios in the latter, take a break in the lovely café that serves up a wonderful range of home-made treats. Take an afternoon drive out to the Daan Viljoen Game Park, easily signposted from the city centre. Enjoy a couple of hours of walking or driving around this small but very pretty park, where there are good opportunities to spot a number of antelopes, other small mammals and abundant bird life. In the early evening head for a sundowner at either the bar at the top of **Hotel Thule**, or the hugely atmospheric rose garden terrace at the **Heinitzburg (Castle) Hotel**; both offer outstanding views of the city and nearby hills. Those with cash to splash can stay on at the **Heinitzburg** for a gourmet dinner and fine wine, easily Windhoek's, if not Namibia's, best restaurant. Those on a cheaper budget should head for beer and steak at **Joe's Beerhouse**, or try an authentic African meal at either **Restaurant Africa** or **La Marmite**. For live music, check out what's on at the **Warehouse Theatre** on Tal Street, or head for the **Tower** nearby for a late night drink.

The roots of today's city, however, lie in the settlement established by the Oorlam leader Jonker Afrikaner in the 1840s and 1850s at *Ai-gams*, stretching along the ridge of the Klein Windhoek Valley. In 1836 Jonker urged the British explorer Sir James Alexander, who called the settlement Queen Adelaide's Bath, to organize a missionary for him. In 1842 the Rhenish missionary Hahn arrived to find a well-established settlement, which he called Elberfeld after a centre of the Rhenish mission in Germany. He was so impressed by the settlement that he was drawn to comment, "The location of Elberfeld is superbly beautiful... seeing the extensive thorntree forest with its delicious green and curious forms, the lovely gardens, and the beautiful greensward..."

Jonker himself, in an 1844 letter to the Wesleyan Mission Station, referred to the settlement as *Wind Hoock*, and despite much speculation that he named the settlement after *Winterhoek*, his ancestral home in the Cape, there is no solid evidence to suggest this. However, it is certain that Windhoek was the original name given by Jonker and his followers when they settled here around 1840.

Under Jonker, the settlement flourished and served both as a trading station between the Oorlam/Namas and Herero, as well as a headquarters from which Jonker and his commandos launched cattle raids on the Herero living north of the Swakop River. Following Jonker's death at Okahandja in 1861, Windhoek was temporarily abandoned until the missionary Schröder installed himself in the remains of the original buildings in the 1870s.

War memorials

All over Windhoek there are memorials, dating back to the early German colonial occupation, which remember German losses during wars with the different Namibian peoples. Among these are the Kriegerdenkmal in Zoo Park, the plaques on the walls in the Christuskirche, the Rider Memorial outside the Alte Feste and the Owambo Campaign Memorial next to the railway station. As with all such memorials the victors have commemorated their own dead without any acknowledgment of those conquered or defeated. Since independence, a debate has raged about what should be done with these relics of the country's colonial past, and in particular with the war memorials. Some argue that these symbols of oppression and occupation have no place in a free, independent Namibia and should be removed. Others maintain that the statues and memorials are part of history and therefore should remain. Inevitably these conflicting opinions reflect the different emotions and views of the descendants of those involved in the wars. Nevertheless, whilst wandering around Windhoek it is worth keeping in mind what the monuments represent to the majority of Namibian citizens.

In 1890 the Germans, under Curt von François, were still not well established in Namibia, and having been effectively driven out of Otjimbingwe and Tsaobis by the Nama leader Hendrik Witbooi, made a strategic retreat to Windhoek. This move neatly coincided with the death of Herero leader Maherero, and by the time his successor Samuel Herero sent envoys to Windhoek a few weeks later, the Germans were already halfway through the completion of the original fort. This served as the headquarters for the **Schutztruppe** (colonial troops) and is known as the **Alte Feste** (Old Fort). It now houses the historical section of the State Museum and is the oldest surviving building in Windhoek.

The German colonial settlement of Windhoek emerged around the Alte Feste and the springs surrounding it. The settler John Ludwig established substantial vineyards and fruit and vegetable gardens which fed the small settlement; the modern suburb, Ludwigsdorf, is named after him. The Klein Windhoek Valley continued to be agriculturally productive until the beginning of the 1960s with the hot springs below the Alte Feste 'smoking away'.

With the completion in 1902 of the railway to Swakopmund on the coast, the settlement was able to expand and develop as the economic and cultural centre of the colony. In 1909 Windhoek became a municipality and this period saw the construction of a number of fine buildings, including the **Tintenpalast**, the present site of Namibia's Parliament, and the **Christuskirch** with its stained-glass windows donated by Kaiser Wilhelm II.

During the 1960s the South African government pursued a policy designed to incorporate Namibia into South Africa as the fifth province, and this period saw a further era of rapid development and growth, not just in Windhoek but in the country as a whole. In Windhoek, the government started forcible movements of people from the 'Old Location' in 1959, and as the black population was gradually obliged to settle in Katutura, the white suburbs of Hochland Park and Pioneer's Park were developed on the western side of the city.

The period since independence has seen further growth characterized by some distinctly post-modern buildings in the city centre. The still very much low level skyline is dominated by the **Kalahari Sands Hotel** and the **Namdeb** (formerly CDM) building, but new office blocks, the new **Supreme Court Building** and other Ministry buildings recently completed are quickly changing the face of the city.

On a more modest scale, the last decade has seen a rapid explosion of medium- to low-cost housing developments around the western and southeastern outskirts of the city. These new developments have helped to extend the city far beyond its old boundaries and are bringing Namibians of all races together, as upwardly mobile young black and coloured (originally of mixed European and African descent) Namibians seek to move out of the townships and young white Namibians, no longer able to afford property in the expensive former white suburbs, look elsewhere.

Sights

There is an interesting mixture of architecture along Independence Avenue and a number of museums and galleries to visit. The numerous street cafés and outdoor restaurants lining the side streets running into Independence Avenue are pleasant places to sit, eat, drink and watch people going about their business. The shopping is good with several quality curio shops and modern shopping malls. The streets themselves are generally busy without being intolerably crowded, even at the end of the month when long queues of Windhoekers form at the banks waiting to cash their pay cheques before going off on the monthly spending spree. Note that the city centre virtually closes down at the weekends from around 1300 on Saturday and all day Sunday, when most of the shops, restaurants and attractions close; so weekends are not the best time to explore. Traffic pollution has yet to become a serious issue and gridlock is, for the time being, unheard of.

As virtually all the sites of interest are in the city centre, the most obvious way to see them is on foot. One full day will allow visitors with limited time the opportunity to appreciate the German colonial architecture and visit a couple of the museums. For people with two or three days to spare, a fairly thorough exploration of the city will be possible.

Clock tower and Zoo Park

A good place to start a walk around the city is by the clock tower on the corner of Independence Avenue and Post Street. The tower itself is modelled on that of the old Deutsch-Afrika bank built in 1908, but now long-since gone. Cross the road, turn right and walk along Independence Avenue as far as Zoo Park. Here there is a children's playground, open-air theatre and a café. Adjacent to the park there is a small open-air crafts market specializing in excellent baskets from the north and wood-carvings from the Kavango – with the 2-m-tall giraffes the stars of the display! Before walking into the park itself, look back across the road and you will see three buildings designed by Willi Sander, a German architect responsible for the design of a number of Windhoek's original colonial buildings.

The **Erkrathus Building**, the furthest right of the three, was constructed in 1910 and is typical of this period, incorporating business premises downstairs and living quarters upstairs. Two buildings to the left is **Gathemann House**, commissioned by the then Mayor of Klein Windhoek, Heinrich Gathemann, and now home to Gathemann's restaurant. The stepped roof was of European design intended to prevent the roof from collapsing under the weight of a build-up of snow! The third building bears the inscription **Kronprinz**, the name of the hotel which occupied the building until 1920, and the date of its completion in 1902 can also be seen carved in the stone. The photo shop here has a fine collection of turn-of-the-century photographs of Windhoek, which can be bought as souvenirs.

Walk into the park about 20 m and you will see a **sculptured column** depicting scenes of a prehistoric elephant kill believed to have taken place some 5000 years

Independence Avenue

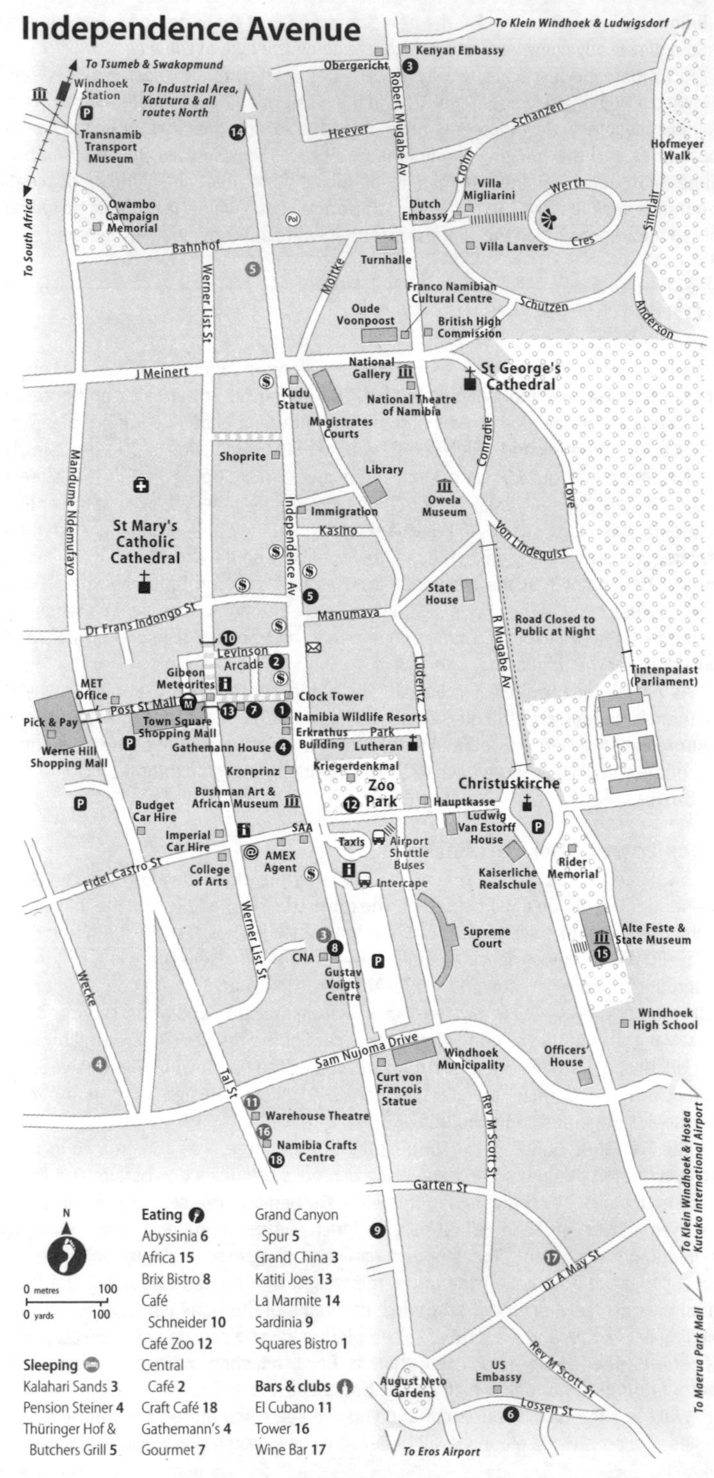

ago on this site. The fossilized remains of two elephants and a variety of Stone Age weapons were found when the park was reconstructed in 1962, evidence that the hot springs were already attracting game to the area in pre-historic times. A message to that effect is carved into the side of the column. On top of the column is part of a fossilized elephant skull, however, the rest of the bones and tools were removed to the State Museum's research collection in 1990. Also in the park is the **Kriegerdenkmal**, unveiled in 1907, a memorial to the German soldiers killed between 1893 to 1894 whilst fighting the Namas led by Hendrik Witbooi.

If you're interested in African arts and crafts, **Bushman Art and African Museum**; *187 Independence Av, T061-228828, www.bushmanart.com, Mon-Fri 0830-1730, Sat-Sun 0900-1300*, is a trendy boutique opposite the park and is worth a visit as it has probably the best selection of souvenirs anywhere in Windhoek. Local curios include items from the Bushmen and Himba and carpets woven from the wool of the karakul sheep. In the back of the store there's an interesting display of carvings, metalwork, jewellery and pottery from all over the continent.

Post Street

Right in the heart of Windhoek, you can't miss the **Gibeon Meteorites** or **Meteor Fountain**, claimed to be the largest collection of meteorites anywhere in the world. Fashioned into a series of sculptures sitting on top of steel columns set around a fountain, they dominate the middle of Post Street. The meteorites get their name from the area in which they were found, southwest of Mariental, and are believed to have belonged to the world's largest ever meteor shower which took place some 600 million years ago. Although they look like fairly ordinary rocks, the meteorites are in fact made from solid metal, mostly iron, with nickel and some smaller amounts of cobalt, phosphorus and other trace elements. The average weight of the meteorites is an impressive 348.5 kg; in total 77 rocks were originally recovered of which a total of 33 are on display here.

The **Crafts Market**, running most of the way down Post Street, is an enjoyable place to wander around, whether you're planning on buying any souvenirs or not. If you do decide to buy, be prepared to bargain over the price. You should be able to pick up some objects at considerably lower prices than in the boutiques around town.

Fidel Castro Street

Back at Zoo Park, the road that crosses Independence Avenue to the south of the park is Fidel Castro Street. One block to the west and on the left of Fidel Castro is the **Windhoek Conservatoire**, built in 1911-1912, which was formerly the Regierungsschule (Government School) and today is the home of the College of Arts, and has an impressive ornamental weather vane perched on top of its pyramidal tower.

Heading east, at the top of the steep hill, on the corner of Lüderitz Street, is the **Hauptkasse**, the former home of the German colonial government's finance section. The building now serves the Ministry of Agriculture's Directorate of Extension Services. Directly opposite is **Ludwig Van Estorff House**, named after the former Schutztruppe commander who, between campaigns, lived here from 1902 to 1910. Over the century it has housed senior officers, a hostel and a trade school until the National Reference Library, usually referred to as the Van Estorff library, moved here in 1984. It is now the **Namibian German Foundation Goethe Centre** in affiliation with the British Council, a centre of cultural exchange with multi-media facilities open to the public. On the far side of the library stands the **Supreme Court Building**, opened in October 1997, which looks down over the parking area and over to the **Kalahari Sands Hotel**.

South of Fidel Castro Street, the statue of **Curt von François** (see page 80) stands outside the Windhoek Municipality on Independence Avenue, and was unveiled in 1965 on the 75th anniversary of the 'founding' of the city.

Townships

Most people with a rudimentary knowledge of South Africa have heard about the Johannesburg township Soweto, usually in the context of violent crimes or civil unrest between rival ANC and Inkatha Freedom Movement urban guerrillas. What is perhaps less well known is that all towns in South Africa and Namibia have their own townships. Usually far from the town centre and well hidden from the white suburbs, the townships are home to the vast majority of black and coloured Namibians in the central and southern regions.

In keeping with the apartheid policy of separateness, it was not sufficient to merely reserve the most desirable parts of town for whites, a policy of divide and rule required that the black and coloured communities also be separated. On the apartheid scale of civil rights, the coloured community enjoyed better educational and employment opportunities than the black community. The construction of separate townships for the two groups in the late 1950s and 1960s was a further expression of the divide and rule strategy of apartheid.

Towards the end of the 1950s the white community in Windhoek decided that the 'non-whites' were living too close for comfort, and so the black and coloured communities were evicted from the 'Old Location' on the western side of the city centre, and relocated further away to the west and northwest. Resistance to the forced removals was mobilized by the then two recently formed liberation movements, Swanu and Swapo, and culminated in the December 1959 uprising when police shot dead 13 protestors and wounded many others. In the Namibian context this massacre signalled a landmark in the liberation struggle comparable to the events that were to take place in Sharpeville, South Africa, a few months later.

Two new townships were built, Khomasdal for the coloured community and Katutura (variously translated as 'we have no dwelling place' or 'the place where we don't want to stay') for the black community. The black township was itself divided along tribal lines with different sections for the Damara, Herero, Owambo and so on. Whilst no expense was spared when it came to providing facilities for the white community, the opposite applied to the creation of Katutura. Thousands of uniform shoe-box houses were built, lining the dirt and dust roads of the township and, until the late 1970s, black people were not even entitled to own property and businesses in their own communities!

After the scrapping of this legislation and of the Group Areas Act restricting freedom of movement, Katutura saw both an influx of newcomers from rural areas and an upsurge in black-owned businesses. This emergent class of business people was soon profiting enough to build some fancy houses in areas such as Soweto and Wanaheda.

Nowadays, in theory, anyone can live where they want; but little has changed since independence, with the overwhelming majority of black Windhoekers livin in Katutura in cramped accommodation.

You can visit Katutura but because of safety issues it is best to go on an organized tour; driving through the area unaccompanied is not recommended. A walk through Katutura is interesting and worthwhile, not least when one bears in mind that this former township is now larger than the main part of the city and is, additionally, a melting pot for Namibians from all parts of the country. For recommended companies that offer half-day tours, see Tour operators, page 99.

Nearby, the **Namibia Crafts Centre** ⓘ *40 Tal St, T061-242222, Mon-Fri 0830-1700, Sat 0830-1330*, is located in the old breweries building next to the Warehouse Theatre. This is a small indoor market on two floors, selling a variety of Namibian carvings, pottery, basket, leatherwork, jewellery and artwork. It also

Windhoek centre

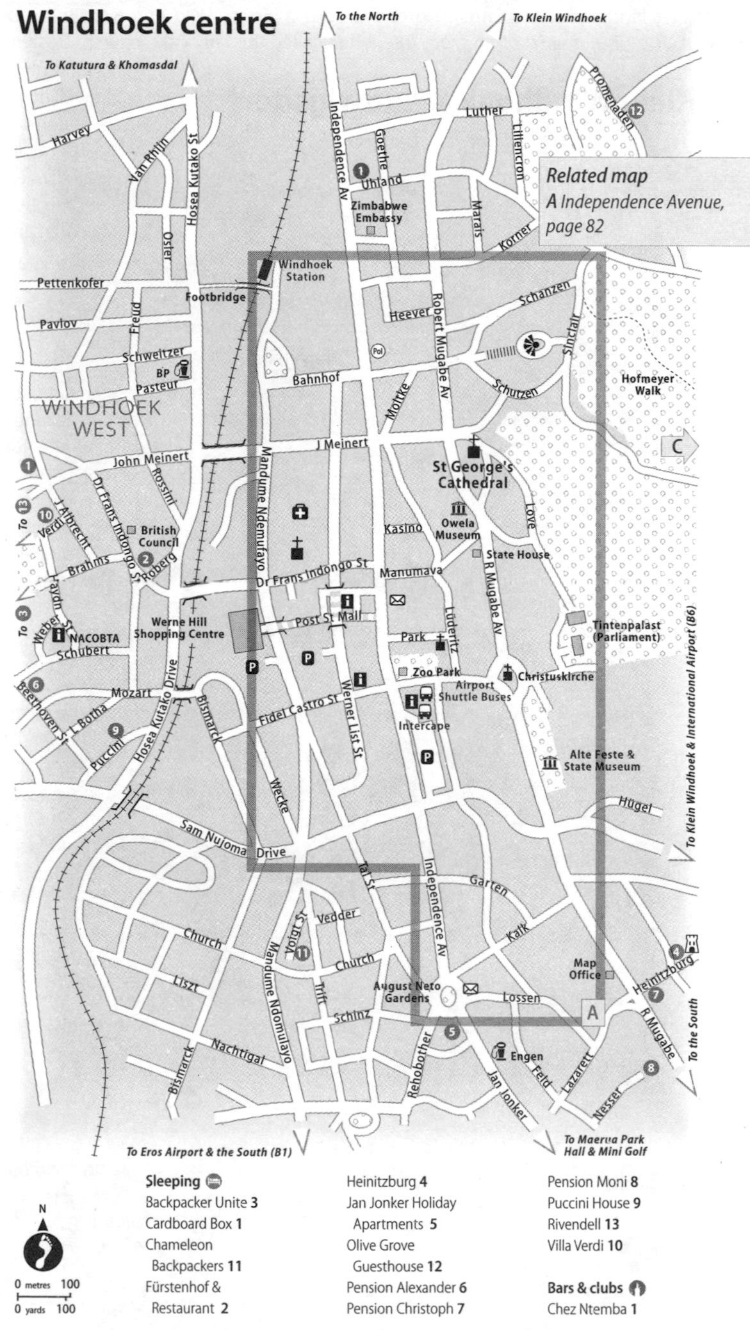

Sleeping
Backpacker Unite **3**
Cardboard Box **1**
Chameleon Backpackers **11**
Fürstenhof & Restaurant **2**
Heinitzburg **4**
Jan Jonker Holiday Apartments **5**
Olive Grove Guesthouse **12**
Pension Alexander **6**
Pension Christoph **7**
Pension Moni **8**
Puccini House **9**
Rivendell **13**
Villa Verdi **10**

Bars & clubs
Chez Ntemba **1**

 houses an earthy café frequented by tourists as well as some of Windhoek's arty crowd (see Eating, page 96).

Christuskirche and Rider Memorial

At the top of the hill on an island in the middle of the road is one of Windhoek's striking landmarks, the **Christuskirche** ⓘ *T061-236002, Wed and Sat 1100-1200, Mon, Tue, Thu, and Fri 1400-1700, free*, often called the fairy cake church. Designed

Klein Windhoek & Ludwigsdorf

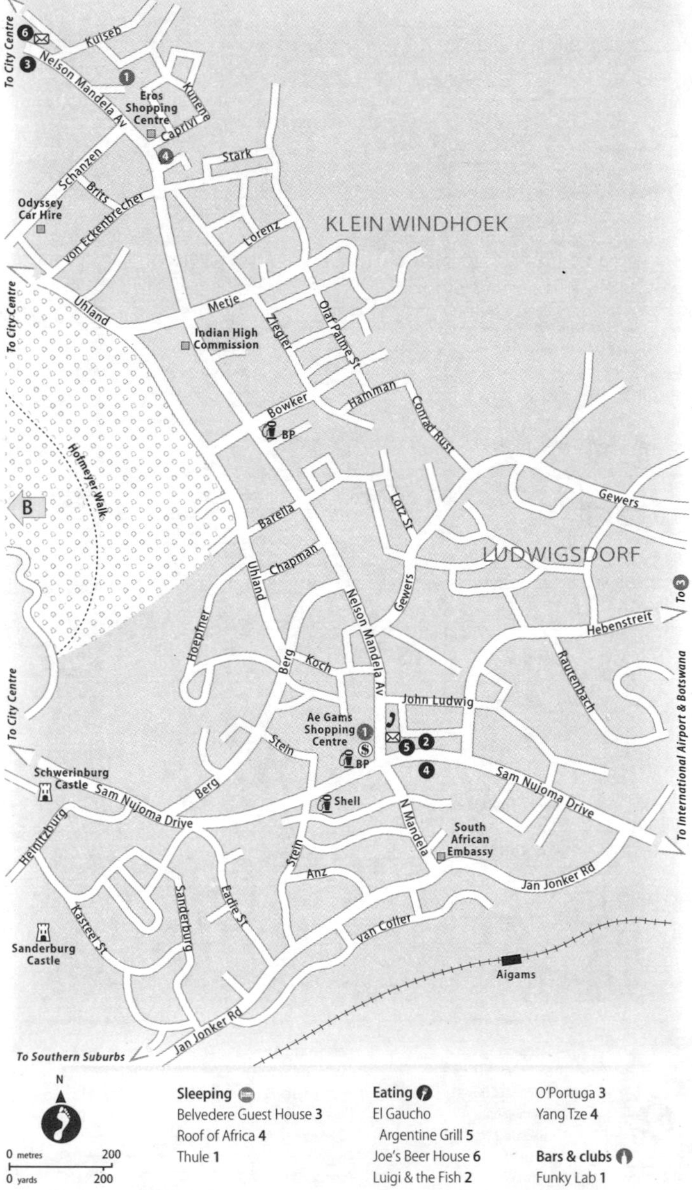

Sleeping
Belvedere Guest House 3
Roof of Africa 4
Thule 1

Eating
El Gaucho Argentine Grill 5
Joe's Beer House 6
Luigi & the Fish 2
O'Portuga 3
Yang Tze 4

Bars & clubs
Funky Lab 1

“” As the sun moves across the sky, the colours on the church walls change to reflect the colours on the mountains...

by Gottlieb Reddecker, the church's foundation stone was laid in 1907 and the building itself finally consecrated in 1910. The church was built by the Germans to commemorate the 'peace' between the Germans and the Nama, Herero and Owambo peoples, and inside there are seven plaques bearing the names of German soldiers killed during the wars. Of the Nama, Herero and Owambo dead there is no record.

This Lutheran church was constructed from local sandstone and its design is an interesting mix of neo-Gothic and art nouveau styles. As the sun moves across the sky, the colours on the church walls change to reflect the colours on the mountains of the Khomas Hochland to the southwest. The church looks most striking at sunrise and sunset which are probably the best times to take photographs. The stained-glass windows were donated by Kaiser Wilhelm II and the altar bible by his wife Augusta, and although not particularly impressive looking from outside, it is well worth climbing the steps to the balcony to get a better look.

The walk along Robert Mugabe Avenue, running south from the church, takes you towards the whitewashed walls of the Alte Feste (the Old Fort), see below, which has looked over central Windhoek for the past century. Before reaching the steps leading up to the fort's entrance you can't fail to notice the enormous Reder Denkmal, the **'Rider Memorial'**. The statue of a mounted soldier depicts General von Trotha, the German Commander who succeeded in 'pacifying' the rebellious Herero and Nama peoples during the 1904 to 1907 uprising. These victories allowed the colonizers to consolidate their control over Namibia and in turn subjugate the indigenous Namibians.

Alte Feste area

The Old Fort itself was built in 1892 as the headquarters of the first Schutztruppe (protection troop) to arrive in Namibia (in 1889) and is Windhoek's oldest surviving building, an impressive sight shimmering in the sunlight on top of the hill. The plaque on the wall outside the entrance states that the fort was built as a 'stronghold to preserve peace and order between the rivalling Namas and Hereros'. This statement was a convenient justification for the colonization and subjugation of Namibia, and typical of the European rhetoric of the time.

The Alte Feste now houses the **State Museum's Alte Feste Display and Education Centre** ⓘ *Robert Mugabe Av, T061-2934362, Mon-Fri 0900-1800, Sat and Sun 1000-1300, 1500-1800, free*, which is interesting and well worth a visit to get a feel for Namibia's colonial heritage and fight for independence. The first room has an exhibition of photographs depicting significant events in Namibia over the last 100 years and includes photographs of important Namibian leaders such as Hendrik Witbooi, Maherero and more recently President Sam Nujoma. One of the most powerful photographs is of Owambo King Mandume Ndemufayo's dead body being recovered by South African troops in 1917. One story has it that the South Africans cut off his head and took it to Windhoek to serve as a warning to other 'rebellious' leaders.

In other rooms there are displays of the early household implements, tools and musical instruments of the first missionaries and European settlers. Arranged alongside these are similar objects used by the different ethnic Namibian peoples, making for an unorthodox, but nevertheless interesting, display.

The **Independence Exhibition** contains photographs, flags, uniforms and other memorabilia of the transition period from South African colonial rule to independence, monitored by the United Nations Transitional Assistance Group (UNTAG). In addition there are interesting sections looking at the various sectors of the economy and their respective roles in Namibia's future development. One prominent section focuses on SWAPO, Namibia's governing party since independence.

The rest of the museum is a modern complex which displays exhibits on natural history and ethnic crafts, and the library has a good collection of early books on Southwest Africa.

Climb the turret before leaving and you'll be rewarded by a splendid view of Windhoek and the hills of the Khomas Hochland to the west.

Windhoek High School is next to the fort and across the road opposite the school is the old **Officers' House** built in 1906-1907 to house senior officers of the Schutztruppe, now serving as the Office of the Ombudsman. The highly decorative and rather attractive brickwork is a recreation of Putz architecture which was fashionable in Germany at the time. The architect, Gottlieb Redecker, designed the building after returning from a year's visit to Germany, and this was the first building of its style in Namibia. Walking back in the direction of the Christuskirche you'll pass the former **Kaiserliche Realschule**, which opened in 1909 as the first German high school in Windhoek. After the Second World War the building became an English-speaking school and now functions as the administrative part of the National Museum.

Schwerinburg, Heinitzburg and Sanderburg castles

A short distance from the city centre, sitting atop a series of hills to the southeast of the museum, between Robert Mugabe Avenue and Sam Nujoma Drive, are Windhoek's three elegant castles. All three were designed by the architect Willi Sander, the first for Graf Schwerin in 1914, and the second for his wife as her residence. The design of Schwerinburg incorporates an original stone structure built by Curt von François and used as a lookout post in the early days of the Schutztruppe's presence in Windhoek. Sander designed the third castle for himself in 1917. Heinitzburg Castle, on Heinitz Strasse, is open to the public as a luxury hotel (see page 90), although anyone can go and have coffee on the terrace, which offers one of the best views of central Windhoek and the mountains of the Khomas Hochland to the west. The terrace coffee shop is open from 1000-1800 and it is well worth the effort of walking up from the city centre to enjoy the views. Sanderburg Castle is privately owned and Schwerinburg Castle is used as the Italian Embassy.

Robert Mugabe Avenue

Walk back in the direction of the Christuskirche and down Robert Mugabe Avenue until you see some gardens on your right. These gardens were laid out in the 1930s and contain an olive grove consisting of 100 trees and a bowling green. More significantly, they surround the home of Namibia's Parliament, the **Tintenpalast**, an impressive yellow and white double-storied building with a veranda running around it. This building was also designed by Gottlieb Redecker, and first opened for business in 1914 as the German colonial government headquarters. It reputedly acquired its name, the 'Ink Palace', from the amount of paper work that went on here. Over the course of the 20th century the palace housed successive governments, before being renovated at independence, in preparation for its role as the home of an independent **Namibian Parliament**.

Further down Robert Mugabe Avenue you will find **State House** on your left-hand side. Currently home to President Pohamba, this grandiose building was formally the official residence of the South African Administrator-General.

Next to State House, the **Owela Museum** ⓘ *Robert Mugabe Av, Mon-Fri 0900-1800, Sat and Sun 1000-1300, 1500-1800, closed public holidays, free*, a section of the State Museum, is located just below State House and houses the ethnology hall. The exhibition consists of a series of diaromas intended to provide a picture of the lifestyles of the inhabitants of the country within their various environments. They include depictions of the cultivation of *omahangu* (millet), fishing in the Kavango, the Kalahari Bushmen (San) and the Owambo *oshanas* (water pans). The foyer of the museum has an ever-changing temporary display. There is also has a permanent cheetah exhibition which seeks to educate people about Africa's most endangered cat, the largest population of which is found in Namibia.

In contrast to the plethora of German-inspired architecture, **St George's Cathedral** in Love Street offers a taste of rural England with its solid brown brickwork and exposed beams inside. It is the smallest functional cathedral in southern Africa and is the spiritual home of the Anglican community in Namibia. Designed by GHS Bradford and dedicated in 1925 the bell tower houses a bell cast in 1670, one of a set made for St Mary's Church in Northwall, Canterbury. Love Street starts opposite the Owela Display next to the Engen garage. On Werth and Sinclair streets, round the corner from the cathedral, are a pair of fine houses, **Villa Migliarini** and **Villa Lanvers**, both dating back to 1907.

The **National Theatre of Namibia** (NTN) building lies at the bottom of Robert Mugabe Avenue on the corner of John Meinert Street. Turn left onto John Meinert Street to the **National Gallery** ⓘ *T061-231160, Mon-Fri 0900-1700, Sat 0900-1100, free*, a permanent display reflecting a spectrum of both historical and contemporary Namibian art, including the work of well-known artist John Mufangeyo.

Opposite the gallery on John Meinert Street is the **Oude Voonpoost**, formerly the survey offices and now home to the National Theatre's offices, with a fire-proof archives room.

Cross over Lüderitz Street where the **Magistrates Courts** are located until you find yourself back at Independence Avenue. The bronze statue of a kudu on the corner is a familiar Windhoek landmark, commemorating the kudu which died during the 1896 rinderpest epidemic.

Bahnhof Street

A short walk north up Independence Avenue and west along Bahnhof Street will take you to the **Owambo Campaign Memorial**, a stone obelisk in the garden next to the railway station. The head of King Mandume is reputed to be buried beneath the memorial.

Upstairs in the Old Railway Station Building is the **Transnamib Transport Museum** ⓘ *Mon-Fri 0900-1300, 1400-1700, closed weekends and public holidays, US$0.75 adults, US$0.50 children (under 18)*, a well-laid-out and extensive collection depicting the history of rail and other transport in Namibia over the past 100 years. The **Railway Station** itself is an interesting building, as is the **Turnhalle Building**, further east on Bahnhof Street, which was built in 1909 for the Gymnastic Society and later played a role in the process of Namibian independence.

Windhoek suburbs and around

Avis Dam ⓘ *on the B6 road east to the airport beyond the suburb of Olympia*, is a popular spot for birdwatchers, particularly just before the first summer rains fall, when sightings of more than a hundred different species have been reported in a day. There is a car park at the entrance.

Namibia Breweries ⓘ *Iscor St, Northern Industrial Area, T061-3204999, www.nambrew.com*, brew the very tasty **Windhoek Lager**, amongst other brands, under the German Purity Law of 1516. To sample the golden nectar, which is made with spring water, and to watch the beer-making process, you can visit the brewery by appointment only on Tuesday and Thursday.

Heroes' Acre ⓘ *15 km to the south of the city off the B1, not far after the police check on the road*, a monument dedicated as a symbol of nationalism and patriotism, was inaugurated in 2002 by the then president Sam Nujoma. It took 13 months and almost US$10 million to build and covers about 733 ha, surrounded by a 3-km fence. As well as being the resting place for 174 war graves, there is a platform, a pavilion that is capable of seating up to 5000 people, and various bronze statues of soldiers and notable figures from the period leading up to Namibia's independence. One of its main features is a frescoed wall which exhibits scenes of the various uprisings throughout Namibia's history including the forced removal of blacks to the Katutura township during the era of the Group Areas Act, and the SWAPO armed liberation struggle in the years leading up to independence. There isn't really much here for the visitor and the site is expected to be used for major local political and celebratory functions such as Heroes' Day which is celebrated on 26 August each year.

Penduka Crafts (Penduka means 'to wake up') is an initiative by women in Katutura township which combines a number of small local enterprises from a craft shop to accommodation. A visit to Penduka, with or without spending the night, is the perfect opportunity to get out of the city and see a local community project. The well-stocked shop has a range of locally produced craft items and you can watch the women at work. There is also a *boma* restaurant and you can spend the night in a simple rondavel, for around US$25 (T061-257210). This is a **NACOBTA** project, see box page 41, or visit www.nacobta.com.na. To get to Penduka, follow Independence Avenue through Katutura, cross Otjimuise Road and continue into Eveline Street past the Queen Supermarket. Turn left into Green Mountain Dam Road and left again at the Penduka sign. However, it is best to go into Katutura on an organized tour. **Face to Face** is recommended, see Tour operators, page 99, and for more information about Katutura see box, page 84.

Sleeping

Windhoek *p76, maps p77, p82, p85 and p86*
As a general rule 2 people sharing a double room get a much better rate than 1 person alone as most places don't actually have single rooms. Windhoek offers a good range of hotel and guesthouse accommodation, from the 4-star luxury of the **Windhoek Country Club** to dormitories for backpackers at the **Cardboard Box**. Unless you need to be near either of the airports there is no need to look for accommodation outside the city centre whilst you are in Windhoek. The larger hotels, apart from the **Safari Hotel** by Eros Airport, are all either on or close to Independence Av, whilst most pensions and guesthouses are found in suburbs close to the city centre.

Making a choice between staying in a hotel or a guesthouse is less about price than about atmosphere. Broadly speaking hotels have over 20 rooms; pensions have 10-20 rooms; and guesthouses have 10 rooms. For further information, see page 43.

Hotels

AL Hotel Heinitzburg, 22 Heinitzburg Strasse, T061-249597, www.heinitzburg.com. Stylish olde-worlde rooms with all mod cons in this turn-of-the-20th-century castle set high on a hill with magnificent views over the city, very atmospheric and professionally run. A member of the international **Relais et Chateaux** hotel group. Rooms are charming and spacious with 4-poster beds and brilliant white bedding. Facilities include a swimming pool, a very good and elegant restaurant, **Leos in the Castle**, run by a French chef and serving superb gourmet food (see under Eating). There is a well-stocked wine cellar that is perhaps the largest in Namibia. Recommended.

AL Kalahari Sands Hotel, Independence Av, T061-2800000, www.suninternational.com. A Windhoek landmark right in the centre of the city. Large, rather impersonal modern luxury hotel. Rooms have a/c, TV, there are several restaurants and conference rooms, swimming pool on the roof, gym, casino; all you'd expect of a 4-star hotel, very popular with both local and overseas business people. Good views over Windhoek.

A Hotel Fürstenhof, 4 Frans Indongo St, T061-237380, fursten@united-hospitality.com. 33 comfortable rooms with a/c and TV, in a

For an explanation of the sleeping and eating price codes used in this guide, see inside the front cover. Other relevant information is found in Essentials, see pages 43-51.

block with balconies overlooking the swimming pool, secure parking, within easy walking distance of the city centre. Best known for the quality continental-style restaurant, **Chef Max Gourmet Bistro**, which specializes in French and German cuisine accompanied by a very good wine list.

A Hotel Thule, 1 Gorges St, T061-250146, www.thulenamibia.com. Fairly new hotel behind imposing gates and a row of flags, perched on the lip of a hill above Eros with fantastic views. Rooms are very stylish and modern with lots of glass and chrome fittings, a/c and heating, and there's a restaurant and bar which is rather special (see Eating, below), swimming pool, and a number of shops. A drink in the **Sundowner Bar** at the top of the complex is recommended, but not for those who have a fear of heights as the steep hill seems to literally fall away beneath you.

A Windhoek Country Club, Western bypass, south of the city centre just beyond Eros Airport, T061-2055911, www.legacyhotels.com. The hotel offers regular bus transfers to the city. A modern hotel with 152 a/c luxury rooms (all spacious and comfortable), 2 quality restaurants, poolside snack bar and casino. This is the best of its kind in Namibia but it may not suit someone planning a quiet holiday. It is completely surrounded by an 18-hole golf course, there's a swimming pool and tennis courts. Recommended.

B Safari Court & Hotel Safari, Rehoboth Weg (B1 S), T061-2968000, www.safari hotel.com.na. Well located for Eros Airport. 2 hotels in 1 on a 5-ha plot, nearly 500 rooms in total with TV and a/c, and made-for hotel furnishings, several restaurants and bars, swimming pool and free transport 0700-1900 into city centre every ½ hr. **Avis** also has a car rental office here and there are several conference halls.

B Thüringer Hof Hotel, Independence Av, T061-226031, www.namibiasunhotels. com.na. Very centrally located opposite the main police station. Best known for its beer garden which offers daily changing menus of both traditional African food and German cuisine. This is a comfortable old-style hotel close to the city centre, the staff are friendly and the 40 rooms have en suite bathrooms, a/c and TV. Popular with German tourists and business travellers. The **Butcher's Grill**, see page 95, is also located here.

C Roof of Africa, 124-126 Nelson Mandela Av, corner with Gusinde St, T061-254708, www.roofofafrica.com. A neat, fairly new, set-up in the northern areas of Klein Windhoek. 24 double rooms, a restaurant and bar under thatched roof, very attractive with trees growing through the roof, secure off-street parking, helpful travel centre that can arrange car hire and airport transfers, e-mail facilities, swimming pool that is heated in the winter in lovely gardens and sauna. Free pick-up from town centre. Recommended.

Pensions

B Hotel Pension Christoph, corner of Henitzburg St and Robert Mugabe Av, T061-240777, christoph@mweb.com.na. Close to the city centre, 12 double rooms with showers, fans, TV, disabled access, phone, price includes an extensive buffet breakfast, secure parking and swimming pool. An excellent small, family-run pension that has won a lot of awards in Namibia, and judging from the amount of repeat trade and readers' recommendations, it is a firm favourite for most guests. Nearly always full – book well in advance to avoid disappointment.

B Hotel Pension Moni, 7 Rieks van der Walt St, T061-228350, www.pensionmoni.com. 12 double rooms, with minibar, TV and radio, some family rooms, swimming pool, good cooked buffet-style breakfasts.

B Hotel Pension Steiner, 11 Wecker, T061-222898, www.steiner.com.na. 16 clean en suite rooms with DSTV, swimming pool, *braai* and bar area, lounge, breakfasts are very good with unusual sweet and savoury crêpes, friendly staff. Recommended. French spoken as well as the usual German and English.

C Hotel Pension Alexander, 10 Beethoven St, T061-240775, hotelale@iafrica.com.na. Behind the Werne Hill Park shopping centre close to the city centre, has 13 en suite rooms which are quite well spread out, with DSTV, and fan, very attractive gardens and swimming pool, bar and parking.

Guesthouses

AL Olive Grove Guesthouse, corner of Promenaden Rd and Ngami St, T061-234971, www.olivegrove.com.na. Stylish upmarket small guesthouse, each room has a large veranda, lovely bathrooms with stone sinks, very nice decor, comfortable communal lounge with fireplace, internet access, the pretty gardens have a plunge pool and spa bath, rates include breakfast, other meals on request.

B **Belvedere Guest House**, 78 Gever St, T061-258867, www.belvedereguest house.com. Lovely group of bright white buildings surrounding a heated swimming pool with wooden decks, very new and fresh looking, the 6 en suite rooms decorated very nicely with African touches, each with coffee maker, DSTV, minibar and internet access for laptops, floodlit tennis court, good breakfasts and on Wed the family has a *braai* that guests are invited to join.

B **Casa Blanca**, corner of Gous and Fritsche Sts, T061-249622, www.casablanca-hotel-namibia.com. Built in the style of an old Moorish castle, large a/c rooms, swimming pool and jacuzzi, romantic dinners served on the patio, reasonable selection of South African wines, library and lovely tropical gardens.

B **Kleines Heim**, 10 Volans St, T061-248200, www.kleinesheim.com. The name comes from its function as a maternity home during the days of the 'Old Location', 14 smart English-cottage-style rooms facing attractive gardens, all individually and nicely decorated with showers, TV, under-floor heating, phone and coffee-making machine, bar, conference facilities built around small pool. Rates include breakfast, and dinner is available on request. Recommended.

B **Villa Verdi**, 4 Verdi St, T061-221994, www.villa-verdi.com. Within easy walking distance of the city centre, offers 14 African-theme rooms with lovely wooden beds and tasteful curios hanging on the walls, with TV and phone, swimming pool, comfortable lounge and secure parking, restaurant and bar serving good Italian-inspired food, the set up is all very elegant. Recommended. Smoking is not permitted here.

C **Rivendell**, 40 Beethoven St, T061-250006, ahj@iafrica.com.na. Simple and affordable guesthouse in the west of the city with 8 rooms, 4 with en suite bathrooms, swimming pool, breakfast not included but there is a kitchen for guests to use, readers have reported that the owner is very helpful and can organize all travel arrangements.

Backpackers' hostels

C-E **Cardboard Box**, 15 Johan Albrecht St, T064-228994, cbbox@iway.na. Long-time first choice with backpackers, is close to town and has double and triple rooms and dorms, weekly rates also available, TV, bar, good restaurant, swimming pool, cooking facilities, car hire is one of the cheapest around, notice board with travellers' information, internet, laundry, free pick-up and drop-off to the Intercape bus (arrange before you arrive).

C-E **Chameleon Backpackers**, 5-7 Voigt St North, T/F061-244347, www.chameleon backpackers.com. 10-15 mins' walk from city centre, very neat en suite rooms in the more upmarket guesthouse section, smart singles and doubles and 6-bed dorms with shared bathrooms in the backpackers, a small space for camping, communal kitchen and common room with TV, phone/fax and internet, swimming pool, thatched bar and *braai* area, secure parking, popular with backpackers, older travellers and overlanders. Chameleon's new location has proved to be a good move and this is an excellent place to stay. Can arrange free pick-up and drop-off for the Intercape bus with notice, and runs its own hugely popular tours of Namibia (see Tour operators, page 99).

D **Puccini House**, 4 Puccini St, T/F061-236355, puccinis@mweb.com.na. Budget guesthouse with dorm beds, double rooms, camping, rates include breakfast. Kitchen, laundry, secure parking, lockers, swimming pool, sauna, nice bar area with open fire and pool table and pretty gardens. Close to city centre.

E **Backpacker Unite**, 5 Grieg St, T/F061-259485, magicbus@iafrica. Room for up to 22 people, dorms and double rooms, kitchen, TV lounge, swimming pool, sauna, pool table, *braais* are held on Sat night, internet access. Run by Hermann and Erica. Can assist with car rental and tours.

Self-catering and camping

B **Jan Jonker Holiday Apartments**, 183 Jan Jonker Weg, T061-221236, janjonker@ natron.net. Fully equipped modern flats sleeping up to 4, plus a house that can sleep 10, very nice decor and each unit has been individually decorated, has a homely feel and recommended for families, cooking facilities include toaster, 4-plate stove, fridge and coffee machine, phone, TV, video, secure parking, close to city centre.

B-F Arebbusch Travel Lodge, Rehoboth Weg (B1 S), outskirts of town on the way to the **Windhoek County Club**, T061-252255, www.arebbush.com. A large attractive and very secure site with 2- and 5-bed bungalows, en suite double rooms, TV and small kitchenette, and camping/caravan sites with spotless ablution and kitchen blocks with cooker, pleasant bar, shop selling basic food items, ice, firewood and beer, laundrette and pool, closest camping to centre of town. **Note** If you are camping, avoid the dry riverbed at the bottom of the site in the rainy season, there have been flash floods here previously and tents have been washed away. Overlanders should note that there is a truck stop at the entrance that sells discounted diesel. Recommended.

Windhoek suburbs and around *p89*

Guest farms and lodges

L Goche Ganas Nature Reserve and Wellness Village, 20 km south of Windhoek on the B1, turn left onto D1463 for 9 km, T061-224909, www.gocheganas.com.. New all-inclusive luxury resort on a private 6000-ha nature reserve which is home to several species of game including rhino and giraffe. 16 superb suites under thatch, with a/c, DSTV, DVD/CD players, internet access and lovely stone bathrooms, a stunning indoor heated swimming pool in a Moorish stone-arched building plus outdoor pool, gym, yoga and fitness facilities, 11 treatment rooms for a full range of pampering, sauna, hilltop restaurant and sundowner decks, detox or weight loss meals can be arranged. Children under 12 not permitted. Very nice top-of-the-range option, rooms start at US$440 for a double and include everything except beauty treatments and alcoholic drinks.

A Auas Game Lodge, 45 km from Windhoek, T061-240043, www.auas-lodge.com. Follow B1 23 km south of Windhoek, turn onto D1463 for 22 km to the farm; they can collect from the airport. Award-winning lodge with 15 large double rooms with patios, swimming pool, restaurant and bar. Activities include a tennis court, hiking and game drives on the well-stocked game farm that is home to giraffe, wildebeest, eland and blesbok. There's also a nearby dam that is good for birdwatching. It offers game drives and walks and has some caged cheetahs. A lovely spot to open your itinerary.

A Midgard Lodge, follow the B6 towards Gobabis for 20 km, turn onto D2102 for 60 km, T062-503888, www.nambisunhotels.com. A 3-star lodge with en suite double bungalows, organic dining under poolside *lapa*, tennis, volleyball, badminton, fitness centre with sauna, hiking, horse riding, game drives in Otjihavera Mountains; an all-round resort with good facilities for families but rather large and impersonal.

B Airport Lodge, 20 km from the airport on the road towards Windhoek, T061-231491/2, airportl@mweb.com.na. 7 thatched self-catering chalets with 2, 3 or 6 beds with TV and minibar, conference facilities and swimming pool, and pleasant views of the surrounding hills. It is one of the few lodges in the country not run by whites. A good bet if you don't fancy staying downtown.

B Düsternbrook, follow the B1 north towards Okahandja, after 30 km take the D1499 and follow it for 10 km and then follow signs for farm, T061-232572, www.duesternbrook.net. 13 comfortable en suite rooms in an old German colonial farmhouse built in 1909, restaurant, swimming pool. The game farm has resident rhino, giraffe, eland, wildebeest, and you are guaranteed to see leopard. Rates include all meals, the game drive and leopard viewing. For a small fee day visitors are welcome for the game drive that begins daily at 1430 in winter and 1530 in summer. Birdwatching and hiking trails are also on offer to guests staying overnight.

B Eagle's Rock Leisure Lodge, follow the C28 west towards Swakopmund for 38 km, then take the D1958 for Wilhelmstal, turn off at the sign for **Eagle's Rock**, T/F061-257116, www.eaglesrocklodge.com. 4 double bungalows, 1 family unit, restaurant, swimming pool, TV, video, hiking trails, horse riding, game drives in Khomas Hochland close to Daan Viljoen, kudu and martial eagles are common around here, choose B&B or full board. The lodge is involved in a project training young women from impoverished backgrounds from all over southern Africa for the hospitality industry.

Eating

Windhoek *p76, maps p77, p82, p85 and p86*
There are plenty of places to eat out in Windhoek, although many restaurants offer the same meaty fare of steak, ribs, schnitzel and hamburgers. Many are chain restaurants, all serving more or less the same type of food for similar prices with the odd speciality here and there. The portions tend to be generous, the meat good quality, the service American style and the atmosphere relaxed and informal. Some are also popular drinking holes with young (white) Namibians and get pretty crowded and loud later in the evenings. There are a small number of restaurants offering a more varied menu, but vegetarians are unlikely to find anything to write home about. There are numerous fast food outlets all over central Windhoek including **KFC, King Pie** and **Nando's Chicken**. In addition most Portuguese corner shops and many garages also have fried chicken, sausages and chips to take away. This may well be your only option late at night as most restaurants close by 2300. Restaurant prices are not unreasonable by European/North American standards, from around US$15-20 for 2 for a light meal with drinks to US$60-80 for a serious meal and wine in one of the better establishments.

African

ΨΨ **Abyssinia**, Lossen St, T061-254891. Tasty ethnic Ethiopian food, interesting place where you can eat seated on the floor the traditional way or at tables, there are also performances of the Ethiopian coffee ceremony, but a touch costly. Tue-Sat 1200-2300.

ΨΨ **La Marmite**, 383 Independence Av, T061-240306. Very unusual for Windhoek, this is a West African restaurant run by Cameroonian chef Marital. Try chicken, fish and meat cooked in spicy tomato sauces or peanut butter, *ndolé* (a spinach dish), okra stew, pepper soup, accompanied by Senegalese rice or couscous, washed down with delicious and very refreshing home-made non-alcoholic ginger beer. West African masks adorn the walls and there is a pretty garden out back under the arms of a mulberry tree. Marital is presently writing a book of peanut butter recipes. The name means 'cooking pot' in French. Daily 1200-1500, 1730-2330.

ΨΨ **Restaurant Africa**, Alte Feste Museum, T061-247178. A good range of African dishes including some from Morocco, Ghana, Nigeria and Mozambique, and the balcony overlooking the city is a great spot for sundowners. The very brave can try the *mopane* worms here. Tue-Sun 1800-2300.

Chinese

ΨΨ **Grand China Restaurant**, Kenya House, Robert Mugabe Av, T061-225751. Authentic mainland Chinese cooking and decor, large portions, friendly service, though not sure about the karaoke bar. Recommended. Daily 1200-2200.

ΨΨ **Yang Tze Restaurant**, Sam Nujoma Drive, just after the Klein Windhoek crossing, T061-224040. The oldest Chinese restaurant in the city but newly relocated to a modern shopping complex, Mr Lee cooks up Mandarin dishes catering for both western and eastern palates. Closed Sun and Mon lunchtime.

Continental

ΨΨΨ **Fürstenhof Hotel**, Frans Indongo St, T061-228751. Before the arrival of Leo's at the **Heintizburg Hotel** (see below) this was the best restaurant in town renowned for its high quality food and good service. Not as good as it was amongst the competition, but nevertheless the food is imaginative and nicely presented in a smart dining room. Daily, 1200-1430, 1800-2200.

ΨΨΨ **Gathemann's Restaurant**, Gathemann Building, 139 Independence Av, T061-223853. Upstairs dining with terrace overlooking the street, busy, smartish German restaurant specializing in hearty meat dishes and expensive wines, tea and cake in the afternoon, bookings recommended for the evening. Mon-Sat 1200-2200.

ΨΨΨ **Leo's**, in the **Heinitzburg Hotel**, T061-249597. Expensive but very good with crystal glassware, silver cutlery, fine linen, and a wonderful atmosphere in this renovated castle. Wonderfully presented haute cuisine dishes created by talented head chef from Bordeaux and sous chef who won the 2005 Namibian Chef of the Year award. A sample menu to whet your taste buds could be crayfish and prawn tails; potato and bacon soup with truffle oil; springbok loin with merlot and cranberry sauce; and almond, chocolate and citrus parfait. There are a staggering 13,000, mostly South African wines to choose from, budget US$60-100 per head for dinner depending on what wine you choose. A recommended gourmet eating experience and remember to dress up for the occasion. Daily 0700-1030, 1200-1400, 1830-2200.

TTT **O'Portuga**, 151 Nelson Mandela Av, Eros, T061-272900. Great Portuguese cuisine, good wine, popular with well-heeled Angolans for the traditional coastal dishes, tables inside or on the small terrace, though it can get windy outside. Daily 1200-2300.

TTT **Thule**, in **Hotel Thule**, 1 Gorges St, T061-250146, www.thulenamibia.com. Located in this fairly new stylish hotel which has dramatic views from its position on top of a steep hill, food includes hung beef and game meat, seafood such as oysters and crayfish shipped in from the coast, local staples like *mahangu* (pearl millet) or *waterblommetjie* (an edible South African plant) and more exotic fare such as truffles. Presentation is very delicate – small servings/big plates – but very tasty food and impeccable service. Daily from 1830 for dinner, reservations necessary. Recommended for another expensive but quality night out.

TT **The Gourmet**, Kaiserkrone Centre, Post St Mall, T061-232360. Excellent and very popular restaurant with outside tables beneath giant palm trees in the shady courtyard or dining room of the historic Kaiserkrone building, with a varied menu including healthy breakfasts, fresh seafood and a range of vegetarian dishes, good service and relaxed atmosphere. Mon-Fri 0900-2200, Sat 0800-1400.

TT **Luigi & The Fish**, 320 Sam Nujoma Drive, T061-256399. Bar and restaurant with a sundowner deck and very pleasant garden courtyard, mostly meat and fish, their mussel pot is recommended, good value and popular with families. Tue-Sat 1200-2200.

TT **Sardinia**, 39 Independence Av close to August Neto Gardens, T061-225600. Good value Italian family run café/restaurant specializing in great pizzas, pasta and a small number of traditional Italian dishes, excellent espresso, cappuccino and ice creams in the café at the front, dining in the popular restaurant at the back. Good range of wines, though as you would expect the Italian ones are far more expensive than the South African ones. Daily 1000-late. Recommended.

Steakhouse restaurants

TTT **Butcher's Grill**, at the **Thüringer Hof Hotel**, Independence Av, T061-226031. Good-quality South African restaurant with branches in Johannesburg and Cape Town, superb hung melt in the mouth steaks with fabulous rich sauces, only the best cuts of meat are used, good wine selection and relaxing decor. Daily 1200-2230.

TT **Cattle Baron**, Maerua Park Mall, Centaurus Rd, opposite the cinema, T061-254154. Despite being in a shopping mall, this has a cosy dark-wood interior and a vast menu with every kind of meat dish imaginable including steaks, ribs, burgers and a variety of sauces. If you want to sit in the smoking section, you may need to book in advance. Mon-Thu 1130-1530, 1730-2330, Fri-Sun 1130-2330.

TT **El Gaucho Argentine Grill**, Sam Nujoma Drive, T061-255503. Quality fairly formal steak house with occasional live music, open kitchen where you can watch the steaks being slapped over the flames, though it can get quite hot if sitting too close. The lamb dishes cooked by the Argentine chef are recommended. Mon-Sat 1200-2300, Sun 1200-1600.

TT **Grand Canyon Spur**, 251 Independence Av, T061-231003. Chain restaurant with good-value steaks and hamburgers as well as a variety of spicy Mexican dishes, though once you have eaten at one **Spur** there are no surprises. Children will like it and the cost for a family meal is reasonable.

TT **Joe's Beer House**, Eros Shopping Centre, Nelson Mandela Av, T061-232457, www.joesbeerhouse.com. A very popular spot complete with mock olde worlde interior with barbecue patio and bar area. Great atmosphere, a Windhoek institution; this is the favourite good-value venue for many residents. The menu is varied, though lots of meat dishes. The owner, Joe Gross, is also an accomplished photographer and his photographs of Namibia's landscapes are for sale in the gallery next door. Mon-Thu 1500-late, Fri-Sun 1100-late.

🍴🍴 **Brix Bistro**, 117 Independence Av, at the Elephant Crossing next to the Gustav Voigts Centre, T061-259110. Very pleasant café/bistro with modern decor, wide range of affordable well-cooked meals such as pastas and salads, exceptionally good breakfasts with a Sun special of *maffioso*, an Italian-style omelette with ham, parmesan cheese and olives, with orange juice, coffee and a glass of sparkling wine for US$8. Mon-Tue 0900-1800, Wed-Fri 0900-late, Sat-Sun 0900-1300.

🍴🍴 **Craft Café**, at the **Namibia Crafts Centre**, Tal St, T061-249974. Light meals amongst all the crafts, quiches, omelettes, open sandwiches, salads, muffins, cheesecake, trendy coffee, yoghurt shakes and unusual juices made from wild figs and plums. Note that the glasses here are made from recycled bottles. Fully licensed and there are some organic wines on offer. You can also buy preserves, chutneys and olives. Mon-Tue 0830-1700, Wed-Sat 0830-2100, Sun 0830-1330.

🍴🍴 **Squares Bistro**, corner of Post Street Mall and Independence Av, T061-272324. Popular spot in the heart of town with seating inside and out under umbrellas, offering good cooked breakfasts, pizzas, pasta, *gyros* for lunch and supper, after-work drinking spot for young Windhoekers. Mon-Sat 0800-2100.

🍴 **Cafe Schneider**, Levinson Arcade, Independence Av, T061-226304. German-style restaurant popular at lunchtimes with office workers, pies, cakes, takeaways; look out for daily specials. Mon-Sat 0700-1730.

🍴 **Café Zoo**, Zoo Park, Independence Av. Lovely setting on the edge of the park, a café has been on the spot since 1910, light meals, snacks and drinks, and a special sundowner menu from 1700. Daily 0800-1830.

🍴 **Central Cafe**, Levinson Arcade, Independence Av. Busy breakfast and lunchtime spot, schnitzels, *bratwurst*, plus takeaway rolls and coffee, large menu but slow service. Mon-Sat 0700-1730.

🍴 **Katiti Joes**, Post St Mall. Small daytime pub with beer barrels outside, counters inside serve up an excellent range of chicken wings, meatballs, slices of wholesome meat loaf, sandwiches, spare ribs and there's an excellent salad bar. Great for lunch with a beer, recommended. Mon-Sat 0830-1800.

Bars and clubs

Windhoek *p76, maps p77, p82, p85 and p86*

Most of the restaurants and cafés already mentioned also serve as bars. In the evening after a meal there is not a massive choice of drinking places, and many double as nightclubs/disco bars charging between US$2-4 entry. Since in Namibia a liquor license is required before a gambling permit is issued, small bars often have slot machines lining the walls. Opening hours vary, but all are open until late.

Chez Ntemba, 154 Uhland St. Popular bar with dance floor in a 1-storey building spread over a block, also serves food, mostly attracts the trendy city set. Open most nights until 0200.

Club Pamodze, Antiochie St, Wanaheda, Katutura. Plays up-to-date dance music until late; you'll need to take a taxi or a local guide to find it.

Club Thriller, Katutura. Authentic African disco which plays a mixture of the latest club sounds and African dance music, with the occasional live band outside in the courtyard, open until very late, a taxi is the best way to get there and it's best to go with a local or a guide. This place has been pumping tunes since before independence. Recommended.

El Cubano, corner of Sam Nujoma and Tal St. Very trendy bar and lounge popular with the media and advertising set, good atmosphere, offers Cuban cigars and light snacks, drinks pricey though and there is limited parking.

Funky Lab, Ae Gams Shopping Centre, Sam Nujoma Rd. Disco with numerous bars that gets incredibly crowded on weekend nights. Wed-Sat 1900-late.

The Tower, Tal St, next to the **Namibia Crafts Centre** in the top of the old brewery building so expect to climb up a lot of stairs. Popular with the Afrikaner crowd. Daily 1800-0200, live music Wed, Fri and Sat.

The Warehouse Theatre, 42 Tal St, T061-225059. The most popular live music venue in Windhoek featuring rock, jazz and African bands from Africa and Europe, excellent atmosphere, late bar, recommended, check local press for details.

The Wine Bar, 3 Garten St, T061-226514. Situated in a historical house built in 1927, a vast range of South African wines and wine-based cocktails, light Mediterranean-inspired meals and snacks, good cheese board with olives, often live jazz or classical music, has its own Wine Club with regular tastings and shop. Tue-Thu 1630-2300, Sat 1700-2230, Sun 1700-2200.

Entertainment

Windhoek *p76, maps p77, p82, p85 and p86*

Art galleries

National Gallery, Robert Mugabe Av and John Meinert St, T061-231160. Exhibitions and permanent display of Namibian and other African art. Mon-Fri 0900-1700, Sat 0900-1100. See page 89.

Cinema

Sterkinekor, Maerua Park Mall, Centaurus St, T061-248980. 5-screen cinema with showings from 1200-2200. Wed tickets are less than half price so you need to buy them early as it gets crowded.

Gambling

There are numerous bars with slot machines as well as bookmakers covering horse racing from South Africa. In 1995 casinos were legalized and there has been a steady development of venues. The larger and smarter casinos are found at the **Windhoek Country Club Resort**, Western Bypass, T061-205911, **Kalahari Sands Hotel**, Gustav Voigts Centre, Independence Av, T061-2800000, and the **Hotel Safari**, on the B1 heading south towards Rehoboth T061-2968000.

Theatre

The College of Arts, Fidel Castro St, T061-225841. Has classical music concerts, ballet and modern dance.

The National Theatre of Namibia, Robert Mugabe Av, T/F061-374400. Stages plays, opera, dance, mime.

The Warehouse Theatre, 42 Tal St, T061-225059. Regular plays and live music. Many of these events are performed by students at the College of Arts, the Performing Arts Department of the University of Namibia, and the Nedbank of Namibia Theatre School.

Festivals and events

Windhoek *p76, maps p77, p82, p85 and p86*

Apr **Windhoek Carnival**, a 2-week traditional German festival, culminates with a parade of floats and dancing troupes down Independence Av. During the festival there are various cabaret evenings and an all-night masked ball. Check press for details, or contact Chris Stock, T061-237656.

May **Namibia Holiday and Travel Expo**, Predominantly a trade fair held at the Windhoek Show Grounds, but open to the public; the country's biggest showcase for its tourism industry, plus a food and wine festival with a chefs' competition. Contact T061-2972009.

26 Aug **Herero Day in Okahandja** commemorates fallen war heroes and involves a parade through town to the graves of former leaders.

Late Sep/early Oct **Windhoek Industrial and Agricultural Show**. Local business fair but with side stalls, food and entertainment, especially for kids. Again at the Windhoek Show Grounds, contact T061-224748.

Late Oct The **Oktobberfest Festival** is held on the last week of Oct with beer, very large sausage consumption, and 'oompah' bands from Germany. Organized by Sport Club Windhoek, T021-235521.

Shopping

Windhoek *p76, maps p77, p82, p85 and p86*

Arts and crafts

African Curiotique, Gustav Voigts Centre, Independence Av, T061-236191. Very stylish crafts, jewellery, decorated ostrich eggs, textiles and clothes, glassware and ornaments. There is also a branch in Swakopmund.

Master Weaver, Werne Hill Shopping Centre, stocks a wide range of southern African carpets, wall hangings and other crafts.

Namibia Crafts Centre, 40 Tal St, T061-242222, located in the old breweries

For an explanation of the sleeping and eating price codes used in this guide, see inside the front cover. Other relevant information is found in Essentials, see pages 43-51.

building next to the Warehouse Theatre. This is a small indoor market on 2 floors (see page 85) selling a variety of Namibian carvings, pottery, basket, leatherwork, jewellery and artwork. It also houses an earthy café frequented by tourists as well as some of Windhoek's arty crowd (see Eating, page 96). Mon-Fri 0830-1700, Sat 0830-1330. **Post Street Mall outdoor market**, sells all sorts of souvenirs, daily except Sun.

Books, magazines and newspapers

The Book Den, Guthenberg Platz, Werner List St. Novels and autobiographies.
Bücherkeller, Fidel Castro St. T061-231615. Specialist books on Namibia, coffee table, wildlife, history in both German and English.
CNA, Gustav Voigts Centre, Independence Av and Werne Hill Shopping Centre. Basic South African stationary/magazine chain, limited choice on just-released books.
Key Executive Books, Town Square Shopping Mall on Post St, T061-258269. Modern mall bookshop with a full range of new and souvenir books, and a few tables for coffee and browsing.

Camera equipment

Nitzsche-Reiter, corner of Fidel Castro St and Independence Av, T061-231116.
Photo World, 246 Independence Av opposite Fidel Castro St, T061-223223.

Camping

Just about all the car hire companies will hire 4WD vehicles fully equipped with camping equipment – see Car hire, page 102.
Adventure Camping Hire and Sales, 27 Schopenhauer St, T061-242478, adventure@natron.net. Everything needed for a camping trip for hire from tents, tables and jerry cans to shovels, chemical toilets, and frying pans. Prices are reasonable with tents costing about US$6 for 3 days and small items such as axes or pillows for as little as US$0.25.
Camping Hire Namibia, 78 Malcom Spence St, Olympia, T/F061-252995, www.natron.net/tour/camping/hire. Again anything from a tent to a teaspoon.
Cymot/Greensport, 60 Mandume Ndemufayo Av, T061-2957000, www.greensport.com.na. Quality company selling a full range of camping and outdoor equipment.

Diamonds and jewellery

See Shopping, page 52, for information about buying diamonds, and also Namibia's diamonds, page 325. Namibia's diamonds are the world's best quality and the designs are outstanding. Namibian jewellers consistently come in the top 10 of the annual De Beers Shining Light Award – the world's leading diamond jewellery competition, as well as the PlatAfrica design competition for platinum jewellery. The jewellers listed below have all won numerous awards.
Adrian Meyer, 250 Independence Av, T061-236100, www.adrian-meyer-jewellers.com.na. Mr Meyer began selling diamonds in Namibia in 1907and Mr Adrian joined the company in 1957, very modern designed jewellery is made in a state-of-the-art workshop.
Canto Goldsmith, Levinson Arcade, T061-222894. Again very modern and unusual designs, staff here speak French, Spanish and Portuguese as well as English and German.
Jeweller Horst Knop, Kaiserkrone Centre in Post Street Mall, T061-228657. A Knop piece of jewellery is very distinctive, many are styled in geometric shapes, a great deal of thought has gone into the displays in this shop where the jewellery is exhibited amongst African art.

Maps

Detailed maps are available from the Surveyor General's office on Robert Mugabe Av. The office is a short walk from the junction with Lazarett St. All types of maps can be bought here. The 1:50,000 are useful if you're planning on hiking. The 1:250,000 are useful for the remote areas where some of the road signs can be confusing. The best road maps are available from the Namibia tourism office.

Shopping malls

There are a number of shopping malls in the city where you can find not only craft and curio shops, but clothes shops and cafés. The most central is **Levinson Arcade** off Independence Av. The **Kaiserkrone Centre** and the adjacent **Werne Hill Shopping Centre,** off Post St, feature mostly South African chain stores, whilst the **Gustav Voigts Centre**, Independence Av, is home to the

Wecke & Voigst department store, supermarket and delicatessen. The **Post Street Mall** not only has shops, but is lined with stalls selling crafts and clothes. The **Maerua Park Mall**, to the south of the city centre in the Suiderhof suburb, has a number of shops, restaurants and cafés, a post office, internet cafés, an enormous **Checkers** supermarket, as well as the 5-screen **Ster Kinekor cinema** and a **Virgin Active** gym. At the time of writing the whole complex was being extended.

Supermarkets

Pick and Pay, Werne Hill Shopping Centre, end of Post St Mall. **Checkers**, Gustav Voigts Centre, Independence Av. **Shoprite**, Independence Av.

Activities and tours

Windhoek *p76, maps p77, p82, p85 and p86*

Football and rugby

Both sports are played at their respective Independence Stadia just off the B1 heading south. Matches can be lively and exciting to watch, and in particular all Africans love their soccer, but do not take anything of value with you as the stands get very crowded and theft is rife. Check local press for match details.

Golf

Windhoek Country Club, south of the city on the B1, T061-258498. An 18-hole course surrounds the hotel.

Swimming and fitness

At the time of writing a new complex housing an Olympic-sized swimming pool was being built in the southern suburb of Olympia, close to the big athletic and rugby stadium. When finished it will have the pool, club houses for the **Namibian Underwater Federation**, **Namibia Swimming Club** and the **Namibia Canoeing Federation**, plus a restaurant, fast food outlets, children's playground, gym, climbing wall and squash courts.

Nucleus Health and Fitness Centre, 40 Tal St, T061-225493. Smaller than **Virgin Active** but with a good range of weight machines and also aerobic classes. Mon-Thu 0600-2100, Fri 0600-2000, Sun 0900-1900.

Virgin Active, Maerua Park, Centaurus Rd, T061-234399. The largest and best-equipped gym in Windhoek with indoor swimming pool, squash courts, a full range of weights machines, aerobics classes and saunas and a warm pool all year round. Monthly membership is available. Mon-Thu 0500-2100, Fri 0500-2000, Sat 0700-1900, Sun 0700-1200.

Tour operators

See also Planning your trip, page 14. All tour operators in Namibia are required to be members of the **Tour and Safari Association** (TASA), so check that the TASA logo is displayed on the websites. Members of TASA have to go through a 2-year probation period to prove their professionalism before being accepted as full members. The TASA website, www.tasa.na, has more information about the organization and links to all its members. See also box, page 16.

Acacia Namibia, T061-229142, www.acacianamibia.com. Tailor-made tours and arrangements, deals with the upmarket lodges and camps.

Africa Tourist Info.cc, run by David at the **Rivendell Guest House**, T061-228717, www.infotour-africa.com. Can organize self-drive safaris and guided tours.

African Wanderer, office at the Windhoek Country Club, T061-233394, www.africanwanderer.com. All arrangements geared towards the top end of the market using the luxury lodges, tailor-made fly-in tours and guided or self-drive itineraries.

Albatros Travel and Safaris, T061-221656, www.albatros-travel.com. Multilingual operator offering scheduled and tailor-made tours and self-drive itineraries.

ATC Namibia, T061-250191, www.namibia-safaris.com. Special interest and small guided groups.

Cardboard Box Travel Shop, Kaiserkrone Centre, Post St Mall, T061-256580, www.namibian.org. Good friendly drop-in shop for all travel arrangements and tours especially for budget travellers.

Chameleon Safaris, based at **Chameleon Backpackers**, T/F061-247668, www.chameleonsafaris.com. Good-value and well-run camping safaris using 4WDs, excellent budget option, assisted camping, great guides. Regular departures between Windhoek and Livingstone (12 days) via many of the highlights of Namibia plus the Okavango Delta in Botswana, and 8-day trips to the north of Namibia that can be combined with Sossusvlei for a 10-day tour. There are also 4-day trips to both Etosha and Sossusvlei. Recommended.

Cheetah Tours and Safaris, T061-230287, www.cheetahtours.com. Scheduled and tailor-made munibus tours, guided 4WD self-drive itineraries, hotel bookings, fly-in safaris.

Crazy Kudu Safaris, T/F061-222636, www.crazykudu.com. Long-established tour operator that cover just about all of Namibia on regular scheduled camping tours using minibuses that carry 10 people maximum, affordable and fun and aimed at the backpacker/adventure travel market. Regular departures for the 10-day **Namibian Explorer**, 6-day **Northern Highlights**, and 3-day **Sossusvlei Express**. If you don't have a sleeping bag you can hire one from them.

Dunas Safari Tour Operator, T061-231179, www.dunassafari.com. Self-drive itineraries and tailor-made safaris.

Elena Travel Services, T061-244443, www.namibweb.com. Day trips including Arnhem Cave and the Ibenstein Weavery (see page 114) and tours further afield, airport shuttles and transport to Sossusvlei.

Face to Face Tours, T061-265446. Daily half-day tours to Katutura township usually departing at 0900 and 1400 and lasting about 3 hrs, US$25 per person.

Focus Travel, T061-257825, www.namibia-adventures.com. Day trips around Windhoek including city centre walk, Katutura Township tour, and a 1-day safari to a game farms to see cats.

Foxtrot Tours, T061-229941, foxtrot@iway.na. Can provide shuttles from the airport to many of the lodges, also short lodge and camping safaris to **Harnas Guest Farm**, Etosha and the Namib-Naukluft Park.

Gourmet Tours, T061-231281. Local tours in and around Windhoek including a half-day city tour which finishes with a coffee at Heinitzburg Castle, half-day tours to Katutura township or Daan Viljoen Game Park, and visits to guest farms in the region.

Hinterland Safaris, T061-252662, www.hinter.com.na. Small guided tours, fly-in safaris, exclusive camping 4WD tours for 4-10 people. Goes further afield to Botswana and Victoria Falls.

Kidogo Safaris, T061-243827, www.kidogo-safaris.com. Very exclusive lodge safaris with all the trimmings for 2-6 people, also camping for 4-6 people, and can make arrangements for disabled travellers.

Namibia Travel Connection, 4 Lorentz St, T061-246427, www.namibiatravel.com. General travel agent for all flights, car hire and accommodation reservations.

NatureFriend Safaris, T061-234793, www.naturefriend.com.na. Specialists in upmarket fly-in safaris in Namibia, Botswana and Zambia, also operates the **Dune Hopper**, the daily air taxi to the upmarket lodges at Sossusvlei and the Namib Rand Nature Reserve (see page 287).

Nawa Safaris, T/F061-243103, www.nawa.iway.na. Guided driving safaris with the flexibility to design your own trip, as well as fly-ins and small group guided tours.

Ondese Travel & Safaris, Kunene Court, Heliodore St, T061-220876, www.ondese.com.au. Tailor-made safaris in Namibia and beyond, self-drive or escorted tours, professional company dealing with the upper end of the market, not camping.

Pasjona Safaris, T/F061-254606, www.pasjona-safaris.com. Tours for groups of 4 or more, 10-day camping tour in northern Namibia, 10-day hotel/lodge/guest farm tour to Swakopmund and Etosha and environs, 10-day self-drive itinerary.

Profile Safaris, T061-224358, www.profilesafaris.com. Quality company offering upmarket fly-in safaris to the more remote locations.

Royal Tours, T061-255940, www.royaltours.com.na. Minibus and self-drive tours, also agent for cruise ships.

Sense of Africa, T061-275300, www.sense-of-africa.com. Scheduled and tailor-made tours, fly-in safaris, self-drive, car hire, activities and excursions, a good all- round operator.

Skeleton Coast Safaris, T061-224248, www.skeletoncoastsafaris.com. Fly-in safaris from 3-6 days. Run by the Schoeman family who are experts on Namibia.

Southern Cross Safaris, T061-251553, www.southern-cross-safaris.com. Well-established operator with over 20 years' experience in Namibia, tailor-made trips, also covers Botswana.

Springbok Atlas, T061-215943, www.springbokatlas.com. Large coach company offering comprehensive tours of Namibia and South Africa, probably best suited to the older traveller who doesn't mind being in a big group. Its **Classic Namibia** covers all the major highlights.

Sunbird Tours, T061-272090, www.sunbirdtours-namibia.com. Fly-in safaris and small group tours to lodges in Namibia, Botswana and Zambia.

SWA Safaris, 43 Independence Av, T061-221193, www.swasafaris.com.na. Another large coach tour company with a comprehensive brochure and over 50 years' experience in southern Africa.

Trip Travel , T061-285570, www.trip.com.na, reasonable quotes for guided tours, self-drive, fly-in safaris and trips to Victoria Falls.

Visit Namibia Tours & Safaris, 4 Lorentz St, T061-250377, www.visitnamibia.com. Tour operator specializing in French visitors, all guides and reservations staff speak French and there's an office in Paris, T+33-1-42975595.

Wilderness Safaris, T061-274500, www.wilderness-safaris.com. Exclusive and upmarket camps in remote areas of the Skeleton Coast, Damaraland, Etosha and Sossusvlei (dealt with under the relevant sections), also arranges air charters, vehicles and guides, and self-drive. Recommended for the very top end of the market, its properties are super luxurious in wonderful locations. In January 2003, **Wilderness Safaris** won **National Geographic Traveler and Conservation International**'s coveted *World Legacy Award for Nature Travel*. Also worth a commendable mention is the **Children in the Wilderness** programme which was established in Namibia in 2002 by **Wilderness Safaris**, after the US actor Paul Newman approached the company to assist underprivileged kids in the region after his visit to Namibia and Botswana. The idea is to introduce disadvantaged and orphaned Namibian children to their environment and their own natural resources, and each year since 2002 150 children (and their teachers) have spent 5 days at the **Wilderness Safari**'s camps to learn about wildlife and nature, art and sport, and topical issues such as HIV/AIDS awareness. Most of the workshops and activities are run by Namibians (not well-meaning foreign whites) who provide superb role models for the kids.

Transport

Windhoek *p76, maps p77, p82, p85 and p86*
Windhoek is in the centre of the country, all the surfaced highways and railways radiate out from here. The pattern of the road network makes it difficult to do a circuit of the country without having to return to Windhoek at some point – unless you want to spend a lot of time driving on gravel roads of variable condition.

Distances It is 1218 km to **Katima Mulilo**; 482 km to **Keetmanshoop**; 850 km to **Lüderitz**; 533 km to **Namutoni** (Etosha NP); 786 km to **Noordoewer** (South Africa border); 435 km to **Okakuejo** (Etosha NP); 350 km to **Swakopmund**; 1435 km to **Victoria Falls** (via the Caprivi Strip).

Air

See pages 26 and 35 for more information; see page 72 for the **Air Namibia** timetable.

Hosea Kutako International Airport (T062-540315/6), 45 km east of the town centre, is used for flights to/from Europe and South Africa and **Air Namibia** flight to Victoria Falls departs from here. Inside the airport there is a bank, post office, car hire offices and a mobile phone hire bureau as well as facilities for making international calls. The departure lounge has a small duty-free shop and a bar which also serves snacks.

Eros Airport, T061-2955500, is used by **Air Namibia** for domestic flights, by tour operators, charter companies and private flights. The airport is next to the **Safari Court Hotel**, 3 km south of the town centre.

International Air Namibia flies direct from London (Gatwick), 10½ hrs, and Frankfurt to Windhoek, 9 hrs. **LTU**, a German charter company, flies between Düsseldorf via Münich to Windhoek from May-Oct. It also flies between Canada and the US to Germany. **Angola Airlines/TAG** flies between Windhoek and Paris, via Luanda, but by far the most frequent service to Namibia is via South Africa, using either **South African Airways** (SAA) or your national carrier from Europe to Johannesburg or Cape Town, and adding the final hop to Windhoek with a local airline such as **Air Namibia** or **South African Express** (a regional subsidiary of SAA). **British Airways** has 2 overnight flights from London to Johannesburg every day, with later connections to Windhoek. It also has a daily overnight flight from London to Cape Town, but no connection on to Windhoek so you would have to use another carrier. **Lufthansa** flies between Frankfurt and Windhoek, 13½ hrs, again via Johannesburg.

Domestic Air Namibia serves all the regional centres such as Johannesburg and Victoria Falls and has regular services between Windhoek and Lüderitz, Mpacha, Ondangwa, Oranjemund, Swakopmund and Walvis Bay, and between Walvis Bay and Lüderitz and Swakopmund. Check when booking which airport your flight departs from. Most domestic flights and a variety of private and charter companies fly from Eros Airport.

Airline offices Air Namibia, corner of Independence St and Bahnhof St, T061-2996170, Hosea Kutoko International Airport, T061-2996600, Eros Airport, T061-2996500, central reservations, T061-2996333, www.airnamibia.com.na; **British Airways**, Carl Lis Building, Independence Av, T061-231118, www.britishairways.com; **LTU**, T061-238205, www.ltu.com; **Lufthansa**, T061-226662, www.lufthansa.com; **SA Express**, T011 978 5577 (South Africa), www.saexpress.co.za; **South African Airways**, T061-273340, www.flysaa.com.

Bus

Intercape, T061-227847, www.inter cape.co.za, see timetable page 70. The coaches from South Africa and Swakopmund direction all terminate by the car park and Tourist Information Office on the corner of Independence Av and Fidel Castro St.

Car hire

For further information, see page 38.
A full range of vehicles is available from small sedan cars from US$50 per day to fully equipped to go 4WDs with rooftop tents, kitchen and cooking equipment, tools, first-aid kit, jerry cans, extra fuel tanks, spare parts, bedding, fridge, lights and towels. The latter option works out about US$140 a day for 2 people but when you consider how much money you will save by camping instead of staying in hotels, this represents good value. Many of the companies also hire out campers and motorhomes.
Advanced 4x4 Car Hire, 74 Aschenborn St, Pioneers Park, T061-246832, www.advancedcarhire.com.
African Tracks, T061-245072, www.africantracks.com. Allows vehicles to go to South Africa, Botswana, Zimbabwe and Zambia, though this means rates are

higher than normal; if you are only staying in Namibia there are cheaper options.

Andes Car Rental, 25 Voigt St, Southern Industrial Area, T061-256334, andescar@iafrica.com.na.

Asco Car Hire, 10 Diehl St, Southern Industrial Estate, T061-233064, www.ascocarhire.com.

Avis, Aviation Rd, T061-233166, airport T062-540271, www.avis.co.za.

Britz Africa, T061-250654, www.britz.com. Allows vehicles to go to other countries.

Budget, 72 Mandume Ndemufayo Av, T061-228720, airport T062-540225, www.budget.com.

Camping Car Hire, 36 Joule St, Southern Industrial Area, T061-237756, www.campingcarhire.com.na. Good-value, fully equipped vehicles with excellent back up. Recommended.

Caprivi Car Hire, corner of Mandume Ndemufayo Av and Fiedel Castro St, Southern Industrial Area, T061-256323, www.caprivicarhire.de.

Classic Car Hire, T061-246708, ccarhire@iafrica.com.na.

Etosha Car Hire, T061-236037, www.etoshacarhire.com. Also allows vehicles into South Africa and Botswana.

Europcar, T061-247398, airport T062-540041, www.europcar.co.za. Now also rents mobile phones with its cars.

Hertz, T061-540115, airport T062-540116, www.hertz.co.za.

Imperial, 43 Werner List St, T061-227103, airport, T062-540278, www.imperialcarrental.co.za.

Into Namibia, T061-253591/2, www.intonam.com.na. 4WD rental and all camping equipment for hire.

Kea Campers, T061-252298, www.keacampers.co.za. A leading camper hire company in Australia and New Zealand, now operating in southern Africa, again can take vehicles out of the country.

Maui Motorhome Rentals, T061-250654, www.maui.co.za.

Namibia Car Hire, T061-255700, www.namibiacarhire.de.

Pegasus Car and Camper Hire, 81 Daan Bekker St, T061-251451, pegasus@mweb.com.na.

Savanna, Trift St, T061-229272, scr@iafrica.com.na. Probably the best deal in Windhoek and recommended by several readers. Limited cars, so book well in advance. Fully equipped pick up-and-go 4WDs start from US$130 per day.
Sixt/Tempest, 49 John Meinert Av, T061-239163/4, www.sixt.com.

Taxi

The taxi rank is on the corner of Independence Av and Fidel Castro Ruz St. It is not usual to hail taxis in the street.
Dial-a-Driver Services, T061-259677, www.namibiasafaris.com. Offers transfer services with drivers and cars or minibuses from the airport and anywhere in Windhoek to the outlying game farms and lodges, plus minibus and bus rental for larger groups.

Train

Transnamib Starline Passenger Services, central reservations T061-2982032, www.transnamib.com.na. The office at the station is open daily 0600-2000. **Gobabis** (7½ hrs), Tue, Thu, Sun, 2150. **Keetmanshoop** (11 hrs 20 mins), via Rehoboth and Mariental, daily except Sat, 1910. **Swakopmund** (9½ hrs) and **Walvis Bay** (11 hrs), daily except Sat, 1955. **Tsumeb** (15 hrs), via Omaruru and Otjiwarongo, Tue, Thu, Sun, 1745. See also timetable on page 68.

The **Desert Express**, T061-2982600, www.desertexpress.com.na, bookings at the Railway Station, Mon-Fri 0800-1700. This is Namibia's answer to luxury train travel. There are 2 classes, the *Starview Sitter* and the *Spitzkoppe Sleeper*. A superb service with cuisine and care to match. En route the train stops for a game drive and a visit to the sand dunes. It departs Windhoek on Tue and Fri at 1130, and it departs Swakopmund on Wed and Sat 1430. Good value when compared with similar luxury trains in the region. Expect to pay in the region of US$550 for a double sleeper, all inclusive. The train can also take your car, but this must be organized in advance. Packages to Etosha have recently been introduced and several run throughout the year. Check the website for dates. For further information, see page 38.

Directory

Windhoek *p76, maps p77, p82, p85 and p86*

Banks

There are 4 main banks in Namibia, **Standard Bank, Bank Windhoek, Nedbank** and **First National Bank**, all of which have a number of branches in central Windhoek which change money and have 24-hr ATMs.

Cultural centres

Franco-Namibian Cultural Centre, 118 Robert Mugabe St, T061-225672, fncc@mweb.com.na. Exhibitions and film shows, check press for details.

Embassies and consulates

Angola, 3 Agostino Neto St, T061-227535. **British High Commission**, 116 Robert Mugabe Av, T061-223022, bhc@mweb.com.na. **European Union**, Sanlaam Centre, 4th floor, 154 Independence Av, T061-202600, www.delnam.cec.eu.int. **Egypt**, 10 Berg St, T061-221501. **Finland**, 5th floor, Sanlam Building, Independence Av, T061-221355. **France**, 1 Goethe St, T061-276700. **Germany**, 6th floor, Sanlam Centre, 154 Independence Av, T061-223100, www.german-embassy-windhoek.org. **Ghana**, 5 Nelson Mandela, T061-220536. **India**, 5 Nelson Mandela Av, T061-221341. **Italy**, Anna/Gevers St, T061-228602. **Kenya**, 5th floor, Kenya House, 134 Robert Mugabe Av, T061-226836. **Netherlands**, 2 Crohn St, T061-223733. **South Africa**, Nelson Mandela/Jan Jonker St, T061-2057111, sahcwin@iafrica.com.na. **Spain**, 53 Bismarck St, T061-223066. **USA**, 14 Lossen St, Ausspannplatz, T061-221601, www.usembassy.namib.com. **Zambia**, Sam Nujoma/Mandume Ndemufayo, T061-237610. **Zimbabwe**, Independence Av/Grimm St, T061-228134.

Emergencies

T10111.

Immigration

Department of Civic Affairs, Cohen Building, corner of Independence Av and Kasino St, T061-2922011.

Internet
Tourist Junction, 40 Fidel Castro Ruz St, T231246, info.ritztours@galileaosa.co.za. Coffee shop, telephones, internet access, bus reservations, bookings. **The Office Shop**, Gustav Voigts Centre, lower floor, T061-245558.

Libraries
Public Library, 18 Lüderitz St, T061-224163.

Medical services
Mediclinic Windhoek, Private Hospital, Heliodoor St, Eros, T061-222687, is the best and most expensive hospital in Windhoek. **Roman Catholic Hospital**, 92 Werner List St, T061-270291. **Rhino Park Clinic**, Rhino Park, Hosea Kutako Drive, T061-225434. **International SOS**, 24-hr evacuation service, T230505, rescue T911222255.

Police
Main station, Bahnhoff St, T061-2094111.

Post office
Windhoek Post Office, Independence Av, T061-2019311. Open 0800-1600 for parcel service round the side on Munamava St as are phones. Phone cards can be bought in the main hall of the post office.

Around Windhoek

To the north of Windhoek along the B1 is the small town of Okahandja which is worth a brief stop if passing through, especially for its two craft markets. Nearby are a couple of worthy distractions for birdwatchers and campers, the Gross Barmen Hot Springs Resort and the Von Bach Resort Recreation Area, both of which can also be visited on a day trip from the city. To the east of Windhoek, the main B6 road heads through the fringes of the Kalahari Desert to Botswana, and a drive along the Trans-Kalahari Highway through the flat, dusty cattle-rich scrubland offers a glimpse of the scenery that lies across the border. Throughout this region are a number of guest farms which make a more peaceful and rural accommodation alternative to the city hotels.
»» *For Sleeping, Eating and other listings, see pages 111-113.*

Daan Viljoen Game Park »» *pp111-113. Colour map 1, C5.*

ⓘ *Entry US$6, vehicle US$1.50.*
The Daan Viljoen Game Park is west of Windhoek at an altitude of 1000 m in the Khomas Hochland Hills. Although small, at 3953 ha, the park is a fabulous resource, with walks through pretty hills and past dams with game and abundant bird life. It is a good spot to enjoy nature close to Windhoek. Formerly a reserve and home to a group of Damara people, the park is named after Daan Viljoen, the former South African administrator to South West Africa. Recently, however, the park has obtained a reputation for being run down, expensive, noisy (particularly the campsite) and generally 'complacent'. As with almost all the NWR sites, investment in facilities over the past few years has been low, but it is clean, the hot water and electricity work and there is a reasonable restaurant and bar with nice twinkling views of Windhoek in the distance. So get a good fire going, watch the sun set by the Augeigas Dam and enjoy the tranquillity.

Ins and outs

Getting there The park is 24 km west of Windhoek on the C28. From Windhoek, simply find Sam Nujoma Drive and follow the signposts which take you all the way to the park's entrance. The road is a scenic meander through seemingly endless hillocks. If you continue along the road it will take you further into the Khomas Hochland Hills and eventually down into the Namib Desert via the Spreethoogte Pass, just about the steepest in Namibia.

Getting around A 6.4-km gravel circuit is designed to take you to where the animals are and there are a few nicely positioned viewpoints on the way. There are also a couple of viewpoints – worth a pause – on the tar road from the entrance gate to the main office. The real beauty of Daan Viljoen is that there is no big game, so the area can be safely explored on foot. The walking trails will probably reward you with better game sightings, and certainly gives you more of a feeling of being in the bush. Bring warm clothes as the temperature drops sharply at dusk.

Park information The park is open year round and is very popular with both Windhoek residents and travellers passing through the area who don't wish to stop in Windhoek. It's a relaxing place to come and swim (in the summer), enjoy a *braai* and a few cold beers; at weekends and on public holidays the campsite and *braai* areas are busy. If the dams are full enough you can try your hand at fishing; permits are obtainable from the office or at the gate. The entrance gate is open until midnight for those with reserved accommodation, and until sunset for everyone else. Out of season, just turn up, or book through **Namibia Wildlife Resorts**, see page 46.

Wildlife and vegetation

The park is well stocked with various species of antelope and other medium-sized game. Chances of seeing mountain zebra, blue wildebeest, springbok, gemsbock, kudu, red hartebeest and impala are good. Smaller mammals such as baboons and rock dassies can also be seen. There is an abundance of bird life in the park including the colourful rollers and bee-eaters, hornbills and weaver birds. By the small Augeigas Dam there is a fantastic assortment of waterbirds.

The vegetation in the park is typical of that of the central highlands area, with an abundance of thorn trees such as blue, mountain and red umbella, and thorn bushes such as trumpet and honey thorn. After the summer rains the hills are covered with new grass, but as the months pass they turn from green to yellow and then become barren just before the next rains. The views over the highlands and Windhoek itself are spectacular whatever the time of year.

Hiking trails

There are three hikes that can be undertaken. The 3-km **Wag-'n-bietjie** (Wait a While) **Trail** is undemanding provided you don't set off in the middle of a summer's day; it is suitable for anyone, whatever their level of fitness. The 9-km **Rooibos** (Red Bushwillow) **Trail** is more demanding, but for anyone who is in reasonable shape it's a very enjoyable experience. The first part of the trail takes you steadily uphill to a triangulation point at 1763 m, before descending into a riverbed which meanders back to the main camp area by way of a final, particularly vicious hill.

The 32-km two-day unaccompanied **Sweet-Thorn Trail** is supposedly for groups of three to 12 people, although unaccompanied couples have reported their enjoyment (and difficulty in locating the path) in the visitors' book. This trail should be booked in advance if possible,

Daan Viljoen Game Park

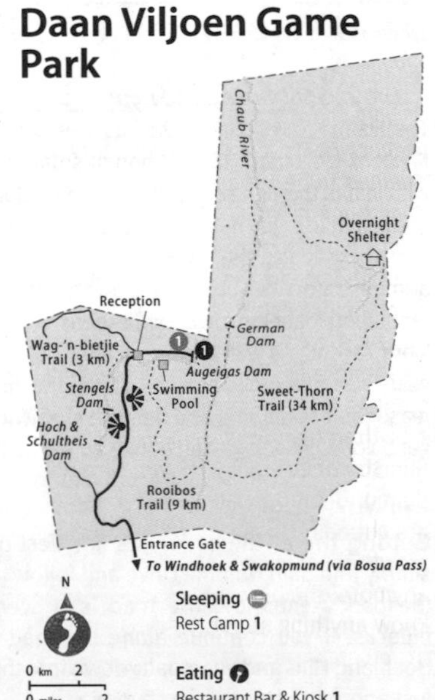

and costs US$10 per person. A 0900 start from the main office is advised. Ask ahead regarding water; you must be self-sufficient for the overnight stop at a picturesque shelter. These trails are a good introduction to walking in the bush for those who intend to take on the more strenuous walks such as the Ugab River, Fish River Canyon or Naukluft Park Trails. It's important to have decent walking shoes, at least two litres of water per person per day, and adequate sun protection for all walks. Poor-quality photocopied maps are all that the office will provide. It is certainly possible to get lost on any of these walks, so it is worth having a chat with the staff before you set out, and keeping alert on the way.

North to Okahandja ›› *pp111-113.* *Phone code: 062. Colour map 1, C5.*

The B1 north out of Windhoek leads first to Okahandja (72 km), where it branches into the B2 for Swakopmund (350 km) and the B1 north for the Waterberg Plateau, Otjiwarongo and the 'triangle' towns of Otavi, Tsumeb and Grootfontein.

For the first 15 km the road is an impressive four-lane highway but then, just before the turn-offs for Döbra and Brakwater, it slims down to a more modest two lanes. As well as being the main route to Swakopmund and the north, this road is a commuter route between Windhoek and Okahandja. It therefore gets very busy during daily 'rush' hours and on Friday and Sunday afternoons with traffic leaving and returning to Windhoek. Care should be exercised when driving this stretch.

The light industry surrounding Windhoek is soon left behind and the road then snakes its way through the attractive mountainous **Khomas Hochland**, with cattle ranches and guest farms situated on either side of the road. About 10 km before Okahandja the road passes the Osona Military Base and soon after on the right is the turn-off for **Von Bach Dam**. Just before the turn-off for Okahandja itself, the road passes over the Okahandja River, a dry, wide sandy riverbed with some market gardening practised along its banks.

Okahandja and around ›› *pp111-113.*

Phone code: 062. Colour map 1, C5.

The small town of Okahandja is one of the oldest-established settlements in Namibia and is the administrative centre of the Herero-speaking people, with a number of its former leaders buried here. The official founding of Okahandja is deemed to be 1894, though oral traditions suggests that Herero-speaking peoples have been living in the vicinity since the end of the 18th century, coinciding with their migration south from the Kaokoland from around 1750. A yearly procession through the town to the Herero graves commemorates Herero dead during various wars against the Nama and the Germans.

As a crossroads between the routes west to the coast and north to Etosha, Okahandja is a busy, bustling place with a railway station, shops, banks, petrol stations and two large outdoor craft markets. The last couple of years have seen a growth in light industry in the town and the relocation of the research arm of the Ministry of Education as part of the decentralization process in the country. A new diamond-cutting factory opened here in 1998 and an increasing number of people are choosing to live in Okahandja and work in Windhoek; as a result, the town's growth is set to continue. There used to be a tourist information centre here, but not anymore; the best bet is to ask the carvers at the two craft markets if you need to know anything about the area.

Sights

The period of German rule saw the construction of a number of attractive early 20th-century buildings scattered around the town.Unfortunately none of them has yet been turned into a museum and, apart from a casual glance, there is not much to see. The **Old Fort**, situated just along from the post office on Martin Neib Street, was started in 1894 (the year Okahandja was officially founded), and served for many years as the local police station. It now lies empty and rather forlorn and the various schemes to put it to use (perhaps as a museum) have so far come to nothing.

There is a cluster of buildings at the southern end of Kerk Street, including the **Rhenish Mission Church**, which was built in the 1870s and contains the grave of Willem Maherero, the eldest son of the late 19th-century Herero leader. Opposite is the **Church of Peace**, consecrated in 1952, which contains the graves of three influential Namibian leaders: the 19th-century Oorlam leader Jonker Afrikaner, who died in 1861; Herero leader Chief Hosea Kutako, widely credited as the leader of post-Second World War resistance to South African rule in Namibia; and Chief Clemens Kapuuo, Kutako's successor and former Democratic Turnhalle Alliance (DTA) President, who was assassinated in 1978.

Behind the Church of Peace is the former house of **Dr H Vedder**, a pioneer in linguistic studies and oral history in Namibia during the first half of the last century, and viewed by some as an important Namibian historian and by others as an apologist of white, colonial rule in the country. Just round the corner from here is the old **Experimental Tobacco Station** where in 1906 the planting of tobacco and making of cigars was started. Although quite an attractive building it is now overgrown and stands empty.

Across the railway line at the end of Bahnhof Street is the Library, another attractive early 20th-century building, constructed for the First District Official Fromm. Leaving town north on Voortrekker Street, next to the National Institute for Educational Development, stands the **Reit Club** with its old-fashioned green corrugated-iron roof. Originally the 1909 home of Dr Fock, the first Mayor of Okahandja, today the house and grounds serve as stables, with one large and impressive building and spacious courtyard forming the **Horseshoe Bar and Grill**, a pleasant lunch stop on your way north.

During the 1840s, the Herero chiefs Tjamuaha and Katjihene both established themselves at Okahandja, having moved away from Oorlam leader Jonker Afrikaner's base in Windhoek, and in 1850 missionary Kolbe set up a mission station here. The establishment of this mission ran contrary to the

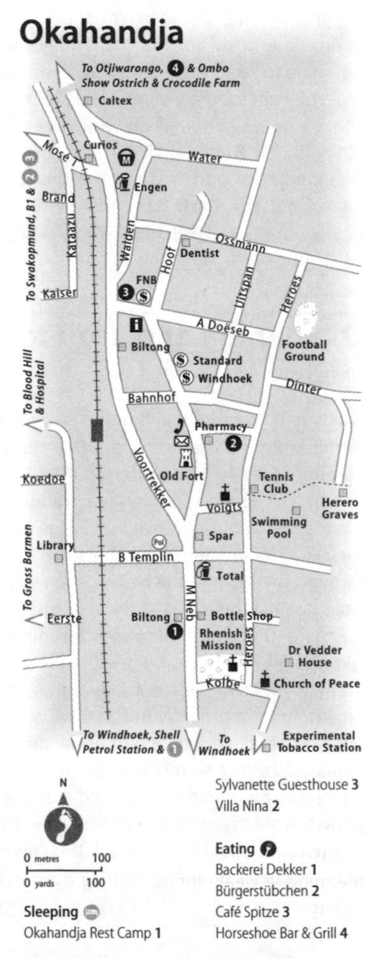

wishes of Jonker Afrikaner, at the time the most powerful leader in central Namibia, as he felt that European influence over the Herero would interfere with his self-declared rights over Herero cattle. In August 1850 he raided the settlement, destroying the mission and killing men, women and children indiscriminately. The site where most of the atrocities took place was named **Moordkoppie** or **Blood Hill** in memory of those who fell there.

Jonker Afrikaner himself settled at Okahandja in 1854 – using the settlement as a base from which to launch his cattle raids in Hereroland – and lived here until his death in 1861. The site is just west of town.

Every year on 26 August, **Heroes' Day**, the Herero gather to honour their forefathers and those fallen in battle. The procession (numbering perhaps a couple of hundred) begins on the outskirts of town, and women in traditional Herero dress and men in military uniforms march to the graves of the 19th-century leader Maherero and his son Samuel Maherero, who led the Herero into exile in Botswana in 1904 after a final pitched battle against the Germans at the Waterberg Plateau (see page 351). It is a colourful ceremony, but fairly low key. The turn-off for the **Herero Graves** is at the northern end of Kerk Street, just after Voigt Street by the tennis courts; however, it is not possible to go into the graveyard.

Entertainment (for children, at least) is available 2 km north out of town (turn left onto D2110). The **Ombo Show Ostrich and Crocodile Farm** ⓘ *daily 0830-1700, US$3 per person*, offers a 45-minute tour to see a few young Nile crocodiles and trained *ostriches. There's a good craft shop with ostrich egg items, restaurant/coffee shop, pony rides for kids, and a small Herero and Himba rural life display.*

Von Bach Recreation Resort ›› *5 km south of town signposted off the B1.*

ⓘ *Day and overnight visitors need to book in advance, T061-2857200; angling licences are available at the gate; US$6 adults, children under 16 free; US$1.50 per car.*

The dam is the main water supply for Windhoek. For residents it is a reasonably popular place for bass, barbell and carp fishing, watersports (BYOB, bring your own boat) and picnics; sadly there are no walking trails. Apart from swimming in the blue water and birdwatching, the dam offers little for overseas visitors. The dam and surrounding reed beds attract large numbers of birds, in particular waterbirds such as moorhen, teal and coot. There are also large numbers of Monteiro's hornbill, lilac-breasted roller and crimson-breasted shrike with their distinct black and crimson markings. Benches on the edge of the dam are excellent places from which to twitch.

Gross Barmen Hot Springs Resort ›› *Colour map 1, C5.*

ⓘ *T061-2857200 (direct) or through Namibia Wildlife Resorts, Windhoek, T061-2857200, www.nwr.com.na. Both overnight and day visitors need to book in advance. Open all year. Entrance to resort US$6 for adults, children under 16 free. US$1.50 cars. Entrance to thermal baths US$2.30 adults, US$1.50 children under 16.*

In 1844 Hugo Hahn and Heinrich Kleinschmidt established a mission station here, the first amongst the Herero-speaking people, and named the station **Neu Barmen** after Barmen, the headquarters of the Rhenish Missionary Society in Germany. Growing numbers of impoverished Herero came to settle by the new church at Gross Barmen and the mission station also became a trading post. Following the 1904-1907 Herero-Nama uprising against the German occupation of Namibia, the colonial government approved the sale of land to white settlers, and in 1907 Gross Barmen was sold off. The Hot Springs Resort was opened in 1966 and is popular with locals as a weekend getaway and is a good place to relax for a day en route to the coast or after a dusty trip in the north. Gross Barmen was known by the Herero as Otjikango, meaning 'a weak spring running over rocky ground', an apt description for the hot spring which bubbles up here and leaves its salty residue around the resort. The main reasons for visiting the resort are these hot spring baths and the outdoor swimming pool, both supplied by the thermal spring (although the outdoor pool is still quite chilly in winter). The indoor thermal hall consists of a large sunken bath and artificial fountain, somewhat out of date and tired now, but still a good place for a relaxing soak during the cooler winter months (June-August). The water temperature is roughly 50°C. The outdoor swimming pool and children's pool are shaded by large palm trees, there are picnic sites, *braai* pits, a restaurant and drinks/ice cream kiosk; the area gets quite animated on summer weekends.

As well as the hot springs, the resort also has two tennis courts, a children's play area, a well-stocked shop, restaurant and petrol station.

To get to the resort, turn off the B2 near Okahandja onto the C87. Follow the road for 25 km to the resort entrance; keep an eye out for the enormous termite mounds, as tall as small trees.

Hiking

Although no trails have been laid out, there are some enjoyable walks along paths and dry riverbeds around the resort, where it is possible to see kudu, warthogs and baboons. As always, keep an eye out for snakes. A prominent rocky outcrop offers views back over the resort and across the arid plains. The salty spring itself, by the campsite, makes an interesting geography lesson for the kids.

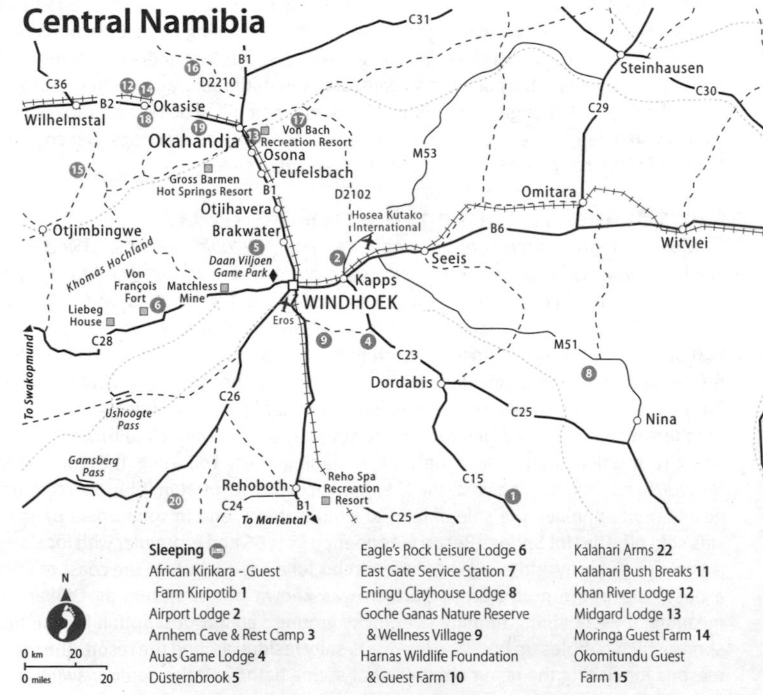

Sleeping

Daan Viljoen Game Park *p105, map p106*
Reservations through **Namibia Wildlife Resorts**, Windhoek, T061-2857200, www.nwr.com.na.
A **Luxury suites**. 4 beds in 2 en suite rooms, with fridge, kitchen, kettle, stove, cutlery and crockery.
C **Bungalows**. 2 beds, fridge, hot plate, wash basin, *braai* pit, communal toilets, and showers, ask for view over dam, all are in fairly poor condition.
D **Caravan and campsites**. Grassed, no privacy, lights, *braai* pit, electricity, maximum 8 people, 2 vehicles per site, communal ablution blocks, field kitchens. there is a swimming pool.

Okahandja and around *p106, map p108*
There is a bewildering array of accommodation in and around Okahandja; pick your price bracket and check the location; there are some nice places just off the main roads.

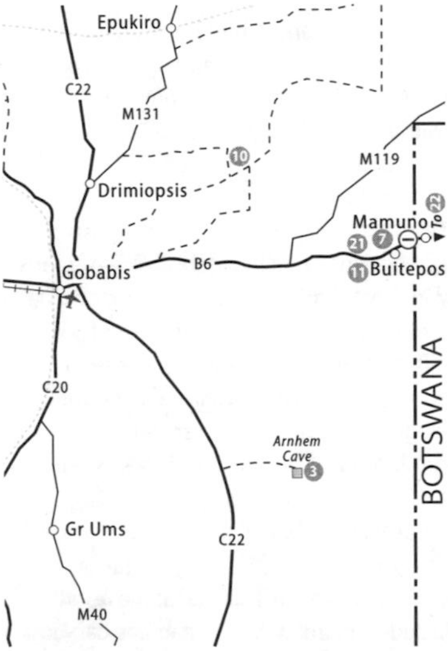

Oropoko **16**
Otjisazu Guest Farm **17**
Ozombanda Guest Farm **18**
Rock Lodge **19**
Weissenfels Guest Farm **20**
Zelda Game & Guest Farm **21**

C **Horseshoe Bar and Grill**, next door to the **Riet Haus** on the B1/Voortrekker St, about 500 m north of town, a few metres after the curio market, T062-501678. One 4-bed and one 2-bed room, B&B, shared ablutions with the basic **camping** (**E**, with electricity, though this is a dry and exposed area). The bar gets lively at night and it does a good buffet lunch on Sun.
C **Okahandja Lodge**, 2 km north of town on the B1, T062-504299, www.okahandja lodge.com. 22 thatched en suite doubles and 2 family rooms, all with fan and TVs, tastefully decorated in African style, restaurant serving buffet and à la carte meals, bar, conference facilities, swimming pool, game drives available. Very nicely done, but lacking in intimacy due to size. **Camping** (**E**, US$8 per person) available with good shared ablutions and cooking facilities.
C **Sylvanette Guesthouse**, 311 Hoogenhout St, 2 blocks west of the railway line, between Kaiser St and Peter Brand St, T062-505550, www.sylvanette.com. Comfortable and pleasant, fairly central. 7 en suite doubles, s/c and a/c, lovely shaded garden, swimming pool, secure parking.
C **Villa Nina**, 327 Conradie St, T062-502497. Pretty guesthouse with kitchen, 2 bathrooms, satellite TV and swimming pool, preferably for a stay of longer than 1 night.
D-E **Okahandja Rest Camp**, opposite Shell station at the B1 turn-off for town (immediately north of the bridge over the Okahandja River), T062-504086. 9 rondavels/chalets with fan, kettle, sink, with or without full bathroom, each has outdoor *braai* area, table and seating. **Campsite** with good communal ablutions and camp kitchen, and individual sites with *braai* area, table, seating, light and electricity. Clean, nicely laid out with established shade trees, the best value option.

Guest farms

A **Moringa Guest Farm**, B2 44 km west, turn north, following signs for 20 km, T/F062-503872, www.moringasafaris.com. 5 en suite bungalows with minibar and kitchen, small dining room, lounge, bar, swimming pool, well-established garden with shade trees, cacti and succulents, plentiful game (as for Oropoko, below, but without the rhino) mingling happily with cattle, easily seen on game drives, landing strip, intimate and peaceful. This guest farm has made a conscientious effort to reintroduce game on to its land, initially for for hunting, although it is presently turning the tide towards simple tourism. Check first if you are from the anti-hunting fraternity.

A **Oropoko**, 44 km west of Okahandja on the B2, turn south on to the D2156, and follow signs for 18 km, T062-503871, www.oropoko.com. 30 double rooms and 3 family units in tastefully built, thatched, en suite bungalows, each with a/c, bar, safe and telephone. A fabulous resort on a granite outcrop with commanding views over game-stocked plains. 15 rhino are in a 1000-ha adjacent area and can be viewed from the restaurant terrace with binoculars. Other game includes giraffe, oryx, kudu, eland, springbok, game drives (they have 11,000 ha in all, and parts are so well stocked it's like visiting a zoo). Bar, large restaurant (buffet and à la carte), TV room and library, a new activity is clay pigeon shooting. Almost recommended, but lacking intimacy; call ahead, they occasionally fill up with a bus-load of tourists.

A **Otjisazu Guest Farm**, D2102 southeast from Okahandja for 27 km, the farm is about 90 km northeast of Windhoek, T062-501259, www.otjisazu.de. The original farm house was built in the 19th century as a mission station, though the 12 en suite doubles and 2 family units are purpose-built, swimming pool and thatched poolside *lapa*, horse riding, mountain bike and hiking trails, game drives, there are a number of antelope species on this farm, rates are all inclusive of buffet breakfast and 3-course lunch and dinner.

A **Ozombanda Guest Farm**, B2 west, 28 km from Okahandja, T062-503870, ozombanda@natron.net. 4 thatched en suite double bungalows, rather palatial decor so reasonably good value for the price, swimming pool, game drives, hiking trails and game viewing from blinds, all inclusive, on a 120-sq km farm; a number of antelope and the more elusive leopard are present, and the owners will drive you around and give you an insight into Namibian farm life.

B **Khan River Lodge**, from Okahandja 63 km west on the B2, then 20 km north, follow signs, T062-503883, www.khanrivier.com. 5 very comfortable en suite rooms with private terrace, a HAN award winner (see page 16), swimming pool with poolside dining *lapa* and bar. Recommended.

B **Okomitundu Guest farm**, 63 km west on the B2, 35 km south on the D196, T062-503901, www.okomitundu.com. HAN award-winning lodge (page 16), with 8 en suite spacious double rooms, set on 11,000 ha offering game drives, horse riding, hiking, swimming in a heated pool and stargazing from an observatory. The highlight here is a drive to the top of the Kuduspitze, a nearby mountain where the views of the surrounding countryside are spectacular.

B **Rock Lodge**, just off the B2, 11 km west of Okahandja, T062-503840, www.rock.lodge.na. 16 en suite doubles and 5 houses each with 2 a/c and en suite bedrooms and open-plan kitchen and lounge, many with fine views of the 'Rock', attractive wooden and stone walk-ways, game walks, drives and a quad-bike trail. Good conference facilities, team-building activities such as abseiling, paint ball, obstacle courses; there's no reason why a group of friends on holiday cannot enjoy these activities.

Von Bach Recreation Resort *p109*

D **Campsites and 2-bed huts** with shared cooking facilities, ablutions blocks, no power points or bedding. Reservations through **Namibia Wildlife Resorts**, Windhoek, T061-2857200, www.nwr.com.na.

Gross Barmen Hot Springs Resort *p109*

Reservations through **Namibia Wildlife Resorts**, Windhoek, T061-2857200, www.nwr.com.na.

A **Luxury suites**. 4 beds with a/c and DSTV.

C **Bungalows**. 2- to 5-bed standard and economy bungalows, well equipped with fridge, cooker and kettle, varying degrees of comfort but all with military barracks 'feel'; reveille at 0600 (only joking).

D **Caravan and campsites**. 16 good, large sites with communal ablutions, *braai* areas, laundry and ovens. Facilities at the resort include a petrol station, restaurant, bar, kiosk, tennis courts, outdoor swimming pool and indoor hot pools.

Eating

Daan Viljoen Game Park *p105, map p106*
The restaurant serves decent meals 0730-0830, 1200-1330, 1900-2030. There is a charge for each picnic site, although it is on your conscience to pay, as no one checks. A small kiosk, open 0900-1700, sells soft drinks, snacks, some *braai* supplies and firewood.

Okahandja and around *p106, map p108*
If you are just driving through there are coffee shops attached to both the 24-hr Shell and Engen petrol stations, both of which also have First National Bank ATMs.
Horseshoe Bar and Grill, 500 m north of town on the B1/Voortrekker St. An active late-night spot, with big-screen TV for sports and reasonable food in big portions, popular with local farmers so expect the likes of enormous T-bone steaks and chips.
Backerei Dekker, Martin Neib St. Pleasant bakery serving fresh rolls, pies, cakes and coffee during the day with a few plastic tables and chairs outside under a green shade cloth.
Bürgerstübchen, Post St, in a small shopping centre built to resemble a fort, behind the **Okahandja Pharmacy**, T062-501830. Small restaurant with outdoor terrace offering steaks, game, schnitzel, reasonably priced, friendly service. Recommended, closed Sun evening.
Café Spitze & Bakery, Voortrekker St. Shady terrace and a/c dining room, serving variety of light meals such as pies and hamburgers with chips, does deals for pizzas and cokes, licensed so there's plenty of cold beer.

Shopping

Okahandja and around *p106, map p108*

Crafts
There are 2 outdoor **craft markets** in town. The bigger one is on the corner of B1 as you turn into town from the south, opposite the Shell Ultra. (The **Namibian Carvers** Association specializes in carvings of animals, masks and drums.) The smaller market is on Voortrekker St by the railway crossing, good quality, and bargains to be had, but beware of crafts from Zimbabwe being sold at inflated prices. Ask for locally crafted goods to get a feel for what is produced where in the country.

Food
Closwa, Vortrekker St, sells excellent *biltong* and dried *wors*, ideal for car journeys; also available at **Kewcor**, Martin Neib St (there is a bottle shop across the road).

Transport

Okahandja and around *p106, map p108*
Okahandja is 68 km to Windhoek and 278 km to Swakopmund.

Bus and taxi
For **Intercape** coaches to **Swakopmund**, **Walvis Bay** and **Windhoek**, see timetable on page 70. All bus transport starts and finishes at the Shell Ultra, by the B1 entrance to town from the south. Taxis can be taken here or at the junction of Voortrekker St and Martin Neib St.

Train
For trains to **Swakopmund**, **Tsumeb**, **Walvis** Bay and **Windhoek**, see timetable on page 68.

Directory

Okahandja and around *p106, map p108*
Banks Standard Bank, Martin Neib St, First National Bank, A Doeseb St, Bank Windhoek, Martin Neib St. All change money and have ATMs. There are also ATMs at the Shell and Engen petrol stations.
Police B Templin St, T062-10111.

For an explanation of the sleeping and eating price codes used in this guide, see inside the front cover. Other relevant information is found in Essentials, see pages 43-51.

East to Botswana

The main road, B6, east out of Windhoek passes through the suburb of Klein Windhoek before it starts to weave its way through the Eros Mountains and out onto the plains past Hosea Kutako and on to Botswana. After passing the airport the road is a dull straight drive to Gobabis, the regional centre and the last settlement of any note before you reach the Botswana border. If you are planning on exploring the Kalahari in Botswana, this is the best place to stock up with supplies. Keep your eyes peeled for warthogs, baboons, antelope (including kudu) and birds of prey. There are rest stops clearly signposted every few kilometres for a picnic or to relieve boredom or yourself. The terrain is relatively flat and, as you near Witvlei, there are few trees. Most of the country is owned by large commercial cattle and sheep farmers. After good rains the countryside turns a beautiful green, but for most of the year it is a dull burnt brown covered with scrub vegetation. ▸▸ *For Sleeping, Eating and other listings, see pages 116-118.*

Ins and outs

Traffic is only heavy on the B6 when there is an international flight arriving or departing from the airport, 45 km out of town. Drive carefully along here, especially at dusk, there are often loaded taxis who will overtake on blind stretches in a mad rush to the airport. The airport was built here because of the need for level land and a clear approach for larger aircraft such as Boeing 747s. Closer to Windhoek there are too many mountains.

Windhoek to the border ▸▸ *pp116-118.*

You'll go past **Seeis** in the blink of an eye and **Witvlei** is a godforsaken, dusty place in the dry season, but it does have a petrol station and a *biltong* factory; the latter is opening up a factory shop with good value dried beef, kudu and gemsbok as well as fresh farm produce. There are bottle stores and small shops, the train stops here, and there is a police station and clinic. Rather than staying in town, choose one of the guest farms along the way (book ahead for all of them) or push through to Gobabis or the border.

Dordabis → *Colour map 1, C6.*

The tiny settlement of Dordabis makes an interesting detour to see the **karakul** carpet weavers. **Ibenstein Weavers** ⓘ *T/F062-573544, www.ibenstein-weavers.com.na, Mon-Fri 0800-1200, 1430-1800, by appointment only*, offer tours of the farm and weavery. They produce a range of animal and African designs in varying sizes as carpets and wall hangings. They don't come cheap; as a measure, a metre square rug will cost you roughly US$200, but it will certainly last your lifetime. The weavery has been going since 1952 and today it supports 20 weavers. The sheeps' wool arrives in varying colours of grey, fawn, black and white, some of it is then dyed, before being spun and weaved by hand. The weavery is just south of the village (ie left at the T-junction); don't be confused by the private farm of the same name.

Arnhem Cave

ⓘ *T/F062-573585, arnhem@mweb.com.na.*

Remember to wear old clothes as a visit to the caves gets rather messy.

If you have plenty of time or are particularly interested in caves and bats then a detour to Arnhem Cave can be recommended. The cave is situated on a private farm in the Arnhem hills south of the B6. Contact Jannie Bekker in advance. He drives groups to the entrance at 1000 each day (given demand). The farm is 4 km (signposted) from the junction of the D1506 and D1808. Entrance to the cave is US$12 per person in a minimum group size of four (reductions for guests of the rest camp); helmets and torches are available for hire.

The cave system is 4500 m long, making it the longest in Namibia. The entrance is divided in two by a thick column of rock; both sides lead down into an enormous cavern measuring 122 m long and 45 m wide. This leads down to smaller crevices and passages. It is a dry cave and thus there are few of the typical cave formations such as stalagmites. After it was discovered in 1931 by Jannie's grandfather, it was exploited as a source of bat guano; today the cave remains a home to six different species of bat: the Egyptian slit-faced bat, leaf-nosed bat and giant leaf-nosed bat, horseshoe bat, and the long-fingered bat. The best time to visit is just after the first summer rains, when the insect-eating mammals are at their busiest; sitting by the cave entrance overnight is a spectacular experience.

Gobabis ›› *Phone code: 062. Colour map 2, C1. Altitude: 1442 m.*

Gobabis is a typical Namibian town; it is the capital of the Omaheke Region, surrounded by important cattle country, which produces a third of all Namibia's red meat. Allthough arid, the region has excellent grazing (and browsing for small game) especially after a few years of good rains. Visitors might find the monthly stock sales interesting (at the *kraal* on the left of the B6 as you approach from Windhoek). The town's name is derived from a Nama word meaning 'the place where people had quarrelled', although many locals believe it comes from *goabbes*, meaning 'the place of the elephants'; this is plausible, as a white hunter's cache of tusks was found nearby. The first Europeans to settle in the district were Rhenish missionaries and, in August 1856, Amraal Lambert decided to move to Gobabis and build a church and small school, and for many years the settlement was a popular stop-over point for hunters and traders between what are now Namibia and Botswana. However, once all the profitable wild animals had been killed the trade and interest moved elsewhere and it was difficult to persuade people to come and settle in this dusty region on the edge of the Kalahari. The future of the town was only secured when the railway service was opened in November 1930, which greatly facilitated the export of cattle from the district to Windhoek and South Africa. In more recent years the prosperity of the town and region has been buoyed by the Trans-Kalahari Highway, which has greatly increased the number of tourists, hauliers and businessmen to the region. There are

Stock up with provisions in Gobabis before heading into Botswana.

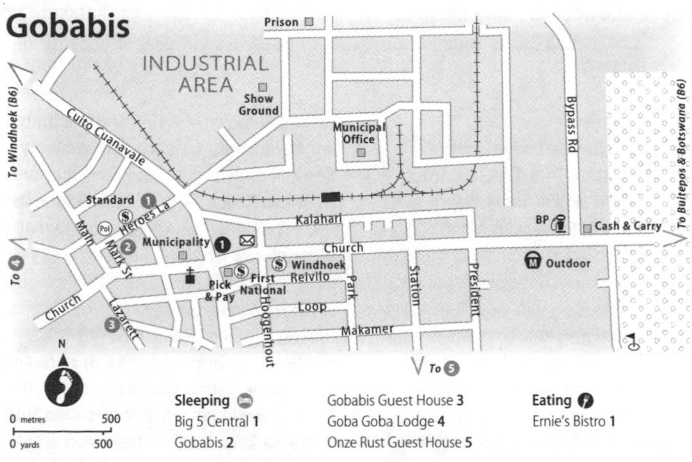

plans to extend the railway alongside the road all the way to Johannesburg, allowing bulk goods to be transported from Walvis Bay to landlocked Botswana and onto Johannesburg.

The town itself has little to recommend it beyond its pretty churches (the greatest density in Namibia). For visitors driving across the Kalahari from Botswana this will be your first introduction to urban Namibia. Afrikaans is the very much the spoken tongue, and despite some inter-racial mixing in the hotel bars, the white clientele is very conservative in its outlook. On your way through, a quick stop at the churches and a glimpse of Herero women and their 'traditional' costumes will probably suffice. It is a place for stocking up on supplies or a base for exploring the surrounding farms, which offer Bushman art and 'experiences' (game viewing on foot and, for those interested, cattle ranching). In town there are banks (**First National Bank** and **Bank Windhoek**) and a good range of shops (including **Pick and Pay** and **Shoprite** supermarkets).

Buitepos-Mamuno border

The road to the Botswana border is straight and dull all the way, but it is in good condition, with a good number of guest farms and rest camps to tempt the weary; many will provide a decent breakfast or lunch.

Traffic volume has increased considerably with the opening of the Trans-Kalahari Highway (tarred all the way), the best and quickest way to reach Namibia from Johannesburg. Just before you arrive at the border there are a couple of petrol stations and, on your left, the East Gate Service Station which has accommodation and a campsite (see Sleeping, below).

The border Open 0700-2400. A Cross Border Certificate is required to take vehicles **not** registered locally out of Namibia, obtained from the police station. All foreign vehicles entering Botswana are charged a small (10 pula) road tax. Vehicles registered outside the Southern African Common Customs Area (SACCA) are required to obtain third party insurance, this can be purchased at the border post.

Onward into Botswana By starting your journey early you will be able to make good progress before the heat becomes a factor. The roads on the Botswana side have all been upgraded as part of the Trans-Kalahari Highway. It is now possible to drive all the way to Johannesburg via Kang, Sekoma and Lobatse on tarred roads. At present there are only a few petrol stations along the Botswana stretch, so make a point of filling your tank at the border. Fill up with fuel at either or Jwaneng in Botswana, as there is no fuel between these two towns except at Kang, 350 km from Jwaneng and 400 km from Buitepos.

Sleeping

Dordabis *p114*

A **Eningu Clayhouse Lodge**, 1 km southwest of the D1471/D1482 junction, just off the M51, 65 km from Hosẹa Kutako Airport, T062-581880, www.eningu.com.na. A superb guest lodge which blends into the dry landscape, built by the owners using local clay bricks, 8 en suite doubles, attractive decorative designs enhance this peaceful location, central dining and lounge area, solar-heated swimming pool, outdoor whirlpool, roof deck with telescope for stargazing, craft shop, very good food and extensive choice of wine, ideal for hiking and birding plus some game viewing. Recommended.

B **African Kirikara – Guest farm Kiripotib**, 160 km southwest of Windhoek; take the B6 east for 28 km, turn south on the C23 for 63 km to Dordabis, take the MR33 for Uhlenhorst for 55 km and follow signs for 10 km from the turning onto the D1488, T062-581419, www.kirikara.com. A colourful, multi-faceted jewellery workshop, spinning/ weaving factory, working sheep farm and guest farm with 5 en suite doubles, cheaper en suite tents, swimming pool, good home cooking, bar, hiking trails, informative, friendly hosts.

Arnhem Cave *p113*

C-E **Arnhem Cave & Rest Camp**, T/F062-581885, arnhem@mweb.com.na. 4 chalets with 2 or 4 beds, fully equipped for self-catering, plus a campsite and swimming pool, excellent meals are available on request. The owners will take guests on tours of the caves which are also on their property.

Gobabis *p115, map p115*

Gobabis is roughly half way between Johannesburg and Swakopmund.

C **Big 5 Central Hotel**, around the corner from the **Gobabis Hotel** on Heroes Lane, T062-562094, www.big5namibia.com. 15 rooms with DSTV, restaurant, bar, bottle store, *braai* area, rooms not quite so comfortable as the **Gobabis**, but little to choose between the 2. Neither can be recommended for more than an overnight stop. Camping (**E**) very cheap at US$3.50 per person.

C **Goba Goba Lodge**, Elim St (follow signs 1 km out of town), T062-564499, goba@mweb.com.na. The best guesthouse in town and a HAN award winner (see page 16), with 7 en suite doubles, a/c, TV, a decent tennis court, big swimming pool, restaurant and plenty of africanalia such as dugout canoes and carvings dotted around. It's in the Nossob riverbed, and there is good birdwatching from its hide.

C **Gobabis Guest House**, 8 Lazerette St, T062-563189, gghnam@iafrica.com.na. 11 en suite rooms, DSTV, a/c or fan, B&B, tasty dinner available on request (it has to be steak, really), self-catering facilities also available, swimming pool and secure parking.

C **Onze Rust Guest House**, 95 Rugby St, T062-562214, www.natron.net/tour/onzerust. 5 neat rooms with a/c and DSTV, private *braai* facilities, doubles, singles and family rooms, B&B and can arrange supper with notice.

C-D **Gobabis Hotel**, Mark St, T062-562568, F562641. 17 rooms with satellite TV, shower, a/c or fan, clean and airy but very square, shaded courtyard, restaurant, bar, pool tables, swimming pool, off-road parking. This is the focus of most activity for the local white community, particularly at weekends.

Buitepos-Mamuno border *p116*

B-D **Kalahari Arms Hotel**, Ghanzi. The first comfortable accommodation across the border. Chalets and space for camping, there is also a swimming pool to help you cool off and a menu that will warm the carnivore's heart.

C-E **East Gate Service Station**, T062-560405, eastgate@namibnet.com. Camp or stay in comfortable bright blue 3-bed bungalows. This is a pleasant spot and a surprise in such a desolate region, there is a bar and restaurant, swimming pool, it sells *braai* packs (meat), ice and firewood, and basic provisions are available at the petrol station. If you wish to drive through to Maun in Botswana in one hit then it is advisable to spend the night here and cross the border as soon as it opens. Also camping with good facilities on bright green lawns.

Guest farms

There are some lovely farms in the district which welcome visitors. In addition to providing a peaceful overnight stop, these farms give an insight into life on the arid fringes of the Kalahari Desert. **Note** Trophy hunting is a popular and lucrative pastime in this region. We have done our best to omit the establishments that offer hunting, but if you don't wish to share the dinner table with hunters, call in advance to double-check. Some of the following are a considerable distance from Gobabis.

AL-D **Harnas Wildlife Foundation and Guest farm**, T062-568788, www.harnas.de (German), www.harnas.org (English). Take the B6 for the border, turn north on the C22, it's a further 94 km, follow signs. There is a variety of accommodation here to suit all budgets from luxurious stone and wooden chalets with en suite bathrooms, fans and *braai* pits, cheaper self-catering tented igloos, to camping with ablutions. Restaurant, very good bar, swimming pool, trampoline, volleyball. The focus of the foundation is rehabilitating injured and orphaned game, and it has many tame predators that arrived as cubs, which it allows adults to 'play' with. There are some

For an explanation of the sleeping and eating price codes used in this guide, see inside the front cover. Other relevant information is found in Essentials, see pages 43-51.

tame cheetahs that have been stars of a number of movies, leopard and a large lion enclosure. The drives and walks around the centre are educational and you can see a large variety of animal and bird species in generous enclosures and it's not too zoo-like. The night-time walk offers a glimpse of the nocturnal creatures and includes a short drive out from the main farmhouse to see porcupine. Recommended especially for children, not quite as impressive as Okonjima.

A Kalahari Bush Breaks, on the B6, 26 km before the border, T062-568936, www.kalaharibushbreaks.com. The architect owner and his wife (who leads the game drives) have built a fabulous 3-storey thatched lodge with 5 doubles, dining room and bar, or guests can stay in 4 double rooms in the main house, in the 10 permanent tents at the tented camp with electricity, *braai* pits and clean, thatched ablutions block, or in 4 self-catering cottages overlooking a waterhole. Full board, dinner is served on a stunning outdoor wooden deck, plunge pool, Bushman paintings nearby, hides for bird/game watching – you can in one overnight for a wilderness thrill. Also good-value **camping (E)** available with open-air ablutions. Recommended.

B-E Zelda Game and Guest Farm, on the D6, 23 km before the Botswana border, T062-560427, www.zelda-game-and-guest farm.com. Picturesque place that caters for larger groups, including overlanders. 16 rooms with en suite bathroom, 3 permanent tents, camping, swimming pool, volleyball, aviary, trampoline, restaurant and bar. It can arrange dancing and walks with Bushmen, in groups of 10 or more. There are also leopard and cheetah on the farm and guests can watch them being fed each evening.

Eating

Gobabis *p115, map p115*

Ernie's Bistro, Church St. Central with a bar and some tourist info, a good option if you don't wish to eat or cook. A white farmer enclave with the formidable Ernie in charge, good hearty food includes a variety of steaks and pork, and bubblegum flavour milkshake.

Shopping

Dordabis *p114*

There is a store/bottle store and petrol station, open sunrise to sunset.

Gobabis *p115, map p115*

If you are travelling towards Botswana this is a good place to stock up with fresh produce and Namibian beer. On the Botswana side of the border you will only come across village stores until you reach Ghanzi. Selection of chemists, supermarkets, 24-hr petrol stations, a hardware store and a large cash and carry on the main road as you leave town for the border.

Activities and tours

Gobabis *p115, map p115*

Gobabis Golf Course, US$4 for 9 holes, but it does not have clubs for hire. Keep an eye for the faded sign 1 km east of town, on the B6, turn south opposite the cash and carry.

Transport

Gobabis *p115, map p115*

Windhoek, 330 km, Botswana, 122 km.

Road If you are trying to **hitch** into Botswana you would be best advised to wait for a through lift as far as the border, if not Ghanzi.

Train See timetable, page 68; it's a very slow service which more or less follows the main road all the way into Windhoek.

Directory

Gobabis *p115, map p115*

Banks The big 3 are all represented, with ATMs. The **Bank of Windhoek** and **First National** are on Church St and the **Standard Bank** is on Heroes' Lane.

Hospital Private hospital, T062-562275.

Police: T10111, or T062-562718.

Etosha & the Northeast

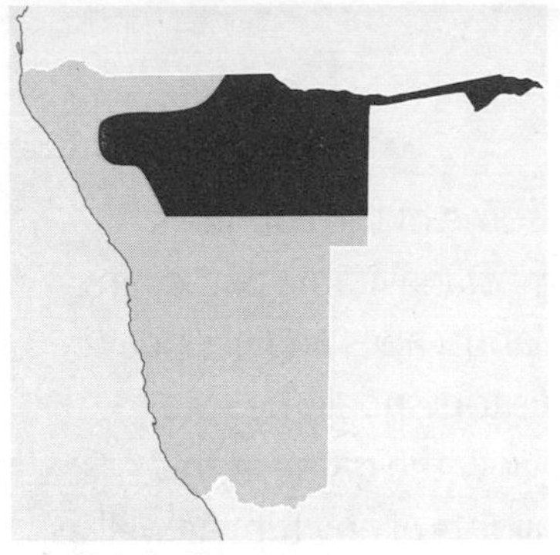

Footprint features

Introduction

The north of Namibia is home to some of the country's principal attractions, and is an almost inevitable part of any tour, due largely to the stunning landscapes and abundant wildlife in Etosha National Park. Visitors should be sure to allow at least a couple of days to view the game at this magnificent park, one of the highlights of any trip. As well as comfortable accommodation within the park, a number of the country's most luxurious lodges are located on its perimeter, providing an unforgettable and upmarket bush experience.

The two other game reserves in the region should not be overlooked. Waterberg Plateau Park offers some excellent hiking in a well-stocked park, across an unusual limestone terrain. To the northeast, Khaudum Game Park is one of Africa's more remote areas, deep in the flat and dry wilderness known as Bushmanland.

Also in the northeast, the Kavango and Caprivi regions provide a welcome change from the relentlessly dry landscapes for which the rest of the country is famous. The landscape in the northeast is dominated by rivers and green forests and, for overseas visitors, it offers something of 'real' Africa and presents a new range of vegetation and wildlife. Souvenir hunters will find some of Namibia's finest local crafts at the community-run markets and roadside stalls. The northeast is certainly a long drive from Windhoek but many hail it as their favourite corner of the country, and it provides easy access to attractions over the border in Botswana, Zambia and Zimbabwe.

★ Don't miss...

1 **Africat Foundation** Predators never seemed so cuddly, page 124.
2 **Waterberg Plateau** Have a sundowner beer at the escarpment edge, overlooking the endless plains below, page 125.
3 **Etosha National Park** Bring a book, beer and binoculars and join the masses watching elephants at Okaukuejo's floodlit watering hole, page 135.
4 **Caprivi rivers** Join the *mokoro* fishermen on any of the region's perennial rivers, either in your own canoe or escorted by a skilled oarsman, page 160.
5 **Impalila Island and Lianshulu Lodge** Relive the days of colonial splendour at a justifiably famous riverbank lodge, pages 172 and 174.
6 **Caprivi Arts Centre** Pick up a souvenir in Katima Mulilo, page 176.

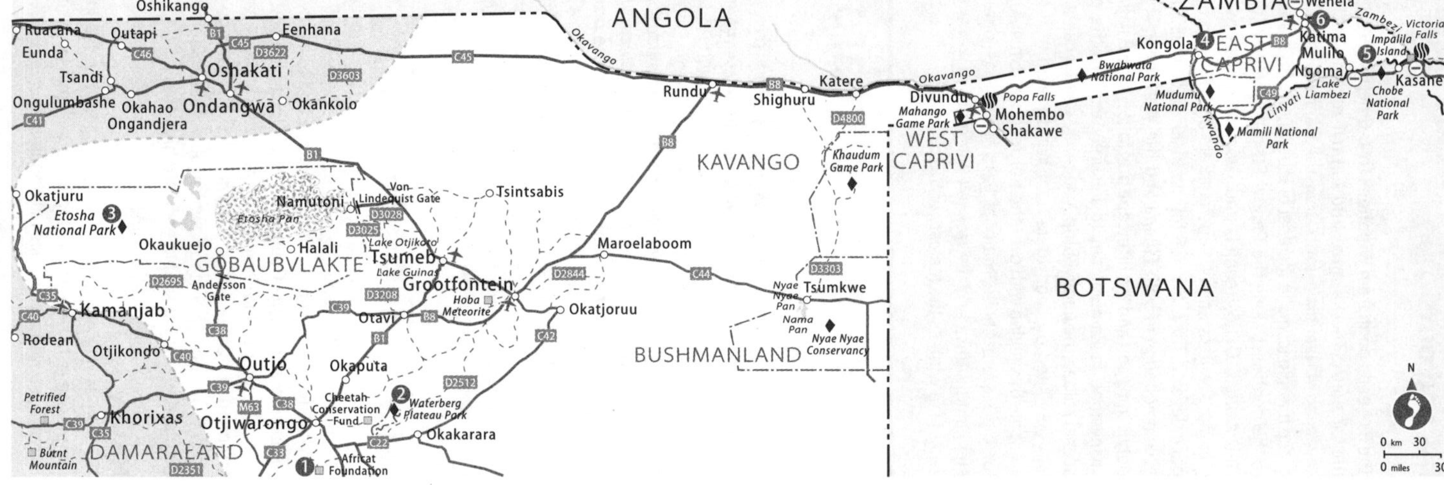

Ins and outs

The B1 heads north from Windhoek to Tsumeb where it branches off to Ondangwa in the far north. The Kavango and Caprivi regions are all within reach of the open savannah of Namibia's north along the B8 and at the sleepy settlement of Otavi, one of the triangle towns to the east of Etosha, the B8 branches off to the east and heads to the northeast along the Caprivi Strip all the way to Katima Mulilo. The towns of Otjiwarongo, Outjo, Tsumeb and Grootfontein are well served with tarred roads, plentiful service stations, supermarkets and a good supply of accommodation at all price levels. They are useful restocking centres on the way to self-catering accommodation in both Etosha and the Waterberg. The region can be accessed by public transport and the **Intercape** bus follows the B1 and then the B8 on its journey to Livingstone in Zambia; but to leisurely explore the parks and the lush riverside scenery along the Caprivi Strip, you really need a car. If you are short of time, Etosha can be visited on short tours from Windhoek; but if time's not an issue, you can combine this region with over-the-border hops to neighbouring countries – Botswana for the superb Chobe National Park which has one of the greatest densities of elephant in Africa and the tranquil wilderness Okavango Delta; and Zimbabwe and Zambia to witness the majesty of Victoria Falls.

Otjiwarongo and around

▸▸ *Phone code: 067. Colour map 1, B5.*

The town of Otjiwarongo is a fast-growing commercial centre, strategically located in the centre-north of Namibia, serving the farming communities in the surrounding area. It is also a regular stopping-off place for people travelling to Etosha and the Waterberg Plateau, with a wide range of reasonably priced accommodation. Nearby are the Cheetah Conservation Fund and Africat Foundation which are both important organizations in the protection of Namibia's big cats and are well worth supporting. A day or overnight visit to the Africat Foundation's guest farm, Okonjima, is highly recommended; it is the best place in Namibia not only to get close to cheetah and leopard, but also to learn about the plight of these creatures in Africa.

Otjiwarongo means 'place of the fat cattle' or 'beautiful place' in Herero. Given the central role that cattle play in their culture, both meanings are appropriate.

▸▸ *For Sleeping, Eating and other listings, see pages 132-135.*

Otjiwarongo ▸▸ *pp 132-135.*

Ins and outs

Ojiwarongo is easy enough to get around and is neatly disected by the B1 as it runs through town as **Hage Geingob Street**. Along here you will find all the town's petrol stations, shops and banks. **Tourist information** can be found at the **Omaue Information Office** ⓘ *St George's St, T/F067-303830, Mon-Fri 0800-1300, 1400-1700, Sat 0800-1300*, which also sells minerals and crafts and is run by a helpful ex-geologist shopkeeper and his wife.

History

The town is officially deemed to have been founded in 1906 upon the arrival of the narrow-gauge railway linking the important mining centre of Tsumeb with the coast. However, as with many places of Namibia, there is evidence that Bushmen were living in the area thousands of years ago. It is believed that groups of Damara settled here in the late 14th century where they lived as hunter gatherers until the arrival of the Herero in the early part of the 19th century. The land was ideal for cattle grazing and the Herero gradually forced the Damara off the land and into the surrounding mountainous areas.

In 1891 the Rhenish Mission Society secured the agreement of Herero Chief Kambazembi, and a mission was established, opening the way for adventurers and traders to move further north. The Herero 'revolt' of 1904 and their eventual retreat from the German troops into the Omaheke *sandveld*, where thousands died of thirst and hunger, provided the colonial authorities with the opportunity to take control of the area. German (and later Afrikaner) cattle farmers were the principal benefactors.

Sights

The **Narrow Gauge Locomotive 'No 41'** sits outside the railway station. The locomotive is one of three manufactured by **Hensel & Son** in Germany in 1912 for Namibia's original narrow-gauge railway and remained in commission until 1960, when the track was widened from 600 to 1067 mm.

The **Crocodile Ranch** ⓘ *near the Acacia Park campsite to the east of town, T067-302121*, was a family business started in 1985, primarily rearing the beasts for their skins. It is the only one of its kind in Namibia. The skins are exported to Europe and North America for use in making expensive leather shoes, wallets and briefcases. The ranch was recently taken over by new management and it remains to be seen whether tours will resume; phone first.

Otjiwarongo Museum ⓘ *T067-302238, Mon-Fri 0900-1230, 1400-1600, entry US$1.50 per person*, was opened in 2003 and is located in a new building on Libertina Amathila Avenue. Two large rooms display a collection of items which demonstrate the area's cultural history and seemingly the advance of technology in the region, judging by the old washing machines, irons, spinning machines and biscuit tins. It does rather resemble a bric-a-brac shop but there are some interesting items on display. These include the old telephone exchange from Kalkfeld, and children's toys

made from animal bones in the days before plastic ones were available. One is an ox wagon where the body is made from a jaw bone and the wheels made from smaller knee joints. Outside in the yard are a number of agricultural implements and an old train carriage that used to be used by numerous foreign dignitaries in its heyday. Of interest next to the museum's front door is the town's **automatic weather metre**, with a rain gauge, a wind metre that measures speed and direction, and a thermometer that records air temperature. Every four hours, the woman in charge of the museum takes a reading of the weather and sends the information to the Weather Bureau in Windhoek. You'll find these weather metres in several of Namibia's regional towns.

Around Otjiwarongo » pp 132-135.

Cheetah Conservation Fund

ⓘ *Elands Vreugde Farm, 44 km east along the D2440 from Otjiwarango, T/F067-306225, www.cheetah.org, daily 0900-1700, no entry fee but donations greatly appreciated.*

The Cheetah Conservation Fund is a non-profit organization which was established in 1990 to research and conserve cheetahs and to provide information on their plight in Namibia. Among other things, the CCF monitors numbers and keeps an up-to-date health/gene pool database, it advises on predator management and relocation techniques, and works with all parties to promote awareness of their sleek protégés. They have large numbers of enthusiasts through their eight chapters in the USA, and indeed in 2001 President Nujoma sent 10 cheetahs to US zoos as a present. You can visit the Field Research Centre where there is a very interesting museum dedicated to cheetah and the ecology of Namibia, plus a gift shop selling drinks.

Africat Foundation

ⓘ *www.africat.org.*

Namibia is home to 25% of the world's cheetah population, 90% of which live on commercial farmland.

The guest farm at **Okonjima** (www.okonjima.com), meaning 'the place of baboons', in Herero, just south of Otjiwarongo, is home to the **Africat Foundation**, a non-profit organization dedicated to the conservation and protection of Namibia's wild carnivores. The foundation works in partnership with farmers – who have traditionally regarded the cats as pests – to find ways in which to preserve the wild cheetah and leopard population. It also houses and attempts to reintroduce, where possible, orphaned, injured or captured carnivores. By offering to remove and relocate cats from farmland to Okonjima, **Africat** provides the farmers with an alternative to shooting the cheetahs and leopards that may be causing problems on farms, killing livestock such as goats, for example. **Africat** says that there is a marked increase in the number of calls from farmers about problem cheetahs each year between July to December, which corresponds with Namibia's dry season. It is thought that when water is less scarce there is a decline in prey for the cats and they go after the livestock on commercial farms and the antelope on game farms. Since the project started in 1991, over 800 cheetahs and leopards have moved through Okonjima, so **Africat** has greatly contributed to saving a large number of these cats from being killed. The foudation also carries out research on the cats and has contributed to our understanding of these animals. Wherever possible the cats are reintroduced into the wild in a location where they will not cause problems to farmers; some 80% of the cheetah and over 90% of the leopard have been rehabilitated in the wild. The ones that cannot be re-released live at Okonjima; these are mostly cheetah that were orphaned at an early age and never learned hunting skills from their mothers and, as these survival skills are not instinctive and need to be learned, they do not have the ability to survive on their own in the wild.

Overnight guests have a full, informative agenda, including viewing and feeding leopard and cheetah. Some of the cheetahs can be tracked on foot, there are guided Bushmen trails, and after dinner guests can watch nocturnal creatures such as porcupine and honey badgers from a hide. Despite Okonjima not guaranteeing leopard sightings, they are often seen and one of the highlights here is watching leopard in the early evening, a wonderful opportunity for photos. For information on staying overnight at Okonjima, see Sleeping, page 132. Day visitors are permitted by prior arrangement and the excursion costs US$100, though visitors will have to drive themselves or fly there at additional cost. Arrival is expected no later than 0700 and departure no later than 1630. Included in the price is tracking cheetahs on foot, a visit to the **Africat Welfare Project**, brunch and afternoon tea.

Waterberg Plateau Park » *pp 132-135. Colour map 1, B6.*

ⓘ *Entry fees into the park are US$13, children under 16 free, cars US$1.50. The park is open year round. For accommodation in the park, see page 133. The resort has a shop, restaurant (0700-0830, 1200-1330, 1900-2100), bar, filling station (no diesel) and swimming pool with pleasant views.*

Known to the Herero-speaking people as *Oueverumue*, or 'narrow gate', the Waterberg Plateau, between the Kleine and Grosse Waterberg, is Namibia's only mountain game park. The plateau rises up to 200 m above the surrounding plain, extending some 50 km by 16 km. The sharp barrier of the plateau presents a stark contrast to the monotonous, scrubby, bushveld plain below, and has operated as a game sanctuary for endangered species since 1972. Today, it is of interest to naturalists and geographers for its rare animal populations, atypical flora and striking sandstone topography, as well as being the scene of a historic encounter between German and Herero troops.

Ins and outs

Turn off the B1, 22 km south of Otjiwarongo, onto the C22. Follow this road for 41 km before turning left onto the D2512. Follow this for a further 27 km to **Bernabé de la Bat Rest Camp,** the entrance to Waterberg Plateau. There is no public transport to

the park and once off the main road, there is little local traffic and hitch-hiking may involve a long wait.

Open-top game-viewing vehicles set off early morning and mid-afternoon from the rest camp, and provide the opportunity for those unable or unwilling to hike on the plateau with the chance to see game. The tours stop at game-viewing hides, often well frequented with game. Bookings should be made at the camp office, wrap up in winter (US$42 adults, US$25 children). Book on arrival since this is a popular drive, lasting three hours and taking you to an area of the plateau that is closed to the public.

History

In 1873, two missionaries from the Rhenish Mission Society, G Beiderbecke and H Brincker, established a mission station at the largest fountain at the Waterberg, although they had been instructed only to assess the situation. Their congregation consisted of Herero, Damara and Bushmen and were described by the missionaries as living in mutual distrust. In 1880 during a dispute between Damara and Herero groups, the mission station was looted and burned to the ground, and lay deserted until 1890, when Missionary Eich was sent to resurrect it. Over the next 10 years a school, church, trading post and post office were established.

However, events elsewhere in Hereroland were leading to a major confrontation between the Germans and the Herero. Unscrupulous traders encouraged and forced Herero-speaking people to buy goods against credit, and when the latter couldn't pay, the traders took land to cover these debts. Certain Herero chiefs, such as Samuel Maherero of Okahandja and Zacharias of Otjimbingwe, sold off large tracts of tribal land to meet their growing desires for European manufactured goods and alcohol. Both promised their people that the land would be recovered at a later date.

In January 1904, facing increasing pressure to take action over the lost lands, or to stand down as Paramount Herero Chief, Samuel Maherero gave the order to drive the Germans from Herero land. Initial Herero attacks were successful, but following the appointment of General von Trotha as German commander in the middle of the year, the tide started to turn against the Herero. As a growing number of Herero men, women and children retreated to the Waterberg with their cattle, the scene was set for the crucial battle of the war.

Throughout 11 August, skirmishes took place between the German and Herero forces. The Germans had a total of about 1500 men, as well as 30 cannons and a dozen

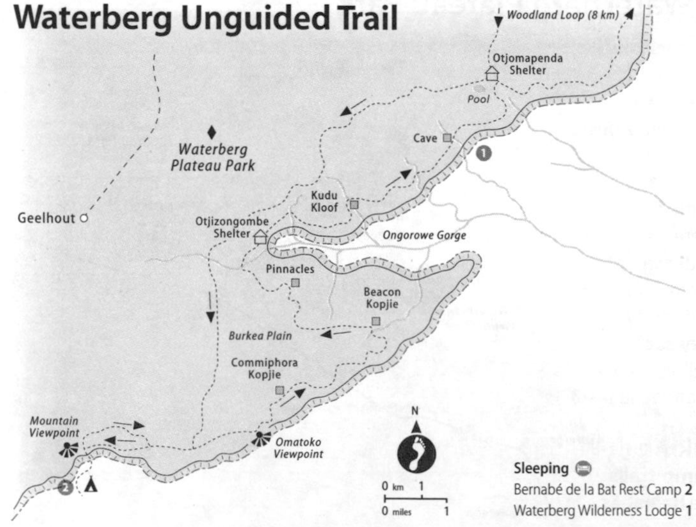

machine guns. Estimates of the strength of the Herero forces range from 35,000 to 80,000 with between 5000 and 6000 guns at their disposal. As the day progressed, the battle moved deeper into the bush, stretching over a 40-km front, with neither side able to establish a telling advantage. However, on the morning of 12 August, a German signal unit on the plateau noticed a huge cloud of dust heading southeast. The Herero were retreating into the Omaheke sandveld rather than surrendering to the enemy.

Over the next months thousands of Herero men, women and children, with their cattle, died of hunger and thirst on the trek into exile in Botswana. In the years immediately following the battle and the exodus of the Herero, the land around the Waterberg was sold off to European settlers. The small graveyard near the rest camp is testimony to some of those who fell during the battle.

Vegetation and wildlife

Originally part of a much larger plateau which extended as far southwards as Mount Etjo, the sediments which make up the Waterberg were originally laid down in Karoo times (290-120 million years ago). The break-up of the super-continent Gondwanaland 150 million years ago caused an upswelling of lava which compacted underlying sediments into rocks. At the same time, the huge pressure caused by the break-up of the continent gave rise to the uplifting of Africa's edges.

This uplifting started an erosion cycle visible today at Waterberg, Mount Etjo and Omatako, which are remnants of the old land surface, and which are slowly being eroded down to the level of the surrounding plain. Finally, in the late Karoo period, a thrust fault on the northwest side of Waterberg covered a section of the plateau with debris, thereby protecting it from further erosion. This part, the **Okarakuvisa Mountains**, is the highest region of the plateau today.

Vegetation on the plateau is lush-green, sub-tropical dry woodland, with tall trees, grassy plains and a variety of ferns. This is in stark contrast to the acacia savannah at the base of the plateau, against which aggressive anti-bush encroachment measures are being taken. The mixture of very sandy soils and the Etjo sandstone cause the plateau to act like a sponge, absorbing any water that falls. The water is sucked into the soil until it reaches a layer of impermeable stone, from where it runs off underground to emerge on the southeast side of the plateau as springs. It is from the springs that the plateau gets its name.

The 40,549 ha area was proclaimed a park in 1972, originally as a sanctuary for rare and endangered species, including buffalo and roan and sable antelopes which were relocated from the Kavango and Caprivi regions. The aim was to breed these animals and then restock the areas from where they originated. Blue wildebeest were brought from Daan Viljoen Park, near Windhoek, and white rhino from Natal, South Africa, followed. Black rhino were reintroduced to the area from Damaraland in 1989. Today, it is possible to see 25 species of game including, leopard, gemsbok, eland, giraffe, kudu, jackal, hyena and baboon, as well as those animals mentioned above.

In addition to the game, the park has an estimated 200 species of bird, and in particular, is home to the only breeding colony of Cape vultures in Namibia (although there are now thought to be only three pairs left). An intensive awareness campaign is underway, aiming to educate farmers to limit the use of poisons, and to reverse bush encroachment on the plateau and thus increase grazing land for species such as kudu and gemsbok, upon which the vultures feed. Other common species are birds of prey such as the black eagle, the booted eagle and the pale chanting goshawk, as well as smaller birds such as the red-billed francolin (whose distinctive call can be heard at sunrise), five different hornbills, and the pretty rosy-faced lovebird.

Hiking in Waterberg Plateau Park

Camp trails ⓘ *See map, page 128.* There are 10 demarcated walking trails around the **Bernabé de la Bat Rest Camp** and up onto the plateau. Photocopied maps should be available from reception; if not, get your bearings using the three-dimensional display at reception and strike out along the well-marked trails. These gentle one- to three-hour walks are an excellent way of seeing the ruins of the **Old Mission**, as well as enjoying the flora and fauna, without undertaking a major expedition.

We recommend you make the effort to walk up to the plateau following the 'Mountain View' trail. It takes 30 to 45 minutes to the top, with plenty of rock hyrax (or 'dassies') to keep you company. This is an enjoyable hike and the view from the top is superb, particularly at dawn and dusk. You will need to be reasonably agile in parts and not dawdle for too long after sunset.

Waterberg Wilderness Trail ⓘ *US$35*. This is a recommended four-day, 50-km guided wilderness trail in the Okarakuvisa Mountains, starting at 1400 on every second, third and fourth Thursday of the month, and arriving back on the Sunday afternoon (April to November only). The hike, which is led by an (armed) expert on the region's flora and fauna, overnights at the rustic base camps in the wilderness area. Only one group (six to eight people) is permitted per week and reservations should be made in advance at the NWR Windhoek Reservations Office, see page 78. Hikers must bring their own food and sleeping bag.

Book ahead for these spectacular four-day hikes.

Bernabé de la Bat Rest Camp

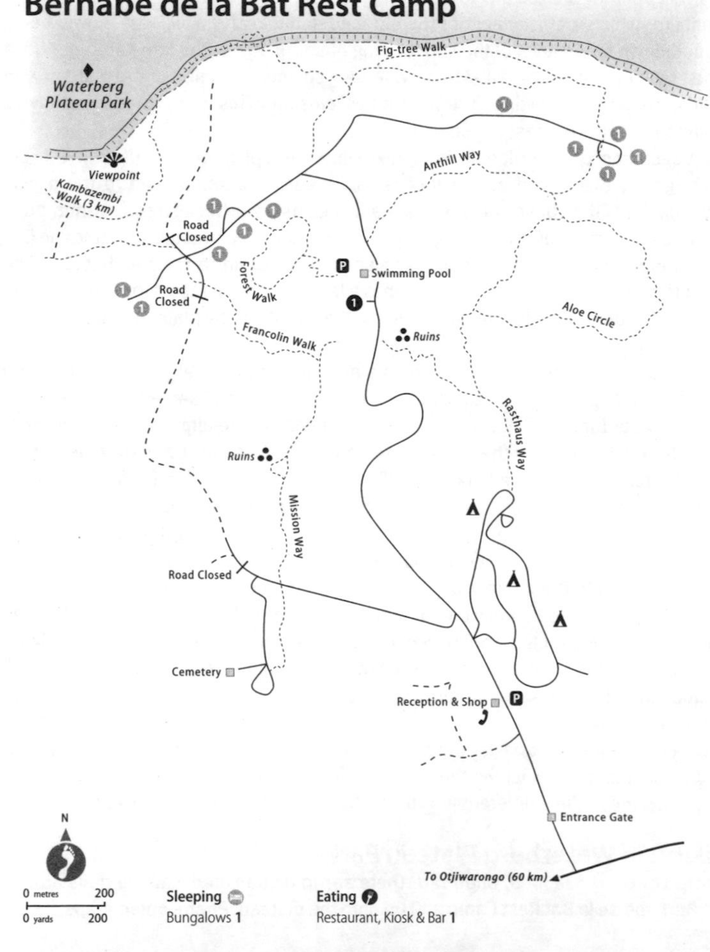

Waterberg Unguided Trail ⓘ *US$16 per person, see map, page 126*. This unaccompanied trail, also recommended, starts at the **Bernabé de la Bat Rest Camp** office before heading up onto the plateau for four days. It is aimed at reasonably fit, self-sufficient hikers and nature lovers who want to enjoy the scenery and wildlife and to have an adventure.

Once up on the plateau itself, the trail winds around the sandstone *koppies* on the southeastern edge of the plateau, through glades of weeping wattle, silver bushwillow and laurel fig trees. Everywhere there are signs of the close presence of game, the dung piles of the white and black rhino, and the spoor of kudu, giraffe, gemsbok and baboon. It is important to take care to walk relatively slowly so as not to surprise any rhino or buffalo, which might charge if frightened. If this happens, your best bet is to climb the nearest tree; failing this, turn and face the onrushing beast and sidestep at the last moment. Then change your pants.

The trail is divided into four stages of 13 km, 7 km, 8 km and 14 km respectively, each of which can be completed in a morning's walk. Day one takes you along the edge of the plateau. There are several good viewpoints, notably Omatoko view close to Commiphora Koppie. Your first night is spent in Otjozongombe shelter. For the second day the path skirts along the rim of Ongorowe Gorge. There is no need to push yourself along this stretch, the overnight shelter – Otjomapenda – is only 7 km away. The third day can also be taken gently; the path follows an 8-km loop bringing you back to the same shelter. Day four follows a different path all the way back to Bernabé de la Bat rest camp. The trail is generally well marked, but in the odd place it is necessary to look for the footprints of previous trailists, adding to the adventure of the walk. Although the distances are not great, and the walk is not nearly as demanding as the Naukluft and Fish River Canyon trails, it can get very warm during the daytime, especially carrying a pack with provisions, sleeping bag, water and camping stove. Nights can be cold with sub-zero temperatures not uncommon, so take warm clothes. Accommodation is in stone shelters with pit latrines; water is provided, hikers must take everything else.

As the early morning and early evening are the best times to see game, a good plan is to walk each stretch early in the day, drop your bags and rest up at camp during the midday heat, and then go for an exploration of your site before dark. After four days of the solitude and silence of the plateau it can feel strange going back down the mountain into civilization again.

Hikes start every Wednesday (April-November). Only one group of three to 10 people is permitted each week and reservations should be made well in advance at the Windhoek Reservations Office (see page 78). Hikers must provide their own food and equipment and the trail is undertaken at the hiker's risk.

Outjo

» *pp 132-135. Phone code: 067. Colour map 1, B5. Altitude: 1300 m.*

Outjo serves as a commercial centre for the large white-owned farms of the region and more recently has developed as a staging post for tourists on their way to Damaraland and the famous Etosha National Park (see page 135). If you have been travelling in the south of the country, or have come up from the coast, you will notice a far greater number and variety of trees in the landscape. This is an area of woodland savannah supporting both cattle and abundant game. As you continue north towards Etosha, keep an eye out for antelope sheltering in the shade of the trees.

The town's name is a Herero word meaning 'little hills'.

Ins and outs

Most visitors to Outjo are en route to or from Etosha and travelling on the C38. The town is 73 km northwest of Otjiwarongo and 114 km south of Okaukuejo rest camp in Etosha National Park. Outjo is also a good jump-off point for Damaraland and Kaokoland (see pages 180 and 192), with both Kamanjab and Khorixas within easy striking distance on good roads, the C40 and the C39, respectively. **SWA Gemstones** ⓘ *8 Hage Geingob Av, T067-313072, Mon-Fri 0900-1700, Sat 0900-1200*, doubles as the tourist office and is very helpful on local information and also has a few maps for sale. You will also find a decent spread of Etosha information and souvenir books available in the park itself.

Sights

The first Europeans to settle here were big game hunters and traders in around 1880. By 1895, part of the German army was stationed here when they constructed several solid buildings, some of which still stand today. One of the more important roles for the army when they were not at war was to help to try and prevent the spread of rinderpest from the Kaokoland and Angola. They also acted as early anti-poaching units.

Overnighters won't miss much if they head off first thing in the morning, but anyone with an interest in local history might enjoy a visit to the museum as well as admiring the old Water Tower. The **Town Museum** ⓘ *Franke House, Mon-Fri 1000-1230,1430-1630, free*, contains an account of the local history and a collection of gemstones, examples of which can still be picked off the ground if you know where to look. The museum building is also known as Franke House. This was one of the first homes to be built in Outjo and dates from around 1899. Its first occupant was the commander of the German garrison, Major von Estorff. Major Victor Franke was one of the last local commanders who made a name for himself in leading a punitive raid against the Portuguese in Angola in 1914.

In 1900, the settlement ran into its first water supply problems; the natural fountain could no longer provide for all the extra people and livestock. At the end of the year the German troops started to dig a well in the dry riverbed, while concurrently beginning construction of the **Water Tower**. The role of the tower was to house a wooden pump powered by wind sails. In March 1902 the first water started to flow, it was lifted into a concrete dam and was then carried over 600 m by pipes to the army barracks, a hospital and the stables. The 9.4-m-high tower remains, being made from local stone and clay, but the sail mechanism has not survived. Today the tower stands on a stone platform between the **Etosha Garten Hotel** (who own the land it stands on) and the dry riverbed; it is protected as a national monument and is an important local landmark, rather like the Franke Tower in Omaruru (see page 269). A less well-known monument

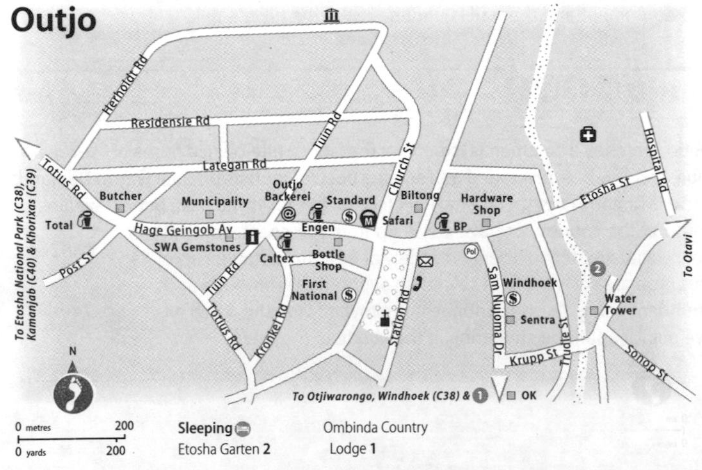

from the past is the **Naulila Memorial** standing in the old German cemetery. In October 1914 a group of German officials and accompanying soldiers were massacred by the Portuguese near Fort Naulila on the Angolan side of the Kunene River. More troops were killed a couple of months later, on 18 December 1914, when a force under the command of Major Victor Franke was sent to avenge the earlier loss of life. In 1933 the Naulila Memorial was built in memory of both expeditions.

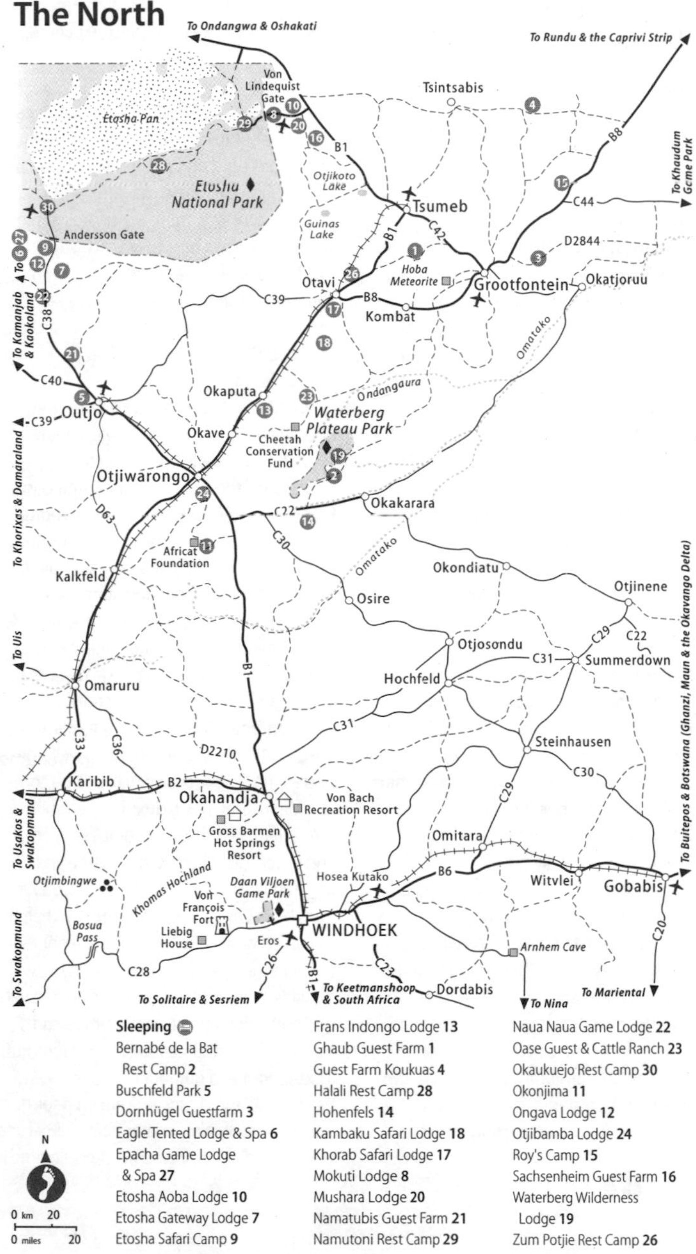

Otjiwarongo *p122, map p123*

B **C'est Si Bon Hotel**, Swembad St, turn left between the BP petrol station and the church if entering town from Windhoek, T067-301240, sibon@iafrica.com.na. The nicest accommodation downtown, laid out like a leisure complex with 20 large, en suite doubles in thatched bungalows, a central grassed courtyard with swimming pool, tennis courts by the car park, a cosy restaurant over 2 floors, and bar. TV, telephone and a/c in each room. Immaculately tended, friendly welcome, tasty à la carte food, not unreasonably priced.

C **Falkennest Guest House**, 21 Industria St, T/F067-302616, otjbb@iafrica.com.na. 10 tidy rooms with TV, a/c or fans, phone, communal kitchen and *braai* area for self-catering in the evening, B&B, small pool in well-tended garden with interesting cacti, decoration and aviary, secure parking.

C **Out of Africa B&B**, 94 Tuin St, T067-303397, www.out-of-afrika.com. An immaculate guesthouse with 21 en suite rooms with TV, fridge, writing desk and comfortable chairs. Friendly hosts, well focused on tourists' needs and willing to answer your questions. Dining room serves breakfast only, lounge, 2 swimming pools, family flat, overnight parking attendant. It also runs the lodge of the same name below. Recommended.

C **Out of Africa Town Lodge**, on the B1 at southern edge of town, T067-302230, www.out-of-afrika.com. 20 en suite doubles with a/c and DSTV, in a modern, bright white, Cape colonial-style building, swimming pool, bistro restaurant, lounge bar and coffee shop. Good hosts and friendly service.

D **Bush Pillow B&B**, Son St, T067-303885, www.bushpillow.hypermart.net. Run by Neville Neveling and his wife. Neville is heavily involved in the Otjiwarongo's tourist promotion effort and is very knowledgeable about the town and area. 7 en suite rooms with fan and TV, welcoming lounge with leather seats, small library, drinks, food and fabrics for sale, restaurant and bar, small swimming pool, secure parking. Also has 1 car available to rent for local excursions.

D **Pension Bahnhof**, Bahnhof St, T067-304801, F304803. 17 en suite rooms with a/c, TV, kettle and phone, B&B, small dining area; has the unwelcoming feel of an overnighting truckers' halt, but the rooms are unexpectedly attractive with African touches, 24-hr reception, secure parking.

Camping

E **Acacia Park**, T067-302121, large campsite to the east of town, which is cheap and central but ugly, and potentially unsafe (crime). However, new management has fenced it properly, there are guards at night, and it is doing its best to add attractive touches; each site has electricity and light, communal ablutions and there is a laundry.

Around Otjiwarongo *p129*

Guest farms

AL **Kambaku Safari Lodge**, 60 km north of Otjiwarongo off the B1 towards Otavi, T067-306292, www.kambaku.com. Situated on the 7600-ha Okariuputa Game Farm. 10 nicely decorated en suite rooms in a lovely thatched structure surrounded by an immaculate lawn, swimming pool, full-board rates, dinner and sundowners are taken on the veranda. Activities include game drives, and there are a number of well-schooled horses on the game farm and it can organize multi-day rides.

AL **Okonjima**, 48 km south of Otjiwarongo on the B1, 24 km along private road, well sign-posted, T067-304566, www.okonjima.com. The Main Camp has 10 luxurious en suite rooms and 3 en suite twin tents, with ornate and tasteful locally crafted furniture and decoration. The separate Bush Camp, 3 km from Main Camp, has 8 large, luxury, thatched rondavels where the beds look straight through the open walls on to the bush, with similarly lavish facilities. There are individual bird baths that attract small animals and a *lapa* made from camelthorn trees. Gourmet food, indoor and outdoor dining areas and bar, lounge and library, swimming pool, game drives, birdwatching, hiking trails, animal and vulture feeding, all-inclusive. Check-in time is

For an explanation of the sleeping and eating price codes used in this guide, see inside the front cover. Other relevant information is found in Essentials, see pages 43-51.

1200, activities begin at 1500, and again the following morning after breakfast. You really need at least 2 nights here to appreciate all it has on offer. An excellent, informative experience for a worthwhile cause and the best place in Namibia to get close to cheetah and leopard, the highlight of many visitors' time and a very special place. It has won several awards including Namibia's Leading Safari by the World Travel Awards in 2004. Note that children under 12 are not permitted. Highly recommended.

A-AL **Oase Guest and Cattle Ranch**, 46 km from the B1 on the D2804, T067-309010, oase@natron.net. A regular HAN award winner, 5 en suite doubles around a colourful garden courtyard with swimming pool. Friendly hosts, a good place to unwind for a couple of days in comfortable surroundings with excellent farm food, but somewhat overpriced and there's little to do beyond informative farm drives.

A **Frans Indongo Lodge**, 43 km on the B1 towards Otavi, T067-687012, www.indongolodge.com. 12 very comfortable modern rooms in either the main house or chalets with TV and a/c, coffee-making facilities and minibar, some with wheelchair access, swimming pool, lovely central *lapa* area under thatch with pretty gardens, all meals available and guests can go for walks in the area which is home to a number of antelope.

B **Otjibamba Lodge**, 3 km south of town on the B1, T067-303133, www.otjibamba.com. 20 large en suite doubles in chalets with TV, a/c, telephone and veranda, swimming pool, the main building houses a lounge, restaurant and bar popular with locals. A gentle introduction to the 'wild', with maps and flora/fauna identification charts available for self-guided walks (up to 3 hrs) through the 220-ha fenced game park, with numerous antelope and abundant bird life. Swiss owner; clean, welcoming and good value, if a little square and lacking in African feel.

Camping

E **Hohenfels**, off the B1, 28 km south of Otjiwarongo), take the D2476 (towards Waterberg) 5 km, then follow sign down farm track for 3 km, T067-304885, T081-2503252 (mob). Individual grassed sites with tables, seating and fabulous views from the hillside, *braai* pits and lights, swimming pool, bar and dining area in a converted stable for eating meals and communing with fellow campers. Well located for Waterberg, with better facilities and greater intimacy than camping in the park. Recommended.

Waterberg Plateau Park

p125, maps p125 and p126

Overnight guests with reservations may enter the park up until 2100, though day visitors must leave by 1800.

A-B **Bernabé de la Bat Rest Camp**, reservations through **Namibia Wildlife Resorts**, Windhoek, T061-2857200, www.nwr.com.na. 5-bed luxury bungalows with DSTV, 5-bed standard bungalows , 3-bed bungalows and 2-bed standard room. Fairly densely packed alongside each other but clean and recently refurbished (an improvement on the standard national park 'barracks') with hot showers and a/c; all fully equipped aside from crockery and cutlery. The resort has a shop, restaurant, kiosk, petrol station and swimming pool, and game drives can be organized. **Caravan and campsites** (D) with ablution blocks, cooking rings and *braai* pits.

Guest farms

AL **Waterberg Wilderness Lodge**, well signposted 8 km past the entrance to the Waterberg Plateau Park on the D2512, T067-687018, www.natron.net/wpl. 6 large en suite doubles and a family unit, very stylish minimalist decor, set beside a small river at the foot of the plateau within the Waterberg Conservancy, with good shade and peaceful ambience. It has some short guided walks and drives (although not on the plateau, as these are currently only available through the national park). Swimming pool, rates are full board, breakfast and lunch are buffet style, afternoon tea, and at dinner everyone eats together with the hosts Joachim and Caroline Rust. Certainly the greatest luxury in the area, but steeply priced.

Outjo and around *p129, map p130*

A **Namatubis Guest farm**, 16 km north of town on the road to Etosha, T067-313061, namatubi@iway.na. 23 large but dull rooms, many with fridge, table and kettle, swimming pool in lovely garden that attracts a lot of birds, excellent and plentiful home-cooked food, rates are dinner B&B, a restful overnight spot, but with little charm.

B Etosha Garten, Krupp St, T067-313130, www.etosha-garten-hotel.com. 20 spacious and colourful en suite rooms, most set around the tranquil and shady garden with well-established jacaranda trees. A HAN award winner, the restaurant is excellent, for all meals, one of the best rural menus in the country, bar, swimming pool, it can advise on (indeed organize) excursions to Damaraland and Etosha and is a good base to explore from, returning to a grand evening feast. Recommended.

B Ombinda Country Lodge, signposted 1 km south of Outjo on the C38, T067-313181, ombinda@namibnet.com. 15 en suite chalets, most thatched with reed walls, electric lighting and colourful fabrics, some have bathrooms partially open to the sky, tasty à la carte menu served in a large thatched *lapa* by the swimming pool, 2 tennis courts and a 9-hole golf course (rackets and clubs can be hired). Basic **campsite** (**E**) at US$7 per person.

B-C Buschfeld Park, 2 km from town on the C38, T067-313665, www.gateway-africa.com/buschfeld. Affordable rest camp, with 6 bungalows with veranda and *braai*, and nice views over the Outjo Valley. Restaurant offers generous breakfasts and farm-style dinners, or you can self cater. Facilities include a swimming pool and a small waterhole; walking trails and horse riding are on offer.

Also **Bambatsi Holiday Ranch** and **Vingerklip Lodge**, see page 189 for details, or the lodges on or around the C38 between Outjo and Etosha.

Eating

Otjiwarongo *p122, map p123*

The hotels in town all have very good restaurants and if you are staying overnight this is where you are likely to eat as they are the only places open in the evening.

If you are self-catering the town has 2 major supermarkets that also sell ice and firewood. The main shopping centre is situated at the eastern end of St George's St which has a large branch of **Shoprite**, and **Pick and Pay** is in the centre of town on Hage Geingob St.

Eden Gardens. Small roadside nursery between the **Caltex** and **Shell** petrol stations on the main road, with a tea room serving light refreshments and a kids' playground, open during the day.

Kameldorn Garten, opposite the BP petrol station is a pleasant café/bistro, with tables outside under shade, basic breakfasts and light meals though limited choice, coffee and cold drinks, Mon-Fri 0730-1800, Sat 0730-1300.

Outjo *p129, map p130*

The town is well served with small grocery stores and butchers, and is the last place to stock up (although you should really have done so in Otjiwaronga as there is a better choice of larger supermarkets) before the wilds (and inflated prices) of Damaraland or Etosha.

Etosha Garten Krupp St, see Sleeping, above. For excellent 'continental' cuisine (with local touches). The best restaurant in town, run by an Austrian couple. Serves game specialities, seafood, home-baked bread and cakes, worth stopping here even if it's just for afternoon tea.

Outjo Bäckerei, Hage Geingob Av, great for breakfasts and light lunches, cake and coffee, takeaway German pastries and pies, and doubles as the internet café.

Transport

Otjiwarongo *p122, map p123*

It is 249 km to Windhoek; 190 km Okaukuejo (Etosha); 375 km to Swakopmund.

Road For Intercape coaches to **Windhoek** via **Okahandja** and north to **Katima Mulilo**, see timetable on page 70. Buses stop at the BP petrol station. It is also well served by **shared taxis** on the **Windhoek-Oshakati** route, though there is a limited service towards Outjo.

Rail For trains to **Windhoek**, **Tsumeb**, **Swakopmund** and **Walvis Bay**, see timetable on page 68.

Outjo *p129, map p130*
It is 318 km from Windhoek; 114 km to Okaukuejo (Etosha NP); 145 km to Kamanjab; 133 km to Khorixas; 73 km to Otjiwarongo; 688 km to Ruacana.

Road There are several very different routes from Outjo; whichever you choose make sure you have refuelled and have plenty of water, all the routes lead into remote regions, where there is minimal traffic and supplies in small village centres cannot be relied upon. Take the C40 for **Kamanjab**, the C35 then continues north into the **Kaokoland**, **Opuwo** and **Ruacana**.
To complete a circuit follow the C46 from Ruacana to **Ondangwa** where you rejoin the B1 which leads back to **Tsumeb** and **Otavi**. Due east from Outjo, the C39 takes you into the heart of **Damaraland**, to **Khorixas** and the tourist sights around the **Brandberg**. Follow the C38 north for **Etosha National Park**, this is the main route into the park; after 96 km the road reaches Andersson Gate, from here it is a further 18 km to Okaukuejo, the main rest camp.

Rail Outjo is at the end of a disused branch line. The Windhoek-Tsumeb train stops at **Otjiwarongo**, from where passengers for Outjo have to travel by road. There are relatively frequent **shared taxis** available for the connection, but no regular bus service.

Directory

Otjiwarongo *p122, map p123*
Banks Bank Windhoek, Hage Geingob St. First National, St George's St. Standard Bank, Hage Geingob St. All have ATMs and change money. There is an FNB ATM in the Shell station on Hage Geingob St (south). **Internet** Communication Centre, opposite Spar, T067-303852, which also does mobile phone repairs, and at the Internet Café on the corner opposite the Pension Bahnhof. Both open shop hours only. **Medical services** The State Hospital, T067-300900, Hospital St, on the eastern outskirts of the town. Medi Clinic Otjiwarongo Private Hospital, T067-303734/5, Son St, is a costlier option. **Police** St George's St, T067-302081, emergencies T10111. **Post office** Van Riebeeck St, Mon-Fri 0800-1630, Sat 0800-1130.

Outjo *p129, map p130*
Banks All 3, and all except First National with ATM. **Internet** Internet café at the Outjo Backerei, Hage Geingob Av, with 2 computers, US$2 per ½ hr. Worth emailing home from here, if only for an excuse to tuck into the pastries; there is no public internet access north or west of Outjo.

Etosha National Park

Phone code: 067. Colour map 1, A4.

Etosha is one of Africa's great national parks; the game viewing here is on a par with Kruger, Hwange, the Masai Mara and Serengeti. Some 114 mammal species, 110 reptile species and more than 340 different bird species have been identified, and three well-appointed rest camps cater for the hundreds of daily visitors. Each rest camp has a floodlit watering hole, which offers overnight visitors the chance to see good numbers of game in an unusual environment. A large proportion of the park is either closed to the public or inaccessible by road, which has enabled conservationists to carry out important studies of wildlife.

The central feature of the park is the Etosha Pan, a huge depression which in years of exceptional rainfall becomes a lake again, although even then the majority of the water sits only a few centimetres deep. There are no roads across the pan, but along the southern fringe a network of gravel roads offers some exceptional views of this natural feature which can be seen clearly from space. A visit to Etosha is rightly one of the highlights of any visit to Namibia. For Sleeping, Eating and other listings, see pages 139-142.

Ins and outs

Getting there There are two entrances open to the public, **Andersson Gate** to the north of Outjo, and **Von Lindequist Gate** at the eastern end of the park. All other gates are currently closed to the public. The shortest route from Windhoek, 447 km, is to follow the B1 north as far as Otjiwarongo; from here, take the C38 for Outjo and continue north to Andersson Gate. For visitors approaching from the Caprivi, follow the B8 south as far as Grootfontein; from here take the C42 to Tsumeb where the road joins the B1, follow the signs for Etosha, Ondangwa and Oshakati. The turn-off for the Von Lindequist Gate and **Mokuti Lodge** is clearly signposted 74 km from Tsumeb. Namutoni camp is just inside the park.

Each of the three camps within the park (Okaukuejo, Halali and Namutoni) have their own **airstrips** which are used by tour operators and charter companies. Most of the smarter lodges on the edge of the park can arrange **fly-in safaris**.

While most people travel in their own **vehicle**, either self-drive or as part of a tour, it is possible to take the luxury **train** service from Windhoek to the outskirts of the park, and enter for day visits. The **Northern Desert Express** started running in 2001 and there are several departures throughout the year. It leaves Windhoek in the morning, with a long afternoon stop (and wine-tasting tour) at Omaruru, and continues overnight before arrival in Tsumeb. Transfer by bus to Namutoni, afternoon game drives, overnight at Namutoni, morning game drive, lunch and back to Tsumeb to catch the train back to Windhoek. Price from US$400 per person, sharing, for the round trip, depending on season. **Reservations** ⓘ *T061-2982600 (Windhoek), www.desertexpress.com.na, Windhoek station, Bahnhof St, Mon-Fri 0800-1700.*

Best time to visit The park is open year round, but there are three distinct seasons which affect the game-viewing experience. Many regard the best time to visit the park as the cooler, drier winter months, August and September, as shortage of natural

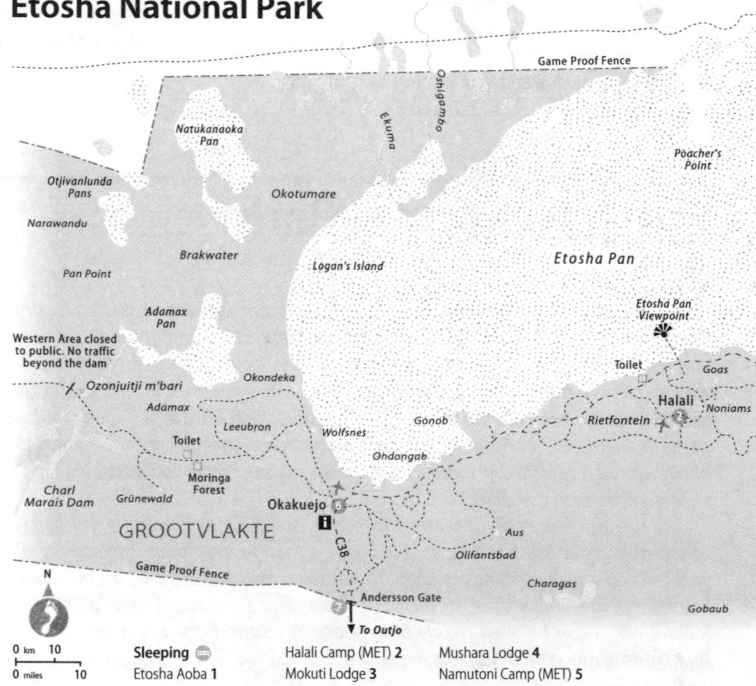

“” You can expect to see large herds of blue wildebeest, gemsbok, Burchell's zebra, springbok and elephant...

pools elsewhere in the park draws animals to the artificial water points, many of which are visible from the rest camps or reachable by car. The other popular time of year for visitors is during December and January (when it is very hot); this is more to do with local school holidays than any particular condition within the park. It may be difficult to book accommodation during the most popular periods, especially at weekends, and during school holidays bookings are limited to three nights per rest camp. If visiting from overseas, consider booking your accommodation prior to your arrival in Namibia (see page 46 for details). For **bird enthusiasts** the best time to visit the park is during and after the rains, November to April.

Background

The name Etosha is usually translated as 'Great White Place' or 'Place of Emptiness'.

The central feature of Etosha is the large pan which covers 23% of the park and is 130 km long and 72 km wide; a fantastic and most unusual natural feature. The first Europeans to see the pan and write about it were Charles Andersson of Sweden and Francis Galton from Britain, who came here in 1851 en route to Owamboland. Having been told it was a large lake, they were very disappointed to find it was bone dry.

There is a San legend which tells of a group who strayed into Heiqum lands only to be surrounded by brutal hunters who killed all the men and children. One of the young women rested under a tree with her dead child in her arms; she wept so much that her tears formed a giant lake. After the sun had dried her tears the ground was left covered in salt – and so the Etosha Pan was formed. The pan is indeed very alkaline, sediment samples have a pH higher than 10, with a sodium content of more than 3%. This attracts the local wildlife, which requires salt in its diet. The first European interference in the region came in the 1890s when the German administration was faced with the rinderpest outbreak. To try and control the spread, a livestock-free buffer zone was established along the southern margins of the pan. In order to enforce the restrictions on the movement of cattle, two small military units were posted in tiny forts at Namutoni and Okaukuejo. The park was created in 1907 by Governor Friedrich von Lindequist. Since its proclamation, the boundaries have been significantly changed on a number of occasions but the park has covered today's area of 22,912 sq km since 1970. The German forts at Okaukuejo and Namutoni were converted into police posts to help

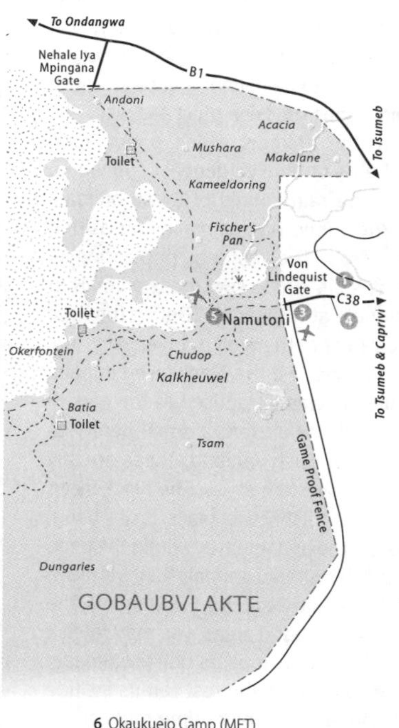

6 Okaukuejo Camp (MET)
7 Ongava Lodge

establish control over the Owambo kingdoms to the north. The fort at Namutoni was made famous after it was attacked on 28 January 1904 by several hundred Ndonga warriors serving King Nehale, and was burnt to the ground. The present building at Namutoni dates from 1906 when a new and larger fort was completed. The last troops stationed here surrendered to the South African forces under the command of General Coen Britz on 6 July 1915. In 1957 the fort was restored as a tourist camp.

Visiting Etosha National Park

ⓘ *Entry for adults is US$13 per day; children under 16 free; US$1.50 per car.*
Gates are open from sunrise to sunset; visitors staying in the park must reach their respective camp before sunset and day visitors must leave by one of the exit gates by sunset. Do not stay out in the park after sunset, you may find yourself in serious trouble if you fail to time your return to the camp by sunset. In the event of a breakdown or a puncture do not leave your car, you may be attacked; stay in the vehicle until help arrives. The distance between **Halali** in the middle of the park to both Namutoni and Okaukuejo is 70 km. The speed limit throughout the park is 60 kph, but you will probably driving an average of 20-30 kph with plenty of stops to watch the game. The roads are gravel but in very good condition and perfectly negotiable in a normal car. It is prohibited to get out of your car except at the toilet stops. An ideal recommended itinerary would be to spend one night in each camp entering the park at either **Okaukuejo** or **Namutoni**, and exiting the park at the opposite end to which you first entered. This way you will not only see all the camps, but you will avoid doubling back on your route too much. Alternatively, in peak season, you might enjoy exploring the routes to the west of the pan, where there are a number of man-made water points and, usually, fewer tourists.

There are countless drives and waterholes that you can visit for game-viewing purposes, they all have their different merits, but it is impossible to recommend any one point ahead of another. The wardens are the best source of advice as to where game is congregating and where the cats and large mammals have been spotted each day. Also at each camp reception is a game-viewing book where visitors write up the location of the most recent sightings. As a tip, remember it always pays to be patient – once you have found a waterhole that appeals to you just turn the engine off, keep quiet and wait.

The most commonly occurring species are the animals which prefer open savannah country. You can expect to see large herds of blue wildebeest, gemsbok, Burchell's zebra, springbok and elephant. After the rains many of these animals migrate to pastures which are in areas closed to the public. A good reason for visiting Etosha is to see the endangered black rhinoceros. The resident population is reckoned to be one of the largest in Africa. While it is difficult to spot these animals in thick bush, they frequently visit the floodlit waterhole at Okaukuejo. During the heat of the day they tend to lie up and you are unlikely to spot them on a drive.

The park is home to three uncommon antelope species: the black-faced impala, Damara dik-dik and roan antelope. The roan antelope was introduced to the park in 1970. In one of the earliest cases of moving animals by aircraft, a small herd was transported by Hercules from Khaudum Game Park in Bushmanland. These are shy animals and tend to be only seen in the inaccessible western areas. The black-faced impala is easily recognized as an impala but with a distinctive black facial band. Originally from Kaokoland, a large herd was translocated and released within the park. The largest groups used to occur near Namutoni, but like all wild animals they will move to the water and pasture. The Damara dik-dik is the smallest antelope in Namibia, the adult only weighs 5 kg. They are shy animals favouring wooded areas; you may catch a glimpse of family groups, but such a small animal often disappears quickly. Smaller animals that are often spotted at night within the confines of the rest camps include jackal and banded mongoose who slip through the fence on night time raids of the rubbish bins, and at Halali honey badgers are often seen within the camp.

Sleeping

Rest camps There are 3 rest camps in the park, each managed by Namibia Wildlife Resorts. The central booking office is on Independence Av near the clock tower in Windhoek. Open for information: Mon-Fri 0800-1700; for reservations: Mon-Fri 0800-1500; T061-236975/8, pro@nwr.com.na. In Cape Town, the NWR office is Ground Floor, Pinnacle Building, (beneath the Tourist Office), Burg St, Cape Town, T+27 (0)21-4223761, ct.bookings@nwr.com.na. Alternatively you can book online at www.nwr.com.na.

The park headquarters is at **Okaukuejo**; the other 2 camps are **Halali** and **Namutoni**. The facilities at each rest camp are similar: there is a parks office which you will have to visit first to find which accommodation unit you have been allocated, a shop which sells a few craft items and food and drink for campers, a restaurant which serves 3 meals per day (and kiosk serving drinks and snacks open when the restaurant is shut), a bar, a filling station (you can cover a surprising distance while game viewing), a swimming pool and a post box (Okaukuejo has a proper post office, Mon-Fri 0830-1300, 1400-1630). The shops are open Mon-Sat 0730-0900, 1100-1400 and 1730-1930; Sun 0800-0900, 1200-1400 and 1800-1900. Restaurant meal times: **breakfast** 0700-0830, US$8; **lunch** 1200-1330, US$10; **dinner** 1800-2030, US$14. During peak season the restaurants can get crowded in the evening; you may have to wait until after the initial rush before you can get a table.

All accommodation must be vacated by 1000, rooms can be occupied from 1200. During local school holidays visits to Etosha are limited to a maximum of 3 nights per camp.

Although you are encouraged to book accommodation in advance, it is possible to obtain a bungalow on the day if there is space. Check at the office at Namutoni or Okaukuejo for availability, either of these offices can advise you of the situation in all 3 camps. Also, if you want to change pre-booked accommodation from 1 camp to another, the office can help with this too. If **camping**, be aware that even in peak season, they rarely turn away last-minute campers, and there seems to be little control over what constitutes 'full'. While there can be frustratingly long queues at the ablutions, and you may find yourself sharing cooking facilities with your neighbours, a full camp has its own distinctive, excited atmosphere, which all adds to the fun.

All bungalows are en suite with towels and bedding, some have hotplates but not all have crockery and cutlery.

Booking All accommodation must be paid for in advance, credit cards are accepted. Bookings by telephone will be accepted 11 months in advance. Written bookings can be made up to 18 months in advance, and will be processed 12 months in advance. All applications should include details of accommodation required (see below for details), date of arrival and departure (give alternative dates for popular periods, see above), number of adults and children (with age), 1 passport number and full home address with contact telephone numbers. While the process is clearly designed for local residents there is no reason why one should not apply from abroad several months prior to your arrival in Namibia.

Okaukuejo *p138, map p136*
18 km from Andersson Gate, 70 km to Halali, 140 km to Namutoni, T067-229800.

This is the largest of the 3 camps and serves as the administrative hub and houses the **Etosha Ecological Institute** from where conservation management is conducted. The central feature of the camp is a circular limestone water tower close to the administration block. A few minutes at the top is well worthwhile, both for the views of the plains and Etosha Pan in the distance, and to help orientate yourself within the camp. In addition to luxury bungalows and simple rooms, there is a camping and caravan site with (barely sufficient) communal facilities. There are 2 swimming pools next to the restaurant (with little shade). The attractive thatched bar is open 1830-2130.

For an explanation of the sleeping and eating price codes used in this guide, see inside the front cover. Other relevant information is found in Essentials, see pages 43-51.

The restaurant is sensibly priced with a choice of dishes for each meal. The whole complex was rebuilt after a fire in 1997. Unfortunately the service, while polite, can be slow and disorganized. Away from the offices and shops is a floodlit waterhole which can get quite busy but is always rewarding for game viewing. Bench seats are arranged behind a protective wall and there is a thatched miniature grandstand. Please refrain from talking loudly when in the vicinity of the waterhole, it is very easy to startle a shy animal, especially at night, and you will not make yourself popular with other guests. There is a good chance of seeing black rhino and elephant with young at this waterhole and the 3 big cats also often drink here.

National parks accommodation

AL- C Staying in the park is less comfortable than in some of the nearby lodges, but you'll have the chance to visit the waterhole after sunset, as well as enjoy being surrounded by the full, rumbling and shrieking African night-time chorus. Adjacent to the waterhole (with thatched roof) are bungalows 3, 5, 7, 11, 13, 18, 19 and 20. Although they tend to offer less privacy, as the rest of the camp arrives at dawn and dusk, you may be rewarded with your own private views in the middle of the night. All rooms and bungalows have en suite bathroom, fridge, kettle, bedding and towels. **Luxury suite** (AL), 4 beds, 2 rooms, a/c, stove, DSTV, cutlery and crockery provided. **Luxury bungalow** (B), 2 rooms, 4 beds, a/c, hotplate, cutlery and crockery provided. **Bungalow** (B), 2 rooms, 4 beds, a/c, as for the luxury version but less spacious though cheaper. **Bungalow** (C), 1 room with 3 beds, a/c, hotplate. **Bungalow** (C), 1 room with 2 beds, a/c, hotplate, the cheapest option for bungalows. **Standard room** (C), 1 room with 2 beds, no hotplate. **Campsite** (C), dusty but shaded, electricity available, pricey at US$37 per site per day for up to 8 people (it is reasonable for groups but not for a couple). Communal facilities are good with clean, hot showers and baths and camp kitchens with hotplates and sinks for washing up but they can develop queues in busy periods, take your chance for a shower when you can; popular with overland trucks. **Day visitors** can hire out picnic sites for US$12, although it is on your conscience to pay as no one checks; day visitors have use of all facilities, including communal kitchens and ablution blocks.

Private lodges and camps

On and around the C38 between Outjo and Andersson Gate are a number of lodges catering for visitors looking for more comfort and attention than you will find within the park. **L Eagle Tented Lodge and Spa**, from Etosha's Andersson Gate, drive south 44 km to the turning to the right along the D2695, then 27 km to the turning to the lodge which is 4 km from the road, T067-697047, member of **Leading Lodges of Africa**, www.leadinglodges.com. Located on the 21,000-ha **Epacha Private Game Reserve**, very close to Epacha below, animals on the reserve include 21 species of antelope including the rare sable and black rhino. Luxury lodge built of natural rock and thatched roofs, 8 spacious canvas en suite tents with balcony and splash pool. There are 2 restaurants, main bar and pool bar, swimming pool and fully equipped spa offering mud baths, aromatherapy, manicures, yoga and all sorts of other treats, activities on offer include game drives in the region as well as into Etosha, quad-biking and horse riding. **L Epacha Game Lodge and Spa**, also a member of **Leading Lodges of Africa**, reservations and directions as above or visit www.epacha.com. Located on the 21,000-ha **Epacha Private Game Reserve**. New luxury lodge with 18 wonderful thatched chalets decorated with specially commissioned antique Victorian furniture, very stylish, each with spacious en suite bathroom, outside shower, private balcony, tea and coffee makers and a/c, the Presidential Suite has 5 en suite bedrooms. The communal areas feature comfortable lounges overlooking waterholes, cigar lounge, library, billiards room, swimming pool and pool bar, the spa has a jacuzzi, steam room, sauna and splash pool and there are all sorts of pampering treatments on offer. Activities include day and night game drives, bush walks, horse riding, clay pigeon shooting, and wine tasting in the extensive cellar. Both this and the **Eagle Tented Lodge and Spa** are recommended for the top end of the market. **L Ongava Lodge**, entrance by Andersson Gate, then 9 km to the lodge, 18 km to the tented camp, reservations **Wilderness Safaris**, Windhoek, T061-274500, www.wilderness-safaris.com. 12 beautifully crafted, en suite, thatched doubles, furnished to an exceptionally high standard, with views from the swimming pool that are hard to tear yourself away from, excellent food; part of the highly regarded **Wilderness Safaris** operation, and usually fully booked. If you prefer to be closer to nature, there is a separate canvas/thatch tented camp with 8 luxury tents known as **Ongava Tented Camp**, and another even more exclusive camp with only 3 tents each with private plunge pool and outdoor shower called **Little Ongava**. All camps offer morning excursions into Etosha, brunch, siesta, afternoon tea and drive within the reserve (30,000 ha, bordering Etosha) sealed with a sumptuous evening meal. They offer day and night guided walks (and rhino tracking), which can be a pleasure after being confined to your vehicle within the national park. Recommended.

AL Naua Naua Game Lodge, 26 km south of Andersson Gate, then a further 15 stony km off the C3, T067-687100, www.nauanaua.com. A beautiful camp with 13 very spacious, en suite, thatched rooms. Small swimming pool with lovely views over the plains, cosy restaurant and bar in large central building, cheetah-feeding and walking trails, game and sundowner drives, airstrip with air safaris available in vintage plane. Great care and attention to detail in the building of this lodge, and limited numbers, means an intimate and close-to-nature experience. If **Ongava** is full, this is your best bet.

A Etosha Gateway Lodge, 26 km south of Andersson Gate then signposted off the C38, T/F067-333440, www.hinter.com.na. 16 large en suite rooms (most can fit 4 people) with own seating area outside, some self- catering, restaurant, swimming pool, new terrace for sundowners. Good value alternative to the accommodation in Etosha, game drives into the park available if you don't have your own vehicle. **Campsite** (C) with good facilities. This has recently been taken over and refurbished to a very good standard.

B Etosha Safari Camp, 10 km from the Andersson Gate on the C38. Reservations, Windhoek, T061-245847, www.etosha-safari.com. 22 en suite safari bungalows perched on a small hill, restaurant and bar serving buffet meals and South African wines, swimming pool, internet café, short walks in the region. **Camping** (D) is also available or you can hire 2-bed igloo tents which, at US$10 per person, are good value if you don't have your own tent.

Halali *p138, map p136*

More or less midway, 75 km, between the other 2 camps, T067-229400.

This was the third camp to be opened in the park. While it is less developed and visually less attractive than the other 2, it has an excellent restaurant and a refreshingly large (20 m) swimming pool. The floodlit waterhole is beautifully located (although not regularly frequented by game) at the base of a *koppie*. There are walks all around the camp, including up and over the small *koppie*; make sure you are quiet as you approach. One of the advantages of staying at this camp is that you are in the centre of the park, thus there are more waterholes within a short driving distance. It is also less popular with overland trucks and the campsite is quieter.

National parks accommodation

A-B All rooms and bungalows have en suite bathroom, kettle, bedding and towels. Some of the accommodation blocks are a bit close together, so when the camp is full you have limited privacy; at the back of each bungalow is a *braai* area. **Luxury suite** (A), 2 rooms, 4 beds, a/c, stove, microwave, fridge, cutlery, crockery and DSTV. **Luxury bungalow** (B), 2 rooms, 4 beds, a/c, hotplate, fridge, cutlery and crockery. **Economy bungalow** (B), a/c, hotplate. **Standard room** (B), Single room with 2 beds, a/c, stove, fridge. **Campsite** (C), dusty but fairly well shaded, clean communal facilities with plenty of hot water, electricity; pricey at US$37 per site but accommodates up to 8 people; day visitors can hire out picnic sites for US$12, although it is on your conscience to pay as no one checks, visitors have use of the communal kitchens and ablution blocks. Recommended restaurant, shop selling basic provisions, bar open 1800-2130.

Namutoni *p138, map p136*

Some 140 km from Okaukuejo, T067-229300. Allow at least 3 hrs to drive between the 2 camps, you are always likely to stop for something, even if it is to allow an elephant to cross the road. For many visitors, this is their favourite camp, with its striking, whitewashed, converted fort, palm-fringed swimming area and picturesque, thatched game-viewing point. However, during the day there are frequently large tour groups stopping for lunch and a look at the museum in the fort. There is a floodlit waterhole surrounded by tall grasses and reeds. The camp was last refurbished in 1995, prior to hosting part of the Miss Universe contest.

As a reminder of its military past, a bugle accompanies the hoisting of the Namibian flag on top of the fort each day at sunrise and sunset.

Tourist office and petrol station are open sunrise to sunset, shop 0700-1830, kiosk 0830-1200 and 1330-1800, bar 1400-2130. It is pretty strict about closing time in the bar to keep the noise impact down.

National parks accommodation

A-C All rooms and bungalows have en suite bathroom, fridge, kettle, bedding and towels, and either a/c or ceiling fans. **Luxury suite** (**A**), in the historic fort, 2 good-sized rooms, 4 beds, a fully equipped kitchen (with stove, cutlery and crockery) and a private bathroom. Unfortunately, it is located by the museum, so you will have to endure a steady flow of visitors peering in. **Luxury flats** (**B**), 2 rooms, 4 beds, stove. **Standard chalets** (**B**), 2 rooms, 4 beds, stove. **Standard room** (**B**), single room with 2 beds. **Economy room**(**C**), single room with 2 beds, some have shared bathroom. **Campsite** (**C**), a greener site than at the other 2 camps but with less shade, electricity available; pricey at US$38 per site for up to 8 people; communal kitchen and excellent ablution blocks, can get crowded, popular with overland trucks.

Outside the park *map p136*

Many of the visitors to Etosha who enter via Andersson Gate leave via the Von Lindequist Gate in the east of the park. From here it is 35 km to the main Tsumeb-Ondangwa road, the B1, and there are a few luxury lodges in the region.

Private lodges and camps

AL Etosha Aoba Lodge, turn off 10 km from Von Lindequist Gate, then 10 winding km further to lodge, T067-229106, www.etosha-aoba-lodge.com. 10 small, thatched en suite bungalows with veranda, a much more 'natural' feel than most upmarket lodges, comfortable, without being pristine, hidden among indigenous *tamboti* trees. Small swimming pool, large thatched bar/restaurant area and pleasant sundowner drives to nearby Fisher Pan. Rates are B&B; dinner is an additional US$23.

AL Mushara Lodge, 1 km from the main road then 7 km to Von Lindequist Gate, T067-229106, www.mushara-lodge.com. 10 doubles, 1 family room and 2 singles in pristine, thatched en suite bungalows with a/c, fridge/minibar, telephone and mosquito net. Highly rated restaurant, bar with comprehensive wine list, decent-sized swimming pool, guided game drives, walks around the property, airstrip. Unusually for this area, the lodge is privately owned by a young and energetic German couple, it is immaculately tended, with not a blade of grass out of place, and yet still intimate, your best bet east of the park.

AL-A Mokuti Lodge, about 2 km from the main road just outside Von Lindequist Gate, T067-229084, www.namibsunhotels.com.na. This is an enormous and impressive set-up, the main complex is in a huge, thatched barn, beautifully rebuilt after a fire in 1997. 106 en suite, a/c, thatched rooms of varying size, set in a small woodland area with neat gardens; restaurant has a very good reputation, bar, pool bar, 2 swimming pools, playground, 2 tennis courts, small museum about the 1997 fire, large curio shop, game drives in open-sided overland trucks and walks on the property available. An impressive place, it loses out to other establishments because of its size, but if you like to be anonymous in large, impersonal establishments, this could be for you.

C Sachsenheim Guest Farm, B1, 3 km north of the C38 for Etosha, 30 km from Von Lindequist Gate, T067-230011, sachse@iway.na. 11 simple doubles with fan, shaded gardens, swimming pool, dining area, rates include breakfast, dinner on request, small waterhole with hide, there are a number of antelope, warthog and zebra on the farm as well as the farm cows. **Camping** (**E**) for cars and overland trucks. This is the closest campsite outside the east end of the park. A hunting farm, not recommended in mid-summer, otherwise it's a pleasant spot.

Eating

See Sleeping, above.

Directory

See Sleeping, above. **Medical services** International SOS, see under Grootfontein, page 153.

The Triangle

When you look at a map of northern Namibia, the roads which link the towns of Otavi, Tsumeb and Grootfontein quite clearly form a triangle. They are part of a prosperous region which produces a significant proportion of the country's maize crop and is also an important mining centre. Because of their proximity to Etosha and the Waterberg Plateau, and being en route to and from the Caprivi, a significant number of visitors pass through these small, simple towns. The museum in Tsumeb and the Hoba Meteorite are worth a detour, and there are some beautifully located guest farms to accommodate you. This is the last outpost of German colonial influence – north of here the countryside and the atmosphere is totally different to that in the centre and the south of the country. All three towns are suitable (although Otavi only barely) for stocking up with supplies and cash, but none merit a stopover of any length.

» *For Sleeping, Eating and other listings, see pages 150-153.*

Road to the Triangle

The B1 goes through Otavi and Tsumeb and then heads northwest to Ondangwa and Oshakati. If you choose to travel north you will experience a Namibia that is totally different from the rest of the country, the most noticeable fact being the people: over 50% of the country's population live in this area. This region used to be known as Owamboland, but it has now been divided up into four new regions (see page 209 for details of the Far North). From Tsumeb the road takes you past Otjikoto and Guinas Lakes, which are found in the bush close to the main road. After 73 km there is a left turning, C38, to Etosha National Park (Von Lindequist Gate). An alternative, more scenic route to Etosha (and taking a similar time), is to head northwest on the D3028 for 44 km, turn left at the D3025, and rejoin the D3028 before meeting the tar road close to Namutoni. The road passes quite close to the southeast border of the park offering an appetizer of game viewing before you enter the park proper. From Tsumeb you are also faced with another choice. If you are heading for the Caprivi Region follow the C42 to Grootfontein (92 km) and then the B8 to Rundu. Before you reach Grootfontein there is a sign to the left for the Hoba Meteorite (see page 149). Visitors travelling from the north have another 426 km to go from Tsumeb to Windhoek on the B1 via Otjiwarongo and Okahandja.

Lake Otjikoto and Lake Guinas » *Colour map 1, B6.*

ⓘ *Lake Otjikoto is 24 km north of Tsumeb, well signposted off the B1, open daily sunrise to sunset, US$1.50, there is a carpark and kiosk selling curios and cold drinks. Lake Guinas has no facilities or entry fee.*

Lake Otjikoto is set back 100 m from the main road amongst the trees, but it is well signposted. When the sun shines the water looks very blue and clear. It is possible

The name Otjikoto is said to come from the Herero and can be loosely translated as 'the place which is too deep for cattle to drink water'. The San named it 'Gaisis' which means 'very ugly', as it was probably the only lake they had ever seen and they were afraid of its deep waters.

to climb down to the lake shore via a rock stairway; this is not encouraged and swimming is forbidden. Just before you reach the lake there is another turning on the right, the D3043.

If you follow this for 19 km and then take a turn onto the D3031 you will find yourself beside Lake Guinas. It is clearly signposted, but the site has not been developed. There is no easy access to the lake shore as the sides are precipitous. If you are able to visit Lake Guinas in May you will see it at its best, surrounded by flowering aloes on the rock faces. The rusty remains of a large steam pump lie nearby, a legacy of efforts in the 1920s to irrigate local citrus orchards.

Both the lakes lie on private farms and, as you can imagine, they are popular with scuba divers. This is a very complex form of **diving** and should not be attempted by inexperienced divers. Prior permission is required from the farmers and you need to contact the **Namibian Underwater Federation** (NUF) ⓘ *T061-238320, theo@schoemans.com.na.*

Each of the lakes was formed by the collapse of a ceiling in a huge dolomite underground cavern. They are technically known as sink holes. The caverns were formed after water leaked into the dolomite rocks, following a minor earthquake which fractured the rocks. Once in contact with the limestone, the water slowly dissolved the rock. The cross-sectional view of the lake can be described as an upside-down mushroom. A popular myth is that Lake Otjikoto is bottomless; this is not so, but the flooded cave system extends for much further than was originally believed. Lake Guinas is considerably deeper; it has been measured to over 200 m. The levels in both lakes fluctuate as water is pumped for irrigation.

Lake Otjikoto is home to an interesting range of fish, most of which are 'alien' species. A sub-species of the common tilapia was introduced to the lake in the 1930s, and the lake is home to a very unusual type of bream. The bream has a protective habit of carrying the eggs and when they are first born, the young fish, in its mouth. The dwarf bream, *Pseudocrenoolabrus philander disperses*, live in the dark depths of the lake too. Scientists have postulated that these fish moved to the depths after the shallower waters became overpopulated due to the absence of predators.

The first Europeans to come across these lakes, Francis Galton and Charles Andersson, camped beside Lake Otjikoto in May 1851. In 1915 the retreating German army took the decision to dump their weapons in Lake Otjikoto so the South Africans could not make use of them. There are mixed accounts about what was actually thrown in, but there is no doubt about the pieces which are on show in Tsumeb Museum. A large ammunition wagon is also on display in the Alte Feste Museum in Windhoek. In 1916, a team of divers under Sergeant G Crofton and J de Villiers of the Special Intelligence Unit of the Union forces was sent to try and recover some of the armaments. They managed to find a mix of small arms and ammunition, five cannons, 10 cannon chassis and three machine guns. In 1970, an ammunition wagon was found at a depth of 41 m, in surprisingly good condition. In the early 1980s, divers recovered some more pieces, including a Sandfontein cannon. All of the most recently discovered items have been carefully restored and are now on show in the Khorab room in the excellent Tsumeb Museum.

Otavi

» *pp 150-153. Phone code: 067. Colour map 1, B6.*

Otavi is the first of the three 'triangle' towns you reach when driving north from Windhoek on the B1. It is also the smallest and offers little of interest to the tourist. In the past it was an important mining centre and the scene of many feuds between the Ovambos, Hereros and Bushmen.

It was the **copper** that brought the boom period to the town. Work on a narrow-gauge railway began in November 1903 and was completed in August 1906, after being interrupted by the Herero-German war. The railway was built to carry copper ore to Swakopmund. The German colonial company which ran the mine and built the railway was the **Otavi Minen-und Eisenbahn-Gesellschaft** (OMEG); there are some excellent photographs of the railway on show in the museum in Swakopmund (see page 218). Very few mining operations continue today, and what are left are based near Tsumeb, leaving Otavi with a run-down feel. Other minerals found in the Otavi Mountains are lead, vanadium, cadmium and zinc.

The only local site of any note in Otavi is the **Khorib Memorial**, 2 km north of the town. Unlike some memorials in Namibia this one is particularly plain. There is a small stone plaque close to the railway. It was unveiled in 1920 to mark the end of German rule in South West Africa in July 1915, when local officials surrendered to the Commander of the Union Forces, General Louis Botha. The German officials were the Commander of the German forces in South West Africa, Colonel Victor Franke and the Governor of South West Africa, Dr Seitz.

Tsumeb » *pp 150-153. Phone code: 067. Colour map 1, B6.*

Tsumeb is the largest of the three triangle towns in northern Namibia and was developed as a major mining centre in about 1905. The name Tsumeb derives from the Hain/Ohmbushman word *Tsomsoub* meaning 'to dig a hole in loose ground', and the Herero word *Otjitsume* meaning 'place of frogs'. The reference to frogs derives from the green, red-brown and grey streaks of copper and lead ores found in the local rock. These are supposed to resemble frogspawn scooped out of a waterhole and sprinkled around on the surrounding rocks! The town's coat of arms acknowledges both Tsumeb's mining and frog connections by depicting a pair of frogs squatting alongside mining tools.

Thanks to the wealth generated by the mines, Tsumeb is an attractive town with some fine old colonial buildings and a palm-tree-lined central park with wide lawns. It is also the last stop before passing north of the so-called **'Red Line'**, separating the enclosed commercial cattle farms to the south from the communally owned lands to the north.

Travelling north across the Red Line one moves away from 'European' Namibia and into the heart of Owamboland, where almost half of all Namibians live.

Ins and outs

The first stop any visitor should make is at **Travel North Namibia** ⓘ *OMEG Allee, T067-220728, Mon-Fri business hours, Sat morning*, a helpful and efficient tourist office next to the backpackers of the same name; there is little you cannot organize from here, including good-value car hire deals with **Imperial** or **Europcar** to visit Etosha. It is also an agent for **Intercape Coaches** and the bus stops outside (though in the middle of the night). If the office is closed, you can drop into the backpackers at any time as it has 24-hour reception.

History

There is evidence of the smelting and mining of copper in the Tsumeb area as long ago as the Stone Age, and certainly both Damara and Owambo communities were known to be skilled smelters and workers of the metal. As the different Namibian tribes came into increased contact with each other during the second half of the 19th century, so disputes arose over the ownership of the land around Tsumeb. White traders, active in Namibia by this time, were also interested in the minerals in the area and a number succeeded in gaining land concessions around Tsumeb.

Serious European interest in the area was signalled in 1892 when the London-based **South West Africa Company** obtained a mining concession, and early the following year the geologist Matthew Rogers visited Tsumeb to carry out further investigations. In

 1900, a new company, the Otavi Minen-und Eisenbahn-Gesellschaft (OMEG), was formed in order to raise more money to develop mines in the area.

Following the construction of a road between the settlement and the mines and the sinking of two new shafts, the first nine tonnes of copper left Tsumeb for Swakopmund at the very end of 1900. Although this first copper was carried by ox-wagon, by August 1906 the narrow-gauge railway to Swakopmund had been constructed. This improved export channel proved a massive boost to the efficiency of the whole operation, and by 1908 the company was already generating significant profits.

This was to signal the start of almost a century of mining at Tsumeb, interrupted only by the two World Wars and the more recent miners' strike. Ownership of the mines passed into the hands of the **Tsumeb Corporation** (TCL) following Germany's defeat in the Second World War, and it continued to develop mining capacity. However, by 1996 the costs of deep mining were exceeding output and that, coupled with a miners' strike in 1996, forced the mines to close (see box, page 147).

Sights

Located in the old German Private School building, dating back to 1915, the **Tsumeb Museum** ⓘ *T067-220447, Mon-Fri 0900-1200, 1500-1800, Sat 1500-1200, US$0.80*, has a fine display of the town's mining history including a display of minerals. There

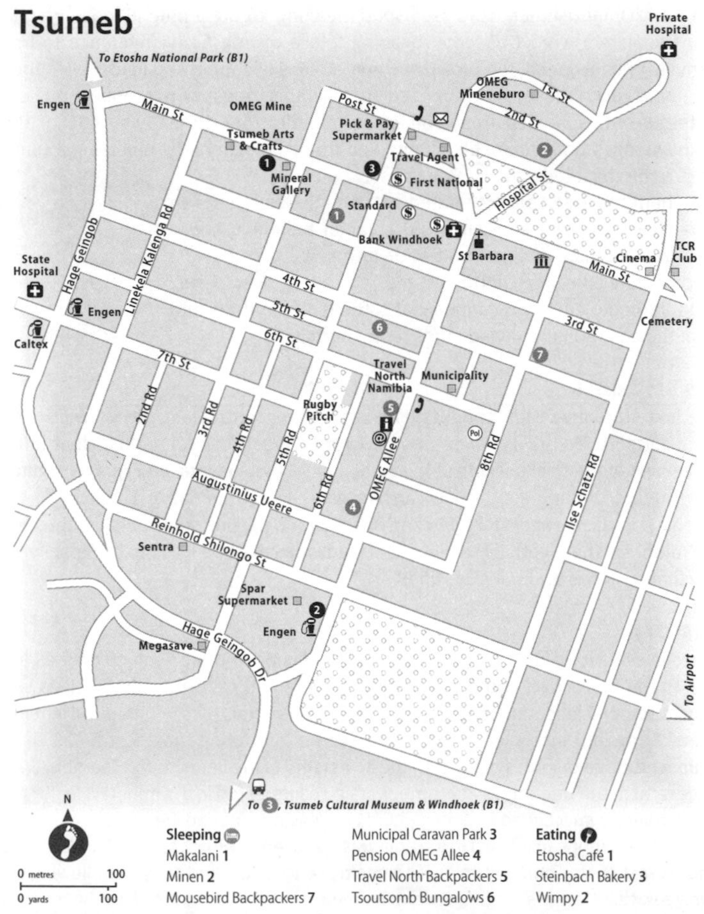

Trouble at TCL

In August 1996, miners working at three TCL-owned mines downed tools, starting Namibia's largest ever industrial dispute. The strike, which was to last for 45 days, started because of a wage dispute; however, over the course of the seven-week stoppage it became clear that the miners were fighting for much more than this: "In view of the magnitude of the dire exploitation at TCL, I do not know what the outcome of this strike will be", said Peter Nholo, Mineworkers Union Of Namibia (MUN) Secretary-General, one day before the start of the strike. "But I can assure you that when the strike ends, TCL will never be the same again", he concluded.

In effect the miners were claiming gross discrimination between white and black employees at the mines, and the payment of near slave wages to black miners. Some were taking home N$541 (US$82) a month after 30 years' service at the mine. In reply TCL claimed that with a 30-35% drop in world copper prices in Jun 1996, the company could not afford to pay its miners the 13.5% increase demanded by the MUN.

The dispute was eventually settled with the help of government mediation and a wage increase of 10.5% was agreed upon, however the MUN did have to agree to the retrenchment of some workers. On the other side, a commission of inquiry was appointed to investigate labour practices at the mines: "There are no two ways about it ... Apartheid and Broederbond TCL must be destroyed and buried 20,000,000 km down the earth so that it never rises again", vowed Labour Minister Moses Garoeb.

Overall the strike cost TCL an estimated N$70 million and the company never really recovered. Mining activities limped on into 1998 when the company announced that it could no longer sustain the losses being incurred.

As it turned out, the effects of the strike were far greater than anyone imagined. Suddenly on 16 April 1998, a provisional liquidation order was filed. For over a year there were rumours that a buyer had been found for the mine. Sadly though, the mine finally closed in April 1999 with the loss of 2000 jobs. For the Tsumeb community it was a devastating blow, one that is still felt today as the town struggles to find jobs for the ex-miners. However, since then the Khusib Springs Mine has opened between Tsumeb and Grootfontein which produces about 3000 tonnes of copper per month, and some of the miners have found gainful employment again.

are also exhibits of traditional costumes, artefacts and photographs, and a fascinating collection of German First World War weapons and ordnance retrieved from Lake Otjikoto, where they were dumped prior to the German surrender to South Africa in 1915. This is one of the best museums in the country.

Each year on the first weekend of August Tsumeb holds a German Carnival and on the last weekend of September it holds the Copper Festival with stalls selling crafts, gemstones, food and wine.

The **St Barbara Catholic Church**, on the corner of Main and Third streets, consecrated in 1914, was dedicated to the patron saint of mine workers, and for 13 years served as the town's only church. It dominates the centre of the town, and the unusual tower above the entrance is particularly eye-catching.

On First Street, the OMEG Mineneburo looks remarkably like a church; however, it was designed in 1907 by Joseph Olbrich to symbolize the wealth and power of the MEG company at the time. The building is currently used as a gymnasium. In the early 1970s it served as the local kindergarten.

The **Tsumeb Cultural Village** ⓘ *T067-220787, Mon-Fri 0800-1600, Sat 0800-1300, US$1.50*, is on the southern outskirts of town, another (in this instance, Norwegian-backed) project trying to harness tourism to benefit the local community. The aim is to have families from each of the eight Namibian tribes living here in traditional huts, wearing traditional dress, and each 'contributing' by either making crafts for sale or dancing, playing music, cooking and selling traditional food. The crafts are priced reasonably (no need to haggle); proceeds are split between the individuals and the project. It's worth stopping by if you are passing. They can also offer simple meals by arrangement, as well as providing accommodation (E), in three basic huts, for a sense of living like they do/did, with mats (or camp beds, for softies), sink and communal ablutions. Again, funds benefit the community, so do take a look. Many tour groups stop here.

Grootfontein

» *pp 150-153. Phone code: 067. Colour map 1, B6.*

Blessed in Namibian terms by a high annual rainfall (450-650 mm), the Grootfontein area supports a wide range of agriculture on its predominantly white-owned farms. Apart from the usual livestock farming of cattle, sheep and goats, the farms here produce most of Namibia's commercially grown maize, sorghum, cotton, peanuts and sunflower.

The northern market town of Grootfontein is a pleasant enough place with limestone buildings and tree-lined streets, and is particularly attractive in September and October when the purple jacaranda blossom and red flamboyants appear. With two reasonable, small hotels, supermarkets, a good municipal campsite, and the nearby Hoba Meteorite, Grootfontein is a good place to stop between Windhoek and the Kavango-Caprivi regions. However, it is worth remembering that there have been problems of theft from vehicles in Grootfontein, especially cars belonging to tourists who stop here to stock up on provisions before heading to Etosha. Do not leave your car unattended and be wary of being distracted while someone else steals from the other side of the car.

History

With an abundant supply of water and good grazing, the area has been home to both game and humans for many thousands of years. In pre-colonial times the town was known to the Herero as *Otjiwandatjongue*, meaning 'hill of the leopard'. The

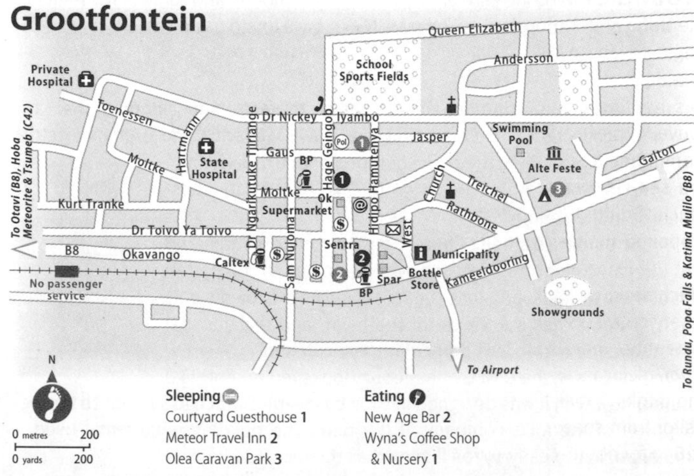

earlier Nama and Berg Damara inhabitants called the area *Gei-ous*, meaning 'big fountain', from which the Afrikaans name Grootfontein is derived. The fountain and the Tree Park, planted by the **South West African Company**, can both be seen today on the northern edge of town close to the municipal swimming pool and adjacent Olea Caravan Park.

In the 1860s, two elephant hunters, Green and Eriksson, used the fountain as a base from which to launch their hunting expeditions. However, the first Europeans to settle in the area arrived around 1880, followed soon after by the so-called 'Dorsland Trekkers' who in the mid-1880s established their own republic on land purchased from Owambo chief, Kambone. The Republic of Upingtonia, as it was called, survived for a mere two years before collapsing.

In 1893 the **South West Africa Company** established its headquarters at Grootfontein and in 1896 the settlement was enlarged by a group of settlers from the Transvaal. In the same year the *Schutztruppe* constructed a fort and administrative centre, and in 1904 a tower was constructed, providing the garrison with an excellent vantage point from which to survey the surrounding area. In 1922 the limestone extension was added.

Between 1923 and 1958 the fort served as a school hostel, after which it was abandoned. A public appeal in 1974 saved the building from demolition, and in 1975 it was declared a national monument, and also served as an assembly point for Angolan refugees. In 1977 it was renovated and in 1983 the Alte Feste (Old Fort), Museum was opened, with a local history exhibition inside and a display of industrial items outside.

Grootfontein itself officially became a town in 1907, and the following year the narrow-gauge railway linked the town with Otavi and Tsumeb. The town has subsequently grown to become the centre of Namibia's maize industry, evidenced by large silos at the end of the railway line, with a significant cattle industry.

The history and character of the town are personified in its coat of arms which features the Hoba Meteorite, a palm tree, a kudu, an eland and a cheetah.

Sights

The **Alte Feste Museum** ⓘ *just west of Olea Caravan Park (municipal campsite), T067-242456, Tue and Fri 1600-1800, Wed 0900-1100, phone for access at other times, free*, is worth visiting for its history of the town and the local area. Exhibits include local minerals, restored carpenter's and blacksmith's shops with working machinery, and traditional crafts.

Around Grootfontein

The **Hoba Meteorite** ⓘ *US$1.50*, is an impressive lump of metal, the largest known single meteorite in the world, weighing in at around 60 tonnes and measuring 2.95 m by 2.84 m. It was discovered by Johannes Brits in 1920 whilst he was hunting in the area. After various people tried to get a souvenir piece of it, the meteorite was declared a national monument in 1955. Made of 82% iron (which really shows when you see it up close), the meteorite also contains 16% nickel, which South West Africa Company manager, T Tonnessen, proposed mining in 1922 – fortunately he never got round to it. There are suggestions that the Hoba Meteorite is merely the largest fragment of an even larger meteorite which broke up during entry into the earth's atmosphere, in which case there may be other fragments lying around in the area waiting to be discovered. Next to the meteorite, there are some panels with information, a basic nature trail, good *braai*/picnic facilities, toilets and a small shop selling information leaflets, souvenirs and drinks. It really is an unusual lump, worth the short detour to see this mysterious visitor from space. To get there, follow C42 towards Tsumeb for 3 km, then take the D2859 for about 15 km, following the sign to the meteorite.

The meteorite is believed to be between 190 and 410 million years old; it fell to earth at least 80,000 years ago.

In the hills around Grootfontein there are reputed to be a number of underground caves on private farms. One such cave is known as **Dragon's Breath Cave,** located on Haraseb farm, 41 km from Grootfontein, 61 km from Tsumeb. It is reputed to be the largest discovered underground lake in the world. While attracting caving teams from all over the world, the cave is closed to the general public. The entrance to the underground system is via a narrow crevice in some dolomite rocks. The first obstacle to negotiate is a 4-m drop, managed with the use of a cable ladder. At the bottom you find yourself in a sloping cavern, which you exit onto a narrow ledge, from where it is a further 18 m down to the point where you can first see the lake. This viewpoint is an opening in the cavern roof directly above the lake waters. A rope is used for the final 25 m to the water. The surface area of the lake is almost 2 ha – the equivalent of four rugby pitches. The water in the lake is crystal clear and very deep. Divers have reported finding huge boulders on those parts of the lake bottom they have actually been able to reach, but they haven't yet found the very deepest part. A small raft is required to cross the lake to a small stone beach. Groups of divers who are interested in exploring the lake must organize their own gear, transport and permission and, needless to say, should be highly experienced. Contact the **Namibian Underwater Federation** (NUF), ⓘ *T061-238320, theo@schoemans.com.na.*

Sleeping

Otavi *p144*

C Palmenecke, 96 Hertzog Av, T/F067-234199. A friendly and comfortable palm oasis (literally 'corner') with 5 large and bright en suite doubles with a/c, TV and desk, price is B&B, all meals available, there are occasional *braais* in the welcoming and cosy thatched *lapa* surrounding the tiny swimming pool. Recommended.

D Otavi Gardens Hotel, Unie St, T/F067-234334. Nice thatched bar/restaurant with pool table, which is worth a visit for a beer or meal, and 7 en suite doubles in square brick blocks in pretty gardens, though on our visit white owners' not very friendly, though black staff very friendly.

If you're **camping**, opt for the decent municipal campsites in Tsumeb or Grootfontein rather than the grim site here.

Guest farms

A Khorab Safari Lodge, 3 km south of Otavi on the B1, T067-234352, khorab@iafrica.com.na. 10 en suite doubles in thatched bungalows, each with fan, fridge and desk; swimming pool with *lapa*, good restaurant, bar and lounge in large thatched barn popular with tourists and local farmers in the evenings. There are also a few well maintained **camping sites** (E) with a neat ablution block.

A-B Ghaub Guest farm, 4 km west of the D2863/D3022 junction, T/F067-240188, www.namibsunhotels.com. Located in the middle of the triangle, this is your best bet in the region. Set in the lovely Otavi Mountains Conservancy, well worth a drive through even if you aren't planning to stay the night (plan your own loop along the D2863 and D3022). 10 large en suite doubles, each with veranda and great views over a huge lawn, the swimming pool and across the valley. The main house is an old Rhenish Mission Station (established 1895), and the impressive trees date from that time, giving the feel of an English country estate, but with African touches everywhere. Full board, including drives, guided walks in the hills (they have Bushman engravings), an excursion to the nearby bat caves (the third largest in Namibia) or large underground reservoir/cave for those interested. Worth staying a couple of nights to enjoy the tranquillity of the spot as well as the activities on offer. Recommended.

C Zum Potjie Rest Camp, 8 km north of Otavi, 2 km off the B1, T/F067-234300, www.zumpotjie.com. 5 basic but clean en suite bungalows, swimming pool, and small farm museum. The attraction is the home-cooking, the resourceful Afrikaans

For an explanation of the sleeping and eating price codes used in this guide, see inside the front cover. Other relevant information is found in Essentials, see pages 43-51.

hosts source most of their ingredients from the farm, including fruit from the orchards to make juice and jams, and the *potjies* (stews cooked in iron 3-legged pots) are very good, non guests can stop for lunch between 1230-1400. **Campsite (E)** with simple ablutions and camp kitchen.

Tsumeb *p145, map p146*

There is a style choice to be made between the 2 excellent hotels in Tsumeb: the modern chic of the **Makalani** or the fading colonial grandeur of the **Minen**.

B-C Makalani Hotel, 3rd St, T067-221051, www.makalanihotel.com. Central location, 18 clean en suite rooms, DSTV, phone, a/c, tea- and coffee-making facilities, secure parking, swimming pool, tastefully decorated, restaurant and pub/bar with attractive beer garden.

B-C Minen Hotel, Post St, T067-221071, minen@mweb.com.na. German-owned hotel with pleasant mature gardens, 49 en suite rooms, a/c, telephone, TV, pub lunches served in the garden, restaurant with extensive menu, and attached bar, swimming pool. An atmospheric old-style hotel, full of character.

C Pension OMEG Allee, OMEG Allee, T067-220631, F067-220821, 6 clean en suite doubles in smart Cape Dutch replica buildings with a/c, TV, fridge, safe and kettle, weird and wonderful cacti in the front garden, secure parking.

C-E Travel North Backpackers, OMEG Alee, T067-220728, T081-1246722 (mob) after hours. Clean but very simple doubles with or without bathrooms, 2 flats with several beds that can be booked as a dorm arrangement for as little as US$11 per person with use of kitchen, 3 **camping** sites in the garden, the **Intercape** bus stops right outside at about 0100 in the morning, so usefully 24-hr reception though still best to call in advance, breakfast on request. Also agent for **Imperial** and **Europcar** car hire, **Intercape** buses and it sells cars too.

D Tsoutsomb Bungalows, between 4th St and 5th St, T067-220404, F220592. Choice of 4-bed or 6-bed, square, blue and white bungalows with tin roofs, *braai* pits and parking outside under shady jacaranda trees, central, quiet location, good value, though very uninspiring and plain.

D-E Mousebird Backpackers, corner of 4th St and 8th Rd, T067-221777, info@mousebird.com. Smart house near the museum with dorms, doubles and some space for camping, bar, self-catering kitchen, internet access, TV lounge with videos and play station, cheerfully decorated and helpful owners.

E Municipal Caravan Park, B1 southern edge of town, T067-221056, muntspro@mweb.com.na. 21 green, shaded and spacious caravan/campsites, each with own *braai* area, table, seating, electricity and water, communal ablutions. Also the best spot for a picnic.

Grootfontein *p148, map p148*

B Courtyard Guesthouse, Hidipo Hamutenya St, T067-240027, platinum@iway.na. 6 plain but spacious en suite rooms, a/c, TV, fridge, swimming pool, secure parking, access for wheelchairs, email for guests, small gardens. Some tasteful touches to the fairly square rooms; not a place to write home about, but still your best bet in town.

C Meteor Travel Inn, Okavango Rd, T067-242078, dirkv@namibnet.com. 24 reasonably comfortable rooms with a/c and phone, arranged around a courtyard, bar/beer garden and restaurant are popular with locals, especially pizza night (Fri) and Sun buffet (1200-1400), large screen TV for watching sport.

C-E Olea Caravan Park, T067-243101, F242930, the municipal campsite, reception open 24 hrs. 4, 4-bed bungalows and 9 pleasant, shaded camp/caravan sites with electricity, water, table and seating and *braai* area, shared ablution block; care should be taken with valuables as the campsite is close to town and, although guarded, not secure. Traffic from Okavango Rd can be heard through the night, but it's not oppressive.

Guest farms

There are some good options north of Grootfontein off the B8.

A Dornhügel Guest farm, T067-240439, www.dornhuegel.com. 11 km north of Grootfontein take the D2844 (through Berg Aukas, where the tar ends), the farm is signposted 24 km from the B8. 3 doubles, 2 singles, all en suite, small but decorated with African touches, large *lapa* with bar and restaurant by the swimming pool, tennis court, lounge with small library. A friendly and tranquil spot, if a little overpriced. Interestingly they breed Basotho ponies here, originally from Lesotho.

C **Guest Farm Koukuas**, T067-232033, 85 km north of Grootfontein, on the D3016, by the D2855 junction. An attractive fort-style building, with en suite rooms, pleasant gardens, bar, restaurant and natural swimming pool among the rocks, walking trails. **Campsite** (E) with good shared ablutions. Recommended for families.

C-E **Roy's Camp**, at the Tsumkwe junction (C44), 57 km north of Grootfontein, 1 km from the main road, T/F067-240302, royscamp@iway.na. 4 thatched en suite huts intriguingly created with indigenous materials, green, shaded campsite with *braai* sites and communal ablutions. Nice bar by swimming pool set into rock, restaurant (book meals in advance), short hiking trail, it is sometimes possible to see zebra and small antelope in and around the camp. Recommended.

Eating

Otavi *p144*

Camel Inn, at the Total petrol station on the B1. Lovely thatched building surrounded by palms with a wooden bar inside sporting very tall stools, cosy tables, expect the likes of rump steaks and all things meaty, daily specials. Mon-Sat 1300-2000, though opening hours are erratic depending on business.

Tsumeb *p145, map p146*

Makalani Hotel and **Minen Hotel** both have good restaurants serving lunch and dinner.

Etosha Café, Main St. Pinafored waitresses, excellent cakes and coffee, light meals plus tourist shop selling books, cards and gifts, beer garden, popular stop for coach groups. Recommended.

Steinbach Bakery, Main St. Light meals, pizza, coffee and cold drinks in an old building with a tin roof, 1 token plastic table on the pavement, open Mon-Sat during the day, bottle store next door.

Wimpy at the Engen petrol station on the approach to town on the B1. The usual burgers, recommended for breakfast and Wimpy mega-coffee in a whoosh of a/c.

Tsumeb is the self-caterers' final chance to stock up with fresh meat, fruit and vegetables en route to Etosha and there are large branches of both **Spar** and Pick and Pay in town.

Grootfontein *p148, map p148*

Meteor Travel Inn, see Sleeping, above. Easily the best place to eat in town with a quiet ambience, broad menu including fish, steaks, ribs and game dishes, pizza specials on a Fri, attractive outdoor seating beneath palms, fully stocked bar, open daily for lunch and dinner.

New Age Bar, Hidipo Hamutenya St, T067-242414. Decent bar with large TV for sports; restaurant specializes in steaks and fish from the nearby lakes, beer garden. Open daily.

Wyna's Coffee Shop and Nursery, Moltke St. Open during the day for light lunches, very Afrikaner menu though some pastas and cakes such as black forest gateau, daily changing menu, pleasant surroundings in the plant nursery under the shade of enormous trees.

Shopping

Tsumeb *p145, map p146*

For those interested in buying unusual rocks and semi-precious stones, Tsumeb is a good place to do your shopping. The **Mineral Gallery** is next to the **Etosha Café** on Main St, which has a good range of stones and minerals for sale. Outside are a number of old railway carts from the mine which now have plants growing in them. A couple of doors along on the other side of the Etosha Café is the **Tsumeb Arts & Crafts Centre**, which supports and displays the work from people in the local community, and there are some nice items for sale.

Transport

Tsumeb *p145, map p146*

427 km to Windhoek, 107 km to Namutoni, 247 km to Ondangwa.

Air West Wings Charters, reservations, Windhoek, T061-221091, charters@westwing.com.na. This company runs a service Mon-Fri between **Windhoek** and Tsumeb.

Flight times are seasonal, and on Mon there is 1 flight from Eros Airport in Windhoek to Tsumeb, on Tue 1 flight from Tsumeb to **Eros**, and Wed-Fri 1 flight in both directions.

Bus Intercape, T067-220728, **Travel North**, OMEG Allee, T067-220728, are agents and the bus stops outside. See timetable page 70.

Car The possibility here to keep car hire costs down, is to get the **Intercape** bus to Tsumeb and hire a car from here to explore **Etosha**. **Avis**, Jordan St, T067-220520. **Europcar**, and **Imperial**, at **Travel North**, OMEG Allee, T067-220728.

Train See timetable, page 68.

Grootfontein *p148, map p148*
460 km to Windhoek, 280 km to Tsumkwe, 807 km to Katima Mulilo.

Bus **Intercape**, see timetable, page 70.

Directory

Otavi *p144*
In town there's a **First National Bank** and **Standard Bank**, both with ATM, a **Spar**, **post office** and **telephone**. On the main road, the 24-hr **Total** has an ATM, a good shop which also does takeaways, stalls selling fruit and vegetables, and a restaurant (see Eating, above). There is also a BP 30 km south of town. **International SOS**, see under Grootfontein, below.

Tsumeb *p145, map p146*
Banks Bank Windhoek, **First National Bank** and **Standard Bank**, all on Main St, with ATMs and money-changing facilities. **Internet** On OMEG Allee, US$2.30 per ½ hr, very slow connection (bring a book), Mon-Thu 0900-1900, Fri 0900-2200, Sat 0900-1300, 1600-2100, Sun 1100-1300, 1700-1900. **Teleshop**, OMEG Allee, close to the Municipality. **Medical services** Jacobs **Pharmacy**, Main St. **Private Hospital**, T067-221001. **International SOS**, see under Grootfontein, below. **Police** 8th Rd, T10111. **Post office** Post St, Mon-Fri 0800-1630, Sat 0800-1130.

Grootfontein *p148, map p148*
Banks **Bank Windhoek**, Sam Nujoma Drive; **First National Bank**, Dr Toivo Ya Toivo St and **Standard Bank**, Bismarck St, all have ATMs, and there is a further **Bank Windhoek** ATM next to the Spar. **Medical services** The **State Hospital**, Hartmann St, T067-221082, **Private Hospital**, T067-240064, **International SOS**, T067-285501, 24-hr response, covers Tsumeb, Grootfontein, Otavi, Etosha and Ovamboland. **Plice** T10111. **Post office** Bismarck St, Mon-Fri 0800-1630, Sat 0800-1130.

Bushmanland and Kavango

Bushmanland is a very remote area, even by Namibian standards. In a wilderness of over 18,000 sq km there is only one settlement of any note – Tsumkwe. The countryside is flat and dry, the few roads that are marked are no more than tracks in places and there aren't many signposts. South of the C44 are a couple of pans, Nyae Nyae Pan and Nama Pan, which tend to flood after rain and then attract wildlife from all over the Kalahari Region. It is very difficult to travel in these areas after the rains, known as the Panveld, since the roads turn into impassable slippery mud. Dotted about this level landscape are the occasional baobab tree and patches of savannah forest, as well as remote San communities.

> *There is no petrol available here and you will need to carry jerry cans of extra fuel.*

Further north, the arid lands are left behind as you enter the the Kavango Region, between Grootfontein and Rundu. This is the wettest part of Namibia where the average annual rainfall is more than twice that of the south, although most of the rain falls between November and March. There is a marked shift in both vegetation and human influence. Even more striking is the contrast in the style of farming, from the commercial low-intensity farming south of the Red Line to the subsistence living of the small farmers and communities of the north. Almost all the tourist lodges and camps are located in strategic positions along the lush riverbanks, where the scenery is at its most beautiful and game and bird life is at its most plentiful. » *For Sleeping, Eating and other listings, see pages 158-160.*

Bushmanland » *pp158-160.*

Ins and outs

Some 57 km north of Grootfontein there is a turning east (C44) for Tsumkwe (222 km) and Khaudum Game Park. When you look at a road map of Namibia there is a large blank area in the northeast with very few roads or settlements. This is the region commonly known as Bushmanland. Like Kaokoland in Namibia's northwest, this is tough country to travel in – you should not even consider exploring here unless you are familiar with 4WD in soft sand and off-road. There are no facilities for tourists and visitors must be completely self-sufficient: food, water, petrol, tents and so on must all be brought with you. On Namibia's border with Botswana is the remote and little-visited Khaudum Game Park. Visitors to Khaudum should have at least two vehicles travelling together. Elsewhere in the region it would also make sense to travel with another vehicle.

Tsumkwe » *Colour map 2, B2.*

Tsumkwe may be the regional administrative centre, and the largest settlement in the region, but it is no more than a ramshackle collection of shops, trading stores and bottle shops. You may find Bushman art for sale in stalls or small shops: ostrich egg bracelets and necklaces and colourful beaded bags are the most common items. If you plan to explore the area make sure you have sufficient fuel for your planned mileage. There is a police station and **Nature Conservation office**, which is useful for anyone travelling on to the Khaudum Game Park; the office will be able to advise on the condition of the roads and location of the wildlife. Look out for a large baobab tree close by.

Nyae Nyae Conservancy » *Colour map 2, B3.*

ⓘ *Nyae Nyae Conservancy Office, Tsumkwe, near the police station, T067-244011.*

The Nyae Nyae Conservancy is 9003 sq km in size and stretches from about 30 km west of Tsumkwe and 55 km east to the Botswana border. From north to south it extends for

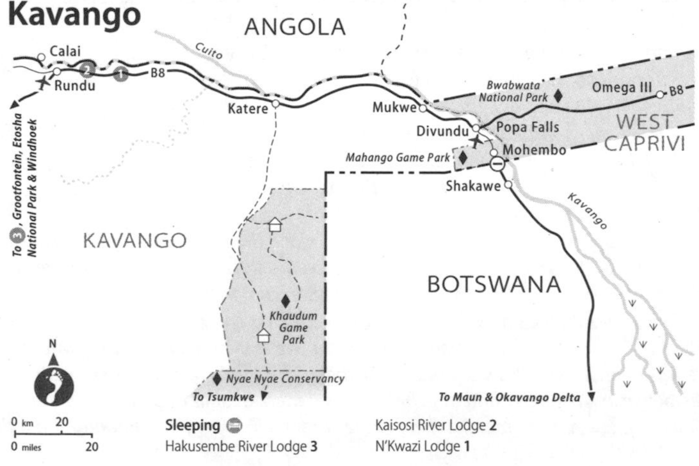

about 100 km. It was registered in 1998, giving the Ju/'hoansi Bushmen the right to utilize the wildlife in the area by receiving the income from a hunting concession. The less than 1000 members of the conservancy (total number of Ju/'hoansi residing in the area are about 3000) receive US$10,000 a year from the concession. They may also hunt traditionally in the area. The WWF (Worldwide Fund for Nature) has sponsored the reintroduction of game such as eland, springbuck, blue wildebeest and oryx to increase game numbers. The Ju/'hoansi have always lived in the Nyae Nyae area as well as across the border in Botswana, north in what is now the Khaudum Game Park, and south in what is now Hereroland. Archaeologists claim they've lived here for at least 40,000 years (ash from their fires have been found below the calcrete layer). Tsumkwe lies in the centre of the Nyae Nyae Conservancy, but is not part of the conservancy. This means that people from any language group can live in Tsumkwe, but not inside the conservancy borders. Since the 1950s the Ju/'hoansi have had contact with the outside world, and they no longer wear traditional clothes. They are also now settled in about 37 villages in the conservancy, each with its own borehole. In recent years simple campsites have been developed close to these villages for tourists and visitors; you can camp here for a small fee which goes back into the local community. A few years ago you could camp for free anywhere in Bushmanland; these days this is discouraged and it's very important that the local people benefit from tourism to the region. Employment opportunities in the area are limited and most people don't have any income. They receive a yearly payment from the hunting concession and also earn money from the selling of crafts; those over 60 get a government pension. However, people still collect food and hunt game to supplement their modern diet of maize meal porridge. If you are interested in learning about the Bushman culture – tracking, bush food, hunting and traditional dancing – you can enquire at the Nyae Nyae Conservancy Office. It can arrange a guide from the community. Always arrange payment before going on an outing, and the office will give you an idea of fees. Expect to pay around US$10 per person for a guide on a short walk or US$3 per peson for a demonstration of traditional dancing. Crafts are also usually for sale. If you do come into contact with the Bushmen communities be courteous at all times and respect their traditions. Tourism has only just started to find its way into this region, the first people who pass through must be careful to leave the right impressions.

Khaudum Game Park

» *Colour map 2, A3.*

ⓘ *Entry US$5.90 per person, US$1.50 per car.*

This is a desperately remote reserve but with a fairly wide variety of animals and bird life. There are no facilities in the park, visitors have to be totally self-sufficient, and many of the tracks are very sandy and it is easy to get stuck. Driving from Grootfontein on the gravel C44, take a left just before entering Tsumkwe, follow the road behind the village school and look out for the signs to the park and Klein Döbe. If approaching from the north from the B8, take the D4800 south off the B8 at a village called Shighuru, 90 km east of Rundu. Once you are on the road driving south, check with people at regular intervals that you are on the right route; there are plenty of tracks, masses of sand and no signposts. Note that a minimum of two vehicles per group is allowed to travel in the park.

This is a tough region to travel in and should not be explored by inexperienced off-road drivers, even if you have the right vehicle.

There used to be two camps in the park, but in 2004 they were closed down by **Namibia Wildlife Resorts** because of the poor and deteriorating condition of the huts

About 2400 San or Bushmen live in the vicinity of Tsumkwe over an area of 13,200 sq km. They are the oldest inhabitants of Africa and once roamed an area several times the extent of the current 'Bushmanland' living as hunter-gatherers.

and campsites. It remains to be seen if they will reopen again after some refurbishment, though you can still camp there but have to be totally self-sufficient. The climate of the area has two distinct seasons: the rainy season extends from late November until March, which is also the hottest time of the year. The rest of the year, April to November, is a long dry season. It's best to avoid late summer, December to March, when rain renders the vegetation very dense and the roads impassable. This is, however, the best time for birds. During the winter, June to October, game numbers seem to improve in the park, particularly close to the artificial waterholes along the *omuramba* (fossil rivers), see below.

Vegetation and wildlife

Khaudum was proclaimed in 1989, covering an area of 384,000 ha along the Botswana border on the edge of the Kalahari. The park was established to conserve one of the few true wilderness areas in Namibia. The vegetation is a dense mix of short and tall dry woodland; in winter, most trees shed their leaves and game viewing is much easier. The dominant trees are wild teak, wild seringa and copalwood. The shorter trees, those less than 5 m in height, include the Kalahari apple-leaf, silver cluster leaf and the shepherd's tree. All of these trees are able to grow on the thin sandy soils of the Kalahari. Running through the park are several fossil rivers known as *omuramba*. In the north of the park are the Khaudum and Cwiba *omuramba*. The soil along the margins of these *omuramba* have a high clay content and therefore support a different range of trees, a mix of thorns – camel, umbrella and candle as well as leadwood. After the first summer rains look out for the flowering knob thorn.

The *omuramba* no longer flow as rivers, but they fill up and store water which is gradually released during the dry season. They are made up of peat beds and are often identifiable by the abundant reed beds. The lush vegetation within them and along their margins make them a natural east-west migration route for game.

If you wish to see animals around each corner when on a game drive, then this is not the game park for you. Here, game viewing is a real skill; you have to be patient and know something about the animals – what they eat, when they eat, where they prefer to be at different times of the day, and so on. Since very few people visit the park the animals are not used to the sound of engines and they are more likely to bolt than ignore you. There are no fences around the park so all the animals are free to move along traditional migration routes during the year, meaning that at certain times of the year there are quite a few animals in the park.

The park is an excellent place to see roan antelope and wild dogs are regularly spotted. Other animals you can expect to see on a good day are kudu, eland, steenbok, gemsbok, blue wildebeest, giraffe, elephant, hartebeest, reedbuck, tsessebe, jackal, spotted hyaena, lion, leopard and perhaps cheetah. The mix of vegetation habitats provides a wide variety of birds: over 320 species have been recorded, with more than 70 migrant species after good rains.

Kavango » pp158-160.

North from Grootfontein

After the Tsumkwe turning, there are no other junctions of note before the B8 reaches Rundu. You will encounter a checkpoint at the **Red Line**, the fence dividing the north and south of the country, built to prevent foot-and-mouth disease and rinderpest from migrating south into the large commercial ranches. At the checkpoint, 131 km south of Rundu, there is a small shop, takeaway and petrol station. The change in landscape and roadside activity north of this divide is striking, you are entering... Africa!

Malaria is a risk in the northeast: you should take prophylactic drugs, especially during the wet season.

Depending on the season, between the Red Line and Rundu you will probably see by the roadside heaped piles of watermelons, contorted gourds or bowls of monkey oranges, as well as some local handicrafts. Avoid driving this stretch after dark as goats and cattle regularly stray into the road; in daylight, enjoy the homesteads, perhaps purchase crafts or fresh produce from roadside stalls. While the road is tarred all the way, beware of potholes and roadworks.

Rundu and onwards » *Phone code: 066. Colour map 2, A2.*

After the long straight drive northeast from Grootfontein the sprawl of Rundu is a welcome sight. The town spreads inland along the banks of the Okavango River, the opposite bank is Angola. Since 1993, Rundu has been the provincial capital of the Kavango Region and consequently is home to an impressive number of municipal offices, schools, hospitals and banks, as well as supermarkets and petrol stations. You will see far fewer white faces than in the south, and almost none after dark; at the weekends the town gets very lively around the gambling and drinking dens.

Rundu was at one time a thriving border town, but the independence struggle brought most commercial activity to a halt. The character of the town is quite different from other Namibian towns; the Portuguese influence from across the border is strong, and there is no legacy of the German past. There are lovely views over the Okavango River, particularly from the **Kavango River Lodge**, and there are opportunities for fishing, watersports, quad-biking and 4WD driving to entertain more active visitors. An annual river carnival, with colourful and noisy floats processing downstream, has established itself on the calendar. A yearly trade fair has taken place since 1998, which is helping to promote the Kavango Region for businesses and institutions. Rundu is certainly picking up as a commercial centre and looks set for further growth as peace and stability become ingrained on both sides of the border and tourists and businesses return. However, most tourists use Rundu as a staging post to the quieter and longer- established destinations further east, where the abundant rivers and plentiful game offer a compelling package.

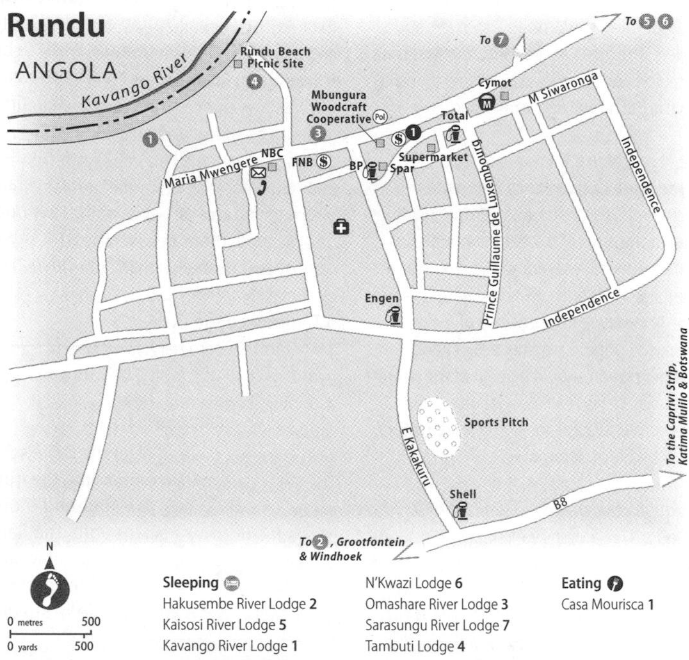

Sleeping
Hakusembe River Lodge 2
Kaisosi River Lodge 5
Kavango River Lodge 1
N'Kwazi Lodge 6
Omashare River Lodge 3
Sarasungu River Lodge 7
Tambuti Lodge 4

Eating
Casa Mourisca 1

There are several options available for continuing your journey. It is possible to drive straight through to **Katima Mulilo** (518 km). If you have already driven from Grootfontein, this would make for a tough day's driving, and you should ensure there is sufficient time to arrive in daylight. At the small village of **Katere**, 120 km east of Rundu on the B8, is the well signposted turning south to Khaudum Game Park (4WD only, see above). Once at Khaudum, the intrepid might want to exit via the south and complete a circuit back to the main road just north of Grootfontein (see page 148). Another popular option is to drive as far as **Popa Falls** and spend the night at the **Nambia Wildlife Resorts** campsite, **Ngepi Camp**, or one of the private lodges along the banks of the Okavango River. The next day you have the option of exploring the **Mahango Game Park**, entering Botswana, or continuing east through Caprivi towards Katima Mulilo. Of course, you could stay a while in Rundu – there are some excellent lodges and the sun setting over the Okavango River is a sight that's hard to beat.

Remember to refuel in Rundu before continuing, supplies east of here are limited and far between.

Sleeping

Tsumkwe *p154*

B Tsumkwe Lodge, reservations T/F067-244028, www.tsumkwel.iway.na.
This is the only place to stay, with 9 thatched, en suite bungalows, restaurant with set menu, bar, swimming pool, accessible by 2WD, but you'll need to hire a 4WD to explore any further or go on one of the lodge's very informative tours. It offers walking trails and traditional crafts and rituals, and can arrange a visit to the nearby Ju/'hoan Bushman village, plus game drives to Khaudum Game Park, 50 km away, and fly-in charters. There's a small **camping site** (**E**) with 2 showers and 2 toilets. The hosts are very informative about the region and have an excellent relationship with the Bushmen. Recommended.

The Nyae Nyae Conservancy *p154*

E Nyae Nyae Conservancy Campsites.
These campsites are basically simple clearings beneath the arms of baobab trees with no facilities. There are several in the region and to get directions and GPS coordinates go first to the **Nyae Nyae Conservancy** office or **Tsumkwe Lodge**. Camping fees of about US$4 per person should be paid at the nearest village, where you can also get water and firewood. All rubbish, including toilet paper, should be burnt or removed.

Rundu and onwards *p157, maps p154, p157*

The lodges are all fairly well signposted. Many of them advertise boat trips on the Okavango River, but be warned that these may well not be possible between May and Nov when water levels are too low. However, if you're energetic you may enjoy a paddle in a canoe.

B Omashare River Lodge, T066-256101, omashare@iway.na. 20 spacious en suite rooms with satellite TV, à la carte restaurant, long wooden veranda, 'ladies' bar, conference facilities, take-aways from adjacent coffee shop. Swimming pool set in large lawn, views of river in the distance. A modern hotel, owned by De Beers, better suited to the business traveller or government official than the tourist, though they can arrange boat trips and microlight flights from here.

B Sarasungu River Lodge, T066-255161, www.sarasunguriverlodge.com. 2 km from town. 14 en suite thatched brick and reed cottages, restaurant, bar, small swimming pool. Excellent location by the river for birdwatching and canoeing, and fishing can be organized. There are several shady **campsites** (**E**) underneath the trees, with electricity, *braai* sites and clean ablution block.

B Tambuti Lodge, T066-255711, www.tambuti.com.na. A fairly new place by the river, with 5 pretty, large bungalows, including a honeymoon suite with jacuzzi. Grassed lawn with well-established trees, swimming pool, good, small restaurant/bar. The Swiss owner enjoys quad-biking and canoeing and will lead an excursion if booked, can also organize traditional singing and dancing.

For an explanation of the sleeping and eating price codes used in this guide, see inside the front cover. Other relevant information is found in Essentials, see pages 43-51.

B-C **Kavango River Lodge**, T066-255244, F255013, kavlodge@tsu.namib.com. 14 en suite rooms with a/c, TV and kitchens, the minibars are also stocked with breakfast items in case you haven't brought your own food, decorated in African style, set high above the river looking west, with fabulous river views in the evening. Tennis court in good order, and there's a reasonable restaurant on site. Discounted rates available at weekends when government/business reps are not in town.

Guest farms

A **Hakusembe River Lodge**, 16 km west of Rundu, T066-257010, hakusembe@mweb.com.na. Take the B8 towards Grootfontein, after 2 km turn northwest on the C45 towards Nkurenkuru, turn right after 10 km at the signpost and follow signs for a further 4 difficult km, call ahead for road conditions, after heavy rain the only access is by boat from Rundu. Stunning riverside location, 6 beautiful en suite thatched huts with river views, excellent restaurant, stylish wooden bar, swimming pool and sundowner pontoon on the river. Long activity list includes powerboat and canoe 'safaris', fishing (the lodge will 'mount' your tiger fish), watersports, horse riding and mule safaris. Price is half board with very good food, but activities are extra. The **Rundu Barge Carnival** (first weekend in May) begins from here – participants build their own rafts and drift down to Rundu town. Recommended.

B **Kaisosi River Lodge**, 7 km east of Rundu, signposted, 2 km north of the B3402, T067-255265, www.namibia.co.za. 16 large, thatched, en suite chalets, square and simply decorated, restaurant, bar, 2 swimming pools, green, shaded area by the river. **Camping and caravanning** (D) available on a good site with thatched *braai* areas and clean ablution blocks. Each night there's a sundowner cruise on the river, and it can also arrange breakfast cruises on request.

B **N'Kwazi Lodge**, 17 km east of Rundu off the B8, well signposted, then 3 winding km towards the river on the D3402, T066-686006-7, nkwazi@iafrica.com.na. 13 spacious, thatched, en suite bungalows tastefully decorated with African touches and wooden walls, restaurant, bar, swimming pool, good selection of river activities, good birding. The whole camp – and its **campsite** (D) – is set in neat, well- kept grounds with plenty of shade and lawns. Offers 3- or 4-day safaris to the Khaudum Game Park which include interaction with the Bushmen; can also arrange visits to local schools. Recommended.

Eating

Rundu and onwards *p157, maps p154, p157*

The supermarkets in town stock everything for self-caterers. Eating out is limited, only the lodges cater regularly for tourists. Of these, **Hakusembe** (although a challenge to get back from in the evening), **Tambuti Lodge** (small and intimate) or **Omashere**, in order, are your best bets. See Sleeping, above. The adventurous might enjoy the street food available through the day behind the main market (near **Casa Mourisca**).

¶¶ **Casa Mourisca**, T067-255487. Daily 0800-late. It has a restaurant, steakhouse, 2 bars and a disco. Probably your best of a poor choice in town.

Shopping

Rundu and onwards *p157, maps p154, p157*

A large number of Angolans cross the border to do their shopping (for food) in Rundu, although officially only the military are allowed to. There is quite a collection of supermarkets, but in particular the **Spar**, next to the **BP** petrol station, sells a very broad range of products. Rundu's bottle stores have some of the most extensive ranges in the country, there are numerous clothes and 'From China' shops, and enough furniture shops to supply half of Namibia. There's also a useful **Cymot** to stock up on camping/fishing supplies. The region is also known for its woodcarvings and these can be purchased for not unreasonable prices at the **Mbungura Woodcraft Cooperative**, T067-256170, in the centre of town. Carvings from here are transported down south to the other craft markets.

Transport

Rundu and onwards *p157, maps p154, p157*

257 km to Grootfontein, 518 km to Katima Mulilo, 438 km to Mudumu NP (for Lianshulu Lodge), 186 km to Popa Falls.

Across the Okavango River is the Angolan town of **Calai**. The **Rundu-Calai border** is open daily 0800-1600.

Bus For **Intercape** coaches from Windhoek on their way to **Livingstone**, see timetable, page 70.

Taxi There are plenty of shared taxis arriving and leaving from the **Shell** garage on the B8, roughly 2 km south of the town centre.

Directory

Rundu and onwards *p157, maps p154, p157*
Banks First National, with ATM.
Emergencies T10111. **Medical services** State hospital, 1 block south of First National Bank, T066-255025. **Police** T066-255622.

Caprivi

The Caprivi Region is a land of fertile, flat flood plains surrounded by perennial rivers, a far cry from the arid lands of the Kalahari or the Namib-Naukluft. The regional centre is Katima Mulilo, a busy commercial town on the banks of the Zambezi. Don't dwell in town: the attractions of the region are the tranquil lodges, plentiful game and bird life and beautiful river scenery, centred in the rarely visited game parks. All four parks – Mahango, Mudumu, Mamili and the new Bwabwata – offer a similar experience, with few tourist facilities, made up for by pristine woodland and riverine flood plain with abundant local and migrant wildlife. The national park along the narrowest part of the Caprivi Strip (the one-time Caprivi Game Reserve) has recently been deproclaimed to make way for the communities that live there to develop their subsistence farming existence; it is now called BwaBwata National Park. Activities from the lodges in this region include sunset river cruises on pontoons, canoeing, watersports, fishing, four-wheel driving and game viewing, before carrying on into Botswana and Zimbabwe for the magnificent Chobe Game Park and famous Victoria Falls. It is only a three-hour drive from Katima to Victoria Falls. ▸▸ *For Sleeping, Eating and other listings, see pages 172-176.*

Ins and outs

The eastern part of the region is verdant and lush, with very little development, and it is blessed with some fabulous forests and rivers and a wide variety of wildlife. Visits

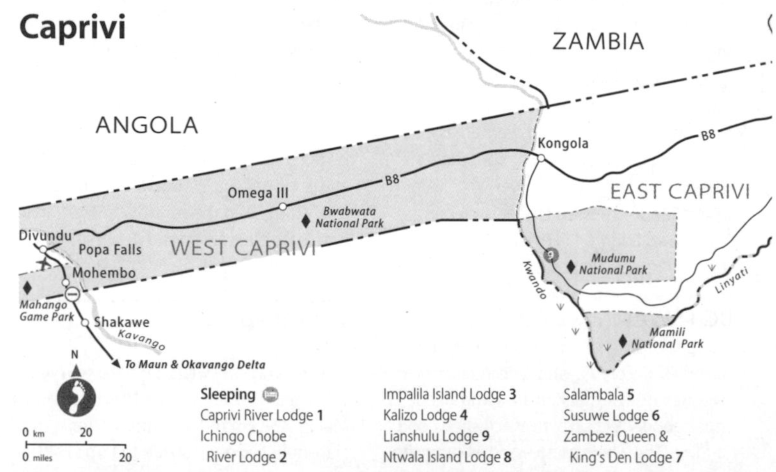

Basket making in Caprivi-Kavango

Baskets are an important part of daily life in both Namibia and Botswana and are used to carry possessions and collect and store grains and vegetables. Traditionally they are woven from *makalani* palm fronds and the most common are the bowl-shaped flour baskets made by the Geiriku, Yei, Subiya and Few women in the Caprivi-Kavango region of Namibia. Many of these round baskets have geometric patterns created with natural dyes in mauves, pinks, greens and blacks. The region's basket weavers are partners with **Namibia's Community Based Natural Resource Management** (CBNRM) programme, along with other institutions dedicated to community tourism such as the **Rossing Foundation** and the **Caprivi Arts and Culture Association**. Through these associations, the women benefit from their natural resources by selling their baskets to tourists. They make very attractive souvenirs and many lodges in Namibia and Botswana use them as decorations on walls.

to any of the game parks will always be remembered for their remote beauty, great variety of flora and range (if not head count) of game. The regional capital, Katima Mulilo, is well served by banks and shops and has a good range of accommodation. Elsewhere, basic homesteads are dotted infrequently along the roadsides and the parks have few or no tourist facilities whatsoever. Regular rainfall and floods support a riverine and *omuramba* ecosystem, sometimes as much as 80% underwater, with plentiful game and bird life but accessible only by boat and 4WD for much of the year. All the attractions in the region are on or off the B8 but beware when driving off the main tarred road: sand, mud or water can slow progress and fray nerves.

The lodges make the most of their riverbank settings and are well worth settling into for a few days to enjoy the scenery and activities they offer.

Background

The Caprivi Strip is a classic example of how the former colonial powers shaped the boundaries of modern Africa. The strip is 500 km long, at its narrowest only 32 km wide, while at the eastern end it bulges to almost 100 km wide before narrowing to a point at the confluence of the Zambezi and Chobe rivers where the boundaries of Zimbabwe, Namibia, Zambia and Botswana meet.

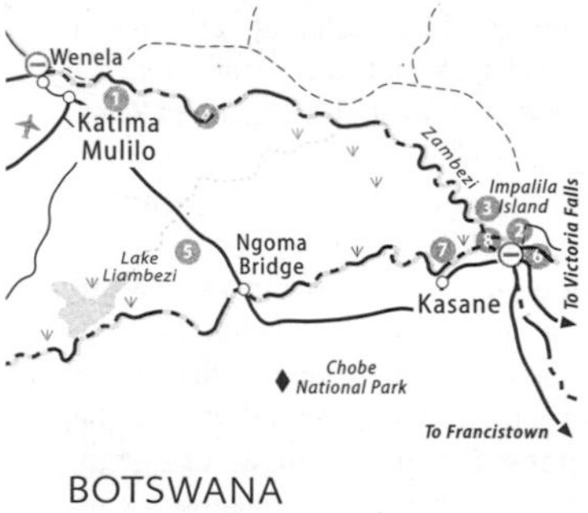

During the struggle for independence, the Caprivi Region was home to the South African Army and police and, as a consequence, no one really knows what went on up here. There were secret army camps, the airfield at Mpacha (now Katima Mulilo) was used for air strikes into Angola and Zambia, and the region was closed to anyone who didn't live here or have a legitimate reason for visiting. From the early 1960s until 1990 the region was in a constant state of war. There was a brief resurgence of 'trouble' in late 1999 following a discovery by the Namibian government who claimed to have unearthed a plot, led by former DTA opposition leader Mishake Muyongo and others, to launch an armed rebellion aiming to secede the Caprivi Region from the rest of Namibia.

Also during this period in a series of separate incidents, tourists were regularly being mugged while driving along the Kongola to Divundu Strip, and an increasing number of cars were flagged down by people posing as military before having their contents liberated. This came to a peak in December 1999 with a tragic incident in which three French tourists were not just robbed but brutally murdered. No one claimed responsibility and no one was caught and brought to trial. The government's claim that it was the work of UNITA rebels from Angola (however unlikely, given the proximity to Namibia's main military base on the strip, Omega III) underlined the sense of lawlessness in the area and caused all western governments to declare it a no-go zone. Virtually overnight, the number of tourists visiting the area fell to zero. Added to this is east and west Caprivi's geographical situation: its common borders with Angola, Botswana, Zimbabwe and Zambia has meant that the territory is particularly vulnerable to unrest within neighbouring states. West Caprivians, in particular, have lived for most of the past decade with the Angolan war on their border, until the April 2002 ceasefire. However, the region has been without incident for a number of years now and peace has been restored in Angola, flights and road travel are operational again and the extreme north of the country is safe and rewarding to visit, although the local communities remain poorly off, economically, as a result of the last few years of conflict.

West Caprivi » *pp172-176.*

Divundu » *Colour map 2, A4.*

The town is signposted both east and west every 10 km for nearly 200 km; when you arrive all you will find is an Engen petrol station (0600-2100) and a fairly well-stocked supermarket. From here, it is 35 km south on the D3430 to the border, passing through the Mahango Game Park (no motorbikes permitted). Along the road is a good range of accommodation as this is a popular route into Botswana and the Okavango Delta.

Popa Falls » *Colour map 2, A4.*

ⓘ *US$6.40 per person, children under 16 free, US$1.50 per car, fishing permits available at the office for a small charge.*

The **Namibia Wildlife Resorts** camp at Popa Falls has long been a popular overnight destination, dating from the days when the road between Rundu and Katima Mulilo was all gravel and an overnight limb-restoring rest was a necessity. Be warned, Popa Falls are not falls at all, rather a series of rapids, waterways and islands on the Okavango River. When the river is low the highest visible drop is about 3 m. There is a walkway into the middle of the river, after this you are free to scramble over the rocks in the middle of the river. At this point the channel is about 1 km wide with the river split into a series of channels making their way through the rocks. The adjacent accommodation is among the finest under NWR control in Namibia: comfortable, in good working order, cheap and very much in tune with the natural environment. The campsite suffers from the inflated park charges, but is set among lovely grassed lawns, by the water's edge. This is a popular spot for travellers on the way to Botswana and a convenient stopping place when travelling between Kavango and East Caprivi. The area is protected as a national park but is very small and apart from bird life, a few hippo and some crocodile there is little wildlife to be seen.

> *Don't swim in the river (except perhaps in the falls themselves, and only after taking local advice); in addition to crocodiles, there is bilharzia in the water.*

Mahango Game Park ›› *Colour map 2, A4.*

ⓘ *Entry fees, which are US$6.40 per person, children under 16 free, US$1.50 per car, are paid at the northern park gate. If you are just passing through en route to/from the Botswana border you do not have to pay.*

Ins and outs The northern gate of the park is 12 km from Popa Falls, 232 km from Rundu and 310 km from Katima Mulilo. Just before the B8 crosses the Okavango River into the Caprivi Strip turn south on the D3430 following the numerous signposts for lodges on the way. The area is served by a relatively busy (and rutted) gravel road and, as well as being a destination in itself, this is the shortest route from northern Namibia via the Mohamebo border with Botswana to **Maun** and the **Okavango Delta**. If approaching from Botswana through the Mohembo border post, you will be in the thick of the park immediately. Within the park there are few roads for game-viewing purposes. In addition to the main road running through the park, there are two side tracks, one for ordinary cars and the other only suitable for 4WD vehicles. The ordinary track to the east follows the river. When in full flood it can be impassable, but the gate attendants will let you know. This track is about 15 km; there is a large baobab and a picnic spot overlooking the river at Kwetche. The western trail is 31 km and follows the course of the two *omurambas* in the park. These roads are very sandy in the dry season, and slippery after the rains. Nevertheless, this is a special drive through unspoilt bush country, though if you have limited 4WD experience it is best to stick to the ordinary road which offers game (and driving challenge) enough. There is **no accommodation** in the park, but there's the NWR rest camp at Popa Falls, plus the lodges and camps off the D3430, detailed below.

There are two distinct seasons. Between 500 and 600 mm of rain is expected in the **rainy season** (December to March) when it gets hot, with the average daily maximum over 30°C. The **dry season** extends from April to November with no rain

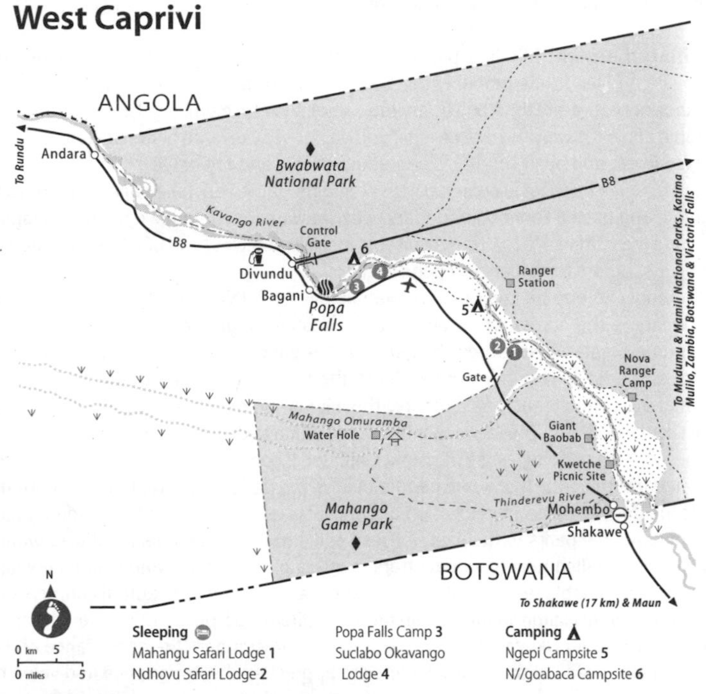

Berlin Conference – carving up the strip

The Caprivi Strip owes its origins to the Berlin Conference when the European colonial powers decided how to carve up Africa between themselves. On 1 July 1890, Britain traded Heliogoland and the Caprivi Region for Zanzibar and parts of Bechuanaland, present-day Botswana. Germany planned to use the strip as a trade route into central Africa, but even before the outbreak of the First World War this plan was thwarted by the activities of Cecil Rhodes in modern-day Zimbabwe.

The strip was named after the German Chancellor, General Count Georg Leo von Caprivi di Caprara di Montecuccoli. Unlike the rest of Namibia the region has little to show from the German period of rule. The strip returned to British control at the outbreak of the First World War, less than 25 years after the Germans had assumed control of the region. The return to British control came about in a most unusual fashion. The story goes that the German governor was having afternoon tea with a senior British official from Rhodesia, when a message arrived saying that war had just been declared between the two countries. The German governor was placed under arrest and the territory under his control annexed.

In 1918 the land was incorporated into Bechuanaland and thus ruled by the British. In 1929 it was handed over to the South African ruled South West Africa, and at independence it remained part of Namibia.

expected and evening temperatures falling to around 7°C. The best time to visit during the winter months is from June to October, when game will be found close to the river and waterholes. Bird life is prolific from November to March, after the rains, when insects are abundant and many of the trees flower and carry fruit.

Visiting the park This is a pleasant, small reserve which borders the perennial Okavango River. It has probably the best birding in the country, as well as a good chance of seeing rare antelope (roan and sable). Visitors travelling through the region should allow a day by the river; even if you do not see the large herds of elephant, the mixed forest and bush country is beautifully scenic and full of life.

Mahango has a lot in common with Khaudum Game Park (see page 155). Both are remote and have a common boundary with Botswana, neither have been developed beyond the cutting of a few tracks suitable for 4WD vehicles, and both were created in 1989 just before Namibian independence.

At only 28,000 ha (20 x 14 km); Mahango is a relatively small park. Its southern boundary is the border with Botswana, its eastern boundary the Okavango River. Year-round water ensures regular game in the park, and there are large seasonal influxes, particularly of migrant elephant. There are no fences, but the presence of man at the perimeter acts as a barrier. The migrant herds move between Angola and the Okavango Delta. They tend to inflict some damage on crops, trees and structures in passing, an ongoing cause of conflict with local communities.

It is worth noting that some people believe the parks were created for the wrong reasons (for example, the relocation of Caprivi secessionists), but like Mudumu and Mamili national parks to the east, if these parks had not been declared they would have quickly fallen prey to woodcutters, hunters and poachers and Namibia would have lost a valuable resource. All of the game parks are set in beautiful countryside, with the key attraction being the plentiful wildlife made possible by the perennial (and picturesque) Okavango River. You only have to compare the appearance of the land on either side of the boundary lines to appreciate the importance and value of the parks. The park and the lodges further upstream benefit from the existence of the newly proclaimed Bwabwata National Park on the opposite bank. Herds of elephant regularly come to the far bank to drink in early winter evenings, a stunning site.

Vegetation and wildlife One of the attractions of Mahango is the variety of vegetation in such a small area. There are three distinct habitats, and with each comes different bird life and conditions for the game. The river provides a mix of trees, reeds and grasses along its banks and on the flood plains. The dominant tree species are Kalahari apple-leaf, water pear and jackal-berry; along the flood plain margins you will see the wild date palm. If you visit one of the private camps or **Popa Falls Rest Camp** you will find many of the riverine trees have been helpfully labelled. A tree which every visitor quickly learns to recognize is the baobab. There are several groups within the park, including a distinctive clump just before the Kwetche picnic site, marked on the map, page 163.

Away from the river, the vegetation is predominantly open dry woodland, aside from a couple of *omurambas*, or fossil rivers (see Khaudum Game Park, page 155), which run west-east towards the Okavango River. The *omurambas* are covered with open grassland and tall acacia and bushwillow grow along their margins. For a few months after the rains, pools of water collect in the *omurambas*, offering good game viewing. Between Mahango *omuramba* in the north and Thinderevu *omuramba* in the south the vegetation is dry woodland with some dense patches of Zambezi teak, wild seringa and wild teak.

If you are fortunate you will encounter a wide variety of animals in this small park. It is home to some rare (certainly in Namibia) antelope: sable and roan (both shy but readily indentified by their magnificent curved horns), reedbuck, tsessebe and sitatunga. The sitatunga is very difficult to spot since it is small and lives in thick swamp areas; if you manage to see one, consider yourself very lucky. They are only found in large numbers in the Okavango Delta. Reedbuck are also quite difficult to spot, they tend to inhabit the flood plains. Keep an eye out here for red lechwe. Along the riverbank are good numbers of kudu and Chobe bushbuck, and rather fewer duiker and steenbok.

Apart from antelope, you can expect to see elephant, hippo, crocodile, warthog, baboon and vervet monkey, and you may spot lion and leopard too. Remember, the large herds of elephant are migrants: outside the dry season sightings will be fewer.

Finally, it is important not to forget the bird life in the park. Over 400 species have been recorded throughout the year and twitchers can expect to spot over 50 different species in a couple of hours sitting by the river at Kwetche. The different habitats in the park help attract the wide variety of species; it is interesting to compare the birds you will see along the riverbanks with those that you come across in the woodlands – even amateurs can quickly start to recognize how the species vary between different areas of the park. Along the open river area, look for the rare African skimmer, white-fronted and white-crowned plovers, and white-fronted and little bee-eaters. On the riverine fringe, you may see the rare western banded snake eagle, Meyer's and Cape parrots, swamp boubou and African golden oriole. The *omuramba* environment attracts the rare wattled crane, slaty egret, herons, copperytailed and Burchell's coucals, open-billed stork and long-toed plover. In the woodland areas, look for raptors including Dickson's kestrel, Steppe, lesser-spotted and booted eagles, as well as arrow-marked and black-faced babblers and sharp-tailed starling.

Crossing into Botswana

If you plan on driving straight through Mahango Game Park to the border, you do not need a permit or to pay any park fees. The **Mohembo border post** with Botswana is open 0600-1800. The road on the Botswana side, which used to have a bad reputation, has now been surfaced. The first settlement you reach is Shakawe, 17 km from the border. The road continues south with the 'panhandle' of the Okavango Delta to the east.

Bwabwata National Park

» *Colour map 2, A4.*

The newly proclaimed Bwabwata National Park (formerly the Caprivi Game Park) is wedged between Angola and Botswana on either side of the Caprivi Highway and covers a total of 5715 sq km. It extends for about 180 km from the Okavango River in the west to the Kwando River in the east. The Caprivi Game Park was proclaimed a game reserve in 1968, and was under the jurisdiction of the South African Defence until independence. During the independence struggle, this area was the South African Army Buffalo Base, the training grounds for the infamous 32nd Battalion and Third Force. Sadly, the army hunted out much of the game. It is said that Western Caprivi was kept as the private hunting ground for John Vorster who used to come up here and go hunting from helicopters. In 1999, the Ministry of Environment decided that the park would be renamed as the Bwabwata National Park and certain areas have been deproclaimed and the land given over to the isolated rural communities living along the B8, centred on the old military posts. It is a region of swamps, flood plains and riverine woodland, and is generally flat with a few sporadic sand dunes rising on the horizon. The Caprivi Highway runs through the entire length of the park, and whilst there are no stopping places or viewpoints along the way, keep an eye out for game, particularly elephant, in the morning and evening. More that 300 species of bird have been recorded in the park, so this is a rewarding drive for birdwatchers. There are 4WD tracks on the western bank of the Kwando River, but there are no tourist facilities except for a few basic camping sites (see Sleeping, below).

! There is no fuel available along the B8 as it runs through the park; Divundu is a fairly safe bet, but be sure to fill up in Rundu and Kongola.

East Caprivi

» *pp172-176.*

A closer look at a map of Eastern Caprivi reveals the unusual feature that except for a 90-km strip of land along the northern border, between the Kwando River and the Zambezi River, the region is completely surrounded by rivers. The Kwando-Linyanti-Chobe forms the border to the west, south and southeast, with the Zambezi, the border with Zambia, to the northeast. Enclosed by these rivers is a landscape which is largely flat, with numerous flood plains, oxbow lakes, swamps and seasonal channels.

The hydrography of the area is particularly interesting because in years of good rain the flow of water in stretches of the rivers can be reversed and water can actually spill into the Okavango Delta system, a completely different (internally draining) watershed. Before 2000, these were all thought to be drying up, but the Kwando, Zambezi and Okavango came back in force in 2000 and 2001. With a map in hand, consider the complexities of the river system, starting in Angola, where the **Kwando River** rises in the Luchazes Mountains. As this river flows southeast it forms the border between Angola and Zambia before it cuts across the eastern end of the narrowest part of the Caprivi Strip (the eastern border of the Bwabwata National Park). Where the river cuts through Namibia (past Kongola) it is known as the **Kwando**. Having cut across the Caprivi Strip, the river once again becomes an international boundary, this time between Botswana and Namibia. At Nkasa Island, the southwest corner of Mamili National Park, the river channel turns sharply to the northeast and becomes known as the **Linyati River** until it reaches just south of **Lake Liambezi** (at one time 100 sq km and an important source of food and water for the surrounding villages; since May 1985, dry and prone to fire); from here it becomes the **Chobe**, which flows into the **Zambezi** at Impalila Island. Confused? It's even worse 'on the ground'.

These are all shallow gradient, slow flowing rivers. While it is highly unusual, when the Zambezi is exceptionally high the flow of water in the Chobe and Linyanti can be reversed. Water then flows back up the Chobe and into Lake Liambezi. In the past, water from the Zambezi has been known to flood right across the plains

Border posts

Ngoma (Botswana) *Colour map 2.*
The border is open 0700-2400 and is 62 km from Katima Mulilo on a new tarred road. About 14 km before the border is the well signposted turn-off for an excellent community-run campsite, **Salambala** (see Sleeping). The Botswana border post is at the far end of the bridge after crossing the broad Chobe River valley. Make sure you have a small amount of currency (about US$2-3 worth) to pay the road levy to drive in Botswana (valid for a year). ZAR, USD or Botswanan Pula can all be used for this. Botswana is part of the Southern Africa Development Community (SADC), so you will only need to sign a book to take a vehicle across the border. If in a hire car ensure you have documentation of permission to take a car into Botswana

Kazangula (Zimbabwe) *Colour map 2.*
The border is open 0600-1800, but beware of time changes due to Central African Time. From Ngoma it is 57 km to Kasane (for Impalila Island and Chobe National Park) where there are also a number of upmarket lodges, a bank with ATM, fuel and some shops. It is a further 90 km from Kasane via the Kazangula border to Victoria Falls where there are plentiful money changers and petty thieves too. Travel from Katima Mulilo to Victoria Falls (217 km) takes you through the top of Chobe National Park. Including border crossings, it should take no more than three hours. If you are only transiting though Chobe, you do not have to pay park fees, but keep your speed down as there are often elephant on this road. At the time of writing, most car hire companies in Namibia and South Africa did not permit you to take cars into Zimbabwe. If this is still the case, then taking your car into Zambia is the better option to see Victoria Falls – discuss this with your car hire company. If you are in your own vehicle and travelling on a carnet de passage, then it is here on the Zimbabwe (or Zambia – see below) border that you will need to stamp out your car from the joint customs organization of the Southern Africa Development Community (SADC) as these countries are not members. You will also need to take out a short-term policy for third-party insurance which can be bought on the Zimbabwe side of the border. Note it is not possible to drive a motorbike through the game parks in both Namibia and Botswana. This means that motorcyclists cannot cross the Namibia-Botswana border on the C48 en route to Maun as it goes through the Mahango Game Park; nor can they cross the Ngoma Bridge border as the road goes through Chobe National Park. Options here are to cross into Zambia instead, and to access Botswana from the B6 to Buitepos on the Trans-Kalahari Highway further south.

Wenela (Zambia) *Colour map 2.*
The border is open 0600-1800. The border with Zambia is 4 km from town on a new tar road. The Sesheke Bridge over the Zambezi opened in 2004 completing the 2100-km TransCaprivi Highway that now links the port of Walvis Bay with Zambia's capital city, Lusaka. The TransCaprivi Highway was built by the Walvis Bay Corridor Group which was established in 1998 to coordinate international trade with the Southern African Development Community (SADC) through the port at Walvis Bay. In addition to trade, the bridge has already proved to a boon for tourism and offers excellent access to all the sights in the region. There are some very nice lodges on the Zambian side. The paperwork needed to take a car into Zambia is the same as that detailed above for crossing the Zimbabwe border post.

 between Katima Mulilo and Ngoma Bridge and drain into the northern shores of Lake Liambezi via a depression known as the **Bukalo Channel**.

Similarly, water from the Kwando River can enter the Okavango system via a channel known as the **Selinda Spillway** or **Magwegqana Channel**. Because of the difference in elevation, the waters usually only flow a few kilometres to the west, however, this channel drains into the **Mababe Depression** via the **Savuti Channel** and, in very wet years, water from the Kwando has been known to drain into the Savuti Marsh in Botswana.

Community projects East Caprivi is seeing a rapid growth in communal area conservancy formation, giving communities more rights and responsibilities to manage the natural resources with which they co-exist. In order to develop respect for the national parks, the communities need to see that the park and tourism directly benefits them. Some initial opposition to game conservation came from farmers suffering crop damage by elephant and hippo, and loss of livestock by lion, leopard and crocodile, but it seems that poaching has been reduced as the problem animals become worth more to the community than the damage they cause. The principal income earners for communities are NACOBTA projects (see page 41) promoting arts and crafts and developing basic but well-positioned campsites (see Sleeping, below). Model villages, with displays of traditional crafts and rituals, have also proved popular, Lizauli village (see below) being one that has gained recognition. Additionally, funds are transferred to the community from a tourist bed levy; for example, every visitor to **Lianshulu Lodge** pays an additional US$3.50 per night, with monies jointly administered by local leaders and community-based conservation programmes.

Kongola and around ›› *Colour map 2, A5.*

At the eastern end of **Bwabwata National Park** the B8 crosses the Kwando River. This area was heavily manned during the fight for independence but game is gradually returning, particularly elephant, as it is an important migration route for water. **Namushasha Country Lodge** (see page 174) provides the best access into this underdeveloped region. It transports visitors by boat from the lodge to an open 4WD for game drives.

Kongola itself is little more than a petrol station, a few buildings and a series of signs advertising camps and lodges along the road to **Mudumu National Park** and **Mamili National Park**, two of Namibia's least developed parks. Both of these are set in beautiful countryside, and as with Bwabwata, both are just starting to see the return of wildlife which was displaced and killed during the war for independence and South African occupation.

At the B8/D3501 junction in Kongola, by the Engen petrol station, is the **Mashi Craft Market** ⓘ *T066-252108 or NACOBTA T061-255977, www.nacobta.com.na, May-Aug Mon-Fri 0900-1600, rest of the year Mon, Wed, Fri 0900-1600*. Opened in 1997 as a community project, it sells a range of traditional handicrafts from over 125 makers in 15 different parts of the Caprivi Region. As well as baskets and mats made from the *makalani* palm, there are interesting bracelets, earrings and other pieces of traditional jewellery. Considerable effort has been put into training the craftsmen and women, and there are now also annual competitions, with displays of the finest crafts at the **Omba Gallery** in Windhoek. By spending your money here you can be sure the benefits are going directly to the community.

Lizauli Village ⓘ *daily 0800-1700, US$4 per person, children under 9 free*, a short distance from **Lianshulu Lodge**, is a traditional village in appearance and layout, but one that has been constructed for the benefit of tourists. During the day a group of local people pass their time here waiting to show visitors around and explain a variety of traditional activities. One of the most comforting aspects of a visit here is that you do not feel like an intruder walking around private homes, neither does it have that theme park feel. The complete tour lasts at least an hour, after which you have ample opportunity to ask questions about all aspects of rural life. On a typical visit you will be shown a collection of household objects and how they are used, (including a crude but effective mousetrap), the girls will perform a couple of dances and the village blacksmith will demonstrate how the farm implements are forged. The tour finishes with the whole group acting out a village dispute with the elders being called upon to resolve the matter. This is an enjoyable introduction to a way of life far removed from that of the tourist from overseas.

Mudumu National Park ›› *Colour map 2, A5.*

Mudumu National Park's charm lies in its simplicity, with no residents, few visitors and increasing numbers of game. There are no accommodation options or facilities in the park, though there are some lodges and simple bush camps in the area. The best place to stay is the upmarket **Lianshulu Lodge** (see page 174) just to the south of the park, which is a special place. It is the first upmarket lodge in the area and a pioneer for tourism, conservation and community projects. The original owners have gone, but the charm of the bush, sensitively coupled with luxury, very much remains.

Ins and outs Just east of the Kwando River, turn south off the B8 by the Engen garage at Kongola, onto the D3501. After 35 km you will see a sign indicating the entrance to the park, marked also by the lack of subsistence farmers and land cleared for millet fields. It is 40 km from the B8 to the turning for **Lianshulu Lodge**.

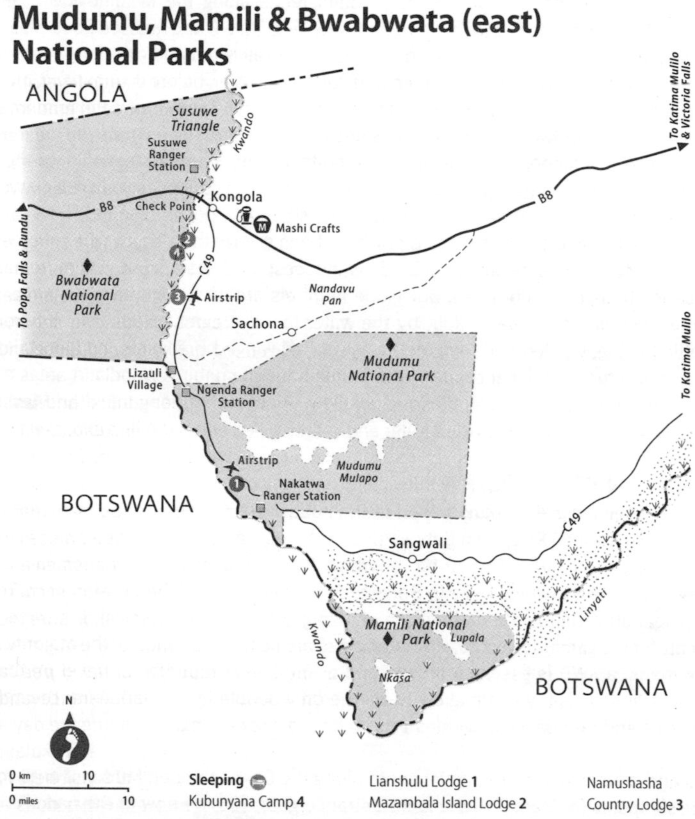

Background Mudumu National Park was proclaimed in 1990, just before independence, and measures over 100,000 ha. In the early 1960s, the Eastern Caprivi had the greatest concentration of wildlife in Namibia. Between 1974 and the early 1980s the region was managed as a private hunting concession and much of the game was shot out. Part of the independence process agreed that no pre-independence proclamations would be changed. While this might appear to be good news for the protection of wildlife in Mudumu and Mamili, it is worth noting that the creation of these two parks was against the will of the local people as there was no proper consultation with the villagers. Since independence, there has been a conscious effort to establish community-based conservation projects in the region, aiming to generate revenue for the local communities (see Community projects, page 168). At present the park remains a backwater as far as the MET (Ministry of Environment and Tourism) is concerned: there are no gates at the entrance to the park, and you are unlikely to meet anyone from the wildlife department (or indeed any human) as you drive along the few tracks in the park.

Before the park was proclaimed, **Lianshulu** obtained a concession to establish a lodge by the Kwando River. Today the lodge is very much associated with the park, although not for day-to-day management. **Lianshulu** continues to play an active role in getting the local community to benefit from tourism.

Vegetation and wildlife A large part of Mudumu is dominated by *mopane* woodland, interspersed with camelthorn, Natal mahogany, mangosteen and mixed acacia. Within the woods are depressions which become flooded after the rains. The western boundary of the park is marked by plentiful reeds along the Kwando River, and remnants of riverine forest (with woodland waterberry trees) and grassed flood plains. Soil is primarily kalahari sandveld with belts of clay and alluvium where the forest occurs.

The best game viewing is in winter, from June to October, before the heat and, more importantly, before the rain comes. After the rains, numerous ponds of water form away from the perennial Kwando and sightings become more rare. The animals you are most likely to see are hippo, crocodile, elephant, buffalo, kudu, impala, steenbok, warthog, Burchell's zebra, southern reedbuck, red lechwe, oribi and baboon. If you are lucky you may catch a glimpse of tsessebe, roan, sable, sitatunga, duiker, spotted hyena and lion. Leopard, cheetah and even wild dog have been seen in the area, but are extremely rare. Hunted out were giraffe, eland, wildebeest and waterbuck. There remain occasional poachers (for food), but game numbers are on the increase, regardless. Birders should be on the lookout by the water for slaty egret, rufous-bellied heron, wattled crane, wattled and long-toed plovers, red-winged pratincole, coppery-tailed coucal and the occasional coppery and purple-banded sunbird. Woodland areas are home to Bradfield's hornbill, mosque swallow, Anrot's chat, long-tailed and lesser blue-eared starlings, broad-billed roller and yellow-billed and red-billed oxpeckers.

Mamili National Park ›› *Colour map 2, A5.*

This is a seldom visited park tucked in the southwestern corner of Eastern Caprivi, across the Kwando River from Botswana. It is the only area of conserved swampland in the country, roughly 32,000 ha, of which 8% is underwater after good rains. It resembles the Okavango Delta in Botswana, but with none of the development. The principal attraction is the bird life (an amazing 430 recorded species), but there is plenty for the game viewer too. However, there are no facilities and, for the majority of the roads, a 4WD is essential (thick sand or mud, year round) – or travel on foot. Whenever you visit, you are likely to be the only people in the park. With the right vehicles and experience (ie guides!) it can be most rewarding.

Ins and outs From the B8, travel south along the D3501 through Mudumu until you see signposts for Mamili. There is no entrance gate, you are now in the park. As at

Mudumu, the MET has a very limited presence here, though there should be a ranger at the Shisinze Station, signposted off the D3501. You can continue via Linyandi (petrol sometimes available) to Katima Mulilo. Ask before attempting the drive; the road is not well or regularly maintained.

Remember, the water is in charge here, and the park is usually flooded between May and August, but this depends in part on how much rain has fallen upstream and what the level of water is in the local rivers (as mentioned above, the area has unusual hydrography); in years of good rains the two large islands, **Nkasa** and **Lupala**, are cut off from the main road for months. During the dry season these 'islands' become part of the picturesque undulating landscape. Henk Coetsee's 1998 *Tourist Map of the Caprivi Region* is recommended for its many maps and good descriptions of parks, roads, flora and fauna.

The park is only accessible by 4WD; whether dry or wet you will require experience to drive in such conditions. **Do not take risks**, if you get stuck it might be a long wait before help arrives. Rangers do patrol the park on the look-out for poachers and squatters, but if you have failed to report to the station it could be several days before you are found. There are no formal camping sites within the park.

Best time to visit Most rain falls between December and March, which is a good time for viewing birds, but the roads can be very slippery. After the rains there tends to be more wildlife in the park, but that's when most of the tracks are likely to be impassable.

Background Mamili was created at the same time as Mudumu. These are the only two protected areas in Eastern Caprivi, an area which 35 years ago had the richest concentration of wildlife in Namibia. While considerably smaller than Mudumu, it has plenty to reward the tourist and, after good rains, the park resembles the Okavango Delta in Botswana.

Wildlife The variety of animals you can expect to see is more or less the same as for Mudumu. The large area of swampland means that you are more likely to see the antelope which favour this environment – red lechwe, sitatunga and waterbuck. If you are lucky you may also see puku, another swamp antelope which is only found along the Chobe River and is quite rare. Unlike Mudumu, you may also come across giraffe in the woodlands. Overall, the game viewing in this park is unpredictable as a large proportion of the animals still migrate between Angola and Botswana. Poaching and hunting have also left their mark. During the dry season the park has a reputation for large herds of buffalo and migrant elephant. Lion and leopard also live in the park, but you are likely, at best, to see only their spoor.

Katima Mulilo and around ›› *Phone code: 066. Colour map 2, A6.*

Katima Mulilo, the regional capital of Caprivi, is an ugly town whose position on the banks of the Zambezi River is easy to forget once you're in town. Mimic a lodge owner and use it to replenish and refuel, and then enjoy the picturesque accommodation and plentiful water and land activities in the Eastern Caprivi, before moving on to the fabulous Chobe National Park in Botswana and the Victoria Falls from either Zimbabwe or Zambia. After you have reprovisioned and made plans for your evening's accommodation, make for the pontoon bar at the **Zambezi Lodge** (see page 174), sadly only open 1600-1900, for that beer you promised yourself way back in Rundu.

Ins and outs Between Kongola and Katima Mulilo the tarred B8 is in good condition. Katima Mulilo airport, served by **Air Namibia** flights, is about 20 km west of town; the Namibian Army's 2nd Battalion has a base and road checkpoint on the way. This was an important military base during the occupation by the South African army (the site is now used by the Namibian army); you can still see the remains of the mortar-proof parking shelters for the South African Air Force beside the runway. If you are arriving by air make sure you have arranged in advance to be collected by your lodge as there are no taxis or buses. There is a card telephone outside the terminal building and a kiosk selling cool drinks. The B8 splits at Katima Mulilo; the Zambezi River is straight ahead; a left turn takes you to Zambia (4 km), right goes through town, then on 57 km to the border with Botswana at Ngoma Bridge.

Your first stop as a tourist should be at **Tutwa Tourism and Travel** ⓘ *T066-252739, www.tutwa.com.na*, just before you reach the T-junction at the Zambezi where the B8 splits. It has numerous maps and is well informed about excursions and lodges, and will happily answer your Caprivi questions and sell you the odd curio. It can also arrange car hire, day trips, airport transfers and fishing excursions. If you haven't already decided what you are going to do in the region, head here.

Sights A visit to the Caprivi Arts Centre in the centre of Katima Mulilo, between the market and the hospital, is recommended. Crafts on offer include a variety of woven baskets, wooden carvings and clay pots, and are brought to the shop by villagers from the surrounding area. Some regional crafts, from neighbouring Zambia and Zimbabwe, are also available. Do the community a favour by picking up a bargain or two. Cold drinks are also for sale. Watch out for closing times, however, as the town is on Central African Time in winter (put simply, your watch will say 1600 when they close the doors at what for them is 1700). This is another **NACOBTA** project, www.nacobta.com.na.

The town has reasonable facilities including 24-hour garages, a post office, pharmacies, a **Bank Windhoek, Air Namibia** office, hardware stores, bottle stores and supermarkets, most of which are situated around a central square which is the centre of all activity.

Impalila Island ›› *Colour map 2, A6.*

At the eastern tip of Caprivi, by the confluence of the Chobe and Zambezi rivers, is the easternmost outpost of Namibia – Impalila Island. The island sits in the Kasai channel between the Zambezi and Chobe. At its eastern end is another small island, Kakumba, which lies opposite the Botswana town of Kazangula where Zimbabwe, Zambia, Botswana and Namibia all meet (officially in the middle of the great Zambezi).

Impalila Island and the banks of Botswana at Kasane are home to a number of upmarket lodges, which offer excellent boat excursions, and all have game drives into the remote riverbank area of Chobe National Park and the abundant game that drinks there. It's strange to think of these lodges as part of Namibia, but that's what their tax bill (if not their phone number) says. They are accessed by boat from Kasane in Botswana, which is 57 km from Ngoma via the tarred road through Chobe National Park, or by plane to the small airfields at Kasane and on the island. There are customs and immigration facilities on the island. In dry periods, with an exceptionally good 4WD and GPS, it is possible to reach Impalila Island overland, remaining within Namibia; an experienced guide is needed for this route. The aquatic attractions include superb **fishing** and **rapids** (Mombova and Chobe), as well as excursions up the Indibi River (western end) for game viewing in the papyrus fringed flood plain. There are several fine walking trails on Impalila Island which will take you past the local villages (picturesque but with associated cattle and rubbish). The stunning location of this island, with its abundant wildlife, tranquil rivers and beautiful lodges makes getting here well worth the effort. En route, if you have come by 4WD, it is certainly worth spending some time along the river in **Chobe National Park** ⓘ *www.botswana-tourism.gov.bw/attractions/chobe.*

Sleeping

Popa Falls *p162, map p163*
Along the D3430 between Popa Falls and Mahango Game Park is the following riverside accommodation. Light aircraft for any of these lodges use Bagani airstrip, close to the entrance to Popa Falls.

AL **Ndhovu Safari Lodge**, 17 km from the B8, well signposted, about 2 km down track towards the river, T066-259901, reservations@resdes.com.na. Luxury tented camp at a beautiful spot by the Okavango River. 7 en suite, fairly basic, thatched/canvas tents with twin beds and veranda, restaurant, bar, pool, shaded lawn. Lovely wooden deck built out on the river. The main attraction is Roy Vincent's knowledge and love of the area and the bush, he guides game walks and drives into the park and excursions along the river in his boat. Pricey, but recommended.

A **Mahangu Safari Lodge**, next door to Ndhovu (see above), T066-259037, www.mahangu.com.na. 5 thatched huts in a shaded, green spot by the river, very tidy, swimming pool with a view of the river, bar and restaurant, camping available, fishing trips can be arranged for US$18 per hr, maximum 3 people. A little overpriced for what you get and without the personal care of the more expensive lodges.

A **Suclabo Okavango Lodge**, well signposted, 6 km from the B8, 1 km off the D3430, T066-259005, www.suclabo.iway.na. 11 thatched, en suite bungalows with electricity, fan, veranda and river view. Swimming pool in nice shaded lawns, attractive central restaurant and bar, sundowner deck 10 m above the water for safe views of the hippos and crocs, fishing trips and boat cruises to the Popa Falls. Aimed at German tour groups, named after the owner, Suzzie, and her children Clara and Boris.

B **Popa Falls Rest Camp**, on the D3430 south of Divundu, reservations through Namibia Wildlife Resorts, Windhoek, T061-2857200, www.nwr.com.na. Standard thatched clean huts, fairly stylish in a 'natural' way, with 2-4 beds, bedding and gas lamps, communal field kitchen and ablutions.

E **Campsite**, green and picturesque, decent ablutions and bush kitchen, with the sound of the rapids to soothe weary drivers to sleep. Unlike the other Namibia Wildlife Resorts properties, Popa Falls charges per person at US$4.75 and not per site, so camping is cheaper than at most places especially for couples. Day visitors are permitted between sunrise and sunset. Facilities include a shop selling a fairly good range of basic foodstuffs, cold drinks, beer and some wine. Being this close to the river mosquitoes can be a problem – cover up in the evening and use plenty of insect repellent.

E **N//goabaca Campsite**, pronounced 'N (click) goabaca' and meaning 'boiling water', the Kxoe name for Popa Falls, just south of Divundu, 3 km off the D3430, look out for the sign 'campsite' on your left, a NACOBTA project, Windhoek T061-255977 www.nacobta.com.na. Basic but picturesque sites in a prime position on the eastern bank of the Okavango River, overlooking Popa Falls, with 4 large sites, lush and shaded by large riverine trees, grassed areas, flush toilets, hot showers, fireplace and reed chalet kitchens. Boat trips can be organized through the lodges on the western bank. Another local attraction is the Mushangara Rock Pools. If you are not keen on walking, there is good fishing (buy your tackle in Rundu) or birdwatching.

E **Ngepi Camp Site**, T/F066-259003, www.ngepicamp.com. Well signposted 12 km from the B8, 5 km from the D3430. Basic (no lights or electricity) campsite beautifully set by the Okavango River, grassed and well shaded, with hot showers, a central dining/*braai* area and lively bar. Traditional dances some evenings. Daytime activities include canoeing, fishing, boating or trips in a *mokoro*. Well-informed, friendly, young hosts, popular with overlanders, but large enough to combine the occasional party with privacy for the independent traveller. Recommended.

Crossing into Botswana *p165*

B **Drotsky's Cabins**, 11 km south of Shakawe, and then 2 km off the road, accessible by 2WD but drive carefully, T267- 675035. 6 chalets, campsite (E), restaurant and bar in a lovely location on stilts overlooking one of the Okavango Delta's channels. Little game around but an excellent spot for fishing and birdwatching.

B **Shakawe Lodge**, 15 km south of Shakawe, T267-660822. 10 chalets, overlooking the Okavango River, dining room and bar, swimming pool and campsite (E). Prince Harry stayed here in 2005.

For an explanation of the sleeping and eating price codes used in this guide, see inside the front cover. Other relevant information is found in Essentials, see pages 43-51.

Kongola and around *p168, map p169*

L **Lianshulu Lodge**, well signposted off the D3501, 40 km south of the B8, then a further 4 km to main lodge, 8 km to bush lodge, reservations T061-254317, www.lianshulu.com.na. Guests can fly to Katima Mulilo with **Air Namibia**, or by charter plane from Victoria Falls or Kasane, customs and immigration facilities are available at the lodge. Main lodge has 11 thatched en suite chalets, including 1 'honeymoon suite', all comfortable, tastefully decorated, with river views. Bush lodge has a further 6 chalets of similar style, and 2 honeymoon suites. Large, beautiful, central dining area, lounge and bar, swimming pool, attractive gardens by the river, protected from roaming elephants by an electric fence. The excursions, with informative guides, are the main attraction: walks, boat trips and game drives, including a night drive with liqueurs, are offered. To fully enjoy the activities, a stay of at least 2 nights is needed. Full board, swimming pool, game hide. Opened in the early 1990s and still regarded as one of the best lodges in the country. Recommended.

A **Mazambala Island Lodge**, signposted off the B8 2 km east of Kongola Bridge, 4 km to lodge, T066-250405, mazambala@mweb.com.na. Call ahead as 4WD may be necessary, particularly through floodwater. A rustic bush camp with 10 comfortable thatch-and-reed bungalows, the main lodge building with bar, lounge and restaurant is built on stilts with excellent views of the flood plain below, and there's an attractive thatched *lapa* built around a tree. Activities include canoe trips, walking trails, fishing or visits to local villages. **Campsite** (**E**) with toilets and hot showers.

A **Namushasha Country Lodge**, well signposted 20 km south of the B8 on the D3501, 4 km from turning, past its airstrip and a few large baobabs, central reservations Windhoek, T061-374750, www.namibialodges.com. 27 en suite doubles, nicely built of thatch and reed, set in shaded gardens by river, swimming pool, bar, buffet restaurant, power boat and open-top 4WD excursions in the Golden Triangle, short marked walking trail. Mixed feedback from visitors (although the Golden Triangle excursions are recommended); generally caters for German tour groups.

E **Kubunyana Camp**, turn off the D3501 7 km south of the B8, the camp is 4 km further on, a **NACOBTA** project, Windhoek T061-255977, www.nacobta.com.na. On the banks of a tributary of the Kwando River, the final few hundred metres to the site may be underwater, hoot your horn for help, access is possible by canoe (and there's a place above high water to park your car). A community campsite with 3 permanent double tents set up on thatched shaded structures, need to supply own bedding, decent communal ablutions with hot showers, plus 4 campsites with simple field kitchen. Note there is no electricity and you need to bring your own drinking water. Guided walks along the riverbank are available on request.

Katima Mulilo and around *p171, map p160*

There is a good selection of lodges in the Katima Mulilo area. Note that while the fishing is excellent, boat trips for game viewing are better in Kasane or Victoria Falls, assuming you are travelling in this direction, or **Lianshulu** (see page 174) or **Namushasha** (see above) lodges on the Kwando River – there is little wildlife on this wide stretch of the Zambezi.

A **Kalizo Lodge**, far from town, on sweep of the Zambezi: take the B8 for Ngoma Bridge for 18 km, then the D3508 signposted for Kalambesa, next signpost after 20 km, 5 km to the lodge (4WD needed after rain), T066-686802-3, www.natron.net/kalizo. 7 en suite rooms in A-frame, wood, reed and thatch chalets overlooking the river, plus 3 family self-catering cottages with 2-3 bedrooms, restaurant with excellent food, bar, shop, pool, plenty of river and riverbank activities including fishing for tiger fish and bream, sunset cruises to see hippo and crocs, and at certain times of the year elephants. Lovely riverside location, but rooms are perhaps a bit simple for the price. Campsite (**E**) with ablutions, *braai* spots and electric points.

B **Zambezi Lodge**, about 4 km east of town on the banks of the Zambezi to the north of the golf course, T066-253149, www.namibsunhotels.com.na. A fairly square 1970s-style hotel but with pleasant gardens and an excellent riverside location, including a floating moored pontoon bar, open daily 1600-1900. 26 en suite rooms with a/c, floodlit pool, restaurant with good evening set menu, bar, TV lounge. The adjacent golf course is pleasant for a morning or evening stroll (or jog). Note the small cemetery just outside the hotel gate, with its large headstone for the previous magistrate of the Caprivi, LEF Trollope. Grassed **campsite** (**E**) on the riverbank upstream from the main complex, adequate ablutions, some lights, security guards, campers can use the bars and restaurant at the lodge.

C **Caprivi River Lodge**, T066-252288, F253158. Signposted off the B8 for Ngoma, 6 km from town. Has 8 cosy and pretty thatched double chalets, en suite, with fridge, on request it will set up tents outside the chalets for children, shaded lawns, small pool, bar and dining area overlooking the river, lounge with TV and library. Excellent for activities: the owner is a keen kayaker and owns an enormous, ex-military 4WD truck. It offers interesting game drives to remote locations, particularly by the Chobe River.

F **Salambala**, at the Salambala Pan, about 50 km south of Katima Mulilo, off the B8, a signpost points to Salambala on the right on the way to the Ngoma Bridge border with Botswana. The track is sandy in patches but is suitable for ordinary vehicles, except during the rainy season (Oct-May) when it turns muddy and may only be accessible by 4WD. A **NACOBTA** project, Windhoek T061-255977, www.nacobta.com.na. 4 separate sites with room for 4 tents on each, each with its own wash block with hot water and flush toilet, *braai* area and simple camp kitchen. A short walk takes you to **Salambala Pan** and a hide for viewing the regular elephant and small game that come to drink and bathe here. Water is pumped in when it gets low, but it looks as though the local farmers are bringing their cattle to drink here, so they may be putting the game off.

Impalila Island *p172, map p160*

Accommodation here is only at the very top end of the market.

L **Ichingo Chobe River Lodge**, exchange in Botswana T+267-6250143, www.ichingo.com. 8 luxury tents with open-air bathrooms and balcony and tastefully decorated. Attractive dining room serving gourmet food, lounge and bar, boat trips for river fishing or cruising, whitewater canoeing or *mokoro* trips into the Caprivi flood plain recommended, walks around the island, fly fishing for tiger fish and bream, excellent game viewing and birdwatching with over 400 species of birds in the area including the very rare African finfoot. Every visitor will leave feeling most privileged, a beautiful spot.

L **Impalila Island Lodge**, reservations in South Africa T/F+2711-7067207, www.islandsinafrica.com. 8 en suite chalets overlooking the Mombova Rapids, swimming pool, craft shop, lounge, small library. The centrepiece of the dining area which is built around 2 large baobab trees. Elevated bar above the river, with the roar of the rapids in the background. Activities include trips in dug-out canoes, sunset game cruises and tiger fishing. An excellent lodge in a most exclusive location. Closed Feb.

Nearby islands

L **Ntwala Island Lodge**, reservations in South Africa T/F+2711-7067207, www.islandsinafrica.com. This is located on Ntwala Island in the Mombova Rapids at the confluence of the Zambezi and Chobe rivers just to the south of Kongola. Ultra luxurious with only 4 suites with private plunge pools, bath, indoor and outdoor shower. Each of the suites has its own boat and guide for game cruises. The main building has a walk-in wine cellar and sort of sunken kitchen where guests can interact with the chef. Very exclusive and expensive at over US$500 per person per night, but a lovely isolated spot, the island has little white-sand beaches and palm trees.

L **Susuwe Lodge**, reservations in South Africa T/F+2711-7067207, www.islandsinafrica.com. On an island in the Kwando River, guests arrive by boat. 6 beautiful, spacious en suite doubles with plunge pool and balcony overlooking the river, central lounge and dining area, library, curio shop, rates include full board, 4WD and boat excursions and guided walks. Candlelit dinners and bush brunches give guests luxury literally in the middle of nowhere.

AL **Zambezi Queen & King's Den Lodge**, T/F066-253203 (Namibia), T/F+267 62-50814 (Botswana), www.namibsunhotels.com.na. Located on the Namibian side of the Chobe River opposite Kasane, the lodge has 10 wooden en suite chalets with balcony right on the river and individually carved African motifs on much of the furniture, restaurant, bar, shaded lawns, price is full board, river activities included; trips to Chobe National Park can be arranged. The huge riverboat, the *Zambezi Queen* (which is sadly too big to navigate the river in anything but highest flood season) is moored at the lodge and offers alternative, luxurious (but fairly small) cabins as overflow accommodation.

Eating

Katima Mulilo and around *p171, map p160*
Mad Dog Mcgee's, down a side street between the **Zambezi Lodge** and the centre of town. If not eating at the lodge, then this is your best bet for dinner in town, which can get quite colourful once the beer has been flowing. Bar, pool tables, wide range of tasty steaks and burgers, though vegetarians may have an uninspired choice here. Open daily except Sun for lunch and dinner.
Zambezi Lodge, see Sleeping, above. Reasonable restaurant with a good choice though mainly aimed at satisfying tour groups with buffet meals, the highlight here is an early evening drink on the pontoon bar that juts out into the river.

Activities and tours

Katima Mulilo and around *p171, map p160*
Fishing The Zambezi is popular for fishing – bring all your tackle with you (Rundu is the nearest town with a decent range of gear). The rivers support good populations of tiger fish, bream, nembwe and barbel. Boats can be organized at any of the lodges, or through Tutwa Tourism and Travel, see page 172.

Shopping

Katima Mulilo and around *p171, map p160*
Most shops are around the central square. The **Caprivi Arts Centre** is next to the open market, which stocks the fairly broad range of carvings, decorated earthenware, weaving and simple jewellery made in the region. In the last few years, training has been provided, and quality is now reliably good. The arts centre is responsible for the marketing and sale of crafts, with revenue going straight to the craftsman or woman; it is certainly worth a browse for souvenirs. You'll smell the **market** next door, which has limited stock, but you might find seasonal fruit and veg or, in the clothing section, perhaps a colourful *shitenge* (wrap-around skirt).

Transport

Katima Mulilo and around *p171, map p160*
1361 km to Windhoek, 660 km to Rundu, 1485 km to Swakopmund, 3340 km to Johannesburg. The Katima Mulilo area is an ideal stopping place on the way to or from Zambia, Botswana and the rest of Namibia with good accommodation and places to eat. Lifts for hitch-hikers can be arranged near the Shell fuel station.

Air Air Namibia, office in the main square, airport 20 km southwest of town off the B8. There is 1 flight a day between Katima Mulilo and **Windhoek's Eros Airport** in each direction except Sat, see timetable on page 72. There is nothing to see or do at the airport except to sit on incredibly uncomfortable wood and brick seats.

Bus For Intercape Mainliner coaches bound for **Windhoek** or **Victoria Falls**, see timetable on page 70; picks up by the Engen station.

Directory

Katima Mulilo and around *p171, map p160*
Banks Bank Windhoek, Mon-Fri 0900-1530, Sat 0800-1000, with efficient a/c, 2 ATMs (often busy). Buy your ZAR, Botswanan pula (for use at the border) and US$ for use in Victoria Falls/Zimbabwe here. If you are heading for Botswana then it is a good idea to buy some pula here since the officials at the Ngoma Bridge border will not accept Namibian dollars (ZAR, US$ are fine); otherwise the nearest bank in Botswana is 54 km away in Kasane. If you have just entered Namibia the next banking facilities are in Rundu and then Grootfontein.
Medical services Hospital, T066-253012.
Police Police station, T066-253060, T10111 (emergency), at the *boma*, an area of government offices on the B8 towards Ngoma Bridge.

The Northwest & the Far North

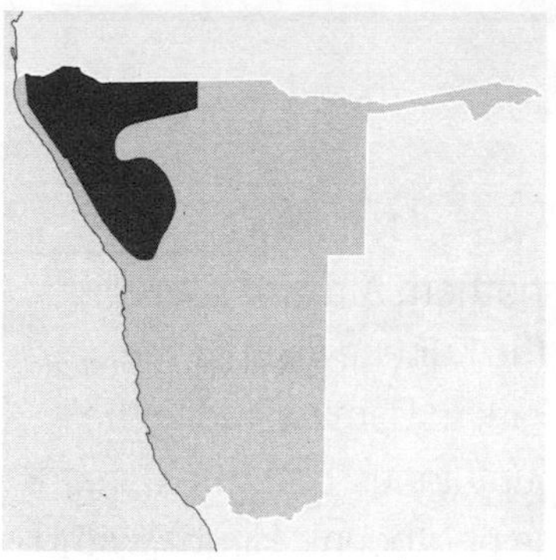

Footprint features

Introduction

Kaokoland, in the extreme northwest of Namibia, is one of the last true wilderness areas in southern Africa. It is a region with stunning landscapes. From the Kunene River to the north, down the Skeleton Coast Park to Damaraland in the south, the area is rugged and mountainous. Both the Damara, with their clicking tongue, and the photogenic Himba, with their ochre-skinned beauty, live in simple villages, mostly subsisting as goat and cattle herders. Namibia's best-known rock art is located in the hills of Damaraland, which also offer some excellent hiking.

In the very north, the Kunene River flows sedately to the sea from the Ruacana Falls hydroelectric power station. For 300 km, this forms the peaceful border with Angola, and offers watersport enthusiasts one- to five-day whitewater canoeing and rafting excursions. The 32-m Epupa Falls are roughly half way to the Atlantic, a beautiful rift in the rock, dotted with precariously perched giant baobab trees and bathed in glorious palm-fringed sunsets. While the game was mostly shot out before independence, there is plenty to entice birders and fishermen. The area is often inaccessible to saloon cars, preserving Kaokoland as a world unto itself. It offers a glimpse into the past, while at the same time being on the verge of massive and fundamental change.

The Far North, or Owamboland, is a dusty, overgrazed, overpopulated area with few attractions for most tourists. However, for those with the time and energy, there is plenty to discover. The towns are an interesting mix of urban and traditional tempered with a vibrant Portuguese/Angolan influence. Out of town, the landscape is dominated by the fascinating geography and agronomy of the *oshanas*, on which so many rely.

★ Don't miss...

1. **Damaraland** Scour the scenic back roads on the hunt for the elusive desert elephant and black rhino, page 180.
2. **Rock art** Dip into this little-known world in some magical locations, especially Twyfelfontein and Spitzkoppe, page 182.
3. **Himba people** Take a sensitively run tour with a local guide to meet this intriguing people, famous for their nomadic lifestyles and striking appearance in the thirstlands of the Far North, page 193.
4. **Epupa Falls** Watch the river tumbling over a dramatic series of boulders, page 201.
5. **Marienfluss and Hartmann's valleys** Intrepid drivers can explore the wastelands and tortured rock of these remote valleys, along the impossibly dramatic and most difficult roads in the country, page 202.
6. **Kunene River** Float down the river on a raft or canoe; many of the northern lodges can organize a trip between Namibia and Angola, page 212.

Damaraland

This sparsely populated region is a highland desert wilderness, home to uniquely adapted animal species such as the desert elephant and the last free roaming black rhinos in the world. Damaraland covers the southern half of the Kaokoveld, the area of northwest Namibia, and together with Kaokoland forms what is now deemed the Kunene political region. A huge area stretching almost 600 km north to south and 200 km east to west, Damaraland is bordered by the Hoanib River to the north, the tar road to Swakopmund to the south and Etosha and the Skeleton Coast to the east and

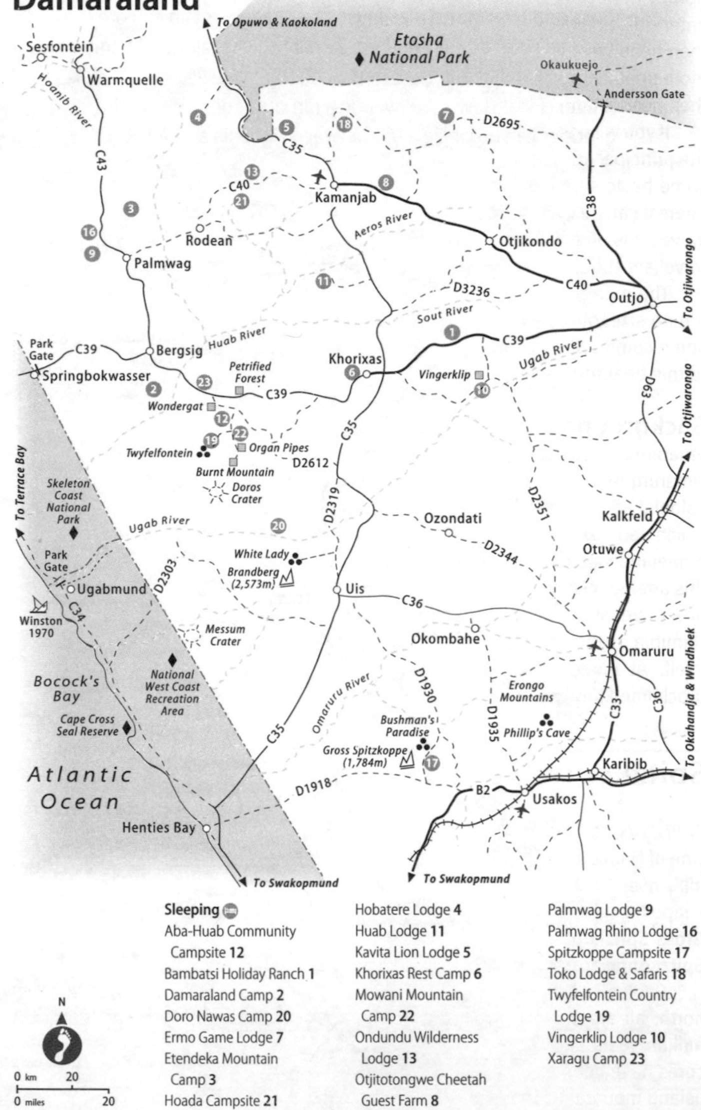

west. The region encompasses some of Namibia's most dramatic natural features such as the Spitzkoppe and Brandberg mountain ranges, which dominate Southern Damaraland and are particularly impressive because they rise out of the flat gravel plains. Both have given rise to community campsites bringing very welcome income to the inhabitants of the drought-affected region. Heading north, the plains give way to rolling hills, dissected by numerous seasonal rivers. Also well suited for exploration on foot with local guides are the Petrified Forest, west of Khorixas, Burnt Mountain, and Organ Pipes near Twyfelfontein, site of Namibia's largest collection of Bushman rock art. ▸▸ *For Sleeping, Eating and other listings, see pages 187-192.*

Ins and outs

Damaraland can be approached from a number of directions. If you headed north from Windhoek and made Etosha National Park your first stop you would be likely to enter via Kamanjab. Another option is to visit a guest farm in the Omaruru Region and then head west into the heart of Damaraland. The following text follows one of the more popular routes, which is to head north out of Swakopmund to Henties Bay and then head inland to either Spitzkoppe (D1918), or via the C35 to Uis.

If you wish to stay at the communal campsites, which tend to be located close to the principal attractions, you will need to have a degree of self-sufficiency and carry some basic supplies, crockery and a sleeping bag. In Damaraland most places of interest can be visited in a saloon car but since virtually all the roads in the region are gravel, it is preferable to have a 4WD. Because of the remoteness and lack of traffic, travellers should carry spare fuel, water and food when travelling in Damaraland.

The majority of Damaras are engaged in subsistence livestock farming. There are no sizeable towns in the region, however a network of lodges and campsites, some community-run, provide comfortable and scenic accommodation for visitors to this beautiful region.

Background

Inhabited for centuries by the Damara people, the area around Okombahe (between Omaruru and Uis) was first proclaimed a 'reserve' for the Damara by the German colonial administration in 1906. Following the Odendaal Commission report in 1964, which led to the creation of Bantustans in Namibia, a separate Damara tribal homeland was proclaimed in this region. Further acts in 1968 and 1969 cemented this arrangement and, in 1971, a Damara Advisory Council was formed. This was part of an overall strategy on the part of the South African government to incorporate Namibia as the country's fifth province and mirrored similar policies in South Africa itself. At independence in 1990, Damaraland was incorporated into the newly proclaimed Kunene Region.

Spitzkoppe

▸▸ *pp187-192. Colour map 1, C4.*

ⓘ *Visitors are charged US$4.50 per person, US$0.80 per car, for entering the area.* One of Namibia's most recognizable landmarks, the 1784-m Spitzkoppe, or 'pointed hill', rises some 700 m above the surrounding plain. The mountain's distinctive shape has given rise to its nickname as the Matterhorn of Africa. The main peak, or **Gross Spitzkoppe**, is one of three mountains in the area, the others being the **Klein Spitzkoppe** at 1572 m and the dome-shaped **Pondok Mountain**.

Geologically, these three mountains are grouped with the Brandberg range to the north; all are ancient volcanoes. The violent break up of Gondwanaland 500-750 million years ago caused explosive activity through these volcanoes; their granite cores have been exposed by millions of years of erosion, creating the **inselbergs** or 'island mountains' that we see today.

The northwest face of Spitzkoppe was first climbed in 1946, the west face in 1960, and today the mountain still attracts climbers. Tourists and students are drawn by a number of Bushman paintings – the best known found at **Bushman's Paradise**. The area is also a great place to hike, camp and enjoy the clear desert air and fine views.

Getting there Turn off the B2 onto the D1918, 23 km west of Usakos. Turn right almost immediately onto the D1930 for 19 km, and left onto the D3716 for 13 km. It's well signposted. Actually in the Erongo Region politically, Spitzkoppe is geologically linked to the mountains further north in Damaraland. The gravel roads are suitable for ordinary vehicles.

Rock art

After checking in at the gate and gathering a map (and possibly a guide), make the short but steep hike from Pondok to Bushman's Paradise; the smooth, precipitous slopes are rendered easily accessible by a well-positioned chain. At the top is a richly vegetated natural amphitheatre and large overhang which protects the paintings from the elements, but unfortunately not the vandals. There are still interesting paintings and the views of the surrounding countryside make the climb worthwhile. Local guides will be able to take visitors to the sites of Bushman paintings, in particular the **Golden Snake** and **Small Bushman's Paradise**.

Brandberg – the White Lady

» *pp187-192. Colour map 1, B3.*

The immense Brandberg Massif lies south of the Ugab River about 40 km northwest of Uis. It has Namibia's highest peak, Konigstein, at 2573 m and is the site of one of Namibia's most intriguing pieces of Bushman art – the so-called White Lady. Like the Burnt Mountain further north, the Brandberg owes its name to its striking colouring, particularly vivid at sunset. Getting to the paintings involves an energetic hike up a well-marked track from the car park at the end of the D2359. You must be accompanied by a guide and depending on your level of fitness the walk to the White Lady will take 30 to 60 minutes. Wear a hat and decent walking shoes and take water with you. The relative cool of early morning and late afternoon is the best time to make this walk.

Getting there From Uis take the C35 north for 14 km then turn west onto D2359 for a further 28 km. You will find the Dâureb Mountain Guides' office at the foot of the mountain. It is part of NACOBTA (see box, page 41), T064-504202, www.nacobta.com.na.

In Khoekhoegowab, the language of the Dama and Nama people, dâureb *means 'the burning mountain'. The Germans translated the name into Brandberg.*

Enjoy the walk up the Tsisab Ravine: the Damara guides are well informed about local fauna and flora, and will happily answer questions and show off their clicking prowess should you be interested in learning a few simple greetings in their language. There is plenty of bird life, but the chance of seeing klipspringer, mountain zebra and the other indigenous mammals is small due to the number of visitors to the valley. The site of the White Lady is protected by some rather unsightly iron railings, made necessary by previous visitors throwing water on the paintings to make them stand out more clearly – at the same time eroding them. Again, the guides are well briefed on what is known of the paintings, although you should not expect a masterful thesis on rock art. While most people are content to turn back at this point, the guides will happily lead the adventurous over boulders to the other more remote and less famous paintings and there are a number of tours on offer including archaeological tours and the three-day-trek to Königstein which is the top of the Brandberg.

The White Lady

The White Lady is the best known of a number of Bushman paintings situated in a 1.5 km radius of each other in the Tsisab Ravine. The first paintings in the area were 'discovered' in 1909 by a German soldier, Hugo Jochmann, however, the White Lady itself was only found in 1918 following a successful ascent of the Königstein peak by three friends, Reinard Mack, A Griess and George Schultz.

Initially the paintings were believed to have been influenced by early Mediterranean art, mainly due to their superficial resemblance to early Cretan art, but also as a result of contemporary European belief that nothing original could possibly have originated from southern Africa. The main authority on rock art at the time, Abb, Henri Breuil, was shown a watercolour of the White Lady at a science congress in Johannesburg in 1929, and concluded that the principal figure in the painting was a woman of European origin. This theory came to be widely accepted. More recently, however, after detailed further research, it has been concluded that the painting is indeed of local origin, most likely the work of Bushmen. In fact, the White Lady is no longer believed to be a woman at all, rather it is thought that the figure is actually a man, probably a shaman or medicine man daubed with white body paint.

Tours

Guides have completed first-aid training and there is a permanent radio link between the office at the mountain and the information office in Uis. **White Lady Tour** (1½ hours, US$4 per person), the shortest of the four tours on offer and relatively easy; **Highlights Tour** (two hours, US$5 per person) which, in addition to the White Lady, goes to other sites in the area; **Archaeology/Geology Tour** (three hours, US$6 per person), similar to the Highlights Tour but with more information about Namibia's archaeological history; **Königstein** (three days, US$33 per person per day, discounts for groups). This tour has to be booked in advance and participants have to be physically fit and must not suffer from vertigo. You'll need good hiking boots, a sleeping bag and precooked food and drinks. The guides take you to the top of Brandberg and the climb is fairly intense. A porter can be taken to carry gear if required. Book via the NACOBTA office in Uis or Windhoek or send an email through the website.

Uis

pp187-192. Phone code: 064. Colour map 1, C4. 128 km from Henties Bay, 121 km from Omaruru.

Uis was once an important tin mining town, but since the principal mine closed in 1990, the town has dwindled to a forlorn shadow of its former self. Tourism is replacing tin as the mainstay of the economy; there are a couple of new places to stay in town, and a fabulous new campsite in the Ugab riverbed just off the road to the White Lady.

Although small-scale tin mining has taken place in the area since the first half of the 20th century, it was not until 1951 that a full-scale mining operation started. In 1958 the South African mining giant ISCOR took over the mining rights and built the town, which flourished until the mine's closure shortly after independence. Today local miners, with overseas donor assistance, are once again mining tin, tantalite and tourmaline on a small scale.

When entering town on the C35 or C36 you will immediately see the natural stone building at the little road-triangle on the main road into town. This is the **Uis Tourist**

 Centre ⓘ *T064-504162, open daily*, where there are displays about the former mining town's history, the surrounding area as well as the flora and fauna. You can pick up information on accommodation facilities and activities in the region. The office of the **Dâureb Mountain Guides** is located in the same building (see under Brandberg above), as is **Vicky's Coffee Shop** (see Eating), an internet café, and the **Dâureb Crafts shop** (see under Shopping). This very useful stop is another NACOBTA project.

Getting there From Swakopmund, either head up the coast via Henties Bay and take the C35 or take the B2 towards Usakos and branch north on the D1918 and D1930. Both are well signposted. From the north or east, take the C35 either to or from Omaruru and Khorixas. The gravel roads are all a little windy in places but in good condition.

Numas Ravine

Located on the southern side of the Brandberg, Numas Ravine is the site of numerous rock paintings believed to be the work of Stone Age inhabitants. Visiting the art is best done as part of a multiple-day hike, carrying all your provisions and with a local guide. Ask at the office for information on best current routes and guides. There are also a number of 4WD routes in the region, and you can pick up GPS coordinates at the tourist office.

Khorixas

» *pp187-192. Phone code: 067. Colour map 1, B4.*

There are no tourist attractions in Khorixas. It is the administrative centre of the Kunene Region and capital of Damaraland, but in truth, it is hard to see much evidence of this. There is a reasonable lodge and campsite run by **Namibia Wildlife Resorts,** the only bank in the whole of the Kunene Region (**Standard,** with ATM), a 24-hour garage, bakery, butchers, supermarket, small craft market and post office. Curio hawkers and beggars regularly pester tourists as they fill up with fuel; it's better to buy your curios at the craft market, or at the Petrified Forest further west.

The town lies just west of the junction between the C39 from Outjo and the C35 between Kamanjab and Uis. The intrepid can reach here from Palmwag in Kaokoland via the C43 and then the C39, or from Torra Bay on the coast via the C39.

West of Khorixas

» *pp187-192.*

Ins and outs

The C39 winds its way through the mountains, following the Aba-Huab Valley into the picturesque heart of Damaraland. If you are lucky, you might catch a glimpse of the desert elephants along the dry river course (and there is usually spoor to be seen on the road). During the heat of the day the beasts tend to remain in the shade of the large trees.

Most tourists are heading for the stunning rock formation and plentiful rock engravings at Twyfelfontein. There are also unusual geological formations of the Petrified Forest, the Organ Pipes and Burnt Mountain. The Wondergat is a little more difficult to find and most organized tours will not bother to stop here. While Twyfelfontein, Organ Pipes, Burnt Mountain and Wondergat are often grouped together (they lie within a few kilometres of each other), it is the paintings, the walk and the geology of Twyfelfontein that are far and away the most interesting attractions in the area. If pushed for time, ignore the other sites and focus your attention on just Twyfelfontein.

From Khorixas, take the C39. The Petrified Forest is well signposted after about 60 km, with a large thatched information hut, plenty of locals and a kiosk selling cold drinks. Continue for a further 15 km and turn left on to the D2612 for Twyfelfontein, clearly signposted. If coming from Uis, head north on the C35 for 58 km, turn left on the D2612, again Twyfelfontein is clearly marked. The D2612 is not very suitable for ordinary vehicles as it may have sandy patches which are difficult to negotiate, especially after rainfall. From either direction you will turn south onto the D3254 and, before you reach any of the attractions, pass the community campsite by the Aba-Huab River (see Sleeping for details). If you are not planning to spend the night at Twyfelfontein, or in Damaraland at least, make sure you start early, as the road needs careful, slow driving, and the distance is considerable.

For 'inner' Damaraland, return to the C39 and continue west. You will pass a sign for the exclusive and highly regarded **Damaraland Camp**, before either heading north towards Palmwag or continuing west on the C39 for 92 km to Torra Bay, via the Spingbokwasser checkpoint. At Palmwag you have the choice of heading north to Sesfontein and Kaokoland, or joining the C40 as it loops east to Kamanjab.

Petrified Forest ›› *Colour map 1, B3.*

ⓘ *There is no entrance fee, instead visitors are obliged to sign the book in the office and to engage the services of a local guide (US$6, tips welcomed), some better than others, to show them around.*

Declared a national monument in 1950, the Petrified Forest lies on a sandstone rise in the Aba-Huab Valley, affording a fine view of the surrounding countryside. Around 50 fossilized trees reckoned to be 260 million years old lie scattered over an area roughly 800 m by 300 m, some of them so perfectly preserved that it is hard to believe that they aren't still alive. The absence of roots and branches suggests that the trees in the Petrified Forest do not originate from this area, rather that they were carried here by floodwaters resulting from retreating glaciers. After being deposited here the logs were saturated with silica-rich water which penetrated the cells of the trees, gradually causing petrification.

Better light and cooler temperatures mean that early morning and late afternoon are probably the best times to visit, if you are able to stay in the area.

The largest trees here measure more than 30 m in length with a circumference of 6 m and belong to a type of cone-bearing plant which flourished between 300 and 200 million years ago. Still alive, scattered among the fallen trees, are some fine examples of *welwitschia mirabilis*, ancient-looking, desert-dwelling plants, some of which are over 1000 years old.

The Petrified Forest is 58 km west of Khorixas on the C39. Beware the many 'false' forests set up by entrepreneurial locals, especially the 'All New Petrified Forest' further up the road! The real one has a large Namibian tourism brown signpost leading off the road. At the entrance are a pile of rocks that might interest the geologist or souvenir hunter, and a few locally made, low-quality crafts.

Twyfelfontein ›› *Colour map 1, B3. 90 km from Khorixas.*

ⓘ *US$4.50 including guided tour, US$0.80 per car. There are a couple of shaded parking places, toilets (fed by water from the original spring), some local curios and a small kiosk. Any money spent here will go back into the local community.*

Early inhabitants of the area must have been attracted to the valley by the small freshwater spring on the hillside and by the game grazing in the valley below. There is evidence of habitation over 5000 years ago. The Damara who lived here named the valley **Uri-Ais** or 'jumping fountain' after this source of freshwater. However, it was renamed Twyfelfontein or 'doubtful fountain' in 1947 by the first white farmer to acquire the land; he considered the fountain too weak to support much life.

The site was declared a national monument in 1952, but sadly this did not prevent many of the engravings being defaced or stolen, and local Damaras are now employed as guides (again through NACOBTA) to protect the rocks and inform visitors. The Namibian government is currently pushing for Twyfelfontein to be declared a UNESCO World Heritage Site, which will grant it further protection.

Over 2500 engravings cut into the rockface of the huge boulders strewn around have been identified. These engravings have been categorized into six phases ranging in age from around 300 BC to as recent as the 19th century. The majority of the engravings depict a wide range of game species, including elephant, rhino, lion and various antelopes. There are, interestingly, far fewer depictions of human figures.

Although experts believe that rock paintings and engravings featured in ceremonies intended to imbue the hunters with the power to catch game, the picture of a seal on one of the rocks is particularly interesting considering that this site is over 100 km from the sea. This suggests that some engravings may literally have been items in a gallery of game the Bushmen were familiar with.

There is a long loop trail which visitors can follow, again a guide must be employed. The trail takes a leisurely two hours to complete; it is advisable to wear a hat, stout shoes and to carry water with you. Before embarking on the trail, it is worth spending a moment looking at the display by the car park. This outlines the geological and archaeological history of the area. There is also a plan of the trail showing where the principal engravings are to be found. Even if you are not especially interested in rock art, Twyfelfontein is still a fantastic place to come and watch the sunset, whilst imagining what life must have been like for earliest inhabitants of the area.

Organ Pipes » *Colour map 1, B3.*

For many visitors the Organ Pipes and Burnt Mountain are of only passing interest, however, for anyone interested in the early history of the earth and its geology, they are fascinating glimpses into the past. The Organ Pipes are a series of perpendicular dolerite columns set at the bottom of a shallow gorge 3 km after the turn-off onto the D3254. These elegant rocks, some up to 5 m long, were formed 120 million years ago when the cooling dolerite split into distinct columns which form the pipes we see today. The easiest way to approach the site is to drive past the small (unsignposted) car park and turn left up a sandy riverbed a little further on. From here you can walk along the riverbed to the pipes without having to scramble down from above.

Burnt Mountain » *Colour map 1, B3.*

The Burnt Mountain or Verbrandeberge is at the end of the D3214, a section of a 12-km-long mountain rising some 100 m above the plain. During the daytime the mountain is bleak and uninviting, however, the distinctive colouring of the rocks appears at sunrise and sunset when the imaginative might contest that the mountain is 'on fire'. The rocks are dolerite and are believed to have been formed over 130 million years ago as a result of volcanic activity.

Wondergat » *Colour map 1, B3.*

The Wondergat, set down a short track off the D3254, 3 km before reaching Aba-Huab campsite, offers an interesting view into the bowels of the earth. The hole is believed to have been created when a subterranean river washed away a chunk of earth. Its depth is still unknown – a team of divers turned back due to lack of oxygen at 100 m, without reaching the bottom.

! There are no signposts or safety barriers, so be careful near the edge.

East of Khorixas

» *pp187-192.*

Also known as the **Kalk Kegel** or 'limestone skittle', the Vingerklip is a 35-m-high limestone rock sitting on a 44-m circumference base. This unusual landmark was formed by erosion of the Ugab River flood plain over a period of 30 million years. There is no fee to explore the site, and there are numerous walks that offer different

Desert elephants

Namibia's desert-adapted elephants have a range that covers 3000 sq km in the north of the country with the elephants trekking up to 200 km in search of water. They have extra long legs that can carry them 70 km in a day. On average normal elephants drink about 100-200 litres of water a day, but desert elephants drink about this amount only every three to four days. During severe drought they use their trunks, feet and tusks to dig narrow holes in the dry riverbeds in search of water. They obviously are aware of the scarcity of food in the arid region, as unlike other elephants, when feeding they hardly ever fell trees, break fewer branches and strip the bark off trees far less than other elephants.

angles to view the unusual skittle. Perhaps the best is from the **Vingerklip Lodge** itself, which will provide the heat-sapped day visitor with a meal or snack and even a swim in one of its pools. The **Ugab Terrace** is visible all along the valley and offers good hiking opportunities. Ask at the lodge for route information. To get there, take the C39 east for 54 km from Khorixas, turn south on D2743 for 22 km.

Northern Damaraland » *pp187-192.*

Loosely defined as the lands to the north of the Huab River, the landscape of northern Damaraland rolls beautifully, with small settlements dotted throughout the flat-topped mountains and valleys. There are plentiful, freely roaming springbok and isolated herds of goats and their goatherds. The authorities have tried to embrace eco-tourism and get maximum return for minimum damage by granting concessions to a few private lodges. To fully appreciate the expertise and knowledge of the local guides, aim to spend at least two nights at any one of the lodges. At **Kamanjab** there is 24-hour petrol, a bakery, supermarket, post office and police station; if heading north, fill up with fuel and provisions since this is the last source before reaching Opuwo or Ruacana. The only place to stay in town is the small but pleasant **Oase Garni Hotel**, which is also your best bet for food.

From **Palmwag**, the C43 continues north towards Sesfontein and into Kaokoland. Ask ahead about road conditions before heading north in a saloon car. This is the border between Damaraland and Kaokoland and travel north of here is preferably undertaken in a 4WD, with a minimum of two vehicles (see page 193). Assuming road conditions allow, continue to **Sesfontein** and call in at the spring at **Warmquelle** (see page 197). Otherwise, take the C40 towards **Kamanjab**. From Kamanjab there is a good tarred road all the way to **Etosha National Park** (see page 135).

Sleeping

Spitzkoppe *p181*

C-E Spitzkoppe Campsite, at the foot of the mountain, now run by NACOBTA, T064-530879, www.nacobta.com.na. Basic bungalows with outside showers and toilets. Bedding is supplied, and there are several secluded campsites around the mountain, in stunning locations amongst the rocks, with *braai* facilities and pit latrines. Bring water and firewood, these are scarce but can usually be bought at reception on arrival if you are without. You can join guided walks to some of the numerous rock art sites or go for hikes on and around the mountain. If you are an experienced rock-climber you might want to attempt the summit (bring your own gear). Donkey-cart rides are available on request. There's a simple bar for cold drinks and a restaurant, which is open for breakfast, lunch and dinner, set meals are cheap but must be booked in advance.

Brandberg – the White Lady *p182*
L **Doro Nawas Camp**, www.wilderness-safaris.com. Brand new luxury camp which was opening during the writing of the book so we have not been able to visit. On the edge of the dry Aba-Haub riverbed, 16 natural walled units, with outdoor showers and verandas where you can also sleep. There's a bar, indoor and outdoor dining areas, swimming pool, small art gallery, some of the fees go towards the empowerment of the local community.

Uis *p183*
A **Haus Lizenstein**, 15 4th Av, T064-504052, www.lizenstein-uis.com. 8 doubles in a detached bungalow, which are clean and reasonably decorated, though a bit frilly and overpriced, B&B, TV lounge, *braai* area, waterhole that attracts birds. **E** camping facilities available for US$7 per person.
B **White Lady**, T/F064-504102, whitelady@iway.na. A long, thatched bungalow with 6 spacious en suite doubles (B&B) with fridge and tea- and coffee-making facilities. There is a large *braai* area, *lapa* and swimming pool, the best rooms in town. **Campers** are welcome (E) at a site behind the main building with adequate ablutions, a separate splash pool and *braai* facilities. There's also a small waterhole at the campsite that attracts a number of birds.
C **Brandberg Rest Camp**, T/F-064-504038, brandberg@africaonline.com.na. 4-bed self-catering flats and doubles, all en suite but with an institutional feel, restaurant, bar, swimming pool. **Camping** (E) with electricity also available. Can arrange tours of the nearby mines and mineral-rich areas, notice required. It offers internet access, and is your best bet for getting to Spitzkoppe or Brandberg if you have no transportation of your own.

Khorixas *p184*
The **Khorixas Rest Camp** is the only place to stay in town and is a pleasant enough place. For those on their way to Twyfelfontein, the **Twyfelfontein Country Lodge, Mowani Mountain Camp** or **Aba-Huab Campsite** are much better options (see below). So, too, is the luxurious **Huab Lodge**, situated between Khorixas and Kamanjab (details under Kamanjab, see page 189).
C-D **Khorixas Rest Camp**, 1 km north of town, T067-331111, www.nwr.com.na. Well signposted on your way west. 38 en suite, a/c but plain bungalows, some with kitchens, set in green gardens with large swimming pool, restaurant and bar with large lounge, pool table and TV, small food/curio shop, plus a dusty campsite with communal facilities.

West of Khorixas *p184*
AL **Mowani Mountain Camp**, signposted off the D2612, just southeast of the turning (D3254) for Twyfelfontein, reservations T061-232009, www.mowani.com. A fairly new exclusive, intimate camp with 12 thatched en suite tents, imaginatively constructed on stilts among huge boulders, each with balcony and lovely views, some have outside baths and showers amongst the boulders, full board, swimming pool, hot-air balloon rides, trips in search of desert elephants. Very elegant in a wonderful setting. Recommended.
AL **Twyfelfontein Country Lodge**, well signposted off the D3214 just before the entrance to Twyfelfontein rock art, central reservations, Windhoek, T061-240375, www.namibialodges.com. Opened by Prime Minister Hage Geingob in 2000 with great fanfare, this is a luxury spot, which has been built with natural materials to blend in with the landscape (which it does, by and large). Very popular with upmarket tour groups. 56 tidy but fairly simple en suite doubles, large restaurant and bar with excellent views and hefty prices, swimming pool for residents, airstrip (charter flights available) and good curio shop. Not an intimate place, but certainly smart, and with a fabulous location.
B **Xaragu Camp**, just to the east of the Petrified Forest on the C39, at the turn-off to Twyfelfontein, T061-256770, www.xaragu.com. Rustic camp opened in 2003 with lovely views, 2 km from the main road, en suite self-catering chalets and 10 spacious **campsites** (E), no electricity, lighting

For an explanation of the sleeping and eating price codes used in this guide, see inside the front cover. Other relevant information is found in Essentials, see pages 43-51.

is provided by oil lamps. In the main building is a bar, dining room and curio shop and outside is a swimming pool and fish pond.
B-E **Aba-Huab Community Campsite**, another NACOBTA project located by the (usually dry) Aba-Huab River, 5 km before Twyfelfontein, on the D3254, T067-331104, www.nacobta.com.na. Small, thatched, open A-frame shelters where you can lay out your sleeping bag, and plentiful campsite space equipped with fireplaces, tables, benches which are scattered along the seasonal Aba-Huab River, running water, ablutions have flush loos and hot water. There's also a rustic bar and restaurant where traditional dishes of the Dama people can be prepared on request, along with a small 'exclusive' campsite over the road with huts and permanent tents with bedding. The camp is busy and very popular with overlanders, but is in a fantastic sandy location and is (usually) a peaceful spot for recovering from the rigours of the awful road to get there. Caution may be required during the rainy season, as the river floods on rare occasions. Walks in the surrounding valley may provide a sight of the desert elephants, and the management will also be happy to arrange performances of traditional singing and dancing. Recommended. **Note** Watch for scorpions here, especially in the A-frames and never leave shoes outside your tent.

East of Khorixas *p186*
AL **Bambatsi Holiday Ranch**, signposted on the C39, 70 km from Outjo, T067-313897, bambatsi@natron.net. 7 simple but pleasant en suite doubles, swimming pool, tennis court, game drives, range of hiking and mountain-biking trails in nearby hills, superb location with magnificent views. A good example of a well-run family guest farm, with day trips to local rock art and tourist sites in the region, returning to the ranch for afternoon tea. Rates are all-inclusive. Recommended. It also runs the neighbouring **Gasenairob** guest farm, with 3 doubles in an older farm house.
A **Vingerklip Lodge**, next to the entrance to the Vingerklip (35 m high limestone rock), reservations T061-255344 (in Windhoek), www.vingerklip.com.na. 24 en suite thatched rooms, tastefully decorated, with veranda and views, 5 of the units have loft space to sleep 2 children, 2 swimming pools, walking trails to the striking Vingerklip (2 km away) and for the adventurous on the nearby Ugab Terrace. Bar, restaurant and separate sundowner hut all have lovely views. Recommended.

Northern Damaraland *p187*
There's a huge selection of places to stay in the Kamanjab area, many making use of their proximity to Etosha and interesting natural geographical features to create a beautiful experience for the visitor.
L **Damaraland Camp**, signposted at the C39/C43 junction, 110 km west of Khorixas, reservations T061-274500 (**Wilderness Safaris**, Windhoek), www.wilderness-safaris.com. Guests leave their vehicles in a car park by the road and are transferred 12 km to the camp by 4WD. 8 en suite twin tents with shady verandas overlooking the valley, central bar and dining area, rock swimming pool and curio shop. Price is full board and includes activities: stargazing, 4WD excursions to rock art and guided walks (recommended) with the hosts/experts who bring the desert landscape to life. If you are very lucky you might just see the elusive desert elephants and there is the option to track black rhino. Often full, book in advance. The local community gets 10% of the lodge's revenue for development projects.
L **Huab Lodge**, 46 km north of Khorixas on the C35, look for a left turning to Monte Carlo (D2670), then a further 35 km. Reservations T061-224712 (Windhoek) www.huablodge.com. A luxurious award-winning lodge set in an 8000-ha private nature reserve, run by the **Haub Conservation Trust** which provides protection for the desert elephant in a buffer zone between commercial and communal land on the border of Damaraland. 8 large thatched en suite bungalows with tasteful decor, private balcony and views across the Huab River, delicious farm cooking and good wine list, swimming pool plus a hot spring to enjoy in the cool evenings, reflexology and massages, game drives, guided hiking and horse riding to rock paintings. Recommended.
L **Palmwag Rhino Lodge**, off the C43, a short distance north of the veterinary control gate, clearly signposted, 140 rutted km from Khorixas (150 km from Kamanjab). Reservations T061-274500 (Wilderness Safaris,

Windhoek), www.wilderness-safaris.com. Very close to **Palmwag Lodge** (below), this semi permanent camp is run in conjunction with the **Save the Rhino Trust**, and although very expensive (over US$600 per night for a couple) some of the fee goes towards the rhino charity and a stay here includes rhino tracking and game drives as well as all meals. The 6 tents are very comfortable with adjoining flush loo and bucket shower.

AL Etendeka Mountain Camp, off the C43, see directions to **Palmwag Lodge**, above. By the veterinary control gate is a petrol station (daylight hours) and puncture repair shop. From the signpost for the camp on the main road, it's another 1½ hrs to the camp (4WD only). The camp can arrange to pick guests up from the main road, usually at 1530-1600, or there's an airstrip. Reservations T061-226979 (Windhoek) www.natron.net/tour/etendeka. 10 double en suite tents, located by the Grootberg Mountain, providing a genuine bush experience. There is a fair amount of game in this region including the last free-roaming black rhino in the world. The camp collects a voluntary bed-levy from visitors for local nature conservation and development projects, directed towards promotion of non-consumptive tourism, with local community involvement. The rates include all food and drinks, game drives and guided bush hikes.

AL Hobatere Lodge, C35 north from Kamanjab for 80 km then follow the signs for 16 km, T067-330261, hobatere@mweb.com.na. 12 en suite thatched bungalows and 1 rustic treehouse overlooking a waterhole, central lounge, bar and restaurant, swimming pool. A relaxing lodge overlooking the Otjivasondu River. Trips into the western part of Etosha can be organized from here, as well as hiking and game drives on the ranch itself which has a fair amount of game including giraffe and elephant. Recommended though a little pricey.

AL Kavita Lion Lodge, C35 north of Kamanjab (for Ruacana), well signed after 35 km, T067-3302244, www.kavitalion.com. 8 comfortable en suite double cottages and 1 family cottage, restaurant, swimming pool. Evenings are spent around a campfire, nature trails and game drives around the farm and food are all included in the rates; trips into the west of Etosha can be arranged for extra. The lodge is home to the new **Afri-Leo Foundation**, which raises funds for lion protection and territory conservation. It is at present home to several lions that were relocated from Rundu Zoo when it closed in 1997, and guests can visit the enclosures.

AL Palmwag Lodge, off the C43, see directions to **Palmwag Lodge**, above. Reservations T064-404459, www.palmwag.com.na. Can sleep 40 people in simple en suite bungalows or more expensive luxury tents among *makalani* palm trees, restaurant, 2 pleasant swimming pools, a restaurant and poolside bar which will also serve snack meals for guests staying at the campsite. Exposed campsite (**D-E**) with privacy but few grassy pitches, peg carefully against the wind. Game drives and hiking trails, a good base to explore the area. Accommodation and tours are usually fully booked, so reserve well ahead.

A Ondundu Wilderness Lodge, 48 km east of Kamanjab off the C40, T067-697038, www.ondundu.com. Overlooking the Haub Riverbed, which is a popular haunt of desert elephant, this lodge has 4 large en suite bungalows with 4-poster beds, fridges, DSTV and corner baths, 4 luxury tents and a central building with high thatched roof, all built into the granite rocks, swimming pool, hikes, horse riding.

B Ermo Game Lodge, 55 km from Kamanjab, take the C35 north, after 8 km turn east, follow signs from junction with D2763, T067-330220, info@ermo-safaris.com. 11 thatched bungalows, farm cuisine with game a speciality of the house, swimming pool, game walks and drives and floodlit waterhole with viewing platforms that is visited by kudu, oryx and eland. Can also arrange a night's camping in the nearby hills.

B Oase Garni Hotel, Kamanjab, T/F067-330032. 6 en suite doubles and a family unit, excellent lunches for those en route and larger evening meals for overnighters, friendly hosts, bar, tiny plunge pool, curio shop selling locally made wares.

B Otjitotongwe Cheetah Guest Farm, 24 km east of Kamanjab, signposted from the C40, T/F067-330201, www.cheetahpark.com. 6 en-suite thatched bungalows lit by gas lamps, thatched bar/restaurant and small swimming pool, hiking trails through interesting fossil rocks and trees, half board and game drives included. Large, well serviced **campsite** (**E**) with separate 'bush bar' that is run by the affable Mario and popular with overland trucks. 4 tame and 21 wild cheetahs live in large enclosures next to the campsite and organized feeding sessions afford good photo opportunities, you can pat the tame ones at the main house on the front lawn, these activities begin at 1500 in winter and 1600 in summer and for a small fee day visitors are permitted to join in. Recommended.

B Toko Lodge and Safaris, Rusting Farm, take C35 north for 8 km, turn right on to D2763 and, after 13 km, take D2695 sign-posted to farm, T067-330250, www.toko lodge.com. Award winner with 10 thatched en suite bungalows, swimming pool, garden, meals in the farm house, family atmosphere, hiking trails. Game drives and longer day trips to see Bushman paintings around Kamanjab are on offer for additional costs; longer safaris to Epupu Falls or Etosha can also be arranged. **Camping** (**E**) available at shaded site with communal ablutions.

E Hoada Campsite, **from Kamanjab**, drive towards Palmwag on the C40 and, after passing the village of Anker, it is another 8 km to the campsite on the left. **From Palmwag** drive through the Grootberg Pass and past the D2659 turning on the right; after about 20 km Hoada is on the right. Reservations through T061-255977 (Windhoek), www.nacobta.com.na. The entrance gate is made from elephant bones. Another NACOBTA camp, very simple, but in a stunning spot, managed by the local people, 3 campsites each with its own flush loo and outside shower, and communal kitchen area, bring all provisions, hiking trails to the Grootberg Plateau.

Eating

Uis *p183*

Vicky's Coffee Shop, part of the NACOBTA tourist centre on the main street, T064-504212. Small café that can seat 12 people at any one time on the pretty veranda, (from where you can watch the donkey carts go up and down Uis's main street). Light meals such as toasted sandwiches and omelettes, muffins and cakes, coffee and tea, open daily until late afternoon.

Khorixas *p184*

Khorixas Rest Camp, see Sleeping, above. The bar and restaurant has good café-style service with an à la carte menu and there is a pool table.

There's also a small shop here selling some food items and a small bakery selling coffee and cake.

Shopping

Uis *p183*

Dâureb Craft Shop, NACOBTA tourist centre. A stylish craft shop in the new tourist centre building selling picture frames, candles, colourful prints, mirrors and mobiles. Everything is made from local materials and the artists will be happy to tell you more while you are browsing in the shop.

Activities and tours

Damaraland *p180*

Tour operators

There are a number of tour companies offering guided hiking and driving trips in the region. Damaraland is often included in longer tours of the country. See also Tour operators and Car hire companies in Windhoek (pages 99 and 102). Budget travellers should consider **Chameleon** or **Crazy Kudu** safaris which run camping trips into Damaraland.

Damarana Safaris, T064-463277, www.damarana.com. Upmarket operator offering 4WD guided tours from between 2-6 days from Swakopmund to remote regions of Damaraland using mobile camps.

Desert Adventure Safaris, 38 Bismarck St, Swakopmund, T064-403274, www.das.com.na. Fly-in and 4WD safaris from 2-12 days.

Nawa Safaris, T/F061-243103, www.nawa. iway.na. Guided driving safaris with the flexibility to design your own trip, as well as fly-ins and small group guided tours.

Directory

Uis *p183*

Desert Computer Line, NACOBTA tourist centre, perhaps one of the remotest internet cafés there is! NACOBTA has plans to open more in other parts of rural Namibia. Understandably access is on the expensive side for around US$1 for 5-10 min. Uis also has a post office, payphone, basic shop, butcher, bottle store and a petrol station (0500-2100). It is advisable to fill up here given the scarcity of petrol stations in the region. If any of these shops are closed during the day ask at the tourist centre and someone will fetch the owner who will open up. This is how they do things in Uis.

Kaokoland

Kaokoland is often described as one of the last truly wild areas in southern Africa. The attractions are the simple beauty of the mountain landscape, the ruggedness of the access routes and the tranquillity enjoyed by those reaching the northern and western corners. These days the region is administrated as the Northern Kunene Region but it is still referred to as Kaokoland, especially in tourist literature. En route, as well as 4WD challenges, is the opportunity to see the unique and photogenic Himba villages

Dos and don'ts of travelling in Kaokoland

- Do not travel on east-west running water courses as these are migration routes for animals. Approaching vehicles will frighten animals and may cause stress or even injury to game which cannot escape up steep slopes out of the river course.
- Do not camp in river courses, to avoid both night-time encounters with large game and the risk of flash floods in summer during the rainy season.
- Ensure that all rubbish is taken out of the area. Do not bury or leave anything for scavengers.
- Do not camp at waterholes or springs. Animals travel long distances to reach water and if you are camped there game will be too scared to drink. Likewise, never wash anything in the springs or waterholes as they provide local inhabitants, both people and animals, with drinking water.
- Respect the customs of the Himba and never enter seemingly deserted settlements. As a semi-nomadic people, the Himba move around with their animals to return later to villages which may appear abandoned but in reality are not.
- Do not enter a *kraal* uninvited and when inside never walk between the sacred fire and the main hut. Never take photographs without first having obtained permission and, if you must take photos, negotiate payment beforehand.

and people. The Kunene River rewards weary travellers with the beautiful Epupa Falls, watersport possibilities and numerous riverside lodges and camps.

Kaokoland is bounded by the Skeleton Coast Park on the west, the perennial Kunene River to the north, the C35 gravel road to the east and Damaraland to the south. There are no tarred roads in the region and no banks; basic supplies are only available in the main centres. Visitors to the area need to have a degree of self-sufficiency, but allowing time in your schedule to visit the region will be amply rewarded. » *For Sleeping, Eating and other listings, see pages 202-205.*

The people of Kakaoland

Kaokoland measures roughly 40,000 sparsely populated square kilometres, with just under 30,000 mainly **Herero** and **Himba** inhabitants. The much-photographed Himba people are a semi-nomadic, pastoral people who follow their cattle and goats in search of good grazing. They are descendants of the earliest Hereros, who migrated into this area early in the 16th century from Botswana. Around the middle of the 18th century the pressure of too many people and not enough cattle in this dry, fragile environment led to the migration of the main body of the Herero to the rich pasturelands further south, leaving behind the Himba in the north. After this separation the Himba were first given the name Tjimba-Herero; the word *Tjimba* being derived from *ondjimba*, meaning bush pig; a reference to them looking for food in the ground like bush pigs because of the scarcity of cattle. Some of these impoverished people went across the Kunene River where they lived with the Ngambwe people in Angola. Here, they were named Himba, which in the Ngambwe language means beggar, simply because they begged for a place to live.

Today it is believed the Himba in Namibia number around 16,000. They live off mostly the meat and milk of their livestock and, like the Masai in East Africa, their animals are the central most important feature of their lives. In particular, cattle are the most important symbol of status and wealth. Their beehive huts are made from *mopane* tree saplings covered with a mixture of mud and dung; surrounded by a *kraal* where their animals are protected overnight against predators. Many settlements are often deserted as these pastoral people continuously wander with their herds in search of water and grazing, and visitors to the region may often meet a family on the move carrying all their worldly goods wrapped in only animal skins. Many of them maintain traditional dress, language and behavioural codes, which has made them an attraction both to anthropologists wishing to study their customs and culture and tourists with a 'romantic' notion of Africa. Perhaps they have managed to keep their traditional lifestyles intact for so long because the land they occupy is so harsh and unyielding that it has rarely been coveted by the colonialists and commercial farmers who have affected so much of the continent. The Himba plaster their skin and hair with butter, ash and red-hued ochre, a primitive protection against the sun and to keep their skins looking younger. The result is quite breathtaking and dramatic, and the treatment must work as even elderly Himba women have incredibly smooth skin. They also wear elaborate, heavy, metal-studded jewellery and weave their hair in complicated and intricate tresses. To signify their status, married women wear a small soft-skinned headpiece on top of their braided hair and an additional heavy ornament around their necks that includes a conch shell that hangs in the front and a metal-studded leather plate that hangs down the back. They are without doubt strikingly beautiful and an evocative image of Namibia. Today the Himba way of life is threatened by the intrusion of traders, tourists and the proposed Epupa Dam Scheme (see box, page 200). More Himba are starting to live in permanent settlements, such as the regional 'capital' Opuwo, and many are adapting their customs and lifestyles as they come into contact with the rest of the world and attempt to meet the demands of living in the 21st century.

Just as the Nama and Herero peoples were exploited by European traders who introduced strong, mass-produced alcohol during the 19th century, today Himba communities are vulnerable. As well as the food staples, metal beads (for jewellery), fat and ochre (for skin colouring) and basic medicine, Angolan and Owambo traders bring liquor, often bartered for goats or cattle. As alcohol tolerance is so low, unscrupulous traders threaten to damage the structure of village life.

Tourists, too, pose a threat as they come into contact with a culture they know little or nothing about; by encouraging the Himba to sell their images for the tourist camera in exchange for cigarettes, sweets and tobacco, a proud and highly successful people are turned into a cliché of the 'noble savage'. Whilst there is undoubtedly a place for tourism in the Kaokoland and for contact with the Himba, caution and sensitivity should be exercised at all times. If possible, a local guide should liaise between tourists and the Himba to ensure that local customs and people are respected. A number of community projects (see Purros Conservation Project, page 198, and box on NACOBTA, page 41) have developed in response to this need for controlled and non-exploitative forms of tourism. Visitors to Kaokoland may well want to support these local initiatives. If you are driving through the region and see the Himba walking along the roads, by all means stop and offer them a lift if it will help them get to their destination. As a thank you, it may possible that you will be granted permission to take a photograph. Another tip is when meeting the Himba don't just stop and stare but interact and share; in many ways they are just as interested in learning about the people who have come to visit them, as the visitors are about the Himba. Talk to them; show them things. Children are delighted to see pictures of themselves on the back of a digital camera, or what it's like to look through a pair of sunglasses. The Himba women may want to see what other women's hair feels like or take a moment to admire and compare items of jewellery with them. It

The Himba will happily pose for photos but they do expect payment, and this must always be arranged in advance – do not under any circumstances take photos without permission.

“” The Himba plaster their skin and hair with butter, ash and red-hued ochre, a primitive protection against the sun and to keep their skin looking younger...

was our experience that the children were mesmerized by how buttons and zips operated. Our earrings, tattoos, velcro sandals, and the contents of somebody's wash kit were scrutinized (and in most cases laughed at!).

Travelling in Kaokoland » pp202-205.

Wildlife

The range of wildlife in Kaokoland is more limited than you may have come to expect in Namibia. The efforts of hunters and poachers, and the inevitable slaughter for food during the struggle for independence rendered many areas devoid of game. However, the legendary **desert elephant**, still roams the remote western river valleys (see box, page 187). The **black rhino** also survives here, the last place in the world where it roams uninhibited. There are small herds of gemsbok, zebra, giraffe and springbok, as well as lion, leopard and cheetah. Despite the inhospitable conditions, game survives. These animals are not accustomed to human presence; if you have come from Etosha, the place will appear barren and the game you do see very skittish. Plans have been afoot for a number of years to declare the western part of Kaokoland (to the Skeleton Coast park) a conservation area and allow game numbers to improve; if successful, at least one part of this great wilderness area will be preserved for the future.

Tours

If you are unable or unwilling to make an independent trip to Damaraland and Kaokoland, consider an organized tour. These are not cheap, but having a guide familiar with the terrain and practicalities can enhance your enjoyment of the holiday, particularly if you are an inexperienced or unlucky driver. And it may not be much more costly, given the expense of hiring two 4WD vehicles. There are a number of tour companies offering guided hiking and driving trips in the region. » *For a list of tour operators, see page 205; see also Windhoek tour operators, page 99, and car hire companies, page 102.*

Self-drive tourism

This is becoming increasingly popular. With it comes the risk that the under-prepared may venture into the region and expose themselves unwittingly to danger. Maps of the area give the misleading impression that there is a well-established system of roads allowing free access to many parts of Kaokoland. Nothing could be further from the truth. Roads are often little more than dirt tracks, which become impassable bogs during the rainy season. The rocky, mountainous terrain of much of the region makes all travel extremely slow and hazardous. Outside Opuwo and Ruacana, the region is devoid of amenities, with no fuel, very few shops with limited supplies and almost no telephones. And this is a large part of the attraction; a vast wilderness and small isolated communities living a subsistence existence off the land.

While many roads, in the dry season, are passable by careful driving in a 2WD car, it is advisable to travel by 4WD, and ideally in convoy. All vehicles should carry two spare tyres and puncture repair kits, basic spares such as oil and fuel filters, at least 160 litres of fuel, water and food and a decent medical kit. Wherever you are, stick to

The Dorsland Trekkers of Kaokoland

In the remote northwestern corner of Namibia there are several monuments to one of the most unusual and hardy group of trekkers to leave South Africa during the 19th century. The origins of this trek date back to 1872 when the Reverend Thomas Burgers was elected president of the Transvaal. On hearing the election results, a highly religious group known as the 'doppers' decided to leave the Transvaal because they opposed the teachings of their new president.

The term 'doppers', meaning dampers, was used because the group had a reputation for opposing all forms of social progress. One of their arguments that is frequently quoted was their claim that the construction of railway lines was the work of Satan. So in 1874 a group suddenly abandoned their homes, packed the wagons and set off into the Kalahari Desert with absolutely no idea of the climatic and physical perils that lay ahead. They were driven by the belief that the trek was necessary to bring them to the land of Beulah (after the biblical land of rest). As they journeyed further into the Kalahari many of the women, children and livestock died from fever, heat exhaustion and dysentery. They came to be known as the 'Dorsland Trekkers' – or the thirstland trekkers. By 1876 part of the group had reached the grasslands that are now part of Etosha National Park. Close to the perennial spring, which they renamed Rietfontein (reed fountain), is a lone *mopane* tree providing the shade for the grave of a trekker woman, Johanna Alberts (1841-1876).

Eventually a group of trekkers reached Humpata in Angola, having passed through Kaokoland. Within Kaokoland there are a couple of monuments to the trek, one at Otjitunduwa, 90 km north of Hobatere Lodge, and a second at Swartbooisdrift where they crossed the Kunene into Angola. In between the two monuments are the ruins of a small church at Kaoko Otavi in the Joubert Mountains. Within a couple of years the trekkers were quarrelling amongst themselves and the group started to fragment. Some of the party decided to return to the Transvaal, others returned as far as Grootfontein where they bought some land from a local Owambo chief and set up the capital of the Republic of Upingtonia. The republic was abandoned in 1893 when the South West Africa Company started to prospect for minerals in the area. The Dorsland Trekkers never fulfilled their dreams of Beulah but they are a tremendous example of the toughness and the will-power required of people if they wished to travel in Namibia before the arrival of the Germans at the end of the 19th century.

existing tracks, as pre-Second World War tyre tracks are still visible in some coastal valleys. There are a few lodges and campsites in the area (see Sleeping, below); bush camping is forbidden in the Marienfluss and Hartmann's valleys.

Before you drive yourself in the area, be sure at least to read a 4WD guide, and preferably take a course. Jan Joubert's *Practical Guide to Off-Road Adventures in Southern Africa* is a recommended introduction to the challenges faced, and there are many similar books. Read up also on the flora and fauna of the area to more fully appreciate your environment. Buy the *Shell Kaokoland Kunene Region Tourist Map*; while some of the roads marked no longer exist, it is the best map of the region and provides information, both practical driving advice and regarding the wildlife and vegetation in the area. Most importantly, stock up well, allow plenty of time and get advice from lodge owners and fellow travellers as to the conditions ahead before embarking on each stretch of your journey. » *See also Essentials, page 38, for more tips on driving in Namibia.*

Planning your route in Kaokoland

» *pp202-205.*

The routes outlined below assume visitors arrive via Damaraland from Swakopmund. However, self-drive visitors who entered Namibia via the Caprivi Strip are likely to follow all the routes in reverse – entering Kaokoland in the north from Oshakati and Ruacana, and then working their way south into Damaraland.

One of the most important considerations when visiting Kaokoland is to carefully plan your route in advance, and calculate distances, fuel consumption and the number of nights camping. Always make sure you have at least two additional jerry cans of fuel above your estimated needs, especially if you are heading for Hartmann's Valley.

While distances may look small from the map, on the ground you will average no more than 50 kph. It takes on average two hours to cover the 73 km between Okongwati and Epupa Falls. You need to allow at least three hours just to cross **Van Zyl's Pass**.

Note This can only be driven east to west. Only very experienced 4WD drivers should even contemplate the route. If heading for Hartmann's Valley, you will have to camp one night in the wild when travelling in each direction, whether you start from Opuwo or Purros. Finally, if you find yourself exploring the area during the rainy season be prepared to wait several hours, even days, before being able to cross certain riverbeds (there are no bridges in the region); do not attempt to drive up river courses if they have recently flowed. Allow at least four days after rain before driving along riverbeds. Never camp in dry riverbeds if there's any sign of rain as flash floods can occur.

Do not be put off from visiting this region but do come prepared and take heed of all local advice. One of the most important points to remember is the degree of isolation and lack of services. It may not be the end of the world if you suffer a broken axle or run out of fuel, but it may take a week or more to get going again. During this period you are going to need to be self-sufficient, particularly in food, water, fuel and medicine.

Khowarib » *Colour map 1, B3.*

This small village and Warmquelle, below, are of little interest in themselves to the passing tourist, however, they have each started a community campsite in recent years. These are worth patronizing since it is one of the few ways in which these marginal communities benefit directly from tourism.

Driving north, the first village you will reach is Khowarib, about 77 km from Palmwag. The village is spread out along the banks of the perennial Khowarib River, which irrigates local agriculture and attracts tourists to the riverside campsite, signposted by the crossing.

With the help of a local guide it is possible to drive up the gorge and explore upstream. However, if you choose to drive up the riverbed remember to observe all the rules concerning minimizing your impact on the local environment, and only do so in convoy.

Warmquelle » *Colour map 1, B3.*

Unfortunately for Khowarib, the campsite at Warmquelle, 11 km further on up the road, has an even more enticing water feature – a year-round natural pool which is large enough to swim in and it's an impossibly pretty spot. Like Khowarib, the village of Warmquelle has little to offer the visitor beyond refreshing patches of green in this dusty environment. Worth a quick look, however, are the remains of a **Shutztruppe Fort**: there is a stone entrance with tower, stables with stone cribs and the prison with two cells, dating from 1895. Warmquelle is also the place where Bondelswarts leader, Jan Christiaan Abrahams, was shot, which led to their uprising in 1903. This event is re-enacted every year around 25 October. Skirmishes continued until peace was agreed in December 1906; the local cemetary houses numerous interesting gravestones.

Water from the spring, which feeds the Warmquelle pool, is piped for domestic needs and to irrigate a few small fields growing maize and vegetables, following the efforts made by a Greek farmer who, long before tourists started visiting the area, built a series of irrigation channels to nearby fields. A few sections of this aqueduct still remain hidden in the scrub bush.

Sesfontein » *Colour map 1, B2.*

The name originates from six springs which surface in the area. In 1896, following the devastating rinderpest epidemic which killed off huge numbers of both livestock and game, the German colonial authorities established a number of control checkpoints across the country; these now form the so-called **Red Line** which demarcate the boundary between commercial and subsistence livestock farming in the country. Sesfontein formed the most westerly in a string of such checkpoints. It lies 31 km north of the Hoanib River on the C43 and is the northernmost point in Damaraland. There is an Engen garage just before the lodge gate, with a small shop.

Following the construction of a road between Outjo and Sesfontein in 1901, the German authorities transported materials to build a military outpost. This was designed to assist in the prevention of poaching and gun-running in the area and although a fort (complete with vegetable garden) was built, by 1909 Sesfontein had been relegated to the status of police outpost before being finally abandoned in 1914. The fort fell into disrepair but was given a reprieve in 1987 when the former Damara administration renovated it. Today it has found a new role as home to the **Fort Sesfontein Lodge** (see page 203).

North from Sesfontein

If you are in a saloon car, ask about the road conditions before continuing north on the D3705 from Sesfontein to Opuwo, as there is a very steep pass on this road. Alternatively, in a 4WD, head 10 km southeast to Anabeb and take the C43 north to Opuwo. Another option is to continue north on the D3707 towards Purros and Orupembe. This is the shortest route to Hartmann's Valley; ensure you have sufficient supplies and fuel before leaving Sesfontein.

Sesfontein to Purros

Follow the D3707 to Purros along the Hoanib River (4WD essential). It is about 107 km northwest of Sesfontein and this is one of the best places to view the desert elephant as well as other wildlife in the area. However, it can be dangerously difficult to find your way without a guide, so we have elected not to provide sufficient detail to navigate through this corner of the region without one. If you are sufficiently well prepared and guided, allow yourself most of the day to reach Purros. With reference to the **Kaokoland Shell Map, Dubis** is a narrow gorge which one can drive through, **Amspoort** is the furthest point to which you can drive. At this point the river passes through another narrow rocky gorge, you are only about 40 km from the Atlantic Ocean. However, this is part of the Skeleton Coast, which is closed to the public.

Purros conservation and eco-tourism project » *Colour map 1, A2.*

This is a joint project between the local community at Purros Village and **Integrated Rural Development and Nature Conservation** (IRDNC) based in Windhoek. The project's aim is to develop sustainable tourism in the area to benefit tourists and the local community and to preserve the environment and the wildlife. Community game guards, funded by the **World Wide Fund for Nature** (WWF) through IRDNC, help to protect the game from poachers using camel patrols. To get there follow the signboards to **Purros Campsite,** but do not turn off to the campsite. Instead continue for about 5 km, until you reach a small group of houses where there is another sign. Drive carefully as there are patches of very deep sand.

The area supports populations of desert elephant, black rhino, giraffe, gemsbok, ostrich and small numbers of predators such as leopard, cheetah and lion. Local guides offer game drives or hikes into the surrounding area and there is a plant trail intended to educate visitors about plants used in traditional medicines.

Guides are available for about US$4 for visits to local Himba or Herero villages where the emphasis is on tourists behaving as guests, spending some time talking with local people, rather than treating them as if they were attractions in a zoo. Visitors learn about Himba-Herero culture through crafts made by local women, traditional food and utensils, building methods and materials or daily chores like the milking of cows.

North of Purros

North of Purros is the part of Kaokoland where all the advice and warnings about travel come into play. Driving sensibly you can expect to get just beyond Red Drum before having to pitch camp in the wild. **Red Drum** is literally a painted drum full of stones and bullet holes. Take a left for Hartmann's Valley and a right for Marienfluss Valley. Remember it will not be possible to return from Marienfluss Valley via Van Zyl's Pass. However, there is an alternative route to Opuwo and Epupa Falls (be very careful about carrying sufficient fuel). From Red Drum, drive back towards Orupembe and take the road marked to Otjihaa on the Shell Map. Although not shown, this joins the D3703 south of Otjitanda. There is no campsite at Orupembe.

Most visitors drive back as far as Orupembe and then take the D3707 and D3705 to Opuwo. This is a very long day's drive and you should make an early start from your camp near Red Drum if you expect to reach Opuwo before dark. This is the most sensible route to take since one can refuel and purchase fresh food before continuing north to Epupa Falls.

Opuwo ›› *Phone code: 065. Colour map 1, A3.*

Surrounded by low-lying hills, Opuwo, which means 'the end' in Herero, is a small and uninspiring town in the middle of the bush, 235 km from Khorixas and 290 km from Oshakati. The town grew into a permanent settlement and administrative centre for the region during the bush war prior to independence, when the South Africa Defence Force used it as a base from which to launch expeditions into the surrounding area. A smart lodge and decent community campsite provide lodgings for tourists passing through to the more isolated, attractive spots in the region.

Opuwo's name is indeed appropriate as it is both the first and last place offering supplies, fuel, accommodation and telecommunications in the region, although there are at present no bank facilities. Along or just off the main street are the two petrol stations, the few shops, post office, a helpful BP and Shell petro stations for emergency repairs and petrol (though they have been known to run out at times), an information centre and the town's bars. The residential areas are a few streets of bungalows built during the bush war for army and government personnel; these now house government officials and the few business people in the area. Not far away are the Himba and Herero settlements and their beehive huts surround the town.

If you fancy a walk around a nearby Himba settlement/township, or further out to one of the outlying villages with a guide if you are in your own vehicle, then go to the **Kaoko Information Office** ⓘ *opposite the offices of the Regional Council, T065-273420, (Mr Kemuu), a NACOBTA project, www.nacobta.com.na.* The guides speak English and will be able to translate for you. It is also a way of putting a little money into the local economy as crafts and other

You will learn about the culture and way of life of the Himba through the eyes of your guide.

Epupa Dam project

The proposed Epupa Dam and hydroelectric power plant project has been the subject of controversy in Namibia since 1996, and has rallied politicians, civil servants, anthropologists, civil engineers, community leaders and conservationists against each other.

The Epupa scheme is intended to meet Namibia's energy needs for the next 25 years, reducing her dependency on importing energy from South Africa. Power generated by the hydroelectric plant will also be used to pump water through the proposed pipeline from the Okavango River to Windhoek, which cannot grow further without solving its water problems.

Much of the Himba community opposes the scheme, fearing that the dam will destroy their way of life as pastures and ancestral graves will be flooded and an influx of thousands of construction workers will overwhelm this semi-nomadic community. Despite these fears, senior government officials have repeatedly come out firmly in favour of the scheme, claiming that the project will bring much-needed development in the form of schools, clinics, roads and businesses to this underdeveloped region.

Consultations between the Himba community and the government have been bedevilled from the start as the Himbas felt that the government was never really interested in their views. The politicization of the project saw the Himbas employ the services of the Legal Assistance Centre and a tour of European capitals by Himba leaders seeking overseas support.

The whole project has been further complicated by the findings of the feasibility study which has considered two alternative sites for the dam. The Baynes site is less environmentally damaging but not economically feasible without the reconstruction of a war-damaged dam further upriver in Angola. The Epupa site would displace 1100 people, affect 5000 occasional users of the site, and drown 95 archaeological sites and 160 Himba graves. In addition, the Namibian and Angolan governments have yet to reach agreement as to which site to move ahead with.

Yet another uncertainty is where the financing for the project will come from. At a cost of around US$550 million, it is clear that the Namibian government will need to raise funds from overseas. At the same time, an alternative source of energy is under consideration off the southwest coast of the country. The Kudu gas field – a vast reserve of natural gas situated under the seabed – has also been the subject of a feasibility study. If the cost of building a 1000-km pipeline from the gas field to South Africa's Cape Province is deemed affordable, the Epupa scheme would not be necessary on energy grounds.

Perhaps more than anything else, the Epupa debate highlights the conflict between those who see grand projects to fuel industrial development as the way to survive in an ever-changing world, and those who seek to preserve the last remnants of the old Africa.

souvenirs can be bought directly from the people themselves. Do not take photos without negotiating first.

Driving out of Opuwo can be a bit confusing. The C41 will take you the 60 km to the C35 Ruacana-Kamanjab on a good gravel road; well signposted, turn right out of the Shell garage and immediately left past the BP garage, sports stadium and airfield. The C43 to Okongwati is also a good gravel road, after this the Epupa Falls road needs to be driven with care. The shortest route to Hartmann's Valley is via the D3703 through the Steilrand Mountains, but this involves negotiating Van Zyl's Pass, very much 4WD only.

Okongwati ›› *Colour map 1, A2.*

This small settlement marks the end of the reasonable C43 from Opuwo. There is a police station, basic store and a scattered collection of houses. There is a small sign for **Epupa Camp** (for Epupa Falls), which takes you across a wide sandy riverbed shortly after leaving the village.

By the time you reach Okongwati you need to have already decided which route you are going to follow. The reason for this is simply the availability of fuel and the distances you plan to cover. Opuwo is the most northeasterly source of fuel. There are three possible routes you can follow, each will take you through beautiful country, and each demands advance planning.

Okongwati to Epupa Falls and Ruacana

The most straightforward route is to continue 76 km north to Epupa Falls, spend a couple of nights here and then return by the same road. However, if you have sufficient fuel (and experience and clearance, it is a rocky road) you can follow the Kunene River upstream from Epupa Falls to Ruacana on the very basic D3700, whose course is vague in places. Note this road does not follow the river as closely as some people expect. It is a narrow track and very hard going in places. If you wish to visit Ruacana and drive along the river we would recommend you drive back to Otjiveze on the D3700 and take theD3701/3702 signposted **Kunene River Lodge.** While this road is not smooth or easy, outside the rainy season it is usually navigable by saloon car. Check both your rental agreement and lodge owners' advice before setting out on this route. It is essential to take sufficient fuel as there is none at Epupa. There are, however, a couple of small shops selling fresh bread (the clay oven is outside) and whatever stocks have been brought in from Opuwo. Cold drinks and beer are available to refresh those without an onboard fridge.

The adventurous and well equipped can take the D3703 west from Omuhonga towards **Otjitanda**, **Van Zyl's Pass** and Hartmann's Valley (see below for further details).

Epupa Falls ›› *Colour map 1, A3.*

About 10 km before the Epupa Falls are a couple of colourful Himba graves, with impressive piles of cattle horns.

The falls are a beautiful series of cascades where the Kunene River drops a total of 60 m over a distance of about 1.5 km. The main drop is roughly 32 m. As the river drops, it divides into a multitude of channels creating hundreds of small vegetated islands. While most people content themselves with a quick peek at the falls by the road, there is a track along the rocks high above the river, downstream of the falls, affording fine views back towards the falls. From here you can appreciate their extent and beauty, and see the range of vegetation (particularly the precariously placed baobabs). Beware of snakes on land and crocodiles in the water. Just before sunset, drive a short way back towards the airfield and take the only track to the right. This leads up to the top of the hill where you are presented with a magnificent view of the falls and all the islands. An ideal spot for your sundowner.

Do not be tempted to swim at the bottom of the falls here; crocodiles are present and the water is very rough. There was a fatality here in 2005.

Over the past few years, Epupa has welcomed a considerable amount of tourist activity. There are thatched structures by the approach to the falls which house collections of local crafts. You will encounter a few (mostly South African) self-drive visitors and the occasional tour group being ferried from airstrip to Himba village to Epupa Falls to lodge; but this is a truly beautiful spot and one can only hope that too much tourism doesn't spoil it. Part of its charm lies in the effort required to get here, and the feeling of remoteness once here.

Don't be put off by the Himba who will approach soon after your arrival. These people are not thieves, but friendly and poor. They rely on tourists, and are happy to earn by selling you a curio item, showing you around or collecting firewood for you.

Okongwati to Marienfluss and Hartmann's valleys

As noted, the crossing of **Van Zyl's Pass** is not to be treated lightly. If you reach here with less than three hours of daylight remaining, camp by the road and cross the pass in the morning. As you negotiate the precipitous road keep an eye out for large rocks – either remove or replace them. The road gets very little maintenance from the authorities. The pass was built by Van Zyl with the help of a few Himba and an ox cart and is a tremendous feat of engineering. Many of the tracks in the area still follow the routes taken by Van Zyl and his team. **Note** Don't expect all the routes on the Shell map to actually exist, some are just the old trails left by Van Zyl. If you started your day's journey in Opuwo you will not manage to cross the pass before nightfall.

Marienfluss and Hartmann's valleys – the Kunene River

▸▸ *Colour map 1, A1.*

Having got this far, both valleys are worth visiting but you will need to be completely self-sufficient. The **Marienfluss Valley** is very scenic and relatively greener than Hartmann's Valley. As the Shell Kaokoland map notes, the valley is known for its 'fairy circles' – round patches without any sign of vegetation thought to consist of hard ground that is impenetrable by moisture. If you are interested in seeing such circles but can't get here, then a couple of days spent at the **NamibRand Nature Reserve** (see page 287) near Sossusvlei will teach you all that is currently known about their origins. No camping is permitted in either valley. Keep to existing tracks.

Hartmann's Valley is closer to the Atlantic and yet much more arid. It has a strange atmosphere when the sea mists drift inland, rather like at Swakopmund. The drive is a tiring one and you should allow three hours to complete the 70 km to the end. Here the road meets a bank of sand dunes, which are part of the Skeleton Coast Park proper, and you are not permitted to continue. You will have to turn back on the same road.

As you drive up each of these valleys it is difficult not to feel a certain sense of achievement and good fortune to be able to visit such a beautiful and fragile environment. Somehow nothing else in Namibia has quite the same impact as a week or more discovering the beauty of Kaokoland. There is only one campsite in this region, though there are a couple of upmarket lodges in the upper reaches of the Skeleton Coast Park which can only be reached by plane (see Sleeping in Skeleton Coast Park, page 263). One final comment from us: please observe all the advice on how to behave in these areas otherwise they could well end up like much of the Skeleton Coast – a private concession area which only the wealthy can afford to visit.

Sleeping

Khowarib *p197*

E Khowarib Rest Camp. Very basic campsite plus traditional Damara huts with *braai* pit and water, but the setting more than makes up for it. There is one 'exclusive' camping spot by the river, with no facilities (4WD only). There is always a small flow of water over the high weir and one can carefully climb down and enjoy a natural shower or bathe in one of the small pools. Next to the campsite is a small camel ride operation run from the **Save the Rhino** camp. These camels were given to the community after they had been used for an adventure along the Namibian Coast through the Namib Desert, and are presently used for poaching patrols.

Warmquelle *p197*

E Ongongo Campsite, 6 km from Warmquelle up a narrow track, if you fail to see the signs just keep following the water pipe (this is navigable, with careful driving, in a saloon car though the track is very stony). 6 shaded campsites with *braai* pit, basic

For an explanation of the sleeping and eating price codes used in this guide, see inside the front cover. Other relevant information is found in Essentials, see pages 43-51.

communal toilets and showers, set in picturesque limestone valley. Firewood and cool drinks for sale, walking trails, swimming in natural pool. At one end there is a waterfall which flows during the rainy season (Nov-Apr). Look out for the turtles which live in the pool; they have been known to attach themselves to men's nipples in the water! This is a wonderful stop, particularly if travelling during summer, and if you climb to the top of the hills behind the camp the views over the gravel plains are tremendous.

Sesfontein *p198*

A **Fort Sesfontein Lodge**, T065-275534/5, www.fort-sesfontein.com. 13 en suite rooms in a historical fort which in the past has been a police station and veterinary checkpoint, wheelchair friendly, cool spacious restaurant, bar, large swimming pool, pleasant shaded gardens with palms and bougainvillea, the lodge can pick you up from the airstrip at Sesfontein and arrange local 4WD trips in the region; simple **campsite (E)** with communal facilities outside the fort. Book ahead for tours and hikes in Damaraland and Kaokoland. Mixed reports about the level of service here.

Purros *p198*

E **Purros Community Campsite**, a NACTOB project, central reservations, Windhoek, T061-255977, www.nactob.com.na. 4 shaded, private sites each with flush toilet, shower, *braai*, water and room for 4 tents. Bar, walking trails, firewood for sale. **Note** The desert elephants pass through the camp if in the area. Exercise caution if you are visited; campers have been forced out of their camp in the past. A percentage of the fee goes to the **Purros Development Committee Fund** used for development projects in the area. If you have time it is worth spending a couple of nights here in order to fully appreciate the beauty and appeal of the region. This is one of our favourite camps in Kaokoland.

Opuwo *p199*

Options are limited as most tourists are en route in or out of the region.

AL **Opuwo Country Hotel**, reservations, T061-374750 (Windhoek), www.namibia lodges.com. Located on a hill to the northwest of the town, this lodge is currently under construction but when finished will offer the best accommodation in the region probably in the **AL** price bracket. There will be 28 luxury, and 12 standard rooms, the main thatched building will house a restaurant, bar, craft shop and conference facilities, and there will be a swimming pool. Once it is open reports are welcome. It is part of the **Namibia Lodges** group so will probably be used by tour groups.

B **Mopane Camp**, 2.5 km from Opuwo on the C41, T065-273031, ohakane@iafrica.com.na. A nice spot under the arms of giant *mopane* trees, 15 comfortable and fully furnished walk-in tents, shared ablutions located in Himba-style huts, cultural exchanges can be arranged with the Himba, breakfast (US$6.50) and dinner (US$23) extra, meals are taken on wooden benches outside lit by lanterns.

B **Ohakene Lodge**, T065-273031, ohakane@iafrica.com.na. The best place to stay in town but not well located and very noisy, behind the Shell garage. 13 en suite rooms, a lovely bar and good restaurant around a floodlit swimming pool, rates do not include any meals. It arranges trips to Epupa Falls and the Himba villages and is accustomed to tour groups, and is the best place to ask for information or help. It also runs **Mopane Camp** (above) which is in a much nicer setting.

E **Kunene Village Rest Camp**, a NACTOB project, central reservations, T061-255977 (Windhoek), www.nactob.com.na. An excellent community campsite set in a sheltered valley, well signposted down a bad road 2 km from Opuwo, the other side of a hill. There are 4 simple rooms with en suite showers, plus 6 grassed sites, each with a *braai*, table and seating under thatched shelter. The central wash block is very basic but clean and fitted with solar lamps (the hot water soon runs out). The reception area has a pleasant bar with a seating area overlooking the camp. The camp is surrounded by a fence to keep goats out, but is still vulnerable to theft, keep your belongings with you in the tent or locked in your car.

Epupa Falls *p201*

AL **Epupa Camp**, about 1 km from the falls, follow the track upstream past the village. Reservations, T061-232740 (Windhoek), www.epupa.com.na. Award-winning camp with 9 canvas tents with en suite shower and toilet, a *lapa* with eating area and bar. Price is full board, and includes a trip to a Himba village and sundowner drive. The smartest accommodation in the area, expensive, but with informative and friendly hosts. Originally built for the experts involved in the feasibility study for the Epupa Dam project (see box, page 200). Despite being very much a going concern, the agreement with the Himba (who own the land) permits no fixed structures, which is perhaps just as well given the considerable flooding in 2000. Reservations are essential as the camp is frequently full.

A **Omarunga Camp**, reservations through **Eden Travel**, T061-234342 (Windhoek), www.camelthorn.com.na. 11 comfortable and spacious canvas dome tents with twin wooden beds and outside wash basin, communal showers, open dining area and bar next to the river with good views into Angola. However, given that accommodation is in normal tents and dinners are simple and heavily overpriced at US$25, this is an expensive option. Good campsite (E) with hot showers and plenty of shade, also located by the river. The whole complex is fenced. Visits to a Himba village with a translator can be organized.

E **Epupa Community Campsite** and **Hot Springs Campsite**. These large campsites have *braai* pit and running water, many (cold) showers and flush toilets. Both have lovely locations on the river, close to the falls. People used to camp here long before any facilities existed, but now the local communities benefit from the camping fees.

Marienfluss and Hartmann's valleys *p202*

L **Serra Cafema**, run by **Wilderness Safaris**, reservations through any agent or at www.wilderness-safaris.com. A private camp in the extreme northwest on the Angolan border used only for clients of fly-in safaris and probably one of the most remote camps in Africa. Luxurious tented camp with 6 self-catering double tents, beautifully furnished with 4-poster beds and wooden decks, swimming pool in shaded, grassed riverside site. Excellent for birding, good fishing, walking and quad-bike and 4WD trails. Visits Himba villages nearby.

AL **Camp Syncro**, reservations through **Kaokohimba Safaris**, T/F061-222378, kaohim @mweb.com.na. This is a wonderfully remote safari camp situated right on the banks of the Kunene River at the end of the Marienfluss Valley. It can be reached only by 4WD and it is a day's drive from either Opuwo or Sesfontein, though most guests fly. 4 stone cottages sleeping 2 with thatched roofs, under a grove of ana trees, solar power, 2 sets of toilets and showers, tends to be booked on a an all-inclusive base for a group rather than separate couples, which the camp prefers. The host, Koos Verwey, has been living in the Marienfluss for several years and has intimate knowledge and respect of the local Himba who he will take you to meet.

E **Okarohombo Campsite**, by the Kunene River at the northern end of the Marienfluss Valley, a NACTOB project, central reservations, T061-255977 (Windhoek), www.nactob.com.na. Run by the local Himba, very little English spoken, although you might find someone who understands Afrikaans. 5 simple campsites with communal flush toilets, showers, taps and shade provided by a few camelthorn trees, a scenic camp which helps make the long and tiring journey worthwhile, the more provisions you have the more you will be able to relax and enjoy this special spot. Bring firewood/charcoal, and be sure to ask the locals the safest spot for swimming in the river – there are crocodiles.

Eating

Opuwo *p199*

Ohakene Lodge generally only provides food to guests but it is worth asking – smart clothes may help.

Bakery Takeaway hamburgers and tasty meat pies. Your best bet after **Ohakene Lodge**.

Otherwise you'll have to resort to the supermarkets and takeaways specializing in goat and chips, a few tinned goods, crisps and not much else.

Bars and clubs

Opuwo *p199*

Don't be put off by the rather seedy-looking bars. People in town are generally friendly and interested in visitors and chatting over a beer or 2. At the T-junction for the C41, next to the information centre, is a decent bar and **Verona Bar** and **Cuvelai No 1** have pool tables where strangers are welcome to take on the locals.

Shopping

Opuwo *p199*
The local crafts shop, set up by missionaries, is on the main street and sells locally made and used baskets, jewellery, dolls, carvings, clothing and ornaments. These, thankfully, are no longer the family heirlooms of the vendors, but are now produced for sale, with designs sometimes adapted to be more appealing to tourists. If you intend buying these kinds of souvenirs this is the place to do so, as the money goes directly to the craftsmen and women, at a fraction of the price you pay in Windhoek.

Activities and tours

Kaokoland *p192*
Tour operators
Desert Adventure Safaris, 38 Bismarck St, Swakopmund, T064-403274, www.das.com.na. Fly-in and 4WD safaris from 2-12 days. Tours to the Kunene River region including Epupa Falls; also fly-in tours with 4WD trips to Damaraland and other parts of the region.
Kaokohimba Safaris, T/F061-222378, kaohim@mweb.com.na. Runs the private, thatched **Camp Syncro** in the Marienfluss Valley by the Kunene River (see page 204), most guests fly there directly from Windhoek and it must be booked in advance.
The company organizes hiking trips from 2-12 days in way-off-the-beaten-path locations, and 4WD cultural tours using local guides. Educationally you will learn about the region and the problems facing the Himba today. Recommended.
Kunene Tours and Safaris, T064-402779, zanberg@iafrica.com.na. Guided 4WD trips to the more remote corners of Kaokoland and Damaraland with experienced guide Caesar Zandberg. You travel in your own vehicle but are joined by Caesar in his own vehicle, recommended to really get off the beaten track. If you don't have you own car, can also operates tours for 6-8 people.
Ohakane Safaris, based in Opuwo, T065-273031, www.natron.net/tour/ohakane. Tours to way-off-the-beaten-track destinations by 4WD, including remote Himba villages, some off-road driving and camping in dry riverbeds, prices include meals and all camping equipment, a chef comes along though you will be expected to pitch your own tent.

The Far North

Formerly known as Owamboland, the far north of Namibia is is a dusty, overgrazed, overpopulated area with few attractions for tourists. The region is now divided into four political regions (Oshikoto, Ohangwena, Omusati and Oshana). This area is home to almost half the country's population (over 800,000 people), with much the greatest population density (over 10 people per square kilometre on average, against a national average of just over two). This part of Namibia is typified by a different relationship between man, animal and land: you will notice a significant increase in traffic (cars, bicycles and donkeys); herds of goats and cattle criss-crossing the roads; rows of wooden, fenced homesteads;, strings of children making their way to and from school; and the tireless collectors of water going about their daily grind. After the vast, uninhabited expanses of the south, it is a striking reminder of how much life the land supports. A great deal of money is flowing into the region from government and overseas aid expenditure on education, health care, the civil service, police and military and there are significant visible infrastructure investments. The area is evidently booming, but visitors will quickly appreciate that tourism is not the engine for this growth. ▸▸ *For Sleeping, Eating and other listings, see pages 212-214.*

Ins and outs

The unnatural division in the structure of life in the country is the **Red Line**, located 120 km south of Ondangwa on the B1, a fence which separates the animals of Etosha and the large commercial farms of the south from those of the communal small farmers of the north. The movement of livestock, meat and animal products from north to south is forbidden, ostensibly to prevent foot-and-mouth disease and rinderpest from infecting the commercial herds of the south. For the tourist, this means any meat, skins, horns, trophies or other animal products either need not to be brought north in the first place, or require a veterinary note specifying the health of your souvenir before being allowed to return south.

While few overseas visitors travel to the Far North, those who do are rewarded with an insight into a unique and highly fertile ecosystem.

Best time to visit Although they seem to be increasingly unreliable, the rains are expected at the beginning of the year, making March to May the most colourful, verdant months to visit. The yearly average (about 500 mm) usually falls in heavy thunderstorms, with resulting damage to crops and flooding; the surface water flows to the *oshanas*, on which the local agronomy relies. Crops are planted, grown and reaped before July or August, when most of the *oshanas* have dried up. This is the time to witness the bizarre spectacle of groups of women with handmade fishing baskets wading in shrinking muddy pools, doing their best to catch an addition to the supper pot. For the remainder of the year, expect dust, heat and breath-sapping hot winds. The dust can be like a mist, requiring headlights for driving, and the landscape becomes surreal and moon-like. For your comfort this period is best avoided.

Ondangwa

▸▸ *pp212-214.* *Phone code: 065. Colour map 1, A5.*

686 km from Windhoek, 256 km from Tsumeb, 35 km from Oshakati.

This is the principal centre in the region where there are small roadside shops and bottle stores, and a couple of smart new malls with banks and supermarkets. This is the second largest town in this populous region and fairly well provisioned. The only tourist attraction is the informative and well-presented Nakambale Museum at Olokonda, signposted off the B1 before you reach town.

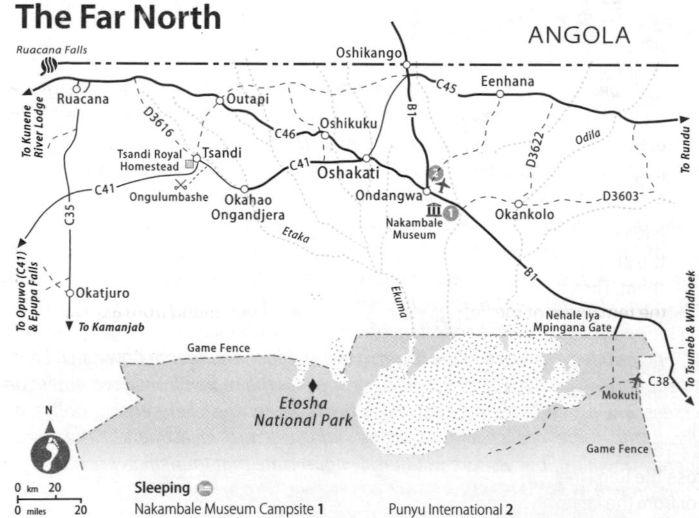

The Oshana environment

The *oshanas* are a system of shallow watercourses and *vleis* which first appear in south-central Angola and reach as far south as the Etosha Pan. Most of these 'rivers' are several hundred kilometres long, but they only flow for a few months each year after the rains. In years of exceptionally heavy rainfall there can be widespread flooding. These floods are known as the *efundja*. The last major *efundja* was recorded in 1954. Recent (2000 and 2001) plentiful rain has meant that the *oshanas* have not dried out until September, extending the productive season for a few more valuable weeks. But the high water levels also highlighted that many homesteads are now vulnerable to floods, should there be exceptionally heavy downpours in coming years.

Aerial photography reveals a pattern of watercourses akin to a river delta emptying into the ocean, but in this case they drain internally into pans, the largest of which is at Etosha. The watercourses are mostly empty, left over from earlier fluvial periods, with alluvium deposits and high salt concentrations. An optimal season sees the rains start in November and fall regularly from December to March. There is water in the *oshanas* from January until July. Farmers prepare their fields and cattle are herded back from distant grazing to benefit from the new pasture near home, enriching the farmers' diet. Crops are reaped before the water evaporates, and this is the peak fishing season as the fish have reached a reasonable size and the ponds are small enough to catch them. Then it's back to mealie pap for the remainder of the year.

Given the large number of people subsisting directly off the land in this region, the *oshanas* play an important role in the well-being of the population. The government is struggling with population increases and erratic rainfall to protect the environment and manage it sensibly. Water is pumped from the Calueque Dam in Angola, but this is for drinking, and there are very few irrigation schemes (Ongwediva being an exception) that can compensate for poor rains. Without rain, the basic crops such as *omahangu* (millet) fail and there are no fish. Additionally, the groundwater level drops and boreholes run dry, pastures remain barren and cattle have nothing to eat. Quickly, a land of plenty becomes a desolate, desperate, disaster zone, an embarrassment for the government in what is its home territory. The visible overgrazing, erosion and deforestation, added to increasing soil salinity and frequent water shortages, put in question the continued balance of the ecosystem. Its successful management is one of the government's greatest challenges. They cannot afford to get it wrong as relocation of so many people (even ignoring the social issues) is virtually impossible in a country as dry and poorly suited to subsistence agriculture as Namibia. Put simply, everyone prays for rain.

Driving through the region, one can't help wondering where the money comes from. While many grow and rear a good deal of their consumption needs, very few produce an excess to sell for income. Principally, money comes from the government and migrant labour, with traders benefiting from a good number of Angolans heading south for supplies.

You can get here either from Tsumeb and the triangle towns along the B1 which cross the Red Line – where there is a 24-hour Engen garage, bottle store and takeaway – or from the far north from the fairly good gravel road C46 from Rucana and Oshakati.

Overgrazing, deforestation and lack of regular rain has reduced the surrounding area to a desolate, sandy rubbish tip, with forlorn cattle wandering and wondering where their grazing has gone. This is communal land buckling under population pressure. The *makalani* palm trees have survived in the harsh landscape, perhaps because of their inefficiency as firewood, and offer attractive silhouettes at sunset, the *mopane* having long since been cut down for firewood or used to build homesteads. For a few weeks after heavy rains, the *oshanas* fill with water and pale pink and white lilies miraculously appear; you may also see the cone-shaped fishing baskets in use. The open markets in July and August are evidence that the fish grow to an impressive size in their shrinking *oshanas* – often little more than big puddles.

While there is nothing for the tourist in town, there is a sense of having 'arrived'. Activity of people and traffic flow increases dramatically, there are more roadside stalls, and developments extend further away from the road. There is more litter, more abandoned, gutted cars and less vegetation. In town, modern shopping centres – with banks and insurance companies, supermarkets and furniture stores – have been developed, and a four-star hotel has appeared on the northern edge of town catering mainly to business travellers.

Nakambale Museum and Campsite

ⓘ *T065-245668, US$0.80, guide US$1.50 per person, visit to a local homestead, US$4.*

The Nakambale Museum is the tourist highlight of the area and another NACOBTA project (see box on page 41). Housed in the original (1893) mission house, much of the collection is devoted to the lives and impressive work of the Finnish missionaries in northern Namibia since the 1870s; in particular, to Martti Rautunen, who translated many (particularly religious) works into local languages and was given the Owambo name 'Nakambale'. There are some excellent and informative displays of traditional musical instruments, household utensils, clothing, tools, snares and clothing. Surrounding the house are a large church and a cemetery with beautifully maintained marble graves for the Rautunen family, which is now a national monument, and a traditional Ndonga homestead. Everything is explained on a guided tour and if you want to learn more about everyday life of the Ndonga you can visit one of the inhabited homesteads nearby. With pre-booking, you can watch demonstrations of Ovambo life and culture: eating, singing, dancing and even sleeping in the traditional way (see Sleeping, below, for details).

The museum and campsite are located 13 km southeast of Ondangwa, off the B1. A signpost, 8 km southeast of Ondangwa, points right onto the gravel road D3629. After about 5 km you will see the settlement of Olukonda to your left. The old church, Nakambale Museum and campsite are situated about 500 m from the junction. The road is suitable for all vehicles.

Ondangwa to Angola » pp212-214.

The ceasefire between the Angolan Government and Unita in 2002 marked the end of the civil war in Angola, and there has been no recent 'trouble' near the Namibian border in the past few years. Economic links with the north of Namibia are improving; many Angolan traders head south for supplies, and wealthier Angolans come to spend their US dollars in this land of relative plenty. With Angolan businesses taking an ever higher profile, you may hear Portuguese being spoken in the border region. Some Namibians venture north, mainly for cheaper petrol, cattle and goats. Angola is most certainly making moves into the African tourism market, and it now has its own tourism website (www.angola.org). Many overlanders have successfully gone into Angola in the last few years, mostly adventurous South African 4WD owners, but also trans-Africa overland trucks which have successfully crossed en route from central Africa to southern Africa;

reports so far seem very positive. It is, however, a very new place to visit so get expert up-to-date advice before crossing into Angola. **Note** Despite extensive de-landmining activity, the roads in Angola are in a dreadful state, though reconstruction is expected to start soon. On the internet you will find a number of South African tour companies that offer guided tours into Angola starting from Johannesburg or Windhoek.

Ondangwa to Oshikango

From Ondangwa, the border with Angola at Oshikango is 68 km north of town along the B1. The road from Ondangwa to the border is busy with Angolan trucks and for the last kilometre it is lined with traders.

For six months of the year there is a time difference between Namibia and Angola, and although there are no signs to warn you, vehicles drive on the right.

The border The customs and immigration offices on the Namibian side are a bricks-and-mortar statement of national pride. The buildings on the Angolan side of the border show all the evidence of war damage. It is possible, with a minimum of red tape, to go over to Santa Clara, the town on the Angolan side of the border, for a few hours. But it is advisable to walk the short distance; you may invite unnecessary problems by taking your car. There do not appear to be formal immigration checkpoints so respond helpfully to officials who may approach you. The border is open 0800-1800.

Ongwediva

At Ongwediva, 10 km southeast of Oshakati on the B1, there is a small concentration of a shops, a **Standard Bank** with ATM, **Spar** and **Engen** garage. Many education and environment ministry offices are located here, and the annual Trade Fair takes place in a huge, new conference facility. The few shops include the **Traditional Shop**, set back from the road, for Owambo and Himba jewellery, traditional dresses and skins.

Oshakati

Phone code: 065. Colour map 1, A4. 35 km to Ondangwa, 152 km from Ruacana.

Oshakati has many faces. There is the 'town', the former South African military base, where government employees, expatriates and the 'successful' live in detached

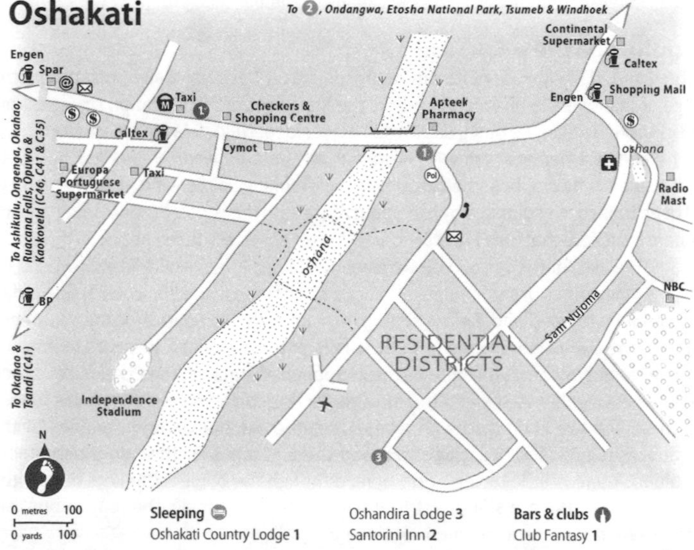

houses set in leafy gardens close to the video shops, private schools and public library. Then there are the various 'locations' where shanty-type dwellings of corrugated iron and scrap metal are dotted with NGO and municipally built public lavatories and stand pipes. In between these extremes are those with housing and services of a basic standard, mostly lowly government workers of some kind.

The commercial centre of Oshakati and the north happens where the high street, banks and the open market, **Omatala**, face each other across the dusty main road. The **University of Namibia** has its Northern Campus in town, and you will notice a major influence of municipal buildings and services including several petrol stations and a branch of **Checkers** supermarket. But, while there is certainly money in the area, the impression remains that life for the majority in Oshakati is hard.

Northwest of Oshakati

Continuing north from Oshakati, the sense of being somewhere becomes elusive as the ribbon development peters out. Only the scattered homesteads and schools are a reminder that this is still one of the most densely populated parts of Namibia.

The direct route from Oshakati to Ruacana follows 160 km of good tar road, the C46, along the Ogongo Canal. This route will take you through **Oshikuku**, 28 km, and Outapi, 100 km. Depending upon the time of year you will either pass through flood plains (usually March to May), or dry sandy pans, dotted with clusters of *makalani* palms, homesteads and *mahangu* fields. The most striking feature of the landscape is its flatness, where *makalani* palms dominate, interspersed with wonderful baobabs.

Ex-President Sam Nujoma was born in a small homestead in the village of Ongandjera, a few kilometres to the south of the main B1.

While there are many around, keep an eye out for the huge baobab tree as you head north for **Ombalantu**. This is not as well known as the one at Outapi (see below).

Outapi » *Colour map 1, A4.*

Outapi, the main town of the Ombalantu Region along the C46 between Oshakati and Rucana, is developing rapidly. As you approach from the south you will notice the large number of newly constructed government buildings and shops, including some small roadside restaurants and a supermarket. There is an exceptionally large baobab tree with a wide girth which in the past has served as a prison and is now a church. To visit the baobab, obtain permission at the police station; it is something of a national monument.

Ongulumbashe » *Colour map 1, A4.*

To the south of Outapi about 36 km along the gravel D3612 and signposted from the village of Tsandi is the historic site where the first shots of the liberation struggle were fired in 1966. Deep in the bush, southwest of President Nujoma's birthplace, a group of PLAN (Peoples Liberation Army of Namibia) combatants were ambushed by South African soldiers having been betrayed by a high-ranking soldier who, it later emerged, had been trained in espionage by the South Africans in the 1950s. When visiting the site it is hard to believe that the PLAN combatants were not totally taken aback by the South Africans' precise knowledge of their whereabouts. It really is the middle of nowhere; far from any main routes or settlements and not a hint of landscape, the countryside is flat, scrubby *mopane* woodland. Before setting their ambush, the South Africans apparently harassed the civilian population in their search for the 'terrorists'. It is hard to imagine who they found to harass. In spite of their opponents' surprise, the PLAN fighters won the battle of Ongulumbashe and the struggle for Namibian independence was born.

Today the site is marked with a monument to the heroes and heroines of the liberation struggle (see box, page 211) and there is talk of setting up a permanent exhibition. There is little to see or do here, although the original bunkers dug by the combatants in 1966 are still intact in the vicinity. Interestingly, the replica bunkers constructed in 1990 as a commemoration have collapsed.

Heroes' Day

Lasting one full day, with visitors to Ongulumbashe camping out before and after the event, the occurrences of 1966 are commemorated and those who fought during the struggle for independence are honoured. Performance and cultural presentations are made by representatives of the 13 regions – traditional songs of praise and colourful dances in traditional costumes. The most popular of these is a dramatic re-enactment of the battle of Ongulumbashe complete with carved wooden AK 47s. The victorious combatants end by raising the Namibian flag just as the real fighters did after each victory in the bush; the flag was flown then lowered and carried with the unit wherever they went. As far as is known, at no point during the bush war did the SAD succeed in capturing the Namibian flag.

Along with the performances, speeches are made and prayers said, before the people – civilians, heroes, heroines and politicians – all sit down and eat together. Away from the pompousness of Windhoek, the bush is a great leveller and you are likely to find yourself filling your plate shoulder to shoulder with some of the most powerful men in the country.

Tsandi Royal Homestead

ⓘ *One of the NACOBTA projects; you can arrange a visit through the office in Windhoek (see page 41) or by phoning direct, T065-258025. Tour costs US$5.90 per person, which includes a performance of traditional dancing and a visit to Ongulumbashe. Best to arrange this in advance.*

In Tsandi is the local royal homestead which is the home of the king of several tribes in Owambo and for centuries has been the place where cultural and traditional values and customs have been passed down through the generations. Here visitors can join a tour of Tsandi Royal Homestead and look at the collections of traditional weapons and clothes, meet some of the homestead's residents and possibly the king himself. A number of craft outlets sell woven baskets and clay pots.

Ruacana Falls » *Colour map 1, A3.*

Ruacana Falls are not the destination they once were. The Calueque Dam in Angola has stopped any flooding and the steady stream that does come through is deviated through the hidden turbines of the hydroelectric power station. However, this corner of the country is still worth a visit; the Kunene River continues to flow, there is a range of watersports including excellent whitewater rafting and canoeing, beautiful riverside accommodation and the chance to see the photogenic Himba and their villages.

Ruacana Falls are 15 km from Ruacana, well signposted from the C46. The falls can still be spectacular, but this requires consistent heavy rains (ie summer). For views of the falls, March to April are your best bets to see water crashing over the rocks. Year-round, the flow of the river is increased with demand for electricity (weekdays in the morning and evening) and it takes roughly four and eight hours for the flow to reach **Kunene River Lodge** (for rafting) and Epupa Falls respectively.

Below the falls is a gorge which ends at **Hippo Pools** where there are a couple of small islands in the middle of the channel. There was a campsite here, but with the lack of water, the attraction of the area has disappeared. It used to be possible to climb the 500 steps to the bottom of the gorge, check in Ruacana at the police station. The border runs down the middle of the river below the main falls.

Kunene River

From the Ruacana Falls to the Atlantic Ocean the Kunene River constitutes the border between Namibia and Angola. It is a pleasant and welcome sight as it weaves its way through the Ehomba Mountains, and then the Zebra Mountains, before plunging over the smaller (but still impressive from ground level) **Epupa Falls**, 162 km west of Ruacana. There are also two sets of rapids at **Enyandi** and **Ondorusu**. The river enters the Atlantic Ocean along the northern extremity of the Skeleton Coast Park, this also marks the northern limits of the giant sand dunes which first appeared 1700 km south, along the banks of the Orange River. The name Kunene was given to the river by the Hereros. In their language it means, 'right-hand side'; the name refers to the land north of the river. The lands to the south are known as the **Kaokoland**, 'land on the left-hand side'. In Angola the local name for the river is *Omulongo*, 'the stream'. Most visitors to Kaokoland approach it from the south via Kamanjab and Sesfontein, or they fly in on excellent, but expensive, organized safaris (see Windhoek tour operators, page 14, or Kaokoland tour operaters, page 205).

Ruacana ➤ *Phone code: 065. Colour map 1, A3. 152 km from Oshakati.*

Ruacana itself is a useful supply stop for those planning to explore northern Kaokoland. The town only came into being as a camp for workers involved with the construction of the Ruacana Hydroelectric Project. The Kunene River provides both an important source of power for Namibia and water for irrigation in Owamboland, the water being carried by the **Ogongo Canal** alongside the C46 to lands beyond Oshakati.

Ruacana is well signposted, 5 km south of the C46; the airport is 3 km east along the C46. A legacy of the armed conflict in the area is that there is only one entrance into the settlement. This was an important South African military base; the barbed wire and bomb shelters are hard to see, but there is the feel of a military camp. There is a BP garage, the only fuel in the area, with a well-stocked shop (open 0800-1800), a small supermarket 200 m further along the same road, hospital and post office. The BP garage is also the place to ask about accommodation, though its best to press on to the attractive sites/lodges on the banks of the Kunene.

There are no banks in Ruacana or in Opuwo.

From Ruacana there are a few options. If you have approached through Oshakati you can avoid backtracking by returning south via the C35 past the western end of Etosha National Park to **Kamanjab**, a 272-km drive. This road is navigable with a saloon car. For **Epupa,** 4WDs can take the D3700 westward along the banks of the Kunene the entire 162 km of the journey, which is very challenging west of the **Kunene River Lodge**. A 4WD vehicle is required (plus experience and plenty of time); the Shell road map of Kaokoland is your best companion for the journey (also see the Epupa Falls section on page 201).

Sleeping

Ondangwa *p206*

During the week, accommodation may be booked with government officials, trade fair visitors, businessmen and NGO staff.

B **Pandu Ondangwa Hotel**, just off the B1, at the northern end of town, by the Oshikango turning, T065-241900, www.unitedhospitality.com. 90 en suite rooms with a/c, TV, radio, telephone, desk and kettle, restaurant, bar, coffee shop with good cakes and savouries, large conference facilities, a very clean, international standard hotel, fairly square and impersonal but with some interesting African carvings and wall hangings.

C **Punyu International**, well signposted off the B1, 4 km southeast of town on the B1, turn for Eenhana (D3622), 1 km from the junction, T065-240556, F240660. Simple urban hotel with little intimacy, 30 en suite rooms with a/c, TV, phone and desk. Restaurant with pleasant outdoor seating, 2 bars. **Punyu** (Owambo for 'generosity') has a finger in many pies, you'll see his sign everywhere, including a bakery (with no bread!) opposite.

Nakambale Museum and Campsite *p208*
D-E **Nakambale Museum Campsite**, at the museum, T065-245668, www.nactob.com.na. Campsite, plus 5 permanent tents to hire with beds and bedding, and a traditional Ndonga mud hut with reed mats on the floor and thatched roof. Very basic ablutions, water, electricity, *braai* pit, small craft shop. By prior arrangement traditional meals and music can be arranged.

Oshakati *p209, map p209*
A **Oshakati Country Lodge**, T065-222380, www.namibialodges.com. 45 large, en suite rooms with a/c, TV, desk and kettle. Nicely built with African touches to good standard, central reception and bar in huge thatched barn, restaurant serving good food around swimming pool in pleasant lawned garden. Easily the nicest place in town, popular with tour groups, can also organize car rental.
B **Oshandira Lodge**, T065-220443, oshandira@iway.na. Follow signs, located at the edge of town by the airstrip. 17 double or family a/c rooms with TV and phone. Set in well-watered green gardens with a few caged parrots. Popular restaurant and bar, with seating either indoors or around the swimming pool; this is the best place to eat in town with some traditional food on the menu, but again the whole place looks rather tired.
B **Santorini Inn**, on the main road, on right if approaching from Tsumeb, T065-220506, info@santorini-inn.com. 29 en suite rooms and chalets each with a/c, satellite TV, telephone and kettle, set around a pool and garden courtyard, bar, restaurant (with good pizza), squash court. Looking very faded these days.

Ruacana Falls *p209*
Both the lodge and campsite are wonderfully positioned on the banks of the Kunene, reached by taking the C46 as far as Ruacana Falls, where the tar runs out and the gravel D3700 winds its way along the southern bank of the river, past small Himba homesteads. Outside the rainy season, this route is navigable (with care) by ordinary saloon cars, but only as far as the lodge.
B-E **Kunene River Lodge**, 56 km west of the C46 junction for Ruacana, on the D3700, T065-274300, www.kuneneriverlodge.com. Simple, stone and thatch bungalows, permanent tents and campsite, swimming pool, bar, restaurant; year-round activities include excellent guided rafting and canoeing, fishing, quad-biking, mountain biking and bird-watching. There's a lovely wooden deck here that goes right over the river. Recommended for people looking for adventure.
E **Hippo Pool Campsite**, close to the falls, just 200 m behind the hydroelectric power station, where the D3700 forks off from the C46, a NACOBTA project, T065-270120, www.nacobta.com.na. The camp has 10 sites under *mopane* trees and acacias right on the riverbank (there's a lot of hippo here), each has a *braai* area, communal ablution block with hot showers and eco-toilets. At the reception you can buy firewood and borrow paraffin lamps. Guided walks are offered to Himba settlements and cattle posts, or to the Nampower Hydroelectric Power Station.

Eating

Oshakati *p209, map p209*
In addition to the more formal places listed below, there is a **KFC** in the Yetu Centre, **Jotty's Fish and Chips** on the main road, and many takeaways/bars and market stalls where you can get a taste of what the locals eat.
¶ **Garden Restaurant**, at the **Oshandira Lodge**, see Sleeping, above. A good option and deservedly popular in attractive surroundings. Outside tables, swimming pool, sports bar with large-screen DSTV, pub fare and some Ovambo dishes on the menu.
¶ **Oshakati Country Lodge**, see Sleeping, above. Your best bet for food, serving good and not overpriced à la carte meals at tables by the swimming pool, or a snack menu at the airy indoor bar under a thatched roof, with TV, pool table, gaming machines and draught beer.

Ruacana *p212*
C-E Ruacana Eha Lodge, Springbok Av, T065-270031, info@ruacanalodge.com.na. 20 double en suite rooms, with cool tiles, a/c and TV, restaurant and swimming pool, gym, squash court, 15 campsites with good shared ablution blocks, a reasonable option but aimed at conference delegates with little atmosphere, owned by Namibia's electricity company.

Bars and clubs

Oshakati *p209, map p209*
There are several bars in town where you can enjoy a beer with the locals, as long as you are not expecting anything too lavish. Of these, try **Club Fantasy**, a long- established party place, arranged around a collection of armchairs and low tables, frequented by businessmen, and good for mixing and finding out what is going on in town; expect South African disco hits, a good dose of *soukous* – the infectious Zairean dance – and the Angolan *kazomba*. Open Wed, Fri and Sat.

Entertainment

Ondangwa *p206*
Cinema The small cinema, **Paradiso**, takes up to 50 people and shows relatively recent films.

Shopping

Ondangwa *p206*
Crafts Approaching Ondangwa from the south, as well as the bottle stores aplenty, you should see roadside stalls selling traditional baskets woven from the *makalani* palm leaves, bowls and calabashes. The revenue derived from these items is important to the individual craftsmen and women who produce them. The stalls may look unattended, but stop your car and someone will be there in a flash. The markets in Ondangwa and Oshakati, also worth browsing, may have carved cups, bowls, snuff containers, knives and colourful material. None of these crafts is produced for tourists; they are the preferred implements and materials of the homesteads.

Oshakati *p209, map p209*
Local magnate and powerful Namibian figure Frans (Oupa) Indongo has his **Continental Supermarket** in Oshakati, selling everything you need for rural survival – cast-iron cooking pots, car stereo systems, saddles, water drums, nylon leopard-skin underwear, curtain hooks and plenty more. It also has a cheap and amazingly well-stocked bottle store. The range of spirits and special liqueurs is final evidence, if necessary, of Namibians' love of drinking. There cannot be many places in Africa which offer 5 different brands of Tequila! There is a **Continental No 2** in **Ongwediva** and the old **Continental No 3** is the new **Spar** in the centre of Oshakati, which has a good coffee bar inside. Try the **Europa Portuguese Supermarket** for **camping supplies**. There is also a branch of the **Checkers supermarket** on the main street.

Transport

Ondangwa *p206*
Air **Air Namibia**, Windhoek, T061-2996333, www.airnamibia.com.na. The airport (and Air Namibia office) is 5 km northwest of Ondangwa on the B1. There are 2 flights a day between Ondangwa and Windhoek (Eros) airport. Ondangwa-Eros (1½ hrs), 0700 and 1500, Windhoek-Ondangwa, 0900 and 1700.

Taxi There are numerous taxis plying south to Windhoek and destinations en route.

Oshakati *p209, map p209*
Car hire **Cheetah Car Hire**, T065-222053.

Directory

Ondangwa *p206*
Medical services Hospital, T065-220211, is 7 km south of town on the D3622 for Eenhana. **Police** T065-210111. There's also a **post office**, all 3 **banks** (with ATMs), numerous **petrol stations**, and a **vet** (for clearance to cross the Red Line with any animal skins, horns, etc, that you may have).

Oshakati *p209, map p209*
Internet Internet café by the Spar, excellent connection speed, Mon-Fri 0900-1900, Sat 0900-1300.

The Coast & Namib-Naukluft

Footprint features

Introduction

For many visitors to Namibia the coast could easily be passed over as they go in search of wildlife and the romance of the African bush portrayed in so many brochures and television programmes. But for Namibians and many South Africans, the coast provides a relaxing and cool contrast to the heat and dust of the interior. Each year thousands descend on the resorts for a few weeks' fishing and boating and, increasingly these days, adventure sports.

The coast provides a series of striking contrasts between the dunes of the desert and the wild South Atlantic Ocean, epitomized by the rusting hulks of sunken ships lying along the Skeleton Coast. Further inland is the Namib Desert, which has the oldest and most evocative desert scenery in the world. Here giant sand dunes march determinedly towards the sea in a dune field 300 km wide. The ever-changing landscape supports gravel plains, rugged canyons, towering walls of volcanic rock and vast dune seas. The dunes are best appreciated in the Namib-Naukluft Park around Sossusvlei or, if you have the extra cash, from the air on a scenic flight from Swakopmund or a balloon ride from Sesriem. Witnessing the changing colours of the shifting sands at sunset or sunrise is easily one of the highlights of Namibia.

★ Don't miss...

1 **Walvis Bay lagoon** Take a cruise or paddle a kayak and check out the dolphins, seals, flamingos and pelicans, page 236.
2 **Sandwich Harbour** Embark on an adventurous 4WD trip to the abandoned whaling settlement, where the towering dunes meet the sea, page 237.
3 **Sandboarding** Get an adrenalin rush quad-biking or sandboarding through the dunes near Swakopmund, or get a bird's-eye view from the Swakop skydive, page 247.
4 **Skeleton Coast National Park or Namib-Naukluft Park** Take a sightseeing flight over the eerie and barren coastal park to witness the forbidding Atlantic Ocean or the dramatic sea of sand, pages 258 and 275.
5 **Sossusvlei** Explore at dawn when the rising sun paints the landscape in vibrant reds and oranges; scramble up a giant dune and slide down, page 284.

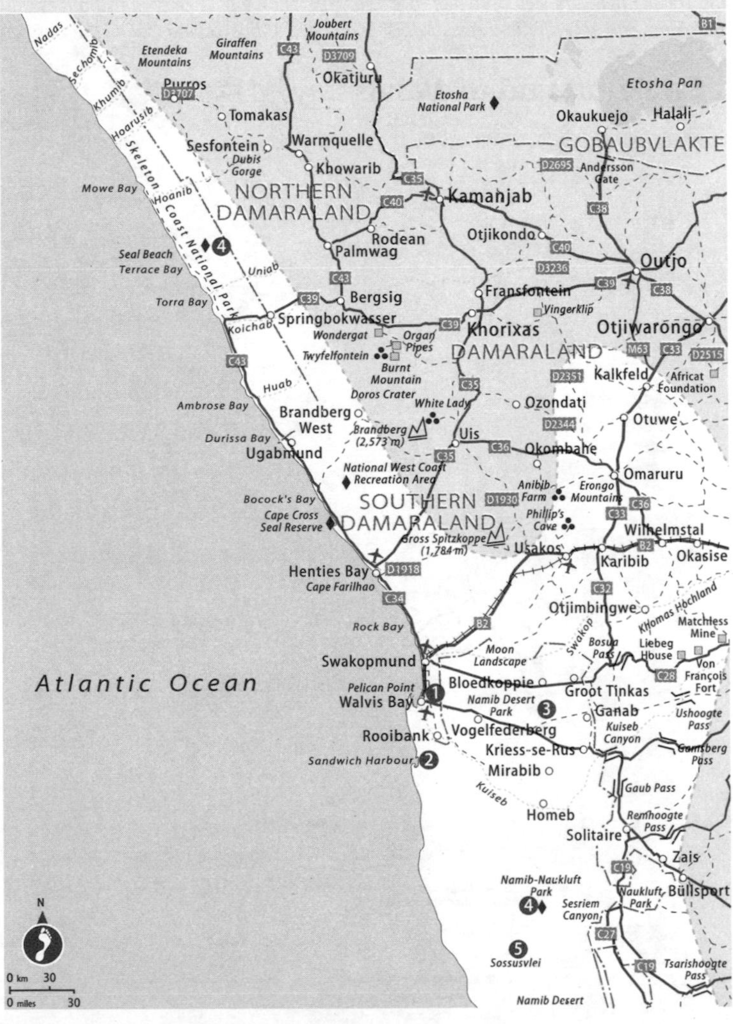

Swakopmund and around

▸▸ *Phone code: 064. Colour map 1, C3.*

Surrounded on three sides by the arid Namib Desert and on the west side by the cold waters of the South Atlantic, Swakopmund is surely one of the most unusual and fascinating colonial towns in the whole of Africa. In a period of a little more than 25 years the German Imperial Government built a succession of extravagant buildings which today represent one of the best-preserved collections of German colonial architecture still standing. When approached from the desert, especially during the morning fog, the turrets, towers and pastel-coloured buildings on the skyline appear as a hazy mirage, and the quirky town comes as quite as surprise on the barren coastline. Today, because of its olde-worlde charm and relaxed atmosphere, Swakopmund is Namibia's premier holiday resort, with a steady flow of visitors all year round, culminating in December and January when thousands descend from the hot interior to enjoy the temperate climate of the coast. There are lots of things to do, a wide choice of hotels, guesthouses and pensions, and several good restaurants and coffee shops selling traditional German

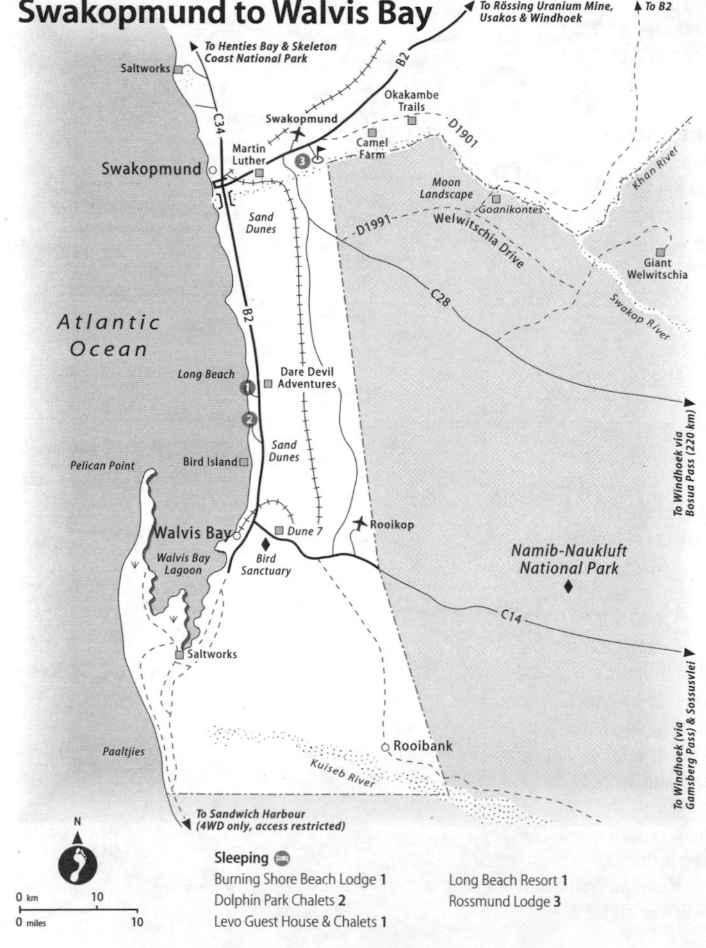

pastries. You will not have a problem finding an apple strudel or a flagon of beer in this town. » *For Sleeping, Eating and other listings, see pages 237-253.*

Ins and outs

Getting there

Swakopmund, the principal town on the coast, is on just about any tour itinerary there is, so if you are on an organized tour, at least a couple of days in town will be included. It is easily reached from Windhoek along the tarred B2 via Okahandja. This route, which can be covered in half a day, is well served by the regional towns of the Hinterland with plenty of shops and petrol stations along the way. However, there are more scenic approaches from the interior to the coast on the gravel roads. From Windhoek the C28 goes to Swakopmund through part of the Namib-Naukluft Park, and this is a very scenic drive though you will require a permit for part of it. Another route that goes through the park is the C26 and then the C14 from Windhoek to Walvis Bay, 30 km to the south of Swakopmund; this route goes over the Gamsberg and Kuiseb passes and again offers a wonderfully scenic drive. For more information on these routes see the Hinterland section on page 264. **Intercape Mainliner** bus runs a daily service from Windhoek to Swakopmund and **Air Namibia** has flights between Windhoek and Swakopmund airport (although nearby Walvis Bay airport is better serviced for flights). There is also the option of taking the luxury (expensive) **Desert Express** train from the capital to the coast. » *See Transport, page 251, for more details.*

Getting around

Swakopmund is entirely negotiable by foot, although at night it is advisable to catch a taxi back to your hotel even over short distances. The town is dissected neatly in a grid pattern and signposts are clear. The main road that runs from east to the coast on the west and is the extension of the B2 is Sam Nujoma Avenue which has, like many streets in Swakopmund and Windhoek, recently undergone a name change from the former Kaiser Wilhelm Street. A move to reflect more contemporary figures in Namibia's history than the old colonial names. To reach the outlying regions of Swakopmund, you need to be on a tour or have a car. All the operators provide pick-ups in town to go to their sites (eg to the Swakopmund Airport for skydiving), which are almost always included in the price.

Swakopmund is fairly quiet over the weekend; most shops are closed from 1300 on Saturday until Monday morning and most restaurants are closed on Sunday night.

Tourist information

Ministry of Environment and Tourism (MET) ⓘ *Woermannhaus Ankerplatz, Bismarck St, T064-404576, Mon-Fri 0800-1700, permits can be obtained from 0800-1500 on weekdays and 0900-1200 on weekends, though the service is erratic on Sat and Sun when the staff may decide not to come in*, is the place to go to get permits for the Welwitschia Plains drive if you are driving yourself and not on a tour. Remember all other permits are available at the gates of the parks. The exception is the Kolmonskop Ghost Town near Lüderitz in the south. These permits can also be obtained at the MET office in Windhoek, Lüderitz, and the Sesriem office at the entrance to the campsite. Avoid the MET office in Walvis Bay which borders on useless. The desert is well patrolled by MET staff, make sure you observe all the regulations and respect the fragility of the local environment. Do not litter (and that includes cigarette butts). There is no excuse for not having a permit if stopped. If you are caught without a permit the fine is US$45 per vehicle.

Namibia Wildlife Resorts ⓘ *Woermannhaus on Bismarck St, T064-405513, www.nwr.com.na, Mon-Fri 0900-1630*, is a helpful office where you can now make

Swakopmund

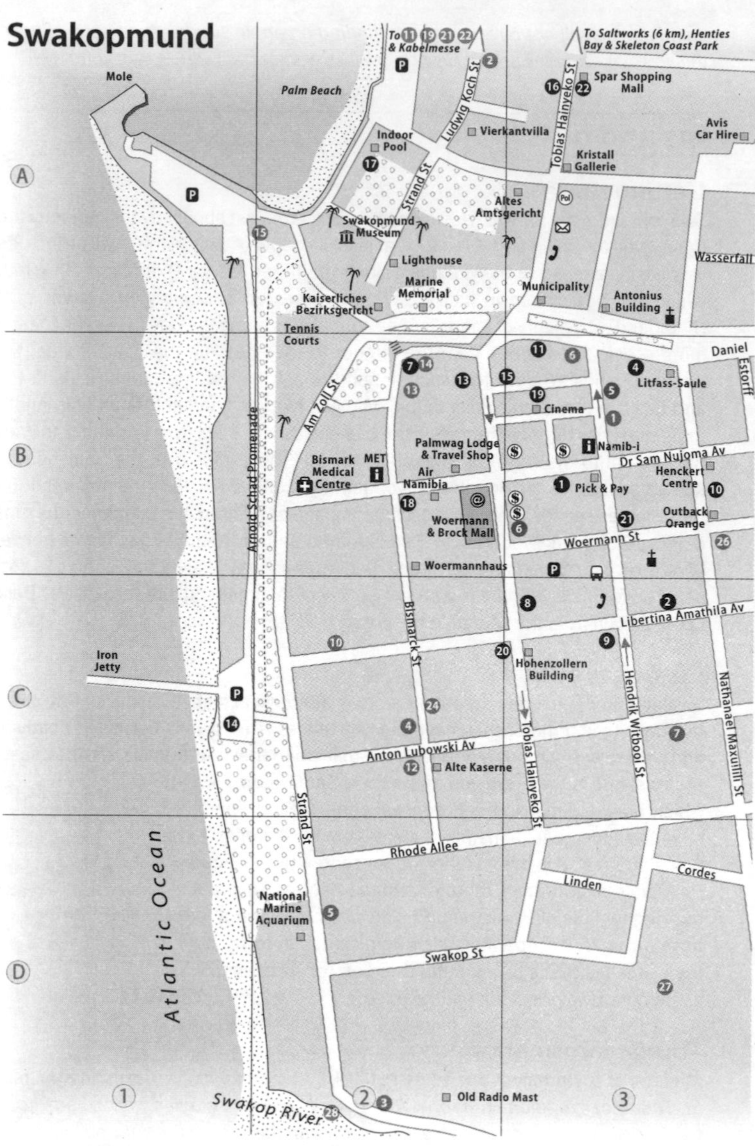

Sleeping

Alte Brücke Resort **3** *D3*
Alternative Space **20** *B4*
Atlanta & Chili Peppers **1** *B3*
Beach Lodge **22** *A2*
Brigadoon **2** *A2*
Desert Sky Backpackers **7** *C3*
Deutsches Haus Pension **8** *B4*
Dunedin Guest House **9** *A4*
Eberwein **17** *B4*
Europa Hof **4** *C2*
Garni Adler **5** *D2*
Hansa **6** *B3*
Intermezzo **21** *A2*
Pension a la Mer **10** *C2*
Pension Prinzessin Rupprecht Heim **12** *C2*
Pension Rapmund **13** *B2*
Restcamp Sophia Dale **18** *D4*
Sam's Giardino **23** *B4*
Schweizerhaus & Café Anton **14** *B2*
Sea Breeze Guesthouse **19** *A2*
Seagull **11** *A2*
Secret Garden Guest House **24** *C2*
Stiltz **28** *D2*
Strand **15** *A2*
Strauss Holiday & Overnight Flats **25** *A4*
Swakop Lodge & Cape to Cairo **26** *B3*
Swakopmund Hotel & Entertainment Centre, Platform One & Station Grill **16** *A4*
Swakopmund Municipal Restcamp **27** *D3*
Villa Wiese Backpackers Lodge **29** *A4*

Eating

Café Tref **1** *B3*
Erich's **4** *B3*
Gelateria Bella Italia **13** *B2*
Grapevine **2** *C3*

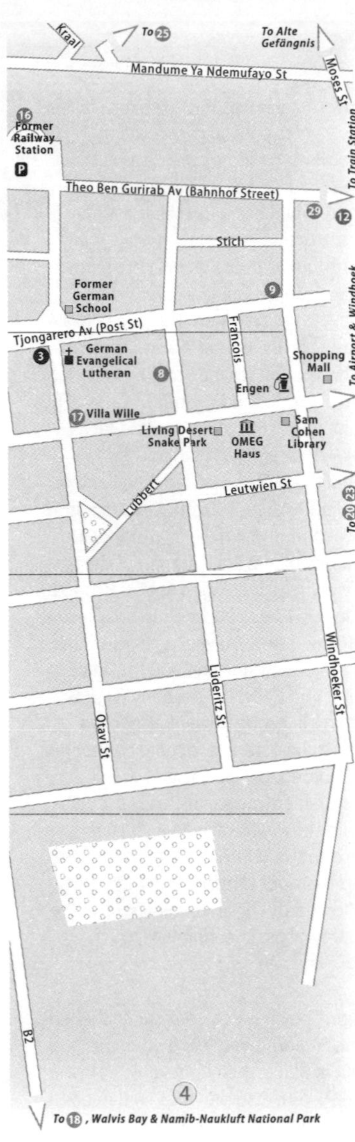

Il Tulipano **3** *B4*
KFC **21** *B3*
Kücki's Pub **8** *C3*
Kuperferpfanne **16** *A3*
Lighthouse Pub **17** *A2*
Mandarin Garden **9** *C3*
Napolitana **10** *B3*
Out of Africa **11** *B3*
Pandora's Box **18** *B2*
Swakopmund Brauhaus **19** *B3*
Tiffany **20** *C2*
Tug **14** *C1*
Western Saloon **15** *B3*
Wimpy & Debonairs Pizza **22** *A3*
Zur Weinmaus **7** *B2*

Bars & clubs
Casablanca **12** *A4*
Fagin's **5** *B3*
Rafters Pub **6** *B3*

bookings for any accommodation it manages in the parks, including the Skeleton Coast National Park (Torra and Terrace Bay), and the Namib-Naukluft desert. The office can provide a little local information too. **Namib-i** ⓘ *Sam Nujoma Av, T064-403129, www.namibi.org.na, open 7 days a week*, is the best source for specific tourist information and is centrally located. Almuth and Elizabeth are helpful and enjoy their work. In addition to local tourist information covering accommodation, they will make reservations for you and book local tours and transport.

Best time to visit

Although the town lies in a true arid desert, the cold Benguela Current which flows from south to north along the coast acts as a moderating influence. The climate on the coast is temperate, temperatures range between 15-25°C. The sea temperature ranges between 14-18°C, too cold for swimming for any period without a wet suit. Swakopmund receives less than 15 mm of rain per year as the rain clouds have to travel all the way over Africa from the Indian Ocean. As you walk about the town note how most buildings have no gutters or drain pipes; on the rare occasion the town gets a lot of rain it floods. The only moisture comes in the form of a sea mist that can reach up to 50 km inland (see box on page 234).

There are occasional sandstorms between October and March, when JCBs are out and about shifting sand off the road between Swakopmund and Walvis Bay.

Safety

On the whole Swakopmund is fairly safe, though, like Windhoek, tourists have been targeted by muggers and robbers in the past. Make use of hotel safes and try to avoid carrying valuables around. At night always take a taxi or walk home in a large group. Ensure that room windows are locked at night, especially in self-catering accommodation that is known to be let out to tourists. Always lock your car and do not leave any valuables on show. Make use of the car guards in the street

Roads, railways and the desert

Much of Swakopmund's early history was a battle to establish a port that could effectively supply the settlements inland. Like all colonial regimes of the period, the colonies were regarded as an important source of raw materials and new territories for trade. If they were to exploit the interior effectively, the Germans had to somehow overcome the inhospitable Namib Desert, which in age before railways and motorcars represented a tremendous natural barrier.

The first road to be constructed between the coast and the interior was known as the '**Baaiweg**'. It was built by the local leader Jan Jonker in 1844. Most of the early traffic consisted of ox wagons carrying copper from Matchless Mine to Walvis Bay, but the 350-km journey proved to be uneconomic and the route was seldom used. All this changed when a harbour was built at Swakopmund, and records show that in 1896, the road was used by 880 ox wagons. But this heavy traffic quickly exposed the local weaknesses: each year more than 12,000 oxen had to be fed and watered across the Namib Desert; there were no waterholes and no suitable pastures; losses were very high. In 1897 the government was forced to turn to the railways to try and overcome the problems posed by the desert.

Work on the first railway started in September 1897, and like the Mole construction project the work greatly contributed to the growth of the town as workshops, supplies and storage sheds were provided. This first railway was a narrow gauge (60 cm), a great achievement for the times considering the obstacles and the remoteness of the colony. The first stage went as far as Jakalsswater, 100 km inland; by July 1900 the railway had reached Karibib, and on 19 June 1902 the first train from Swakopmund arrived in Windhoek, a journey of 382 km. This part of the state railway remained open until March 1910.

In 1903 work had begun on a second narrow-gauge railway, known as the Otavi railway line. In 1900 the Otavi Mine and Railway Company (OMEG: Otavi Minen-und Eisenbahngesell-schaft) had started to mine copper ore in Tsumeb, but because of the unreliable state service they opted to build their own railway line. Their chosen route into the interior proved to be a more sensible one than that followed by the state railway, and the quality of engineering was much

who usually wear yellow work vests and an ID badge. They'll watch your car and when you return to it, a N$2 tip is about right (more at night and if you leave your car for a lengthy period of time). Since the car guards were put in place, theft from vehicles in the town is reported to have been reduced by 90% (the system also provides well-needed jobs). Try and ensure that your accommodation has secure off-street parking.

History

"The municipality since 1909 has made every effort to create an up-to-date township. The water supply is the best in the whole Protectorate and shortage is never felt in the town. There is an Electric Power Station, Ice and Mineral Waters Factories, a first class Hospital and Nursing Home, Public Library, German, Dutch and English Churches, High-class Schools and Hostels and a lot of Corporations and Clubs" (Swakopmund Publicity Association, 1924-1925).

This is how the town proudly promoted itself during the inter-war years, yet less than 30 years earlier no more than 30 Europeans lived in the newly established town.

higher. When the full line opened on 12 November 1906 it was the longest narrow-gauge line in the world at 567 km. The running of the line was taken over by the government when the state railway was closed in 1910. The stretch between Tsumeb and Usakos was only widened in 1960.

Up until 1914 all the German efforts had been concentrated on connecting the port of Swakopmund with the rest of the country. But once the colony had been taken over by the British, Swakopmund quickly fell into disuse since the far more favourable site of Walvis Bay could be exploited. During the First World War the troops from the Union of South Africa built a railway line between Walvis Bay and the Swakop River in just over two months, but unlike the German-built railways this was a broad-gauge track, measuring 106.7 cm. The problem proved to be crossing the Swakop River; the first railway bridge was washed away in 1917. As the German army retreated inland they destroyed the existing narrow-gauge railway, but this merely paved the way for the South African engineers to replace the tracks with a broad-gauge railway. Following the Treaty of Versailles the railway network was taken over by the South African Railways and Harbour Administration. While the network was improved and extended in the interior the problem of crossing the Swakop River remained unaddressed. A railway bridge was built between 1925 and 1926, but in January 1931 the structure was washed away by the river in flood. It was not until 1935 that a secure bridge was built across the river, a short distance inland from the current road bridge. If you visit Swakopmund today, you may well wonder what all the fuss was about, but during the town's early years, the river caused great damage as well as loss of life. The dry riverbed may well look innocuous today, but with sufficient rainfall inland the flood waters can drastically alter the current landscape.

As you drive along the surfaced road between Swakopmund and Walvis Bay it is worth remembering that this stretch of road was first opened in August 1959, and was only surfaced in 1970. The railway that ran between the two towns had to be re-routed in 1980 when the sand dunes finally reclaimed another transport route. You will feel very safe driving between the two towns today, but 100 years ago the Namib was a real threat.

As a visitor to this modern town it is always worth pausing and questioning why and how the town came to be here. If ever there was a town in Africa that owed its origins to colonialism it was Swakopmund.

The first Europeans to encounter the barren Namibian coastline did not stop here; the Portuguese sailors left monuments to mark the points where they had ventured ashore, but there was no attempt made to settle anywhere along this section of the Atlantic coast. But when the German protectorate was proclaimed in 1884 the British had already claimed possession of Walvis Bay, forcing the Germans to look elsewhere for a suitable coastal port. The choice of Swakopmund had a lot to do with the immediate availability of fresh water. While there were other more suitable sites along the coast, the Germans selected Swakopmund as the point to develop a future harbour and settlement because, first, the immediate hinterland was not a mass of sand dunes which inhibited the inland development of transport routes, and second, a short distance up the Swakop River valley there was a fresh water supply.

In August 1892 the German gunboat, *Hyena*, landed just north of the Swakop River and two beacons were raised by the crew to mark their position. At the time this was one of many possible locations for a port along the coast that the Germans were looking for. Today history recounts that the landing in 1892 marked the origins of Swakopmund, however, it was a combination of chance and a tough spirit that saw the establishment and growth of a town at this point on the coast. The first 40 settlers were landed in 1893 by four boats, but thereafter they had to fend for themselves. There was no accommodation, there was nothing; many of these early settlers ended up living in what have been described as 'caves' on the beaches. Today the town can be a grim place on a misty day, so imagine how it was for the first settlers at the turn of the last century. Gradually a town developed and people were able to move inland and establish trading posts and mission stations, but it was the resilience of the earliest settlers that set the pattern. After the First World War the town fell into decline as the nearby port of Walvis Bay assumed the role as the main town on the coast. Many businesses and government offices also moved.

Until the 1970s Swakopmund may have been a forgotten town, but many of the citizens made their mark – today it is one of the most unusual and vibrant communities along the western coast of Africa; what's more, it has a special place in German history. Tourism is now an integral part of the local economy, and many people in the area depend upon the thousands of visitors each year. During the month of December the population on the coast is said to double, hotels are full, restaurants require a booking and to the frustration of local residents there are no parking places in the town centre. Today Swakopmund is witnessing development on a large scale, and the modern town is experiencing a building boom that is taking many people by surprise. Already a number of resorts and holiday homes have been built at Long Beach between Swakopmund and Walvis Bay. To the north of Swakopmund the former bleak campsite at Mile 4 is long gone and the region is now part of the built-up area of the town. Building (mostly apartments) is going on everywhere: both Namibian Breweries and the Swakopmund Tannery have been closed down for new development; a new apartment and shops complex is scheduled to replace the present site of the municipal swimming pool near the Mole; and to the north of town blasting has started, and rocks are being quarried to build a new marina as part of a waterfront development that will also include apartments, shops, restaurants and two hotels, one a five-star establishment.

Sights

For Namibian residents, Swakopmund is popular as a beach resort which provides a comfortable contrast to the hot interior. International visitors come here for the sea, the desert and the fine collection of German colonial buildings. Although most of these old buildings are closed to the public, much of their elegance lies in their exteriors and can be enjoyed whilst strolling around town. The buildings are listed in a sequence that could be followed on a walk starting from the **Strand Hotel**. If you choose to follow the route allow a couple of hours and avoid the hottest part of the day; there are plenty of cafés and bars to call in on along the route. Alternatively, guided walking tours of Swakopmund are worthwhile if you are interested in the town's history and related anecdotes, though not necessary if you just want to see the colonial architecture as most of the interesting buildings are centrally located and easy to find.

Beach area

The **Strand Hotel** was built close to the point where the **mole** joined the mainland. Swakopmund was never the ideal place for a harbour or port, as there was no natural bay or sheltered spot, so, in 1898 the government decided that a mole should be built in order to create an artificial harbour basin. The whole project acted as a great stimulus for the fledgling settlement, such a giant engineering project required a lot of preparation and additional facilities; these took more than 10 months to put in place and included a piped water supply for making cement, a small railway line, the opening up of a quarry and the provision of housing for the labour force. The foundation stone was laid on 2 September 1899, and the mole officially opened on 12 February 1903. It had proved to be a far greater job than imagined; the 375-m construction had cost 2.5 million marks. Along the mole were three steam-powered cranes that could transfer the freight from ships to barges. Unfortunately the planners were totally ignorant to the ocean currents and within two years of completion large amounts of silt started to build up on the south side of the mole. By July 1904 the tugs could only enter the artificial basin at high tide. By 1906 the whole basin had silted up and in the process created Palm Beach that is so enjoyed by today's tourist. After the Herero War the government looked for an alternative solution and plans were drawn up for the construction of a jetty. A wooden jetty was quickly built, which in turn was replaced by the iron jetty which can still be seen today (see below). These days the mole is used as a launch point for pleasure boats and the original harbour basin is a pleasant sheltered swimming area. If you are lucky you may see a dolphin or two swimming around in the bay as you walk out to the end of the mole.

Close to the **Strand Hotel**, by the mole, is the **Swakopmund Museum** ⓘ *T064-402046, Mon-Fri 1000-1300, 1400-1700, adults US$3.20*, founded in 1951 by Dr Alfons Weber and transferred to its present site in 1960. The collection is very strong on local German history and the geography of the Namib Desert. A small museum shop stocks a wide selection of historical leaflets (mostly in German) plus the usual choice of postcards, slides and books on Namibia. Visitors interested in rocks and minerals will find an impressive collection to the right of the entrance. Next door to the uranium mine show cases are a series of shops and rooms recreating the days of German occupation, and this is one of the most interesting displays in the museum. There is also a section devoted to transport and photography in and around Swakopmund during the German occupation. Note the diving helmets that were used during the construction of the jetty, each weighing 15 kg. Overall this is a worthwhile museum and, given that there are not that many museums worth visiting in Namibia, an hour spent here should be of interest to most visitors young and old.

Tucked away in the gardens behind the museum is the port **lighthouse**. The first version, built in 1903, stood at only 11 m; in 1910 a further 10 m was added. The lighthouse marked the harbour as well as warning ships off the treacherous Skeleton Coast – the light can be seen more than 30 km out to sea. Next to the lighthouse is the **Kaiserliches Bezirksgericht** that serves as the presidential holiday home. The presence of heavily armed soldiers will alert you to his presence and it is advisable to keep well clear during such visits. The building was originally the first magistrates court in Swakopmund.

Close to the lighthouse is the **Marine Memorial**, a monument to members of the First Marine Expedition Corps who died during the Herero War, 1904-1905. The statue was designed and cast in Berlin, and presented to the town by the crew of the German gunboat, *Panther*, in July 1908. The figure represents a marine standing by his wounded colleague, ready for action.

As you walk north along the beach look out for Ludwig Koch Street just beyond the municipal swimming pool. There are a couple of contrasting colonial buildings along the seafront. At No 5 is **Vierkantvilla**, the last house assembled by the 'Hafenbauamt' for the construction of the harbour mole. The interesting thing about this building is that it was prefabricated by Fa Zadek in Germany for the Kaiser government. It was shipped out to Africa and erected on a stone foundation in 1899. Further along the street is a solid double-storey building built in 1901 for the **Eastern and South Africa Telegraph** company. **Kabelmesse** was the principal office for the employees who installed the undersea cable from Europe to Cape Town.

Alte Gefängnis

Away from the centre of the town, in Garoeb Street, is the Alte Gefängnis (Old Prison). When the prison was completed in 1909 it stood right out of the town. The building has such a fine façade that it has frequently been mistaken for a hotel or private mansion. There is a tale which recounts the first visit of an official in the South West Africa administration who on seeing the solitary building for the first time exclaimed: "I wouldn't mind staying there." Local dignitaries politely replied, "That, your honour, is the prison." Currently undergoing a facelift, the building is still used as a prison today so be very discreet when trying to take a photograph!

Theo-Ben Gurirab Avenue (formerly Bahnhof Street)

Close to the police station on the corner of Theo-Ben Gurirab Avenue and Tobias Hainyeko Street streets is a lemon yellow building in a well-kept garden full of succulents and palm trees. This is the **Altes Amtsgericht**, built in 1906 as a school but then used as the magistrates office after the state had to complete the building when the private source of funds ran out. After falling into disrepair the building was restored in 1976. During office hours you may be able to get a glimpse of the interior. The building was designed by Otto Ertl who was also responsible for designing the prison and the Lutheran church; notice the similarities of features, such as the gables and turrets, of these buildings.

A short walk along Theo-Ben Guriab Avenue will bring you to the **Swakopmund Hotel and Entertainment Centre**, one of the most comfortable hotels in town. Until the early 1990s this was the **Railway Station**, and passengers from Windhoek would alight here into this fine colonial building. While all the building work has destroyed any trace of the railway line, there are plenty of old photographs on display in the hotel restaurant and reception area which capture the scene perfectly. Before the conversion took place there was only one structure here, the building which is now the hotel reception and evening bar. The original platform is the terrace which overlooks the swimming pool. The building was designed by the architect C Schmidt, and built in 1901, whilst the central tower was added at a later date by W Sander. In 1910 the main railway line was closed, but the station continued to act as a terminus for the narrow-gauge railway, of the **Otavi Railway Company**. After the First World War the broad-gauge railway was once again opened and continued to terminate here until a new station was built a short distance inland on the other side of Garoeb Street. In October 1972 the building was declared a national monument, so guaranteeing its future.

Daniel Tjongarero Avenue (formerly Post Street)

Daniel Tjongarero Avenue is a pleasant wide road with some palm trees on the centre island, and a variety of old buildings to admire all along this street. It may not be the most interesting sight but the **Litfass-Saule** on the corner of Daniel Tjongarero Avenue and Nathanael Maxilili Street has an unusual background. This rather tatty looking pillar is an original advertising post dating from the days before radio and television. There were similar posts all over the town to which people used to stick their promotional posters. This is the only post still standing. Litfass was a printer in Berlin who first thought of the pillars in 1855.

The **Municipality** dates from 1907 when it started life as a post office, telephone exchange and living quarters for the personnel. Perhaps the fact that this and many other buildings are still standing is due to the high standard of craftsmanship and attention to detail that was typical of the period. The architect, Redecker, included the following clause in the contract with the builders: "the building must be built as stipulated in the contract and associated plans; all wood must be seasoned and dry; qualified artisans must be engaged for each task; the roof nails must be 4 cm apart and countersunk."

A short distance along Daniel Tjongarero Avenue is the **Antonius Building**. Over the years there have been many additions to this building, but between March 1908 and 1987 it was Swakopmund's only hospital. In the early days it was staffed by sisters of the Franciscan order, later on it was run by the Roman Catholic church.

The neo-baroque **German Evangelical Lutheran Church** was designed by the government builder, Otto Ertl, in 1909, and built by FH Schmidt. The parsonage was completed in 1911 and, as with several other important buildings and homes of the wealthy, the church roof was covered with copper. On 7 January 1912 the inaugural dedication service was held in this grand building. At the time the white population of Swakopmund was about 1400.

Across the road from the Lutheran Church is the **Old German School** building. Still in use as a school, its new extension to the right has none of the baroque style of the original building which was opened in 1913 and was designed to fit in with the church.

Central Swakopmund

Villa Wille, Otavi Street, now enjoying a renaissance as a Victorian period-piece hotel (see Sleeping, below), is a fine example of a comfortable private residence of the colonial period. This was the home of Hermann Wille who was responsible for building some of the most elegant buildings in Swakopmund. Originally he designed it as a bungalow but then decided to add a second floor and today it is one of the most noteworthy buildings in Swakopmund with a fine balcony and a turret (a popular feature of the time) with a copper roof. Unfortunately, Wille only enjoyed a short life in Swakopmund; he was killed in action in 1915.

If you walk along Sam Nujoma Avenue for a couple of blocks you will reach the **OMEG Haus** and museum next to a small botanical garden and snake park. **Living Desert Snake Park** ⓘ *opposite the Engen petrol station on Sam Nujoma, T064-405100, Mon-Fri 0830-1700, Sat 0830-1300, small entry fee*, is home to over 25 species of Namibian snakes as well as small lizards, chameleons and scorpions. It doesn't take long to walk around and children especially will be curious about these creatures.

Around the corner in Windhuker Street is the excellent **Sam Cohen Library** ⓘ *Mon-Fri 0900-1300, 1500-1700, Sat 1000-1430, free*, which will fascinate anyone with a keen interest in Namibian history. Here you will find most of the material that has ever been published on Swakopmund; of particular interest is the collection of historical photographs and old newspapers. Those able to read German will find plenty of fascinating reading here.

One of the finest colonial buildings in Swakopmund is the **Hohenzollern Building**, on the corner of Libertina Amathila Avenue (formerly Brücken Street) and Tobias Hainyeko Street. The most obvious feature, on the roof above the front door, is the statue of a kneeling Atlas holding up a globe of the world. In 1988 the original cement figure had to be replaced with the present plaster-of-Paris version. The building dates from 1909 when it started life as a hotel but in 1912 it was taken over by the municipality after the hotel licence had been revoked by the local magistrate. The hotel had become a well-known gambling den. When the municipality moved out, the building was converted into private flats.

The **Alte Kaserne (Old Schützenhaus)** was built in 1906 as a fort for the Second Railway Company who were involved with the construction of a wooden jetty. The style of the fort was considerably different from other forts of the period, notably Fort Namutoni. The front of the building measured 55 m with a tower in the centre facing out to sea, the other sides measured 45.5 m. A turret was built at each corner; the turret loopholes were included more for decoration than practical purposes.

On the opposite corner of Bismarck and Anton Lubowski Avenue is another original colonial building, now a pension for visitors. The **Prinzessin Rupprecht Heim** is a fine single-storey building dating from 1902. It was first used as a military hospital, but in 1914 it was taken over by the Bavarian Women's Red Cross who renamed the building after their patron, Princess Rupprecht, the wife of the crown

Lappiesdorp – tent city on the beach

In 1947 the municipality set aside an area, close to the present-day Municipal Restcamp, as a temporary campsite with 10 tents to cope with the large number of holidaymakers. This proved to be a great success and the following year 50 tents were erected on the site which became known as 'Lappiesdorp'. In 1949 the site had swollen to 400 tents occupied by an estimated 2000 people. Each year the council was faced with the same problem of providing enough accommodation for the Christmas influx of holidaymakers.

In 1952 the council built the first small bungalows (which are still in use today); by 1972 more than 200 bungalows had been built, ranging from luxury self-catering units to the most basic of shelters. The camp continues to be very popular, particularly since most hotels in Swakopmund are too expensive for the average Namibian. Just below the camp is the sandy bed of the Swakop River, where the original concrete pillars from the first railway bridge can still be seen leaning in all directions after being washed away by the great flood in 1932.

prince of Bavaria. For many years the building served as a peaceful nursing home until it was converted, and some outbuildings added, into a private guesthouse.

Bismarck Street

Heading back along Bismarck Street, the **Woermannhaus** ⓘ *US$1.50, open daily 1000-1200, 1500-1700*, is easily recognized as the building on the high ground with a decorated tower. Housing the reservation office of **Namibia Wildlife Resorts**, visitors can still climb the tower and visit the **Swakopmund Arts Association** on the first floor, which has exhibits of traditional Namibian art alongside some contemporary European art and the local library. The Woermannhaus dates from 1905 and was designed by Friedrich Höft as an office for the **Damara and Namaqua Trading Company.** In 1909 the building was bought by another trading company, **Woermann, Brock and Co.** The Damara Tower was used as a lookout position to see when ships arrived at sea, and when ox wagons arrived from the desert. Between 1924 and 1972 the building served as a school hostel. When it was closed in 1972 it was in such a poor state of repair that the municipality planned to demolish the building. Fortunately a successful campaign saved the building; restoration was completed in 1975 and the public library moved into part of the building.

At the lower end of Libertina Amathila Avenue you can view the town from a different angle by walking to the end of the jetty. In 1910 the German government decided that it was time to build a permanent **Iron Jetty**. A contract was entered with the bridge builders, Flender, Grund and Bilfinger to complete the jetty in 3½ years at a cost of 3½ million marks. Before work on the jetty could start, workshops and storage rooms had to be built on the shore; these were only finished in November 1911. The original plans were to build a bridge reaching 640 m out to sea, carrying two parallel railway lines of 490 m. These lines would carry a loading platform with two cranes; a third crane was planned for the shipping of marble from the Karibib Region. Each of the iron posts supporting the jetty were filled with cement. Progress was slower than planned and by September 1912 only 100 m had been completed.

At this stage the contractors ran into the first problems with shifting sandbanks. When work stopped at the outbreak of the First World War a third of the jetty had been completed for a cost of 2½ million marks. In 1919 one side of the jetty was covered with planks so that it could be used by visitors and fishermen. In 1931

Martin Luther – the steam ox

Just out of town, in a brand new brick and glass shed, beside a clump of palm trees on the Windhoek road, stands one of Swakopmund's most famous historical monuments, an old steam engine known as 'Martin Luther'. In 1896 a First Lieutenant Edmund Troost of the Imperial Schutztruppe on a trip back to Germany came across a mobile steam engine at the engineering works in Halberstadt. Aware of the heavy losses suffered by the ox wagons he saw this new machine as the answer to Swakopmund's problems. He was so sure of the idea that he paid for the steam engine out of his own pocket and arranged for its transportation from Hamburg to Swakopmund. But when the ship arrived in Swakopmund the offloading equipment could not cope with the 280 cwt iron machine, so the boat proceeded to Walvis Bay where the engine was successfully landed. Troost was forced to leave the machine at the harbour for four months because of his military obligations elsewhere. When he finally returned to Walvis Bay he found that the engineer he had retained to drive the steam engine had left and returned home when his initial five-month contract had expired.

The first attempt to drive the steam engine to Swakopmund was undertaken by an American who, it quickly became apparent, knew little about such machines. The going was very tough, the machine continually got stuck in the sand, and by the time a Boer had completed the journey for Troost a further three months had elapsed. The whole venture was never that successful – apart from the problems of weight, the machine consumed vast amounts of water and there was no one able to carry out regular maintenance and repairs. In all, about 13 tonnes of freight were transported inland; two trips were made to Heigamchab and several journeys to Nonidas, the first source of water inland. In 1897 the engine broke down where it stands today and Troost was forced to give up his venture. Fortunately by now the government in Germany had released funds for the construction of a railway.

One of the most frequent stories you will come across in Swakopmund is how the steam engine got its name. The tale goes that shortly after it had ground to a halt a Dr Max Rhode said during a meeting at the Bismarck Hotel: "Did you know that the steam ox is called 'Martin Luther' now because it can also say – 'Here I stand; I cannot do otherwise'?" The original statement was made by the German reformer, Martin Luther, in 1521 in front of the German parliament in Worms.

In 2005, the steam engine got its new home in a glass and brick shed to protect it from the elements and vandalism. It was completely renovated by students of the Namibia Institute of Mining and Technology as a class project. The students – young black Namibians, not older white people with a penchant for German history – spent a lot of time researching and got original sketches of steam engines from all over the world. They discovered, somewhere in Russia, the only other engine type similar to the Martin Luther in the world today. They matched the steel and repaired the rust and followed the original design to the letter. In the future there is talk about adding a transport museum and a craft market to the site. For now, visitors can stop at any time and peer through the glass to look at the engine.

Radio mast

At the southern end of Strand Street behind the new Fisheries and Marine Centre are three small buildings which were once the anchor points for the radio mast used by the Germans until 1914. In December 1911 the Germans erected a strong transmitter which could communicate with Windhoek, ships along the coast as well as a similar transmitter in Duala, in the German Cameroon. This 85-m-high steel tower became of great strategic importance at the outbreak of the First World War since it enabled the German navy to operate in the South Atlantic and threaten all the allies' shipping. When the British government asked the Union of South Africa to invade German South West Africa it was to both silence this radio and gain control of it for themselves. On 14 September 1914 the British auxiliary cruiser, *Armadale Castle*, started to bombard the radio mast, but failed to score a hit. At the time they did not know that on 13 August the Germans had dismantled the equipment and moved the radio inland. To try and stop the bombardment, the remaining personnel cut two of the cables causing the tower to collapse, no more shots were fired at the town that day. Ten days later the British cruiser *Kinfauns Castle* bombarded the town hitting the customs shed by the lighthouse with a lucky shot. Forty years later these ruins were converted into Swakopmund Museum.

and 1934 the Swakop River flowed for more than four months after exceptionally good rains in the interior. In 1934 parts of the town were destroyed by the floodwaters and silt from the Swakop River pushed the sea 3 km back from the present coastline. The jetty stood high and dry with a set of steps added at the end to help people get to the ocean. Slowly the sea washed away the silt and the present coastline was restored. A rather delightful story surrounding the jetty is about what happened to the first women settlers who arrived from Germany in the early days. The men had already been on the coast for a number of years, when German women aged between 18 and 20 (an age that was considered past the prime for marriage at home), were shipped out to the new colony as nurses. The young male settlers would line the jetty in wait for the boat carrying the women and when they landed on shore, the women were grabbed and whisked away immediately, some marrying within a few short days. Many of Swakop's residents tell how their great grandparents were married to complete strangers in this way. The story also goes that those women who did not quite live up to the young men's expectations of a wife, ended up in the town's first brothel!

In 1985 the jetty had to be closed for safety reasons. The following year an appeal raised money for the necessary repairs but unfortunately it would seem the work done was inadequate. In 1997 the Save the Jetty Fund was established to raise funds for renovation and by the time this book comes out, it should have been completed. The first 140 m of the jetty to the 17th polder has been restored with the rest of it being left to decay at the mercy of the ocean. Once finished you will be able to walk to the end and it will provide a platform for anglers.

The new **National Marine Aquarium** ⓘ *Strand St, T064-405744, Tue-Sun 1000-1600, closed Mon, US$2.40, fish are fed daily at 1500; on Tue, Sat and Sun they are hand-fed by divers*, has a large central tank 12 m by 8 m with a walk-through tunnel. The tank contains some sharks and stingrays plus a mix of smaller fish, and the overall theme is typical of a west coast reef with related flora. There are 17 smaller tanks with a variety of fish and some with lobster, crabs and prawns which you can pick up if you so desire. It's a fascinating glimpse at marine life, but you only need allow about 30 minutes unless you are there during feeding time.

If you have been following the recommended walk this marks the end of the tour. **The Tug** by the jetty is as pleasant a place as any for a sundowner and a good fish meal. Alternatively you could walk along the cool **Arnold Schad Promenade** back to the **Strand Hotel**.

Around Swakopmund

» pp 237-253.

Swakopmund Saltworks

Located 6 km to the north of town off the Henties Bay road, the C34, the saltworks should be on the itinerary of any keen birder. Follow the dirt track around the salt lakes; on the coastal side is the **Seabird Guano House**, and drivers in a saloon car will have to stop by the fence. The terrain is a mix of ponds and canals surrounded by a gravel plain, off the sandy beach is a guano platform. It is advisable to arrive here in the early morning before human activity at the works and on the beach disturb the birds. In addition to the resident population of waders, many migrants can be seen between September and April. A comprehensive bird list has been put together by Dr G Friede whose small booklet can be bought at the museum. Species recorded at the saltworks include: (resident) avocets, chestnut-banded plover, oyster catcher, Cape teal, Cape shoveller, grey heron and black-winged stilts; the pelicans and cormorants breed on the guano platform; (migrants) whimbrel, turnstones, little stint, knot, ringed plover, sanderling and bar-tailed godwit. Salt no longer naturally occurs in the area, but water is pumped from the ocean into the shallow pans and during the following 15 months evaporation results in the formation of salt crystals which are then collected. The whole area is a private nature reserve.

For details of activities and tours in and around Swakopmund, see page 246.

Other birdwatching sites include the **Swakop Estuary**, just beyond the aquarium. It can easily be visited by foot from the centre of town. Here there is a mix of reed beds and sandy beach; find a sheltered spot and you should be rewarded with a variety of waders and land birds.

Welwitschia tour

Another popular excursion is to follow the **Moon Landscape and Welwitschia Tour** drive in the Namib section of the Namib-Naukluft National Park. The full route is about 135 km long and can be covered in four or five hours. However, if you take a picnic this can be turned into a pleasant, leisurely day trip. Follow the B2 out of town for the airport and Windhoek, take a right turn on to the C28 signposted for Windhoek via the Bosua Pass. Alternatively, join a tour as the guides will point out much more than you can see on your own. **Note** Permits for the Namib Desert and Welwitschia Plains must be purchased in advance from the **Ministry of Environment and Tourism** (MET) office on Bismarck Street. A map of the route can be bought from **Namib-i**. » *See Tourist information, page 219, for full details.*

Rössing Uranium Mine

ⓘ *T064-402046, every first and third Fri of the month, 0800-1200, except during mine holidays, US$3.50, bookings must be made in advance at the Swakopmund Museum, see page 225; note that tours are conducted in English only.*

Once a fortnight, a tour to Rössing Uranium Mine departs from the **Schweizerhaus Hotel**. While this is undoubtedly a fascinating glimpse into a major mining operation and one that provides much-needed employment in this part of the country, like everything associated with the nuclear industry there is a sense of 'look how good and safe we are'. Even if this is the case, the giant scar on the landscape could never be passed off as environmentally sound.

Mondesa

ⓘ *Hata Angu Cultural Tours, T081-1246111, www.natron.net/hata-angu, or book through the Namib-i office; prices start from US$50.*

Just outside central Swakopmund is Mondesa, the town's township created in the 1950s during Apartheid to house the local black people. Mondesa has established itself as the more African part of town and despite people these days being permitted to live where they like, it has been home to many generations of black families for decades. This well-organized excursion is recommended for tourists wishing to see all aspects of Namibia through the eyes of the different ethnic groups. You will visit areas where the Damara and Herero live, and be invited to sample local food and drinks. It takes you out to the new low-cost housing developments on the edge of Swakopmund, and can also organize evening tours, meals and visits to a *shebeen* (pub). Half the fees go towards community projects and the company is currently building a local football pitch.

Desert tours

The **Namib Desert tour** is one of the most worthwhile trips on offer. Most tours criss-cross the country to the north of the Swakop River, where you will drive through the amazing moonscape, be introduced to many of the unusual plants which manage to survive in this arid environment, such as the 1500-year-old Welwitschias, lithops, hoodias and mist-gathering lichens, and see some spectacular rock formations. Some desert tours include a visit to Goanikontes Spring.

Other excursions

Tours to **Cape Cross Seal Reserve** involve a lot of driving and limited sightseeing. The landscape of the National West Coast Recreation Area to the north of Swakopmund where the reserve is located is typical of much of the Skeleton Coast, but after a while it becomes very repetitive. The outing should include a stop at the Saltworks, a good location for birds (see above), and the fishing resort, **Henties Bay**. If you have no plans to travel in Damaraland then a tour to **Spitzkoppe** should be considered. This is a long day trip and you can expect to spend a lot of time in the vehicle. The tour will start by driving up the coast as far as Henties Bay before turning inland towards the mountains. Around the Spitzkoppe are a number of interesting rock paintings. Some companies will include a visit to a small mineral mine where you can buy semi-precious stones.

Walvis Bay

» *pp 237-253. Phone code: 064.*

Colour map 1, C3.

Had it not been for two colonial powers seeking to gain a foothold on this remote coastline, it is unlikely that both Swakopmund and Walvis Bay would have thrived. Nevertheless, today, Walvis (as it is affectionately known) represents a pleasant alternative if the Disneyesque charms of Swakopmund leave you cold, particularly if you enjoy birdwatching or just want a convenient base from which to explore the Namib-Naukluft Park. However, it is not as pretty as Swakopmund and there is less choice of accommodation and fewer eating options. In truth, much of the town is a grid of characterless modern buildings, although it is currently enjoying a renaissance after the quiet years following its return to Namibia. The highlight is the Walvis Bay Lagoon, which is home to hundreds of thousands of birds throughout the year, most notably flamingos. It has been declared a Ramsar site for its importance as a wetlands area and a feeding ground for many of species of bird on migratory routes from Africa to the Arctic Circle.

Ins and outs

Getting there Visitors from Cape Town in South Africa can fly direct to Walvis Bay, and it is a 40-minute drive to Swakopmund. The 30-odd-km drive down the coast from Swakopmund snakes between the rolling sand dunes inland to the east and the Atlantic Ocean to the west, making this one of the prettiest drives in Namibia. On your way, you will pass the holiday resorts of Long Beach or Langstrand and Dolphin Beach. Opposite the beach are the dunes where adrenaline seekers can try out quad-biking or parasailing. Finally, the two townships of Narraville and Kuisebmond appear on either side of the road just before a roundabout which signals the start of Walvis Bay proper. The town is well serviced by public transport with an international airport, and both the train and the **Intercape** bus which service Swakopmund terminating in Walvis Bay. » *See Transport, page 232, for further details.*

> *If you want to ship a vehicle from Europe to Africa, Walvis Bay is a good option.*

Getting around The town is laid out in a large grid pattern, and apart from the few shops in the centre that you can walk around, you really need a car to get around, especially to reach the Yacht Club at the western end and to explore the lagoon. If you don't have your own wheels, there are plenty of taxis in Walvis Bay.

Tourist information **Walvis Bay Tourism** ⓘ *Shop No 6, Spur Complex, Theo Ben Gurirab St, off Nangolo Mbumba Drive opposite the Civic Centre, T064-209170, www.walvisbay.com.na, Mon-Fri 0800-1700, Sat 0900-1200*, is supported by tourist companies in the town and is also a source of up-to-date and useful information.

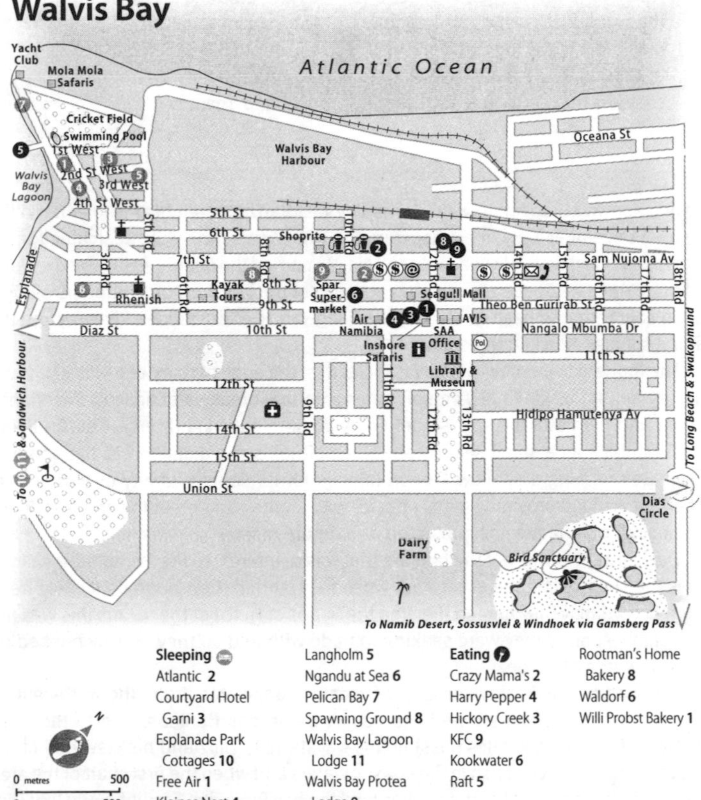

The amazing Benguela Current

The Benguela Current flows from Antarctica to the southernmost tip of Africa where the Atlantic steers it up the western coast as far as Mossamedes in Angola. As the current flows so close to the coast, sea temperatures are colder next to there than further out to sea. On most days a dense belt of sea fog hangs over the ocean on the Namibian coast that is generated by the cool air of the Benguela Current meeting the warmer air inland. During the night when the desert surface cools, the humid sea air of the day is transformed into visible clouds of mist because of condensation and each morning the coast wakes up in a fog. On most days the fog penetrates inland for about 50 km, some days reaching 100 km. As the sun rises and the land surface warms up, heat is radiated into the fog and it gradually disperses into a hazy belt along the coast. As the day progresses, the sea breezes blow away any remaining moisture over the desert. It is because of this mist that the coastal strip of the Namib Desert has a unique living environment. There is sufficient moisture to support over 50 different lichen species and many other larger plants. These plants in turn provide food and water for hardy animals such as the gemsbok and springbok that also live in the desert. Without the fog the desert would otherwise be almost completely devoid of life. The Benguela Current also plays a very important role the economy of Namibia. The current provides ideal conditions for fish to breed in, as it is rich in nitrogen which supports an excess of plankton, the favourite diet of whales and pelagic fish such as pilchards and anchovies, which live in giant shoals. The fishing sector provides about 22% of all exports and remains a large source of employment.

History

The first known European to visit Walvis Bay was **Bartholomeu Diaz** who entered the bay on 8 December 1487 in his flagship, the *São Christovão*, while searching for the tip of Africa and a possible sea route to Asia. He named the sheltered lagoon the Golfo de Santa Maria de Conceição. The bay was one of the finest natural harbours along a barren coast, having been formed by the floodwaters of the Kuiseb River, before the natural silt load blocked the delta.

The modern town of Walvis Bay is located on the edge of this deep-water bay and tidal lagoon. An 18-km-long sandspit forms a natural breakwater against the Atlantic Ocean, and the tip of the spit is marked by an automatic lighthouse, Pelican Point, which doubles as a small seal colony. The spit joins the mainland to the south of Walvis Bay forming a shallow lagoon famous for its superb variety of bird life, an important wetland providing many species with feeding and breeding grounds. In all, a total of 45,000 ha are now protected as a nature reserve.

Back in 1487 it was not the bird life that was of interest to the Portuguese sailors, it was the shelter from the ocean, but when they landed they found no surface fresh water. Accordingly Diaz named the area the Sands of Hell. For the sailors this was not the wealthy country they were seeking to trade with and so they quickly pushed on further towards the cape.

The name Walvis Bay, or bay of whales, originates from the 16th-century Portuguese maps which showed the bay as Bahia das Bahleas, due to the large numbers of migratory whales passing this way. In 1487 Diaz and his crew had taken note of the abundance of fish in the coastal waters and when the first chart of the area was drawn up he had called the area around the bay Praia dos Sardinha, the 'coast of sardines'. During the 17th century, British and American ships frequented the area in search of whale meat and seals, from time to time using the natural harbours at Walvis Bay and Sandwich Harbour, but no attempts were made to explore the interior. Eventually the Dutch in Cape Town decided to investigate the hinterland, prompted by the rumours of great cattle and copper wealth. On 26 February 1793 Captain F Duminy, in the ship *Meermin*, landed and annexed the Bahia das Bahleas, renaming it Walvis Bay. But the land remained in Dutch hands for only a few years; in 1795 the British occupied the cape and Captain Alexander travelled up the coast to Walvis Bay, where he hoisted the British flag.

The growth of the settlement was very slow; a few traders made the epic journey from Cape Town and some missionaries passed through for the Rhenish Missionary Society. Up until the time that the Germans started to develop Swakopmund, the small community at Walvis Bay prospered on the cattle trade, and copper from the Matchless Mine in the Khomas Hochland close to Windhoek. The coast at this time was linked with the interior by a road known as the **Baaiweg**, built by Jan Jonker in 1844. Most of the early traffic consisted of ox wagons.

During the 1870s, unrest in the interior led to the British government in the Cape being asked to intervene to protect missionaries and traders. However, the British concluded that the lands were too poor and not worth adding to the territory of the British Empire. Instead they decided to consolidate their position at Walvis Bay: by controlling the movement of goods and people to the interior they hoped to be able to influence or even control the events inland. On 12 March 1878 Commander RC Dyer formally annexed the area, the boundaries being described as follows: "on the south by a line from a point on the coast 15 miles south of Pelican Point to Scheppmansdorf; on the east by a line from Scheppmansdorf to the Rooibank, including the Plateau, and thence to 10 miles inland from the mouth of the Swakop River; on the north by the last 10 miles of the course of the said Swakop River". Rooibank had been included since it was the closest place with fresh water and greenery. The rest of the 750 sq km enclave was desert.

For the next 50 years the fortunes of Walvis Bay were influenced by the development of the German colony of South West Africa; as Swakopmund grew and prospered so the amount of traffic using Walvis Bay declined. The outbreak of the First World War was to change everything for good. Once the South African troops had built the broad-gauge railway the port was quick to develop, and in 1927 a newly dredged harbour was opened by the Earl of Athlone, Governor-General of South Africa. At the same time a new source of fresh water was discovered in the bed of the Kuiseb River, which helped guarantee the future of the town.

At the end of the First World War, Walvis Bay was given to South Africa to govern as part of the mandated territory of South West Africa. This remained the case until 1977 when South Africa declared Walvis Bay to be part of the Cape Province. Despite pressure from the United Nations, South Africa refused to give up the small enclave as it served both as an important commercial port and as location of a South African military base. In 1992 South Africa relented and agreed to a joint administration without any border controls; on 28 February 1994 South Africa returned Walvis Bay to Namibia.

The port represents a great asset for Namibia which, if properly developed and well managed, can challenge ports such as Durban and Maputo for trade destined for countries such as Zimbabwe, Botswana, Zambia and even Malawi. In 1996 the private **Walvis Bay Export Processing Zone Management Company**, was established to attract more businesses to Walvis Bay and to take advantage of the port and its improved access to the hinterland. Both the Trans-Kalahari and Trans-Caprivi highways have been completed, thus reducing the transport time of commodities to and from Zambia, Zimbabwe, Botswana and South Africa by up to 14 days. The port now handles about 150 ships per month. If you would like to visit the port, entry permits to the harbour are available at the police office at the harbour entrance on 13th Road. Slowly the town is

...as you approach the towering, wind-sculptured dunes at the edge of Sandwich Harbour, there is a sense of entering a different world...

starting to benefit from the improved economic climate, and this and the increased volume of tourists choosing to visit the town and surrounding area are providing the local population with grounds for optimism.

Sights

Despite its long history the town has surprisingly few old buildings. For most visitors the attractions here are in the sea, not on the land. The earliest building in Walvis Bay is the **Rhenish Mission Church** ⓘ *5th Rd*, a small structure surrounded by modern private homes. It was made in Hamburg as a prefabricated kit in 1879 and in 1880 the wooden building was erected on the waterfront. As the harbour grew in importance it was decided to move the church to its present site. Once reassembled, the wooden walls were plastered to help prevent wood rot. The last service was held here in 1966.

Just before you reach the outskirts of Walvis Bay look out for a large wooden platform in the sea. This is known as **Bird Island** and was built to provide a nesting site for seabirds from which man could collect guano. Still in use today, the platform can yield close to 1000 tonnes in a single year. There are always plenty of seabirds to watch in the vicinity. Beyond the platform you may occasionally see one of the drilling platforms which are being used to look for off-shore gas fields, and you will certainly see the ships lining up out to sea waiting to get into Walvis Bay port.

The **Walvis Bay Lagoon** to the southwest of town is regarded as one of the most important wetlands for birds along the southern African coast and since 1995 it has been a proclaimed Ramsar site (an important wetland area for birds). This site covers the shallow lagoon, the beach and the inter-tidal areas of Pelican Point and the saltworks. The region is a feeding site for around 80% of all the lesser flamingos found in southern Africa and about 50% of greater flamingos. It also attracts large numbers of chestnut plovers, pelicans, damara, Caspian and swift terns, white-fronted plovers and Hartlaub's gulls. There are an estimated 170,000 resident birds around the lagoon, with some 200,000 more stopping off on migratory routes. On the inland side of the town is a small **Bird Sanctuary** built around several freshwater ponds. Follow 13th road inland and take a left by the signpost close to the dairy farm. The track climbs over a couple of dunes before you reach a hide on stilts overlooking two pools. There are often flamingos and pelicans to be seen here. If you follow the road past another pool you will join the main surfaced road to the airport. The lagoon can also be explored by boat or kayak; most of the tour operators (see page 250) can organize trips around the lagoon, to Bird Island and to Pelican Point which forms the most westerly lip of the lagoon, and it is also a popular spot for windsurfing.

The lagoon is tidal – low tide is the best time for birdwatching.

Other minor attractions include **Dune 7**, on the outskirts of town, on the C14, the highest dune in the area. A small picnic site has been set up amongst some palm trees. The best time of the day to visit the dune is close to sunset, when the views are spectacular but the sand is not so hot for walking on.

The Cape gannet detects fish from the air and then dive bombs into the ocean at speeds of up to 160 kph. If it were not for an air bubble that surrounds its tiny brain, the birds would kill themselves when hitting the water at this speed.

Sandwich Harbour ›› *Colour map 3, A1.*

Sandwich Harbour is 48 km south of Walvis Bay. Do not attempt this road without a 4WD as much of it goes through soft sand; the last bit can only be tackled on foot and permits are required. You will have to go on a guided tour and many of the tour companies listed on page 246 offer day-long trips. However, the drive down is long and tough and the journey is as dramatic as the landscape, and it soon becomes clear why Sandwich Harbour is often described as inaccessible! Spring tides and shifting sands ensure an unpredictable route, but as you approach the towering, wind-sculptured dunes at the edge of Sandwich Harbour, there is a sense of entering a different world. All that is left of the old whaling station is a solitary deserted building and the strange greenery around the lagoon. Some 40,000 birds (34 different species) have been recorded in this area during recent surveys. There is time to take a leisurely walk around the lagoon and you may also see seals, dolphins and even whales.

For details of activities and tours in and around Walvis Bay, see page 250.

Sleeping

Swakopmund *p218, map p220*

Swakopmund has a wide choice of rooms covering all budgets and the number of establishments seems to increase each year as the economy comes to depend more and more heavily on tourism. Whilst some of the older establishments still cater for predominantly German-speaking tourists, the majority now cater for the needs of visitors from Europe, North America and from countries further afield such as Taiwan and Japan. There is a vast range of hotels, pension (or *garni*) hotels, guesthouses, rest camps and self-catering apartments – indeed far too many to list. Because of Namibia Tourism Board's confusing grading system, we have listed recommended establishments by type; it is personal preference whether you want the anonymity of a large hotel, the intimacy of a pension or hosted guesthouse, or the independence of a fully equipped self-catering apartment (many of which are on or close to the beach).

Note that all accommodation in Swakopmund is likely to be fully booked around the peak Christmas period. Even at other times of the year occupancy rates may be very high. You are therefore strongly advised to book in advance or at the very least to check on availability before arriving.

Camping Because of the cool fog that collects over the coast each night, camping can be cold and you may want to consider treating yourself to a bed whilst on the coast.

Hotels

AL **Hansa Hotel**, 3 Hendrik Witbooi St, T064-400311, www.hansahotel.com.na. 55 rooms arranged around a garden courtyard with palm trees. The restaurant has a good selection of Namibian and continental dishes, bar, spacious and comfortable guest lounge. A smoothly run hotel in the centre of town which many still regard as the best in Swakopmund. Recommended.

AL **Swakopmund Hotel and Entertainment Centre**, Theo-Ben Gurirab Av, T064-4105200, www.legacyhotels.co.za. 89 a/c, light and airy rooms with DSTV. There are 2 hotel restaurants (See Eating, below) heated swimming pool, shops, hair salon and car hire. The casino and amusement arcade tend to appeal more to the Swakopmund residents than any of the guests at the hotel. The front building is the original railway station built in 1901 (see page 226); look at the old photographs to see where the trains used to pull up. An excellent hotel that caters primarily for international visitors. The service here is of a higher standard than most Windhoek hotels. Recommended.

A **Hotel Garni Adler**, 3 Strand St, T064-405045, adler@iafrica.com.na. 14 rooms, TV, breakfast room, but no evening meals, residents' bar, indoor heated swimming pool and sauna, private and sheltered sun deck on the roof. A very clean and neat hotel. Secure off-street parking. The new fisheries building has partly spoilt the location but this remains

For an explanation of the sleeping and eating price codes used in this guide, see inside the front cover. Other relevant information is found in Essentials, see pages 43-51.

a pleasant and peaceful hotel. Popular with German tour groups, but recommended outside busy periods.

A Sam's Giardino Hotel, 89 Anton Lubowski Av, Krammersdorf, T064-403210, www.giardino.com.na. Located on the edge of town facing the desert, this award-winning, Swiss-owned hotel has been built in the style of Swiss mountain chalet. With 10 stylish and pleasant rooms facing the garden, breakfast is included and a 4-course dinner is also offered. An excellent bar well stocked with fine South African wines and regular wine-tasting evenings, mini-library/ reading room with plenty of information on Namibia, a selection of fine cigars and friendly relaxed atmosphere, this hotel is recommended for people wishing to avoid the formality of the bigger hotels but still enjoy the same level of service. Consistently recommended by readers.

A-B Strand Hotel, on the beachfront close to the lighthouse, T064-400315, www.namibsunhotels.com.na. 23 sea-facing and 22 garden-facing rooms, restaurant, a shady terrace bar serves light lunches. Popular family holiday hotel with comfortable rooms, often used by tour groups on a Namibia circuit using the other quality **Namib Sun Hotels**.

Note A completely new **Strand Hotel** is about to be built next to the original. When it is finished the old one will be knocked down.

B Beach Lodge, 1 Stint St, Vogel Strand, 5 km from the town centre, T064-414500, www.beachlodge.com.na. Excellent location on the seafront, all rooms en suite with fireplace, TV, phone and sea view, a very unusual building constructed to look like ships with enormous circular porthole-style windows; choose B&B or units with self-catering facilities. If you are looking to be out of the town centre and enjoy some serious sea breezes, then try this one.

B Europa Hof , 39 Bismarck St, T064-405898, www.europahof.com. 35 plain rooms, with DSTV and phone, cool but gloomy restaurant with a menu anyone from Germany will feel at home with. Secure off-street parking, popular with organized tour groups. The whole building looks out of place in Swakopmund – the timber frame and flower boxes seem more suited to the Alps.

B Hotel Eberwein, Sam Nujoma Av, T064-463355, www.eberwein.com.na. Splendid colonial-era home which has been tastefully converted into a Victorian-style hotel with underground parking. The 17 rooms, including 4 luxury doubles, are comfortably furnished and equipped with all mod cons including under-floor heating. Breakfast included, dinner on request, nice bar with a good range of South African wines, recommended for those who want the colonial experience.

C Atlanta Hotel, Hendrik Witbooi St, T064-402360, allantah@iafrica.com.na. 14 rooms, en suite bathroom, TV, secure parking, reasonable restaurant next door, **Chili Peppers** (see Eating, below), where guests of the hotel have breakfast (included in the room rate) and get 10% discount on other meals. **Fagin's Bar**, a lively local drinking haunt, is also in the same block.

C Rossmund Lodge, 6 km east of Swakopmund at the **Rossmund Golf Club**, T064-404459, roslodge@palmwag.com.na. New lodge built of natural rock with 20 en suite rooms in chalets with DSTV and phone, mostly aimed at golfers, breakfast on the nearby veranda, lunch and dinner at the club house restaurant and bar, bowling green, swimming pool, shuttle service to town, guests get reduced rates for the 18-hole golf course.

Pensions and guesthouses

AL The Stiltz, T064-400771, www.oasys.com.na/thestiltz. Brand new to Swakop are these 8 lovely thatched chalets built high up on stilts overlooking the Swakop riverbed, sand dunes and the ocean. All polished wood, the en suite rooms are interlinked by wooden walkways and have minibar, balcony, furniture made from tree trunks, and breakfast is taken in a dining area with wonderful views. Despite being above ground, there is access for wheelchairs.

B Deutsches Haus Pension, 13 Lüderitz St, close to the town centre, T064-404896, www.deutsches-haus-swakopmund.com. Family-run establishment with 18 rather plain double and 2 single rooms. Room rates include breakfast with lunch and dinner available for extra at the restaurant, there is a sauna and small indoor heated swimming pool, bar and TV lounge. Despite the name the hotel also caters for non-German speakers. Popular with tour groups, good value for money.

B **Intermezzo**, 9 Dolphin St, T064-464114, www.swakop.com/intermezzo. Small guesthouse in a modern building, 6 spacious rooms, all very bright white, with en suite bathrooms, DSTV and tea- and coffee-making facilities, secure parking, good and filling buffet breakfasts.

B **Schweizerhaus Hotel**, 1 Bismarck St, T064-400331, www.schweizerhaus.net. 24 rooms on the 1st floor, some with ocean views, short beds, clean and spacious rooms, bath and shower, TV. Rooms on the inside overlook a courtyard which is also an aviary for parrots: unfortunately this means the balconies are not very clean. Restaurant, private residents' bar in the back garden. While this is a fully fledged hotel the reception area doubles up as the popular **Café Anton**. A good-value hotel still under family management, helpful and friendly young staff. Recommended.

B **Sea Breeze Guesthouse**, 48 Turmalin St, T064-463348, www.natron.net/tour/seabreeze. Italian-run establishment offering 4 self-catering flats and a selection of en suite single and double rooms. Great location about 3 km from the town centre, from the dining room there is a terrific view down the beach to the town centre, very new and exceptionally modern and clean, one reader rates the breakfasts as the best in Namibia.

B **Secret Garden Guest House**, 36 Bismarck St, T/F064-404037, sgg@iway.na. Attractive orange building surrounding a courtyard with flowers and giant palms, 8 en suite rooms, and 2 suites with additional kitchens and living rooms, each with DSTV, phone and internet connections for laptops, *braai* areas outside, lounge area with TV and honesty bar, and a jacuzzi, recommended by the tourist office.

C **Alternative Space**, 46 Dr Alfons Weber St, T/F064-402713. This used to be a backpackers' hotel, but has now reinvented itself as an intimate guesthouse with just 4 en suite rooms decorated with an extensive collection of Namibian art. Facilities include a small library and outside play area with toys for children. A welcome peaceful location though a long walk from the centre of town.

C **Dunedin Guest House**, corner of Daniel Tjongerero St and Wondhoeker St, T064-403437, villawiese@compuscan.co.za. 15 spacious en suite rooms with either 1 double and 1 single, or 1 double and 2 single beds, ideal for families as rooms work out cheap per person. Modern decor, rates include a cooked breakfast and laundry is available, parking behind a gate, named after one of the shipwrecks on the Skeleton Coast.

C **Pension Rapmund**, 6-8 Bismarck St, T064-402035, rapmund@iafrica.com.na. Good central location near the **Café Anton**, 25 simple rooms, breakfast available overlooking the garden and ocean but no restaurant. One of the most welcoming and friendly pensions and therefore often full. Call in advance. Recommended.

C **Seagull**, 60 Strand St, T/F064-405287, www.seagullbandb.com.na. Bed and breakfast in a smart house, 5 double rooms with en suite bathroom and TV, varying size and price depending on whether they face the ocean or not, lounge, secure parking. Short walk from the shops and beach.

C-D **Brigadoon**, 16 Ludwig Koch St, T064-406064, brigadoon@iway.na. 3 comfortable self-catering cottages with small garden overlooking Palm Beach, and 4 en suite rooms, breakfast included. Ideal for a family or visitors wishing to avoid hotels. Secure parking, a short walk from the museum and post office.

C-D **Pension Prinzessin Rupprecht Heim**, 15 Anton Lubowski Av, T064-412540, www.prinrupp.com.na. 20 rooms, 5 of which are singles with shared bathroom, located in a historic building (see page 227). A quiet and somewhat staid pension, good value for anyone on a medium budget, off-street parking and a sheltered garden at the back, breakfast included, wheelchair friendly.

Self-catering and rest camps

Apartments can be booked through a number of agents acting on behalf of the owners. Try **Namibia Holiday Services**, 23 Sam Nujoma Av, T064-404400, www.henric-estates.com, or **Nel's Estates**, T064-405226/8, www.nels-estates.com.na.

B **Alte Brücke Resort**, 200 m from the beach at the southern end of Strand St, T064-404918, accomod@iafrica.com.na. Family resort with good-value (rates are for a group of 4) 1- or 2-bed chalets with sofa beds in the lounge suitable for children, TV, kitchens, *braai* spots, minibar, fully equipped for self-catering including an ironing board, (though breakfast is available). Also very nice **camping spots** (D) on green lawns, each with its own bathroom, *braai* spot and power point. The whole complex is surrounded by an electric fence.

B-D **Swakopmund Municipal Restcamp**, Hendrik Witbooi St, T064-402807, www.swakopmund-restcamp.com. Advance reservations through the office, open 1730-1300 and 1400-1600. A mix of bungalows which can sleep 2-6 people: the most basic are known as 'Fisherman', these have bunk beds, shower, a small seating area plus a hot plate, thin walls. At the other end of the scale are luxury bungalows with 2 bedrooms, bathroom, lounge/dining area, kitchen with crockery (no glasses or towels provided). In between are 4-bed bungalows and flats which are good value, and A-frames with a lot of character. Out of season the camp is frequently recommended as a good value self-catering set-up. During peak periods it is unlikely that a visitor from overseas will get in since the bookings open months in advance, and for many Namibians this is the only comfortable accommodation they can afford in Swakopmund. The camp is to the left of the main road after crossing the bridge coming into town from Walvis Bay. **Note** Checkout time is strictly 1000 and you must pay a deposit for keys. Rates are US$21 for the smallest unit sleeping 2 up to US$80 sleeping 5.

C **Strauss Holiday and overnight Flats**, 10 Hidipo Hamutenya Av, T064-412350, straussholidays@iway.na. 7 fully equipped apartments in a brilliant pink block, with 2 double bedrooms, 1 with en suite facilities, TV, telephone, *braai* facilities. A bit of a walk from town, not especially friendly and rather chintzy decor but good value for money.

C-E **Restcamp Sophia Dale**, Street 1901 (12 km outside town on the B2), T/F064-403264, www.sophiadale.com. Bungalows with self-catering facilities, *braai* areas and carports; **caravan and camping sites** with *braai* places, wash block. An alternative to staying in town, with great views of the desert and the Erongo Mountains on a clear day. Offers unusual guided skiing trips in the dunes for US$30 per person.

Backpackers

C-D **Desert Sky Backpackers**, 35 Anton Lubowski St, T064-402339, www.swakop.com/dsb. Reasonably new option but already popular, 13 dorm beds, 3 doubles and camping, parking behind an electric fence, luggage lockers, self-catering kitchen, bar, internet access, pool table, the owners are helpful with organizing local activities.

C-E **Swakop Lodge**, 14 Nathaniel Maxuilili St, T064-402030, www.swakoplodge.com. This is a great all-round place to stay. 30 smart en suite rooms with satillite TV, 8 dorms rooms each with their own bathroom and 4-6 beds, laundry, kitchen for self-catering, 24-hr reception, secure parking, **Cool Bananas Pub** upstairs with pool tables, long wooden bar with thatched roof, large screen TV, and on the roof is a wooden deck with tables and sun loungers. Next door to the pub is a briefing room with a bank of TV screens where the tour operators for the adventure activities can show videos and talk about quad-biking, sandboarding, etc. Downstairs is **Roxy's Café** and the **Cape to Cairo** restaurant (see Eating, below). The whole place is decorated with some brightly painted African art and lovingly polished wood, the staff are great, and there's a real holiday/adventure atmosphere about the place. Recommended.

C-E **Villa Wiese Backpackers Lodge**, corner of Theo Gurirab St and Windhoeker St, T064-407105, www.villaviese.com. Well-run and established backpackers in a lovely house originally built in 1905, very friendly owners Johan and Tinkie, kitchen and dining area, some parking space behind a gate, doubles, twins and dorms, the latter have a minimum of 4 beds in each, all rates include cooked breakfast, very comfortable bar upstairs with TV, laundry, lovely fish pond with giant lilies in the courtyard, an old tree has been cleverly incorporated into the decor, complimentary pick-up/drop-off from bus or airport, good all-round place to stay for those on a budget. Recommended.

Around Swakopmund *p231*

Long Beach

There are a string of resorts roughly midway between Swakopmund and Walvis Bay which is known as Long Beach, or Langestrand in German. They offer good-value accommodation with modern facilites and are especially attractive for families. However, you will need a car to get to and fro and you may want to avoid them at the height of the season when they are fully booked.

A **Burning Shore Beach Lodge**, 152 4th St, Long Beach, T064-207568, burningshore@namibnet.com. A fairly recent addition to the accommodation available at this resort with 4 suites and 3 luxury rooms and great views over the ocean and the desert. Despite the modern exterior, the furniture is very elegant with large wooden beds, standard lamps and high-back armchairs, meals and afternoon tea are taken on the outside terrace or if it's cold in the lounge next to a roaring fire.

B-C **Levo Guest House and Chalets**, 3rd St, Long Beach, T/F064-207555, www.levotours.com. Self-catering chalets on 2 storeys, suitable for 4 people, with sea views, DSTV and lock-up garages, swimming pool. A small, well-run establishment. A full range of fishing trips and cruises can be organized from here.

C **Dolphin Park Chalets**, Long Beach, the turning is beyond the main turn-off to Long Beach towards Walvis Bay, reservations through **Walvis Bay Resorts**, T064-215500, www.wbresorts.com.na. 20, 1-bedroom en suite self-catering chalets, though can sleep 4, swimming pool, hydroslide and recreation area, no restaurant but shop for basic provisions. Popular with families.

C-E **Long Beach Resort**, Long Beach, reservations through **Walvis Bay Resorts**, T064-215500, www.wbresorts.com.na. A choice of 2- or 4-bed flats, plus 120 camping sites with electric points and shade on tiers that can get very overcrowded in season, though very quiet at other times. Within the complex are 2 restaurants, a very nice bar at the end of a jetty, shop and modern coin-operated laundromat. This is a very popular holiday centre during local school holidays, as it is close to the beach with plenty of watersport facilities for children.

Walvis Bay *p232, map p233*

The choice of accommodation in Walvis Bay has improved in recent years, reflecting the mini-boom the town now enjoys. There are a number of comfortable options for tourists and business travellers, as well as several good-value guesthouses and small hotels and a choice of self-catering accommodation. There is even a good backpackers for anyone who finds Swakopmund too busy!

A **Pelican Bay Hotel**, the Esplanade, at the edge of the Walvis Bay Lagoon, T064-214000, www.united-hospitality.com. Lovely new hotel with white walls and bright blue roof, very modern decor throughout, lots of slate and marble floors, 50 a/c rooms with a deck overlooking the lagoon, 1 with disabled access, some with 4-poster beds, each has DSTV and minibar. Facilities include a very smart restaurant and comfortable bar area, a 24-hr coffee shop that serves light meals, and full conference facilities. A highlight here is the pelican feeding from the jetty at the front of the hotel.

B **Courtyard Hotel Garni**, 6 3rd Rd, T064-206252, www.courtyardhotel.com. Situated close to the lagoon this new and comfortable addition to Walvis' guesthouses has 13 en suite double rooms and 4 en suite single rooms with TV, phone and a mini kitchen for self-catering, arranged around a neat green courtyard with a little shade, an indoor swimming pool, sauna and a pleasant garden, rates include full English breakfast.

B **Hotel Atlantic**, Sam Nujoma Av, T064-202811, www.namibsunhotels.com.na. 12 en suite rooms in an ugly squat brick block, bar, the restaurant had a good reputation but has failed to respond to changing times in Walvis Bay; better suited to business travellers than tourists.

B **Kleines Nest**, on the lagoon, T064-203203, wmlcoast@iafrica.com.na. 4 en suite rooms in a modern pink block with excellent views over the lagoon, each has mini kitchen with fridge, DSTV, phone, and balcony, secure parking, breakfast included and restaurants within walking distance. The owners can organize windsurfing on the lagoon.

B **Langholm Hotel**, 24 2nd St West, T064-209230, www.langholm.com.na. A clean new building with 12 rooms, en suite bathrooms, DSTV, plus 1 self-catering suite that can sleep 5 people, lounge and bar, no restaurant, but you can walk to or order in from local restaurants, bike hire. Ideal if you are looking for a quieter option. On the display in the bar here is the owner's collection of over 500 peaked caps!

B **Ngandu at Sea**, corner of 1st Rd and Theo Ben Gurirab St, close to the lagoon,

T064-207350, theart@mweb.com.na. 13 en suite double rooms, some with kitchenettes, a penthouse with a breathtaking view over the lagoon and a self-catering family unit, all equipped with TV, phone and individual alarm system. Restaurant, bar and beer garden, launderette, parking garages can be hired, popular with local visitors.

B **Walvis Bay Lagoon Lodge**, 2 Kovambo Nujoma Drive, T064-200850, www.lagoon lodge.com.na. Established and run by French couple Wilfred and Helene Meiller, 8 comfortable, individually styled rooms all with excellent views, in a bright yellow building, lovely decor, swimming pool, the warm hospitality make this one of the most pleasant places to stay in town. Rates are B&B or full board. Bikes and fishing rods available on free loan. Recommended.

B-C **Walvis Bay Protea Lodge**, corner of Sam Nujoma Av and 10th Rd, T064-209560, www.proteahotels.com. Part of a large, quality South African chain, very striking modern building painted in a variety of pastel colours, 26 a/c rooms, M-Net TV, no restaurant. A functional, smart hotel located in the centre of town, more suited to business travellers than tourists and the first hotel in the region to provide wireless internet access, laptop-sized safes in the rooms and fully equipped office facilites.

C **Esplanade Park Cottages**, reservations through **Walvis Bay Resorts**, T064-215500, www.wbresorts.com.na. 27 self-catering bungalows set amongst shaded lawns overlooking the lagoon. Suitable for up to 5 people, simple but clean. Each unit has a fully equipped kitchen, bathroom TV, garage, fish cleaning and *braai* area. Good-value holiday accommodation provided by the municipality, advance booking essential during school holidays.

C **Free Air**, Esplanade, T064-202247, www.free-air.net. Lovely new spot overlooking the lagoon in a bright yellow building, striking architecture with pointed walls and floor-to-ceiling windows, 10 en suite rooms, bar with large screen TV, trendy furnishings, wireless internet access, restaurant with pizza oven, an excellent friendly set-up. It has equipment and can arrange lessons for kitesurfing and windsailing.

C-D **The Spawning Ground**, 84 Hage Giengob St, T064-204400. Dwayner@hotmail.com. The only true backpackers' in Walvis Bay, which moved location in 2003. 3 doubles and 8 bunk beds in a dorm, communal TV lounge and a well- equipped kitchen. **Camping** possible in a simple bare garden. Good source of local info for budget traveller. Given that there is less to do in the town itself many visitors tend to stay here for some R&R. Eugene is the owner. Recommended if you find yourself in Walvis on a tight budget.

Eating

Swakopmund *p218, map p220*

Most of the major hotels have attached restaurants but after several meals their menus can seem a little limited. However, Swakopmund has the best choice of restaurants in Namibia outside Windhoek, including a number of restaurants offering high-quality affordable seafood. Check opening times as quite a few will be closed Sun or Mon evenings. During the day there are plenty of cafés offering cakes, pastries and German-style sandwiches, some of which also serve beer; a Swakop must-do is to have coffee and cake at the famous **Café Anton**. Fast food can be found at **KFC** on Nathaniel Maxuilili St, **Wimpy** and **Debonairs Pizza** in the Spar Shopping Mall.

TTT **Cape to Cairo**, adjoining **Swakop Lodge**, T064-463310. Very stylish, African decor, tables arranged on roped wooden decks, African dishes fused with European presentation, try the Algerian salad, Tunisian meatballs or Somalian spiced lamb, also game meat including crocodile, steaks and seafood, South African wine. Open daily 1800-2200, reservations recommended as it's quite small, during the day you can make a reservation at **Roxy's Café** a couple of doors along.

TTT **Erich's**, 21 Daniel Tjongarero Av, T064-405141. A dull tiled interior, but a vibrant seafood restaurant during the season, which also serves game meat such as kudu, springbok and eland, and a fair choice of vegetarian dishes, though somewhat pricey. Mon-Sat 1800-late; the adjoining takeaway and coffee shop is open Mon-Sat 0830-1630.

TTT **Grapevine**, Libertina Amathila Av, T064-404760. Lovely intimate and romantic restaurant offering superb gourmet food with a heavy emphasis on the wine as the owner is a real connoisseur. Rather than read through a wine list, guests are invited to peruse the bottles in the wine rack and taste a few before making a selection. Food includes fresh fish, steak and duck, with rather special desserts such as crème brûlée or a deep-fried ice cream doughnut. Each cup of coffee is individually ground. Reservations recommended for dinner. Mon-Sat 1130-1400, 1800-2130.

TTT **Il Tulipano**, 37 Daniel Tjongarero St, T064-400122. Authentic Italian food run by an Italian woman, bright modern decor, kilims on the wooden floor, gold and silver plates, art on the walls, Italian and South African wines, home-made pasta. Daily 1700-2200, also at lunchtime during high season.

TTT **Kücki's Pub**, 22 Tobias Hainyeko St, T064-402407. A long-time favourite with all visitors to Swakopmund and has been going strong for 25 years, this popular local haunt is a great place for eating seafood. Traditional restaurant arrangements downstairs and pub-type seating upstairs. It is advisable to make a reservation if you are planning to eat here in the evening. Mon-Sat 1800-late, closed Sun.

TTT **Kuperferpfanne**, 13 Tobias Hainyeko, T064-405405. Very large menu and excellently presented food, unusual dishes such as crayfish tail with asparagus, or cold game meat platter. Good food and comfortable, though mostly German clientele and the decor is a little plain. Tue-Sun 1800-2130.

TTT **Platform One**, Theo-Ben Gurirab Av. **Swakopmund Hotel** restaurants, T064-400800. A smart room which has been decorated with railway memorabilia. The Sun evening buffet is to be recommended, plenty of fresh seafood and a wide selection of meat dishes, limited à la carte choice. Booking is necessary during busy periods, attentive service. Open daily 1230-1430, 1900-2200.

TTT **Station Grill**,Theo-Ben Gurirab Av, **Swakopmund Hotel**, T064-400800. Formal hotel grill restaurant, good but expensive seafood platters, mixed grills, steaks with unusual toppings such as fried egg or pineapple, plus sauces, if you manage to get through a 1 kg steak, you get a free T-shirt! Mon-Sat 1900-2200.

TTT **The Tug**, Strand St, by the iron jetty, T064-402356. Cool beers, a great sunset with an ocean view. A good place to relax and enjoy fantastic seafood and Irish coffees, sister restaurant to **The Raft** in Walvis Bay. Bookings required. The bar is in part of an old ship complete with portholes, whilst the dining area is built around the ship with chunky brick walls and heavy wooden furniture. Very good atmosphere and service and thoroughly recommended.

TT **Chili Peppers**, part of the **Atlanta Hotel**, Hendrick Witbooi St. Friendly informal restaurant that's more like a café although it does sell beer, Mexican snacks and sandwiches for lunch, with a more extensive range of dishes for dinner, a few tables outside on the pavement. Daily 0800-2100.

TT **Lighthouse Pub and Restaurant**, Pool Terrace, Main Beach, next to the Swakopmund Museum, T064-400894. Outdoor terrace overlooking the sea and inside bar and dining. Offers a wide range of dishes from excellent fresh seafood to steaks, burgers and pizzas. Good atmosphere, sensible prices and great views. Recommended, booking advised. Daily 1100-2200.

TT **Mandarin Gardens**, 27 Libertina Amathila Av, T064-402081. Owned and run by a mainland Chinese from the northeast, this restaurant offers as close to authentic Chinese cuisine as you will find in Namibia. A pleasant change to the range of dishes on offer elsewhere with a takeaway service. Try the dumplings! Mon-Sat 1800-2200.

TT **Napolitana**, Nathanael Maxilili St, T064-402773. Real pizzas prepared in a wood oven and a range of pastas and meat dishes. Popular with locals and tourists from the Mediterranean, prices are very reasonable and the atmosphere friendly and relaxed. Recommended. Tue-Sun, 1200-1400, 1800-2200.

TT **Swakopmund Brauhaus**, Brauhaus Arcade, Sam Nujoma Av, T064-402214. Bistro pub offering traditional German dishes, Namibian game and fish and a great cooked breakfast. Tables under umbrellas outside, plenty of German beer on tap. A good place to stop and relax during a walk about town. Mon-Sat 1000-1430, 1800-2130.

TT **Tiffany**, Libertina Amathila Av, T064-463655. Small bar to one side and tables in the next-door room, friendly German owners and relaxed atmosphere, rather different cheese fondue with meat and fish, fresh and salted fish available, also schnitzels and all things beef, imported German beers from Munich plus draft beer. Tue-Sun 1700-late, Sat and Sun also open from 1000 for 'breakfast at Tiffanys'.

ŸŸ **Western Saloon**, 8 Tobias Hainyeko St, T064-405395. The name sums up the Wild West theme. The seafood is good and so are the steaks, specials include game meat and oysters, easy-going medium priced restaurant. Daily from 1700.

ŸŸ **Zur Weinmaus**, Bismarck St, T064-400098. With heavy dark furniture and wooden beams, the interior could be described as cosy and private or small and dark depending on your mood, German cuisine, seafood, South African wine, though a short menu. Daily 1730-2200.

Cafés

In recent years several new street cafés have opened, providing Swakopmund with a pleasant alternative to the quiet, enclosed a/c cafés of old. These all serve light snacks and some excellent coffee – a rare luxury in Namibia.

ŸŸ **Roxy's Café**, at the **Swakop Lodge**, build your own breakfasts from a variety of items from bacon to fried fish, light meals such as salads and filled pancakes, pasta dishes, toasted sandwiches and hamburgers. There are also a few terminals for internet access here. Open daily 0630-1900.

Ÿ **Café Anton**, 1 Bismarck St, T064-400331. A very popular bakery in the lobby of the **Schweizerhaus Hotel**. A good range of cakes and pastries to takeaway or eat in, delicate German cream cakes, sandwiches and drinks, some tables outside, the **Anton** was established in 1966 and is a Swakop institution. Recommended.

Ÿ **Café Tref**, Sam Nujoma Av, coffee, cakes, bit of a ladies-who-lunch meeting place, completely refurbished with modern and swish glass and chrome decor, closed evenings.

Ÿ **Gelateria Bella Italia**, 32 Tobias Hainyeko St. Ice cream and deli counters, coffee, cakes, home-made muffins, soup, sandwiches, fully licenced for drinks, closed evenings.

Ÿ **Out of Africa**, Daniel Tjongarero Av. A very popular café which spills out onto the palm-shaded street. Excellent coffee and cappuccino. The ideal place to write a few postcards. Recommended.

Ÿ **Pandora's Box**, Ankerplatz, Bismarck St, doubles as a café and curio shop. A great place to catch the sun in the morning at the outside tables next to a babbling water feature whilst enjoying a traditional Namibian fry-up breakfast! Also offers the likes of schnitzel, goulash, lemon meringue pie and beer for lunch. Mon-Fri 0900-1800, Sat 0900-1300.

Walvis Bay *p232, map p233*

With the exception of a couple of notable options, restaurants in Walvis Bay are not nearly as varied or interesting as those in Swakopmund, and few stay open in the evening. Most are cafés or bakeries that cater for the passing trade at lunchtime, and again there is a KFC in town for fast food.

ŸŸŸ **The Raft**, Esplanade, T064-204877. A fantastic structure built on stilts in the lagoon with a long boardwalk to reach it. A wide selection of dishes, seafood, pasta, fresh salads and the usual choice of steaks. Popular with the local business community. Always worth a visit to watch the sunset from the bar and the pelicans flying into the lagoon. Sister restaurant to **The Tug** in Swakopmund.

ŸŸ **Crazy Mama's**, Sam Nujoma Av, T064-207364. Good-value steaks, seafood as well as excellent pizzas and pasta dishes. Popular amongst locals and budget travellers alike, and a meal with a beer or glass of wine works out very reasonably. Closed Sun.

ŸŸ **Hickory Creek**, 140 Theo Ben Gurirab St, T064-207990, part of the **Spur** chain. Solid South African fare, always good value, filling and friendly service, children well catered for, salad bar, similar menu throughout the region.

Ÿ **Harry Pepper**, near the information office, corner of 11th Av and Nangolo Mbumba Dr, T064-203131. Informal modern pizzeria, great cheap pizzas, Mexican decor, licenced, takeaway and delivery, open daily 1000-late.

Ÿ **Kookwater**, 10th Rd, coffee shop and café with wooden tables in a relaxed atmosphere, good place to settle down with breakfast and the newspaper, warming hot meals for cool days, closed evenings, though one of the few to open on Sun.

Ÿ **Rootman's Home Bakery**, Sam Nujoma Av, milkshakes, cakes and pastries, breakfasts and light lunches, simple café but cheap and tasty food, Mon-Fri 0700-1700, Sat 0800-1300.

The Waldorf, 10th Rd, T064-205744. An alternative for lunches and daytime snacks. Typical Namibian grilled fare, also serves beer and does takeaway. Closed evenings.
Willi Probst Bakery and Restaurant, corner of Theo Ben Gurirab St and 12th Rd, T064-202744. A popular German bakery, recommended for breakfasts, light lunches and snacks, wide variety of cakes, bread and rolls. A good place to start the day for early fishermen, and also it makes up picnic baskets. Mon-Fri 0615-1800, Sat 0615-1415.

Bars and clubs

Swakopmund *p218, map p220*
All the restaurants are licensed and most have a small bar area where you can enjoy a beer before going to your table. In some, such as the **Lighthouse** and **The Tug**, you can go just for a drink (both of these are recommended for sundowners as they have great ocean views). A couple of more lively bars cater for an odd mix of overlanders, the young hip Swakop crowd who look too young to drink, and an older crowd who just like bars.
Casablanca, in a white building to the west of town near the **Villa Weise Backpackers Lodge**. Currently the only nightclub in town, large bar and dance floor, stays open very late, check with the reception at the **Swakop Lodge** (who own it) for opening days as these change depending on season.
Cool Bananas, **Swakop Lodge**. The most popular bar in town at the time of writing. A great place with an enormous TV screen, cool sounds and pool tables, so if you are in the mood for a party, try your luck here. Particularly busy at the weekends when the overland trucks are in town.
Fagin's Bar, Hendrik Witbooi St, close to the **Atlanta Hotel**. Swakop's version of an Irish pub, but without the draught **Murphy's**. The T-shirts overhead tell their own story. A popular bar where most are welcome and at weekends you can enjoy a late lively evening. Recommended.
Rafters Pub, 18 Tobias Hainyeko St. Pub with large windows so you can look in on the action before deciding to go inside, loud music, comfortable seating, huge range of drinks, opens at 1600 and stays open fairly late if there is the demand, occasionally they sell fresh oysters over the bar.

Shopping

Swakopmund *p218, map p220*

Crafts

As Namibia's principal domestic resort Swakopmund has a particularly good selection of shops selling tourist items, not all of these are as tacky as you might imagine; there are some excellent cloth shops and some interesting art studios.

Crafts are sold at 2 street markets in town, one opposite the old prison building on Moses Garoeb St and the other on the pavement below **Café Anton**.
African Curiotique, Nedbank Arcade, close to the Brauhaus Arcade, T064-461062. Very stylish crafts, jewellery, decorated ostrich eggs, textiles and clothes, glassware and ornaments. There is also a branch in Windhoek.
Henckert Gallery, Sam Nujoma Av. A new showroom with its sister branch in Karibib, carpets, wall hangings, minerals and semi-precious stones, wood carvings and drums, can buy polished stones by weight. One of the few shops open 7 days a week, 0830-1900.
Karakulia, Brauhaus Arcade, T064-461415. Good selection of karakul rugs and wall hangings, some of the finest Namibian products to take back home, all of a high standard. Alternatively, go to the factory on Rakotoka St and take a tour around to see how the carpets are made.
Kirikara, Ankerplatz Arcade, www.kirikara.com. Excellent variety of quality crafts, fabrics and jewellery in a very brightly painted orange shop, also has a branch in Cape Town.
Peter's Antiques, 24 Tobias Hainyeko St, a must for anyone interested in German colonial history, excellent collection of Africana books, as well as some genuine tribal antiques. Not cheap but the quality is excellent and the knowledgeable owner is worth talking to.

Books

CNA, Hendrik Witbooi St, stationers, magazines and books, though it doesn't carry a very inspiring range. Good for foreign magazines, though.
Die Muchel Book & Art, 10 Hendrik Witbooi St, T064-402874. Professional bookshop with a charming art gallery to the back and soft music playing, full range of intelligent books

in English and German and a good selection of books on Africa.

Die Swakopmunder Buchhandlung, 22 Sam Nujoma Av, between Nedbank and Standard Bank, T064-402613. A full range of coffee-table books, calendars, local guides and maps, also sells postcards and stamps.

Camera

Photo Studio Behrens, 7 Tobias Hainyeko St, T064-404711. Cameras, binoculars, film, repairs, 1-hr photo development.

Camping and fishing equipment

Cymot, very large branch on Sam Nujoma selling a full range of camping equipment, car accessories and hardware.

Tide Out Fishing, 42 Nathaniel Maxuilili St, T064-405920. Good range of outdoor equipment including fishing rods and tackle, tents, sleeping bags and camp kitchen items.

Jewellery

Desert Gems, Hendrik Witbooi St, opposite the Hansa Hotel. For anyone interested in buying gem stones, polished or in their natural state.

Kristall Gallerie, corner of Tobias Hainyeko Av and Theo-Ben Gurirab Av, T064-406080. A modern gallery with a display of crystals and other semi-precious stones and replica of the original Otjua Tourmaline Mine as the hook to get you to come into the jewellery boutique. Worth it if this sort of thing appeals to you. Mon-Sat 0900-1700, entry fee is US$3.20 but you get this back if you buy something.

Rolf Schmidt Goldsmiths, in the Brauhaus Arcade, precious stones and jewellery.

Shopping malls

There are several shopping malls in Swakopmund. For specialist tourist shops try the Brauhaus Arcade accessed off Hendrik Witbooi St, which is also home to the Atlanta Cinema and restaurants; the Ankerplatz off Sam Nujoma Av which backs on to the Woermann House; and Woermann and Brock Arcade again accessible from Sam Nujoma Av. For food and clothes, standard South African chain stores and supermarkets can be found at the Pick & Pay Mall on Hendrik Witbooi St close to the Namib-I office, or at the Spar Shopping Mall to the north of the centre on Thobias Hainyeko St. Opposite here, the Engen petrol station has a shop which is open 24 hrs. To the north of town near the police station on Tobias Hainyeko St is the Spar supermarket and centre with several shops and takeaways.

Walvis Bay *p232, map p233*

There is nothing too much to write home about the shops in Walvis Bay, but it has the useful chains, such as CNA for books and stationary and the Pick & Pay supermarket, which are in the Seagulls Mall in the centre of town.

Activities and tours

The very many activities available on land and at sea are the highlight of this region. In the last decade Swakopmund and its environs has seen a growing list of adventure and adrenalin activities and sports – so much so that these days Swakopmund is giving Victoria Falls a run for its money as Adventure Capital of Africa! Regional tourists tend to stick to angling, *braaing* and relaxing in their self-catering accommodation for the length of the annual holiday, whilst foreign tourists arrive throughout the week on tour buses and overland trucks to throw themselves into a couple of days of action- packed frenzy by quad-bike, sandboard or skydive. There are also numerous half-day, full-day and longer sightseeing tours that can be taken with one of the many tour operators listed below.

Swakopmund *p218, map p220*

Camel riding

One of the more interesting ways of enjoying the desert landscape is to ride on a camel.

Camel Farm, about 12 km from the town centre, off the B2, T064-400363. Rides can be organized every afternoon 1400-1700, advance notice advised, US$9 per 15 mins. As you drive out to the farm there is a large pipeline visible to the right of the main road, this is the water supply for Swakopmund; the pipe supplies over 11.5 million cubic metres per year, most of the water comes from the Omaruru and Kuiseb rivers.

Fishing

The coastline either side of Swakopmund is famous for its superb fishing. Many of the local cars seem to have a set of rods permanently attached to the roof. Check at the MET office for details of the strict regulations which control angling. Clients have the choice to fish from boats or remote beach locations, always remember to protect yourself from the sun. The principal angling season is Nov-Mar, though some fish can be caught all year round. If you've never tried fishing before, this is a superb introduction. There is a variety of species in the ocean including shark, kob, West Coast steenbras, blacktail, galjoen and catfish. If you are successful, the operators will clean and gut the fish for you, and if you are staying in self-catering accommodation you can cook it for dinner over the *braai*. Expect to pay in the region of US$100 per day for shore angling or deep-sea fishing. All equipment, transport and refreshments are included.

Golf

Rossmund Golf Course, 6 km east of Swakopmund on the B2, T064-405644. A par 72, 18-hole course with grass greens, palm trees and shrubs that add to the character. There is a restaurant in the club house and golf clubs can be hired. Avoid playing in the heat of the day.

Horse riding

Okakambe Trails, 12 km from town centre, follow the B2 towards the airport, take a right turn on the D1901, the stables are close to the camel farm, T064-402799, www.okakambe.iway.na. A variety of short 2-hr rides or pony rides for kids to ½-day, day or longer overnight rides which include camping out in the desert. If you are an experienced rider this is one of the most pleasant ways to explore the amazing desert landscape – good fun, recommended. If you are not a rider, it can also organize hikes in the region. Prices start from US$60 for a 2-hr ride.

Quad-biking

An excellent way to explore the dune field south of Swakopmund is by quad-bike (a 4-wheel all-terrain motorbike). This is one of the best ways to access parts of the Swakopmund sand dunes that even 4WD cars can't reach. There are 2 types of bike you can choose from. For those who are a little unsure of their biking prowess there are 160 cc semi-automatic bikes. Those who wish to go hell for leather and have some idea of what they are doing can ride the 200 cc manual quad-bikes. Helmets, goggles and gloves are provided. Tours are multi-guiding with slow and fast groups in the same tour, catering for both the adrenalin seeker and the complete novice. They start on the edge of the Swakop Riverbed, cross flat gravel plains before going into the dune belt where the fun starts. Trails follow the crests of the dunes and there are some very steep ascents and descents where your bikes plough through the sand. Although there are variations between the companies, the standard full ride takes about 2½ hrs and covers 35 km. Take something warm to wear later in the day as the ride back to Swakop can be cold. Expect to pay in the region of US$70-80.

Desert Explorers, on the main road to Walvis Bay just before the bridge over the Swakop River, T064-406096, www.swakop.com/adv. Book through any agent in town or just rock up, it will run a trip for a minimum of 2 people. Daily 0800-1800. Offers a 2-hr, 35-km round trip of thrills through the desert. It can also organize overnight or multi-day safaris using tented camp accommodation in the desert. There's a bar and lounge area at the office, and videos of your trip can be arranged with prior notice.

Outback Orange, 42 Nathaniel Maxuilili St, T/F064-400968, outbackorange@yahoo.com. Fun company that is thoroughly recommended for this excursion, Dave has been operating quad-bike rides for 5 years. Departures are daily at 0930, 1130, 1330 and 1530. Videos available. It also runs tours on 2-seater beach/dune buggies, departing daily at 1030, 1330 and 1500. The 2½-hr trip goes into the Swakop Riverbed and out to the dune field and the guide will point out some of the desert fauna, US$95 per buggy that seats 2.

Sandboarding

There is no better way to conquer the towering dunes than to zoom down them head first on a traditional Swakop sandboard, or carve up the dune with style and skill on a snowboard adapted for sand. The dunes are constantly shifting and can move 10 m in a week; sandboard tracks soon disappear. The beauty about sandboarding is the sand is not abrasive, and as it's obviously not cold, you can board in shorts and T-shirts. The worst that can happen is that you walk away covered in sand. For the lie-down option you're supplied with a large flat piece of waxed hardboard, safety hat, elbow guards and gloves before heading off to climb a dune. The idea is to lie on the board, push off from the top and speed headfirst down the sandy surface. Speeds easily reach 80 kph and some of the dunes are very steep though first you'll do a few training rides on the lower dunes. No experience is necessary; it's exhilarating and lots of fun. Stand-up boarding requires more skill. It is exactly the same as snowboarding, but on sand, using standard snowboarding equipment to surf your way down the dunes. If you've got snowboarding experience then this is an opportunity to try out those turns, free-style jumps and big spray curves. Prices are about US$40-50. All trips include lunch and a few drinks.

Alter Action, T064-402737, alteraxn@iafrica.com.na. Beth invented sand boarding at Swakopmund and has taken thousands of people through the dunes over the years. A fun half-day excursion with a lot of laughs.

Dune 7, T064-204400, dawayner@hotmail.com. Stand-up boarding and with a quad-bike to take you up to the top of the dune, professional instructor.

Scenic flights

For those visitors short on time but long on cash a number of companies offer flying safaris. Flights vary from 1½-hr flips along the coast to all-day safaris to northern Namibia that include landings and 4WD adventures. From the air you can clearly see Namibia's desert landscapes, dried up riverbeds, moonscapes, rock formations, mountains and gravel plains. Strongly recommended if you wish to appreciate the Namibian landscape from the air, the views are just tremendous.

Most flights are high-winged, single- engine, 6-seater Cessnas, which have the wings above the windows for better sightseeing.

The most popular trip is a 2¼-hr flight from Swakopmund to Sossusvlei, which goes over the massive dune field and returns along the coast over the flamingos, seals and shipwrecks. Other sample flights include a 1½-hr trip along the coast; a full-day trip over Sossusvlei and the Fish River Canyon which includes a stop in Lüderitz to visit Kolmonskop; a day trip over Sossusvlei, the coast and a stop in the Kalahari for lunch and a visit to the bushmen; or a day trip ovet the Skeleton Coast in the north and a stop to visit the Himba in the far north. Costs vary enormously depending on the length of the trip and the number of people in the plane, but the cheapest and shortest flights of about 1½ hrs are about US$140 if there are 5 people in the plane. Obviously the prices increase significantly if there are less people though the companies will endeavour to find other people to fill the plane. The companies listed below also can arrange fly-in safaris to the remote lodges.

Atlantic Aviation, 5 Hendrik Witbooi St, next to **Hansa Hotel**, T064-404749, www.flyinnamibia.com.

Bush Birds, Woermann Centre, T064-404071, www.bushbird.info.

Pleasure Flights and Safaris, corner of Sam Nujoma Av and Hendrik Witbooi St, T/F064-404500, www.pleasureflights.com.na. Now also has a helicopter. Look out for the blackboard outside the office which posts what spaces it has left on each flight.

Wings Over Africa, office at the **Swakopmund Hotel**, T064-403720, www.flyinafrica.com.

Skydiving

Ground Rush Adventures, at the **Swakopmund Skydiving Club** at Swakopmund Airport, T064-402841, www.skydiveswakopmund.com.na. Extremely popular tandem free-fall jumps for novices. Jumps take place daily, normally after the fog has lifted in the morning. After a brief safety chat, you board a small plane for a 35-min scenic flight over Swakopmund and the surrounding coast and desert as you prepare yourself for your jump. This involves being strapped between the thighs of your tandem jump master and shuffling to the door of the plane. At 12,000 ft you both tumble into the sky for a mind-blowing 30-sec free-fall at around 220 kph – a totally exhilarating experience. Then the parachute opens and you float to the ground for a 10-min ride enjoying the breathtaking desert scenery. A cameraman jumps with you with either a hand-held camera or a camera strapped to his helmet; videos and T-shirts are for sale and the clubhouse is a good place for a celebratory drink after jumping. The jump costs in the region of US$250-270. The club also runs static line courses which involve 6 hrs of ground school before the initial jump at 3000 ft.

Swimming

Indoor heated pool and sauna, next to the museum, Strand St. Mon-Fri 0700-1900, Sat-Sun 1000-1800, US$1. You can also rent umberellas from here to take on to the beach. At the front of the complex is a paddling pool for kids and a curly water slide. In 2006 the swimming pool is rumoured to be moving to a new site at a new sports complex (presently being built in town), which will also include an athletics track and football pitch; the present site, which includes the **Lighthouse** restaurant, is to be developed to include apartments, shops and a new location for the restaurant.
Palm Beach Just below the pool is the mole and the adjacent Palm Beach from where you can swim but whilst the ocean is sheltered and calm, it is very, very cold.

Tour operators

All of the companies in Swakopmund, Walvis Bay and Henties Bay offer a selection of similar tours. It always pays to shop around and ask fellow guests at your hotel whether they might recommend anyone. Prices do vary, but then so too does the quality of the guide, the maximum group size, the comfort of the vehicle and the quality of any food and drink that might be included in the tour price. Tours cost approximately US$55-70 per half day, and US$70-120 per full day. Before you make your choice find out how many people will be in the group and, if possible, what their nationalities are as a mixed-language group will get far less out of their guide. As it can also get very hot in the middle of the day, this is not the time to find oneself squashed in the back of a Land Rover with an awkward view. If the tour you wish to go on is not running on the day that suits your timetable don't be persuaded into joining another tour; check first with another company, there is plenty of choice. Finally, if you are not happy with the tour inform the tourist office as some companies are not yet accustomed to providing the level of service and value that international visitors expect. Day tours on offer include **Cape Cross Seal Colony** and **Henties Bay, desert tours** to see welwitschia plants, sand dunes and the **Swakop Canyon** and **Spitzekoppe**. Some companies offer multi-day trips further afield, so if you haven't yet decided what you want to see in Namibia before arriving, then you can discuss longer trips with these companies.

Africa Leisure Travel, T064-463812, www.africaleisure.net. Day tours to Cape Cross and into the desert, town tours of Swakopmund and Walvis Bay, can organize dinner in the desert under marquees for very large groups.

Charly's Desert Tours, T064-404341, charlydt@mweb.com.na. Day and overnight tours from Swakop, as well as tours further afield, well-established company with experience of working with film crews.

Damarana Safaris, T064-463277, www.damarana.com. Upmarket operator offering 4WD guided tours from between 2-6 days from Swakopmund to remote regions of Damaraland using mobile camps.

Desert Adventure Safaris, 38 Bismarck St, T064-403274, www.das.com.na. Slightly cheaper than other companies for day tours, longer tours for small groups can be put together to suit your needs.

Kallisto Tours, T064-402473, www.natron.net/kallisto-tours. Several day tours on offer, including a short 1½-hr tour of historical Swakopmund, can organize longer tours to Etosha for groups in a/c minibuses.

Kunene Tours and Safaris, T064-402779, zanberg@iafrica.com.na. Guided 4WD trips to the more remote corners of Kaokoland and Damaraland with experienced guide Caesar Zandberg. You travel in your own vehicle but are joined by Caesar in his vehicle, recommended to really get off the beaten track. If you don't have you own car, can also arrange tours for 6-8 people.

Living Desert Adventures, T064-405070, or book through the Namib-i office. This is a ½-day tour, usually leaving Swakopmund at 0800, to discover the creatures in the dune belt such as geckos, snakes, insects, dancing lizards, the white lady spider and desert cameleons. This is an excellent tour and whilst many people initially think they don't want to go and see insects and reptiles, they come back from the dunes fully rewarded. The guide also takes out a magnet and draws the iron ore out of the sand in such a way you can write on a dune! You are also taught how to extract moisture from the desert plants and thus drink in the dunes. Expect to pay about US$70 per person. It can also organize tours after dark by spotlight, when these little creatures are out in full and do not have to searched for by digging in the sand. Recommended, and children will love it.

Namib Tours, Hendrik Witbooi St, T/F064-404072. Another option for the full selection of day tours in the Swakop Region, contact Heinz Heuschneider.

Namibia Tours & Safaris, T064-406038, www.namibia-tours-safaris.com. 4WD tours to regions around Swakopmund, camping and lodge safaris for small groups, fly-in safaris.

Nolte Adventure Safaris, 121 Libertina Amathila Av, T064-405454, notltesaf@africaonline.com.na. Half and full day tours into the desert, Spitzkoppe, Cape Cross, etc., can cater for the disabled.

Palmwag Lodge and Travel Shop, 14a Sam Nujoma Av, T064-404459, www.palmwag.com.na. Primarily an office for bookings for **Palmwag Lodge** in Damaraland, but also takes reservations for the new **Rossmund Lodge** at the Rossmund Golf Course 6 km east of Swakopmund, and books day trips in and around the town.

Sunrise Tours and Safaris, 8 Hendrik Witbooi St, T064-404561, www.sunrisetours.com.na. Fishing trips as well as sightseeing, guided lodge/hotel tours using minibuses or 4WDs.

Turnstone Tours, T/F064-403123, www.turnstone-tours.com. Run by Bruno and Kate Nebe, **Turnstone** is the Sandwich Harbour (see page 237) specialist working closely with MET, as well as offering excellent overnight camping trips into the Namib Desert, Damaraland and the Erongo Mountains. Whether your interests are geological, ornithological, botanical or just general you will get individually tailored, in-depth, expertly guided trips. All tours (maximum 7 people) are conducted by Bruno or his assistant Michael and include pick-up from hotel or guesthouse and all snacks or meals including soft drinks. Strongly recommended.

Walking tours

Swakop on Foot, T081-1243329, or **Angelica Flamm-Schneeweiss**, T064-461647, or book through the **Namib-i** office, US$16 for a 2- to 3-hr walk in German or English, minimum 2 people.

Around Swakopmund *p231*

Dare Devil Adventures, Long Beach, T081-1284492, daredev@iway.na. This company offers quad-biking trips through the dunes from 10-40 km, and a children's quad-bike circuit.

Walvis Bay *p232, map p233*

Dolphin watching and fishing

A number of companies offer dolphin and seal tours from Walvis Bay. These are usually half-day tours of the harbour and lagoon areas and you can expect excellent sightings of seals, dolphins, flamingos and pelicans. Boats usually depart from the **Walvis Bay Yacht Club** each morning and go through the harbour and past the fishing factories to **Bird Island** and **Pelican Point** and back via the lagoon. Seals are often fed by hand, and most trips include fresh oysters and champagne. For those contemplating a trip up to **Cape Cross Colony** to see the seal reserve, these tours offer an excellent alternative that avoids both the long drive and the pungent smell! A further possibility – if you are lucky – is the chance of spotting whales as they make their way up and down their migratory routes to and from the Antarctic. At around US$60 per person these tours are good value for money and recommended. Some operators (such as **Eco Marine Kayak Tours**, see Kayaking, below) offer sea kayacking which will enable you to get really close to the marine and bird life – you'll literally float with the seals.

Aquanaut Tours, Walvis Bay Yacht Club, T064-405969, www.aquanauttours.com. Departs daily from the **Walvis Bay Yacht Club** at 0830, 3-hr trip to see dolphins and seals, includes champagne and seafood platter.

Catamaran Charters, T064-205511, www.namibiancharters.com. Trips out to Pelican Point and out to sea to see dolphins and seals on a 12-m catamaran.

By arrangement only but trips usually go out daily from Walvis Bay Yacht Club at 0900 and 1300 and last 4 hrs.

Levo Fishing and Pleasure Tours, at the **Walvis Bay Yacht Club** on the lagoon, T064-207555, www.levotours.com. Seal and dolphin cruises and quality fishing tours with local fishermen who have years of experience. Deep-sea trips also available with sufficient advance notice.

Mola Mola Safaris, office and coffee shop is on Atlantic St, off the Esplanade, opposite the entrance to the Yacht Club, T064-205511, www.mola-namibia.com. Daily 4-hr dolphin and seal tours around the harbour and fishing trips for the enthusiast, can also arrange 4WD trips into the dunes. Ask for Neels or Megan. Well-established and professional company.

Skeleton Coast Charters, T064-404305, www.skeletoncoast.com.na. Sightseeing trips on a 52-ft yacht, the *Devona*, daily at 0900 from **Walvis Bay Yacht Club**, 4 hrs to Pelican Point.

Kayaking

Eco Marine Kayak Tours, T/F064-203144, jeannem@iafrica.com.na. Kayak tours for both the experienced and the beginner. Choose between leisurely tours of the coastal wetlands and longer trips to Pelican Point for the fitter, which also includes a kayak out to the seal colonies off the coast. Guides carry GPS and VHF comms. Contact Jeanne for further details. At US$60 per head for a 5-hr trip this is good value for money and is recommended.

Quad-biking

No previous motorbiking experience is needed.

Kuiseb Delta Adventures, at the **Lagoon Chalets**, Walvis Bay, T/f064-202550, www.kuisebonline.com. Quad-bike trips for older people or children, a much slower pace, with information about the desert flora and fauna.

Tour operators

See also under Swakopmund tour operators, above.

Diamond Rain, Circumferential Rd, Industrial Area, Walvis Bay, T064-217200. Guided diamond manufacturing tours daily at 0900, 1100, 1400, and 1600, book in advance. On the tour you are shown the diamond cutting and polishing process and can buy loose diamonds direct from the factory. A little bit of history of Namibia's diamonds is included and this is the only place in Namibia where you can visit a diamond factory.

Transport

Swakopmund *p218, map p220*

30 km to Walvis Bay, 395 km to Windhoek, 76 km Henties Bay, 120 km to Cape Cross.

Air

Air Namibia, Sam Nujoma Av, T064-405123, central reservations, Windhoek, T061-2996333, www.airnamibia.com.na. It has 1 daily flight (except Sat) between Swakopmund and Windhoek's Eros Airport. This departs Eros at 1500, arrives at Swakopmund at 1600, departs again at 1630 and arrives back in Windhoek at 1730. Walvis Bay is much better served with flights (see below). **Swakopmund Airport** is a small room with some seats, there is a public telephone, toilets and boxes to deposit hired car keys at the end of your trip. These flights are rarely fully booked, but if the plane has a lot of baggage it will take fewer passengers to keep to a safe weight. See **Air Namibia** timetable, page 72 (the schedules are continually changing so if you are planning your holiday on a tight schedule check before arranging car hire and hotel accommodation).

If you have not booked a hire car for your arrival, arrange for your hotel to collect you from the airport. Local taxis do not make a habit of going to the airport to meet each flight. The local **Avis** representatives may give you a lift into town, assuming they are meeting the flight. If you get stranded, go to **Ground Rush Adventure**'s (skydiving operator) clubhouse right at the airport; you can get a drink and food here and they are always ferrying people in and out of town. You might even be persuaded to jump!

Bus

There is a daily **Intercape Mainliner** coach, www.intercape.co.za, between Windhoek and Walvis Bay in both directions that stops in Swakopmund. It drops off and picks up passengers by **The Talk Shop**, on Hendrik

Witbooi St. (This was a café where you could make telephone calls from, but on our visit it was firmly shut.) For **Windhoek** (4½ hrs) via Karibib and Okahandja, and **Walvis Bay** (25 mins) see timetable on page 70. Namibia daylight-saving service departs 1 hr earlier between the first Sun in Apr and the first Sun in Sep.

Transnamib also runs a weekly coach service between **Walvis Bay** and **Khorixas** that stops in Swakopmund (see Walvis Bay, below). **Welwitschia Shuttle**, T081-2631433, or book through Namib-i office. Daily shuttle using micro/sprinter bus that usually departs from Swakopmund at 0700 and arrives in **Windhoek** at 1100, then departs Windhoek at 1400 and gets back to Swakopmund at around 1700. This costs US$12 one way and given that this is the same as the set price between Windhoek and Windhoek airport which is only 40 km away, this is excellent value.

Bicycle

Cycle Clinic, 10 Hendrik Witbooi St, T064-402530. Hires out mountain bikes for around US$15 a day.

Car

Some of the major car hire companies have an office in Swakopmund, staff will meet flights at either Swakopmund or Walvis Bay airports where you will be able to pick up your car. Note, however, that if you want a fully equipped car with camping gear there is a much better choice in Windhoek.
Avis, Theo-Ben Gurirab Av, in the Swakopmund Entertainment Centre, T064-405792, www.avis.co.za. **Budget**, Shop 6, Woerman and Brock Centre, Tobias Hainyeko St, T064-463380, www.budget.com. **Tempest/Sixt**, T064-461924, www.sixt.com.

Taxi

There are taxis all over Swakopmund, if you find a driver you like, get his mobile phone number.

Train

The railway station is on the desert side of Garoeb St; reservations, T064-463538. If time is not an issue then the **Transnamib Starline Passenger Service**, T061-2982032 (central reservations), www.transnamib.com.na, between **Windhoek** and Swakopmund/Walvis Bay is a comfortable alternative to the coach. But note, Namibian railways must rate as one of the slowest services in Africa. For timetables for services to Windhoek, Tsumeb (via Omaruru and Otavi), Walvis Bay and Windhoek, see page 68.

The Desert Express, T061-2982600 (reservations), www.desertexpress.com.na, departs **Windhoek** on Tue and Fri at 1130, and it departs Swakopmund on Wed and Sat 1430. The train and whole service has been modelled around existing luxury services in South Africa. En route the train stops for a game drive and a visit to the sand dunes and arrives at the respective destination the following morning (see page 104 for further details).

Walvis Bay *p232, map p233*

Air

Airport at Rooikop, 10 km east of town off the C14, T064-202867. **Air Namibia**, T064-202938, central reservations T061-2996333, www.airnamibia.com.na. There are direct flights to **Windhoek** and **Cape Town** via Lüderitz and Oranjemund. See timetable, page 72.

SA Express, T+27 (0)11 978 5577 (South Africa), www.saexpress.co.za, has 1 flight a day (except Sat) between **Cape Town** and Walvis Bay, and 1 flight a day (except Sat) between **Johannesburg** and Walvis Bay.

Bus

30 km to Swakopmund, 389 km to Windhoek.

For **Intercape** luxury coach service, www.intercape.co.za (book online), to **Windhoek** (5 hrs) via Swakopmund, see timetable, page 70. Coaches arrive and depart from outside the Omega Service Station, corner of Sam Nujoma and 15th Rd. Namibia daylight-saving service departs 1 hr earlier between 1st Sun in Apr and 1st Sun in Sep.

Transnamib Starline Passenger Services, central reservations T061-2982032, www.transnamib.com.na, also runs a weekly coach service from Walvis Bay train station on Fri at 1300, via Swakopmund, 1400, Henties Bay, 1530 and Uis, 1800, to **Khorixas** 2030. It departs from Khorixas on Sun at 1300, Uis, 1530, Henties Bay, 1800, Swakopmund, 1930, and arrives back in Walvis Bay at 2030.

Car

Avis, T064-207520, www.avis.co.za, Rooikop Airport. **Budget**, T064-204624, www.budget.co.za, Rooikop Airport. **Coastal Car Hire**, T064-205345, cch@iway.na. Double cab 4WDs with all camping equipment including rooftop tents, from US$130 per day with unlimited mileage and insurance. This is excellent value. **Europcar**, Rooikop Airport, T064-203651, www.europcar.co.za. **Hertz**, Rooikop Airport, T064-461854, www.hertz.co.za. **Imperial**, T064-207391, www.imperialcarrental.co.za, Nangolo Mbumba Drive. **Triple Three Rentals**, Rooikop Airport, T064-206686, oliver@iafrica.com.na.

Train

For information, T064-208504. If you are not in a hurry there is an overnight train service to **Windhoek**. This train is a useful way of returning to Swakopmund if you have been visiting Walvis Bay without your own vehicle, though you will have to stay overnight as the train arrives in Walvis Bay late morning and departs back to Swakopmund almost immediately. For trains to Tsumeb via Usakos and Otjiwarongo, and Windhoek, see timetable on page 68. Both services stop at Swakopmund (90 mins). **Transnamib Starline Passenger Services**, central reservations T061-2982032 (Windhow, www.transnamib.com.na.

Directory

Swakopmund *p218, map p220*
Banks All the main banks are in the centre of town, all with 24-hr ATMs, and a foreign exchange desk inside. **First National Bank**, Tobias Hainyeko St. **Nedbank**, **Standard Bank** and **Windhoek Bank**, all 3 on Sam Nujoma Av. There are also ATMs at many of the Engen petrol stations. **Emergencies** International SOS, T064-463676, 24-hr response. Police, see below. **Sea Rescue**, T064- 203202. **Internet** Compucare, next to Pleasure Flights on Hendrik Witbooi St, T064-463775, US$1.60 per ½ hr, also downloads of digital photos on CD, scanning, cold drinks and coffee, Mon-Sat 0800-1800, Sun 1000-1700. Also has dial up for laptops. **Swakopmund I-Café and Coffee Shop**, Tobias Hainyeko St, in the Woerman and Brock centre, T064-464021. Plenty of computers with quick links, can also access with your own laptop, international fax and phone, can download digital photos on to CD, photocopying, and a coffee and cake counter. This is very popular with overseas visitors, particularly groups from the overland trucks. Mon-Fri 0700-2000, Sun 1000-2000. US$1.90 per ½ hr. The quad-bike operator **Outback Orange**, on Nathaniel Maxuilili St, and **Roxy's Café** in Swakop Lodge, opposite, also have terminals for internet access. **Medical services** Bismark **Pharmacy and Medical Centre**, 17 Sam Nujoma Av, T064-405894. For foreign visitors with good medical insurance, this is the best bet for doctor's visits, medical and dentistry emergencies. **Cottage Medi Clinic**, private hospital, T064-412200. **Police** T064-402431, emergencies T10111. **Post office** The main post office is in Tobias Hainyeko St, next to the police station. Mon-Fri 0830-1300, 1400-1630; Sat 0900-1200. **Telephone** Outside the post office are some public telephones and a booth selling phone cards, this is the cheapest place to make international calls from.

Walvis Bay *p232, map p233*
Banks All the main banks have an office in the centre of town next to each other on Sam Nujoma Av, all with 24-hr ATMs. **Emergencies** International SOS, T064-400700, 24-hr response. Police, see below. **Internet** Computerland, computer shop with a few terminals for internet access, Sam Nujoma Av, Mon-Sat 0800-2000, Sat 0900-1900. **Medical services** Welwitschia Private Hospital, T064-218911. **Police** T064-219048, emergencies T10111.

North of Swakopmund – Skeleton Coast

To the north of Swakopmund, Namibia's bleak coastline follows its course to the Angolan border. Firstly it passes through the not very inspiringly named National West Coast Tourist Recreation Area and then through the more evocatively named Skeleton Coast National Park. To the east of the coast are the inhospitable mountains and gravel plains of Damaraland and Kaokoland. The Skeleton Coast got its name from the ships and unlucky sailors who perished after being shipwrecked on the barren shores over the centuries. The first stretch of coast through the Recreational Area is open to all and, although flat, foggy and featureless, the beach is hugely popular with anglers in search of the Benguela Current's big game fish. The only settlement of note is Henties Bay, primarily a regional centre that supports the fisherman, and the nearest town to the Cape Cross Seal Colony to the north. Here, one of the largest breeding grounds of seals in the southern hemisphere, thousands of Cape fur seals unfathomably decide to sit on the same overcrowed rock. Further north and in the Skeleton Coast Park proper, permits are needed for any stay longer than a transfer through to the interior, though staying overnight in the park offers the chance to experience complete isolation in this eerie and desolate environment. ▸▸ *For Sleeping, Eating and other listings, see pages 262-264.*

Ins and outs

Driving from Swakopmund north through the Recreational Area, takes you through flat monotonous stoney plains to Henties Bay. From here there are three different routes to explore. The easiest route is the D1918 inland, which passes close to the Klein Spitzkoppe (1572 m) and Gross Spitzkoppe (1784 m) before joining the B2 near Usakos. The other two routes will take you into some of Namibia's finest wilderness areas. Just north of the town, the C35 turns east into the heart of Damaraland; this is the road to Uis and the Brandberg (2573 m). Finally, you can follow the C34 along the coast. It is possible to drive as far north as Terrace Bay; once you have crossed the Ugab River you are in the Skeleton Coast National Park (southern section). To travel through the park on the C34 and then the C39, you need to pay entrance and vehicle fees at the gate. Both roads that lead inland from the coast go through a sparsely populated region; care should be taken when driving on these gravel and sand roads. If you have an accident or a breakdown you may have a long wait before the next vehicle comes along.

National West Coast Recreation Area

▸▸ *pp262-264. Colour map 1, C3.*

The National West Coast Recreation Area stretches from the northern boundary of the Namib-Naukluft National Park to the Ugab River. It extends for around 200 km along the coast and covers an area of 16,400 sq km. The Ugab forms the southern boundary of the Skeleton Coast Park. Although part of the protected Skeleton Coast, this area is not subject to quite the same stringent controls as those that apply to areas of the Skeleton Coast National Park. The area is open all year round and there are no restrictions on when you can travel through here. For most visitors the only area of interest is the seal colony at Cape Cross; the rest of the coastline is flat and monotonous, and most visitors come for the fishing. If you are not visiting the

Hentie's Bay

In 1929 Major Hentie van der Merwe, a motor dealer in Kalkveld, discovered a freshwater spring in an old delta of the Omaruru River while on a rhino hunt/expedition in the desert. He immediately fell in love with the place and returned there on his next December holiday and built himself a wooden shack from crates used for the importation of motor cars in those early years. For years it was his own private spot that he escaped to every December. Later, he started inviting his friends along who referred to it as Hentie's Bay, which eventually became Henties Bay as more people claimed their own little place amongst the dunes. In 1966 it was decided that the people must move out of the riverbed and 27 people were given land to the north and south of the dunes, either side of the riverbed. In 1967 the **De Duine Hotel** was built and after that the town started to develop.

Skeleton Coast National Park there is no point travelling beyond Cape Cross – shipwrecks such as the *Winston* are very disappointing and the **Messum Crater** can only be visited with a guide and a 4WD vehicle.

Henties Bay and the coast road ›› *Phone code: 064. Colour map 1, C3.*

Named after Major Hentie van der Merwe who started fishing here in 1929 (see box, page 255), this is the most northerly settlement of any note on the Namibian Atlantic seaboard. For much of the year it is just a quiet collection of bungalows on a windswept, sand-blasted coast, with a resident community of about 2700 people. During the summer season it comes to life with around 10,000 visitors. Traditionally, most of these visitors have been Afrikaans-speakers, either from the interior or from the Jo'burg/Pretoria areas, intent on some serious fishing. Apart from the splendid coastline and fine sandy beach, there is little to do here, and the majority of international visitors are unlikely to find much of interest, unless it's solitude you want!

Make sure you fill up with petrol in Henties Bay as well as with drinking water and food.

Henties Bay Tourism ⓘ *Jakkalsputz Rd, T064-501143, www.hentiesbay.com, Mon-Fri 0900-1630, Sat 0900-1200*, is at the **Total Service Station/Grobler Motors**. The first main road to the left and north of the tourist office, Duineweg, leads to the best and oldest hotel in town, the **Hotel de Duine** (see box, page 255, and Sleeping, page 262). As you turn left look out for Benguela Street on the left, where all the shops are. Opposite the hotel is a dramatic nine-hole **golf course** set in a valley leading down to the beach. It extends over a distance of 2.7 km and has very well-tended grass greens and tees while the fairways are virgin desert sand. Visitors can play for a minimal fee, but have to provide their own golf clubs. A round here will test your ability to cope with windy conditions.

There are two walking trails that start from town. The **Jakkalsputz Trail** (18 km) heads south either along the beach or the dune road, past some tidal pools which are visible at low tide, past Cape Farilhao where the ruins of an old lighthouse can be seen, to the Jakkalsputz camping site. The way back to Henties Bay further inland is through a wetlands area (where jackal may be spotted) and through the dunes. The **Omaruru River Trail** (20 km) goes north along the beach up to the Omaruru River mouth, then along the river before turning back to town on an existing track through the desert where various species of lichen can be seen. Maps of these trails are available from the tourist office. If you are in a 4WD there are several routes in the region. Again information and GPS coordinates can be found at the tourist office.

Driving between Swakopmund and Henties Bay will quickly make you realize how repetitive and dull much of this coastline is, but once you get out of the vehicle and start to explore the dry rivers and the occasional salt pans on foot, the park can be enjoyed at a different level. The peace and solitude is amazing, the air is clean and fresh and at night the stars are like you've never seen them before. If this does not sound like fun then go no further north than Henties Bay, where you can take the C35 and head inland for a different area of Namibia.

Cape Cross Seal Reserve ›› *Colour map 1, C3.*

ⓘ *A short distance into the reserve is the office where you pay the fees and can pick up some leaflets, To64-501143, daily 1000-1700, US$6.50 adults, US$1.50 car; the only facilities here are some toilets and fresh drinking water.*

Pick up any tour brochure in Swakopmund and you will see advertisements for trips to Cape Cross. There are 23 breeding colonies of Cape fur seals, *Arctocephalus pusillus*, along the coast of South Africa and Namibia (16 are in Namibia) and this is reputed to be one of the largest and best known. It is also the most easily visited. Apart from being the location of an important seal colony the reserve has had an interesting history.

If you think that the rank smell and the sight of dead, squashed seal pups during the birthing season might rattle your senses, avoid a visit here during November/December; instead, view seals from a boat excursion in Walvis Bay (see page 250).

In 1485 the Portuguese navigator, Diego Cão landed at Cape Cross. This was the furthest any European had reached down the coast of Africa, and to mark the event he erected a stone cross on the isolated stony headland, inscribing it thus: "Since the creation of the world 6684 years have passed and since the birth of Christ, 1484 years and so the Illustrious Don John has ordered this pillar to be erected here by Diego Cão, his knight." Diego Cão died at Cape Cross and was buried in some high ground close by. His original cross was later removed and taken to Berlin by the Oceanographical Museum. In 1974 the whole area was landscaped and a couple of replica crosses now stand amongst the rocks.

As you walk to the shoreline from the office you pass a small graveyard which dates from the turn of the last century. Between 1899 and 1903 there was a small thriving community at Cape Cross which was involved in the collection of guano from a salt pans on nearby islands. The records show that 124 people died and were buried here. Around 1900 this was a busy little port which was even served by a railway. The guano industry was so prosperous that a 16-km railway track was laid across the salt pan to facilitate the collection of guano. In its heyday there were steam locomotives working here.

Estimates as to the number of seals here vary between 80,000 and as many as 250,000 during the breeding season (November/December). The second largest colony covers Wolf Bay, Atlas Bay and Long Island, south of Lüderitz. Most of the other colonies are offshore on small islands. The bulls, which can weigh up to 360 kg, start to arrive here in October to claim the land for their cows. Ninety per cent of seal pups are born over a 34-day period in November and December. The female produces a single pup that begins suckling immediately after birth. Approximately a week later when a bond has been established between mother and pup, the mother will go into the sea to feed. When she returns she will bark for her pup who responds by bleating until they find each other again, usually by detecting scents. The whole scene during the birth of the young pups can be quite distressing as many of the newly born seals get crushed by adults, others drown, and then there is always the threat posed by the predators, jackals and hyenas that come to the colony to nab lone pups. This has to

The Cape fur seal is the largest of the world's nine species of fur seals and is only found on the islands and coasts of southern Africa from southern Angola, down Namibia's coastline and as far south as Algoa Bay in South Africa.

Twitching for a tern

It has been estimated that over 300,000 wading birds seasonally visit the Namib coast and most of the birds live along the coast since there are few areas of wetlands with fresh water inland. Some of the most popular birds are also those that are the easiest to identify: plovers, cormorants, sandpipers, flamingos and white pelicans. Further inland along the riverbeds you will come across birds which favour gravel plains and cliff faces. Along the Ugab River Hiking Trail the augur buzzard, peregrine falcon, black eagle and rock kestrel have all been seen; after a little rain the reed beds are home to a few weavers and warblers. But this stretch of coast is also home to one of the rarest and smallest terns found in the world, the Damara tern (*Sterna balaenarum*).

It has been estimated that of the 2000 breeding pairs left in the world, 1800 inhabit Namibia; the rest are found close by along the coast in South Africa and Angola, where they favour the open coastline and its sandy bays. The Damara tern is only 23 cm long, with a white breast and a black head. In flight it is similar to a swallow. Such a small bird is not able to carry much food for the young so to limit the amount of flying they have to do they tend to nest close to the food supply. Their size also influences the more precise location of their nests. They are unable to defend their nests against jackals and hyenas, so to try and avoid predators they nest on the salt pans and the gravel plains up to 5 km inland. This is another reason for observing the park off-road regulations, for once disturbed a breeding pair will abandon the chick.

be one of the smelliest places on earth – think pungent rotting fish/flesh – and it really is a relief to get away again after having taken in the sight of tens of thousands of seals basking on the rocks or surfing amongst the waves.

The Cape Cross Seal Reserve is 55 km north of Henties Bay just off the C34. The entrance gate is 3 km from the junction, the colony is located just beyond the crosses, a short drive from the entrance.

About 33 km north of Cape Cross the salt road divides in two. The salt road, C34, continues to follow the coastline towards the campsite at Mile 108 while the side road, D2303, turns inland and then joins the D2342, the back road to Uis. These roads are heavily corrugated and best driven in a 4WD.

Ugab River hike

ⓘ *Apr-Oct, second and fourth Thu each month, limited to 8 people, US$32; more information from the Namibia Wildlife Resorts office, Woermann House, Swakopmund, www.nwr.com.na.*

A pleasant alternative to visiting the Skeleton Coast is to join the Ugab River hike which starts and finishes at Ugabmund and follows the river inland before looping through some hills where there are some caves and natural springs. If you have the time this is a walk worth joining as it is a very interesting way to learn about the environment and life on the Skeleton Coast. The full hike is 50 km long and usually takes three days to complete. Hikers must bring and carry all their own food and bedding for the duration. As with the Fish River Canyon hike (see page 333), a medical certificate must be handed over to the trails officer.

Skeleton Coast National Park » pp262-264. Colour map 1, C3.

ⓘ *Entry adults US$13 per day, car US$1.50.*

The Skeleton Coast is one of the finest and most unusual coastal wildernesses in the world. It stretches between Swakopmund in the south to the mouth of the Kunene River, marking the border with Angola. The strong currents and swirling fogs of this Atlantic coastline had long been a hazard to shipping and when the term Skeleton Coast was first applied to it in 1933 by newspaperman, Sam Davis, the name stuck. Davis had been reporting on the search for a Swiss airman, Carl Nauer, whose plane had disappeared along the coast while trying to break the Cape Town to London solo air record. No trace was ever found. Today it is the elements previously responsible for so much loss of life – the desert, wide-open space, isolation and solitude – that attract the majority of visitors to the coast.

Sleeping
Cape Cross Lodge **1**
Skeleton Coast Camp **2**

Ins and outs

The park can be entered in the south, from the West Coast Recreational Area, or in the east from Damaraland. Whichever gate you enter by you must make sure there are sufficient hours of daylight to either travel through the park or reach your camp. Visitors must enter before 1500 and depart no later than 1700. Two hours is the minimum time it takes to cross the park between the two gates. Day visitors are not permitted to visit **Terrace Bay** or **Torra Bay**, and if you are staying overnight in these places you will need to show proof of your reservation at the gate. The southern gate, by the Ugab River, is known as **Ugabmund** and is about 207 km from Swakopmund; it is a further 162 km to the camp at Terrace Bay. This gate closes at 1500 each day for traffic going as far as Terrace Bay or Springbokwasser. The eastern gate, **Springbokwasser**, is 178 km from Khorixas. The quality of the road heading inland from the gate is not as good as the coast road. Torra Bay is 50 km from the gate, Terrace Bay is 98 km. Driving through is one way! You cannot leave and depart through the same gate unless you are staying overnight. The reason for this was explained to us as sheer laziness on the part of the staff at each of the gates. They fill in a register of vehicles entering the park and at the end of the day simply fax this list to the other gate so staff can check that all vehicles have left the park. If vehicles were allowed to go in and out of the same gate, a lot more work would be involved! No motorcycles are allowed into the park. There are only three places to stay within the national park: Terrace Bay, Torra Bay and the upmarket camp run by **Wilderness Safaris** in the far north that can only be reached by plane, see page 263. Torra Bay is only open during from December to January. Accommodation at Terrace Bay is all-inclusive; Torra Bay is a basic campsite – you will need to bring everything with you, even the water for the showers has to be trucked in. During the Christmas period accommodation gets booked up quickly, mostly by local fishermen. As in Swakopmund it never gets too hot thanks to the cooling influence of the ocean, but during the winter months it can get cold at night.

Petrol is available at Terrace Bay year round and Torra Bay December-January. There is also a basic grocery store at Terrace Bay. All camps have plenty of freezer space for anglers.

In order to get the maximum out of the park it is worth making the arduous journey as far north as Terrace Bay, assuming you have pre-booked accomodation.

Background

For many people the Skeleton Coast is synonymous with shipwrecks – just about every photograph promoting the wild coastline will include a rusting, beached hull. The Portuguese used to call the area the Sands of Hell and before the days of modern communications and transport this 1600-km-long coastline represented a real threat to shipping. Sailors knew that if they did survive a wrecked ship then their problems had only just begun. The land behind them was a dry desert, and there were very few known natural sources of drinking water. The few places that did occasionally have drinking water (the riverbeds) were home to wild animals such as lion, leopard and elephant, which in turn represented another threat to the sailors' lives. A third factor that added to the dangers for survivors was the remoteness. Before 1893, when the first people were landed at Swakopmund, there was no settlement of note along more than 1000 km of coastline. Which way would you head off if you had survived? Unfortunately the most spectacular wrecks are all found in the areas which are closed to the public in the far north. A little background to some of the wrecks has been included in the route description below.

Wildlife and vegetation

Between Ugabmund and Terrace Bay the coastal road crosses four westward flowing rivers: the Ugab, Huab, Koichab and Uniab. These ephemeral rivers only flow when sufficient rain has fallen in the interior, and even then they will only flow for a short period each year. For the rest of the year they represent long narrow oases that are home to migratory birds, animals and the few plants that can flourish under drought conditions.

The animals which may be seen in the park have all adapted in different ways to overcome some of the problems the desert creates. The smaller species such as genet, caracal, baboon, springbok, jackal and brown hyena live in the desert all year round; the larger animals, such as black rhino, elephant and lion, tend to migrate along the channels in search of food and water. The lion may well no longer occur along the coast, but when they were roaming the beaches they were known to have fed upon Cape cormorants, seals and the odd stranded whale. Gemsbok, kudu and zebra are occasionally seen inland in the mountainous regions, while at the coast the Uniab Delta is a good location for viewing gemsbok. During low tide, black-backed jackals can be seen on the beach scavenging on dead birds, fish and seals. There is stiff competition for scraps among the hyena, ghost crabs, crows and gulls.

Like much of the wildlife, most of the plants growing in the park occur in the four major riverbeds which dissect the park. Two of the most common shrubs are the dollar bush, *Zygophyllum stapfii*, and brakspekbos, *Zygophyllum simplex*, both of which can be found in the riverbeds. The former is a semi-deciduous shrub with small leaves shaped like a 'dollar' coin. It will only grow where there is some groundwater as it has not adapted to make use of the sea mist. Brakspekbos, a food source for the black rhino, can be recognized by looking for an off-green carpet in a shallow depression where rainwater would drain.

The only other vegetation you are likely to come across is the amazing variety of lichen. The bright orange lichens, which cling to rock outcrops facing the ocean, add a welcome splash of colour to the grey landscape. Over a hundred different species have been recorded in the Skeleton Coast National Park, all depending upon the coastal fog for moisture; in the moist air the plants become soft and many change colour.

Durissa Bay north ›› *Colour map 1, C2.*

As you approach the entrance gate to the Skeleton Coast National Park there is a signpost for the wrecked fishing boat, *Winston*. Do not drive on the salt pans; despite their dry appearance, it is easy to get stuck here. The boundary between the National West Coast Recreation Area and the Skeleton Coast National Park is marked by the Ugab River which flows into Durissa Bay. The Ugab is one of Namibia's major rivers, rising over 500 km inland, east of Outjo; after good rains it is an important source of water in Damaraland. A giant skull and crossbones adorns the gate by the Ugabmund park office and this is a good spot to have your photo taken.

As you cross the wide river notice the variety of trees and shrubs growing in the sandy bed. Some of the well-established plants are stunted since they have had to survive in windswept conditions with long periods of moisture stress. Whenever you approach these riverbeds try to be as quiet as possible since there is always a chance of seeing a small herd of springbok resting in the shade or a shy family of kudu browsing the acacia trees.

Once across the river the salt road stays close to shore. One of the first shipwrecks you see is the *South West Sea*, wrecked in 1976. Just after you have crossed the **Huab River** there is a signpost indicating an old oil rig. While you will see the remains of various mining ventures along the coast, this is the only case of oil exploration. In the 1960s Ben du Preez went ahead and erected the rig despite numerous warnings that the scheme was unlikely to succeed. Today the rusty rig lies on its side providing the perfect nesting area for a breeding colony of Cape cormorants. Between September and March visitors are asked to stay in the car park so as not to disturb the birds during the breeding season. On the beach you can visit the wreck of the fishing schooner, *Atlantic Pride*.

About 50 km from the park entrance you reach the point marked Toscanini on most maps. This is the site of a derelict **diamond mine** – only a few small diamonds were ever found. Today the legacy of the operations are a few cement slabs which acted as foundations for the buildings and the ruins of the sorting plant. There are a couple more wrecks in the ocean here, but there is little to see.

Soon after crossing the Koichab River, which has more sand than vegetation, there is a junction in the road. This is the only other access road for the Skeleton Coast Park, the C39. A right here leads to **Springbokwasser Gate**, 40 km inland. There are some fine sand dunes along this stretch of road as well as some welwitschia plants growing in the dry riverbeds.

Torra Bay ›› *Colour map 1, B2.*

Continuing north on the salt road you reach the seasonal fishing resort, Torra Bay. In the 16th century, Portuguese sailors named it Dark Hill after the dark-capped hills which they could see while they were looking for fresh water. Anyone planning on staying here must be totally self-sufficient, though during the holiday season petrol and a few basic groceries are available. Aside from the solitude, the great attraction of this site is the excellent fishing. During the few months the camp is open it is necessary to book a pitch if you plan on spending a night here (see Sleeping, page 263). Despite restrictions on where to fish and drive there has been extensive damage caused by vehicles on the beaches.

Uniab River Delta ›› *Colour map 1, B2.*

Between the temporary camp at Torra Bay and the permanent camp at Terrace Bay is one of the most interesting attractions in the southern part of the Skeleton Coast National Park, the Uniab River Delta. The river has split into five main channels plus a number of reed-ringed pools which are formed by seepage from the riverbed. After good rains this is the perfect spot for birders. There are a number of walks in the delta, including a trail to a waterfall and a small canyon, which lie between the road and the beach. Check with the parks authorities what the situation is here from year to year since the amount of rainfall and the size of the flood can change the lie of the land between seasons. But if you hear there is water here, then it is well worth the drive. Within the delta are several hides and parking spaces, each with a different view of the system. Look out for the shipwreck, *Atlantic*, at the rivermouth.

Terrace Bay ›› *Colour map 1, B2.*

Having enjoyed the delta it is a short drive to the final destination, Terrace Bay. The camp and all the outbuildings were once part of the mining operation owned by Ben du Preez. When the company was declared bankrupt, the state inherited all the facilities at the camp. There is a grocery shop with basic supplies and petrol is also available. The camp is built next to an old mine dump. There is an airfield to the north of the complex. Visitors to the park are allowed to drive a further 14 km along the coast to **Seal Beach**, this being the absolute northern limit for private visitors. At this point you are over 380 km from Swakopmund, in the heart of the Skeleton Coast National Park.

Skeleton Coast Wilderness

When reading about Namibia's desert from Oranjemund to the Angolan border, a recurrent theme is fragility of the desert environment and the need to control people's access to the most sensitive areas. When the Skeleton Coast National Park was proclaimed in 1967 the park was divided into two zones, each covering about 800,000 ha. The southern zone is the 210-km-long coastal strip between the Ugab River in the south and the Hoanib River in the north. The boundary of the park extends no more than 40 km inland. Access to the northern zone is tightly controlled and, for the tourist, limited to those who join the exclusive fly-in safaris organized by the sole concessionaire in Windhoek.

Wilderness Safaris is the only company which holds the rights to organize fly-in safaris to its camp in the north of the Skeleton Coast Park, see page 101 for details.

The northern section of the park extends from the Hoanib River (although tourists are only permitted to travel 14 km north from Terrace Bay camp, as far as Seal Beach) to the Kunene River, which forms the border with Angola – a distance of about 290 km. This section of the national park is managed as a wilderness area and is sometimes referred to as the Skeleton Coast Wilderness. While the government has chosen to allow a private operator access to this area, there are still tight controls in place on how the operation must be run in order to guarantee minimal environmental impact from each tour group. In addition to these regulations, most of the area is also off-limits to the concession holder. Access to the northern section is limited to the area between the Hoarusib and Nadas rivers, a strip of coastline measuring about 90 km long by 30 km wide.

National West Coast Recreation Area *p254*
Between Swakopmund and the Skeleton Coast National Park there are 3 campsites, all managed by **Namibia Wildlife Resorts:** Jakkalspütz, Mile 72 and Mile 108. They are very basic sites designed to serve the needs of the angler more than the holidaymaker. Each is in a grim and barren location with very few facilities and, as they are not fenced, security is an issue. Each site has communal toilets and showers and sheltered eating areas. You must bring all your own food, fuel and camping equipment. A simple shop appears at some of the sites during the local school holidays Dec-Jan. Water has to be paid for at Mile 72 and Mile 108, and during the Christmas school holidays it is usually possible to purchase fuel at these 2 campsites. Anyone looking for more comfort in this area should consider **Hotel de Duine** in Henties Bay or try the new **Cape Cross Lodge** (see below) next to the seal colony.

Henties Bay *p255*
Most of the accommodation consists of holiday flats and apartments which get booked months in advance over the peak Christmas period. For the remainder of the year there should be no difficulty in finding somewhere to stay unless you happen to coincide with a fishing tournament or festival.
AL Ocean Pearl Hydro, 1482 Oranje St, T064-500550, www.oceanpearlhydro.com. New boutique hotel right on the beach in a startlingly white double-storey building. This is rather special and quite a surprise for Henties Bay. Just 5 en suite rooms with unbeatable ocean views, which are exceptionally comfortable and lovingly decorated, but it is the facilities that are the real draw here: jacuzzi, indoor heated swimming pool, steam room, therapy baths (underwater massage) and sauna. Use of these is included in the rates which are full board with healthy breakfasts and salads for lunch and a gourmet dinner. Extras include massages, beauty and slimming treatments, and dental work! This is not as daft as it seems, the cost of quality dental work in southern Africa is considerably cheaper than in the US, Europe, Australia and New Zealand.
B Byseewah Guest House (formerly **Fisherman's Lodge**), 200 m from the beach, 2007 Auas St, T064-501177, www.fishermans lodge.com.na. Tidy and neat lodge with 9 en suite modern rooms in a bright yellow building, each room has DSTV, minibar and phone, pleasant restaurant and bar, book food in advance before 1600, also can provide packed breakfasts and lunches for fishermen, can arrange beach angling excursions from here for around US$95, minimum 2 people.
B Hotel de Duine, 34 Duine Rd, reservations, T061-374750 (Windhoek), www.namibia lodges.com. 20 rooms with TV and en suite bathroom and a restaurant known for its good seafood. Attached bar with slot machines and oddly shaped pool tables; outside there's a swimming pool, squash court, recently refurbished. Clear views across Atlantic from its high perch, close to the beach and golf course. Useful source for local information.
D Eagle Holiday Flats, 175 Jakkelsputz Rd, T064-500032, www.eagleholiday.com. Whitewashed self-catering flats equipped for 4 people at US$13 per person, clean with tiled floors, TV, linen and towels provided, a bit stark, part of the **Eagle Centre** complex where there is a supermarket, restaurant, bottle store and **Total** petrol.

Cape Cross Seal Reserve *p256*
AL Cape Cross Lodge, T064-694012, www.capecross.org. 4 km north of the seal reserve, this new hotel in Cape Dutch style is situated on the beach just north of the seal colony – but out of the 'smell zone' – and has 20 en suite rooms, the ones with balconies overlooking the sea are slightly more expensive than the ones at the back, stylish and modern if not a little overpriced. Tours are on offer into the desert and to the Tsiseb Conservancy comprising the Messum Crater, the Brandberg and Ugab River West.

For an explanation of the sleeping and eating price codes used in this guide, see inside the front cover. Other relevant information is found in Essentials, see pages 43-51.

The rate includes dinner, bed, breakfast and afternoon tea. Lunch is also available for passing trade. Very attractive wine celler with lots of polished wood and comfortable lounge with fire. South Africans can ask for a 20% discount.

Skeleton Coast National Park
p258, map p258
There are only 3 places to stay within the national park and all accommodation, even camping at Torra Bay, must be booked in advance.

L **Skeleton Coast Camp**, run by **Wilderness Safaris**, reservations through any agent or at www.wilderness-safaris.com. The only concessionaire permitted to run accommodation in the restricted northern section of the park, only accessed by plane. **Wilderness Safaris** flies there on Wed and Sat, so a minimum stay here is 4 days. 6 super luxury self-contained tents on raised wooden platforms, lovely decor using items found locally, dining room, lounge and bar. You'll have access to close on 240,000 ha of the Skeleton Coast National Park with its vast sand dunes, towering canyons, seal colonies and shipwrecks. With luck you will see a wide range of desert-dwelling wildlife such as springbok, gemsbok, desert elephants, brown hyena, jackal, ostrich and, if you are extremely lucky, cheetah. The day starts with breakfast in camp and then a day out in the park taking in the scenery and the flora and fauna before returning to camp for sundowner and dinner. This is the Namibia frequently used to promote the country as a tourist destination, yet ironically only a few hundred people get to enjoy it each year.

A **Terrace Bay**, **Namibia Wildlife Resorts**, T061-2857200 (Windhoek), www.nwr.com.na. Economy bungalows with 2 bedrooms and en suite facilities, the price includes all 3 meals plus freezer space for anglers. Recently reported as being dirty and run down, and only suitable for serious fisherman, though to sleep in such a remote environment may make up for the lack of comfort. There is, however, the much nicer Presidential Suite – the former president Sam Nujoma is a great fisherman and often takes his holidays up here. The suite, which has 8 bedrooms, can be booked by large groups when not in use by the esteemed guest. Facilities include a petrol station and a small shop selling booze and *braai* meat.

D **Torra Bay**, managed by **Namibia Wildlife Resorts**, T061-2857200 (Windhoek), www.nwr.com.na. Only open Dec and Jan. Torra Bay is a very basic campsite primarily aimed at southern African anglers – you will need to bring everything with you, even the water for the showers has to be trucked in. The small shop sells firewood and a few basic goods and petrol is available.

Eating

Henties Bay *p255*
As well as the 2 main restaurants in town, there are also a number of early-morning/ late-night snack bars, takeaways and petrol station shops that sell food and drinks, including beer.

TT **Hotel de Duine** (see Sleeping, above). Great service and reasonably priced food, steaks and grills, well known for its seafood, a good place to try crayfish, but order in advance to guarantee freshness. Open all day for all meals.

TT **Spitzkoppe**, Duine Rd, T064-500394. Formal restaurant with huge menu, fish meat, chicken, lighter snacks, generous portions, good value, a busy spot in season, but quiet for the rest of the year. Also lively bar with L-shaped and star-shaped pool tables and gambling machines, open daily from lunchtime until late, a very good night out can be had here and the people running it are very friendly. Stop for lunch here if you are visitng Cape Cross from Swakopmund. Recommended.

Activities and tours

Henties Bay *p255*
Fishing
Sea Ace Adventure Angling, T064-206363, www.seaace.com.na. Shore and deep-sea angling.

West & Skeleton Coast Angling, T064-500066, www.africaquad.com. Can arrange all fishing excursions along the coast.

Directory

Henties Bay *p255*
Banks There is a branch of Bank Windhoek just past the information office with a 24-hr ATM. This is the last bank for some distance if you are travelling away from Swakopmund. The next banks are located in Omaruru or Khorixas. **Police** The police station, T064-500201, is east of the post office. **Post office** As you approach from Swakopmund look out for a petrol station on the left just before a right turn to Usakos. Beyond the petrol station is the post office on the corner of Pelican St. A left here will take you to the seafront.

The Hinterland

There are several routes from Windhoek to the coast. The most straightforward is to take the main B2 via Okahandja, Karibib and Usakos, which will take between three and four hours. More interesting though is to explore the hinterland and to travel via one of the three passes – the Bosua, Ushoogte or Gamsberg – and stop along the way to enjoy the spectacular views. Of the three, the Bosua is the quickest and provides the opportunity to stop and see the ruins of Liebig Haus and Von François Fort, while the Gamsberg is certainly the most dramatic. ▸▸ *For Sleeping, Eating and other listings, see pages 270-274.*

Three Passes ▸▸ *pp270-274.*

All three routes – via the Bosua, Ushoogte or Gamsberg Pass – are gravel roads without any petrol stations or shops along the way. Furthermore, they each include some extremely steep sections. If there has been heavy rain you may have difficulty negotiating certain sections in a heavily loaded, low-slung saloon car.

The Khomas Hochland is the rugged, upland area, lying between 1750 m and 2000 m, which joins the central highland plateau with the escarpment, where the land falls dramatically away to the gravel plains of the central Namib. The surface of the Hochland was laid down in Karoo times some 180-300 million years ago; subsequent erosion has carved out the sharp ridges and rolling hills characteristic of the area.

Bosua Pass ▸▸ *Colour map 1, C5.*

Following the C28 out of Windhoek past Daan Viljoen Game Park, the tar road turns to gravel near the first landmark, the **Matchless Mine**. Archaeological evidence suggests that copper mining and smelting was taking place in the Khomas Hochland area some 200 to 300 years ago, although commercial exploitation of the copper reserves only started in 1856. The first manager of the mine, run by the Walvis Bay Mining Company, was Charles John Andersson (see page 346). The mine was closed down for the first time in 1860, reopened briefly but without success in 1902 by the Deutsche Kolonialgesellschaft, and then reopened for the third time between 1970 and 1983 by the Tsumeb Corporation Limited (TCL). The collapse of world copper prices during the 1980s once more forced the closure of the mine, which is now abandoned and closed to the public.

A further 16 km down the road is the abandoned **Liebig House**, built in 1912 for Dr R Hartig, director of the Deutsche Farmgesellschaft. This double-storey house must once have been a splendid place to live, with its fountain in the main downstairs room and fine views over the surrounding rolling highlands. A little further on lie the ruins of **Von François Fort** named after the 'founder' of Windhoek. The fort was one of a number of military outposts built after Von François established his headquarters in Windhoek, and was designed to protect the route between Windhoek and

Swakopmund. It was, however, later turned into a **Trockenposten**, or 'drying-out post', for alcoholic German soldiers!

The pass itself has a 1:5 descent down to the gravel plains of the Namib and is not suitable for trailers or caravans. West of here, the road heads straight as an arrow through the Namib to Swakopmund.

Ushoogte Pass ›› *Colour map 1, C5.*

In Windhoek, take the main road towards the University of Namibia (UNAM) and ignore the turn-off south towards Rehoboth. Continue past the university out of town on the C26 for 32 km until the road branches right onto the D1982. This road continues towards the 1:10 Ushoogte Pass, on past **Niedersachsen Guest Farm** (see Sleeping, page 270) before eventually joining the main C14 highway to Walvis Bay.

Gamsberg Pass ›› *Colour map 3, A2.*

Probably the most popular of the three passes, the Gamsberg is sometimes called Namibia's Garden Route. It certainly offers spectacular scenery, and is well provided

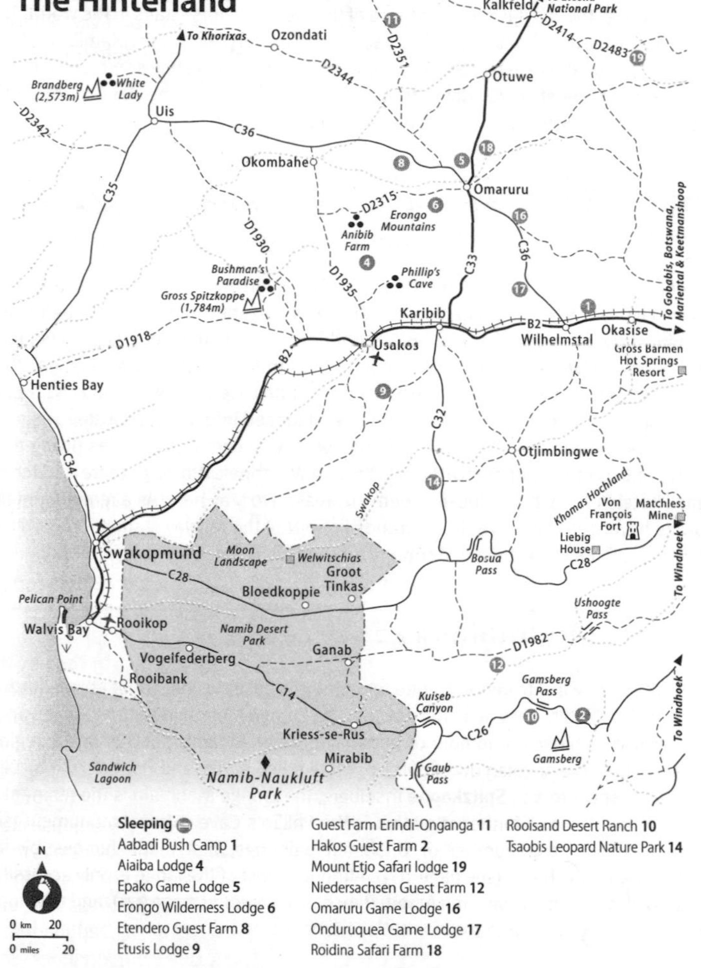

 with accommodation and activities en route. The name is a mixture of the Nama word *gan* meaning 'closed' or 'shut' and the German *berg* meaning 'mountain', and refers to the flat-topped Gamsberg Mountain (2347 m) which dominates the view. This 1000-million-year-old granite mountain rises 500 m above the surrounding highlands and has survived further erosion, thanks to a sandstone cap formed about 200 million years ago when most of this area was covered by an inland sea. It is worth stopping at the top of the pass to enjoy the views of the surrounding hills and to contemplate the snaking descent towards the desert floor. Before reaching the Namib, however, the road must still make its way through the Kuiseb Pass (see Kuiseb Canyon, page 277) after which it joins the C14 for the final 110 km stretch to Walvis Bay.

Astronomically minded visitors will probably already be heading for Hakos Guest Farm (see page 270), a stargazer's paradise with its own observatory and state-of-the-art telescopes.

The Gamsberg Region boasts some challenging terrain, and proximity to Windhoek attracts hikers, horse riders and 4WD enthusiasts. There are hiking trails from most farms: the **Namibgrens Guest Farm** (see Sleeping, page 290) has one of the more popular, the Dassie Trail. **Reitsafaris Namibia** (see page 274) offers the 12-day, 400-km **Namib Desert Ride** that they have completed over 50 times in the past 10 years, though it is ranked as one of the toughest horse trails in the world. The route runs from the Khomas Hochland across the gravel plains of the Namib-Naukluft Park, ending on the beach in Swakopmund 12 days later, covering some 400 km. The **Isabis** and **Weener** 4WD drive trails are signposted off the D1265 and C26 respectively, both within 15 km of that junction.

Usakos

» *pp270-274. Phone code: 064. Colour map 1, C4. 211 km to Windhoek, 147 km to Swakopmund.*

The first town east of the Namib Desert on the main B2 road from Swakopmund, Usakos lies on the southern bank of the Khan River, nestled in the last hills before the Namib, at the edge of a vast expanse of nothingness. The town originally developed around the railway workshops which were built to service the narrow-gauge Otavi line, completed in 1906. Until 1960, the town prospered but when the old steam locomotives were replaced by diesel engines it lapsed into its present sleepy state.

Nowadays the town's main role is one of service centre to vehicles plying their way to and from Swakopmund/Walvis Bay and Windhoek. Although there is a decent small hotel in town, there doesn't seem any reason to stay here. As a reminder of the town's heyday, Locomotive No 40 stands in front of the railway station, one of three Henschel steam trains built in Germany for the colony's narrow-gauge railway.

Erongo Mountains

» *pp270-274. Colour map 1, C4.*

The Erongo Massif of towering granite mountains is easily visible about 40 km north of Usakos and Karibib. They lie in the 200,000-ha Erongo Mountain Nature Conservancy, established to protect a number of endemic or near-endemic species to the region. These include the Angolan dwarf python, white-tailed shrike and Hartlaub's francolin. Like the **Brandberg** and **Spitzkoppe** inselberg, the Erongo Mountain is the remnant of an ancient volcano. A further attraction is the Phillip's Cave national monument (see below), containing a number of Bushmen paintings, first made famous by the prehistorian Abbé Breuil (see page 183). Although most of the range is only accessible by 4WD, it is possible to visit the **Ameib Ranch** (see Sleeping, page 271), and take tours to the following sights and rock formations from there.

Phillip's Cave
» *Colour map 1, C4.*

A short drive from Ameib Ranch, plus a 20- to 30-minute walk over a series of low hills, takes hikers up to the cave. This is in fact an overhang on one of the highest hills in the area and offers excellent views over surrounding countryside, making it easy to see why Bushmen used this place. There are numerous paintings of the Bushmen themselves, as well as buffalo and the famous white elephant.

Bull's Party and **Stone Elephant Head** are two sites with interesting rock formations, in particular the 'balancing' rocks at the Bull's Head.

Karibib
» *pp270-274. Phone code: 064. Colour map 1, C5.*

175 km to Swakopmund, 181 km to Windhoek.

This tiny bustling town lies almost exactly halfway between Windhoek and Swakopmund on the main B2 highway. Although most people zip through on their way to and from the coast, there is more to the town than first meets the eye. There are a number of fine old colonial buildings on the main street, the Navachab Gold Mine just southwest of town and the internationally reputed Marmorwerke, or marble works, lying to the north of the town, though these last two cannot be visited.

In the early years of the 20th century, the train between Windhoek and Swakopmund only travelled during the daytime, so passengers needed hotels for the overnight stop in Karibib. The present-day **bakery**, on the left-hand side coming from Okahandja, was one of these hotels; it survived until 1950 when it was converted into a bakery. The **Rösemann Building**, a little further down the road, was built in 1900 and the façade has remained virtually unchanged since. Originally the headquarters of the trading firm Rösemann and Kronewitter, it was later converted into a hotel. The **granite building** further down the street, resembling a church, was in fact used by a local merchant, George Woll, as both his shop and living quarters. The **Christuskirche**, made partially of marble from the nearby marble works, dates back to 1910.

Out of town, the **Marmorwerke** was started in 1904 and produces high-quality marble, considered to be the hardest in the world. About 100 tonnes of marble is quarried each month. This is first cut up into blocks and then processed into floor and bathroom tiles, ornaments and tombstones. It is hard to believe, but marble from Karibib is exported to Italy. The **Navachab Gold Mine**, lying southwest of town, was started in 1987, two years after gold was discovered on Navachab Farm. The gold is actually of quite low quality; 750,000 tonnes of rock are processed each year.

Otjimbingwe
» *pp270-274. Colour map 1, C5.* *55 km south of Karibib on the D1953.*

Once the administrative centre of German South West Africa, now a forgotten, dusty village in the bush, Otjimbingwe is situated south of Karibib at the junction of the Swakop and Omusema rivers. Opinions on the origins of the name of the town differ, the most common meaning given being 'place of refreshment', referring to the spring in the Omusema River.

History

The town rose to prominence due to its position on an established ox-wagon route half-way between Windhoek and Walvis Bay. A mission station was established here in 1849 by the Rhenish missionary, Johannes Rath, although it was not until 1867 that the first church was built. However, it was Otjimbingwe's role as a trading post that made it an important centre.

In 1854, the Walvisch Bay Mining Company had made the settlement its headquarters after the discovery of copper in the area. A trading post was set up and soon a roaring trade, typical of the time, was going on in arms, ammunition, alcohol and livestock. In 1860, the hunter, explorer and trader Charles John Andersson (see page 346) established his headquarters here, the first permanent trading post in the area. His subsequent involvement in the Herero-Nama wars to defend his trade routes was significant in drawing the small European population into Namibian tribal conflict, and further focused attention on Otjimbingwe.

After Curt von François moved his small garrison to Windhoek in 1890, the town started to decline and, following the construction of the narrow-gauge railway between Windhoek and Swakopmund in 1902 which bypassed the town, Otjimbingwe became increasingly irrelevant. A few historical monuments do still make the town of interest to students of 19th-century Namibian history.

Sights

The **church**, completed in 1867, is the oldest to have been built to serve the Herero community. Although Herero leader Zeraua was not himself a Christian, he arranged for 10,000 bricks to be made for the church. As with other early mission stations, the church doubled as place of worship and mini-fort during the on-off Herero-Nama wars of the time. The tower was only added later in 1899.

The **old powder magazine**, an 8-m tower, was originally built by the Missionhandelgesellschaft, or mission station trading company, to protect its goods during attacks by the Nama. Following the collapse of the company in 1882, the tower passed into the hands of the Hälbich trading firm.

The **wind motor** was put up in 1896 by the Hälbich family in order to generate power for their machinery in the wagon factory next door. The motor also pumped water to the settlement from a nearby fountain.

Omaruru

» *pp270-274. Phone code: 064. Colour map 1, C5.*

242 km to Windhoek, 236 km to Swakopmund.

The C33 tar road heads due north from just outside Karibib and 48 km later arrives at the small, sleepy, historical town of Omaruru. Set in the heart of game-farm country, the town is surrounded by an impressive array of mountains, the most prominent being the Oruwe or Omaruru *koppie* southeast of town. Omaruru is renowned in Namibia these days for having the country's only vineyard, the Kristall Kellerei, and is a centre of mineral production and trading.

Ins and outs

Tourist office ⓘ *Namib-i, W Zeraua St, T064-570261, next to the post office, Mon-Fri 0900-1600, may close for lunch if it's quiet*, provides good information on the many excellent guest farms in the area, with directions and up-to-date prices.

History

The area around the town has been home both to humans and game for thousands of years, evident from the numerous sites of Bushman art found here. The first Europeans reached the area in 1851, but it was only after the missionary, Gottlieb Viehe, arrived in 1870 that the town was 'officially' founded. In 1858, Charles Andersson, attracted by the area's plentiful game, established a hunting camp on the banks of the Omaruru River. In 1870, the hunter Axel Eriksson and brewer Anders Ohissen formed a partnership to exploit the game and by 1880 they had succeeded in wiping out all the elephant, rhino, lion and giraffe that had once lived in the area. Throughout the 1880s, Omaruru was a focal point for Herero-Nama battles

The name Omaruru is derived from the Herero omaere omaruru *meaning 'bitter curd' which is apparently how the milk tasted after the cattle grazed on one particular local bush.*

and, as part of the consolidation of German rule in Namibia, a garrison was stationed here at the end of 1894. The town started to grow and by the end of 1896 Omaruru had the largest population of European settlers in Namibia. However, the great rinderpest epidemic of 1897 wiped out the last remaining game in the area as well as taking a heavy toll on the settlers' cattle; many were forced to leave the area. But the military garrison continued to grow and a new barracks and sick bay were completed by 1901. In 1904 the Herero rose up against the German occupiers and the town was besieged. At the time the military commander, Captain Franke, was away in the south helping to put down the Bondelswart uprising. Nevertheless, he marched 900 km in 20 days and broke the siege by leading a cavalry charge, thereby defeating the Herero. In 1907, to commemorate Franke's victory, work began on the Franke Tower, which was officially opened the following year.

Sights

Franke Tower is on the southern bank of the Omaruru River. The tower was declared a national monument in 1963 and offers a good view over the town from the top. Usually kept locked, the key is available at either the **Central Hotel** or **Hotel Staebe**. Check the staircase inside; it looks a bit fragile.

The **Mission House**, the oldest building in Omaruru, now serves as the town museum, focusing on the early history of the area. Made from clay bricks, the house was built by missionary Gottleib Viehe and completed in 1872, and was where he completed the first translation of the gospel into Oshiherero. Later the house also served as a temporary military post and a meeting place between Herero and German leaders. Collect the key from the **tourist office** ⓘ *Municipality building, Wilhelm Zeraua St.*

The **Kristall Kellerei** ⓘ *T064-570083, Mon-Fri 0900-1800, Sat 0900-1300, book ahead*, the only vineyard operating in Namibia, is certainly worth a visit before you leave town. Helmut Kluge planted 4 ha of Colombard and Ruby Cabernet vines in 1990 and since 1996 has been perfecting his Colombard white (to which he adds oak chips) and Ruby Cabernet red wine. Samples are sent each year to Stellenbosch for quality control. He produces between 4000 and 6000 litres per year, split equally between white and red, distribution of which he carefully controls so that he has a supply available for those coming to enjoy his meals and wine tours, and a few chosen Namibian lodges and guesthouses which sell his wine. Bottling (into 500 ml bottles) takes place every August. He and his wife conduct wine tours personally

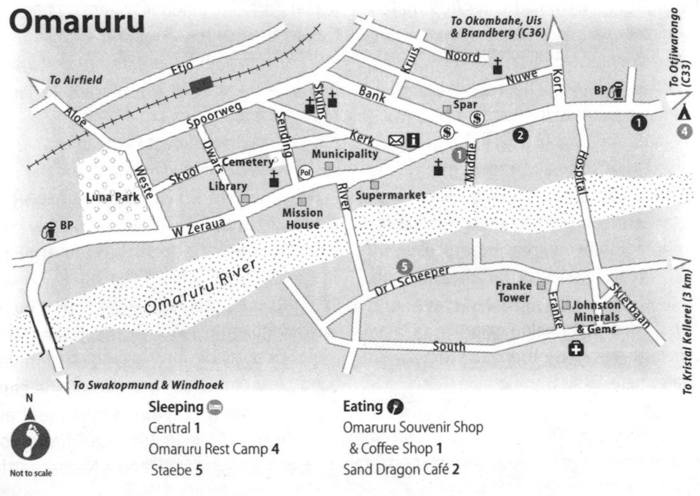

 throughout the year, each one ending in a tasting in his restaurant. The food is recommended, either on its own or accompanied. Also worth a taste are his various schnapps (schnapps, lemon, prickly pear and wine yeast). Before you ask, he will not be able to expand production due to the scarcity of water in the area.

Rock art

Anibib Farm, located 52 km west of Omaruru on the D2315 (follow signs), is said to have one of the largest collections of rock paintings in Namibia. Over an area of 2000 ha are a host of rock paintings depicting both humans and animals, as well as a range of Stone Age tools and jewellery which have been left in their original spots. There are two guided trips per day intended to give visitors a real insight into the paintings and tools and to ensure the preservation of the sites. Bookings should be made beforehand through the **Aiaiba Lodge**, T06622320 (farmline) 1711 (see also Sleeping, page 272).

Kalkfeld

» pp270-274. Phone code: 067. Colour map 1, B5.

Kalkfeld is simply a staging post on the C33 between Omaruru and Otjiwarongo for those looking for the **Dinosaur Footprints**. The village has petrol (not 24 hour), a small general and bottle store, a post office and police station.

About 150 to 200 million years ago, the 25-m tracks of a two-legged, three-toed dinosaur were embedded in the (at the time) soft, red Etjo sandstone. There are some 30 imprints with a distance between them of about 70 to 90 cm, so it is clear the creatures had a big stride. The dinosaur was probably one of the forerunners of modern birds and, much like an ostrich, had powerful hind legs. Declared a national monument in 1951, the site at **Otjihaenamaperero Farm** ⓘ *29 km east of Kalkfeld on D2414, T067-290153, viewing hours Mon-Fri 0800-1300, 1400-1700*, is well worth a visit. Be careful not to turn north to **Mount Etjo Safari Lodge** accidentally. Stop at the farmhouse and ask permission first.

Sleeping

Three Passes *p264*

A **Hakos Guest Farm**, signposted 7 km north off the C26, 135 km from Windhoek, T/F062-572111, www.natron.net/tour/hakos. A stargazer's paradise, Hakos is Nama for 'the place where no-one will disturb you'. The owner was manager of the neighbouring **Max Planck Institute for Astronomy** observatory for 25 years, and it can be accessed. Hakos offers 'star tours' for beginners, and it often has enthusiasts (mostly German) with their own observation and photographic equipment, particularly in winter, when the skies can be relied on to be clear (and cold – it is 1830 m above sea level). The **Internationale Amateur Sternwarte**, www.ias-observatory.org, operates here. If this is something that interests you, its website (also in English) has information all about astronomy from the Gamsberg Mountains. 10 en suite doubles, full board, heated indoor swimming pool. Guided mountain walks and challenging 4WD trails available. Camping (**E**) at US$8. Recommended, for an introduction to the southern hemisphere's night sky.

A **Niedersachsen Guest Farm**, off the D1982, midway between Windhoek and Walvis Bay, T062-572200, niedersachsen@natron.net. 5 en suite, a/c doubles set in rolling hills near the Kuiseb River, farm-style swimming pool, home-grown food, 4WD tours of surrounding landscape are available to enthusiasts. There is also a telescope available for stargazers on a good, clear night. The farm is mentioned in

For an explanation of the sleeping and eating price codes used in this guide, see inside the front cover. Other relevant information is found in Essentials, see pages 43-51.

The Sheltering Desert, a book written in 1957 about the true story of 2 German geologists who spent the entire Second World War hiding out in the mountains.

B **Rooisand Desert Ranch**, about 30 km east of the C14/C26 junction at the base of the Gamsberg Pass, T062-572119, www.rooisand.com. 5 a/c rooms, TV, restaurant, bar with pool table and dart board, good-sized swimming pool, sauna and tennis court. A good base from which to explore the Gamsberg Mountains on foot. Trips to Bushman paintings and the Kuiseb Canyon are on offer and there is an observatory for stargazing with some very sophisticated telescopic equipment. Serious astronomers should check out the website for full details.

Usakos *p266*

B-E **Ameib Ranch**, from Usakos turn on to the D1935 towards Okombahe, after 12 km turn right on to the D1937. Simple farmhouse with 8 en suite double rooms, 2 cottages, 3 chalets, pleasant garden, small plunge pool, restaurant and bar, plus a rest camp with 4 bungalows and campsites, shared communal ablutions, *braai* pits. The owners can organize scenic walks and trips to the rock art in Phillips Cave also on their farm, though we do not wholly approve of the caged animals and birds near the main house.

C **Bahnhof Hotel**, in town, T/F064-530444, www.hop.to/namibia. This is an old hotel that has been extensively rebuilt and refurbished, with 10 large en suite doubles with TV, a/c and telephone, bar with TV for rugby matches, beer garden, restaurant, conference room, secure parking. Young, friendly and informative hosts, the best and only bet in town. Recommended.

D-E **Namib Wüste Farm Stall and Camping**, B2 on the western outskirts of town, T064-530283. 24 beds in a train sleeper carriage (clean and fun, but a little warm in summer), a simple, good menu. A fine place for a lunch/coffee stop (open until 2000, and later for those staying the night), it has excellent *biltong* and rusks for sale, and whatever local produce is in season. Grassy campsite, with ablutions *braai* pits, electricity and a small swimming pool. Look out for the semi-tame peacocks and springboks in the grounds.

Karibib *p267*

D **Hotel Erongoblick**, in town, T064-550009. 15 doubles, 11 en suite, swimming pool, squash court, off-street parking in this former boarding school, which still retains the institutional feel. Very basic and there are more attractive options; best to move on.

Guest farms

AL-A **Etusis Lodge**, T064-550826, etusis@aol.com. 36 km from Karibib, follow the signs from town. An award-winning lodge on the private Etusis Game Reserve, with 7 en suite thatched bungalows and 6 slightly cheaper bush tents, along with the main thatch and stone construction all built entirely of natural resources found on the reserve, restaurant, bar, swimming pool, waterhole which is lit up at night, game drives, 4 well-mapped hiking trails, mountain biking and horse riding, and for those who don't want to get on a horse there are also horse-carriage rides. On the expensive side, but rates are full board and include all activities.

C-E **Tsaobis Leopard Nature Park**, 63 km southwest of Karibib, signposted 11 km off the C32, follow the signs from town, T064-550881, tsaobis@iafrica.com.na. 10, 2-bed simple self-catering bungalows, swimming pool, home-made meals served in a thatched *lapa*, game viewing. Established as a leopard sanctuary in 1969 and has a number of rescued or orphaned leopard and cheetah in large enclosures, offers good hiking in rugged bush country with the chance of seeing the elusive leopard in its natural habitat. You can also **camp** here for around US$7 per person. Book ahead.

E **Aabadi Bush Camp**, roughly 50 km east of Karibib, the turn-off is off the B1 at Wilhelmstal, reservations T061-224712 (Windhoek), www.aabadi-safaris.com. Simple campsite in a peaceful location overlooking a waterhole, with good facilities including a thatched *lapa* area where you can sample local food such as pot-baked bread, local crafts for sale, the highlight here is the interaction with the Bushman and Damara people, guided walks into the bush with the San, guests can also join the ladies making their own jewellery. Day visits can be arranged as well as transport from Windhoek. This is a locally run enterprise, and early reports are very good, but we would welcome feedback.

Omaruru *p268, map p269*

C **Central Hotel Omaruru**, Wilhelm Zeraua St, T064-570030, central@omaruru.na. Recently completely refurbished, 10 double rooms and 2 rondavels are at the back of the original colonial building with a classic shaded veranda, cool rooms, spacious, welcoming bar with TV, beer garden, swimming pool in a very neat garden with palm trees.

C **Hotel Staebe**, Dr Ian Sheeper Av, south of the river, T064-570035, staebe@omaruru.na. 24 stark en suite doubles with phones and kettle, good German cooking, small bar with draught beer, swimming pool, off-street parking. A good-value, clean hotel, recommended by locals.

Game lodges and guest farms

AL **Epako Game Lodge**, 22 km northeast of Omaruru on C33, T064-570551/2, www.etosha.com/epako-game-lodge. Large lodge with 11,000 well-stocked ha, 25 en suite luxury rooms with a/c, telephone and minibar, excellent French cuisine, bar, swimming pool, tennis, TV lounge, guided walks on request, game drives to Bushman paintings, chance to see elephant, rhino, cheetah, leopard and wide range of antelope (a bit like visiting the zoo, actually). Somewhat impersonal, and lacking in 'African' feel, but worth the trip for the food; dinner is served over a floodlit waterhole.

AL **Erongo Wilderness Lodge**, 11 km southwest of Omaruru on D2315, T064-570537, www.erongowilderness.com. Just off the road is a (secure) car park that you must use unless you have a high-clearance 4WD – you will be transported the short distance to the lodge (walk if you arrive unannounced!). Part of the Erongo Mountain Nature Conservancy (200,000 ha), the lodge has 10 very comfortable en suite, stilted cabins with thatched covers, straddling enormous granite rocks. Central *lapa* with restaurant, bar and lounge, lovely evening views of the enormous ruddy granite blocks; small swimming pool built among the rocks, scenic drives to rock art, guided walks and plentiful game. Pricey, but with masses of character and good range of activities. Book ahead. Recommended.

A-AL **Roidina Safari Farm**, 21 km north of Omaruru on C33, then 7 rough km along a farm track, T064-570883, www.natron.net/roidina. Swiss-owned lodge with 5 luxurious, thatched double en suite rondavels with large (mostly 4-poster) beds, 2, 2-bedroomed family units, fan and safe, stunning, large thatched restaurant/bar overlooking waterhole. Swimming pool, game drives, has its own plane and landing strip and can organize flights from Windhoek.

A **Aiaiba Lodge**, in the Erongo Mountains, just south of Omaruru take the D2315 for 45 km, the lodge is 1.5 km from the gate at the road, T064-570330, www.aiaiba.com. This new lodge opened in 2004 also calls itself the **Rock Painting Lodge** thanks to a number of ancient rock art sites on the farm which it will happily show you. 20 comfortable double en suite rooms in neat thatched chalets nestled between giant balancing boulders, nice views from the restaurant and bar area, very good food including game meat, TV room, library and swimming pool.

A **Etendero Guest farm**, 36 km from Omaruru in the direction of Uis on the C36, T064-570927, www.namibiatours.de. Stylish farmhouse with pillared entrance, en suite rooms in the main building or in garden cottages, wholesome farm food and outdoor *braais*, activities include donkey cart rides and drives around the farm, comfortable. Very German orientated.

A **Onduruquea Game Lodge**, 28 km southeast of Omaruru, signposted off the C33, T/F064-570832, www.ondu.com.na. En suite doubles in thatched bungalows with a/c, large swimming pool, game drives, bush walks, horse riding. Food is traditional German and Namibian game dishes, outside *lapa* area with bonfire in the evening, mostly German clientele.

A-B **Guest farm Erindi-Onganga**, C36 towards Uis and after 6 km turn right onto D2344; after a further 35 km turn onto D2351 and drive for 27 km, following signs to guest farm, T067-290112, www.natron.net/erindi-onganga. 4 en suite doubles, good home cooking, swimming pool, hiking, game drives, donkey-cart rides, and archery – a tranquil, remote, low-key guest farm. Rates are full board and children under 7 stay for free.

A-B **Omaruru Game Lodge**, 15 km east of Omaruru on D2329, T064-570044, www.omaruru-game-lodge.com. 30 en suite doubles in pretty thatched bungalows, 5 of which are self-catering and work out a bit cheaper, set in shaded gardens with cactus-lined, lit paths, restaurant and bar overlooking dam, swimming pool and *braai* area. Game drives view all major antelopes, elephant, zebra, giraffe and maybe leopard. Caters for tour groups, but maintains an intimate atmosphere.

Camping

C-E **Omaruru Rest Camp**, next to the Omaruru River on the C33, T064-570516, jdg@iway.na. 6 simple chalets plus campsites with own *braai* facilities and bathrooms, tables, electricity and light, outdoor kitchens, green and clean, with cheap meals available, internet access and a friendly sports bar with DSTV for crucial matches.

Kalkfeld *p270*

AL **Mount Etjo Safari Lodge**, 37 km from Kalkfeld, take the D2414, then D2483 (well signed after 22 km), T067-290173, www.mount-etjo.com.na. Named after the 2000-m, 18-km-long flat mountain that dominates the view. 26 spacious en suite rooms (and one 'presidential suite'), with varying positions and degrees of luxury. Castle-style ramparts and flamingos welcome you, gardens and comfortable lounges overlook the birds and game (including hippo) that come to drink, game drives, escorted game walk. Plentiful buffet dinners served in a sheltered outdoor *boma*. There are 2 further, more intimate lodges, away from the main, rather crowded complex – one for tourists (**Rhino Lodge**), the other for hunters, each with 8 doubles. The surrounding land is well stocked with white and black rhino, lion, leopard, cheetah, elephant and a host of antelope. The lodge has been in the tourist business since the 1970s, and was the site of the historic **Mount Etjo Declaration**, supervised by the UN, which effectively ended the bush war and gave birth to independent Namibia. Rates are half board; an impressive lodge and interesting curio shop with details of animal spoor to improve your skills; perhaps too popular with large tour buses. **Dinosaur Campsite** (C), along the way to its **Safari Lodge**'s own private prints (about 4 km from the main road, 1 km on foot, but you'll need a guide to find them). 6 fully equipped sites amongst the trees overlooking a dam, 3 km from the main lodge; pricey unless you split the site cost between 4.

Eating

Usakos *p266*

Eating is either at the **Bahnhof Hotel** (see Sleeping, above) or from the takeaway at the **Shell Ultra** at the eastern edge, or **Engen** at the western edge, of town. Both are open 24 hrs. There is a supermarket, bottle store, and butchers.

Karibib *p267*

ΨΨ **Western Bar and Restaurant**, on the main street at the Swakopmund end. Your best bet in the evenings, lively with good food including steaks, seafood, ice cold draught beer and nice beer garden. There is a bottle shop next door.

Ψ **Coffee shop**, Henckert Centre (see Shopping, below). Snacks.

Ψ **Die Grüne Ecke**, on the main street in an old building with a tin roof, cool inside if its hot. Serves cakes, coffee and tea and cold drinks to passing motorists during the day.

Ψ **Karibib Bakery & Café**, entrance through the **OK Supermarket**. Pies and cold drinks.

Omaruru *p268, mao p269*

ΨΨ **Sand Dragon Café**, 94 Wilhelm Zeraua St, T064-570707. New and stylish internet café, gallery and restaurant, daily 0800-1900 for breakfast and lunch, Wed and Fri evening for dinner until 2100, daily changing menu including toasted sandwiches, Mexican dishes and pizza, very good coffee.

Ψ **Omaruru Souvenir Shop & Coffee Shop**, Main Rd, serves excellent breakfast, lunchtime snacks, afternoon tea with home-made cakes, and takeaways. It has a good curio shop, plant nursery and a beer garden with swimming pool at the back for patrons. Recommended.

Handmade Chocolates, 9 Industrial Rd, T064-570286. Delicious handmade chocolates with a variety of fillings and liqueurs. This is a family-run business and the chocolates are made with original German recipes and moulds from the 1950s and preservative-free ingredients. Mon-Fri 0800-1300, 1400-1700.

Festivals and events

Omaruru *p268, map p269*

Oct Every year on the last weekend before 10 Oct, the Herero hold a march to and from the cemetery where former leader **Wilhelm Zeraua** is buried. Worth a visit if you are in the area.

Shopping

Karibib *p267*

Henckert Centre, Main St, opposite **Western** Bar, T064-550700, www.henckert.com. Here is a small tourist office, a token but functional weavery where you can watch the women at work, a few curios and an enormous range of (gem) stones, both local and imported. It also does coffee and filled rolls. Open 7 days a week, 0800-1700. There's another branch in Swakopmund.

Omaruru *p268, map p269*

Johnston Minerals and Gems, Franke St, T064-570303. Owned by an American miner/geologist couple who have a good (legitimate) supply of local stones which they work on the premises; fairly priced and beautifully presented. He is a gemstone polisher and she has worked with gold for over 20 years. Open 7 days and worth a visit, they will take their time explaining the trade/stones to you.

Activities and tours

Three Passes *p264*

Reitsafaris Namibia, Gamsberg Pass, T061-250764 www.natron.net/reitsafaris, offers the 12-day, 400-km **Namib Desert Ride**, see page 266.

Karibib *p267*

Klippenberg Country Club, 2 km south of town (well signposted), T081-1248760 (mob). Welcomes visitors to its 9-hole golf course, swimming pool, squash and tennis facilities. Non-players can enjoy good views from the bar/restaurant. Fairly empty except at weekends when it attracts residents of the town on a social.

Transport

Usakos *p266*

Train For trains to **Swakopmund, Tsumeb** via Otjiwarongo, and **Windhoek** via Okahandja, see timetable, page 68.

Karibib *p267*

Bus For Intercape buses to **Swakopmund, Walvis Bay** and **Windhoek**, see timetable, page 70.

Train For trains to **Swakopmund**, and **Windhoek** via Okahandja, see timetable, page 68.

Omaruru *p268, map p269*

Train For trains to **Swakopmund**, **Tsumeb** via Otjiwarongo, and **Windhoek** via Okahandja, see timetable, page 68.

Directory

Usakos *p266*

Post and telecoms office and First National (with an ATM) at the Shell Ultra.

Karibib *p267*

Banks First National Bank with ATM. **Medical services** Private clinic behind First National Bank, T064-550073. **Police** T064-10111. Services 24-hr. Total (as you head west) and Engen (east), small OK supermarket, butchery, bakery, *biltong* shop and post office.

Omaruru *p268, map p269*

Banks First National Bank and Standard Bank, on corner of Bank St and W Zeraua St, both with ATM. **Medical services** Doctor, T064-570033. State Hospital, T064-570037, follow Hospital St south over the river. **Police** Near corner of Sending St and W Zeraua St, T064-570010. **Post office** Corner of Church St and W Zeraua St, Mon-Fri 0800-1630, Sat 0800-1130.

Namib-Naukluft Park

First proclaimed in 1907 and progressively enlarged over the years until it reached its present size in 1986, the Namib-Naukluft Park is the largest nature reserve in Africa, covering an area more than twice the size of Wales. Geographically, the park is divided into four distinct areas of which three are covered here: the gravel plains of the central Namib between the Swakop and Kuiseb rivers, known as the Namib Desert Park; the mountainous knuckle of land stretching inland south of Solitaire to just west of Büllsport, known as the Naukluft Park; and the towering sand dunes south of the Kuiseb River, which we label here simply as Sossusvlei. The fourth area, the seemingly endless sand sea south towards Lüderitz known as the Sperrgebiet ('Forbidden Zone'), has for many decades been declared out of bounds to tourists due to the presence of diamonds and the fragility of the ecosystem. These days this is changing, however, and the Sperrgebiet has recently been declared a national park. For more details on this region, see page 324.

This truly remarkable area attracts geographers, ecologists, hikers and tourists. On the larger scale, flights and balloon trips over the mountains and dunes in light aircraft provide breathtaking views of the magnificent natural formations. At the opposite extreme, researchers analyze and hikers enjoy a glimpse of the fascinating variety of life that survives in the inhospitable sand and heat. ▸▸ *For Sleeping, Eating and other listings, see pages 289-292.*

Ins and outs

Getting there

There are several approaches to the Namib-Naukluft Park, and where you enter it rather depends on where you have come from. From Windhoek, Swakopmund or Walvis Bay, the options are to drive between the capital and the coast through the top of the park on either the C28 or C14. These routes are described on page 264. The most popular access to the park is at Sesriem and Sossusvlei further south, which can be accessed from Windhoek in a day or alternatively from anywhere along the C14 as it heads south through Maltahohe and Helmeringhausen.

Getting around

Most roads in the park are gravel, though normally naviagable in a 2WD. The exceptions are the roads around Groot Tinkas and Gemsbokwater campsites, which require a 4WD. Permits are not necessary for visitors travelling on the public roads through the park (the C14, C26, D1982 and D1998). However, those planning to travel on any of the signposted tourist roads, or stay at any of the campsites here, must obtain permits which are available at all the gates, or from the **MET** offices in Swakopmund and Windhoek. You can also make reservations for all the campsites through **Namibia Wildlife Resorts** at their offices in Windhoek and Swakopmund or through the website, www,nwr.com.na.

Background

The Namib Desert is a narrow strip of land stretching for 2000 km north to south and never extending more than 200 km from west to east. Bounded by the cold waters of the South Atlantic Ocean on its west and an escarpment to the east, the Namib passes through three countries, South Africa, Namibia and Angola. In this chapter, our coverage is limited to the central Namibian areas that are accessible to tourists, namely the portion between the Swakop River in the north and the dune fields of Sossusvlei to the south. The majority of the desert further south is out of bounds to tourists. For the other accessible portion, within Namibia, encompassing the National West Coast Tourist Recreation Area and Skeleton Coast Park, see pages 254 and 258.

The Namib Desert is generally believed to be the 'oldest' desert in the world, having enjoyed or endured arid and semi-arid conditions for around 80 million years. This does not mean that the climate has remained static during that period, nor that the dunes are that old. On the contrary, the desert itself has been changing as a result of climatic shifts, one of the most significant being the development of the cold Benguela Current, about five million years ago, which plays an important part in maintaining the Namib's extremely arid conditions.

The great sand dune fields visible at Sossusvlei are also 'recent' occurrences, probably having developed after the Benguela Current was formed; they are migrating north and west in a constant cycle thanks to the prevailing wind.

The desert is also an archaeological storehouse, abounding in a whole range of stone tools, pieces of pottery or paintings left by the earliest inhabitants of this region. As such they play an important role in informing us how early humans made use of the natural resources of the desert in order to survive. They also beg the question as to why did humans spend periods of time in the desert when there was an abundance of better-watered land further inland?

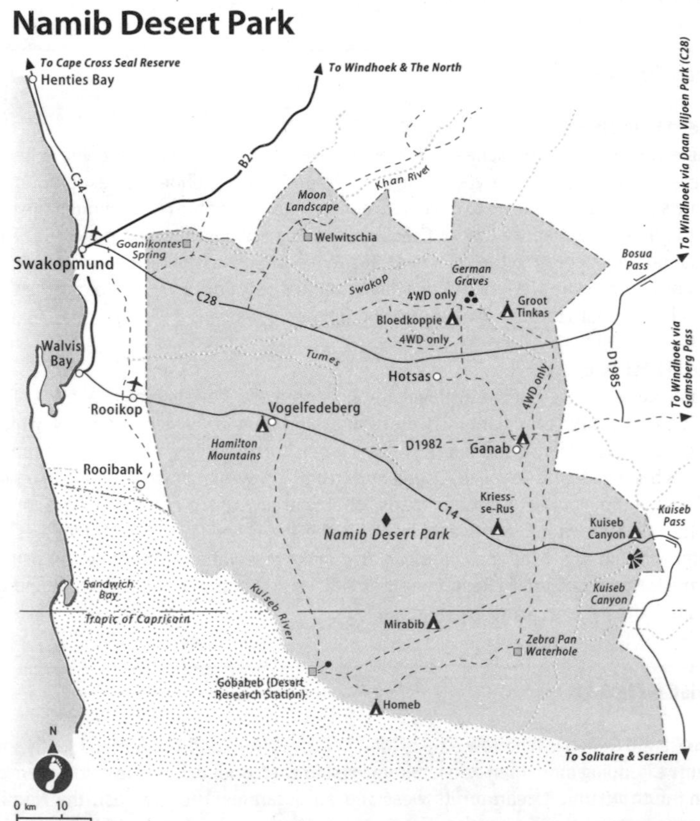

Namib Desert Park » pp289-292. Colour map 3, B2.

Although the common perception of a desert is a hot, dry barren wilderness, the Namib actually has distinct climatic zones. At an altitude of 300-600 m, the desert is watered each morning by a rolling fog caused by the cool offshore air meeting the hot dry air from inland. This fog allows a host of life forms, such as lichens, succulents and small bushes and the insects and animals that feed off them, to exist in an otherwise inhospitable environment.

Closer to the escarpment, beyond the reach of the daily fog, the desert is hot and dry, sustaining only the hardiest forms of life. The gemsbok, for example, is specially adapted to these conditions and has an in-built cooling system to keep the blood flowing to its brain cool enough to survive in these otherwise intolerable temperatures. Ground squirrels position themselves so that their upturned tails serve as sunshades, and a number of species of beetle have extra long legs which afford them 'stilts'. Raising their bodies above the surface of the desert allows them to benefit from cooler air just above ground level. Other insects and animals have developed different strategies to allow them to survive in this environment, some simply retreat below the surface of the desert, either into the dunes themselves or by burrowing into the desert floor.

Kuiseb Canyon » *Colour map 3, A2. On the C14 at the base of Kuiseb Pass.*

"We stared down in fascination. It was an impressive and intimidating sight, landscape inconceivable under a more temperate sky and in milder latitudes. Barren cliffs fell away steeply into deep ravines all around the main canyon like a wild and gigantic maze. They had a name, the *gramadoelas*, and as someone had aptly said, they looked as though the Devil had created them in an idle hour." So wrote Henno Martin, a German geologist, who during the Second World War spent 2½ years with his friend Hermann Korn living in the desert in order to avoid internment. His book *The Sheltering Desert* describes their experiences as they struggled to survive in the harsh and unforgiving Namib environment and is well worth reading before visiting the region.

The Kuiseb Canyon campsite is located by the Kuiseb River bridge in the river course. The river may flood during the rainy season and visitors should check when booking the site.

Kriess-se-Rus » *Colour map 3, A2.*

Named after an early European resident of Swakopmund who was interested in the game in the Namib area, the Kriess-se-Rus campsite, 107 km east of Walvis Bay on the C14, is located in a dry watercourse surrounded by camelthorn trees. Short walks around the area give visitors access to three typical central Namib habitats: the watercourse, calcrete plain and the schist or crystalline rock.

Mirabib » *Colour map 3, A2.*

Off the C14 in the direction of Gobabeb, this is a granite inselberg rising above the desert floor accommodating two groups at a time. Rocky overhangs offer protection from the sun and carbon dating has revealed that early humans took advantage of this site some 8500 years ago. There is also evidence of more recent visits by pastoralists about 1600 years ago. A small waterhole, **Zebra Pan**, located 35 km southeast of here, is visited by mountain zebra, ostrich and gemsbok.

Homeb » *Colour map 3, A2.*

Turn off C14 towards Zebra Pan and continue on the track to the Kuiseb River. Located on the banks of the Kuiseb River, the Homeb campsite – capable of accommodating several parties – offers excellent views of the nearby sand dunes. Although the river

The Dune Sea

The sand dunes of the Namibia south of the Kuiseb River are sometimes referred to as a dune sea. This is because the dunes are not stationary – on the contrary they are ever-moving and ever-changing as the wind blows the sand in different directions.

All the dunes in the Namib are composed of grains of quartz with a few heavy minerals, such as ilmenite, also present. The dunes rest on a base of sand where the so-called 'mega-ripples' are found; these can be as large as 50 cm high and are shaped by the wind. Above this base is the 'dune slope' and then the 'slipface', the area at the top of the dune where the sand is constantly cascading.

Sand dunes come in many shapes. South of Walvis Bay and close to the coast are the **transverse dunes**, so-called because the axis of the dune lies perpendicular to the strong winds blowing mainly from the south. Around Sossusvlei are found **parabolic** or **multi-cycle dunes**, formed by winds of more or less equal strength blowing from every direction. The third kind, the **parallel linear dunes**, are most commonly found in the Homeb area. It is believed that this series of 100-m-high north-south dunes, which generally lie about 1 km apart, are caused by strong south and east winds which blow at different times of the year. The most mobile dunes, the **barchans**, are most visible in the Lüderitz area, especially at the deserted town of Kolmanskop, where they have invaded the abandoned houses.

The distinct, different types of sand found in the Sossusvlei area are the result of wind and water acting together. The yellow sand originates in the Namib itself, but the deep red sand usually found in the Kalahari Desert has reached the Namib by being washed down into the Orange River far to the south before being blown northwards again into the Namib. Standing on top of a dune at Sossusvlei you can see the rippling dune sea extending far into the distance.

The mobility of dunes varies. The largest move perhaps no more than 1 m each year. Barchans, however, can travel more quickly – at up to 50 m per year. Mobile dunes create a hazard for transport since roads can be covered quickly in high wind conditions. Elsewhere, cultivated lands can slowly be inundated with sand.

Stabilizing sand dunes is a difficult matter. The large dune systems are unstoppable and man's attempts to halt their advance have rarely succeeded for long. Smaller dunes can be stabilized by planting them with a close graticule of drought-resistant grass or other plants, which once established can be inter-planted with desert bushes and shrubs. This process is slow and expensive though generally very effective even in very dry conditions. More cheap and dramatic is to build sand fences to catch moving sand, tar-spraying dunes or layering dunes with a plastic net. The results are less aesthetically pleasing than the traditional planting system and are less long-lasting unless combined with planting.

only flows when good rains are received in the highland areas west of Windhoek, this site demonstrates the role of the Kuiseb River in preventing the huge dune field south of here from encroaching onto the gravel plains to the north. Seasonal water from the river and occasional rain means that there is a sufficient supply of underground water to support substantial riverine vegetation and to provide water for animals and humans. The Topnaar Namas, one of the groups of original Khoi living in Namibia,

Leave only footprints

The desert is a fragile environment and both plant and animal species struggle to survive here. It is important that visitors leave the area in the same condition as they entered it, and consider carefully their impact on the environment – take only photographs and leave only footprints. Visitors to the desert should be extra-sensitive and abide by the following rules:

- When driving, stick to existing roads and tracks, as tyre marks can scar the desert floor for decades. Similarly, lichens and other fragile plants which play an important role in the ecology of the desert can be easily destroyed.
- Do not disturb or collect any samples of plant or vegetable life from the desert. Many of these, such as desert melons, are a life-giving source of food and water for many species of animals. Take photos or make sketches to keep as souvenirs.
- When camping in the desert take firewood with you, never collect wood. Many dead-looking trees or bushes come alive again after rain.
- Whatever their condition, always use public toilets when they are available. If it is absolutely essential to go to the loo in the desert, bury everything well away from roads, paths (including those made by animals) and ground water, and burn or take with you any toilet paper used.
- Never drop litter or cigarette butts. Carry all rubbish with you until you reach the next bin, though remember that because of the remoteness of campsites, etc in the desert, it is a difficult process to transport rubbish out of the desert so if possible carry it all with you until you next reach a town.

have their home in a village at Homeb. Sometimes called the Naranin or Nara people, due to their close dependence on the nara melon which grows here, most of the Topnaars now look for work in Walvis Bay or Swakopmund.

There is a good chance at Homeb of seeing game such as steenbok, gemsbok and baboons, as well as a fairly large number of birds. In particular look out for birds of prey such as the lappet-faced vulture, black eagle and booted eagles, as well as the noisy red-billed francolin, the well-camouflaged Namaqualand sandgrouse and the attractive swallow-tailed bee-eater. » *For information on the Gamsberg area, see page 265.*

Ganab » *Colour map 3, A1.*

This site, near a dry watercourse, is named after the Nama word for the camelthorn trees which are found here. Although rather dusty, it gives a good idea of the expanse of the Namib Desert, and the nearby borehole and windmill are an attraction for game. A host of mammals have been spotted here, including gemsbok, springbok and zebra, as well as predators such as spotted hyena, aardwolf, bat-eared fox and caracal. To get here, turn off the C14 onto the D1982 in the direction of Windhoek

Groot Tinkas » *Colour map 3, A1.*

Only accessible by 4WD, this is an ideal place to camp in the Namib. The surrounding area is an interesting place for hikes, although the heat means that early morning and late afternoon are the best times to do this. After good summer rains the nearby dam, an unusual site in the middle of the desert, is full of water and attracts both game and bird life. To get here, turn north off the C28 from Swakopmund to Windhoek, or north on the small track le ading from Ganab.

Nara melons

The nara melon is endemic to the Namib desert, in particular the Kuiseb River area. A member of the cucumber family, the nara grows in sandy places where its roots are able to burrow deep down into the earth as far as the water table. In order to reduce water loss, the stems of the plant are almost leafless, thereby also preventing animals from eating it. The nara is dioecious, meaning it has separate male and female plants. The male plant, which flowers for most of the year, provides a ready source of food for one particular species of dune beetle. One crop of the melons, which grow to about 15 cm in diameter, is produced each year in late summer providing food for desert dwellers such as jackals, gerbils, crickets and beetles. Traditionally the nara has also been a source of food for the Topnaar Namas, who have lived around the lower reaches of the Kuiseb River for several centuries. At harvest time the fruit is collected on donkey carts and carried back to camp, where the flesh and seeds are separated from the rind and roasted over a fire. The seeds are then separated from the pulp which can be eaten as it is or dried and eaten at a later date. Archaeological sites in the Namib provide evidence in the form of seeds that the nara melon was an important source of desert food to prehistoric humans.

Bloedkoppie »› *Colour map 3, A1.*

Close to Groot Tinkas (55 km northeast of the C28 from Swakopmund) stands the 'blood hill' granite inselberg, a popular campsite in this part of the Namib. The sites on the western side of the hill are very sandy, requiring 4WD to get there. It is well worth exploring the immediate area, not least for the fascinating rock formations found here. About 5 km east of the campsite lie the ruins of a **German colonial police station** and the graves of two policemen which date back to 1895.

Vogelfedeberg »› *Colour map 3, A1.*

A smaller inselberg than Bloedkoppie, Vogelfedeberg is nevertheless an interesting place to visit, especially after summer rains. Water collects in a number of rock pools which, for a short while, become home to a host of small invertebrates, such as the crab-like *triops*. The development of all these creatures has to be rapid as the water only remains in the pools for a few weeks. During this brief period the eggs, which have been lying waiting for the rain, must hatch, the creatures must mature, mate and lay eggs for the next generation to emerge when the rain returns. To get here from Walvis Bay, take the C14 east for 51 km and then turn off at the sign.

South of Vogelfedeberg lie the **Hamilton Mountains**, not officially on the tourist route, but nevertheless an interesting place for those with the energy for a hike. This limestone range climbs between 300 m and 600 m above the Namib plain and benefits from enough fog-water to allow a fascinating range of plants to grow here. In particular look out for blooming succulents following summer rains and the occasional lily.

Naukluft Park »› *pp289-292.* *Colour map 3, A2.*

ⓘ *US$13 adults, free for children under 16, US$1.50 cars.*

The Naukluft Park was proclaimed in 1964 as a sanctuary for the Hartmann's mountain zebra before being joined with the Namib Desert Park in 1979 to form the Namib-Naukluft Park. The name Naukluft derives from the narrow *kloof* or gorge on the eastern side of the mountain range. This rugged, mountainous area hides deep ravines, plunging gorges, crystal-clear rock pools and a variety of game totally at odds with the desolate surrounding desert. Accessible only on foot or on horseback the Naukluft Park is an ideal place for hiking and has a number of superb trails, ranging from the 10-km **Olive Trail** to the 120-km eight-day **Naukluft Hiking Trail**.

Ins and outs

The entrance to the park is 10 km south of Büllsport on the D854. From Windhoek take the B1 south to Rehoboth and then immediately south of the town turn west onto the gravel C24. This passes the small settlements of **Klein Aub** and **Rietoog** (petrol during daylight hours) before gradually descending from the central highlands into the semi-desert around **Büllsport**. From the coast, the C14 passes through the central Namib climbing steeply and tortuously through the Kuiseb and Gaub passes past Solitaire to Büllsport. From the south the most direct route is on the **C14** from Maltahöhe.

Geology

The geological history of the area starts between 1000 and 2000 million years ago when the base of the mountains was formed by volcanic rocks, granites and gneisses. Between 650 and 750 million years ago the whole of this part of Namibia was flooded by a shallow tropical sea which formed the next layer of rock – mainly black limestone. The mountains themselves were formed between 500 and 550 million years ago during a period of crustal movement when large sheets of sedimentary rock formed and were set in place. These rock sheets give the tops of the Naukluft Mountains their characteristic nappes or folds. Porous limestone deposits caused by evaporating limestone-rich water are also common all over the range and suggest a much wetter past.

Vegetation and wildlife

For such a harsh environment the mountains are home to a surprisingly large number of plants and trees. These range from common gravel plain species such as corkwood trees and wild raisin bushes to mountain species such as shepherd's tree, quiver tree and mountain thorn bushes. The deep gorges with their perennial streams are home to a wide range of different species such as sweet thorn and cluster figs which attract large numbers of birds.

The park is home to a host of small mammals, many of them nocturnal and therefore easily missed. These include Cape hare, ground squirrel, badger and yellow mongoose, as well as the common and easily spotted rock dassies, which make up the bulk of the black eagle's diet. Of the larger mammals, the Naukluft Park is home to the unique Hartmann's mountain zebra which live only in Southern Angola and Namibia. A zebra sub-species, the Hartmann's differ from plains zebras by being about 14 cm taller and also by virtue of a slightly different pattern of stripes on the lower back. Antelopes such as klipspringers are common and easily spotted as they bounce from rock to rock, as are duiker and steenbok. The mountains with their rocky overhangs, gorges and caves are an ideal home to leopards, shy animals not easily spotted, but nevertheless the most significant predators in the area. Smaller predators like black-backed jackal, bat-eared fox, African wild cats and aardwolfs are also common in the park, although like many of the smaller animals, most of these are nocturnal and therefore difficult to spot.

Due to its position between the desert to the west and the highlands to the east, the park lies at the limits of the distribution of a large number of endemic Namibian species. Furthermore the perennial streams in the deep kloofs attracts birds that otherwise would not be found in this environment. Late summer (February-March) is an excellent time for bird-spotting in the park when species such as the Herero chat, Rüppell's korhan, Monteiro's hornbill, cinnamon-breasted warblers and African black ducks can be seen.

Hiking

Without a doubt some of the most exciting hiking country in Namibia is found here in the Naukluft Mountains, both within the national park and from the neighbouring guest farms. There are hikes to suit just about anyone, but conditions can be hard and all hikers should make sure they come properly equipped with decent boots and a hat as well as ensuring they take enough water with them (minimum 2 litres per person per day). For those people planning longer hikes involving overnight stops in the mountains it is absolutely essential to take warm clothing as the temperature at night, even in summer, can drop close to freezing, and windproof clothing is recommended.

Olive Trail A 10-km, four- to five-hour hike, ideal as a starter for those unaccustomed to the conditions. The walk gets its name from the preponderance of wild olive trees encountered en route. The trail starts from the car park close to the Naukluft Campsite (see page 290) with a steep climb to the top of a plateau giving great views of the main Naukluft Gorge. From here the path continues northwest as far as a huge social weaver nest, and then turns east into a river valley. This valley gradually deepens until a narrow gorge has to be crossed with the assistance of chains anchored into the rocks. Don't be alarmed, with some application this is easily achieved by even the most timid. From here onwards the trail more or less follows a jeep track back to the starting point.

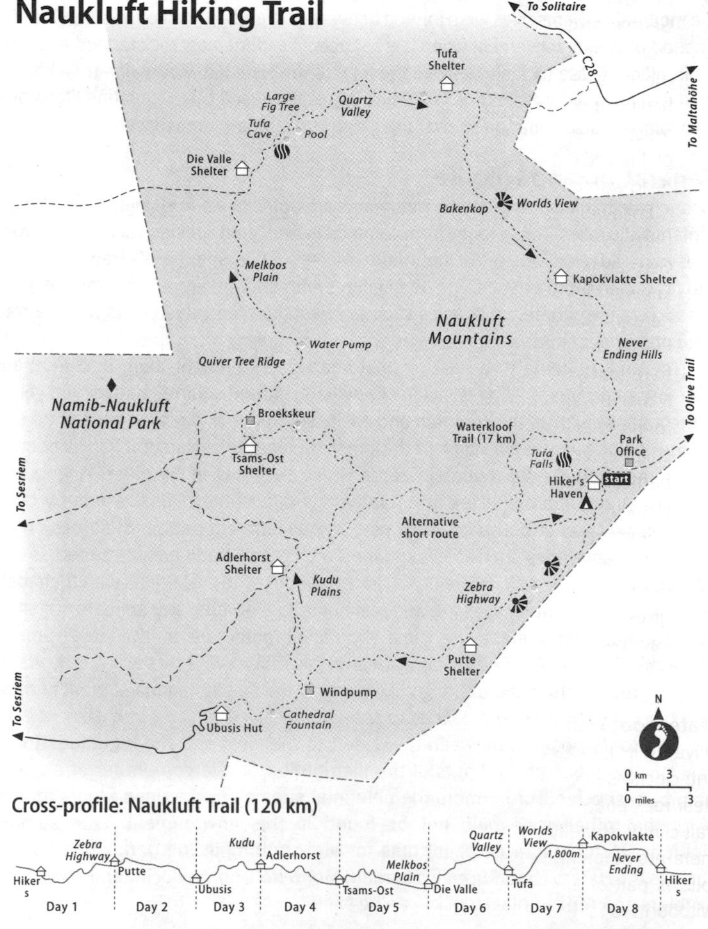

War in the Naukluft Mountains

In 1894 the Naukluft Mountains were the setting for a series of skirmishes and battles between the Nama leader Hendrik Witbooi and the German forces led by Theodor Leutwein. The outcome played an important role in the consolidation of German control over Namibia.

In April 1893 the Germans, led by Captain Curt von François, had attacked Witbooi's stronghold at Hoornkrans west of Rehoboth, forcing Witbooi and his followers to flee. Signed affidavits by survivors of the attack (Hendrik Witbooi Papers, Appendix 3) give a vivid picture of this bloody raid. "A little before sunrise the German soldiers opened fire on us and stormed the place... When we heard the firing we ran out of our houses; we had no opportunity of making resistance but fled. ... Houses were set on fire and burned over the bodies of dead women and children."

Following this attack Witbooi pursued a guerrilla war against the Germans, using his superior knowledge of the countryside to harass and outwit the German forces. Finally, however, Witbooi was forced to retreat and chose the inaccessible Naukluft Mountains as the last refuge for his followers, including women, children and livestock. The decisive battles of the war took place in the Naukluft between 27 August and 5 September 1894.

An account of the fighting by German commander Major Leutwein gives an idea of how tough it must have been for both sides to have waged a war in these mountains: "The troops followed the tracks left by the Hottentots' livestock; more often than not, however, it was extremely difficult to discern these tracks on the rocky ground. For this reason, the enemy could be pursued only during the day...the sun burned down from a cloudless sky, while the temperature dropped to several degrees below zero during the night...no fires could be lit... The troops were exhausted, clothing and shoes in tatters; casualties had reduced their already thin ranks..."

Despite superiority in arms and ammunition these deprivations prevented the German forces from defeating Witbooi; on the other hand Witbooi was not able to successfully break out of the siege. Eventually, the two sides came to a standstill and on 15 September Witbooi signed a conditional surrender which required him and his supporters to return to Gibeon, to accept the paramountcy of the German Empire and the presence of a German garrison at Gibeon. In return Witbooi retained jurisdiction over his land and people, and the right to keep guns and ammunition.

Concluding his account of the battle in the Naukluft, Leutwein wrote, "The enemy had suffered only minor losses... It proved that the Hottentot was far superior to us when it came to marching, enduring deprivation and knowledge of and ability to use the terrain...it was only in weaponry, courage, perseverance and discipline that the troops surpassed the enemy."

Waterkloof Trail A 17-km, seven-hour trail, considerably more demanding than the Olive Trail, although well worth it. This hike starts from the campsite and is an anti-clockwise circular route which first leads past a weir up to a series of beautifully clear rock pools which, although cold, make for wonderful swimming. From here the trail climbs steadily up to a high point of 1910 m just over halfway round from where there are stunning views over the whole mountain range. As the path descends it follows part of an old German cannon road used in the campaign against Hendrik Witbooi in 1894. The last 6 km of the walk follow the Naukluft River back to the campsite.

 Naukluft Hiking Trail Reputed to be one of the toughest hiking trails in southern Africa, the full distance of 120 km is normally completed in eight days, although it is possible to shorten this to a four-day, 58-km trail. Accommodation on the trail consists of a farmhouse on the first, third and last nights and simple stone shelters on the other nights. Water is provided at the overnight stops but fires are not permitted, making a camping stove essential. It goes without saying that this trail is only for fit and experienced hikers! A good map of the trail is available from the Tourist Information office on Independence Avenue in Windhoek. Due to extreme summer temperatures the trail is only open from 1 March to the third Friday in October to groups of between three and 12 people who must book in advance. Bookings can only be made through **Namibia Wildlife Resorts** ⓘ *Windhoek, T061-2857200, www.nwr.com.na, US$17 per person, regardless of hike duration*. The trail starts on Tuesday, Thursday and Saturday on the first three weeks of each month. Visitors must provide their own food and equipment. Demand is high so reservations should be made well in advance.

Naukluft 4WD trail This self-guided trail for 4WD enthusiasts is 73 km long and has to be driven within two days. Groups must have all their own equipment, firewood and fuel, and a maximum of four vehicles and 16 people are allowed on the trail at any one time. The cost (US$37 per vehicle) includes overnight accommodation which consists of simple shelters with basic ablutions (including shower).

Solitaire » *Phone code: 063 Colour map 3, A2.*

Once featured in a Toyota advertisement, and the subject (in fact, title) of a Dutch novel, Solitaire is actually just a dusty, desolate farm between the gravel plains of the Namib Desert Park and the dunes of the southern Namib. The name Solitaire is derived from the lone dead tree standing next to the service station, a motif frequently seen on publicity posters for tourism in Namibia. The mountains to the east are an extension of the Naukluft Mountains, to the north is the flat-topped Gamsberg Mountain and to the west lie the massive red dunes of the heart of the Namib.

Solitaire is usefully placed with fuel, toilets, soft drinks, beer, ice, home-made bread and cake, meat and basic supplies. There are also a number of places to stay in the area. It is useful if the campsite at Sesriem is booked out.

Sossusvlei » *pp289-292.* *Phone code: 063. Colour map 3, A2.*

One of most visitors' highlights of Namibia is a trip to the massive sand dunes surrounding Sossusvlei (actually the pan or valley floor that you will park on). This is one of the world's most striking, well-preserved and easily accessible desert landcapes, and is well worth the effort of getting there.

Sossusvlei is actually a huge pan surrounded by towering sand dunes, reputed to be the highest in the world. While you will quickly realize this is an exaggeration when you arrive (there are towering dunes as far as the eye can see), it is a spectacular region of the Namib Desert. In years of extraordinary rains, such as 1997 and 2000, the Tsauchab River breaks through the sand and flows all the way to Sossusvlei, filling the pan with water and presenting the surreal site of ducks and even flamingos wading amid the dunes. The water gradually seeps into the ground, where it is tapped by the long roots of the camelthorn trees and nara plants living here.

Ins and outs

The C19 gravel road winds south out of Solitaire into the Namib Desert, through a 20-km section of the Namib-Naukluft Park where there is a good chance of seeing wild ostriches, springbok and gemsbok. It continues south through the red earth before turning east to the **Tsarishoogte Pass** in the **Tsaris Mountains** with stunning

mountainscapes either side, and eventually reaching the small town of **Maltahöhe**.
The C27 is the turn-off for Sesriem, approximately 80 km of fairly tricky, undulating, loose gravel from Solitaire, and is well indicated.

The tarred road to Sossusvlei lies beyond a gate inside the rest camp where a permit must be obtained before driving into the park. The gate is open from 0600-1800, or sunrise to sunset. It is 65 km to the pan itself, and it's worth stopping at the photogenic **Dune 45** (coincidentally, 45 km from the gate) and (if you've got the energy) climbing to the top for the view of the surrounding dune sea. This is a lovely spot to watch the sun rise to the east in the early morning or setting over the dunes to the west in the evening before scurrying back to the gate before it closes (and you get fined).

Seeing the dunes

ⓘ *Entry for the day is US$13 per person, free for children under 16, US$1.50 per car.* Access to the *vlei* itself is either by 4WD or or on foot. There is a car park for 2WD vehicles 5 km short of the *vlei* (65 km from the gates), and another 4WD car park just before the main *vlei*. The gates are open from before sunrise to after sunset (and campers within Sesriem get a 15-minute headstart on 'outsiders') to allow visitors to enjoy the more photogenic and comfortable early morning and late afternoon. There is a sporadic shuttle from the ordinary car park throughout the day between 0800 and 1600 (US$13) that will transport you the final 5 km. Alternatively, join a walking tour with **Sossus-on-Foot** (T063-293217, sossusft@mweb.com.na), which start at the 2WD car park each morning. The guide Boesman, will bring the desert to life. Our recommendation here, especially if you are staying in the campsite, is to drive into the park first thing in the morning as soon as the gate opens (remember to drive slowly if it is still semi dark as there maybe game on the road) and stop at Dune 45 to watch the sunrise, before continuing to Sossusvlei. Once there, instead of following the herd straight up the nearest dune, we suggest that you walk a few hundred metres beyond the final car park to the Dead or **Hidden Vlei** to enjoy the tranquillity and scenery of the area, before climbing one of the less-crowded surrounding dunes. Being even one ridge away from the crowds transports you into your own silent and awesome desert wilderness; on clear days your view over the dune sea extends to around 100 km in all directions. There are no restrictions to walkers: orientate yourself from the top of a dune and explore at will. Remember, it very quickly gets warm, but if you set off before the sun gets too high you can quite easily cut straight across the dunes for the 3 km (as the crow flies) to the ordinary car park.

It is extremely important to respect Nature Conservation's request that, while in the park, vehicles must remain on the road in order not to damage the fragile desert environment. Walking is permitted anywhere and good walking shoes with thick socks (going barefoot in summer will blister your soles), snacks and plenty of water are strongly recommended.

Desert flights This is a fantastic way to appreciate the majesty and enormity of the dunes, marvel at their abrupt stop at the coast, see the geological shift at the mountains to the east and be back on the ground in time for breakfast. Any of the more expensive lodges with airstrips will be happy to arrange a flying excursion for you, and there are several pleasure flight companies in Swakopmund that offer a two- to 2½-hour sightseeing flight from Swakopmund over Sossusvlei and back. Flights are rarely cancelled due to inclement weather or wind (unlike balloon trips) and can be arranged at the last minute (even the night before). Obviously, you should book in advance to ensure availability. Budget US$100-120 per person per hour in the air.

Ballooning This is another fantastic way to view the region from the air. The technological limitations of balloons (ask Mr Branson) make this a hit-and-miss way of getting views of the dunes (let alone the sea – panic if you do). They are always cancellable on days of inclement weather or wind direction. This activity is recommended if you would like to experience ballooning, rather than as the best way to see the dunes from the air. In fact, as the support vehicle may not enter the dunes, any risk of sailing over them results in the balloon being immediately grounded. The trip is elegantly concluded with a champagne breakfast while the silk is stowed away. A very memorable start to any day, and can easily be combined in a day with a trip to Sossusvlei itself and a guided desert walk with an expert. Contact **Namib Sky Adventure Safaris** (T063-238580, namibsky@mweb.com.na). Expect to pay US$400 per person. Daily pick-ups before sunrise at **Camp Mwisho, Kulala Desert Lodge, Sesriem** and **Sossusvlei Lodge.**

Desert hikes Far from being a desolate, lifeless landscape, the desert is full of scurrying, clinging life, adapted to survival against the heat and aridity. The desert floor is brought to life with the aid of an informed guide, although, as before, you are advised to carry snacks and water and dress appropriately. The company

Sesriem & Solitaire

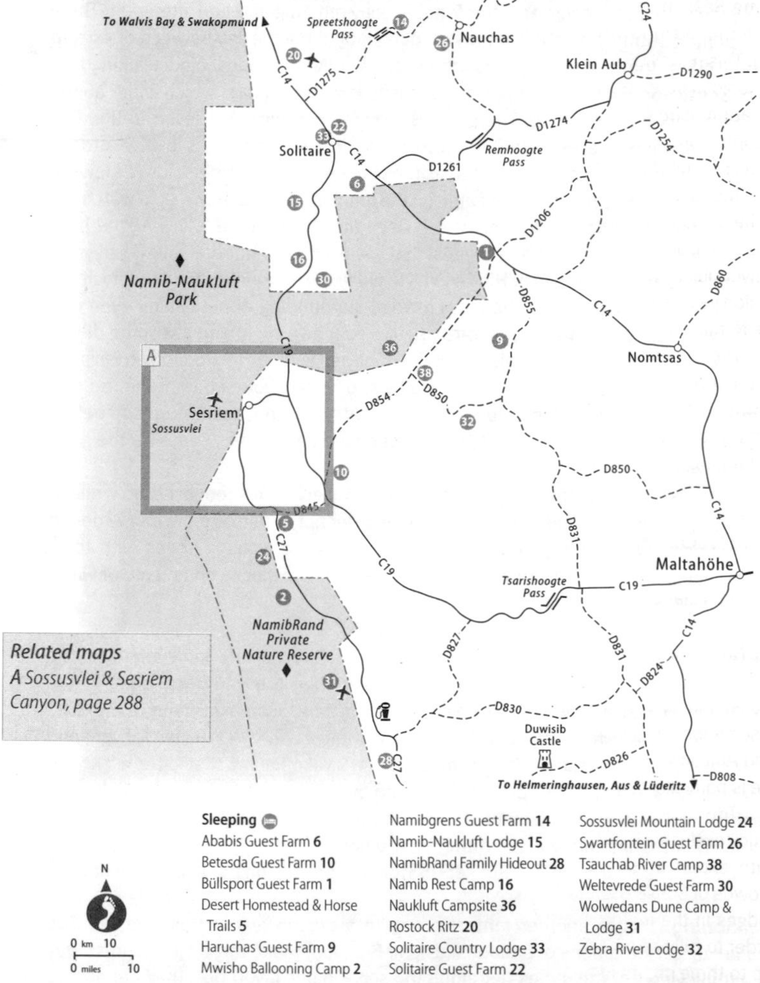

Related maps
A Sossusvlei & Sesriem Canyon, page 288

Sleeping
Ababis Guest Farm **6**
Betesda Guest Farm **10**
Büllsport Guest Farm **1**
Desert Homestead & Horse Trails **5**
Haruchas Guest Farm **9**
Mwisho Ballooning Camp **2**
Namibgrens Guest Farm **14**
Namib-Naukluft Lodge **15**
NamibRand Family Hideout **28**
Namib Rest Camp **16**
Naukluft Campsite **36**
Rostock Ritz **20**
Solitaire Country Lodge **33**
Solitaire Guest Farm **22**
Sossusvlei Mountain Lodge **24**
Swartfontein Guest Farm **26**
Tsauchab River Camp **38**
Weltevrede Guest Farm **30**
Wolwedans Dune Camp & Lodge **31**
Zebra River Lodge **32**

Sossus-on-Foot (T063-293217, sossusft@mweb.com.na) comes highly recommended and offers morning walks of two to three hours. Boseman (bushman) is a dedicated and informative guide and will take walkers through Sossusvlei and Deadvlei, stopping to point out the small creatures and explain the desert flora and fauna along the way. He will meet the people in the 2WD car park about 1½ hours after sunrise, and then drives the group to the 4WD car park, from where the walk begins. After the walk you are taken back to the 2WD car park. The minimum number of people is two at US$70 per person, though he often takes groups of overland truck passengers out when the price comes down considerably to US$24 per person for seven people or more, so it is worth phoning ahead to see when he has another group booked and tag on to that. We have only had excellent feedback on this walk for a complete understanding of what is a unique environment.

For more information about the reserve visit www.namibrand.com.

Sesriem Canyon » *Colour map 3, A2.*

Located near the campsite and entrance to Sossusvlei is another interesting geological feature, the sharp schism in the earth known as Sesriem Canyon. The name Sesriem is derived from the *ses riems*, or six lengths of rope that were needed to haul water out of the gorge from the top. This narrow gorge is a deep slash in the earth 1 km long and up to 30 m deep running west before eventually flattening out as it approaches Sossusvlei. Needless to say, it is not recommended after heavy rain; however, it very infrequently acts as a channel these days.

The Tsauchab River, which today only runs after good rains fall in the Naukluft Mountains, cut the gorge some 15 to 18 million years ago during a significantly wetter period in the Namib's history. The canyon itself was created by continental upheaval somewhere between two and four million years ago, which resulted in the creation of most of the westward flowing rivers in the Namib Desert Region.

The canyon is located 4 km from the campsite; ask at the office and follow signs, it is a poor gravel road and the cars parked in the dust indicate your destination. It is an interesting place to walk and appreciate the multiple rock layers exposed there. After good rains p ools of water form at the bottom of the gorge; take along your swimming gear and enjoy a quick dip.

There is a BP petrol station on the C27, 5 km north of the D827 junction, which is useful, in that it allows you to continue along this beautiful route, rather than heading away from the dunes towards Maltahöhe.

NamibRand Nature Reserve → pp289-292. *Colour map 3, B2.*

A short distance south of the dunes at Sossusvlei lies the largest private nature reserve in the country. It shares a 100-km border with the Namib-Naukluft Park to the west and the Nubib Mountains border the eastern boundary. The special attraction of the reserve is the diversity of the desert landscapes: mountains plunging down on to endless grassy plains which are intercepted by red vegetated dunes. Game species in the reserve include gemsbok, mountain and plains zebra, bat-eared fox, spotted hyena and African wildcats. In the more rocky areas are baboon, kudu and leopard. The bird life is particularly varied for this region, with over 120 species recorded.

The development of the reserve has been carefully controlled and guests can enjoy exclusive insight into the ecology of this fascinating region with expert and enthusiastic guides. For anyone fearing the crowds of Sossusvlei, or the limited offering of some of the other lodges in the region, a stay at NamibRand is recommended. In order to fully appreciate the area it is recommended you spend up to three nights in the reserve.

NamibRand extends over 180,000 ha, incorporating some of the most beautiful and spectacular scenery of the Namib Desert.

Ins and outs

There are currently five camps/lodges in the area and the policy is to limit the number of beds to keep tourism to a minimum and the wilderness area intact – hence the high prices. Some of the fees paid by guests go towards conservation initiatives and have already been used to introduce black rhino into the reserve. Each lodge offers hiking or late-afternoon drives and will happily arrange a breathtaking light aircraft or balloon ride over the dunes, if this is not already included in your agenda.

It is possible to organize fly-in safaris, each including a low-level flight over the dunes at Sossusvlei. Independent travellers wanting to splash out should make their own arrangements with private charter flight companies (see page 36). The lodges in the reserve are serviced by the **Dune Hopper** (see page 292).

Background

In the 1950s, the NamibRand area was allocated to individual farmers (ex First World War soldiers) who introduced sheep to the area, cut roads and put up fences and water points. After 30 years of marginal farming it was obvious that the local environment was just not suited to commercial farming. A series of drought years in the early 1980s forced several farmers to sell their land. It was at this point that the idea of NamibRand started to emerge.

In 1984, Albi Brückner bought **Farm Gorrasis**, and later he bought two neighbouring farms, **Die Duine** and **Stellarine.** It quickly became apparent that throughout the drought years the game had survived and flourished. The reserve today is made up of a series of farms which have had their fences removed in order to allow the wildlife to roam freely; over 200 km of fencing and 120 km of roads have been removed, and pipelines serving waterpoints installed. In order to support and develop the project a series of different operators have taken out 'concessions' on the farms and now offer a range of activities designed to introduce and educate visitors about the wonders of the Namib Desert.

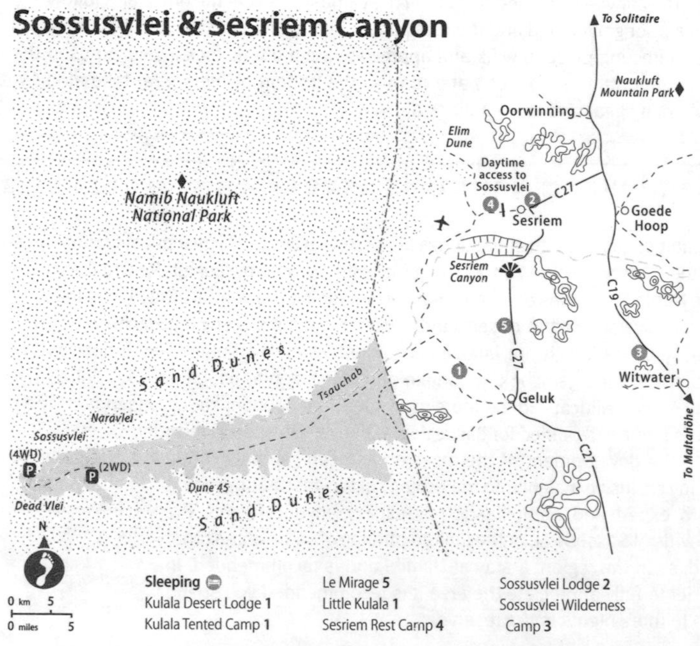

Sleeping

Namib Desert Park *p277*
Accommodation within the park is at the 8 basic campsites detailed on pages 277-280. Visitors to the region unwilling to camp should stay either at the coast (Walvis Bay or Swakopmund) or consider the lodges on the inland fringe of the desert and neighbouring mountains (for suggested route and available accommodation, see Hinterland, page 264-274). All 8 small campsites within the Namib Desert Park can be booked in advance through **Namibia Wildlife Resorts** Central Reservations in Windhoek (see page 46) or through www.nwr.com.na. Visitors to these campsites need to be entirely self-sufficient, taking water and firewood with them. The only amenities are drop toilets, *braai* areas and picnic sites.

Naukluft Park *p280*
There are numerous places to stay in the area north and east of the Naukluft Park, centred around Solitaire and Büllsport. Take a good look at the road map before choosing your accommodation; make sure your overnight stops correspond to your daytime activities to minimize unnecessary gravel road driving. We make the assumption that you will be coming from or travelling to Sossusvlei, and so provide distances to the entry point to the dunes at Sesriem.
AL Namib-Naukluft Lodge, 18 km south of Solitaire off the C36, 70 km from Sesriem, reservations through **African Extravaganza**, Windhoek, T061-372100, www.natron.net/afex. 16 double rooms each with a private veranda, restaurant, swimming pool with adjacent thatched bar overlooking the desert. This was at one time the luxury choice in the area, but the design disappoints and the place feels tired, next to the newer competition. Good-value morning excursion to the dunes, and there are easy walks within the vicinity. Serviced by a daily shuttle from Windhoek.
AL Swartfontein Guest Farm, D1261, 15 km south of the D1275 junction, T062-572004, reservations T061-226979 (Windhoek), logufa@mweb.com.na. 5 tastefully furnished rooms with lovely en suite bathrooms, oil paintings on the wall and a very comfortable lounge and dining area. The Italianhosts offer superb food including home-made pasta and ice cream. There is some game in the area and walks and drives are available. Recommended.
A Ababis Guest Farm, D1261/C14 junction, 100 km from Sesriem, T063-683080, www.ababis-gaestefarm.de. On a working farm, 4 en suite doubles and 3 rooms in the main farmhouse, communal lounge, payphone, swimming pool and pretty, shaded veranda. Game drives and hiking trails in the surrounding Naukluft Mountains, all inclusive, but still pricey, even for this part of the country. Off-road driving courses also on offer.
A Büllsport Guest Farm, C14/D854 junction, 124 km from Sesriem, T063-693371, www.bullsport.com. 8 en suite doubles with facilities for the disabled, swimming pool, petrol station, small store, payphone, hiking trails in the surrounding Naukluft Mountains. Full board. Not as charming or pretty as others nearby and fairly pricey, but there are a number of horses available for outrides, overnight trips and riding lessons, and there's a full dressage and jumping arena.
A Haruchas Guest Farm, D855, 19 km south of the C14 junction, 119 km from Sesriem, T063-683071, haruchas@ natron.net. 20,000-ha farm offering 4 en suite double rooms and a 4-bed, 2-room family chalet, swimming pool, hiking, 4WD and game drives, dinner, B&B included, curios.
A Weltevrede Guest Farm, 35 km south of Solitaire on the C36, 49 km from Sesriem, T063-293374, aswarts@mweb.com.na. 10 en suite rooms, some with self-catering facilities, swimming in a large farm water holder, bar, rates are dinner and B&B with wholesome farm cuisine. A simple but relaxing operation on a working farm. Special arrangements for photographers as it has its own darkroom. **Campsite (E)** with 4 shady sights and communal cooking and ablutions.
A Zebra River Lodge, 91 windy km to Sesriem, T063-693265, www.zebrariver.com. Take the C14 to Büllsport, turn onto D854, after 42 km turn onto D850, farm is signposted 19 km down this road. Deep in a canyon in the Tsaris Mountains. A superb lodge with 7 en suite doubles, and a 2-bed-roomed self-catering cottage 3.5 km away, a sheltered veranda surrounds an imaginatively designed plunge pool. Room rates are full board with plentiful, excellent

food. Knowledgeable, friendly hosts, Rob, is a fount of information on the geology of the region and his farm (on which the oldest known shell fossil, 550 million years old, was discovered in 2000), the moon and stars (explored through his telescope), flora and fauna, local history, and more. Hiking to perennial springs, 4WD drives. Recommended.

B **Desert Homestead and Horse Trails**, C14/D854 junction, 38 km from Sesriem, T063-293243, www.deserthomestead-namibia.com. An excellent, very tastefuly created option. 16 large bungalows with en suite bathrooms and fabulous views. Small swimming pool, shop, restaurant for guests (and lunch for drive-by visitors). Good value for the region. Well located for the dunes, offers sunrise horse rides which include a full breakfast and sunset rides into the desert with gin and tonics. Recommended.

B **Rostock Ritz**, signposted off the C14, just south of the Gaub Pass, 30 km northeast of Solitaire, T064-69400 (reservations), www.desertlodge.web.na. Award-winning lodge with 22 en suite rooms with an unusual 'traditional' adobe design. Restaurant overlooks the plains below, good food, certainly worth a lunch stop. Swimming pool with shaded terrace. Good, long hikes to the nearby canyon, water and day packs provided, all routes clearly marked. Horse and camel trails, Bushman paintings. A tasteful, peaceful lodge. Recommended.

B **Namib Rest Camp**, 27 km south of Solitaire on the C36 then 6 km along farm track, 62 km from Sesriem, T064-293211, namibrestcamp@mweb.com.na. A simple rest camp with 12 bungalows and 4 family units, all en suite, available self-catering or full board. Swimming pool with a shaded bar and *braai* area (restaurant soon), quad-biking, evening trips to the Diep River to view petrified dunes, fuel station. Overpriced, unimaginative design and a little run down, but with 5 good **campsites (F)** with light, water, no electricity, shared ablutions.

B **Solitaire Country Lodge**, new lodge next to the shop and petrol station in Solitaire, reservations T061-374750 (Windhoek), www.namibialodges.com. 25 en suite rooms with stone floors in low blocks surrounding a courtyard with a swimming pool, restaurant and bar. Good food, buffet style, including home-made bread and apple pie. A new spot popular with tour groups and already a HAN award winner. 30 camping sites (**E**) with good ablution blocks.

B-C **Solitaire Guest Farm**, follow signs from Solitaire, 6 km north along a farm track, off the C14, 90 km from Sesriem, T062-572024, solgt@mweb.com.na. Not a working farm but dedicated entirely to tourists. 5 carefully crafted en suite doubles, 1 self-catering house, with a swimming pool, comfortable lounge and peaceful garden. Recommended, a good option in this pricey region, cheaper if you self-cater but the farm cuisine is very good.

C **Namibgrens Guest Farm**, D1275 from the C14 to the Spreetshoogte Pass and follow the signs; it is 130 km from Sesriem, T062-572021, www.natron.net/namibgrens. 47 challenging km from the C14. 9 double rooms, self-catering or full board, around an old farmhouse with huge trees (shade in summer) and a lovely conservatory (warmth in winter). Located at 1760 m on the Spreetshoogte Pass, with superb views of the desert below (it gets cold at night). There are beautiful hiking trails in the mountains (with Bushman art – the Dassie Trail is the most popular) with overnight stops in basic huts (with hot water), and 4WD trails. Maps are provided. **Camping** (**E**) in pretty area with old farming memorabilia, large communal *braai* area, water, decent ablutions, no electricity.

F **Naukluft Campsite**, 12 km within the park from the gate, book in advance through Namibia Wildlife Resorts, T061-2857200 (Windhoek), www.nwr.com.na. 8 sites, *braai* facilities, shared ablution block with hot showers, no shop; drinking water and firewood are available. Information on the park's flora and fauna is available next to the office.

Sossusvlei *p284, map p288*

Check distances from Sesriem before committing yourself to a particular lodge as you should avoid driving before sunrise and after sunset as much as possible. There are an additional 5 upmarket lodges in the NamibRand Nature Reserve (see page 292).

L **Kulala Desert Lodge**, 17 km south of Sesriem on C27, www.kulalalodge.com, reservations T061-274500 (Windhoek), www.wilderness-safaris.com. 12 thatched *kulalas* (en suite double bungalows, with a roof you can sleep on or stargaze from) with veranda, half board, swimming pool, horse riding and ballooning. On a large farm (21,000 ha) with private entrance to Sossusvlei, 4WD trips from the lodge are on offer; this is the closest accommodation to Sossusvlei, with phenomenal views.

L **Kulala Tented Camp**, again in the same region, same contact details as **Kulala Desert Lodge** (above). 9 *kulalas*, the main area is an elevated wooden deck under thatch, and there's another swimming pool and sundeck. Again in a tremendous spot with sweeping views.

L **Le Mirage**, 21 km from Sesriem, T063-293293, www.lemiragelodge.com, member of **Leading Lodges of Africa**, www.leadinglodges.com. Stunning and remote stone castle-style structure in the middle of a wide expanse of gravel desert, with very much the atmosphere of a North African desert medieval castle, 27 super luxury en suite rooms with a/c and sumptuous bedding, gourmet food and wine, jacuzzi and swimming pool. The **Wellness Centre** offers a variety of pampering treatments such as Thai massage and pedicures, activities include quad-biking, balloon rides and guided trips to Sossusvlei. Flights from Windhoek available. If you are in this league; enjoy.

L **Little Kulala**, situated on the same farm as the **Kulala Desert Lodge** (above), same contact details. Very similar in concept and design and offering the same activities, though slightly more expensive as there are just 8 *kulalas* each with its own plunge pool. The main area has a bar, lounge dining room, curio shop and swimming pool.

L **Sossusvlei Wilderness Camp**, about 30 km southeast of Sesriem, off the C36, www.sossusvleicamp.com, reservations **Wilderness Safaris**, T061-274500 (Windhoek), www.wilderness-safaris.com. This is one of the best lodges in the country, built in the style of a wilderness camp with raised wooden walkways linking 9 thatched en suite units; each unit has a private plunge pool, veranda and stunning uninterrupted view. Rooms are built into the rock with plenty of character. Guests are usually part of one of **Wilderness Safaris**' fly-in safaris. Recommended, if money is no object, although you can get similar views, and 'experience' at other nearby, less expensive camps.

AL **Sossusvlei Lodge**, adjacent to **Sesriem Rest Camp**, central reservations T+27 21 9304564 (South Africa), www.sossusvleilodge.com. 45 tent/bungalow structures designed to blend into the desert, comfortable, en suite doubles, restaurant, bar with lovely views, nature videos in the evening, swimming pool, full board. Expensive, but well located and comfortable, the closest non-campers can stay to **Sesriem Camp**, the main entrance to Sossusvlei, making it handy for dawn and dusk views and photography. 4WD excursions to the dunes offered, plus quad-biking, hot-air ballooning, and star gazing through telescopes.

AL-B **NamibRand Family Hideout**, 110 km south of Sesriem off the C27, the turn-off is 400 m north of the junction with the D827, and drive 11 km, reservations T061-226803 (Windhoek), www.hideout.iway.na. 3-bedroomed farmhouse that accommodates up to 10, self-catering, gas fridge, solar lights and *braai* area, bedding by arrangement only, numerous activities available, US$75-200 per night for the hideout, dependent on length of stay and season. Ask about discounts.

B **Betesda Guest Farm**, 40 km from Sesriem on D854, T063-693253, www.betesda.iway.na. En suite rooms and self-catering chalets built from local materials, swimming pool, horse riding, hiking, farm trips, food available if booked. The owner has an interesting collection of racing trophies; small craft shop, lovely mountain views, handily placed for Sossusvlei. Stony **campsite** (**E**) by riverbed; cheap, but poor ablutions and no electricity.

B-D **Tsauchab River Camp**, follow signs 1 km from the D854/D850 junction, 72 km from Sesriem, T/F063-293416, www.natron.net/tsauchab. Run by a young South African couple, Johan and Nicky, who have a huge amount of energy; they offer a broad range of camping sites and en suite thatched chalets in imaginative locations along a 3-km stretch of the river, farm shop selling fresh bread and *braai* packs, bar, will cook if warned in advance, excellent ablutions, firewood and candles, no electricity. There are donkey cart trips, lovely walks and 4WD trails in the area. Recommended.

F **Sesriem Rest Camp**, inside the gates to Sossusvlei, which is 63 km away, T063-693247, reservations also through **Namibia Wildlife Resorts**, T061-2857200

(Windhoek), www.nwr.com.na. Large campsite with room for 26 groups of campers (and an overflow). As the rest camp is already inside the park, campers have a 15-min headstart on 'outsiders' in the morning for those uninterrupted dawn views and photos. Beware of the overflow area where you may be alone, or grouped in with overland trucks. Communal ablutions, each site has some shade with a large camelthorn tree, very nice bar, miniscule swimming pool that gets crowded, fairly well-stocked shop with postcards, films, phonecards, wood, beer, meat, ice and tinned food, petrol station and pay phone. Book in advance, this site is, unsurprisingly, popular. Gates open sunrise to sunset only; no entry after sunset. Camping is more expensive than other NWR sites, at US$38 per site for up to 8 people.

NamibRand Nature Reserve *p287*

L **Sossusvlei Mountain Lodge**, C27, 9 km south of the D845 junction, 26 km from Sesriem, reservations through **CC Africa** T+27 (0)11-8094300 (South Africa), www.ccafrica.com. Competes with the **Sossusvlei Wilderness Lodge** as the smartest place in the area, opened in 2001. 10 stone and glass luxurious double villas, stunning views, excellent food and extensive wine list. Satellite TV, internet access for guests, all game and scenic arrangements possible, including balloon rides and quad-biking. Star-gazing skylight over beds, plus observatory. Recommended, if money is no object.

L **Wolwedans Dunes Lodge**, C27, 40 km south of Sesriem, reservations through **NamibRand Safaris**, T061-230616 (Windhoek), www.wolwedans.com. A stunning set-up, located on the edge of the 250-m-high dunes, superb view over the valley and ancient mountains. 8 beautifully decorated, luxurious, en suite chalets on stilts, with private veranda. The central dining area has a separate bar and a comfortable lounge with fireplace to which you can retreat, should the wind start to howl, library, wine cellar, sundowner decks. Exquisite food and service. Rates are in the region of US$550 for a double all inclusive.

L **Wolwedans Dune Camp**, a short distance from the **Wolwedans Dunes Lodge**, reservations as above. This was the first camp to be built in the dunes. 6 en suite tents all on raised wooden platforms. Wooden walkways link the tents with the central dining and lounge block where guests gather for their sundowner before enjoying an alfresco dinner. This is an unforgettable camp in the perfect location. Aside from the superb views, the principal attraction here is the limited number of guests. Recommended. Rates are in the region of US$370 for a double all inclusive. Both the lodge and camp offer game drives and walks in the reserve and rides in their hot-air balloon.

L **Wolwedans Private Camp**. Wolwedans also has another wood and canvas property in the area that is completely stuck out in its own private patch of wilderness, reservations as above. Again it is sumptuously decorated but with a kitchen, and has 2 bedrooms that sleep 4, though it is designed and located with honeymooners in mind to provide absolute seclusion. You can choose to self-cater and stay there completely on your own (US$550 for a couple) for just pure uninterrupted romantic relaxation in a magnificent desert setting, or be fully catered for with a chef and field guide (US$1000 per couple). The **Private Camp** is seasonal and is open from 15 Mar-15 Dec and the minimum stay is 2 nights.

AL **Mwisho Ballooning Camp**, C27, 20 km south of the D845 junction, 37 km from Sesriem, T063-293233, namibsky@mweb.com.na. An intimate camp set at the foot of the dunes next to a waterhole. Best-known operator of balloon trips over the desert. 4 double tents with en suite facilities, meals in the renovated farmhouse. Afternoon and sundowner game drives, early-morning balloon rides, weather permitting (see page 285).

Transport

Namib-Naukluft Park *p275*

The **Dune Hopper**, www.dunehopper.com, is a daily air taxi that runs a service from **Windhoek** and between the following lodges: **Wolwedans, Sossusvlei Mountain Lodge, Sossusvlei Wilderness Lodge, Sossusvlei Lodge** and **Kulala Desert Lodge**. There are several packages to choose from, from 2-5 days. Alternatively book through **NatureFriend Safaris**, in Windhoek, T061-234793, www.naturefriend.com.na.

The South

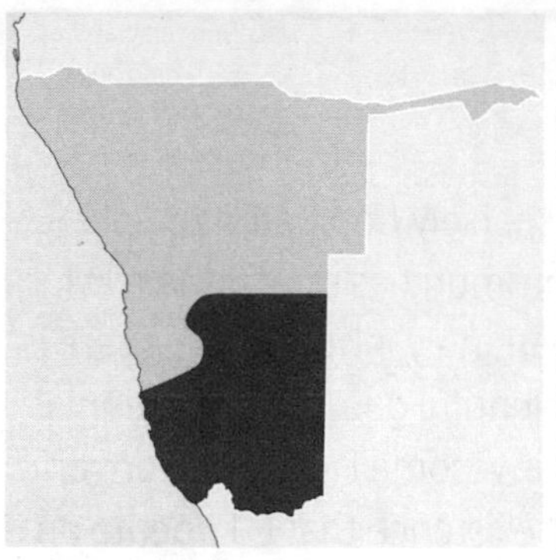

Footprint features

Introduction

The south of Namibia is an arid, sparsely populated region with isolated farmhouses and communities scratching a living from the rocky ground. While seemingly inhospitable, there is widespread cattle farming and plentiful game, two perennial rivers (the Fish and Orange), the awesome Fish River Canyon and the frankly unusual, isolated existence that is Lüderitz on the coast. The distances are vast, but there is plenty to catch the eye, with mountain ranges, red Kalahari sand and quiver trees, herds of kudu and circling birds of prey, pleasant dams for watersports and the sand-enveloped diamond boom town of Kolmanskop. On the edge of the Namib Desert is the delicate Duwisib Castle, an outpost of European elegance in the middle of the veld, and further south lie the brooding Brukkaros Volcano and the quirky Quiver Tree Forest.

Geographically, the south encompasses all the land from Rehoboth to the South African border and from the borders with Botswana and South Africa in the Kalahari Desert to the ancient Namib and cold waters of the South Atlantic Ocean. The central highland plateau runs like a spine down the middle of the region and it is along this narrow strip of land that the majority of the population lives.

★ Don't miss...

1 **Oanob Lake Resort** Soothe and restore your overheated self with a swim and a beer, page 298.

2 **Klein-Aus Vista** Hike, bike or ride in the the rocky hills near Aus and enjoy the isolated beauty of this superb lodge and campsite – you may catch glimpses of the wild horses or gemsbok, page 317.

3 **Kolmanskop** Keep your promise of returning to this ghost town in the early or late hours of the day and watch the shadows play, page 322.

4 **Lüderitz** Devour some of the freshest seafood and shellfish you will ever come across, washed down with superb chilled wine, at Ritzi's or The Penguin, page 328.

5 **Saddle Hill** Tackle a remote corner of the world just north of Lüderitz, by joining the 4WD concession across the dunes and to the coast, page 330.

6 **Fish River Canyon** Watch the sun fill the canyon with colour at sunrise or sunset from the viewpoints at the top near Hobas Campsite, page 331.

South from Windhoek

Physically, the South is a semi-arid region of vast plains stretching as far as the eye can see. To the west lie a series of mountain ranges demarcating the edge of the plateau and the pro-Namib Desert Region. Just north of Keetmanshoop stands the ancient volcano Brukkaros, towering 650 m above the surrounding plain, and in the moonscape of the far south lies the Fish River Canyon, an artery through which the Fish River flows down to its confluence with the Orange River.

Politically, the South is divided into the Hardap and Karas regions, with their administrative centres at Mariental and Keetmanshoop respectively. The only other towns of significant size are Rehoboth and the old German coastal town of Lüderitz. However, all over the south there are a scattering of smaller towns and settlements, many of them dating back to the days of the first European missionaries.

The economy of the south has always been based around livestock farming. In pre-colonial times the Nama people grazed their animals on the vast plains, watering them at the springs of Rehoboth, Hoachanas, Gibeon, Berseba, and Bethanie, now all small settlements. Following the arrival of European missionaries, traders and settlers, the majority of the land was turned into vast white-owned ranches, many of over 10,000 ha, and for much of the 20th century the wealth of these farmers was built on the back of the trade in the wool of the karakul sheep (see box page 352). Although the Basters in Rehoboth managed to hold on to their land, following the Odendaal Commission Report in 1962, the Nama people were forced into a Namaland Bantustan located west of the main road between Mariental and Keetmanshoop. » For Sleeping, Eating and other listings, see pages 299-300.

Ins and outs

Getting there

The B1 is a good, tarred road leading all the way to the two southern border crossings at Noordoewer and Ariamsvlei, 800 km and 855 km from Windhoek, respectively. In places, the road becomes quite narrow and great care should be exercised when overtaking the large trucks which ply their way up and down the highway between South Africa and Windhoek, particularly at night. **Note** Avoid driving the B1 at night. It has acquired the unfortunate nickname of 'the road of death' due to the high number of fatal accidents that take place on it. It's wise to avoid it during morning and afternoon rush hours too, as large numbers of Rehobothers commute in cars, pick-up trucks and minibuses to and from their jobs in Windhoek. At such times this stretch of the road is uncharacteristically crowded, by Namibian standards.

Despite its rather sinister nickname, the road between Windhoek and Rehoboth is a beautiful route, winding through the picturesque ranchland of the Auas Mountains. On this stretch of the road troops of baboons rooting around in the bush for food are a common sight; also keep an eye open for warthogs, mongoose, guinea fowl and yellow-billed hornbills.

Just south of Rehoboth the C24 branches west off the main B1 and leads to the Remhoogte Pass, one of three spectacular routes which descend to the Namib Desert floor. From here you can head west into the Naukluft Mountains or southwest towards Sossusvlei.

Getting around

This region is the size of Germany and, with towns and settlements far apart, it is difficult to explore properly without your own vehicle. The rail network runs through

Mariental and Keetmanshoop as far as Karasburg and the border at Ariamsvlei, and there are some bus services to the major towns. Beyond that, there is a network of relatively frequent shared taxis, mostly to the smaller settlements. However, to get to the sites of interest – in particular the Fish River Canyon – the only alternative to driving yourself is hitch-hiking, which may involve long waits in the hot sun, with lifts few and far between.

Rehoboth

» pp299-300. Phone code: 062. Colour map 3, A3.

Situated 87 km south of Windhoek at the foot of the Auas Mountains, Rehoboth is home to the Basters (literally, 'Bastards'), a fiercely proud and independent people who are the descendants of a group of farmers of mixed European and Khoisan blood. The town has very little to recommend it; some say this is part of a deliberate policy to marginalize the Basters' hometown. A plunge in the Reho-Spa resort pool to cool off (or the hot spring to warm up) is recommended, though whilst you can stay overnight here there are better options in the region. Nearby, Oanob Lake is a stunning spot, with lakeside thatched chalets, well-tended camping sites and a range of watersports and entertainment for families.

The main street of town which turns off the B1 east at the BP petrol station is well equipped with petrol stations (24 hour), supermarkets including a **Spar**, butcher's and *biltong* shops and lots of bottle stores.

History

The hot springs had been known for centuries by the Swartobooi Namas who called the place *Anhes*, meaning 'smoke', which referred to the steam rising from the hot water. A more permanent settlement was established in 1844 by Rhenish Missionary, Heinrich Kleinschmidt. This original mission station lasted for 20 years before being abandoned in 1864 following an attack by the Oorlam Afrikaners under Jonker Afrikaner. Kleinschmidt's congregation dispersed following their defeat and Kleinschmidt and his family walked through the bush for four days before reaching the safety of the mission station at Otjimbinwge, where Kleinschmidt laid down and died.

The Basters migrated to the area from the Cape in 1870 and under the leadership of Hemanus van Wyk established a settlement at the site of the now abandoned Rhenish mission station. The name of the town comes from the Bible: "He moved on from there and dug another well, and no one quarrelled over it. He named it Rehoboth, saying, 'Now the Lord has given us room and we will flourish in the land.'" (Genesis Chapter 26, verse 22).

In the years following the arrival of van Wyk and his people, the mission station was rebuilt. One of the earliest buildings to be completed was the Lutheran Church in Church Street; with its distinctive brickwork it is reminiscent of the Putz architechtural style of the Ombudsman's Office in Windhoek.

The Baster community has traditionally been a farming community, living a more or less self-sufficient farming existence, similar to that of the white Afrikaner settlers. Fiercely independent, Christian and western-oriented in their culture, the Basters have managed to hold on to their land despite attempts by the German and South African colonial governments to take it away from them.

From the 1920s until independence, the Rehoboth community was governed by a *kaptein* (traditional leader) and his *raad* (council) who had jurisdiction over all aspects of community life except for the law. A white magistrate appointed by the colonial government held these powers. Matters concerning agriculture, education, local government and health were all managed by the *raad* assisted by seven *volksraad* or 'people's councils' from around the region. In effect the Rehoboth district existed as a semi-autonomous region within Namibia.

After independence, a section of the Baster community, under the leadership of the former *kaptein*, Hans Diergaardt, fought a court battle with the central government to keep control over the traditional communal land of the town itself and the land in a radius of 10 km around it. The most recent Supreme Court ruling in 1996 handed control of the land to the government, to be administered by the town council, thus depriving the traditional leadership of the right to administer the land. Just before his death in 1998, Diergaardt made peace with PM Hage Geingob, and Rehoboth finally put aside its dispute with the new Namibian state.

Rehoboth Museum

ⓘ *T062-522954, Mon-Fri 0900-1200, 1400-1600, Sat 0900-1200.*

Located in the former residence of the town's first postmaster, built in 1903, the museum houses an interesting record of the community's history and culture revealing the fascinating twists and turns in the history of this unusual 'Lost White Tribe'. There is also information on local flora and fauna, and in the garden a display of traditional huts of the different ethnic groups.

Reho Spa Recreation Resort » *Colour map 3, A3.*

ⓘ *US$6.40 adults, children under 16 free, plus a further US$1.60 for adults and US$0.80 for children to enter the thermal baths.*

Known to the indigenous Nama people for centuries, the hot springs here have been developed into a spa resort run by **Namibia Wildlife Resorts**, but it is not a terribly attractive place. The camp has the look and feel of a military barracks, but there is a fine 20-sq-m indoor thermal bath with huge ceiling in a 1960s-style structure, grassy picnic areas and a 25-m outdoor swimming pool. Picnic/*braai* sites are available for day visitors. The resort is open year round. See also Sleeping, page 299. To get to the resort, follow the signs off the B1 onto the gravel road, turn right immediately after the Catholic Church. The road curves to the left before reaching a crossroads. Turn right here (you will be able to see the military barracks-style buildings on your right) and the entrance to the resort is a further 400 m on the right.

Oanob Lake Resort

ⓘ *US$1.50 entry fee for day visitors.*

The dam, which supplies Rehoboth's water, was completed in 1990. Originally there were plans to set up some irrigated crop cultivation by the dam, but this has not materialized. Unusually, this resort is not in the hands of **Namibia Wildlife Resorts**, and as such is able to respond to growth in demand by providing new facilities and accommodation. This is just what they have done, with two good restaurants/bars, excellent chalets and campsite and a range of facilities for the visitor to enjoy. The blue water of the lake is a welcome sight amidst the arid thorn veld of the surrounding countryside. This is justifiably a popular summer weekend and holiday spot for locals, though tourist numbers have risen, and attractive, comfortable accommodation overlooking the lake has been built.

The resort is well signposted west off the B1 and just north of Rehoboth (on either the D1280 or D1237).

The resort is open all year round, pre-booking is recommended but by no means essential. There are shaded, grassy *braai* sites for day visitors as well as two picturesque and reasonable thatched bar/restaurants, one overlooking the children's pool.

There are a few ostriches, as well as colonies of cormorants, pelicans, darters and other waterbirds living on and alongside the lake, plus some noisy, inquisitive turkeys, hens and a peacock roaming the campsite.

There are a few marked walks laid out around the lake, along which it is possible to spot springbok, baboons and other smaller mammals. Visitors can also hire pedalos, canoes or jet skis or go waterskiing. Windsurfers with their own boards can also make use of the lake, however, there are no boards at present available for hire.

South from Rehoboth

The B1 south from Rehoboth passes through the ranching land of the Baster community, before reaching the village of **Kalkrand** with its Shell garage, bottle store and takeaway stand, small clinic and about 10 houses. About 20 km north of Kalkrand, at the **Duineveld Crossroads**, there are a number of roadside stalls where springbok skin rugs are sold by locals from Duineveld. The skins themselves are bought from commercial farmers and then stitched together and lined with karakul fur before being sold. The sale of these rugs plays an important role in the economy of the village.

About 10 km south of Rehoboth, the B1 crosses the Tropic of Capricorn; there are signs and a gravel patch on both sides of the road where you can pull over and take a photograph.

Sleeping

South from Windhoek *p296*

B-D **Weissenfels Guest Farm**, C26 towards Gamsberg Pass for 114 km, follow signs to farm. T062-572112, www.orusovo.com/weissenfels. 6 en suite rooms, 1 family room sleeping 5 people, 5 double budget rooms with shared bathrooms, camping sites, swimming pool, hiking, horse riding, game viewing, with 7 days' notice can organize birdwatching in Gamsberg Mountains. The **Vortex Wellness Centre** here offers 'spiritual' and holistic treatments such as musical therapy, Japanese reiki, and therapeutic massage. Different, though it won't suit all visitors.

Rehoboth *p297*

B-C **Reho Spa Recreation Resort**, T062-522774, or reservations through **Namibia Wildlife Resorts**, T061-2857200 (Windhoek), www.nwr.com.na. The only option for accommodation in Rehoboth itself are these bungalows, 6-bed 2-room, or 5- and 4-bed 1-room, with bathrooms and kitchen. Also 'VIP' suites with crockery and cutlery. Although recently repainted, they are certainly nothing special or very attractive but amazing as it may seem, the bungalows often get booked up. **Camping and caravan sites** (D) maximum 8 persons per site, communal ablution and cooking facilities, the sites are not especially nice and thanks to all the water around there is a real problem with mosquitoes. However, the attraction here is to go for a late-night dip in the hot pools. People staying overnight can access the pools in the evening when there are fewer people around – after a relaxing wallow you a guaranteed a good night's sleep.

B-E **Lake Oanob Resort**, T062-522370, www.oanob.com.na. A much better option outside of town are these lakeside chalets and camping facilities, 3, 6-bedroomed luxurious, chalets and rooms, beautifully positioned by the lake. The only possible complaint might be of over-exuberance from day visitors during the summer. 20 immaculate grassed, shaded campsites, adequate ablutions. Restaurant and bar, activities include banana boat rides, fishing, canoeing and waterskiing on the lake, and hiking and horse riding in the surrounding hills. Recommended.

South from Rehoboth *p299*

AL **Intu Afrika Kalahari Game Reserve**, reservations T061-248741, www.resafrica.net/intu-afrika. From the north, turn east off the B1 at Kalkrand onto the C21, then right on the B1268, follow signs. From the south, take the C20, left after 12 km on the D1268 and follow the signs. A beautiful collection of lodges set amidst the red sand dunes of the Kalahari. Price depends on the season and degree of elegance of your room; all guests share the swimming pool, restaurant, game drives and birdwatching. A particular attraction of this lodge is !Kung Bushman village, with the opportunity to go on nature hikes with Bushman guides. Book in advance.

AL-A **Bitterwasser Flying Centre and Lodge**, T063-265300, www.bitterwasser.com. 10 km north of the C20/D1219 junction, roughly 75 km from Mariental, or by charter flight from Windhoek. This has been a gliding

For an explanation of the sleeping and eating price codes used in this guide, see inside the front cover. Other relevant information is found in Essentials, see pages 43-51.

centre for aficionados for 40 years; a group of German and Swiss enthusiasts (there are currently 28 partner owners) bought the land in 1994 and after initial construction of some basic rondavels for themselves, the lodge has been extended with some wonderful accommodation for tourists. There are 22 a/c chalets decorated in African style, a swimming pool, and a fabulous thatched central *lapa* containing the bar and restaurant. Thanks to the excellent thermals, the principal attraction is the gliding; a number of world records have flown from here. The expanding agenda for landlubbers, grounded partners and children includes excursions into the Kalahari, mountain biking and ballooning. Call for details, and book as far ahead as possible if in the 'season' (Oct-Jan).

Eating

Rehoboth *p297*
There are no restaurants to recommend in town. There are takeaways including the **Dolphin** fish and chip shop at the corner of the B1 and the turn-off to the Reho-Spa, and simple fare from the shops at the various petrol stations. The **BP** on the B1 serves tea and coffee and snacks such as fried chicken and pies. For a beer you could try **The Pink Palace**, which doubles as the town's casino but this is pretty rough and ready, and there's no doubt from the dubious characters staggering around town even in the early morning, that there is a real problem of alcohol abuse in Rehoboth.

Transport

Rehoboth *p297*
87 km to Windhoek.
Bus and taxi For Intercape coaches to **Cape Town**, **Keetmanshoop**, **Windhoek** and **Upington**, see timetable on page 70. Coaches pick up and drop off at the main service station on the B1, as do local shared taxis (frequent service to **Windhoek**, and south down the B1).

Train For trains to **Keetmanshoop** via Mariental, and **Windhoek**, see timetable on page 68. The station is 10 km from town, but this is a desolate spot and is not recommended.

Directory

Rehoboth *p297*
Banks First National Bank, and Standard Bank on the main street, both with ATMs, and an additional First National ATM at the BP. **Medical services** Hospital, T062-220067, follow signs for Reho-Spa. **Police station** T062-523223. **Post office** Next to the museum. **Telephone** Namibia Telecoms (for international calls) is next to the post office. There is a 'computer centre', which advertises email but can't be relied on for a connection.

Mariental and south to Keetmanshoop

Phone code: 063. Colour map 3, A4.

After Rehoboth and continuing south along the B1 the next major (and we use this term loosely) settlement is Mariental. There is little here to hold your attention but it's a useful stop for provisions, petrol and maybe a coffee at the Wimpy for weary drivers. A much more worthy attraction nearby is the Hardap Dam, which has some interesting birds and animals that can be spotted on the dam's attractive shores. From here you can either head south to Brukkaros Volcano, close to the old Nama settlement at Berseba, or southwest to the quaint, rural villages of Maltahöhe and Helmeringhausen on the edge of the Namib Desert. Also in this region is the German built Duwisib Castle, worth a stop to see what is a rather incredulous location for a sandstone fortress. If you have no pressing need to go to Keetmanshoop, this western route is a pleasant alternative between Mariental and both Lüderitz and the Fish River Canyon. » *For Sleeping, Eating and other listings, see pages 307-310.*

Mariental

» pp307-310. Colour map 3, A4.

Mariental is a small, quietly flourishing market town in the heart of southern Namibia and is the administrative centre of the Hardap Region. The nearby Hardap Dam is the largest reservoir in Namibia and provides water for irrigation, making it possible to cultivate animal fodder, as well as some fruit and vegetables. Nevertheless, Mariental is not the most exciting place in Namibia and is windswept and dusty in spring and autumn, ferociously hot in summer and bitterly cold in winter.

Mariental is home to a large number of Nama-speaking people, descendants of the early Khoi inhabitants of Namibia.

Mariental was officially founded in 1920 following the construction of Namibia's first Dutch Reform Church, however it was well known to the early Nama inhabitants who referred to the place as *Zaragaeiba* meaning 'dusty'. The present name is derived from 'Marie's Valley', bestowed upon the settlement by the first white settler, Herman Brandt, in honour of his wife. Following some rather turbulent early years during the anti-German war of 1904 to 1907 and the arrival of the railway in 1912, Mariental settled down to life as a quiet *dorp* in the middle of the veld.

Hardap Dam

» pp307-310. Colour map 3, A4.

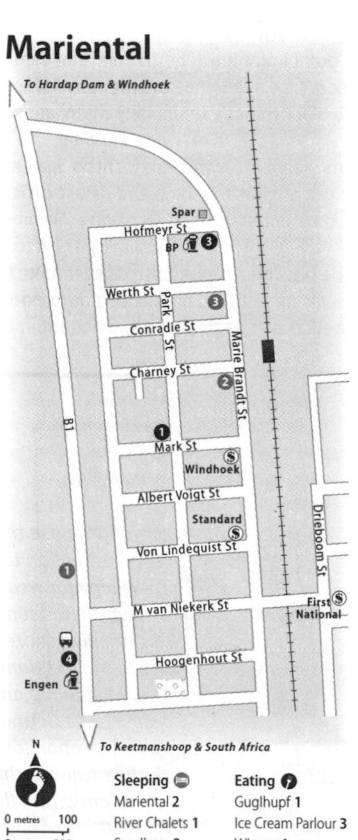

Gates are open from 0600-2300; day visitors are permitted sunrise-1800, later if dining, entrance fee US$5.90 per adult, children under 16 free, US$1.50 per car. The Hardap Dam was first proposed in 1897 by German geologist Dr Theodor Rehbock but it took a number of surveys and a further 63 years before construction began on what is now Namibia's largest dam. The 252-sq-km game reserve that surrounds the dam was later proclaimed in 1968. The name Hardap derives from the Nama word meaning 'nipple' or 'wart', which is how the surrounding area of low conical-shaped hills appeared to the early inhabitants. The resort is off the B1, 15 km north of Mariental. Follow the road 6 km to the resort entrance.

The dam has a surface area of 25 sq km, is the largest dam in Namibia and has a number of functions. It provides water to irrigate 2500 ha of wheat, maize, lucerne, cotton, grapes and vegetables, all cultivated on small holdings. It also provides Mariental with its water and acts as a flood-prevention mechanism, needed in 1997 and 2000, the first years of very heavy rainfall since construction.

As a bonus, the dam is an anglers' paradise, being well stocked with species such as yellowfish, carp, mullet and catfish, and the resort is a popular weekend getaway for people living in the area. There are commanding 180° views from the glass-walled restaurant which has been built on the cliffs by the northern edge of the dam.

Hardap Dam Recreation Resort

The resort is open year round, but experiences very high (35°C+) daytime temperatures in summer (December to March) and very cold (0°C) night-time temperatures in winter (June to July), so these may not be the best times to visit. Accommodation can be booked through **Namibia Wildlife Resorts** in Windhoek (see Sleeping, page 307). The resort has a good, reasonably priced restaurant with panoramic views of the lake, filling station and shop (closes 1800), conference centre, four tennis courts and 25-m swimming pool.

Hardap Dam Game Reserve

Wildlife Geographically, the park is divided into two sections, both of which can be accessed for game drives. A small 1848-ha section is located near the resort along the northern edge of the dam, and this is where the resident population of four **black rhino** lives. These are Namibia's southernmost black rhinos, having been introduced from Damaraland in 1990, though they are seldom seen. In the larger section of the park to the south of the dam is a 15-km game drive. Upon proclamation as a game park, the area was restocked with antelopes, such as kudu, gemsbok, eland, red hartebeest and springbok, and mountain zebra. Leopards, too, have been spotted in the area of the Great Komatsas River.

Angling There are fishing spots at various points along the northern shore of the lake. Permits and a map of permitted fishing spots are available from the resort office. Anglers are advised to watch out for the park's black rhinos, particularly when you get out of your vehicle.

There is a private concession for a ferry service on the lake; **Oasis Ferries**, T063-240805, T081-2494200 (mob), encourages anglers to 'come and catch the big one' from the boat. Follow the signs near the park entrance.

Birdwatching A large number of birds can be observed around the dam, thanks to the diverse habitats on offer. Water birds, such as pelican, cormorant, darter and spoonbill, can be seen on the lake itself, as well as fish eagle and a small number of

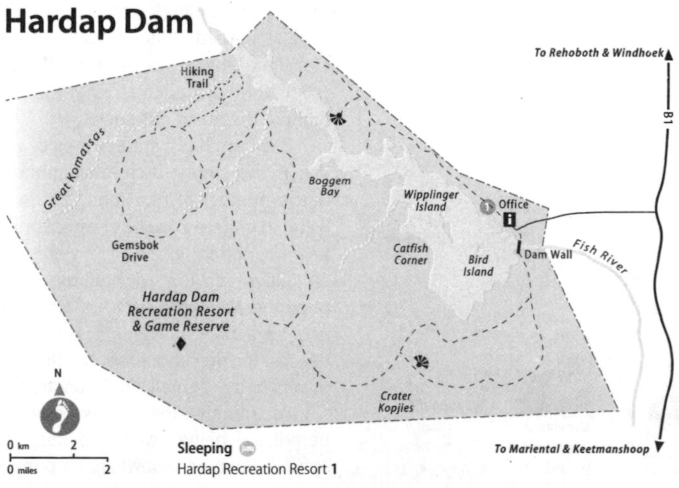

osprey. The reed beds below the dam wall support large numbers of herons and between April and October are home to white dwarf bitterns. Following the roads through the park, there is a good chance of seeing ostrich, kori bustard and the ubiquitous Namaqua sandgrouse.

260 species of bird have been identified here, 20% of which are water birds including pelicans and greater flamingos.

Hiking There is a newly marked 5-km hiking trail in the northwestern corner of the park, which takes roughly two hours to complete. Vegetation along the route consists of dwarf shrub savannah such as shepherd's tree, stink bush, wool bush and brittle thorn, with camelthorn and buffalo thorn found growing in the dry river courses. As the trail passes by the banks of the Great Komatsas River, the ruins of the country's first school for whites can be seen. Shortly after, there is a spring surrounded by shady trees, making a good place to sit down, have a picnic and a break. As with all hiking in Namibia, it is important to take along a minimum of 2 litres of water per person.

Note Hikers should watch out for black rhino along the route, especially when passing through patches of dense vegetation. Should the need arise, standard advice is not to panic and to try to get up a tree or large boulder. Failing that, face any charge and step aside at the last moment. Being virtually blind, the rhino should sail on past!

East of Mariental – Stampriet and Gochas

Colour map 3, A4.

Some 10 km north of Mariental, the C20 heads east into the Kalahari Desert towards the small cattle town of **Aranos**. En route it passes **Stampriet**, a small settlement where thanks to artesian water flowing in from the Kalahari, fruit and vegetables are cultivated. At Stampriet, the C15 heads south along the Auob River towards Gochas. Along this route lie a number of battle sites and memorials dating back to the 1904-1907 war of resistance against the Germans.

South of Stampriet, 20 km along the C15, is the farm **Gross Nabas**, the sight of one of the bloodiest battles of the war. A small monument on the main road commemorates the battle of 2-4 January 1905, during which the Witbooi Nama inflicted heavy losses on the German forces. Another monument, a further 24 km on, indicates where a German patrol was ambushed and killed in March of that year. **Gochas** is a desolate place and lives in hope of a reopening of the Mata Mata border gate into South Africa's Kagaligadi Transfrontier Park which spans the Botswana/South Africa border) for an upturn in its fortunes. There is a 24-hour petrol station, general store, grubby hotel and cemetery with numerous German graves from the early 1900s.

Mariental to Keetmanshoop

Mukurob *Phone code: 063. Colour map 3, B4.*

Close to the settlement of **Asab**, 100 km south of Mariental, lies what was one of Namibia's best-known landmarks. A 34-m pinnacle of rock used to balance precariously on a narrow neck and base of shale; it was known in English as the 'finger of God' and in Afrikaans as the **Vingerklip**. The part sandstone, part conglomerate rock survived the erosion of the Weissrand Plateau to the east, but tumbled from its perch in 1988 as a result of seismic tremors experienced after the Armenian earthquake of 7 December. To get there from Asab on the B1, turn onto the D1066 and follow for 12 km. Turn right onto D620 and continue for a further 10 km.

Brukkaros Volcano ›› Colour map 3, B4.

ⓘ *US$2.40 per person and US$1.50 per car.*

This mountain dominates the skyline to the west of the main road between Mariental and Keetmanshoop. A climb to the top is well rewarded with superb views of the surrounding plains. The name Brukkaros is the German equivalent of the Nama name *Geitsigubeb*, referring to the mountain's supposed resemblance to the large leather apron traditionally worn by Nama women around their waist.

Brukkaros, whose evolution began 80 million years ago, was formed when molten lava intruded into rocks about 1 km below the earth's surface. The lava must have encountered underground water, creating steam which caused huge pressure, raising the overlying rocks into a dome 400 m high and 10 km across. The process was then repeated, but the cover of overlying rock was thin enough to be blown out in a vast explosion. Sedimentation and erosion over several hundred thousand years created the crater floor; simply put, rain washed the finely shattered rock fragments into the crater, which is roughly 2 km across.

In 1930, the American Smithsonian Institute declared the mountain the perfect site to establish a research station to study the surface of the sun, thanks to the incredibly clear desert air. While the observatory has not functioned for years, this point on the northwestern rim of the crater is an ideal place to take in the view over the surrounding plains. The Germans established a heliograph on the eastern rim around 1900. There is a functional VHF radio mast on the rim.

To reach the volcano, turn off the B1 at Tses, 80 km north of Keetmanshoop, follow the C98 for 40 km towards Berseba, then take the D3904 north for 18 km to Brukkaros. The D3904 reaches a gate at the foot of the volcano, where the entry charge is levied. There is a payphone here. Visitors with 4WD vehicles (with good clearance) will be able to drive a further 3 km up to the simple but beautifully located community campsite right on the slopes of the volcano (see Sleeping, page 308).

For those based in Keetmanshoop, set off early in the morning; avoid hiking in the heat of the day in summer. If you plan on looking in on en route between Windhoek and Keetmanshoop be prepared for an early start and a long day.

Hiking the volcano Hikers have a moderate 4-km walk from the parking area to the crater lip. From here the path, such as it is, leads down into the crater and across a dried riverbed, past a number of ancient quiver trees before starting the climb to the radio mast on the northern rim of the crater. There are still signs of the scientists' stay at the volcano – ancient rusting tins, a few old bottles and some graffiti etched into the trunks of the quiver trees. It's all fairly awesome and eerie. At any moment one expects a hungry creature from a Hollywood B-movie to come crawling over the lip of the volcano and gobble you up. The walk itself is not very tough, but there is no water and no shade on the mountain, so it is absolutely essential to take at least 2 litres of water per person.

Keetmanshoop via Maltahöhe ›› pp307-310.

Just south of Mariental on the B1, the tarred C19 crosses the Fish River, and heads west towards the small town of Maltahöhe, on the edge of the Namib Desert, 110 km away. From Maltahöhe there is a choice of roads: west through the spectacular Tsarishoogte Pass before descending into the Namib Desert and on to Sesriem and Sossusvlei; or south past Duwisib Castle and the Schwartzberge, through the hamlet of Helmeringhausen to Bethanie, Keetmanshoop and Lüderitz. The clear desert air and the absolute emptiness of the landscape make this part of southern Namibia well worth the effort of driving through for those with the time and inclination to prolong their journey. Once you have spotted a nice view, stop and turn off the car engine and drink it all in; this is surely one of the reasons you came.

Maltahöhe ›› *Phone code: 063. Colour map 3, A3.*

The small town of Maltahöhe, situated on the edge of the Namib Desert, was founded in 1900 and owes its name to Malta von Burgdorff, wife of the German commander of the Gibeon garrison. The town was once an important agricultural centre; the nearby farm **Nomtsas** was established as a sheep farm of some 100,000 ha by the turn of the century. Later, Maltahöhe became the centre of the karakul trade, but years of drought and the collapse of karakul prices brought hard times to the town. Many of the white commercial farmers were forced to sell up and leave, and the resulting loss of revenue killed off many of the businesses in town. While Maltahöhe does have a hotel, the town is now a run-down and faded reminder of its former self. The area around the town is spectacular, encompassing the Tsaris, Namgorab and Nubub mountain ranges that border the central highland plateau and there are many game farms in the region.

Duwisib Castle ›› *Phone code: 063. Colour map 3, B2.*

ⓘ *Open year round 0800-1700, with cafeteria and small curio shop, US$6.50 adults, children under 16 free, car US$1.50.*

Duwisib Castle, a reminder of Namibia's colonial past, is situated in an improbable location in the rugged, dry veld on the edge of the Namib Desert southwest of Maltahöhe. Designed by the architect Willi Sander who was also responsible for Windhoek's three hilltop castles, Duwisib was commissioned in 1907 by Hansheinrich von Wolf and his wife Jayta, an American heiress. Von Wolf had arrived in Namibia in 1904 to serve in the Schutztruppe as a captain in command of a regiment. It was during this time that he became interested in the area around Maltahöhe. In 1906 he resigned his commission and returned to Germany where he met Jayta. The two were married in April 1907 after which they arrived to settle in Namibia, buying Farm Duwisib from the Treasury.

The castle took two years to build, a remarkably short time considering that many of the building materials were imported from Europe via Lüderitz, from where they were hauled by ox wagon across the Namib Desert. Herero workers were employed to quarry stone from a nearby site; Italian stonemasons were brought from Italy to finish off the stone and actually build the castle; and carpenters from Germany, Sweden and Belgium were responsible for the woodwork.

Von Wolf and his wife soon became known as the Baron and Baroness by the local German and Afrikaner farmers in recognition of the lavish lifestyle they enjoyed. The von Wolfs employed seven Europeans to assist in managing the castle and the business. 'Baron' von Wolf bred horses from imported Australian and British stock and some people believe that the wild horses of the Namib seen today in the Aus area are survivors of his original stud. He also imported Hereford bulls from England and wool sheep from the Cape.

In 1914, just before the outbreak of the First World War, the von Wolfs left for England to buy further stock for their stud. During the voyage war broke out and the boat they were travelling on was forced to seek shelter in Argentina where they were interned. Released a few months later, von Wolf was determined to join the German forces, which he succeeded in doing, only to fall at the Battle of the Somme in September 1916. Jayta never returned to Namibia to reclaim her property or to sell the farm, and died in New Jersey in 1946 at the age of 64. The farm itself was bought and sold twice before eventually, in 1979, the then colonial administration of South West Africa bought the castle with the intention of preserving it as a heritage site.

The castle has elements of both Gothic and Renaissance architecture. In addition there is a collection of antique European furniture on display, as well as old armour, paintings, photographs and copperplate engravings. The courtyard at the rear has an ornamental fountain and a pair of large jacaranda trees, which provide shade during the heat of the day and, when in flower (September-October), fill the courtyard with their scent.

To get to Duwisib Castle from either Maltahöhe or Helmeringhausen, take the C14, then the D831 before turning onto the D826. The roads are rough, but manageable and the route is well signposted from the rutted main roads (drive with extra care), but then poorly signposted; once in the grounds, take the turning away from the campsite.

Helmeringhausen » *Phone code: 063. Colour map 3, B3.*

This small settlement lies 120 km south of Maltahöhe on the gravel C14, en route for Bethanie, Aus and Lüderitz. There is a petrol station (Monday-Saturday 0800-1800), a

The South

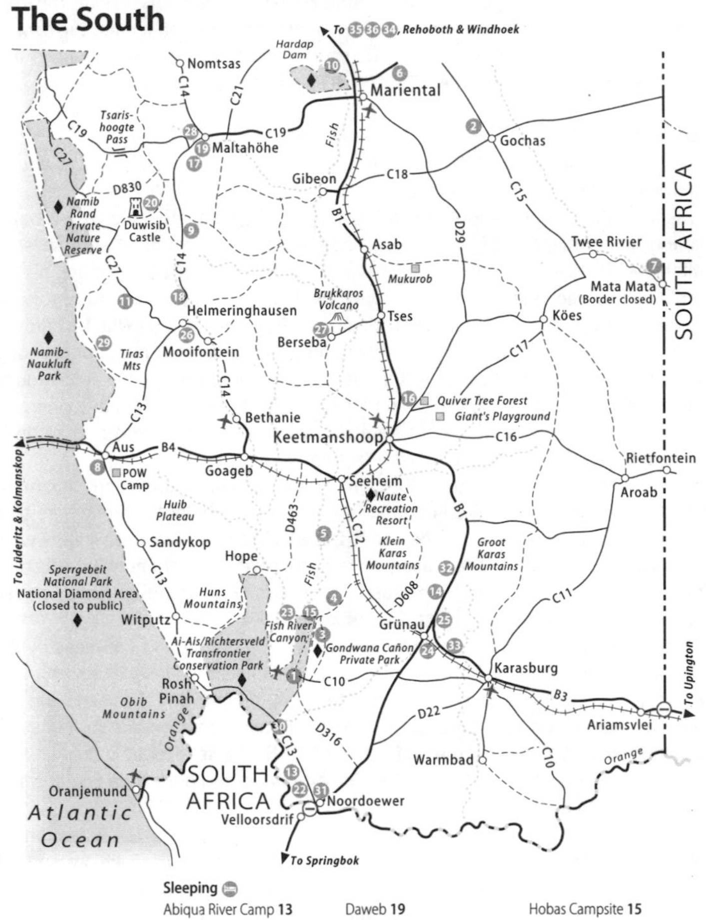

Sleeping

Abiqua River Camp **13**
Ai-Ais Hot Springs Resort **1**
Anib Lodge **34**
Auob Country Lodge **2**
Bagatelle Kalahari Game Ranch **35**
Bitterwasser Flying Centre & Lodge **36**
Brukkaros Campsite **27**
Burgsdorf **17**
Cañon Lodge **3**
Cañon Mountain Camp **3**
Cañon Roadhouse **4**
Cañon Village **3**
Dabis Guest Farm **18**
Daweb **19**
Duwisib Castle Camping **20**
Farm Duwisib Guest House **20**
Felix Unite Cabanas **22**
Fish River Guest Farm (closed for renovation) **5**
Grande View Lodge **23**
Grünau Country House **24**
Grünau Motors Chalet & Caravan Park **25**
Hardap Recreation Resort **10**
Helmeringhausen & Guest Farm **26**
Hobas Campsite **15**
Intu Afrika Kalahari Game Reserve **6**
Kalahari Game Lodge **7**
Klein-Aus Vista **8**
La Vallée Tranquille **9**
Namseb Game Lodge **28**
Namtib Desert Lodge **29**
Norotshama River Resort **30**
Orange River Lodge **31**
Quivertree Forest Camp **16**
Savanna Guest Farm **32**
Sinclair Guest Farm **11**
Vastrap Guest Farm **33**
White House **14**

N

0 km 30
0 miles 30

general store, bottle store and small hotel. It is worth visiting the **Agricultural Museum** to look at the old farming implements, an old fire engine used at Lüderitz and one of the ox wagons used to transfer building materials and furniture from the coast to Duwisib Castle. The key is available from the hotel next door.

Farm Mooifontesin, 19 km south of Helmeringhausen on the C14, was the site of a German military station during the colonial period. The bodies of German soldiers who died while fighting the Nama lie in the graveyard, which contains a memorial in the form of a chapel. The iron gates were forged from the rims of ox-wagon wheels.

The area around the C13/D707 junction is the newly declared **Tiras Mountains Conservancy**, a collection of farms that offer a range of 'back to nature' experiences, principally walking in their remote region. Hikes from their farms take you into dune and mountainscapes that are unimaginable from the dusty roadside, with walks to and through rock art, succulents, quiver trees, plus bird and game viewing. Worth a couple of days in your agenda, as an introduction to Namibia's outback.

Sleeping

Mariental *p301, map p301*

C **Mariental Hotel**, Marie Brandt St, T063-242466/7, mnhotel@iafrican.com.na. The most comfortable place to stay in town, with 18 en suite rooms with a/c and phone, there is a small swimming pool with thatched braai, lapa, gym and secure off-street parking. The restaurant is light and airy, if a little more expensive than average. 2 bars to choose from (lively at weekends), pool table, fruit machines.

C-D **Sandberg Hotel**, Marie Brandt St, T063-242291, F240738. Reasonable option with en suite rooms with a/c and phone, though not as good quality as the Mariental. 14 rooms, an unremarkable restaurant, a bar with a seedy atmosphere and occasionally the lively Basement Disco. Mediocre but worth considering if the other places are full.

C-E **River Chalets**, T063-240515, garbers@iway.na. 6 smart en suite self-catering chalets painted in pastel colours with 2-5 beds with a/c and DSTV, patio with *braai* facilities, shaded parking, also camping sites with ablution block, swimming pool, next to the Engen garage and Wimpy on the B1, walking distance from town (though there's not much there to warrant the effort). The only downside is that, despite being behind a fence, the chalets are a little exposed next to the main road.

Hardap Dam *p301, map p302*

A-C **Hardap Recreation Resort**, T063-240381, or through Namibia Wildlife Resorts, T061-2857200 (Windhoek). A large resort with over 50 bungalows. Accommodation ranges from fully equipped 5-bed, self-catering bungalows with crockery and cutlery, 2-bed bungalows with use of field-kitchen cooking facilities, to a 12-bed dormitory that must be taken as 1 unit with shared ablutions and camp kitchen. All units have a/c or ceiling fans. Camping and caravan sites (D) with shared ablution blocks and cooking facilities. Restaurant (open 0700-0900, 1200-1400 and 1800-2100), petrol, kiosk and swimming pool.

Game ranches and lodges

A **Bagatelle Kalahari Game Ranch**, 50 km north from Mariental, take the C20 and then left on the D1268, T063-240982, www.bagatelle-kalahari-gameranch.com. 4 wooden chalets perched on stilts on bright red dunes with expansive views of the Kalahari, or 6 bungalows in the valley below rather unusually made from hay bales, nicely decorated, the bathrooms in the chalets have claw-foot baths and open windows, swimming pool, bar, dining room and library are at a converted farmhouse, there are 100 videos on African wildlife to watch, and 3 cheetah in a spacious enclosure, nature drives and sundowners in the dunes are available.

B **Anib Lodge**, turn off the B1 10 km north of Mariental onto the C20, follow for 24 km, well signposted, T063-240529, www.anib lodge.com. Has 6 luxurious en suite rooms next to the farmhouse, swimming pool set in

For an explanation of the sleeping and eating price codes used in this guide, see inside the front cover. Other relevant information is found in Essentials, see pages 43-51.

a small lush garden, friendly service and wholesome German home-cooking, curio shop, game drives and birdwatching although not a stocked game farm, all inclusive. You can also **camp** (**D**) here for US$15 per person and each camping site has its own ablution block. **Note** At the time of writing this lodge had just been taken over; renovation is expected, as is a new name, possibly **Namib Desert Lodge**.

B **Auob Country Lodge**, 6 km north of Gochas on the C15, central reservations, T061-374750 (Windhoek), www.namibialodges.com. (**Note** Drive carefully on the C15, it undulates and oncoming traffic can give you a surprise). It is is worth travelling especially to Gochas just to stay at this country lodge situated on the banks of the dry Auob River. It has 52 en suite rooms, swimming pool with outdoor courtyard, squash court, bar, restaurant, horse riding and game drives (to view antelope, giraffe and zebra). It offers excellent deals in the low season – be sure to book ahead, you really don't want to stay in the **Gochas Hotel**.

B **Kalahari Game Lodge**, C15 near the border with Botswana, approximately 100 km to the east of Koes, T/F063-693105, kgl@africaonline.com.na. 8 en suite A-frame chalets, self-catering available or choose full- board rates, plus permanent tents on platforms with shared ablution block, restaurant, bar, shop, swimming pool, petrol. Offers good game viewing, birdwatching, horse riding and hiking trails. Situated on the 27,000-ha **Sandheuwel Game Ranch** neighbouring the Kgalagadi Transfrontier Park over the border in Botswana. The gate at Mata Mata remains closed by red tape, but the game is fairly plentiful on the farm in any case.

Brukkaros Volcano *p304*

E **Brukkaros Campsite**, in a stunning spot on the slopes of Brukkaros Volcano, 80 km northwest of Keetmanshoop, at Tses turn-off the B1 on to the D3901 to Berseba. After about 30 km a signpost saying 'Brukkaros' directs you to the right. From there it is another 8 km to the campsite. This is a NACOBTA project (see box, page 41), T063-257188, T081-2696150. 5 individual campsites, 2 are situated at the foot of the mountain, while the other 3 are higher up on the slope and can only be reached with a 4WD. Each is shaded and has a wind shelter, fireplace, bush shower and toilet. As there is no running water at the mountain, you need to bring all water for drinking, cooking and showering. Here you will be well rewarded with fantastic views of the night sky, particularly around the new moon.

Maltahöhe *p305*

B **Atelier du Désert Guest House**, opposite the petrol station, T063-293304, www.natron.net/genevieve. 5 en suite doubles, a tastefully decorated, more intimate addition to the town's limited offering. Breakfast included, dinner by arrangement. Also sells some pottery and silk paintings by local artists, French spoken as well as English and German.

C **Maltahöhe Hotel**, if coming from Mariental on the C19, turn left at the first stop sign and the hotel is on the right, T063-293013, www.maltahoehe-hotel.com. Established in 1907, this is the main place to stay in town, a regular HAN award winner, well run if a little smug, with 26 simple en suite rooms with fans and phone, swimming pool, shaded garden. The restaurant serves good-value, tasty, home-cooked food and the bar is the only place in town to sit and relax in the evening. Nice enough, but you are better off in one of the many fabulous guest farms in the region (see below).

D **Pappot Rest Camp**, if coming from Mariental on the C19, go over the 1st stop sign and the rest camp is the penultimate plot on the right-hand side, T063-293091, pappot@mweb.com.na. 3 simple bungalows and a **campsite** (**E**) with *braai* pits and electricity. It also serves as the town's bakery, grocery shop and tourist information office, and can organize meals in advance.

Guest farms

A **Daweb**, 2 km south of town on the C14, T/F063-293088, www.natron.net/tour/daweb. 6 comfortable en suite rooms, a working farm since 1896, it offers farm tours, where blesbok, kudu, oryx and springbok share the 18,000 ha grazing with the cattle, and good bird-watching. Available full board or self-catering, nice communal *braai* area. There's **camping** (**E**) with clean ablutions and water.

A **La Vallée Tranquille**, 60 km south of Maltahöhe on the C14, T/F063-293508, valleet@iway.na. Run by pleasant French owner with 9 en suite doubles, good food and tasteful decor, swimming pool, price is for half board, discounts in low season, activities include nature walks and ostrich feeding. Actively promoting the local community's interest in tourism by employing local Nama people who spend time with the guests and demonstrate their culture and environment.

B **Burgsdorf**, 16 km south of Maltahöhe on the C14, then a further 10 km along their bumpy farm track, T/F063-293200, burgsdorf@mweb.com.na. 9 en suite rooms located in an old police station, pretty courtyard with succulents and orange trees, large swimming pool, game drives and walks to animal viewing hide, sundowner drive, internet access.

Duwisib Castle *p305*

B Farm Duwisib Guest House, located beside the castle, reservations T063-293344, duwisib@iway.na. 4 en suite doubles in the main building, 2-bed, 4-bed and 6-bed bungalows with self-catering facilities, swimming pool and landing strip. Full board can be arranged and the food is good home-cooked fare, day visitors and campers can also get tea and coffee, cold drinks and treats such as apple pie at the kiosk here.

E Duwisib Castle Camping, by the entrance to the grounds of the castle, T06638, ask for 5303, reservations also through **Namibia Wildlife Resorts**, T061-2857200 (Windhoek), www.nwr.com.na. 10 large and pleasant pitches under huge camelthorn trees with *braai* pit, water, but no electricity and dingy ablution facilities with haphazard hot water.

Guest farms

A-C Namseb Game Lodge, 17 km from Maltahöhe, take D36 northeast and follow the signs, T063-293166, eden@mweb.com.na. Accommodation in either attractive, square, brick bungalows with self-catering facilities or in 16 en suite double rooms on this working ostrich farm, swimming pool, à la carte restaurant and farm drives.

Helmeringhausen *p306*

B Helmeringhausen Hotel and Guest Farm, at the crossroads, T063-283083, www.helmeringhausen.com. Small, friendly country hotel with 22 newly refurbished en suite rooms, dining room, bar, beer garden with *braai* area, swimming pool, rates are B&B and good and cheap dinners are available. Hotel owner arranges tours to local places of interest.

Guest farms

Note that the local party telephone numbers are likely to change soon.

AL Dabis Guest Farm, 10 km north of Helmeringhausen on C14, T0638, ask for 6362, also reservations T061-232300, (Windhoek), photographer@mweb.com.na. 7 en suite rooms, functional but nothing special, fresh farm food on this working farm, hiking, game viewing, rates are all inclusive and there is the opportunity to learn about the working sheep farm from friendly and informative Jo and Heidi Gaugler; but still expensive for what you get.

A Namtib Desert Lodge, signposted off the D707, northwest of the C13 junction, T0638 ask for 6640, reservations also T061-233597, www.namtib.com. Located on the 16,400-ha Namtib Biosphere Reserve in the Tiras Mountains, about halfway between Lüderitz and Sesriem. Has 5 en suite chalets, very welcoming owners, game drives, hiking trails, horse riding. **Little Hunters Rest** (**E**) is a campsite on the property with 5 sites, simple facilities.

A Sinclair Guest Farm, D407 northwest out of Helmeringhausen for 50 km and follow the signs to the farm, T06362 ask for 6503, reservations, Windhoek T061-226979, www.natron.net/tour/sinclair/sinclair.htm. One of the oldest guest farms in Namibia, 5 en suite doubles, restaurant, bar, game drives, hiking, landing strip and flights over the desert can be arranged. A nearby abandoned copper mine makes for an interesting excursion for the geologically inclined, all inclusive, caters mostly to German guests.

Eating

Mariental *p301, map p301*

For provisions and takeaways pop into the surprisingly large **Spar** supermarket which also has a bottle shop, just off the B1 north of town. Next door at the **BP** petrol station is an ice cream parlour and takeaway shop.

Guglhupf Café & Restaurant. Popular with locals, with tasty, filling, steaks, schnitzel and ribs washed down by local draught beer, reasonably priced, your best bet, though located in a characterless, windowless, yellow building.

Mariental Hotel, see Sleeping, above. Standard fare in decent dining room, plenty of meat, bar, adequate and filling.

Wimpy, at the large Engen garage on the B1 just south of town (telephone, toilets, ATM and shop available), spotlessly clean, as mentioned elsewhere in this book, Wimpys in southern Africa are not too bad, many local people eat here, service is good and although predictable, food tends to look like the pictures on the menu, breakfasts and Wimpy mega-coffee are recommended. Open daily until mid-evening, so you can still do steak, egg and chips or a burger as an early evening meal.

Transport

Mariental *p301, map p301*
264 km to Windhoek, 228 km to Keetmanshoop.

Bus For Intercape coaches to **Cape Town**, **Keetmanshoop**, **Upington** and **Windhoek**, see timetable on page 70. Transnamib Starline Passenger Services, central reservations T061-2982032, www.transnamib.com.na, has 1 bus that goes between Mariental and **Maltahöhe** that takes 2 hrs. It departs from Mariental at 0800, arrives in Maltahöhe at about 1000, departs again at 1300 and arrives back in Mariental at 1500.

Train For trains to **Keetmanshoop** and **Windhoek**, see timetable on page 68. The station dominates the middle of town.

Directory

Mariental *p301, map p301*

Banks Bank Windhoek and Standard Bank are both found on Marie Brandt St. First National Bank is on Drieboom St. All 3 have ATMs and money-changing facilities. **Medical services** State Hospital, T063-242092. **Police** T063-10111, Ernest Stumpfe St. **Post** Khoicas St, Mon-Fri 0800-1630, Sat 0800-1130. **Telephone** (international) next door to the post office.

Maltahöhe *p305*
There are 2, 24-hr garages, payphones, a post office, police station, excellent butcher's, bottle stores, takeaways and a Standard Bank and a First National Bank, with ATMs – all are located on or just off the main street. You may have to use your wits, as every sign appears to point in the wrong direction.

Keetmanshoop and around

Keetmanshoop lies at the crossroads of southern Namibia and is principally a transit stop to and from South Africa, with a wide range of relatively pricey accommodation. However, it is also a convenient base from which to explore the 'deep' south, in particular the Fish River Canyon and the nearby Quiver Tree Forest. *»» For Sleeping, Eating and other listings, see pages 316-318.*

Ins and outs

Getting there The B1 from Mariental and Windhoek is a fairly dull straight run. You will see Brukkaros Volcano to the west and a long, low ridge to the east, atop which is the **Commonwealth War Graves** (on the C18, signposted, quite far out of your way unless you have a specific interest). Heading south, you pass the village of **Asab** (24-hour Shell garage, bottle store, shop and truckers hotel), a signposted turn-off for **Iganigobes Hot Springs**, **Quiver Tree Forest** and camping (all very basic and fairly run down), and the village of **Tses** (Caltex garage open 0700-2000); turn here for Berseba and Brukkaros. The B1 continues for a further 160 km to Grünau where it branches into the B3 heading east through Karasburg to the South African border at **Ariamsvlei**. The B1 itself reaches the South African border at **Noordoewer** after 142 km. From Keetmanshoop, the B4 heads west towards the Aus Mountains before descending to the desert floor, eventually arriving at the old German seaside town of Lüderitz 350 km away.

Tourist office Southern Tourist Forum ⓘ *corner of Fenchel St and 5th Av, T063-221166, munkhoop@iafrica.com.na, Mon-Fri 0730-1630,* has a miniature replica of the toppled Vingerklip (see page 186) in the office; very helpful for information and arrangements for travel and accommodation in the south.

History

Keetmanshoop is effectively the capital of the south and one of the oldest-established towns in Namibia. The settlement, dating back to the late 18th century, was originally known as **Modderfontein** due to the presence of a strong freshwater spring. Nama herders trekking north from the Cape settled here, calling the place **Swartmodder**, after the muddy river which ran through the settlement after good rains.

During the middle part of the 19th century, the Barmen Society gradually established a series of mission stations in the south of Namibia at places such as Bethanie, Warmbad and Berseba. In 1866, following a request by converted Namas living at Swartmodder, Johan Schröder was sent by Reverend Krönlein, the pastor at Berseba, to establish a mission station at Swartmodder. After struggling to build a church and home for himself and his family, Schröder appealed to the Barmen Society for funds to develop the station. Johan Keetman, a rich industrialist and Chairman of the Barmen Society, personally donated 2000 marks to pay for the building of a church, and in appreciation Schröder renamed the settlement Keetmanshoop (Keetman's Hope).

Like many other settlements in Namibia at the time, Keetmanshoop functioned both as a mission station and as a trading post. A successor to Schröder, Reverend Thomas Fenchel, came into conflict with the European traders who bartered liquor,

Sleeping
Bird's Mansions **1**
Bird's Nest Guest House **2**
Canyon **3**
Central Lodge **4**
Gessert's Guest House **6**
Lafenis Lodge **8**
La Rochelle **7**
Municipal Campsite & Caravan Park **5**

Eating
Balaton **2**
Bullring & Sports Bar **5**
Lara's **5**

 usually brandy, with the Nama herders in exchange for livestock which was then sold in the Cape. Once the liquor was drunk the only source of food for the herders was the mission station.

In 1890, a freak flooding of the Swartmodder River washed away the original church, but Fenchel and his congregation had rebuilt it by 1895 from when it served a multiracial congregation until 1930. Abandoned for many years, the church was restored and declared a National Monument in 1978 and today houses the Keetmanshoop Museum.

The year 1890 also saw a wave of German immigrants to the new colony and particularly to this area, and in 1894 a fort was established in the town. In the following years as soldiers were discharged from the army, many bought farms or settled in the town which grew to support the surrounding farms. The growth of the town convinced the authorities of the necessity of improving communications, and the railway to Lüderitz was completed in 1908. In the following year the military handed over the town to a civil authority and Keetmanshoop became the administrative centre for the south of the country.

Economically, the town's prosperity was built upon the karakul sheep industry which reached its peak in the early 1970s; since the decline of the industry (see box opposite) Keetmanshoop has earned its keep more mundanely as a transit point for goods and people travelling between Namibia and South Africa.

Keetmanshoop ›› *Phone code: 063. Colour map 3, B4.*

The old Rhenish Mission Church on Kaiser Street now houses **Keetmanshoop Museum** ⓘ *T063-221256, Mon-Thu 0730-1630, Fri 0730-1600, no entry fee but donations are welcomed*. It was built in 1890 on the site of the previous mission that was washed away during floods. For many years it was left neglected because of the Group Areas Act that forced most of the congregation to live in other regions away from Keetmanshoop. But it was reopened as a museum and declared a National Monument in 1978. The displays focus on the history of the town, information on the surrounding area and a small art exhibition. Outside, by the rock garden of aloes, succulents and cacti, a traditional Nama hut stands cheek by jowl with early trekkers' wagons. The stone church itself is a fine example of early colonial architecture, with its original corrugated-iron roof and bell tower with weathervane, and inside there is an elegant pulpit and wooden balcony. The church looks particularly attractive at night when it is floodlit.

The former post and telegraph office, the **Kaiserliches Poststamp**, designed by government architect, Gottlieb Redecker, and built in 1910, is another of Keetmanshoop's fine early buildings. The building now houses the useful **Southern Tourist Forum**.

Naute Recreation Resort ›› *Colour map 3, B4.*

Located on the Lowen River, surrounded by a series of small conical hills, the focal point of the recreation resort is the **Naute Dam** which is Namibia's third largest dam and a lovely spot to escape the heat of the surrounding sandy hills. It is surrounded by flat-topped ridges and large rust-coloured boulders. The dam provides Keetmanshoop with all its water, in addition to providing water for some small-scale irrigation. Visitors are few and far between though it does attract a few freshwater anglers.

Birdwatchers will find colonies of pelicans, cormorants, darters, Egyptian geese and other water birds on the reservoir. There are no specific **hiking trails** laid out, but it is quite possible to walk around the dam. There is a variety of game in the vicinity, as the animal spores on the sand dunes testify, and kudu, springbok, ostrich and other small animals may be spotted. There is a 10-km 'nature drive' that can be followed, but there are no other facilities here except for rudimentary picnic sites.

Karakul sheep

The use of karakul sheep pelts to make high-quality leather and fur clothes, formed the backbone of the farming industry in southern Namibia from the early 1920s to the mid-1970s. Often called Namibia's 'black gold' the karakul sheep originated in Bokhara in central Asia, from where they were imported to Germany in the early 1900s.

Experimental breeding started in Germany in 1903 and Paul Thorer, a prominent fur trader, started promoting the idea of exporting the sheep to German colonies. The then Governor of German South West Africa, Von Lindequist, supported the idea, and the first dozen sheep were brought into the country in 1907. In 1909 a further consignment of 22 rams and 252 ewes arrived, followed by smaller numbers of the animals in the years leading up to the First World War. After the end of the war an experimental government karakul farm was set up at Neudam near Windhoek, in order to develop and improve the quality of the pelts. Breeders succeeded in developing pure white pelts in addition to the more normal black and grey ones, and although the former Soviet Union and Afghanistan produced larger numbers of the pelts, Namibian karakul fur was internationally recognized as being of the finest quality.

In 1919 the Karakul Breeders Association was founded to consolidate this new industry, and by 1923 thousands of the pelts were being exported to Germany. Over the next 50 years the numbers of pelts exported each year mushroomed to a peak of 3.2 million in 1973, earning millions of dollars for the farmers of the south. However, a combination of severe drought and changing views in Europe during the 1970s about the ethics of slaughtering millions of lambs only 24 hours old for their pelts, sent the karakul fur industry into decline.

In response to this most farmers in the south switched to breeding dorbber sheep for their meat which guarantees a more reliable source of income, not affected by swings in the fashion industry. However, the recent extreme drought in Namibia has forced many farmers to sell all their livestock, creating a severe economic crisis in the farming industry of the south. Ironically however there has been a revival in the price of karakul pelts and demand for karakul wool in order to make carpets at present outstrips availability. Perhaps the hardy karakul sheep, well adapted to conditions of drought, will make a comeback to supply this new demand.

Quiver Tree Forest and Giant's Playground ›› *Colour map 3, B4.*

ⓘ *Both attractions are on private land; the local farmer has a lucrative trade in charging a US$3.20 per person entrance fee. To get there, follow signs from the B1 north from town, turn onto the D29 after 3 km.*

The Quiver Tree Forest is one of the main attractions of southern Namibia. The 'trees' are in fact aloe plants or *Aloe dichotoma* which usually only grow singly, but which in a few places grow in large groups, and are ambitiously called forests. The plant's name derives from the former practice of some of the San and Nama peoples of hollowing out the light, tough-skinned branches of the plant to use as quivers for their arrows. The

A good time to visit the forest is either early in the morning for sunrise, or late afternoon for sunset, when the clear light offers good photo opportunities. The view south over the veld to the Karas Mountains is especially beautiful at these times.

 forest was declared a National Monument in 1955 and the quiver trees themselves are a protected species in Namibia. It is forbidden to carry off any parts of the trees.

The Giant's Playground is 5 km further northeast on the D29. Let yourself in via the farmgate and drive up to a car park. From here there is a short trail through the most striking formations. This is an area covered in huge, black, basalt rocks balanced precariously on top of each other. These strange formations were caused by the erosion of sedimentary overlying rocks 170 million years ago. The playground is a pleasantly eerie place to go for a gentle late-afternoon walk before catching sunset at the Quiver Tree Forest. There is a lodge and a campsite close to the entrance to the Quiver Tree Forest, see Sleeping, page 316.

Do not climb on the rocks, they may be well balanced but they are not necessarily secure.

West from Keetmanshoop » pp316-318.

The B4 heads west from Keetmanshoop over the high veld past **Seeheim**. There's nothing to see here, just two places to stop for lunch or overnight (see listings, below). Next is **Goageb**, a dusty village only noteworthy as the turn-off to Bethanie (not much of an honour), with a village bar, restaurant and petrol pump (not 24 hour). The C14 is tarred for the 15 km to **Bethanie**, another forgotten town that now serves the local community with a garage, takeaway, well-stocked shops, and a hotel dating back to 1880.

Aus » *Phone code: 063. Colour map 3, B2.*

This small settlement perched high up in the Aus Mountains is famous in Namibia for receiving occasional snowfalls during cold winters. After summer rains, the area is also renowned for the beauty of its wild flowers and hiking trails, particularly around **Klein-Aus Vista**, west of town. The village consists of a small hotel (doubling as the bottle store), guesthouse, railway halt, police station, well-stocked shop and garage, and a line of old cottages. The new **tourist information centre** is in a bright pink block on the corner of the turn-off from the B4 to Aus. At the time of writing it had still not opened but should have by the time the book is published. It will be run by **Aus Community Conservation Trust** and will have exhibitions and information about the desert horses, the flora and fauna in the area, in particular the desert succulents, exhibits on the First World War and transport in the region, toilets and a restaurant. Given that this region has a severe shortage of water; it will also have a water-recycling plant. The centre will be run by members of the community and any profits will go back into other community projects.

Aus was established as a prisoner-of-war camp in 1915 following the surrender of the German colonial troops to the South African forces. The site was chosen for its strategic significance, situated as it is on the railway line between Keetmanshoop and the harbour at Lüderitz. This made it possible to ship food and equipment from Cape Town via Lüderitz to the camp.

By 15 August 1915, 22 POWs and 600 guards were stationed here, initially living in tents. At one stage the camp held more than 1500 prisoners, many of these people were German nationals who had never been in the army but had been making their living as farmers and traders. The hot summer days and cold winter nights made life virtually unbearable, and in the face of South African apathy to improve the situation, the inmates themselves set about making bricks which they used to build their own houses. By the end of 1916 none of the prisoners were living in tents and they were even selling their surplus to their South African guards at 10 shillings per 1000 bricks.

By 1916 the prisoners had built their own wood stoves on which to cook and the authorities had provided water for washing and laundry purposes. It seems as if the South African garrison was not so enterprising and continued living in tents until 1918 when barracks were finally constructed.

Wild horses of the Namib

The legendary wild horses of the Namib are probably the only wild desert-dwelling horses in the world, and their origins are a source of much speculation. Romantics suggest that they are the descendants of the stud kept by 'Baron' von Wolf at Duwisib Castle 160 km away, or that they descend from thoroughbred horses shipwrecked on the coast. Other less fanciful suggestions are that they escaped from surrounding farms or that they originate from horses left behind by the German troops when they fled Aus in 1915. The latter is probably the truth, judging by a photograph on display at Klein-Aus Vista which shows Union soldiers and horses that were stationed at Garub for five weeks during the First World War. Allegedly there were 10,000 soldiers and 6000 horses, and during an aircraft battle over the base, some of the horses were dispersed.

These horses live in an area of about 350 sq km and are adapted to survive in their desert environment. They move slowly, sweat less and drink as infrequently as once every five days, their only source of water coming from a borehole at Garub sunk especially for them. A blind here allows visitors to observe the horses close up when they come to drink.

The numbers of horses are constantly fluctuating in response to the grazing conditions – only the toughest can survive the frequent droughts. It is estimated that the number has been anywhere from 50-280 during the 90 years of their existence, and it currently stands at about 150. Deaths of horses during drought periods are a necessary population control method. However, during good rainy seasons grass grows on the dunes and the horses are able to fatten themselves in preparation for the lean seasons ahead. They spend about three-quarters of their time grazing. The horses are now overseen by the Namib Feral Horse Trust, a collaboration between Klein-Aus Vista and the Lüderitz MET. Visit www.namibhorses.com for more information.

Following the signing of the Treaty of Versailles at the end of the First World War, the prisoners were gradually released, the last group leaving on 13 May 1919 after which the camp was closed. Unfortunately little remains of the camp beyond a few weather-beaten walls and foundations and a commemorative plaque.

The site of the old **POW Camp** can be visited and is indicated by a National Monuments plaque on a rock. It really is a desolate place, and as you walk around, images of the place in its heyday are not hard to conjure. To get there, turn off the B4 into the village. Drive up the hill past the hotel and petrol station and continue for a further 3 km to the turn-off for Rosh Pinah. Ignore this, take the left fork, after 500 m the remains of the camp are to the right, drive slowly, the turning by the small trees can easily be missed.

After leaving Aus, the road descends rapidly from the edge of the central highlands plateau to the desert floor, where it cuts a swathe through the sand dunes for a further 120 km until it reaches Lüderitz. The last stretch through the Namib Desert is one of the most stunning drives in Namibia, allow yourself time to stop and to enjoy the calming silence, and stop off at the watering hole for the desert horses too.

Garub/Koichab Concession Area

This concession area around Aus was created by **Klein-Aus Vista** (see Sleeping, page 317) for tours run from the 15,000-ha farm of Klein-Aus. Within the concession area is the Koichab dune belt, a region of high bright red dunes that are partially vegetated and many of Namibia's wild horses migrate through the region. Also in the area are the remains of a heliograph station used by the Germans to maintain contact with Lüderitz from the hinterland. **Klein-Aus Vista** runs half or day trips into the region as well as horse trails.

Garub Plain » *Colour map 3, B2.*

If you fail to catch a glimpse of the famous **desert horses** from the main road it is always worth making a short detour to the Garub Plain. Here you will find an artificial water point and a viewing shelter with information board and visitors book. The site is 1 km north of the B4, 22 km west of Aus. The horses are usually here in the winter, when there is little standing water elsewhere in the area.

Sleeping

Keetmanshoop *p310, map p311*

B Bird's Mansions Hotel, Sixth Av, T063-221711 www.birdsaccommodation.com. 23 en suite rooms with a/c, TV, phone, the rooms off the courtyard at the back are newer than in the main building, parking, lovely courtyard and *lapa*, good restaurant and bar, recently taken over and new facilities added such as a heated swimming pool and internet café.

B Bird's Nest Guest House, 16 Pastorie St, T063-222906, www.birdsaccommodation.com. Under the same management as the hotel above, has 10 en suite a/c rooms with TV, phone and tea- and coffee-making facilities, secure parking, communal *braai* area, relaxing garden, plentiful breakfasts, dinner if booked ahead.

B Canyon Hotel, 5th Av, T063-223361, canyon@iwwn.com.na. Well-managed, friendly 3-star hotel with comfortable en suite rooms with a/c, TV and phone. Built 30 years ago, the hotel has a new wing, a total of 70 spacious rooms, gym, very good restaurant, coffee shop and bar by the swimming pool – a good place to escape from the intense summer heat of the south, and passers-by are welcome to use the facilities free of charge. Recommended.

B Quivertree Forest Camp, T/F063-222835, quiver@iafrica.com.na. Well placed for morning or evening photography of the quiver trees, 16 km from Keetmanshoop on the D29. Accommodation is in 8 a/c en suite rooms with full board or B&B in the farmhouse, 7 fully equipped self-catering 'igloos' with 2-4 beds, or **camping** (**C**) with electricity, lights and basic ablutions by the Quivertree Forest itself, 1 km from the farmhouse. Extras include a swimming pool and 2 pet warthogs, and it has cheetah here which you can watch being fed in the afternoon, but unfortunately they live in a cage.

B-D Central Lodge, 5th Av, T063-225850, www.central-lodge.com. Comfortable lodge with 19 en suite rooms with a/c and TV, 3 with spa baths, also 1 self-catering unit with 1 double and 2 single beds, some of the rooms are in a very elegant refurbished 1910 building, swimming pool, good bar and restaurant and conference facilities. Budget travellers: try to bag room 20, which is small, but still has DSTV, a/c and tea- and coffee- making facilities for only US$25. Recommended.

C Gessert's Guest House, 138 13th St, Westdene, T/F063-223892, www.natron.net/gesserts. A small, friendly, family-run guesthouse in a quiet residential area with 5 en suite rooms, lovely gardens and swimming pool, rates include a good-sized breakfast, slightly out of town in Westdene, follow signs.

C La Rochelle, 12 6th Av, T063-223845. A smart new guesthouse on the side of the hill overlooking the town, 7 en suite rooms, but check that you like the bathroom arrangement as some of the bathrooms are within the bedroom, a/c and TV, small swimming pool, secure parking and an attractive garden.

C Lafenis Lodge, on the B1, 5 km south of town, T063-224316, lafenislodge@iway.na. 19 simple but adequate 4-bed en suite bungalows with DSTV and a/c, each with private *braai* facilities, restaurant and bar decorated in a Wild West theme, pool, and **campsite** (**C**) with adequate facilities.

Camping

E Municipal Campsite & Caravan Park, T063-221265/11. In the centre of town, with pleasant, good-value campsites, electricity, adequate ablution blocks and laundry facilities. As in any town centre campsite, beware of thieves.

West from Keetmanshoopp *p314*

B Seeheim Hotel, Seeheim, signposted off the C12, just south of the B4, T063-250503, www.seeheim.co.za, has cultivated a Wild West hotel feel (which has led to it appearing in 3 feature films), has comfortable en suite rooms, swimming pool, satellite TV lounge, a decent bar and restaurant, petrol, shop, hiking trails, and horse riding. A picturesque spot, but baking hot in summer. The stone and thatch buildings are located at the bottom of a small canyon making it invisible from the road, larger vehicles may have difficulty getting down the steep track. Camping facilities (**E**) with ablutions.

C-D Bethanie Hotel, Bethanie, T063-283013. Built in the 1880s, this is probably one of the oldest hotels in Namibia to still be functioning, although it's old fashioned and gloomy, 10 rooms, 4 with a/c, doubles have en suite but the single rooms share the ablution block with campers outside, bar, restaurant, pool table.

D Konkiep Motel, Goageb, T063-283566. Very basic unremarkable rooms attached to the village bar, restaurant and petrol pump (not 24 hour). Adequate in an emergency, but better to move on to the excellent **Klein-Aus Vista** in Aus.

Aus *p314*

A-E Klein-Aus Vista, well signposted 2 km west of turning off the B4 for Aus, T/F063-258021, www.namibhorses.com. A wonderful spot, worth spending an extra day of your holiday here and as this is only 120 km to Lüderitz it offers an alternative base to explore the region including the coast. In addition to a lovely campsite in the hills (10 sites, some with wind shelters, with water, but no electricity, though there is light in the excellent ablutions block), a dorm cabin with 12 bunks, and 14 large en suite 'luxury' rooms (half-board) in the main house (currently being extended to 24), there are a couple of isolated self-catering cottages 7 km from the farmhouse, built into the rocks, and blessed with superb views across the desert. In the main building is a very tastefully decorated restaurant and bar, with excellent food and lovely wooden decks to enjoy your meal with a view. There are mapped trails in the hills which can be followed on foot, horse or mountain bike, taking from a few hours to 3 days. Recommended. It offers 4WD and horse-riding excursions to see wild horses and can provide information on the **Namib Feral Horse Hiking Trail**, an easy 3- to 4-day trail with well-provisioned overnight huts.

C Bahnhof Hotel, T063-258091. This rather quaint village-centre hotel has adequate but rather tired-looking rooms with and without en suite facilities, a restaurant and bar, which is very long and can get very lively, there's also a full size billiards table. Adequate but in need of refurbishment; **Klein-Aus Vista** offers the best accommodation in Aus.

D-E Namib Garage One-Stop B&B, T063-258029. Reception is at the garage/shop. This was the garage owners' house and it feels as if they only left yesterday, 4 en suite rooms in a small block, self-catering facilities, shady but sandy campsite behind a wall, reasonable ablutions. The well-stocked shop sells meat and fresh produce.

Eating

Keetmanshoop *p310, map p311*

Busy by day, Keetmanshoop becomes a dark and unwelcoming town once the sun goes down; you are best picking a dinner spot and settling in for the evening. Kitchens typically shut at 2100.

Bird's Mansions Restaurant, within the hotel (see Sleeping, above). Serves a good range of meat and fish with tasty sauces in an airy dining room with good service and wide selection of drinks. Open daily until 2200.

Bullring Restaurant and Sports Bar, in a yellow windowless block on the corner of 5th Av and Schmiede St, T063-223322. Reasonably priced and has a well-attended bar in the evenings, expect the likes of burgers and T-bone steaks. Daily until 2100.

Canyon Hotel (see Sleeping, above). The smartest restaurant in town offering Namibian game dishes as well as a wide variety of fish, pasta and other European dishes, with a decent selection of wines to go with the food. Open daily until 2200.

🍴🍴 **Lara's**, corner of 5th Av and Schmiede St, T063-222233. Again all things meaty and everything comes with chips, but big plates of food for the price and friendly relaxed atmosphere in one of the town's most popular bars and grills. Mon-Sat 1200-2100.

🍴 **Balaton Restaurant**, Mittel St. Small restaurant with plastic tables and chairs, serves tasty Hungarian goulash, chicken paprika, etc, as well as the usual light meals and takeaways. Closes at 1700.

West from Keetmanshoopp *p314*

🍴 **Kuibis Restaurant**, about 9 km west of Seeheim, on the B4. This small restaurant is one of the few places you can stop for refreshments on the way to Lüderitz. Tea, coffee and cold drinks, toasted sandwiches and snacks, its shop sells excellent home- made jam and cookies, *biltong* and basic provisions. Mon-Fri 0700-2000, Sat and Sun 0700-1600.

Activities and tours

Keetmanshoop *p310, map p311*

Swimming Excellent 50-m municipal swimming pool, just off 8th Av, open Sep-Apr.

Transport

Keetmanshoop *p310, map p311*

500 km Windhoek, 340 km Lüderitz, 300 km Noordoewer (South African border).

Bus

For **Intercape Mainliner** coaches to **Cape Town** via Upington, and **Windhoek** via Mariental and Rehoboth, see timetable on page 70. Coach picks-up and drops-off at the BP petrol station on 5th Av. **Starline Passenger Services**, central reservations T061-2982032, www.transnamib.com.na, has 1 bus on Mon and Fri between Keetmanshoop and **Lüderitz** which leaves at 0730 and arrives in Lüderitz at 1215, before returning at 1230 and arriving back at 1730.

Train

The station is on the edge of town. For trains to **Windhoek** via Marienthal, Ariamsvlei and Upington, see timetable on page 68.

Directory

Keetmanshoop *p310, map p311*

Banks Bank Windhoek, First National Bank and Standard Bank are all situated on Fenschel St, and all change money and have ATMs. **Emergencies** T10111. **Internet** Access available from the SCT Computer Shop, next to the Birds Mansions Hotel, open office/shop hrs. **Medical services** State Hospital, T063-223388, signposted just off B1, 1 km north of town. There is a very well-stocked pharmacy on the corner of Mittel/7th Av. **Police** 5th Av, T063-223359. **Post** 5th Av, Mon-Fri 0800-1630, Sat 0800-1200.

Lüderitz and around

The small coastal town of Lüderitz is one of Namibia's oddities: a faded, picturesque, German colonial town lying between the inhospitable dunes of the Namib Desert on the one side, and the vast iciness of the South Atlantic on the other. Ironically, both desert and ocean provide the resources necessary for Lüderitz's survival: diamonds from the desert and fish, rock lobster and more diamonds from the ocean.

Twenty-five years ago, the town was as good as dead, but thanks to the reopening of the diamond mine at Elizabeth Bay in 1981 and an improvement in tourist numbers and fishing catches, Lüderitz is currently enjoying a mini-boom. The harbour has been expanded and a smart Waterfront Development has been built with new shops, kiosks, offices and restaurants. Proposals to redevelop around the headland to the excellent Nest Hotel are under consideration. ▸▸ *For Sleeping, Eating and other listings, see pages 327-331.*

Ins and outs ›› *Phone code: 063. Colour map 3, B2.*

Tourist information

The **Lüderitz Info Centre** ⓘ *Bismarck St, T063-202719, ludsaf@africaonline.com.na, summer Mon-Fri 0800-1230, 1330-1700, winter Mon-Fri 0730-1230-1330-1630, Sat 0830-1200, Sun 0830-1000*, a private office run by **Lüderitz Safaris and Tours**, can book accommodation, arrange taxis around town, and issue permits for Kolmanskop. The opening times correspond with the Kolmanskop tours and you need to book here preferably on the previous day, and at least half an hour before the tours start so the office knows how many guides to send out. The office also sells books, postcards and a number of quality curios. The climate in Lüderitz can be harsh and changeable. Arriving from the interior you will notice a distinct change in temperature getting nearer to the coast, and whilst most days are sunny, during September and February there are some severe storms and ferocious winds.

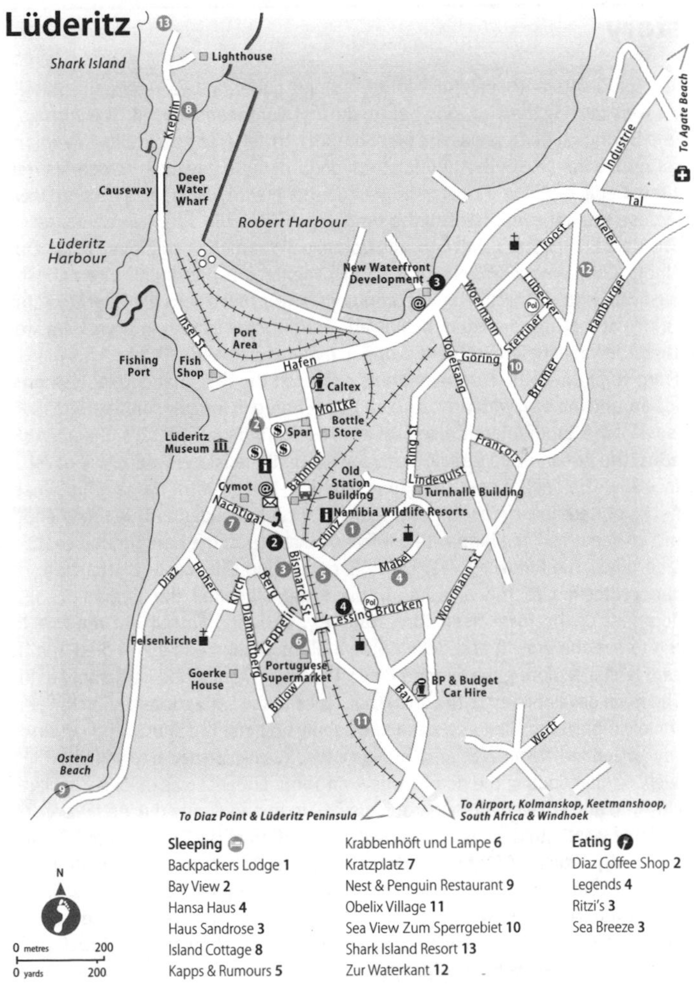

Best time to visit

Like many tourist centres in Namibia, Lüderitz can get busy during the school holidays; book accommodation in advance if possible. The peak tourist season lasts from June through to September, the winter months. However, because of its relative inaccessibility, the town never gets as overrun as Swakopmund. A word of warning – Lüderitz is a very windy town. The worst time is between the end of December and mid-February. During this period the winds enforce a 60-kph speed limit along the approach road for safety. The last 20 km of the main road pass through shifting sand dunes; if you hit a ridge of sand at speed it is like running into cement and can easily cause you to lose control – beware and observe local advice.

One significant aspect of the local climate is the absence of the thick fog that plagues Walvis Bay and Swakopmund. This is thanks to the town's position in a bay, thereby protecting it from this phenomena. Quite often you can see the bank of fog off Diaz Point, but that is as close as it gets to town. In fact, many of the long-time residents who moved to Swakopmund during Lüderitz's decline have returned, unwilling to contend with the terrible fog further up the coast.

History

Stone implements and skeletons found around Lüderitz area testify that Khoisan people were visiting the area long before the first Europeans arrived. The Portuguese explorer Bartholomeu Diaz was the first European to set eyes on Lüderitz Bay when he sought refuge from a South Atlantic storm on Christmas Day, 1487. Upon his return from the Cape of Good Hope in July 1488 he erected a stone cross, following Portuguese seafaring traditions of the time.

The next European to show up was Cornelius Wobma, an employee of the Dutch East India Company, who was sent to investigate the possibility of establishing trading links with the local Nama communities. He failed and although the Dutch authorities at the Cape annexed the bay and surrounding islands in 1593, it was to be a further 200 years before further European influence arrived.

From 1842 onwards, European ships exploited the rich guano resources on the islands around the bay, with up to 450 ships anchored in the bay simultaneously. The cold seas of the South Atlantic also proved to be rich whaling grounds. Between 1842 and 1861, the British-ruled Cape Colony annexed all the islands along the coast.

In 1883, Heinrich Vogelsang negotiated a treaty with Nama chief Joseph Fredericks of Bethanie on behalf of the merchant Adolf Lüderitz. This treaty entitled Lüderitz to acquire all the land within a five mile radius of the harbour and cost £100 and 200 rifles. The following year Lüderitz persuaded Chancellor Bismarck to offer German protection to the area, and this event signalled the beginning of the development of the town itself. Unfortunately, Lüderitz himself did not live long enough to see the growth and development of his settlement, as he died in a boat accident whilst exploring the Orange River. The town was named in memory of him.

The main development of the town took place in the early 1900s during the period of German colonization, first as a base and supply point for the Shutztruppe during the 1904-1907 German-Nama War, and then as a Wild West-type boom town following the discovery of diamonds in the nearby desert in 1908. Lüderitz was officially declared a town in 1909 and enjoyed a prosperous growth up to and during the inter-war years.

Lüderitz went into decline following the relocation of the Consolidated Diamond Mining Headquarters (CDM) to Oranjemund in 1938. Ironically, the stagnation of the economy prevented the development of the town and thus ensured the preservation of the original buildings, which gives the town its quaint turn-of-the-century feel. During the 1980s interest in Lüderitz as a tourist destination grew and rock lobster and fishing industries were developed.

The renaissance of the town is now in full swing with the harbour once again busy with fishing boats and container ships, hotels full and migrant workers arriving from the north of Namibia looking for work. There has recently been much upgrading of the shops with the new Waterfront development and the harbour has new gates.

Sights

Lüderitz has a number of fine old colonial buildings and a small museum which can easily be explored in a couple of hours walking around the town. A walk up Bismarck Street, the main thoroughfare, will take you past what was the **Deutsche-Afrika Bank** building, constructed in 1907 on the corner of Diaz Street, which today is home to **Nedbank**. Further up the street is the **Station Building**, commissioned in 1912 and finished two years later. The railway line from Lüderitz to Aus was completed in 1906 and became important as a means of transporting troops into the interior during the 1904-1907 German-Nama War. Following the discovery of diamonds in 1908 and the subsequent extension of the railway line to Keetmanshoop, the existing station became too small and the German Colonial Administration authorized the building of a new station.

The **Old Post Office**, found on Shintz Street, was completed in 1908, and originally had a clock in its tower, but this was removed in 1912 and transferred to the church. The building now functions as the local **Namibia Wildlife Resorts** offices. The **Turnhalle Building** on Ring Street dates from 1912-1913 and was originally a gymnasium and now serves as a function room.

Two of the town's most impressive buildings, the **German Lutheran Church** ⓘ *daily winter 1600-1700 summer 1700-1800, payment by donation*, or **Felsenkirche** (Church on the Rocks), and Goerke House (see below), are situated on top of neighbouring hillocks in the old part of town. Each has an excellent view of the town centre and harbour area. The foundation stone for the church was laid in 1911 and the building was consecrated the following year. It is notable for its fine stained-glass windows and as with the Christuskirche in Windhoek, the altar window was donated by Kaiser Wilhelm II and the altar bible by his wife. Just below the church in Berg Street is an interesting collection of original town houses. Unfortunately these can only be viewed from the outside. To get a better idea of what they would have looked like inside, visit Goerke House.

Goerke House

ⓘ *Diamantberg St, daily 1400-1600, US$2.40, informative introduction provided.*
The house was named after its original owner Hans Goerke who had been a store inspector in the Shutztruppe and then became a successful local businessman. CDM (Consolidated Diamond Mines) acquired the house in 1920, sold it to the government in 1944 when it became the town magistrate's official residence, and then repurchased the building in 1983. The house lay empty between 1980 and 1983 after the magistrate was recalled to Keetmanshoop (there not being enough crime in Lüderitz to warrant his presence).

From the outside, the house is an array of different architectural styles incorporating Roman and Egyptian, amongst others, and inside it is possible to imagine what many of the crumbling houses at nearby Kolmanskop must have looked like in their heyday. There is a fine stained-glass window above the staircase depicting a flock of flamingos on the beach, as well as an excellent view over the town and harbour from the balcony of the main bedroom. The house operates as an occasional guesthouse for NAMDEB's VIP guests, so it may be shut during your visit.

Lüderitz Museum

ⓘ *Diaz St, Mon-Fri 1530-1700, minimal entry fee.*

The museum was founded by Friederich Eberlanz who arrived in Lüderitz in 1914. Fascinated by the local flora, he started a private collection which grew to incorporate ancient stone tools, rocks and other items he discovered. This private collection attracted a wide interest and the existing museum was established in 1961. Today the museum also has displays of local history, the mining industry and an interesting collection of photos and artefacts of the indigenous peoples of the country. Look for the photo of the group of Bushmen after a big feed, as Laurens van der Post puts it in *The Lost World of the Kalahari*, "made him look like a pregnant woman...in this way nature enabled him to store a reserve against dry and hungry moments."

Around Lüderitz

Kolmanskop Ghost Town » *Colour map 3, B2.*

ⓘ *Guided tours in English and German, Mon-Sat 0930 and 1100, Sun and public holidays 1000, starting at Kolmanskop Museum. US$6.50 adults, US$3.20 children, purchase tickets beforehand from Lüderitz Safaris and Tours, on Bismarck St (it can also arrange transport). These tickets allow you to go on the tour, visit the museum and spend some time exploring the houses and dunes after the tour before Kolmanskop closes at 1300. There is no access in the afternoon unless you obtain a special Photo Permit for US$20 which includes the 0930 tour and allows access between sunrise and sunset for photography.*

For organized tours in the Lüderitz area, see page 329.

The former diamond boom town of Kolmanskop, finally deserted in 1956, is now a ghost town and lies crumbling in the desert 15 km inland from Lüderitz (drive 10 km inland on the B4, turn right and then follow signs; it is clearly visible from the road), gradually being weathered by the wind and buried by the sand. It is a fascinating place to visit, offering as it does a glimpse into an exciting part of Namibia's history.

In April 1908, Zacharias Lewala, a worker on the Lüderitz-Aus railway line, presented a shiny stone to his supervisor August Stauch, who was intelligent enough to obtain a prospecting licence before having it officially verified and thereby starting the diamond rush around the site of Kolmanskop. In the early days, in the nearby Itadel Valley, stones were so accessible that prospectors with no mining equipment would crawl on their hands and knees in full moonlight collecting the glittering stones.

In September 1908, the Colonial Government declared a Sperrgebiet or 'forbidden zone' extending 360 km northwards from the Orange River and 100 km inland from the coast in order to control the mining of the diamonds, and in February 1909, a central diamond market was established.

The First World War effectively stopped diamond production, by which time more than 5.4 million carats of very high-quality stones had been extracted from the region. The recession which followed the war hit the diamond industry badly. However, Sir Ernest Oppenheimer, the chairman of the Anglo-American Company, saw this as an opportunity to buy up all the small diamond companies operating in the Sperrgebiet, and combine them to form Consolidated Diamond Mines. CDM, as it became known, was to control all diamond mining in the area until entering into partnership with the Namibian government in 1995 under the new name of NAMDEB.

Kolmanskop enjoyed its heyday in the 1920s when it grew rapidly to service the diamond miners and eventually the families which followed. A hospital, gymnasium and concert hall, school, butchery, bakery and a number of fine houses were built in the middle of the desert, and at its peak there were as many as 300 German and 800 Oshiwambo adults living in the town. The hospital was ultra-modern and was equipped with the first X-ray machine in southern Africa (used principally for detecting secreted gemstones, rather than broken bones!).

The sheer wealth generated at Kolmanskop (peak production was over 30,000 carats per day) is demonstrated by the way in which water was supplied to the town. Every month a ship left Cape Town carrying 1000 tonnes of water, and each resident was supplied with 20 litres per day for free. Those requiring additional water paid for it, at half the price of beer! The lack of fresh water to power steam engines also forced the building of a power station which supplied electricity, very advanced technology at the time, to power the mining machinery.

However, the boom years in Kolmanskop ended in 1928 when diamond reserves six times the size of those at Kolmanskop (although of lesser quality) were discovered at the mouth of the Orange River. The town of Oranjemund was built in 1936 to exploit these reserves and in 1938 most of the workers and equipment relocated from Kolmanskop to this new headquarters. Following this, the town went into steady decline, although the last people (including the 100 full-time labourers employed to remove the encroaching sand) only left Kolmanskop in 1956, abandoning this once-flourishing town to time and the forces of nature.

Kolmanskop was rescued from the desert in 1979 following a CDM-commissioned report to assess the tourist potential of this ghost town. In 1980,

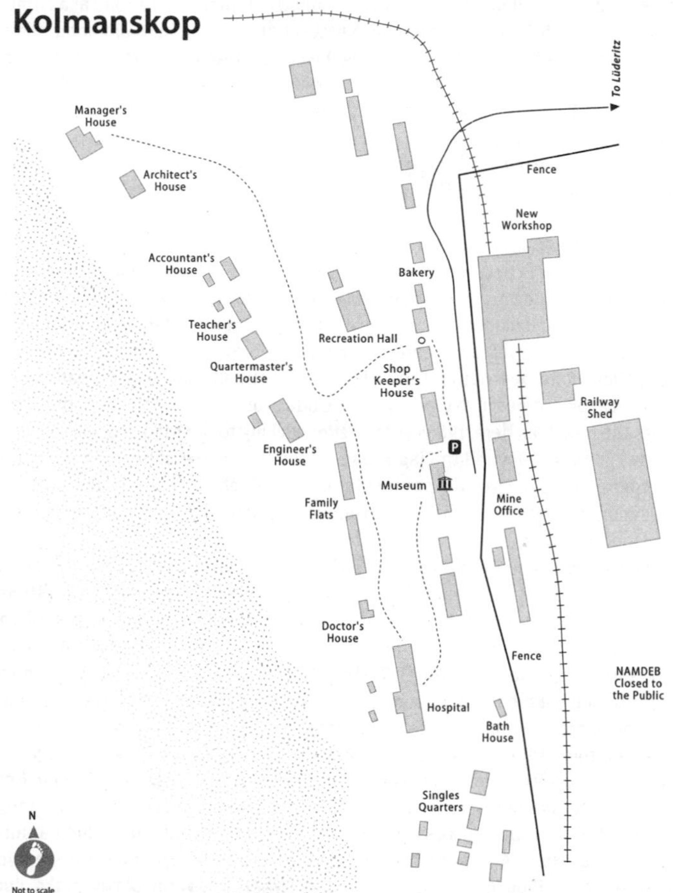

simple restoration began and the town was opened to tourism. At present the most carefully preserved/restored buildings are the **Recreation Hall** and those adjacent to the **museum**, and the lavish **Manager's House**, complete with marble bath, grand piano and sun room. Sadly, following an expensive restoration of the Skittle Alley in the basement of the Recreation Hall, visitors are no longer permitted to play.

Although it is not obligatory to join a tour, it is worth following one to hear some of the historic detail and stories about Kolmanskop. After about 45 minutes you are left to your own devices to explore all buildings at your leisure. There is a pleasant curio shop and café open during tour hours.

National Diamond Area » *Colour map 3, B2.*

Drive 10 km inland on B4, turn right and then follow signs.

Following the discovery of diamonds at Kolmanskop in 1908 and the ensuing diamond rush the German colonial authorities declared a Sperrgebiet, or 'forbidden zone', along the coast. This area extended from the Orange River in the south for 360 km northward to latitude 26S and inland for 100 km, and covers 26,000 sq km and is known today as Diamond Area No 1.

Exclusive mining rights for this area are held by NAMDEB, owned jointly by the Namibian Government and De Beers, and it is forbidden to enter the area without permission. Even where the Sperrgebiet becomes part of the Namib-Naukluft Park, access is strictly controlled and visitors are required to remain on the road at all times.

In 1994 a British-Canadian company NAMCO obtained offshore diamond mining concessions at Lüderitz, potentially breaking the current NAMDEB monopoly. Diamond divers, many from South Africa, Australia and New Zealand, suck up the seabed with powerful vacuum pumps, after which the gravel is sorted for diamonds. It is difficult, unpleasant work, which the divers can only carry out when sea conditions permit. The rewards, however, are potentially huge and consequently a small diver community lives in Lüderitz hoping to strike it rich. Their boats are visible in the harbour.

Lüderitz Peninsula » *Colour map 3, B1.*

Assuming you have your own vehicle and that the winds are not too strong, an interesting excursion can be made around the peninsula south of town. Follow the Keetmanshoop road out of town and look out for a signpost for Diaz Point just after the buildings end. From here a twisting gravel road heads south round the coast through a moonscape of rocky bays, mud flats, beaches and small islands. Shortly after passing the water tower, the Second Lagoon comes in to view. When the tide is out it is possible to cut the corner and cross the mud flats here, but you are better sticking to the road in a saloon car.

A few kilometres beyond the lagoon you have the choice of heading straight to the southernmost point of the peninsula, Grosse Bucht (6 km) via the D733, or continuing on the D701 to Griffith Bay, Sturmvogel Bucht and Diaz Point. Either way, the road loops round.

Most visitors head straight for **Diaz Point** and the viewpoint for Halifax Island, however, if it is late in the afternoon it is worth following the D734 as far as **Griffith Bay** where you can enjoy a distant view of Lüderitz bathed in the evening sunlight. Continuing along the D701, and after a further 5 km or so, look out for a turning to the right. This road leads to **Sturmvogel Bucht**, one of the best bathing beaches in the area. Also of interest are the rusty remains of a whaling station. It doesn't take much imagination to picture what used to occur here.

Just past the turning for **Shearwater Bay**, the road goes over a small ridge and presents a good view of Diaz Point. Take the next right to visit **Diaz Point**, 22 km from town. A large cross stands here, a replica of the original erected by Portuguese explorer Bartholomeu Diaz in 1487 on his way back to Portugal after sailing around the Cape of Good Hope. Access to the cross is via a wooden bridge and some steps up to an exposed position on a rocky headland. When the wind blows make sure

Namibia's diamonds

Diamonds have lured the fortune seekers and enchanted mankind for centuries. The Ancient Greeks believed they were splinters of stars that fell from the sky and these precious stones have been regarded with fascination and intrigue since they were first mined in India 2500 years ago. They are a pure mineral extracted from the earth's crust, the hardest of all natural substances in the world, and inarguably the most beautiful. Africa's diamonds can be found from the Cape to the Congo, with other deposits in Tanzania and parts of West Africa. The combined output of South Africa, Namibia and Botswana produces the greatest volume and value of diamonds on the globe. Namibia contributes some 30% of world output and has produced more than 70 million carats, of which 85% are of gem quality. Once polished, 95% of Namibia's diamonds are sent to the major northern hemisphere diamond markets, such as Antwerp and Tel Aviv, whilst 5% are sold to local Namibian jewellers. A diamond is a crystal of pure carbon, formed by immense pressure 60-120 km beneath the earth's surface. Sixty million years ago, when today's southern continents began to divide, the earth discharged molten mass by way of volcanic eruptions known as Kimberlites (after which the famous South African diamond mine Kimberly is named). Diamonds are usually extracted from Kimberlites below the earth's surface by mining, but in Namibia these hardened masses eroded with time and weather causing them to emerge from the surface, and the debris was washed away and distributed through the deserts and rivers, which in turn washed them into the ocean too. Namibia's diamonds have been largely mined by pushing back the desert's sand to expose ancient beaches rich in diamond-bearing gravel; at sea the ocean floor has been dredged or explored by individual diamond divers.

Despite anything James Bond may have said, though, diamonds are not forever; in fact it is believed that there is only another 15-20 years of diamond production available in the Sperrgebiet. When production stops, Namibia will face the challenge of ensuring that any future use of this near pristine wilderness region is appropriate and sustainable. In 2004 the Sperrgebiet was declared a national park, and although mining is to continue in selected areas, the vast majority of this untamed wilderness has been granted extra protection from any form of human impact. However, the government has also recognized that ecotourism with strict permit controls can contribute to the land use in the non-mining areas. In recent years, the Ministry of Environment and Tourism (MET) has given a selected number of tour operators permission to conduct a limited number of trips along the stretch of coastline between Sylvia Hill northwards to Sandwich Harbour in the wilderness section of the Namib-Naukluft Park. Participants drive in their own vehicles and are accompanied throughout the trip by two or three vehicles and a nature conservator from the MET. Points of interest visited include Saddle Hill, Koichab Pan, Sylvia Hill, Conception Bay, Langewand, the wreck of the Eduard Bohlen, Fischersbrunn and Sandwich Harbour. (See under Tour operators for more details.) Now, with the gazetting of this new park, over 75% of the Namib Desert falls into protected areas.

 everything is securely attached, it is easy to lose a hat or a pair of sunglasses. There is a simple toilet block in the car park. The nearby lighthouse was built in 1910 and the modern foghorn tower was added later.

All along this section of coast there is a profusion of wildlife; just offshore from the cross itself is a seal colony and further down the coast on **Halifax Island** there are large numbers of jackass penguins and cormorants. Pink flamingos flock in the bays and also in small onoshore lakes. The presence of so much wildlife is due to the cold, clean and abundantly fertile Benguela Current, which provides ideal conditions for catching their prey of fish, rock lobster and oyster. The drawback for the tourist is the accompanying persistently strong, cold, southwest wind which makes warm clothes essential.

As you follow the D702 towards Grosse Bucht there are plenty of tracks off to the right which lead up to a variety of vantage points along the coast. Not all are clearly marked and it is easy to find yourself further down the road than your map might have you believe. At **Knochen Bay** and **Essy Bay** there are *braai* sites and basic toilets. If you can find the right road and then the right path there is a small cave cut into the rock face at **Eberlanz Höhle**. A little further on there is a sign for **Kleiner Fjord**, which is nice for a walk, but offers little at the destination.

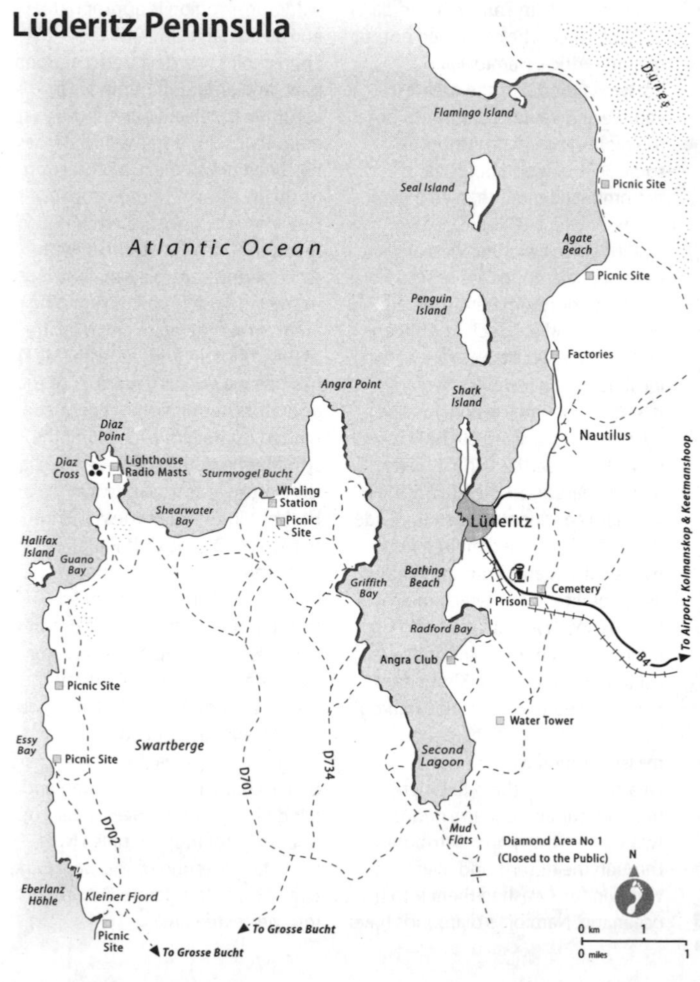

Finally the broad south-facing **Grosse Bucht** comes into view. This is the furthest south you can travel along this part of the coast. When you reach a junction, take a right and this will lead you to the western end of the bay and a *braai* site. Just on the tideline are the rusty remains of a small boat which has an interesting local history. The boat was called the *Irmgard* and was used for cray fishing. When launched it was the first flat-bottomed steel boat to be built in Lüderitz. The builder and first owner was the father of the current manager of the **Nest Hotel** (see page 327). The shortest route back to town is via the D733, about 40 minutes' drive.

Agate Beach

A similarly rocky drive north out of Lüderitz leads to Agate Beach (follow the signs from Hafen Street), a fine, sandy stretch of coast suitable for surfing and swimming, for those willing to brave the cold sea. Small piles of stones and mini-trenches dot the beach, remnants from past diamond and agate diggings. In the late afternoon there is a good chance of seeing wild gemsbok and springbok. **Note** Most of the land on the inland side of the road is part of the NAMDEB concession area and thus closed to the public. It is not advisable to venture into these areas at any time.

Sleeping

Lüderitz *p318, map p319*
Lüderitz boasts an excellent selection of hospitable hotels and guesthouses.

A **Nest Hotel** , Ostend Beach, T063-204000, www.nesthotel.com. This is the smartest option in town, built in 1997, and an award winner several times in local competitions. 70 en suite doubles and 3 suites, with a/c, TV, phone and radio, small balcony and sea views. Very good restaurant, bar with open terrace where you can indulge yourself with oysters and champagne, plus a Sunset bar at the top of the hotel (residents only). Swimming pool, sauna, internet café, conference facilities. Recommended.

A-B **Sea View Hotel Zum Sperrgebiet**, Woermann St, T063-203411/3, www.seaview.luderitz.com. Another award winner on a hill in a quiet residential area, with balconies overlooking the harbour. 22 en suite rooms, TV, phone, sauna, sheltered heated swimming pool, good restaurant and secure parking. Good-value mid-range hotel, discounts for children under 12 and pensioners.

B **Bay View Hotel**, Diaz St, T063-202288, bayview@ldz.namib.com. Another award winner with a friendly small-town hotel charm. 22 en suite rooms, phone, fan, TV, old-fashioned decor but comfortable. Built around 2 small courtyards, 1 with a swimming pool, newly built restaurant and bar, good range of food but not much for vegetarians, secure parking.

C **Kapps Hotel**, Bay Rd, T063-202345, pmk@mweb.com.na. Historic hotel that dates back to the diamond boom days and was built in 1907, now completely renovated. 14 en suite rooms with TV and tea- and coffee-making facilities grouped around the courtyard at the back, **Rumours Grill** restaurant serving excellent steaks and seafood, secure parking. A bit stark, and noisy when **Rumours Pub** gets going.

C **Kratzplatz**, 5 Nachtigal St, T/F063-202458. 10 rooms in an old converted church with high ceilings and whitewashed walls, simple decor but comfortable. 5 en suite rooms, 2 family rooms, and the remaining 3 doubles which share a bathroom and work out a bit cheaper. Most rooms have TV and there's secure parking. Central location, *braai*, laundry facilities.

C **Obelix Village**, on the approach road into town, T063-203456, www.obelixvillage.com. Named after the Asterix character, this smart new guesthouse has 11 spacious en suite rooms with 2-4 beds – 1 wheelchair friendly – ideal for groups of friends or families, car park, spotless modern bathrooms, and a superbly attractive and cosy thatched *lapa* with a fully stocked bar and roaring fire where you can *braai* your meat, meals can be arranged with advance notice.

For an explanation of the sleeping and eating price codes used in this guide, see inside the front cover. Other relevant information is found in Essentials, see pages 43-51.

Self-catering

A-B **Shark Island Resort**, take a left at the end of Bismarck St and follow the road round the harbour and across the causeway onto Shark Island, reservations through Namibia Wildlife Resorts, T061-2857200 (Windhoek), www.nwr.com.na, or in person at its offices on Schinz St in Lüderitz, T063-202752, open 0800-1700. Even if you have a pre- arranged reservation, you are required to check in at this office before going out to Shark Island so will need to be in Lüderitz before 1700. Accommodation here comprises a fabulous **converted lighthouse** (A) with 2 bedrooms, 2 bathrooms, fully equipped kitchen, satellite TV, lounge area, secure parking. It is the panoramic view from the top that makes this place such a pleasure. Access is a little awkward via a ladder and a trapdoor. So long as the wind doesn't blow this is a peaceful setting to watch the sun rise.

There are also 3 standard **self-catering bungalows** (B) that sleep 6, with *braai* areas, and a rocky **campsite** (D) with 20 sites overlooking the harbour and the ocean, with clean ablution blocks. However, camping here is very exposed when the wind blows furiously. Only a couple of pitches have a small patch of grass and any degree of shelter, and tents have been known to blow away; make sure yours is securely pegged down and it is really only advised to put up your tent when you're ready to get into it. In fact if you want to go to the loo in the middle of the night, make sure someone stays in the tent or weigh it down with rocks – it really can get that windy! For a swirl in the wind, day visitors are allowed on to Shark Island from 0800-1700, just ask nicely at the gate.

C **Hansa Haus**, Mabel St, T/F063-203581, is a pretty blue house that was built in 1909 with harbour views, 2 en suite doubles, and 2 doubles with shared bathroom, communal lounge with TV, and fully equipped kitchen, facilities are shared with the family that owns it.

C **Haus Sandrose**, Bismarck St, T063-202630, haussandrose@iway.na. 3 lovely, fully equipped flats, 1 sleeping a family of 5, set back from the street in a private courtyard, *braai* area, friendly owner, good-quality curios in the shop out front.

C **Island Cottage**, on the peninsula just before the boom gate to Shark Island, T063-203626. Self-catering flats in bright red blocks perched amongst giant boulders with airy and spacious balconies overlooking the bay and Shark Island, polished wooden floors, new modern fixtures and fittings, spotlessly clean, suitable for families, garages for parking.

C **Zur Waterkant**, Bremer St, T/F063-203145, www.raubkatzen.de. Choice of B&B or self-catering, a clean modern house in the suburbs, with balconies overlooking the harbour, meals can be organized on request, mostly German clientele.

D **Krabbenhöft und Lampe**, Bismarck St, T063-202466, T081-1292025 (mob), taurus@ ldz.namib.com. Great for comfortable self-catering, though the rooms are plain with no signs of modernization, with a large family flat and smaller luxury flat on the 1st floor, and simpler rooms with shared facilities on the top floor.

D-E **Backpackers Lodge**, 7 Schinz St, T/F063-202000. Dorms and double rooms, kitchen, spacious communal room, washing facilities, *braai* area, small lawn for a few tents. Central location, a welcome alternative for budget travellers to the exposed Shark Island campsite.

Eating

Lüderitz *p318, map p319*

The hotels can be relied on for reasonable fare, and there is a fair choice of restaurants in Lüderitz, most serving fresh seafood and shellfish in season, in addition to the customary Namibian fare. As elsewhere, kitchens close fairly early.

TTT **The Penguin**, T063-204000, located in the **Nest Hotel** (see Sleeping, above). Extensive menu with excellent seafood, smart and formal hotel restaurant, good value US$12 buffets at the weekend plus an imaginative à la carte menu. Ocean view and outside seating area when the wind stops blowing. On the expensive side but very good food and large range of wines. Daily 1830-2200 for dinner; light meals are available throughout the day.

TT **Legends**, opposite the police station on Nachtigal Bay Rd, T063-203119. Popular and relaxed bar and restaurant serving up large portions of meat and seafood, pizzas, burgers and ribs, good value for the very hungry. Wed-Mon 1630-2230.

TT **Ritzi's Restaurant**, at the new waterfront development, T063-202818. Owned by a

South African ex-diamond diver, now settled here with a young family, this restaurant has relocated into modern premises, with great views of the jetty and harbour. Excellent value, both the food and wine, very tasty – aim for the specials, they will have just been landed. Eat inside or on the wooden deck under umbrellas. Mon-Sat 0800-2200.

Ⲯ **Rumours**, at the **Kapps Hotel** (see Sleeping, above). Restaurant and sports bar with TV, popular with tourists and locals, good extensive menu from burgers to seafood, though old-fashioned and uninspiring decor. However, the bar is probably your best bet for 'action' in the evenings. Open daily 1800-late.

Diaz Coffee Shop, T063-203147, corner of Bismarck St. Excellent coffee and lunchtime snacks, daily specials, light and airy central venue. Mon-Fri 0700-1700, Sat 0800-1500, Sun 0900-1300.

Sea Breeze, at the waterfront. Modern, smart café serving breakfasts, omelettes, sandwiches and cakes. Mon-Fri 0700-1730, Sat 0800-1600, Sun 0900-1300.

Shopping

Lüderitz *p318, map p319*

There is a new waterfront development just to the east of the harbour and across the road and opposite another shopping centre in the same architectural style. At the time of writing not all of the shops in the complex had been occupied. However, the square on the sea side of the complex is very attractive and you can walk along to the end of the new public jetty for good views of the harbour.

Camping equipment

A new branch of the camping equipment store **Cymot** is on Nachtigal St.

Food

If you are self-catering there is an **OK** on Hafen St and a **Spar** on Moltke St. Both have a bakery and a butcher's counter and are open Mon-Fri until 1800, Sat and Sun until 1300. The **Portuguese Supermarket** in Bismarck St is also open Sat afternoons 1600-2000. The **bottle store** is just up from Haus Sandrose on Bismarck St, and the **fishmonger** is just outside the gate into the harbour.

Activities and tours

Lüderitz *p318, map p319*

Most of the tours listed below can be booked through the Lüderitz Info Centre at the lower end of Bismarck St. With the exception of Kolmonskop, tours into diamond areas require 5 days pre-booking due to NAMDEB restrictions.

Bogenfels – 'Rock Arch' Tour

This is one of the most interesting tours in the Lüderitz Region but, like the Elizabeth Bay tour described below, it requires a certain degree of forward planning. Because most of the tour is within the Sperrgebiet, permits have to be processed in advance. The tour lasts a full day; the 55-m-high rock arch lies 110 km south of Lüderitz. Most of the drive is across flat gravel plains, but to break the monotony there are also visits to another abandoned mining town, **Pomona**, and the **Idatal Valley** which famously yielded surface diamonds, gathered by crawling prospectors in the moonlight. This is an enjoyable trip and made that little bit special as it allows you to enter an area of the desert that has been closed to the public for most of the last 100 years. US$127 per person, minimum of 4 people. Visitors need to provide the **Coastways Tours**, office in the Waterfront Complex, T063-202001, www.coastways.com.na, with clear photocopies of their passports 5 working days in advance. If at all possible these need to be scanned and sent via email as faxed copies are not always that clear.

Diaz Point and Halifax Island

Diaz Trails, T081-2540808 (contact Gunther). Vehicle tours out to the Diaz Peninsula for US$32 per person to explore the desert flora and fauna. It can also arrange historic walking tours of Lüderitz for US$8 per person.

Sedina Boat Trips, T063-204030, sedina@iafrica.com.na. The red-sailed schooner *Sedina* departs every morning at 0800 from the waterfront jetty, weather permitting, and it carries up to 20 people. The full trip lasts for about 2½ hrs. The route takes you between Shark Island and Penguin Island, past Angra Point and on to Diaz Point.

Under ideal conditions you will sail to Halifax Island to view the colony of jackass penguins. You can also expect to see Heaviside dolphins and the colony of Cape fur seals. US$35 adults, US$18 children; book a day in advance at its office in Goerke House or through the Lüderitz Information Centre; minimum of 6 people, maximum of 20, dress warm, with windproofs.

Sturmvogel runs the same excursion for about the same price daily from the jetty at 0900 and another shorter sunset cruise out to sea that lasts 2 hrs with drinks and oysters for US$16 at 1700.

Elizabeth Bay

Ghost Town Tours, T063-204031, kolmans@iafrica.com.na. This is a ½-day tour to another ghost town where diamonds were mined between 1911 and 1950. Today NAMDEB operates a small mine slightly inland of here, opened in 1991. The tour includes visits to the operations of the old mine, and is a good insight into diamond production. US$45 per person, no children under 14, minimum of 4 people, maximum of 10. Visitors need to provide clear copies of their passports 5 working days in advance.

4WD tours

Selected tour operators have been granted the tourism concession for the spectacular dune and surf area north of Lüderitz (see also box, page 325).

In 2002 the organizers of the 4WD **Eco-Challenge** obtained permission to cross the dunes as part of the competition's finals, and proved that 4WD enthusiasts could visit the region with minimal impact on the environment. Since then Namibian authorities are allowing limited numbers of people with their own 4WD to visit the desert as part of guided convoys with selected tour operators. Participants drive their own vehicles and cater for themselves, using the old mining camp at **Saddle Hill** as a base camp. For many, this kind of off-roading is a new experience and very different to tackling muddy or rocky terrain in a 4WD. But the guides teach drivers the skills necessary to drive in sand from what tyre pressure is needed for soft sand, to what gear you will need to shift into to descend a steep dune face. Excursions total 450 km of beaches with Cape fur seals, shipwrecks and spectacular coastal land and seascapes. In the extreme the route goes into the dunes 170 km from the nearest civilization and also goes along parts of the coast to visit the shipwrecks of the *Otavi* and *United Trader* and abandoned mining equipment. This is an expensive excursion at about US$1000 per person for a 7-day trip but it is certainly the ultimate 4WD trip and a real adventure. The operators can also organize shorter tours of 1-4 days.

For more information contact **Coastways Tours**, Lüderitz, T063-202002, www.coastways.com.na. **JJ 4x4 Adventures**, South Africa, T+27 (0)44-2724576, www.jj4x4adventures.co.za, **Uri Adventures**, Windhoek, T061-231246 , www.uriadventures.com.

Transport

Lüderitz *p318, map p319*

350 km to Keetmanshoop, 650 km to Noordoewer (South African border), 845 km to Windhoek.

Air

Air Namibia, central reservations, T061-2996333, www.airnamibia.com.na, see timetable on page 72. Flights from Windhoek-Eros via Swakopmund and on to Oranjemund and Cape Town.

Note There can be delays if the wind is too strong, always allow yourself an extra day if connecting with an international flight.

Bus

Starline Passenger Services, central reservations T061-2982032, www.transnamib.com.na, has 1 bus on Mon and Fri between **Keetmanshoop** and Lüderitz which leaves at 0730 and arrives in Lüderitz at 1215, before returning at 1230 and arriving back at 1730. At the time of writing the railway was being re-laid and this service has replaced the passenger train between Lüderitz and Keetmanshoop. Buses arrive and depart from outside the Old Railway Station on the corner of Bahnhof St and Bismarck St.

Car

Car hire **Budget** has an office at the BP petrol station on Bay Rd, T063-203477, www.budget.com. Avis, opposite the Total petrol station on the way into town, T063-203968, www.avis.co.za.

Directory

Lüderitz *p318, map p319*
Banks Nedbank, First National Bank and Standard Bank, all have their premises on Bismarck St and all have money-changing facilities and ATMs. Beware of the large queues on Sat mornings after pay day.

Internet Extreme Communications in the waterfront development, 5 terminals, though on the expensive side at US$4.70 per ½ hr, open Mon-Fri 0900-1730, Sat 0900-1300. There is also 1 terminal at the post office and 1 at the Teleshop. **Medical services** State Hospital, T063-202446. There is a surgery next door to the town museum. **Police** T063-202050, emergencies T10111. **Post and Teleshop** Bismarck St, Mon-Fri 0800-1630, Sat 0800-1100.

Fish River Canyon and the Far South

The route south from Keetmanshoop is arguably the most desolate yet most impressive journey in Namibia. If you have ever wondered what the surface of the moon looks like, this is the place to find out, albeit in blinding sunlight. In defiance of the bareness of the arid, rocky landscape, a host of desert plants, cacti, succulents and quiver trees survive and even prosper. The highlight in this region is the huge gash in the earth, the Fish River Canyon, Africa's second largest canyon and one of Namibia's most popular destinations. Drive to the observation point at Hobas to witness the spectacular view and then head down into the depths of the canyon to enjoy the hot spring at Ai-Ais. Alternatively, for the fit and the adventurous, there is a four-day, 85-km hike through the canyon. ▸▸ *For Sleeping, Eating and other listings, see pages 338-340.*

Ins and outs

Leaving Keetmanshoop, the B1 heads south through the Karas Mountains towards the crossroads settlement of Grünau. From here the B1 itself continues a further 147 km to the border at Noordoewer, while the B3 heads towards Karasburg, 51 km away, and continues to the border at Ariamsvlei, a further 108 km.

The route through the **Groot Karas Mountains** is particularly beautiful, especially after rain, when the bright light reflecting off the green veld contrasts with the deep shadows cast by the rocky *koppies*. The D26 (left turn, 70 km out of Keetmanshoop) winds its way through these mountains and provides an interesting detour for those on their way to Karasburg.

An equally lovely route, travels south through the **Klein Karas Mountains**, west of the B1. This gravel road twists and turns, climbs and falls like a rollercoaster and must be approached with caution, however, it takes you through breathtaking, pristine mountain scenery. Turn right onto the D608, 6 km after leaving Keetmanshoop, and continue for 125 km before turning left onto the C12 and into Grünau, which serves as a useful staging post for trucks and Capetonians on long-distance journeys. There are a few pleasant places to stay in the vicinity, a 24-hour breakdown service with telephone and a 24-hour Shell garage just out of town by the B1/B3 junction.

There are two NWR resorts in the Fish River Canyon, **Hobas** (10 km from the canyon rim, with an observation point and campsite) and **Ai-Ais Hot Springs Resort** (by the riverbed, at the southern end). From Grünau, take the B1 south for 31 km, then turn onto the C10 which leads to Ai-Ais and the turn-off for Hobas. From Keetmanshoop take the B4 until the turn for the C12. Follow this for 77 km before the turn-off for the D601. This leads to Hobas and the D324 for Ai-Ais.

66 99 If you have ever wondered what the surface of the moon looks like, this is the place to find out, albeit in blinding sunlight...

Background

The history of the Fish River Canyon begins roughly 1800 million years ago when sandstones, shales and lava were deposited along what are now the slopes of the canyon. Between 1300 and 1000 million years ago, extreme heat caused these deposits to become folded and change into gneiss and granites. About 800 million years ago, dolerite dykes intruded into these rocks and these are now visible inside the canyon.

Between 750 and 650 million years ago, the surface of these rocks was eroded to form the floor of a shallow sea which washed over southern Namibia. The two final pieces in the jigsaw took place about 500 million years ago when tectonic movement caused a series of fractures which led to the formation of the Fish River Canyon. This early version of the canyon was deepened by the retreat southwards of glaciers during the Gondwana Ice Age some 300 million years ago.

However, this was not the end of the process. Within the main canyon a second or lower canyon was created by further movements of the earth's crust as it cooled. Initially a trough, this second canyon became the watercourse which is now the Fish River. The Fish is the longest river in Namibia and plays an important role in both watering and draining southern Namibia. In particular, it feeds Hardap Dam, Namibia's largest artificial lake.

Early Bushman legends suggest an alternative origin to the canyon. Hunters were chasing a serpent called *Kouteign Kooru* across the veld; in order to escape the snake slithered off into this deserted place and in so doing caused the massive gash that is the canyon. Archaeological evidence suggests that the Bushmen, or their ancestors, were here 50,000 years ago, so perhaps they witnessed something...

With a supply of water even during the dry winter months and food in the form of fish and game birds, the canyon has attracted human beings for thousands of years. So far, six Early and three Middle Stone Age sites have been identified in the canyon as well as the remains of a number of pre-colonial herders' camps.

Although all the tourist literature boasts that the Fish River Canyon is second in size only to the Grand Canyon in Arizona, this is not actually the case. It remains unclear as to what criteria are used to measure the size of a canyon, but it is actually only Africa's second largest after the Blue Nile Gorge in Ethiopia.

Hobas Campsite and Observation Point ›› *Colour map 3, A3.*

ⓘ *US$13 per adult, children under 16 free, US$1.50 per car; fees (both for people going to the observation points and hikers on the Fish River Canyon Hiking Trail) are paid at the gate to Hobas Campsite or Ai-Ais Hot Springs Resort.*

About halfway along the canyon at **Hell's Bend** are a series of tortuous curves in the river. Along this stretch, about 80 km north of Ai-Ais, are a number of observation points perched on the edge of the canyon where its awe-inspiring splendour can be fully appreciated. Driving out from Hobas Campsite (see Sleeping, page 338), the first

Each year approximately 35 kg of rubbish left by hikers is removed from the canyon. Recycling bins have been set up at the viewpoints and camping sites to deal with the vast quantities of rubbish accumulated.

viewpoint you reach is known as **Main Viewpoint**. The view from here is the one that appears in most publicity brochures. There are several shaded picnic tables and *braai* sites. Set back from the road are a couple of basic toilets. As the viewpoint is westward facing, early morning rather than late afternoon is probably the best time to come here.

If you continue along the track from the car park, you reach **Hiker's Viewpoint**, the starting point for the 85-km trail. The view from here is equally rewarding and it is well worth visiting both sites if you have time. Returning to Hobas Campsite look out for a turning to the right. This is a track which follows the edge of the canyon southwards for about 15 km. The road to the **Sulphur Springs Viewpoint** is pretty good; beyond this it is only passable in a 4WD vehicle. There is a path into the canyon at Sulphur Springs, being one of the escape routes for hikers unwilling to continue the full four days to Ai-Ais; you are not permitted to enter here. In the past visitors were allowed to hike down to the bottom of the canyon and back up to Hiker's Viewpoint, but this is no longer permitted and the only method of exploring the bottom of the canyon is to go on the Fish River Hiking Trail.

Fish River Canyon

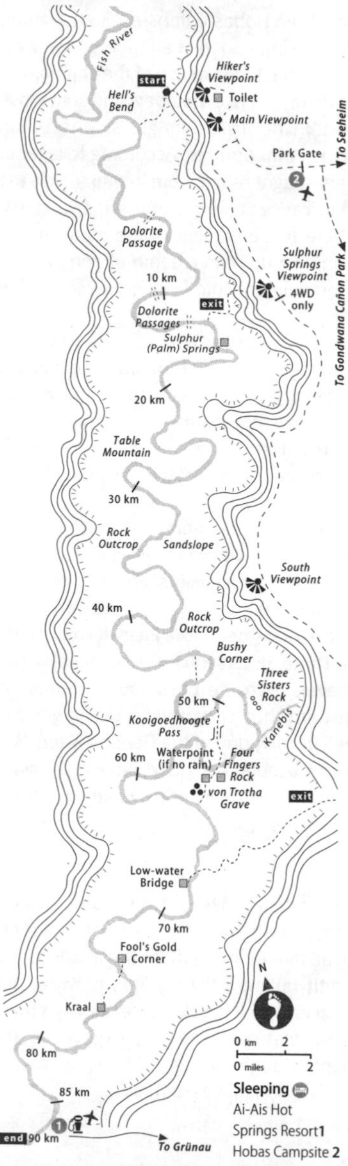

Fish River Canyon Hiking Trail

›› pp 338-340.

ⓘ *For fees, see Hobas Campsite and Observation Point, above.*

This 85-km, four-day trail is reputed to be one of the toughest hiking trails in southern Africa, and is not for beginners or the unfit. Although the trail is more or less flat, loose sand and large boulders make progress tiring, and this, added to the fact that hikers have to carry all provisions with them, cause some to take the option of an early emergency 'escape' route from the canyon. For those who are fit and determined enough to complete the trail, the four days are a magical wilderness experience, offering opportunities for game and birdwatching as well as wonderment at the scale and power of nature.

Trail information

Due to extreme temperatures and the risk of flash flooding in summer, the trail is only open from 1 May to 15 September. Groups must consist of three people minimum, 40 maximum. Medical certificates of physical fitness issued within the previous 40 days need to be shown to the ranger at Hobas before starting. No casual walkers are permitted (one died in January 2001). Bookings must be made at the **Namibia Wildlife Resorts** in Windhoek or through the website www.nwr.com.na. Roughly 2500-3000 people hike the trail each season and bookings should be made well in advance. Hikers are requested to spend at least one night at Hobas before the start of the trail and will need their own transport to get there, though transport is available from Ai-Ais back to Hobas at the end of the hike. If you are staying in one of the nearby lodges, then they should be able to arrange transport to and from the start/finish points.

The route

The route starts from **Hiker's Viewpoint**, 10 km from Hobas Campsite. From the rim, the path descends sharply to the canyon floor, losing 500 m in altitude on the way. Parts of the descent are very steep and it is advisable to make use of the chains. The route at the bottom follows the left-hand side of the river over boulders and soft, loose sand – one of the worst stretches of the walk. The first overnight stop is 15 km downstream at **Sulphur Springs**, also known as **Palm Springs**. According to legend, during the First World War two German soldiers sought refuge from internment in the canyon. One of them was suffering from skin cancer and the other from asthma. However, after bathing in the hot springs here these ailments were miraculously cured. Whether true or not, these springs, bubbling up from a depth of 2000 m at a rate of 30 litres per second, offer much-needed relief for sore feet and muscles after the long first day's trek.

Heading south of Palm Springs the shortest route criss-crosses the river as far as the **Table Mountain** landmark some 15 km on. This section of the trail is extremely tiring and not much fun as it involves struggling through deep sand and gravel. Further on, the canyon widens and the trail becomes firmer with more river crossings, more or less wet depending on the state of the river. If the rains have been good earlier in the year, trailists can expect to find a fair amount of water in the pools. Check with the rangers at Hobas regarding the availability of water.

Close to the 30-km point is Table Mountain, one of the more easily recognizable natural landmarks along the trail. After a further 18 km, you will reach the first of four possible short cuts. At this point the alternative path avoids an area of scrub vegetation known as **Bushy Corner**. Around the next corner of the canyon is the second short cut. Here the path climbs up to the **Kooigoedhoote Pass**. If you choose to take this short cut you will miss seeing the **Three Sisters Rock** and the point where the Kanbis River joins the Fish River. However, from the pass you will enjoy an excellent view of **Four Fingers Rock**. Along the third short cut you will pass the grave of Lieutenant von Trotha, a German soldier killed in 1905 during the German-Nama War and buried where he fell. A couple of kilometres beyond the grave, back in the main canyon, is the second 'emergency' exit path. From here it is a further 20 km to Ai-Ais, a cold drink, soft bed and no more walking for a few days.

Equipment

Hikers must take all their food with them – a camping stove is also needed as wood for fires is scarce during the first couple of days of the hike. Maps can be bought at Ai-Ais and Hobas. Water is almost always available en route (from the river), but for safety should be purified or boiled. It's worth taking a fishing line, provided the river/pools are deep enough; freshly grilled fish is a great luxury after a hot day's hike.

A tent is not necessary but a sleeping mat and sleeping bag is, as the temperature can fall dramatically at night. Tough walking boots, a hat, a comprehensive first-aid kit and plasters for blisters are all essential.

Transfrontier conservation areas

The Fish River Canyon and Ai-Ais Hot Springs as well as the Hunsberg Conservation Area to the west, and Richtersveld National Park over the border in South Africa, are now all part of the newly established Ai-Ais/Richtersveld Transfrontier Conservation Park, the first such transfrontier park between Namibia and South Africa for which the treaty was signed by presidents Nujoma and Mbeki in Windhoek in 2003. The ultimate aim in the future is to link the Ai-Ais/Richtersveld Transfrontier Conservation Park with the newly proclaimed Sperrgebiet National Park along the coast and then to the Lona National Park in Angola. The proposed name for this vast area that will be protected under national park status is the Three Nations Namib Desert Transfrontier Park. For now the Ai-Ais/Richtersveld Transfrontier Park covers 6045 sq km and spans some of the most spectacular desert scenery in southern Africa. There are over 50 species of mammal and it is hoped that this could be a good area to relocate other species such as black rhino or mountain zebra. It is managed jointly by the Namibian Ministry of Environment and Tourism and South African National Parks. Transfrontier parks are being established in Africa with the sponsorship of the Peace Parks Foundation (www.peaceparks.org) which promotes sustainable economic development, the conservation of biodiversity and regional peace and stability. By taking fences down, original migration routes for the game are re-established and park authorities from neighbouring countries are encouraged to work as a team. Other transfrontier parks are the Kalahari Gemsbok Park between South Africa and Botswana and the Limpopo Transfrontier between South Africa and Mozambique. Many others are in the pipeline throughout east and southern Africa.

Bird and game viewing

Small mammals such as rock dassies and ground squirrels are a common sight in the canyon and, with luck, larger mammals such as klipspringer, steenbok and springbok may also be spotted. Kudu, gemsbok and mountain zebra live in and around the canyon but are harder to spot and leopard is the hardest of all. The rock pools and reeds attract a large number of water birds, including the African fish eagle, grey herons and hammerkops; other birds such as bee-eaters, wagtails and rock pigeons are all common.

Ai-Ais Hot Springs Resort » *pp 338-340. Colour map 3, C3.*

ⓘ *Open 0800-2000, US$13 per adult, children under 16 free, US$1.50 per car; entry into the indoor hot springs, US$3.20 adult, US$0.80 child; room rates include entrance to the indoor pools, only campers and day visitors have to pay the extra fees.* The resort is very popular with families from Namibia and South Africa as a place to come and relax and lounge around in the thermal baths and outdoor heated swimming pool. As with all thermal springs the water is supposed to have natural curative properties and is especially beneficial for sufferers of rheumatism. The resort was refurbished after flooding in March 2000, but much of the accommodation remains adequate, rather than luxurious (see Sleeping, page 338).

Open year round as of 2001, the resort offers indoor and outdoor thermal pools (for a cold swim, try the river), tennis courts, good restaurant (0700-0900, 1200-1400, 1800-2200), bar, shop (0800-1800) with basic provisions, firewood and cooking utensils, petrol (0600-1800), horse riding, hiking trails and birdwatching in a beautiful and peaceful setting. There are no banking facilities.

For those feeling energetic there are some enjoyable walks into the canyon, especially pleasant in the late afternoon when the shadows are long and the heat off the rocks contrasts with the cool sand. It is also possible to hire a horse and ride into the canyon. Outside the school holidays, the tranquillity of the resort may lull you into a state of complete relaxation.

Ai-Ais is a Nama name meaning 'fire-water', indicating the extreme heat of the hot springs here. Modern knowledge of the springs dates back to 1850 when a Nama herder discovered the springs whilst searching for lost sheep. However, it is certain that Stone Age people inhabited the area thousands of years ago.

During the 1904-1907 German-Nama War, the springs were used as a base camp by German forces. Following the First World War the site was partially developed but it was not until 1969 that the site was declared a conservation area. The present resort was opened in 1971, but was almost immediately destroyed by the Fish River coming down in flood. Since then flooding has occurred three more times, in 1974, 1988 and again in 2000, on each occasion forcing the closure of the resort for repairs.

Gondwana Cañon Park ›› *Colour map 3, C4.*

Gondwana Cañon Park is a private operation that manages 1120 sq km of land to the east of the canyon, more or less the area between Hobas and Ai-Ais. After being over grazed for many years by intensive sheep farming, the park was established in 1996 and game, reintroduced into the region, can roam freely now that the old farm fences have been removed. Species include small populations of kudu, gemsbok, springbok, mountain zebra, ostrich and a number of smaller antelope. Funding comes from the 5% tourism levy charged on accommodation at the four Cañon lodges in the area (see Sleeping, below), all of them situated about 20 km from the main viewing point at Hobas. Visitors can explore the park on drives, on foot or on horseback.

The Far South ›› *pp338-340.*

The drive from **Grünau** to Noordoewer climbs steadily to a plateau, beyond which it is all downhill to the Orange River, where summer temperatures can reach 50°C. It feels almost as if one is entering hell's kitchen, but the sight of the green irrigated riverbanks soon dispels that notion. For those into canoeing this is the place to start an Orange River Canoe Safari.

Noordoewer and Orange River ›› *Phone code: 063. Colour map 3, C4.*

Noordoewer is a small settlement on the banks of the Orange River, known for being one of the hottest places in Namibia. Fortunately, there is an abundance of water, used to irrigate fruit, in particular grapes. The village consists of the border post, a post office, Bank Windhoek, a couple of petrol stations and minimarkets, and one hotel.

A few kilometres northwest of town along the banks of the Orange River are the base camps for a number of canoeing and rafting companies (see page 54). Spending a few days floating down the river either in (winter) or submerged alongside (summer) your canoe is a fabulous way to unwind from the rigours of the road – book ahead. Most of these companies are based in Cape Town, but you can meet them here and park safely ahead of your trip. The standard trip is four days, starting first thing in the morning after a night in the main camp by the river, a hearty breakfast and safety talk. The groups are pot luck, with a range of ages and backgrounds on each trip, but the same experienced, entertaining guides. Throw yourself in (literally) and you'll have a wonderful time (for details see Sleeping, page 336). Highly recommended.

Crossing into South Africa

Ariamsvlei (Namibia)/Nakop (South Africa), T063-280020. Border open 24 hours and consists of no more than a petrol station and the immigration offices. This is the best border to cross if you are heading to South Africa's Eastern Cape or Johannesburg and it's 149 km to the nearest town of Upington.

Noordoewer (Namibia)/ Velloorsdrif (South Africa), T063-2099111. Border open 24 hours and involves crossing the bridge over the Orange River in no-man's land between the two border posts. Again there are just the immigration and customs offices here and payphones. This is the best border to cross for Cape Town which is 714 km south at the end of the N7. There are petrol stations in Noordoewer on the Namibian side and ensure you have sufficient fuel to get to the next petrol stations 118 km away at Springbok in South Africa.

Just over the Velloorsdrif border, with the Orange River as its northern boundary to the Atlantic, is South Africa's Richtersveld National Park, with its beautiful, unspoilt landscape, challenging 4WD routes and beautiful camping areas. If you can't make it to Namibia's Kaokoland, this area is certainly worth exploring. For more details of this, Namaqualand and further south, see *Footprint South Africa*. However, the first reasonable hotel on the South African side is the **Okiep Country Hotel** (**C**), T+27 (0)27-7441000, www.okiep.co.za, 120 km south of the border and 8 km north of Springbok, which offers pleasant en suite rooms with DSTV, parking and good country cooking in the restaurant and bar.

Apart from over-busy holiday periods it should not take too long to complete formalities at either of these borders. If you are in a hire car ensure you have written permission from the car hire company to take the vehicle into South Africa.

Note Firewood cannot be taken from Namibia into South Africa and it will be taken off you on the South African side.

Karasburg ›› *Phone code: 063. Colour map 3, B4.*

From the visitor's point of view, Karasburg is no more than a small settlement en route to other places. It has a number of 24-hour garages, one hotel, and a Spar and OK supermarkets, but otherwise is devoid of attractions for the visitor.

Warmbad ›› *Phone code: 063. Colour map 3, B4.*

Located 43 km south of Karasburg, Warmbad is the site of the oldest mission station in Namibia. In 1805 the Albrecht brothers Abraham and Christian started working with the semi-nomadic Nama people living in this area. Although Abraham died in 1810, Christian carried on to establish the mission station at Warmbad.

The village is also the site of a series of hot springs which give the place its name. The spring is surrounded by the ruins of the Old Fort and Mission Station and as with a number of such historical sites in Namibia, there are plans to establish a resort here. Until that happens Warmbad remains another tiny settlement stuck in the middle of the veld.

Sleeping

Your sleeping arrangements, if you are not staying at the **Hobas Campsite** or **Ai-Ais Resort**, will probably be in the hands of **Gondwana Cañon Park**. Also in the region is the **Fish River Guest Farm**, www.resafrica.net/fish-river-lodge, signposted off the C12, 18 km north of the turning for the Fish River Canyon (Hobas), 22 km along this track is the farm. At the time of writing this was closed for major renovations, but may open soon. Check the website for more details.

Fish River Canyon Hiking Trail *p333, map p333*

A **Grande View Lodge**, on the rim of the canyon, accessed on the D459 from Goageb, T063-683005, www.canyonnaturepark.com. 6 en suite chalets with fantastic views, modern and comfortably furnished, cosy dining room with fireplace, good food, rates include dinner, B&B, offers fully catered and guided hiking on the **Grande-Fish Hiking Trail** in the region around the top of the canyon over 2-4 days.

D **Hobas Campsite**, T063-266028, reservations though **Namibia Wildlife Resorts**, T061-2857200 (Windhoek), www.nwr.com.na. One of the better NWR sites, located 10 km from the main viewpoint and the starting point of the **Fish River Canyon Hiking Trail** at the top of the canyon, accessible along the D601 from Hoolog which is on the C12. The campsite has 10 shaded pitches with *braai* pit and light, communal ablutions, swimming pool, small kiosk with frozen meat, beer and basic provisions, information centre (read the article on the wall of the 2 marathon runners who completed the Fish River Canyon hike in less than 12 hrs!), cool drinks and T-shirts. This is a welcome oasis after the hot drive from either of the main roads. Being smaller than most, and a popular stop for overland trucks, you are advised to book in advance. Usual form is to arrive by mid-afternoon for a swim in the pool and to set up camp, before filling the cool box with cold beer or a bottle of wine and driving out to the viewpoint at the top of the canyon to watch the sunset. Again in the morning there is the option of watching the canyon fill with light at sunrise. Allow sufficient time to drive the 10 km as the road is stony, and check with the office for times of sunset and sunrise. A 1-night stay is sufficient at **Hobas**.

Ai-Ais Hot Springs Resort *p335*

B **Ai-Ais Hot Springs Resort**, at the bottom of the canyon, just under 60 km south of Hobas along the D324, alternatively it can be reached from the B1 along the C10 which is a distance of 66 km, T063-262045, reservations though **Namibia Wildlife Resorts**, T061-2857200 (Windhoek), www.nwr.com.na. It gets exceptionally hot at the bottom of the canyon, so the flats and restaurant are only open from mid-Mar until the end of Oct. The campsite stays open throughout the year but if the river is especially high during the rainy seasons this closes too on occasion. Always check before setting out. The resort is often fully booked (apart from the campsite); reserve in advance and get confirmation to avoid receiving a surprise at the end of a long drive. Facilities include a restaurant, bar, shop, kiosk, outdoor swimming pools, indoor thermal pools, tennis courts and petrol station.

Luxury flat Modern 2-bed flat, fridge, hot plate, bedding and towels.

Flat Fully equipped 4-bed en suite flats, fridge, hot plate, bedding and towels, rather cramped for 4. **Hut** Simple 4-bed accommodation with own cooking but shared ablution facilities. Some readers have reported that there is some evidence of the damage done by the 2000 floods in some of the rooms such as signs of corrosion and rust on the doors and walls. **Camping** (**D**) in attractive, grassy camp and caravan sites, shared cooking and ablution facilities.

Gondwana Cañon Park *p336*

The lodges here are in stunning locations and cater for both organized tour groups and casual visitors and have become regular HAN award winners. All the **Cañon** properties can be booked through central reservations, T061-230066 (Windhoek), www.gondwanapark.com. Activities on offer

For an explanation of the sleeping and eating price codes used in this guide, see inside the front cover. Other relevant information is found in Essentials, see pages 43-51.

to all guests of the 4 lodges include guided walks, horse riding and game drives, which all start from the **Cañon Lodge**.

AL Cañon Lodge, from Keetmanshoop take the B4 for Lüderitz, after 32 km turn left onto the D545, signposted Naute Dam, follow this road past the dam wall until it joins the C12 after 33 km. Follow the C12 for 50 km towards Grünau, turn right onto the D601, signposted Fish River Canyon. After 20 km you will see the **Cañon Roadhouse** on your right, carry on to the D324, turn left, signposted Ai-Ais and follow the sign for the lodge 8 km down this road. 26 en suite rock chalets built into the huge boulders, each tastefully furnished and with wooden door and thatched roof. The best chalets are 11, 13, 23 and 25. Meals are served in the cool converted 1910 farmhouse, with a shaded terrace with views over the rocks and old farm implements and vehicles dotted around. Evening drives and horse trails on the farm. Day visitors are welcome for coffee, beer, buffet lunch or a refreshing swim in the pool. Before leaving it is worth climbing one of the small hills to view the surrounds. An excellent lodge in a beautiful setting; expensive, but recommended.

A Cañon Village, directions as above, but the turn-off to the village is about 3 km before the turn-off to the lodge on the D324. Opened in 2003 and expanded in 2005, the village caters mostly for tour groups (whilst the lodge, above, mostly caters for individual travellers). Styled like a Cape Dutch hamlet, the main building houses a restaurant, bar, a souvenir shop and a partly covered beer garden. 24 comfortable en suite chalets with veranda and wooden railings in front to tie horses to.

B Cañon Roadhouse, see above for directions. 7 double and 2 family en suite rooms around a pretty, shaded courtyard, swimming pool, excellent restaurant and petrol pump (not 24 hrs). The rooms have recently been renovated with new furnishings, including unusual blinds made out of recycled air filters. A new nursery for quiver trees has been planted near the swimming pool. The **campsite (D)** has *braai* pits and good ablutions but no light or electricity.

C-D Cañon Mountain Camp, 4 km beyond **Cañon Lodge** on the same road (see above); guests must check in at the lodge on the way through. The cheapest of the options, the U-shaped building surrounding a garden courtyard, used to be a sheep shearers hut. It has 8 simple double rooms, separate toilets and showers, communal kitchen and dining area, and shady terrace with *braai* facilities. If you want to eat out, there is a restaurant at the **Cañon Lodge**.

The Far South *p331*

B Savanna Guest Farm, 1 km off the B1, 40 km north of Grünau, T/F063-262070, savannah@iway.na. On 22,000-ha working sheep farm, a historical building (the busy German Shutztruppe again), with family and double en suite rooms and some self-catering units, all with a/c, breakfast included and dinner by arrangement, heated pool.

C Vastrap Guest Farm, 5 km down the B3 from Grünau towards the border, T/F063-262063, www.vastrapguestfarm.com. 6 pleasant rooms in the old farmstead buildings with *braai* and freezer facilities, very nice decor but not all guests will appreciate the animal heads on the walls in the communal areas, swimming pool, bar and farm meals available on request.

C White House, 11 km north of Grünau on the B1, T/F063-2622061, www.withuis.iway.na. 8 simple, en suite rooms in a lovely old white house and 2 more in the farmhouse where the welcoming and informative owners will look after you, cook if you book ahead and even call around their neighbours to find alternative accommodation if they are full. Recommended.

C-D Grünau Motors Chalet and Caravan Park, Grünau, behind the **Shell** garage at the B1/B3 junction, T063-262026, F262017. Reception is in the garage, which is also home to a small restaurant, food kiosk and curio shop. 4 small self-contained, a/c chalets and 4 rock-hard camping pitches, each with private ablutions, light, *braai* pit and electricity. Good value. The garage is also a stop for the **Intercape** bus between Windhoek, Cape Town and Johannesburg.

C-E Grünau Country House (formerly **Grünau Hotel**), 1 Main St, Grünau, T/F063-262001, www.grunauch.iway.na. The only option in the village itself, with 8 en suite double or family rooms, 2 with wheelchair access, 4 cheaper bungalows without bathrooms, a bar, restaurant and small swimming pool, camping facilities with adequate ablutions. The whole place is surrounded by an electric fence. Ownership has recently changed hands, and improvements have been made, HAN award winner in 2004, will pick up from **Intercape** buses by prior arrangement.

Noordoewer and Orange River *p336*
A-D Norotshama River Resort, 50 km northwest of Noordoewer on the C13 on the banks of the Orange River, T063-297215, norotshama@africaonline.com.na. Attractive thatched self-contained chalets or camping next to the river with *braai* areas, electricity and clean ablution blocks. Restaurant and bar, and lovely swimming pool designed around piles of boulders, activities include self-drive mountain bike and 4WD trails, canoeing on the Orange River, and horse riding through the dramatic local canyons.
B Felix Unite Cabanas, 10 km to the west of Noordoewer, turn left at the **Engen** petrol station, T063-297161, www.felixunite.com. Lovely reed, thatch and stone cabanas overlooking the Orange River, en suite, a/c, decorated in African style, landscaped gardens, neat dining room with good views, breakfast included in the rates. **Felix Unite** organize 4-day canoe trips on the river, spending the nights camping under the stars and cooking out bush (see Activities and tours, below).
C-E Orange River Lodge, 1 km north of the border post, the turn-off is at the BP petrol station, T063-297012, www.orlodge.iway.na. Modern, en suite rooms with a/c and TV, plain but comfortable decor, 1 family room and self-catering facilities, *lapa* restaurant and bar for breakfast and dinner, also a campsite on the banks of the Orange River with ablution block and firewood, can arrange 1-day canoe trips.
E Abiqua River Camp, about 15 km from the border post on the C13, T063-297255, abiqua@iway.na. Simple campsite on the banks of the Orange River, clean ablutions with hot water, bar and kiosk at main *lapa*, ice, firewood and *braai* packs available to buy, meals on request, lovely spot with nice views, canoeing can be arranged.

Karasburg *p337*
D Kalkfontein Hotel, Kalkfontein St, Karasburg, T063-270023. 17 rooms, 11 with en suite facilities, telephone and a/c, the furniture and decor is very faded. The hotel has a restaurant serving plain but acceptable meaty fare, a bar and lounge with TV, breakfast included, off-street parking but not secure.

Activities and tours

Noordoewer and Orange River *p336*
Most of the lodges and campsites along the Orange River on both the Namibian and South African side offer relaxing canoeing over a morning or afternoon.
Felix Unite, see Sleeping, above, reservations Cape Town T+27 (0)21-6836433 www.felixunite.com, offers 4-day canoeing trips in 2-person kayaks where every night is spent sleeping under the stars by the banks of the river. Clothes and sleeping bags are squashed into waterproof plastic drums which fit neatly into the boats. The guides take care of everything – navigating the river, choosing campsites and preparing all meals, as well as pointing out the different species of bird and animal living on and along the river. These trips come highly recommended.

Transport

Karasburg *p337*
712 km to Windhoek, 110 km to the border at Ariamsvlei.

Bus Intercape coach to **Windhoek** picks up and drops off in front of the BP petrol station next to the Spar supermerket. See timetable on page 70.

Train For trains, see timetable on page 68.

Directory

Karasburg *p337*
Banks Bank Windhoek, 9th Av, First National Bank, Main St, both offer money-changing facilities and ATMs. **Medical services** State Hospital, T063-270167, signposted on the southern outskirts of town. **Police** T10111. **Post office** Park St, Mon-Fri 0800-1630, Sat 0800-1130. **Telephones** Outside post office.

Background

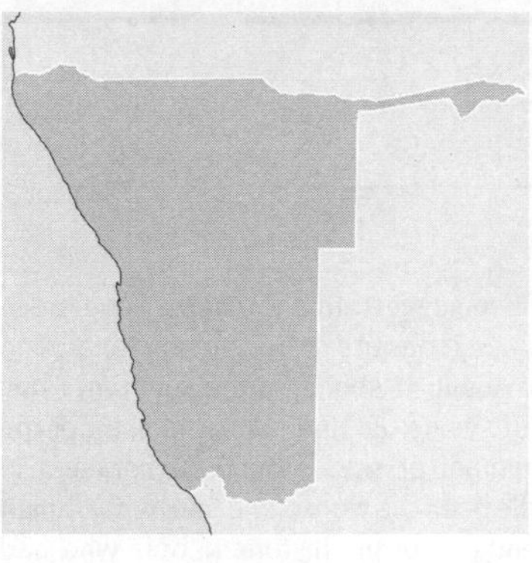

Footprint features

History

Pre-colonial Namibia

Archaeological finds from southern Namibia suggest that humans have been wandering the vast plains, dense bush and harsh deserts of the country for around 45,000 years. Ancient cave paintings at the Apollo 11 shelter in the southern Huns Mountains have been estimated to be 27,000 years old and similar rock art of the same period has also been found at a number of sites around Damaraland in northwest Namibia. These are believed to have been the work of the **San**, or **Bushmen** as they are most commonly known, descendants of pre-historic people who had migrated from southern Africa into East and North Africa before subsequently returning to the tip of the continent.

The San were traditionally hunter-gatherers, extraordinarily successful at surviving in the bush and desert despite their limited technology and weapons. They lived in small bands of up to 50 people roaming across the veld in a continuous search for food and water, rarely coming into contact with other San groups. Rock art all around Namibia, clearly seen at sites such as Twyfelfontein and Brandberg, provides vivid evidence of the widespread distribution of San communities all over the country.

Around 2000 years ago the San were joined by groups of **Khoi-khoi** (**Nama**) who had migrated from Botswana to the middle stretches of the Orange River. From here, it is believed that the group split into two, one group heading north and west into present-day Namibia, the other group moving south into the Cape Province area of South Africa. Unlike the San, the Khoi-khoi were both hunter-gatherers and livestock herders, living a semi-nomadic existence moving around the country with their herds of animals. Despite the differences in lifestyle, it appears as if Khoi and San people co-existed peacefully.

By the ninth century AD a third group was settled in Namibia living alongside the Khoisan (Nama and San); these were the **Damara** people. Sharing common cultural and linguistic ties with the Nama (rather than the Owambo, Herero or other Bantu-speaking tribes in Namibia), the exact origin and migration route of the Damara into Namibia remains a mystery. Some anthropologists argue that they must have originated in West Africa, whilst others maintain that they developed alongside the Khoi-khoin in Botswana and merely migrated later to Namibia.

By the early 19th century the Damara were living all over Namibia both alongside Nama and Herero communities as well as in their own settlements which were reported to be more permanent than those of the Nama. They had also evolved a number of distinct characteristics; they practised communal hunting techniques, the cultivation of tobacco and *dagga* (marijuana), mined and smelted copper and manufactured soapstone pipes.

Bantu-speaking tribes started arriving in Namibia during the 16th and 17th centuries, having migrated south and west from the Great Lakes area of east and central Africa. These tribes settled in the northern parts of the country alongside or close to the perennial Kunene, Kavango and Zambezi rivers which more or less correspond to their distribution in present-day Namibia.

These peoples brought with them a variety of skills such as pottery and metalworking and lived by a mixture of farming, fishing and hunting. This influx of people looking for land to establish semi-permanent settlements inevitably put pressure on existing groups, and the San and Damara in particular were forced to move further south or into less hospitable parts of the country on the fringes of the Namib and Kalahari deserts.

The **Herero** people had arrived in Namibia from east and central Africa during the 16th century and had originally settled in the Kaokoland area in the extreme northwest of the country. As cattle herders they required increasingly large areas of land to feed their growing herds and by the middle of the 18th century the marginal veld of the Kaokoland had become overgrazed and, suffering severe drought, was no longer able to support the Herero.

Gradually the majority of the Herero migrated southwards, and by around 1750 the first groups of Herero came into contact with groups of Khoi-khoi in the Swakop River area. Pressure from the Herero pushing southward more or less coincided with the northwards migration of **Oorlam** groups from the Cape Province. These two opposing movements created enormous pressure which was to erupt into almost a century of upheaval and at times open warfare in central Namibia. It was against this backdrop that the first European missionaries and traders came into the country, and their presence contributed significantly to the eventual establishment of the German colony of Southwest Africa.

Namibia - historical

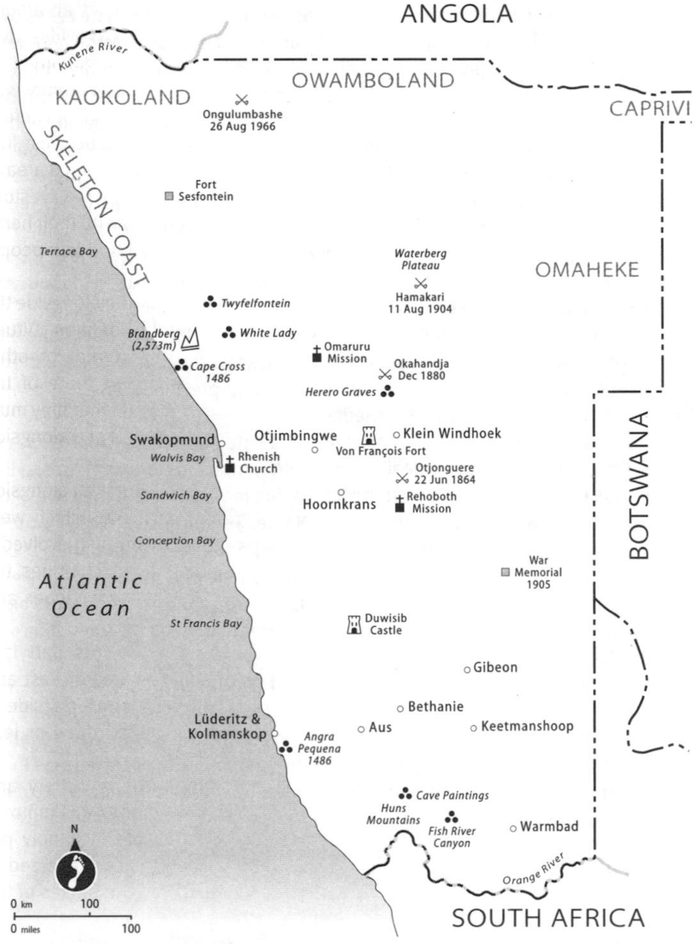

Oorlam migration

The emergence of industrial capitalism in England during the second half of the 18th century drastically changed the economy of the satellite Cape Colony. Urban centres grew and **Boer** farmers moved progressively inland, claiming land and resources further and further away from the reach of the English authorities in the Cape Colony. The Boer farmers' freedoms were won largely at the expense of the local Khoisan population who lost their land, their hunting grounds and livestock, and even their liberty, as many became servants or even slaves of these European farmers.

In the wake of these developments a new group of frontiers people emerged. These were the Oorlams, a mixed bunch of Khoi-khoin, runaway slaves, and people of mixed race descent who worked for the Boer farmers and traders as hunters and guides. They were baptized, had access to guns and horses and had shed the traditional lifestyles of other Nama groups. Some of these formed themselves into commandos, autonomous groups living separate from the European farmers and traders, surviving by hunting, trading and raiding the cattle of the Nama tribes living over the Orange River into southern Namibia.

Early missionary reports at the time described the Nama tribes of southern Namibia to be living in highly organized communities numbering in some cases over 1000 individuals. They had large herds of cattle, sheep and goats, and were completely self-sufficient, producing all their own food and manufacturing the reed mats for their huts, as well as growing tobacco and *dagga*. The different Nama tribes co-existed peacefully, sharing and respecting each other's water and grazing rights.

Initial contact between the first Oorlam groups to cross the Orange River and the local Nama tribes was relatively peaceful, but as more and more Oorlams poured over the river, demanding watering and grazing rights, the level of conflict increased to open warfare. Although the Nama were superior in numbers to the Oorlams, they had far fewer guns and horses and with their large herds of livestock were less mobile than the Oorlams. Consequently the Oorlams were soon able to establish footholds in the region from where they continued to harry and raid the Nama tribes.

Over a 40-year period up until the 1840s, southern Namibia – or Namaland as it became to be known – was in a virtually constant state of turmoil. Traditional patterns of living were disrupted, a new economy emerged and previously pastoral people started to settle in more permanent settlements.

In the 1840s Chief Oaseb, a paramount Nama chief, and **Jonker Afrikaner**, the foremost Oorlam leader, struck a deal that allowed Nama and Oorlam groups to live in peace. This deal was struck against the increasing realization that there was now little difference between the Oorlam and the Nama. The intense struggle for land and water had brought the two groups close together and intermarriage had become commonplace, so that making distinctions between the two groups was increasingly difficult. Furthermore, Herero-speaking groups who had been migrating southwards for almost 100 years were threatening the common interests of both Oorlam and Nama.

Oaseb and Afrikaner divided the land south of Windhoek amongst themselves and Afrikaner was declared overlord of the Herero lands north of the Swakop River up as far as the Waterberg Plateau. By force of arms, Afrikaner was able to maintain his hegemony over these Herero groups with their large herds of cattle, and in so doing was able to control loosely most of central and southern Namibia. Until his death in 1861, Jonker Afrikaner was probably the single most influential leader in this part of Namibia.

Jonker Afrikaner

One of the key figures in Namibia during the first half of the 19th century was Jonker Afrikaner, an Oorlam from the Cape Province who established his authority over the central and southern part of Namibia, and who established the settlement at Windhoek which was to eventually become Namibia's capital.

Jonker Afrikaner belonged to an Oorlam group who, around the turn of the century, crossed the Orange River and established a fortified village in the Karasburg District. The leader of the clan at the time was Jager Afrikaner, Jonker's father, who had killed his white employer, a farmer named Pienaar, in a dispute over wages and had subsequently fled over the Orange River beyond the reach of the Cape Province authorities. After his father's death in 1823, Jonker Afrikaner trekked north with a group of his followers, and by the 1830s had established himself as leader of central and southern Namibia.

Due to the lack of accurate historical records during this period, there are differing accounts of how Jonker established himself as the senior Nama/Oorlam leader. One explanation is that by force of arms and constant cattle raids upon neighbouring Nama tribes, Jonker was able to establish his predominance. Other theories suggest that Nama leaders, fearing the steady encroachment of the Herero on their grazing lands, called in Jonker to force the Herero back. The English explorer Sir James Alexander met Jonker in 1836 in the Rehoboth area and reported that the Afrikaners had defeated the Hereros in three decisive battles in 1835, allowing the Afrikaners to steal the Herero cattle and establish themselves as the dominant power in the area.

By the 1840s an informal but definite alliance between Jonker Afrikaner and other Nama chiefs, such as Oaseb and Swartbooi existed. The basis of the alliance recognized Jonker Afrikaner as an equal of the Nama leaders, gave the Afrikaners sovereignty of the land between the Swakop and Kuiseb rivers and made Jonker Afrikaner overlord of the Herero lands north of the Swakop River. In this way the Afrikaners effectively acted as a buffer between the Hereros to the north and the Nama tribes of the south, ensuring greater security for the Nama lands to the south. This informal alliance was officially confirmed in 1858 in an agreement between Chief Oaseb and Jonker Afrikaner.

During the 1840s and 1850s, Jonker established relations with various Herero leaders, in particular Chief Tjamuaha and his son Kamaherero and Chief Kahitjene. The basis of these relations obliged the Herero to look after Afrikaner cattle and to pay regular tributes in the form of cattle, and in return the Herero leaders were generally spared cattle raids and were able to enrich themselves at the expense of their fellow Herero.

In 1840, Jonker had established the settlement of Windhoek in the Klein Windhoek Valley. In 1842, invited by Jonker, the first two missionaries Hahn and Kleinschmidt arrived to find a flourishing community, boasting a whitewashed stone church capable of seating up to 500 people. There were also well- established gardens where corn, tobacco and *dagga* (marijuana) were being cultivated in irrigated fields. For the next 20 years Windhoek was to flourish as a centre of commerce between the Hereros and the Oorlam/Namas.

Jonker Afrikaner died in 1861 and the years following his death were to see the gradual erosion of Afrikaner hegemony over central and southern Namibia, and the abandonment of the settlement at Windhoek.

Charles John Andersson

Charles Andersson was born in Sweden in 1827 of a Swedish mother and English father. After a short spell at the University of Lund, in 1847 he abandoned his studies in order to hunt and trade with his father. In 1849 he left for England with the intention of pursuing a career of hunting and exploration in Iceland; he sailed for South Africa instead upon the invitation of an Englishman named Galton.

During the 1850s Andersson travelled and hunted for ivory all over southwestern Africa, visiting King Nangolo in Ondongo, exploring Lake Ngami and reaching the Okavango River. By 1860 he was in a position to buy up the assets of the defunct Walvis Bay Trading Company in Otjimbingwe and set up a trading company there. Andersson was interested in ivory and cattle for the Cape trade and was able to set up other hunters and traders to work for him. The fact that Andersson's trading post was permanent made it the first of its kind in Namibia. He could set up the best possible deals and, if required, travel to the Cape himself, leaving his trading partners to look after the business in Otjimbingwe.

The opening of the trading post at Otjimbingwe coincided with the outbreak of lung sickness in cattle in the region. This posed a serious threat to all the groups raising cattle – Nama, Herero and European alike. Determined to protect their herds and pastures from the deadly disease, Jonker Afrikaner and his allies were extremely reluctant to let Andersson drive his cattle south through their lands. Furthermore, by opening up Hereroland to trade, Andersson posed a threat to the hegemony of the Afrikaner clan.

In 1861, while Jonker Afrikaner was in Owamboland, Andersson set off with 1400 head of infected cattle for the Cape. Between Otjimbingwe and Rehoboth he was attacked by Hendrik Zes, a close ally of Jonker Afrikaner, who made off with 500 of the animals.

Missionaries and traders

The first Europeans had appeared off the coast of Africa in the 15th century. In 1486, the Portuguese explorer **Diego Cao** erected a cross at Cape Cross and **Bartholomeu Diaz** planted another at Angra Pequena near Lüderitz in 1486. However, the coast was barren and inhospitable, and the interior of the country at this time would have only been accessible to these explorers by crossing the Namib Desert. No other Europeans are believed to have visited Namibia until the late 18th century when a small number of Dutch settlers trekked north from the Cape Colony and established themselves as farmers. Following them a small number of traders also came to Namibia but without initially having any significant impact.

The earliest missionaries, from the **London Mission Society**, began to operate in southern Namibia at the beginning of the 19th century and were soon joined by the German Rhenish and Finnish **Lutheran Mission Societies**. The appearance of the earliest missionaries coincided with increasing numbers of Oorlams crossing the Orange River, and the presence of these missionaries was crucial to the success of the Oorlam commando groups in establishing themselves in Namibia.

Missionaries were important in 19th-century Namibia as they fulfilled a number of different roles, in addition to their primary aim of preaching the gospel. Indeed one early missionary, Ebner, regretting that he was unable to provide the Nama leader Titus AfrikanThe scene was then set for an escalation of the conflict between Andersson and his traders on the one hand and the Afrikaners and their allies on the other. A series of cattle raids and skirmishes took place during 1863, culinating in an attack on

Although Andersson and his traders were able to force Zes to return the cattle, the incident served as a serious warning to him. Thereafter, Andersson started to recruit and train mercenaries, mainly from the Cape, to protect his trading interests.

By January 1862, five months after Jonker Afrikaner's death, Andersson was established as a successful trader, organizing expeditions north into Hereroland, gradually changing the focus of his interest towards ivory and ostrich feathers. However, his position was not secure, as he noted in his diary on 26 January 1862: "The Hottentots [Namas] are fearfully jealous of me: they got a notion that I am the only person who benefits by my presence. I am not afraid of any Hottentot individually or collectively, but I may have to leave the country unless I resort to bloodshed."

In 1864 Andersson decided to seek an alliance with the Herero chiefs in an attempt to muster a big enough army to settle the conflict in one decisive battle. The Hereros had a long series of grievances going back many years against the Afrikaners and, after a series of negotiations and the election of Kamaherero as chief of all Herero speakers, a joint army of about 2500 men was put together. On 22 June 1864 the two armies met near Rehoboth in a battle that proved to be anything but conclusive. The Afrikaners retreated after a day's battle, neither having been defeated nor emerging victorious. Andersson's shin was shattered by a bullet, a wound he never fully recovered from. He sold his business interests to the Rhenish Mission and retired to the Cape to put together his bird book on Namibia.

He returned to Namibia in 1865 leaving his wife and two young children in Cape Town. However, he was never to return, and died in Owamboland in 1867 of a combination of diphtheria, dysentery and exhaustion.

Otjimbingwe by the Afrikaners in June of that year. Andersson, his traders and mercenaries – the 'Otjimbingwe volunteers' as they had come to be known – routed the attackers, killing about a third of them including their commander Christian Afrikaner. However, the power of the Afrikaners was not broken, and guerrilla attacks on Andersson's cattle trains continued.er with a supply of gunpowder as earlier preachers had done, was driven to write that "it seems to me that he is more interested in powder, lead and tobacco than in the teachings of the gospel".

Until the arrival of the missionaries, the Nama communities in the south of Namibia were semi-nomadic, however, the building of churches and the development of agriculture saw the establishment of the first stable settlements. The stone-walled churches fulfilled the role of mini-fortresses, and the brass bells that the missionaries provided were an effective warning system during raids. Many missionaries also introduced agriculture to the communities in which they lived, and the more stable food supply that followed allowed larger numbers of people to settle in an area. In turn, these larger settlements allowed for improved defence against raids through better organization.

Second, the missionaries acted as focal points for traders from the Cape, who were able to supply the missionaries and their families with the goods they needed. In this way the trade routes to the Cape were established and kept open, thus guaranteeing the Oorlam leaders continued supplies of the guns and ammunition upon which they depended for their supremacy. In the early years of the 19th century it seems as if some missionaries even supplied the guns themselves. Schmelen, who established a mission at Bethanie in southern Namibia, found it necessary to "furnish some of my people with arms". Even in later years when the export of guns and gunpowder from the Cape was prohibited, Kleinschmidt, who operated the mission at Rehoboth, provided Chief Swartbooi with gunpowder.

The almost constant conflict brought about the breaking down of social structures, although the missionaries armed with their Christian rules proved effective control mechanisms for tribal leaders. In 1815, referring to the Afrikaner clan, Ebner noted that "it is only the baptised who are allowed ... to use the gun." Blameless Christian behaviour was also a prerequisite to political positions in communities such as Bethanie, Rehoboth and Warmbad (behaviour defined, of course, by the missionaries). Missionaries also performed the roles of social worker and doctor, and Jonker Afrikaner once explained to Schonberg why he wanted a missionary at Otjimbingwe "... traders come and go, but the missionary stays, and consequently we know where to get our medicines from".

By the 1860s an extensive network of trading posts existed in Namibia, the most important being Otjimbingwe northwest of present-day Windhoek. Set up by the Anglo-Swede **Charles John Andersson**, Otjimbingwe was also a key mission station for the Herero-speaking peoples. Under Andersson's influence the European community of missionaries, traders and hunters were gradually sucked into the escalating Herero-Nama conflict (see box, page 345).

Following the death of Jonker Afrikaner in 1861 and the defeat of the Afrikaners and their allies at Otjonguere south of Windhoek in 1864, the years leading up to 1870 saw a virtual constant jockeying for position amongst the various Nama and Oorlam leaders. Once again the southern and central parts of Namibia were the scene of skirmishes and cattle raids. This infighting amongst the Oorlam/Namas effectively allowed the Herero-speaking people under the leadership of Kamaherero to break free of Afrikaner dominance.

The 1870 Peace Accord

In 1870 Jan Jonker Afrikaner arrived at Okahandja with a large group of armed men with the intention of renewing the old alliance between Kamaherero and the Afrikaners. However, missionary Hahn intervened and when the treaty was concluded in September of that year the Afrikaners had lost their old rights over the Herero-speaking peoples. Furthermore, Hahn obtained permission for the Cape **Basters** to settle at Rehoboth. The Basters were a farming community of mixed Khoi-European descent who, having been forced from their lands in the Cape Province, had been looking for a place to settle. The Baster settlement at Rehoboth acted as an effective buffer between the Herero-speaking peoples and the Oorlam-Namas.

Peace was preserved between the Nama and Herero-speaking peoples throughout the 1870s, and it was not until the beginning of the 1880s that conflict broke out once more. However, this period of relative peace amongst indigenous Namibians also saw the consolidation of the position of the missionaries and traders – particularly the latter. As the Nama leaders developed a taste for manufactured goods and alcohol, the economy of Namaland – virtually all the land south of Windhoek as far as the Orange River – became inextricably linked with that of the Cape. As a result the numbers of hunters, traders and explorers entering Namibia grew uncontrollably, and this in turn saw the over-exploitation of animal and natural resources in the central-southern part of Namibia.

The hunters and traders were chiefly interested in obtaining ivory and ostrich feathers to export to the Cape. At the same time they were selling guns, coffee, sugar, soap, gin and brandy to the Namibians. The only way the Nama chiefs could support their habit for western manufactured goods and alcohol was by granting licenses to the hunters and traders, leading one explorer, A Anderson, to complain to the Cape government that "every petty kaptein claims a license fee" for hunting, passing through and trading.

However, while the Oorlam/Namas of southern Namibia became caught up in this trading network, the Herero-speaking peoples living north of Windhoek remained largely aloof from this burgeoning trade. True, they were the main purchasers of guns, for they had learned during the middle part of the century of the importance of modern weapons, but for the rest, trade with Hereroland was tightly controlled.

Given the vast numbers of cattle which the Herero were breeding, it seems strange that the European traders were not more active in their contact with the Herero. The main reason for this it seems, was a lack of interest on the part of the Herero in exchanging their cattle for western goods.

Unlike the inhabitants of Namaland who were experiencing a spiralling circle of dependency on imported manufactured goods together with the virtual invasion of their territory by Europeans of one description or another, the Herero-speaking peoples retained their traditional kinship-oriented pastoral way of life. In other words the Herero valued their cattle far more highly than any manufactured goods, and rather than exchanging cattle for goods, they actually increased the size of their herds.

Despite renewed raids during the early part of the 1880s by Oorlam/Namas who succeeded in stealing thousands of head of cattle, ex-missionary Hahn – now a full-time trader – remarked that the Herero "will in a few years make up for these losses. There is, perhaps, no people in the world who equals the Damaras (Hereros) as cattle breeders ...".

Namibia becomes a colonial possession

In 1880, after 10 years of relative peace, fierce fighting broke out once more in central Namibia. Once again the disputes were over cattle and grazing rights and they involved all the key players in central Namibia at the time. There were the Herero – led by **(Ka)Maherero** as he came to be known – the Nama Swartboois, the Afrikaners under Jan Jonker and the Rehoboth Basters (relative newcomers to the scene). All through 1880 and 1881 the fighting continued with a number of important leaders falling in battle, in particular Maherero's eldest son Willem in the fight for Okahandja in December 1880. Up until 1884 and the rise of **Hendrik Witbooi**, a bewildering series of shifting alliances, cattle raids and skirmishes characterized the scene in south and central Namibia.

However, it was the arrival of German representatives in 1884, the subsequent treaties with the Herero and the effective subduing of Hendrik Witbooi 10 years later that fundamentally changed the way in which Namibia was governed. Power steadily shifted away from traditional leaders, such as Witbooi and Maherero, into the hands of the German colonial administrators. Furthermore, over the next 25 years vast tracts of Namaland and Hereroland passed into the hands of the colonial government and individual settlers. This fundamental change culminated with the 1904-1907 German-Namibian war which saw the final consolidation of colonial authority over the country, and the subjugation of the Namibian peoples by Europeans.

Between 1883 and 1885, the German trader and businessman **Adolf Lüderitz** negotiated a series of agreements which saw him buy practically the entire coastal strip of Namibia between the Orange and Kunene rivers, extending as far as 150 km inland. A settlement was established at **Angra Pequena**, soon renamed as **Lüderitzbucht**, which helped open the country up to German political and economic interests. German policy in Namibia was that private initiative and capital would 'develop' the country, secured by German government protection.

In order to bring 'order' to Namibia, the German authorities pursued a policy of persuading local leaders to sign so-called protection treaties (Shuzverträge) with them. This they achieved by exploiting local conflicts to serve their own ends, and in the face of continuing conflict between Maherero and Hendrik Witbooi, were able to persuade Maherero to sign a protection treaty with the German authorities in 1885. In the same year Commissioner Göring wrote to Hendrik Witbooi ordering him to desist from continuing with his cattle raids against the Herero and threatening him with unspecified consequences.

However, these threats were empty gestures. During the period 1884-1889 the official German presence in Namibia consisted of three officials based in a classroom at the mission school in Otjimbingwe, plus a small number of business representatives who effected the protection treaties. It was not until 1889 that the first force of 21 soldiers (Schutztruppe) landed in Namibia, to be followed by another 40 the following year, and only after 1894, following the subduing of Hendrik Witbooi, that significant numbers of settlers were able to enter the country.

Between 1894 and 1904 the Witboois sold a third of their land to European settlers, and the treaties that Samuel Herero signed with the German colonial government in 1894 and 1895 ceded Herero land to them. Meanwhile, following the death of old Maherero in 1890, the German administration established its headquarters in Windhoek and during the confusion over the succession of the Herero leader was able to consolidate its position there. However, the greatest sale of Herero land took place in the years after 1896 – the result of the trade on credit systems in operation at the time, the rinderpest epidemic of 1897 and the fever epidemic of 1898.

With the further opening of Hereroland to trade following the treaties signed with the German colonial administration, there was a dramatic increase in the number of traders operating in the country. For Europeans without their own capital but prepared to put up with the hardships of living in the veld, this was a perfect opportunity to make money and acquire cattle and land. Large firms employed these traders to go out to Herero settlements in the veld and sell their goods there. Due to the risks involved, all parties attempted to maximize profit, often adding 70 to 100% onto the value of goods to achieve this. They were also quite happy to give the Hereros credit in order to encourage them to buy more and more, until the situation arrived whereby an individual or community's debt was greater than their assets.

In addition, following the rinderpest epidemic of 1897 in which up to 97% of unvaccinated cattle died, the only way in which the Hereros could pay for the goods they wanted or settle their debts was to sell land. An addiction to alcohol amongst many Hereros, not least their leader Samuel Maherero, also caused large debts which had to be settled through land sales. Although the colonial government attempted to put all business dealings between Europeans and Namibians on a cash basis, the protests of the traders brought about a suspension of this regulation almost immediately after its introduction.

Inevitably tension grew among the Herero as they saw their traditional lands gradually disappearing. The Rhenish Missionary Society petitioned the colonial government to consider creating reserves for the Herero where the land could not be sold, and despite initial resistance both within Namibia and from Germany, so-called paper reserves (because initially they only existed on paper) were created around Otjimbingwe at the end of 1902 and around Okahandja and Waterberg in 1903. However, there were many Herero leaders who were deeply dissatisfied with the land issue, and pressure was growing on Herero leader Samuel Maherero to take some action to recover lost lands – although he himself had been responsible for the sale of much of it.

The 1904-1907 German-Namibian War

The three years of fighting between the German colonial forces and various Namibian tribes ended with victory for the Germans and the consolidation of their colonial rule over Namibia. Thousands of Namibians died either as a result of the fighting or in the aftermath and the effect that this had was to put a stop to organized resistance to outside rule. The trauma of defeat and dislocation meant that 50-odd years were to pass before the emergence of the independence movements in the late 1950s.

The war began following a revolt of the Bondelswarts Namas in the extreme south of the country at the end of 1903. The majority of German soldiers were sent to the south to quell the uprising and in January 1904 Samuel Maherero, under intense pressure from other Herero leaders and fearing for his own position as paramount Herero leader, gave the order to the Herero nation to rise up against the German presence in Namibia. At the same time he also appealed to Hendrik Witbooi and other Namibian leaders to follow suite.

During the first months of the uprising the Herero were successful in capturing or isolating German fortified positions, however, following the appointment of **Lothar von Trotha** as German military commander, the Herero were gradually forced to retreat from around Okahandja and other strongholds in central Namibia. They made a final stand at the waterholes at Hamakari by the Waterberg Plateau south of Otjiwarongo in August of 1904. The German plan was to encircle the assembled Herero, defeat them, capture their leaders and pursue any splinter groups which might have escaped. The Herero objective was to hold onto the waterholes, for without these they and their cattle would either die or be obliged to surrender.

The German troops attacked the Herero forces on 11 August with the battle continuing on a number of fronts all day. By nightfall no clear picture had yet emerged, however, the following day it became apparent that although the Herero had not been defeated, their resistance was broken and Samuel Maherero and the entire Herero nation fled into the Omaheke sandveld in eastern Namibia en route for Botswana. Stories from those who eventually arrived in Betchuanaland (Botswana) tell horrific stories of men, women and children struggling through the desert, gradually dying of thirst.

A section of the German forces initially gave chase but by 14 August they had returned to the original battle site, both soldiers and horses suffering from exhaustion, hunger and thirst. The chase was once again taken up on 16 August but finally abandoned at the end of September as it was impossible to provision both troops and horses in the inhospitable sandveld.

On 2 October Von Trotha issued a proclamation ordering all Herero-speaking people to leave German Southwest Africa or face extermination, and then turned his attention to subduing uprisings in the south of the country. Just over a month later, Von Trotha received orders from Berlin to spare all Herero except the leaders and those 'guilty'. Following the retreat of the Herero, three more years of sporadic resistance to German rule took place in the centre and south of Namibia as the Nama-speaking people continued the revolt.

Much has been written on the German-Namibian War, specifically of the deliberate intention of the German colonial administration to 'exterminate' the Herero nation. Until recently it was widely accepted that the Herero nation was reduced from a population of 60,000-80,000 people before the war, to between 16,000 and 18,000 people after the war. Similarly, the generally accepted view is that the population of the Nama-speaking peoples was also reduced by 35-50% to around 10,000 people.

It is impossible to obtain accurate figures to either confirm or refute the allegations of genocide. Nevertheless, some recent research, especially by the late Brigitte Lau, former head of the National Archives, challenges a number of popular conceptions of the war. In particular questions have now been raised on how the numbers were calculated and on the capacity of the German forces to actually set about the deliberate process of genocide.

The only figures available were based on missionary reports in the 1870s, but the missionaries only worked in a relatively small area of Hereroland. Furthermore, any accurate estimate of the numbers of Herero would have been near impossible, as the Herero were scattered across the veld. In addition, the effects of the rinderpest epidemic of 1897 and the fever epidemic of 1898 were also not taken into account. The suggestion is therefore that there were far fewer Herero than was originally believed.

As far as the capacity of German military to wipe out the Herero is concerned, medical records of the time show that the average military presence during the war was 11,000 men. Of these an average of 57% per year were sick from the effects of lack of water and sanitation, typhoid fever, malaria, jaundice and chronic dysentery. This information suggests that the German military presence was simply not capable of a concerted attempt to commit genocide – even if that had been the intention.

There is no question, however, that following the war both Herero and Nama prisoners of war died in concentration camps; there were executions of captured leaders and many survivors were forced into labour – working on the railroads and in the mines. By the end of the war, the German colonial administration was firmly in control of Namibia from the Tsumeb-Grootfontein area in the north down to the Orange River in the south. In 2004 Germany offered a formal apology for colonial-era killings of tens of thousands of ethnic Hereros, but ruled out compensation for victims' descendants.

Economic development

With the consolidation of German control of central and southern Namibia came rapid economic growth and infrastructural development. Land in the most productive areas in the country was parcelled up and given to settler families, forming the basis of much of the existing white agricultural wealth in the country today. The railway network, already in place between Lüderitz and Aus in the south and Swakopmund, Okahandja and Windhoek in the centre of the country, was expanded to reach the central-northern towns of Tsumeb and Otavi and Grootfontein, Gobabis in the east and Keetmanshoop in the south.

The discovery of diamonds at Kolmanskop near Lüderitz in the south in 1908 financed the economic boom in that part of the country – between 1908 and 1914, German mining companies cut a total of 5,145,000 carats of diamonds. The introduction of the **karakul** sheep (see box, page 313) to the south saw the start of the highly successful karakul wool and leather industry, which brought tremendous prosperity to white farmers in the ranchlands south of Windhoek. Finally, the development of the Tsumeb mines producing copper, zinc and lead brought wealth and development to the Tsumeb-Grootfontein-Otavi triangle in the central-northern areas.

While the wealth that accrued from this flurry of economic activity was concentrated in the hands of white settlers, the labour which built the railroads and worked the farms and mines was predominantly black. A vivid example of this was the estimated 10,000 Oshiwambo-speaking workers who came down from Owamboland in the far north (an area still outside German colonial control, although technically part of German Southwest Africa) to work on the railroads and in the mines. This was the start of migratory work patterns upon which the apartheid era contract labour system was built.

Self-government for the white population was granted by Germany in January 1909 and the following month the main towns including Windhoek, Swakopmund,

Keetmanshoop, Lüderitz, Okahandja and Tsumeb were granted the status of municipalities. In Windhoek this period up to the beginning of the First World War in 1914 saw the building of many landmarks – in particular the **Christuskirche** (German Lutheran Church) and the **Tintenpalast** – now the seat of the Namibian Parliament. Self-government in German Southwest Africa lasted until the peaceful surrender of the territory to South African troops fighting on the side of the British in July 1915. This brought to an end the brief period of German colonial rule and ushered in the beginning of 75 years of South African rule.

League of Nations mandate

Following the end of the First World War and the signing of the Treaty of Versailles in 1919, the newly formed League of Nations gave the mandate for governing Namibia to Britain. The mandate, which was to be managed by South Africa on behalf of Britain, came into effect in 1921 and was the beginning of South African control of Namibia, which was to end only with independence in 1990.

The pattern of South African rule over Namibia was established from the start with the relentless expropriation of good farm land for white farmers and the removal of the black population, first to native reserves and later to the so-called homelands. When South Africa took over control of Namibia about 12,000,000 ha of land were in the hands of white (mainly German) farmers, however by 1925 a further 11,800,000 ha had been given to white settlers.

A great number of these new settlers were poor, illiterate Afrikaners who the Union government in South Africa did not want within their own borders. In this way Namibia effectively became a dumping ground for these unwanted farmers, who were given the most generous of terms. New farmers were not only given land for free, but also received credit in the form of cash, wire fences and government-built bore holes to help them get started.

In contrast, in 1923 the Native Reserves Commission proclaimed a mere 2,000,000 ha for the black population of the country who made up 90% of the total population. At the same time a series of laws and regulations governed where the black population was entitled to live and work, severely restricting their freedom of movement in the white-controlled areas. The most obvious consequences of these laws was the creation of a pool of readily available, cheap labour – the nascence of the contract labour system.

The bulk of the population of Namibia was forced to live in a narrow strip of land north of Etosha and south of the Angolan border, marked by the Kunene and Okavango rivers. The **Red Line**, a veterinary fence established by the Germans to prevent the spread of rinderpest and foot-and-mouth disease, effectively separated the communal grazing lands of the north from the commercial white-owned land of the centre and south of the country. This strip of land was far too small to support the number of people living there, obliging many to put themselves into the hands of the contract labour system by seeking work further south.

In 1925 two recruitment agencies were established to find workers for the mines in the centre and south of the country, and in 1943 these two original agencies were amalgamated into the South West Africa Native Labour Association (SWANLA). Potential workers were sorted into three categories – those fit and able to work underground, those suitable for work above ground at the mines, and the rest only suitable for farm work. Workers themselves had no choice in this and a document of the time stated that "Only the servant is required to render to the master his service at all fit and reasonable times."

The period following the Second World War saw further land give-aways, mainly as rewards to Union soldiers who had served in the war. By the mid-1950s a further

 7,000,000 ha of farmland had been put into white hands and the number of whites in Namibia had increased by 50% to around 75,000. The last viable farmland was given away in the 1960s to white conservatives who supported the South African regime's hard-line apartheid policies.

At the same time the Odendaal Commission of Inquiry formulated a plan for the creation of **bantustans**, or black homelands, around the country, involving the forced removal of the black population from all areas designated for whites. The commission also called for the even closer integration of Namibia into South Africa and stated explicitly that "the government of South Africa no longer regards the original (League of Nations) mandate as still existing as such".

Road to independence

Following the end of the Second World War, the newly formed United Nations Organization assumed responsibility for the administration of the former German colonies, such as the Cameroons, Togo and Namibia. The UN set up a trusteeship system intended to lead to independence for these territories and in response the South African government sought to incorporate Namibia into South Africa. A series of 'consultations' with Namibian leaders during 1946 were intended to convince the UN that Namibians themselves sought to become part of South Africa. Although these efforts were unsuccessful, it was not until 1971 that the South African presence was deemed to be 'illegal'.

Organized resistance to South African rule took off in the 1950s and was initially led by Herero Chief **Hosea Kutako**, who initiated a long series of petitions to the UN. In 1957 the Owamboland's People's Congress was founded in Cape Town by Namibian contract workers lead by **Andimba Toivo Ja Toivo**, its prime objective being to achieve the abolition of the hated contract labour system. In 1958 Toivo succeeded in smuggling a tape to the UN giving oral evidence of South African suppression and for his pains was immediately deported to Namibia. The same year the name of the organization was changed to the Owamboland People's Organization (OPO) and in 1959 Sam Nujoma and Jacob Kuhangu launched the organization in Windhoek.

The same year also saw the founding of Southwest Africa National Union (SWANU), initially an alliance between urban youth, intellectuals and the Herero Chief's Council. In September of that year the executive of the organization was broadened to include members of the OPO and other organizations, thereby widening its base and making it more representative of the Namibian population as a whole.

These new organizations were soon in conflict with the South African authorities and the December 1959 shootings at the **Old Location** (see box, page 84) effectively marked the start of concerted resistance to South African rule. 1n 1960 the OPO was reconstituted into the **South West Africa People's Organization** (**SWAPO**), with the central objective of liberating the Namibian people from colonial oppression and exploitation. SWAPO leader Sam Nujoma had managed to leave Namibia and was to lead the organization in exile until his return in 1989.

In 1966, SWAPO appealed to the International Court of Justice to declare South Africa's control of Namibia illegal. The court failed to deliver, even though the UN General Assembly voted to terminate South Africa's mandate. SWAPO's response was to launch the guerrilla war at Ongulumbashe in Owamboland on 26 August, with the declaration that the court's ruling 'would relieve Namibians once and for all from any illusions which they might have harboured about the United Nations as some kind of saviour in their plight'.

In the early stages, the bush war was by necessity a small-scale affair. SWAPO's bases were in Zambia, close only to the Eastern Caprivi Region, and it was only after the Portuguese withdrawal from Angola in 1975 that it became possible to wage a larger-scale campaign. In response to the launching of the guerrilla war, the South African government established military bases all across Namibia's northern borders, and as the scale of the fighting escalated during the 1980s, life became increasingly intolerable for the inhabitants of these areas.

On the political scene, SWAPO activists in Namibia were arrested, tried and sentenced to long prison terms. Among the first group to be sentenced in 1968 was Toivo Ja Toivo, at that time regional secretary for Owamboland. He was sentenced to 20 years imprisonment on Robben Island where he was to remain until 1984. Following the International Court of Justice ruling in 1971 that "the continued presence of South Africa in Namibia [was] illegal", a wave of strikes led by contract workers broke out around the country, precipitating a further round of arrests of strike leaders.

Although the South African government succeeded in quelling the strikes of late 1971 and early 1972, the rest of the decade saw growing resistance to South African rule of Namibia. Ordinary Namibians everywhere, but especially in the densely populated north, buoyed by the International Court of Justice ruling, became politicized, resisting South African attempts to push forward apartheid policies to create separate bantustans around the country.

In response to pressure from Western countries South Africa struggled to find an 'internal solution' to the deadlock in Namibia which would both satisfy the outside world and at the same time defend white minority interests in the country. In 1977 the **Turnhalle Conference** produced a draft constitution for an independent Namibia based on a three-tier system of government which would change little. Needless to say, no one was fooled and the war continued.

During the 1980s South Africa's position in Namibia became increasingly untenable. The bush war was expensive and never-ending and was seriously affecting the South African economy; at the same time attempts to find a political solution within Namibia which excluded SWAPO were proving impossible. Furthermore, opinion amongst the influential Western nations was swinging away from South Africa, making it inevitable that sooner or later Namibia would have to be granted independence with black majority rule.

The key to the solution was the withdrawal of Cuban troops from Angola in return for the withdrawal of South African soldiers from Namibia. At the same time a United National Transitional Government (UNTAG) was to oversee the transition to independence, with elections taking place in November 1989. The final months leading up to the elections saw the return of SWAPO President **Sam Nujoma** from 30 years in exile along with thousands of ordinary Namibians who had also fled into exile during the long years of the bush war.

The main political parties were SWAPO and the DTA, formed in the wake of the unsuccessful Turnhalle Conference. Support for SWAPO was almost universal in Owamboland where the majority of the population lived, while the DTA looked to the south and much of the white community for its support. Although SWAPO won the elections it did not gain the two-thirds majority required to draw up a new constitution for the country.

Following the successful elections a new constitution was drafted by the various political parties, with the help of international advisers from a number of countries including the USA, France, Germany and the former Soviet Union. Widely viewed as a model of its kind, the new constitution guaranteed wide-ranging human rights and freedom of speech, as well as establishing a multi-party democracy governed by the rule of law. The final date for independence was set for 21 March 1990.

Modern Namibia

Since independence the SWAPO government led by Sam Nujoma has pursued a policy of national reconciliation designed to heal the wounds of 25 years of civil war and over a century of colonial rule. Strongly supported by the various UN agencies and major donors, the Namibian government has set about redressing the injustices of the past and rebuilding the economy, so badly damaged by the war. The mining sector, which is by far the largest sector of the economy, has been further developed and significant growth has also occurred in both the fishing and tourist industries. Nevertheless, Namibia is still largely dependent on South Africa for foodstuffs and manufactured products, and this is one of the weak links in the economy.

The provision of educational and health care facilities to previously neglected sections of the community has also been a priority for the government, but this has placed a heavy burden on the country's finances. Education alone has been consuming around 30% of the national budget since independence, while the combined effects of rapid population growth (around 3.5%) and an inflation rate hovering around the 10% mark have made it difficult for the country to address the problem of massive unemployment.

Elections in 1994 saw SWAPO win with a massive 68% of the vote, which effectively gave the party the right to change the constitution if it had wished to do so. Throughout 1998 a debate raged as to whether or not the constitution should be changed to allow the president to stand for a third term. On the one hand it was argued that allowing the generally popular Sam Nujoma to stand for a third term would contribute to stability and continuity in this young nation. On the other hand, some Namibians and external observers believe that changing the constitution would set a dangerous precedent and set Namibia on the path to becoming a one-party state.

The debate effectively ended in November 1998 when the Namibian Constitution Amendment Bill, allowing President Nujoma a third term in office, passed through the final parliamentary stage. General and presidential elections held at the end of 1999 saw another convincing SWAPO victory, and Sam Nujoma duly commenced his third term in office as president.

Around this time, the bizarre events in the Caprivi – which saw the governor of the region, prominent leaders and ordinary citizens flee to Botswana and apply for political asylum – were the first indications of serious unrest since independence in 1990. In addition, renewed fighting in the Angolan Civil War and Namibian government support for the MPLA government saw incursions by both UNITA and MPLA soldiers from Angola. At the same time well-publicized attacks on foreign tourists in 2000 damaged tourist confidence in the country.

An additional and unnecessary distraction from the serious business of creating economic growth was the country's involvement in the conflict in the Democratic Republic of Congo to prop up the now-assassinated Laurent Kabila. Despite the Prime Minister's explanations that Namibia was "fighting for peace" and "going every inch" for negotiations to end the conflict, the real reasons behind Namibia's involvement remain somewhat murky.

Despite suggestions that another amendment to the constitution might be made to permit a fourth term of presidency, in April 2004, Nujoma announced that he would step down at the end of his third term. In the November elections, **Hifikepunye Pohamba**, the SWAPO candidate and Nujoma's handpicked successor (who uncannily looks just like him), won in a landslide victory and took over the presidency in March 2005. Hage Geingob, Namibia's Prime Minister since independence was replaced by **Theo-Ben Guirirab**, and SWAPO also retained a two-thirds majority parliament. In 2002, President Nujoma began to address the issue of land reform, and said that white farmers must embrace a reform programme. For many blacks who have seen little change in the pattern of land ownership since independence; this is a contentious issue given that half of the country's agricultural land is owned by a few thousand white farmers. Pohamba has been a long-time confidante of Nujoma and plans to follow similar policies to his predecessor and, like Nujoma, is committed to the principle of sale and purchase of land by consent, not by illegal occupation as happened in neighbouring Zimbabwe. By the end of 2005, the government had begun the expropriation of white-owned farms as part of the land-reform programme but faces resistance to change from predominantly the white population.

During the late 1990s and first part of the new century, the Namibian economy has continued to grow, albeit slowly, and the further development of the Walvis Bay port, the completion of the Trans-Kalahari and Trans-Caprivi highways and the opening of the new road bridge across River Zambezi between Namibia and Zambia demonstrates the government's commitment to international commerce and trade. The tourism sector has been a bright beacon as the country has emerged as one of Africa's best-known secrets. Namibia is also an active member of the Southern African Development Community (SADC). Above all else, human rights and freedom of speech continue to be respected in Namibia and for the most part the rule of law prevails.

The biggest challenges facing Namibia as she moves into her second decade of independence and the new millennium are to address poverty and unemployment, find a fair solution to the land debate and get to grips with the **AIDS** epidemic which affects more than 40% of the population in some northern areas. With education and training high on the government's list of priorities and the all-round will to see the country prosper, Namibia's future is potentially bright.

Economy

Since independence Namibia has enjoyed steady but unspectacular economic growth, but this has been checked by periods of drought and low world commodity prices. Per capita income in 2005 was estimated at US$7400, which is high compared to the rest of the region, but disguises the great inequality in income distribution as almost 50% of the population lives below the poverty line. Namibia has one of the most unequal income distribution in the world, with most of the productive ranch land lying in the hands of a minority of white farmers, as it did until very recently in neighbouring Zimbabwe. Similarly, most commerce and industry is controlled by a minority of whites and a small black middle class, while the mass of the population earns a meagre living from subsistence farming, from the service industry and from the informal sector.

Between 1990 and 1995 the economy grew at an average rate of 4.5%, but a 3.2% population growth eroded many of the economic gains and meant that a majority of Namibians actually became poorer during this period. Today the trends have been reversed as the population growth is less than 1% and inflation is put at around 4.2%. In 1982 mining contributed to 26.9% of GDP; by 1995 this figure had fallen to 11% but is presently rising again and is 20% of GDP in 2005. Tourism and the fisheries sector have made significant contributions to recent growth and agricultural output remains more or less constant. However, these sectors have been unable to absorb the increase in the number of Namibians looking for work.

In 2005, 84% of the adult population were literate, and education is compulsory from 6-16. Namibia has placed a high priority on education – since independence the system has been rationalized and the quality and relevance of the education for all Namibian children has been improved. Over 10% of GDP is devoted to education, a proportion exceeded by few countries in the world. In the long run the government is hoping to reap the dividends, assuming sufficient jobs can be created.

The Namibian health care system is one of the government's four priority sectors. Before independence the system concentrated on curative care for the urban elite, while neglecting the majority of the poor. The system was racially based with inequitable quality and access to care. The government has embarked upon a programme to redistribute resources from curative to primary care. Investment in health care has been 14% of government spending, a high proportion by regional and international standards. Improvements have been made but many of the remote rural areas are still without access to clinics and community health workers.

However, the major health issue facing Namibia is the desperately serious AIDS epidemic that will have profound social, demographic and economic consequences for the country. According to the Ministry of Health, the rate of HIV infection has grown from 8% in 1998 to 17% in 2005. This is despite widespread public education campaigns in the media, and a much healthier and open debate than was previously the case about how to tackle this serious problem. The epidemic as in other parts of Africa, fundamentally affects the poorer communities.

Mining

In simple statistical terms Namibia is mineral rich and mining accounts for 30% of GDP and the largest source of corporate tax. Namibia is the fourth-largest exporter of non-fuel minerals in Africa and the country has the world's largest uranium mine at Rössing Uranium Mine near Swakopmund, and Namibia is Africa's second largest producer of zinc, its third largest producer of lead and fourth largest supplier of copper. The diamond mines around Lüderitz are the leading producers of gem-quality diamonds in the world; and then there are significant reserves of silver, gold, tin, cadmium, zinc, vanadium, tungsten and germanium. There are over 40 different operating mines and quarries in the sector, producing a wide range of precious metals and minerals, though the sector only employs 3% of the country's workforce. This has been mainly due to job losses at Rössing Uranium and Namdeb Diamond Corporation and the closure of the Namib Lead Mine.

The April 1994 Minerals Act was promulgated to govern all future prospecting and the government has been working hard to diversify the sector and promote small-scale mining. It will take some time before the sector is not dominated by large-scale foreign-owned companies, which employ a limited number of Namibians, and repatriate a large proportion of their profits overseas. At present many of the locally owned small mines suffer from a lack of financial assistance, technical expertise and administrative skills. Mining also is always vulnerable to demand and world-wide price fluctuations, and during the 1996 industrial dispute at TCL (see box, page 147) it was claimed that the company had had to cope with a 30-35% drop in world copper prices.

Diamonds In recent years the **diamond** industry in Namibia has undergone some major changes, both in means of production and ownership. At the end of 1994 a new operating company, Namdeb Diamond Corporation, acquired the diamond assets of the Consolidated Diamond Mine based in Oranjemund. The new company is equally owned by the Namibian government and De Beers Centenary AG. While the importance of income from diamonds has declined, they remain an important source of income for the government. Namibia contributes some 30% of world output and has produced more than 70 million carats, of which 85% are of gem quality. In recent years, a recovery in prices has led to several operations being reopened but overall the trend around Lüderitz and Oranjemund is to increase the exploitation of offshore diamond fields. The Namibian Minerals Corporation, NAMCO, holds the concession rights to over 1,000 sq km offshore, an area estimated to contain 73,000,000 carats of gem diamonds.

Uranium Some 50 km inland from Swakopmund is the Rössing uranium mine, the world's largest single producer of a low-grade uranium. The mine has been developed by the Rio Tinto-Zinc group. The first oxide was extracted in 1976, since when the mine's fortunes have fluctuated along with world prices. Most of the uranium is sold to Europe, Japan and Taiwan on long-term contracts. In 1994 a deal was struck with Electricité de France which ensured survival through to 2001, and the recent change of management saw promises made to keep the mine open for another seven years. Once the reserves are eventually exhausted the mine is committed to a major environmental clean-up project; while it will not be difficult to dismantle machinery and housing, how best to deal with the giant hole in the ground is another matter.

Oil and gas

Prior to independence there was no investment in the exploration for hydrocarbon potential because of political uncertainty. Since 1990 offshore geological investigations have revealed conditions to be similar to the north, off the coast of Angola, where oil has already been discovered. A World Bank study has indicated that there may be up to 31 billion cubic metres' worth of natural gas reserves in the **Kudu** fields offshore from Lüderitz. In 1993 the exploration rights were awarded to a consortium of Shell and Engen. A proposed project is the US$1 billion Kudu Gas Fields Project or Kudu Power Project (KPP) which entails piping the gas from the Kudu fields to Oranjemund to be used in a gas-fired power station that will generate electricity for both Namibia and South Africa. This project is expected to contribute to providing many rural communities with electricity.

Agriculture

Agriculture is a very important sector in terms of the employment it provides. Despite the fragile environment and constant threat of drought, the sector contributes around 10% to the GDP. The most important component is livestock, beef and mutton production accounting for almost 88% of the gross agricultural income. The livestock population of Namibia is about 2.5 million cattle, 2.4 million sheep and 1.8 million goats. Cattle farming is concentrated in the northern and central part of the country where a variety of breeds freely roam the nutritious grasslands. White farmers have developed Bonsmara and Afrikaner breeds as well as Brahman and Simmentaler to suit local conditions. About 70-80% of Namibia's beef is exported and most beef products are chilled and vacuum packed before being sent frozen to South Africa and the EU. The sector directly or indirectly supports over 70% of the total population. Of all the economic sectors agriculture is the most emotive: under successive colonial governments much of the land was expropriated from the black majority to a few white settlers. This led to a dualistic agricultural sector with just over 4000 white farmers owning 48% of agricultural land under freehold title, though these support up to 70,000 black families through employment.

Namibia's low and erratic rainfall pattern places severe limits on potential rain-fed agriculture and only 2% of the land is considered arable. It is only possible to grow a single rain-fed crop each year and this has to be in areas where the annual summer rainfall is more than 450 mm. The yields for rain-fed crops are affected by the uneven distribution of rains during the wet season and by poor soils. Many of the soils in the north suffer from deficiencies of zinc, phosphorus and organic matter. In order to obtain high yields the government is forced to use expensive imported fertilizers and other chemicals. Namibia remains a net importer of basic food crops and drought has forced the country to appeal for emergency food aid on several occasions in recent years. In 1994 Namibia produced 76,000 tonnes of cereals, in 1995 this figure was only 41,000 tonnes and in 1999 this figure had dropped further to 28,600 tonnes. Faced with this decline in productivity, the only option for the government is further dependence upon imports, particularly from South Africa and in 2005 the country was importing 50% of the cereals it required.

Fishing

Namibia ranks amongst the top 10 in the world in terms of the value of its catch. The fishing industry is in the same league as Norway and Canada and bigger than the UK or Australia. Some 60,000 tonnes of fish and shellfish are landed annually for processing on shore. The cold waters of the **Benguela Current** produce a nutrient-rich system which is very productive and typified by a low number of species being present but with large numbers of individuals per species. While these waters are ideal for industrial-scale exploitation the careful management of the resources is vital (see below).

The recently revived Namibian industry is subdivided into two sectors, white fish and pelagic. The **white fish** species – kingklip, hake, sole, monk and snoek – occur along the continental shelf which stretches from the Kunene River in the north to the Orange River in the south. The total exploitable area is some 60,000 nautical square miles. The **pelagic** species – pilchard and horse mackerel – are found in more shallow waters which stretch from just south of Walvis Bay to Cape Frio in the north. The industry has yet to start exploiting the waters beyond the edge of the continental shelf.

The fishing industry is an excellent example of how conditions have changed to the benefit of Namibia since independence. Prior to independence Namibia had no control over the illegal fishing which took place within the internationally recognized fishing zone of 200 nautical miles (370 km), the exclusive economic zone (EEZ). As Namibia did not exist as an independent nation no foreign fishing fleet was obliged to pay any of the taxes or licence fees that would normally be due when fishing within another nation's EEZ. Without any controls in place this nearly resulted in the total destruction of some of the richest fishing waters in the world. Over-fishing during the 1980s resulted in the closure of five out of nine processing factories and the loss of jobs for four-fifths of the work force. It was estimated that foreign fleets were catching over 80% of the fish within Namibian waters, and that this catch was worth at least 227 million US dollars.

Immediately after independence the new government proclaimed the existence of Namibia's EEZ and instructed foreign vessels to respect the zone and cease fishing within it. The government has been quick to introduce legislation which promotes the conservation of the marine environment and the managed exploitation of marine resources. The National Fisheries Act was passed at the end of 1992. By introducing new quotas and awarding long-term concessions the government has managed to facilitate the recovery of stocks while at the same time seeing its revenue grow each year. In 1992 a government-owned National Fishing Corporation was set up.

Since then over US$63 million has been invested in upgrading the Namibian fishing fleet and the construction of new onshore processing plants. A new factory has been built in Lüderitz and a processing plant in Walvis Bay. The number of people employed by the sector has increased to over 15,000, making the fishing sector the second largest source of private-sector employment behind mining. In the last few years the fishing industry has been worth about US$15-16 million per annum to Namibia's economy, though the rising value of the Namibia dollar and cheaper fish prices in Europe seen since 2003-2004 have had a knock-on effect to the industry.

It is estimated that fish stocks have more than doubled since independence, but the government has been wary not to increase the catch limits too quickly, despite pressure from within the industry, as it is very easy to over-judge the extent of any recovery. A good example of how effective the recovery has been is to look at figures for hake, one of the most important species. Before the Namibian government was able to introduce controls hake was being heavily over-fished. As much as 600,000 tonnes had been caught in a single year. In 1991 the catch was limited to 60,000 tonnes, which allowed for the fish to replenish for a few years before the catch was increased slowly over the years to 120,000 tonnes in 2003.

As long as Namibia is careful in its management of its marine resources the sector will continue to be a valuable source of income. Further investment is required but this will lead to a more efficient industry and greater profits in the long term. But while stocks of white fish, anchovies and pilchards have all shown signs of growing, the tale of the rock lobster is not so good, the 1995 allowable catch was set at 230 tonnes, and in 2003 it was 400 tonnes; in 1990 the figure had been 1800 tonnes, a reminder that not all the components in a damaged ecosystem can recover at the same rate. A final positive point that will help ensure the future success of the industry is that all the fish come from one of the least-polluted coastal seas in the world. There are no perennial rivers polluted by industry and virtually no sewage, either raw or treated, flows into the ocean. With expert quality control the industry should be able to expect premium prices for most of its products.

Other sectors

The **tourist** sector is rightly regarded as having a tremendous potential for growth. Namibia has a wild and varied landscape ideal for upmarket, high-value, low-volume tourism. Since independence the country has enjoyed a peaceful existence, an important factor for the tourist industry. Many tourists from overseas are attracted to remote areas which are essentially 'unspoilt' and Namibia has an abundance of such areas. These are also the areas where the local communities have no employment opportunities and have suffered the most during periods of drought. If the right training can be provided, these people will be able to directly benefit from tourism. Since independence there has been a 50% growth in the hotel and restaurant sector. New hotels and guest farms have opened and continue to open across the country, and **Namibia Wildlife Resorts** alone sell over 500,000 bed nights a year. Currently the country receives about 750,000 tourists with 37% of these coming from South Africa. Today the sector contributes 7% to GDP, the third largest foreign-exchange earner, and the country's biggest employer. For future developments the government is looking closely at community-based tourism and the NACOBTA (Namibia Community Based Tourism Association) today oversees many successful projects where rural communities enjoy the benefits of tourism and conservation policies. Once people start to derive significant benefits from wildlife and conservation policies they are more likely to work with the government and private sector to preserve the environment. Rural households must enjoy a cash income as well as job opportunities.

The **manufacturing** sector provides less than 8% of annual GDP and it remains a small sector based around processing meat, fish and minerals for export. The sector has a high cost structure and operates with a low competitiveness. Many of the businesses were established under an apartheid government where wages were not linked to productivity. Most goods have in the past been produced in South Africa thus the sector remains underdeveloped within Namibia. Small-scale and informal sector industries have limited access to credit and markets, poor management skills and outdated technologies. Future success and growth will depend in part upon these issues being fully addressed in the long term.

Culture

Namibia is a blend of many different peoples and cultures, similar in some respects to the 'rainbow' nation next door. Home to the Bushmen, the oldest inhabitants of southern Africa as well as to the more recently arrived Europeans, Namibia's culture has absorbed both African and European elements and fused them into a blend of the two. The choral tradition brought from Germany has been adopted and modified and is one of Namibia's most vibrant art forms, while cooking in a *potjie*, a traditional three-legged iron pot over an open fire, is a favourite pastime of many Namibians.

Namibia's population of approximately 1,800,000 has doubled in the past 30 years and is currently growing at an exponential 2.6% per year. The population density of less than two people per square kilometre is one of the lowest in the world. While most Namibians still live in the rural areas, practising subsistence farming of one form or another, increasing mobility and a lack of employment opportunities in the rural areas are causing a rapid migration to the towns. As people lose touch with their homes and traditional ways of life and adopt a more urban, western lifestyle, the levels of crime and unemployment experienced in many western cities are unfortunately also becoming a fact of life in Namibia.

In a predominantly rural country where many aspects of culture are closely linked with land ownership, unresolved land issues dating back to pre-colonial, colonial and apartheid days are still live issues for many communities. One recent example saw the blockade of the Etosha Game Park entrance by groups of Bushmen calling for the return of their traditional lands. Other communities, such as the Rehoboth Basters, have been involved in a series of court cases with the government over the issue of ownership of traditional lands.

As in South Africa, and until recently in neighbouring Zimbabwe, the majority of quality commercial farmland is still in the hands of white farmers. The problem of how to satisfy the demands of landless peasants whilst not alienating an important revenue-generating section of the community is yet another unresolved issue facing the government. The events of the last five years or so in Zimbabwe have caused rumblings in Namibia, and while few (at least openly) support a similar appropriation of land in Namibia, this issue will not go away.

People

Namibia's people consist of 11 major ethnic groups scattered around the country. From semi-nomadic cattle herders and hunters to the sophisticated black and white urban elite, ethnicity is an important unifying force in this sparsely inhabited country. Since independence in 1990 there has been a resurgence of support for traditional leaders who the government has banned from becoming political leaders. At the same time there are tensions between different ethnic groups, in part for historical reasons and in part due to the overwhelming numerical superiority of the Oshiwambo-speaking peoples and their strong support for and involvement with SWAPO – the governing party.

Nevertheless, for the time being, unlike some other African countries, Namibia is largely free of tribal conflict. The government's stance on the issue was summarized by Prime Minister Hage Geingob at a 1993 conference on tribalism. "For too long we have thought of ourselves as Hereros, Namas, Afrikaners, Germans, Owambos. We must now start to think of ourselves as Namibians."

Basters

The 39,000-strong Rehoboth Basters are the descendants of a group of Khoi-European mixed-race settlers who arrived in Namibia in 1869. After negotiations with the Herero and the Swartbooi Namas, the Basters bought and settled land in the Rehoboth area, where the majority earned a living through livestock farming.

During the apartheid era, the Basters managed to hold on to their land, enabling the community to retain a strong sense of its own identity; at independence a section of the Basters even called for the creation of a separate Baster homeland. The traditional leadership under former *Kaptein* or leader Hans Diergaardt was engaged in a series of court cases against the government concerning the rights to administer communal land in and around the town of Rehoboth. The matter was finally settled in 1996 with a Supreme Court ruling in favour of the government.

Recurrent drought over recent years has forced many Basters off the land to seek employment in Rehoboth and Windhoek. Today, despite the isolationism of some, the majority of Basters have entered the mainstream of Namibian society working in a wide range of trades and professions.

Caprivi

Stretching from the Kavango Region in the west to the Zambezi in the east, the narrow strip of land that constitutes the Caprivi Region is home to the **Subia** and **Fwe** tribes, the latter including a number of Yeyi, Totela and Lozi communities. An estimated 92,000 people in all live in this well-watered, subtropical region which forms part of the northern Kalahari basin.

Historically the area has been dominated by the **Lozi** tribe from Zambia and the **Kololo** from South Africa. The more recent intervention of Europeans followed the agreement between Britain and Germany in 1890 which gave colonial authority over the land to the Germans, who only arrived, however in 1909.

The Lozi first conquered the area in the late 17th and early 18th century only to be ousted following the migration of southern Sotho tribes from South Africa in the wake of the Zulu wars in Natal. The existing Lozi customs were adapted to suit Sotho institutions in a so-called Kololo Empire – until a Lozi revolt in 1864 restored their control over the area.

During the consecutive periods of Lozi and Kololo rule, Lozi was established as the *lingua franca* of the area and subsequently as medium of instruction in schools. Both Lozi and Kololo empires promoted patrilineal institutions making the patrilineal extended family the basic social unit.

Both Fwe and Subia practise a mixed economy including hunting, gathering, fishing, hoe-farming and pastoralism, with agriculture forming the backbone of the traditional economy. There are few urban centres apart from the regional capital Katima Mulilo and job opportunities outside subsistence farming are few and far between. Inevitably this is leading to many young people moving away from the land to look for work in urban areas in other parts of the country.

In recent years the population of the Caprivi has been hit very hard by the spread of HIV and AIDS and there is considerable concern over how this will effect the community as a whole.

Coloureds

Around 60,000 people in Namibia today regard themselves as 'Coloureds'. These people were originally of mixed European and African descent, but the vast majority today are born from Coloured parents. The apartheid reality of Coloured townships, Coloured schools and Coloured churches means that there is a strong sense of shared community and culture.

Afrikaans-speaking and urban-dwelling, the Coloured community is predominantly Christian and western oriented. Most Coloureds live in the central and southern areas.

Damara

Widely believed to be the oldest inhabitants of Namibia after the Bushmen and the **Nama**, and sharing a similar language and customs with the Nama, the precise origins of the Damara remain something of a mystery. Two conflicting theories suggest first that the Damara migrated from West Africa to Namibia, where they were subjected by the Nama people, and in this way acquired similar language and customs. An alternative theory suggests that the Damara evolved alongside the Nama in Botswana thousands of years ago, thereby explaining the similarities in language and culture, and simply migrated at a later date into Namibia.

By the beginning of the 19th century Damara communities were established throughout the central parts of Namibia, living by a mixture of hunting, livestock farming and limited crop cultivation. The Damara are also known to have been skilled smelters and workers of copper and it seems likely that they were engaged in trade with the Owambo to the north and the Nama to the south.

However, as tension over land issues grew during the 19th century, in particular between the Nama and the Herero, the Damara were squeezed out of many of the areas in which they were settled. Some became servants to the Herero and the Nama, others fled to the remote mountainous areas, earning them the name *Berg* or 'mountain' Damara.

Following the establishment of German colonial rule over Namibia, the first Damara 'reserve' was created in 1906 around the Okombahe area. This original area was enlarged upon the recommendations of the Odendaal Commission of Inquiry in the 1960s, when so-called tribal homelands were created for the different ethnic groups in Namibia. The Damara 'homeland' was established in the northwest of the country, from Uis in the south to Sesfontein in the north, and this remains a predominantly Damara area today.

Today the majority of the estimated 132,000 Damara community actually lives outside of this area, working in the towns of the central part of the country, such as Windhoek, Okahandja, Swakopmund, Walvis Bay, Otavi and Tsumeb. Many Damara are today active in public life, notably the Prime Minister Hage Geingob and Labour Minister Moses Garoeb.

Herero

Like the other **Bantu**-speaking tribes in Namibia, it is believed that the Herero originated in the great lakes region of East Africa, before migrating west and south. Initially settled in Kaokoland in the northwest of Namibia, the majority of Herero started a southward migration from the middle of the 18th century. By the time the first Europeans arrived in Namibia in the early part of the 19th century, the Herero were well established in the central areas of the country.

The second half of the 19th century saw virtual constant low-level warfare between the Herero and the Nama over the question of land and grazing rights for their cattle. Following the German occupation of Namibia late in the 19th century, more and more Herero land passed into the hands of the colonizers, leading to increasing discontent amongst the people.

Finally in 1904 the Herero rose up against the Germans in an attempt to claim back their tribal land. The final

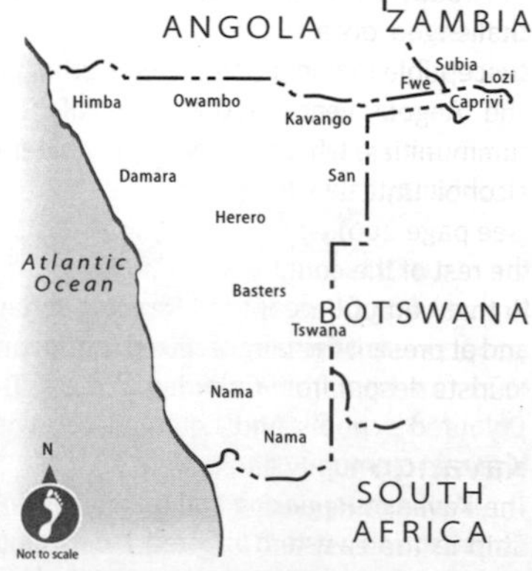

battle was fought at the Waterberg Plateau in August 1904 and in itself was not decisive. However, the subsequent retreat of the Herero into the Omaheke sandveld, in the east of the country, saw the deaths of thousands due to hunger and starvation. Defeat also brought about the further loss of traditional grazing lands and the displacement of the survivors into so-called homelands.

Traditionally, the Herero followed a semi-nomadic pastoral way of life, keeping large herds of cattle and following their cattle around in search of good grazing. However, unlike commercial farmers, the Herero have traditionally seen their cattle as an indication of wealth and status, not to be sold or slaughtered arbitrarily for food. Until relatively recently, in fact, the Herero have largely remained outside of the formal labour market, preferring to focus on their livestock.

During the 20th century there was a resurgence of Herero culture and former paramount **Chief Hosea Kutako** was a key figure in carrying the case for Namibian independence to the United Nations. One important expression of Herero identity is the annual 26 August Heroes' Day parade in Okahandja, when the people march to the grave of their former leaders in order to pay respect to those fallen in battle. Some Herero women are also easily identified by the huge, colourful dresses and hats which they wear. These Victorian remnants of the influence of the 19th-century German missionaries' wives are nevertheless a symbol of pride to their wearers.

Himba

During the Herero-Nama conflict of the second half of the 19th century, the Herero still living in Kaokoland lost much of their cattle to marauding Nama bands. Those dispossessed of their cattle were forced into a hunter-gatherer way of life, considered an inferior way of existence to the pastoral Herero. This led to the branding of such people as **Tjimba** derived from *ondjimba-ndjimba* meaning an *aardvark* or digger of roots.

During the early years of this century groups of Tjimba-Herero who had fled into Angola, and other Hereros who had joined them there following the defeat at the hands of the Germans, united behind a Herero leader, **Vita**. Under his leadership, an effective fighting force operated in southern Angola, building up substantial herds of cattle. Following the German withdrawal from Southwest Africa after the First World War, Vita and many of his followers crossed back over the Kunene River into Namibia. Today their descendants form the bulk of the **Himba** and **Herero** population in Kaokoland.

Elevated to almost legendary status in Namibia, the Himba still live a more or less traditional existence, with their cattle as the centre of their lives. Largely eschewing westernization, they have managed to successfully live in balance with nature in the fragile Kaokoland, pursuing their old customs such as ancestor worship and the keeping of the sacred fire at the homestead.

Today, however, the Himba's independent way of life is being seriously challenged on a number of fronts. Like many traditional peoples the Himba are susceptible to the effects of strong alcohol; unscrupulous traders from both Namibia and Angola are currently spreading this curse to even the remotest Himba communities, while enriching themselves with Himba livestock in exchange for the alcohol. Until two years ago it was also feared that the proposed Epupa Dam scheme (see page 200) which is likely to finally break the Himba's geographic isolation from the rest of the country and introduce whole-scale modernization and westernization to that part of Kaokoland. This plan seems to have disappeared for the time being, and at present the biggest threat to the Himba appears to be people-spotting western tourists desperate for a glimpse of the nomadic past that all human beings share.

Kavango

The Kavango Region stretching from Owamboland to the west as far as the Caprivi Strip in the east and bordered to the north by the Kavango River is home to five distinct tribal groups totalling around 140,000 people. Traditionally the five Okavango tribes – the **Geiriku**, **Shambiu**, **Mbunzu**, **Kwangai** and **Mbukushu** – followed a matrilineal system of leadership and inheritance, however, the growth of livestock farming by men has increased their economic and social status and stimulated a system of patrilineal ties of inheritance.

All of the five tribes live along the banks of the Kavango River and predominantly practise a subsistence economy made up of pastoralism, fishing and hunting. Fishing is a prime source of protein to the Kavango peoples and is practised by both men and women, who specialize in using funnel-shaped baskets to make their catch. Thanks to a rich store of wildlife, hunting has played an important part in the economy of the Kavango communities. However, today no game remains in the inhabited areas of the region and strict control is enforced over hunting in less densely populated areas.

Most Namibian woodcarving originates in the Kavango area and objects such as masks, drums, stools are available in Windhoek curio shops. It is also not uncommon to see the carvers working and selling their products by the side of the road outside towns in the central and southern parts of the country.

As the population grows and more young people become educated, a gradual migration to the urban areas is taking place, although not on the same scale as with the Owambo. At the same time, stimulated by cross-border trade with Angola, the economy of the region is becoming more commodity and cash based, most visible in the regional capital Rundu.

Nama

Ethnically the Nama living in Namibia are descendants of **Khoisan** groups who have been living in southern Africa for many thousands of years. It is believed that the first Nama groups to arrive in Namibia did so about 2000 years ago, having migrated first from Botswana.

Traditionally the Nama were semi-nomadic pastoralists who also continued to hunt and gather food from the veld. The various different clans shared the available grazing and water in southern and central Namibia, moving with their animals as need dictated. Although little is known of the precise relations between Nama and Bushmen, it is assumed that there must have been contact between the two groups, and even some social movement between them.

At the turn of the 19th century the first groups of Oorlam Namas started to cross the Orange River in search of land. These mixed race newcomers were generally Christians, having had extensive contact with white settlers in the Cape, and in most cases having lost their land to them. The Oorlams' contact with Europeans meant that they had acquired guns and horses and were consequently able to establish themselves in southern Namibia alongside existing Nama groups.

Although the first half of the 19th century saw significant conflict between the Nama and the Oorlams, by the end of the century the old differences had largely disappeared. Intermarriage and common enemies in the form first of the Herero and then the Germans had united the two groups so that today no differentiation is made between them.

In the 1890s, the famous Nama leader **Hendrik Witbooi** (see box, page 283), was the first Namibian leader to see that differences between the various ethnic groups in the country were far less important than the struggle against the Germans. Together with other Nama leaders he led resistance to German rule in the south of Namibia during the 1904-1907 war.

Like the Herero, the Nama suffered heavy losses during this period as a result of war and famine and their numbers declined significantly. In addition the loss of traditional land, a process which had begun during the 19th century, continued under German and then South African rule. During the apartheid era, the majority of the

Nama-speaking population was confined to a tribal homeland southwest of Mariental and northwest of Keetmanshoop.

Today the majority of the Nama still live in the south of the country, although small groups live in other parts of the country, such as the **Topnaars** who are in the Kuiseb Canyon area. Their main source of income is derived from livestock farming, especially cattle and goats, but the struggle for survival in the harsh environment of the semi-desert of the south of Namibia means that most Namas today still live a subsistence existence.

The estimated 80,000 Nama are famous for their poetry and singing, in the form of traditional praise poems and their church choirs, and these are an important form of modern-day Nama cultural expression.

Owambo

Made up of 12 tribes in all, of whom eight live in Namibia and four in Angola, the Owambo are the single largest ethnic group in Namibia with an estimated population in 1994 of 670,000. Traditionally the Owambo live in round, pallisaded homesteads built on raised ground between the *oshanas*, seasonal lakes which flood during the rainy season.

The few hectares of land surrounding each homestead is farmed with livestock such as cattle, goats and sheep for which the men are traditionally responsible. Crops are also grown, in particular finger millet, *omuhango*, which is used to make porridge and brew beer; other crops grown are sorghum, maize, beans and pumpkins, and this is traditionally the work of the women.

During the apartheid era tens of thousands of Owambos migrated to the central and southern parts of the country in search of work. In recent years the lack of availability of land and water have forced many more people to abandon subsistence farming as a way of life and instead enter the labour market. This in turn has caused the growth of villages and larger urban centres such as **Oshakati**, **Ongwediva** and **Ombalantu** which function as part of the wider urban cash economy.

Namibia's governing party SWAPO emerged from the Owamboland People's Organization which was constituted in 1957, and originally dedicated to fighting the hated contract labour system. A breakdown of the traditional leadership system among four of the tribes left a political void which SWAPO stepped in to fill. Offering itself initially as the voice of the Owambo nation, the party eventually took the moral, political and military initiative for the whole country in launching the independence struggle against the South African government. Today SWAPO enjoys overwhelming support in the country as a whole and within the Owambo-speaking areas of the north draws over 90% of the vote.

San

The San, or Bushmen as they are often called, are generally accepted to be the oldest indigenous inhabitants of southern Africa, and numerous examples of their rock art, dating back thousands of years, is to be found all over the sub-region.

Traditionally the San were skilled hunter-gatherers living in small independent bands with the family as the basic unit. Different bands had limited contact with each other, although individuals were free to come and go as they pleased, unhampered by possessions or fixed work responsibilities.

Although successful and well-adapted to their environment, about 300 years ago the San started to come under pressure both from migrating **Bantu** tribes and early European settlers. Regarded as cattle thieves and considered as more or less sub-human by these groups, the San were hunted down and forced off their traditional lands, the majority seeking the relative safety of the Kalahari Desert in Botswana and Namibia.

Today, the estimated 45,000 San living in Namibia live a marginalized existence on the fringes of mainstream society. Like other aboriginal peoples in Australia and North America, the loss of their land and traditional way of life has seriously undermined the San people's culture. Human rights groups in Namibia maintain that the San are seriously exploited and discriminated against by other ethnic groups in the country.

However, the San have not given up hope and there are groups who since independence in 1990 have been campaigning for the return of traditional hunting lands. In January 1997 a group of around 70 Hai/Om San demonstrated at the gates of Etosha National Park. The response of the authorities was to teargas and arrest these peaceful protestors, for which they were condemned by human rights groups and various opposition parties.

The future for the San in Namibia does not look good. They are unlikely to be granted significant tracts of land on which to return to their former way of life, and unless educational and employment opportunities can be provided for them, they will remain a poor and marginalized community.

Tswana

The Tswana make up the smallest ethnic group in Namibia, numbering around 9000. Related to the Tswana in South Africa and Botswana, they are the descendants of a group who migrated to Namibia from South Africa during the 19th century. These people eventually settled in the east of the country between Aminuis and the Botswana border where they live predominantly as livestock farmers.

Whites

The majority of the estimated 100,000 whites living in Namibia are of German and Afrikaner descent, with a small group of English speakers. The first Europeans to arrive in Namibia were missionaries travelling with Oorlam groups over the Orange River from Namaqualand. These were followed during the first half of the 19th century by traders and hunters who opened up the interior of the country for further European exploration.

Following the consolidation of German colonial rule towards the end of the 19th century, Europeans started to settle in larger numbers, most earning a living through trading and livestock farming. The discovery of diamonds and other minerals early this century attracted outside investment and led to further European control of the economy of the country.

The period of South African rule from 1917 until independence in 1990 saw the bulk of the viable farmland transferred into the hands of white farmers. Mineral rights were controlled by the multi-national European and American conglomerates and apartheid legislation ensured that all significant commercial activities were firmly placed in white hands.

Following independence, although political power has passed into the hands of the black majority, the bulk of viable commercial farmland is still in white hands. Likewise, most businesses in the towns of central and southern Namibia belong to whites and the majority of the private sector of the burgeoning tourist industry is also in white hands.

While many white people are making an effort to adapt to the realities of living in independent Namibia, an equal number still live as in the past, sticking exclusively to their own communities. Inevitably the barriers of the past will take time to be overcome but, with the integration of the education system, there is hope that the next generation of white Namibians, who have nowhere else to go, will participate fully in the wider society in their country.

Land and environment

Geography

Namibia is located on the west coast of Africa between the 17th and 29th latitudes. The territory stretches from Angola and Zambia in the north to South Africa in the south; most of the eastern border is with Botswana. The total surface area is 824,269 sq km, nearly four times the size of the UK, or twice the size of California.

As you travel around the country you are likely to form the impression that the countryside is harsh and forbidding and that most of the country is either desert or semi-desert in appearance. If you do not like hot, dry and dusty countries then Namibia is not for you. There are only five perennial rivers, the Cuando, Kunene, Kavango and Zambezi in the north and the Orange River in the south, which forms the border with South Africa.

Regions

There are four distinct regions, although only the far north can be truly described as being green in appearance. The dominant feature is the **Namib-Naukluft Desert** which occupies almost a fifth of the total area. The desert varies between 80 and 120 km in width and stretches along the entire Atlantic coastline, a distance of approximately 1,600 km. This whole region receives less than 100 mm of rain per year. The central portion of the desert is an impassable mass of giant sand dunes which are one of the major tourist attractions.

The centre of the country is a semi-arid mountainous plateau, with the capital Windhoek located on this plateau. Most of the annual rains fall during the summer months when the plateau is covered with green grasslands and the occasional flowering acacia tree. The average elevation is 1100 m, the highest mountains are the Brandberg (2573 m) and the Moltkeblick (2446 m) in the **Aus** range. Throughout the plateau are numerous dry, seasonal river courses, the signs of the ephemeral river that only flow for a few days each year if at all. Few ever drain into the ocean, the water disappearing in the sands of either the Namib or Kalahari deserts. The dramatic **Fish River Canyon** in the south of the country is evidence of the presence of a large body of water at some time in the distant past.

The southeastern area of the country is characterized by low-lying plains covered with scrub vegetation, typical of the Kalahari and Karoo regions of Botswana and South Africa.

The far north of the country is the only region which receives sufficient rainfall each year to sustain agriculture and a wooded environment. As you travel north of Etosha National Park the vegetation cover gradually increases and the overall landscape is more green than brown. The **Caprivi Strip** has some magnificent woodlands and lush riverine vegetation along with a wide variety of wild animals.

Climate

Namibia, like so many countries in Africa, eagerly waits for the first rains to fall every year. The country lies within the dry latitudes and depends upon the unpredictable movements of the climatic zones for its rainfall. These zones are known as the Inter-Tropical Convergence Zone (ITCZ), the Mid-Latitude High Pressure Zone (MLHPZ) and the temperate zone. Generally rains can be expected in areas dominated by the ITCZ or the temperate zone, whereas the MLHPZ is associated with little or no rainfall.

 The weather in the north of the country depends upon the southerly movement of the ITCZ, while in the extreme south the rains can be expected if the temperate zone pushes north into the MLHPZ. Predicting the movement of these climatic zones is the key to understanding Namibia's weather.

Namibia is blessed with a climate in which the sun shines for more than 300 days per year, an important consideration for many holidaymakers. Most visitors will enjoy clear blue skies during their visit, and it is only during the height of the rainy season that you might encounter cloudy days. While these warm clear days are what most visitors are looking for it is important that you protect your skin from sunburn. The combined effect of latitude and altitude means that if you are fair skinned you will quickly burn without some form of protection – always wear a hat, sunglasses, apply sun-block on a regular basis and drink plenty of liquid throughout the day, preferably water. The warmest months are January and February, when the daytime temperature in the interior can reach 40°C. This will be far warmer than most visitors from the temperate latitudes will have experienced and clearly is not the weather to walk about in, especially without a hat or protection.

In general the rain season lasts from November to March, although during this period it might not rain for several weeks. However, by February most parts of the country should have received a significant proportion of their annual rainfall. Visitors to Namibia in April and May will see a country far greener than most would imagine or expect. The Caprivi Region receives the most rainfall each year, the annual average for Katima Mulilo being over 700 mm. The isohyets run northwest to southeast, with total rainfall decreasing as you travel from the Caprivi towards the Karas Region in the south. In a good year Lüderitz may receive 20 mm, which is insignificant when you take into account the high evapotranspiration rates. In a good year the first rain in the north may fall as early as October, this can cause havoc with the agricultural system if farmers plant their seed expecting the rains to continue. There is always the danger of planting too early with the young shoots of millet and maize emerging only to die from lack of water because the next rains don't fall until mid-November.

A quick glance at any map of Namibia will clearly show the entire coast to be desert. The three major coastal settlements all depend upon water piped from the interior for their survival. During the height of the summer, December, there is a mass exodus from the interior (especially Windhoek) to the coast and this is the peak tourist season for the coastal resort of Swakopmund. The reason is quite simple: local residents are looking to escape the heat. The cold Benguela ocean current has a modifying influence on the weather, although one negative aspect of the coastal climate is the frequent sea fog which forms when the cool ocean air mixes with the hot Namib Desert air. It really can get very gloomy, but this fog is vital to the survival of plants and animals in the Namib Desert. Do not be fooled into thinking the sun cannot harm you when there is a fog – the UV rays will still penetrate the mist and burn your skin.

The most pleasant weather in the interior is experienced during the autumn (April-May) and spring (August-September), when it tends to be neither too hot, nor too cold. Here the altitude has a modifying influence on temperatures.

A final point to remember when visiting Namibia is that more often than not the country may be suffering from a period of drought. Do not be wasteful with water, it is a valuable commodity which many people have to walk miles for each day. When you are camping or travelling in remote areas make sure you carry extra water with you – there are no guarantees of a clean source in the middle of the bush. Interestingly, rains over the last few years have been surprisingly good over most of the country, to the extent that Mariental – one of the driest and dustiest places in the south – experienced flooding!

Vegetation

While much of the Namibian landscape is characterized by deserts and mountains, the country extends far enough north into the tropical latitudes to have a varied range of plant life. The most interesting ecological area is the Namib Desert where the diverse flora and fauna have had to adapt to a unique set of climatic conditions. Botanists from all over the world have visited the Namib to study some of the more unusual plants and the ways in which they cope with the hot and dry conditions. A good tour of the desert should include an introduction to some of these plants. This is also the only desert in the world where you can see elephant, lion and rhino.

Although a large proportion of the country is desert there are four distinct vegetation zones which together support more than 4000 seed-bearing vascular plants, 120 different species of tree, over 200 endemic plant species and 100 varieties of lichen. These zones are loosely defined as follows: the tropical forests and wetlands along the banks of the perennial rivers in Kavango and Caprivi; the savanna plains with occasional trees in the Kalahari; the mountainous escarpment regions such as Kaokoland and Damaraland, which support a mixture of succulent and semi-succulent plants; and the low altitude coastlands and Namib Desert.

Along the mountainous escarpment most of the plants are either arborescent, succulents or semi-succulents. The most common species are the **quiver tree**, or kokerboom (*Aloë dichotoma*), the spiky tall cactus-like plants known as *Euphorbia* and the **paper bark tree**, or *Commiphora*, which can be seen along the road between Sesfontein and Opuwo in Kaokoland. The vegetation mix in the Kaokoland is largely determined by physical and climatic factors. In the extreme north the Marienfluss and Hartmann's valleys are covered with open grasslands with very few trees and shrubs. Further to the south a few more trees start to appear in the savanna, notably the **mopane** (*Colophospermum mopane*) and **purple-pod terminalia** (*Terminalia prunioides*). Along the Kunene River the dominant trees are **leadwood** (*Combretum imberbe*), **jakkalsbessie** (*Diospyros mespiliformis*) and **sycamore fig** (*Ficus sycamorus*). After the rains look out for the magnificent pink flowers of the **Boesmangif** (*Andanium boehmianum*), a creeper which is found on many of the larger trees. The palm trees along the river are **makalani palms** (*Hyphaene petersana*), a common sight further east in Owamboland. In areas where there is slightly more rainfall there are a variety of flowering annuals which will cover the land with a carpet of colour for a couple of months. Most of these annuals are of the *Brasicaceae* and *Asteraceae* families.

The Kavango and Caprivi regions are the only areas where you will see large stands of forest. Most of the trees are deciduous so, like the rest of the country, the area looks at its best after the rains. Along the riverbeds you can expect to see *mopane*, the **palm** (*Hyphaene ventricosa*) and a couple of **reed** species on the flood plains, *Phragmites australis* and *Typha latifolia*. The woodland areas of the game reserves are dominated by *Terminalia* shrubs, *Boscia albitrunca*, *Bauhinia macrantha* and *Grewia*.

Along the edge of the Kalahari desert the sands gradually give way to trees and tall shrubs, although most of the vegetation is restricted to grasslands – *Stipagrotis* is the dominant grass. The most common flower is the **driedoring** (*Rhigozum trichotomum*).

As noted above, the Namib Desert has the most interesting mix of plants in Namibia, many of which have been subjected to intensive studies. One of the most unusual of all plants is the *Welwitschia mirabilis*, a plant first seen by the white man in 1859. These plants are found in small groups inland from the coast at Swakopmund. Each plant has two long leaves which are often torn and discoloured. Using carbon dating they have been shown to live for over 1000 years in the harshest of conditions. One of the oldest plants in the Namib is now protected by a fence but you can still get close to smaller plants. After the welwitschia it is the lichens which attract the greatest attention in the desert. The lichens are found on west facing slopes and surfaces where they are able to draw moisture from the sea fogs. If it were not for the fog the plants would have no source of water. They are now recognized as a vital component of the Namib environment and most areas are protected. Many of the animals rely upon the lichen as an important source of water after the fog has condensed on the plants. While they can survive long periods of drought they will quickly die when disturbed.

Visitors with a keen interest in the plants of Namibia will find the following publications helpful for background and identification purposes: *Namib Flora (86)*, P Craven & C Marais; *National List of Indigenous Trees (86)*, Von Breitenbach; *Trees of Southern Africa (77)*, KC Palgrave; *Waterberg Flora (89)*, P Craven & C Marais.

Precious stones, rocks and minerals

Every visitor to Namibia will at some point have read or perhaps been told something about the country that sparked their imagination and desire to see the place for themselves. For many holidaymakers it is the beauty and variety of the flora and fauna that initially tempts them to visit southern Africa – few return home disappointed. But Namibia can also prove to be an exciting and interesting destination for a much smaller interest group, for it is a country that has an outstanding assembly of precious and semi-precious stones as well as grand and spectacular rock formations. Throughout the Namib Desert and the surrounding countryside there is a superb record of the events that took place millions of years ago as the landscape was formed and sculptured. The magnificent Fish River Canyon, the isolated Waterberg Plateau, the Spitzkoppe, Etosha Pan, the Naukluft Mountains, the Hoba Meteorite are just a few of the more popular sites. Namibia is often described as a geologist's paradise, and rightly so.

The few notes below are intended for the visitor who has never really taken an interest in rocks and gemstones, someone whose knowledge of semi-precious stones is confined to the jewellery which has been in the family for generations. One stone you are unlikely to be picking off the ground and carrying back home in the suitcase, is a **diamond**. Most of the diamonds are found in the south of the country around Lüderitz, in the Atlantic as well as on land (see page 328). When you look at a map of the Lüderitz district the **National Diamond Areas** can clearly be seen. This area is closed to the public and well patrolled as the diamond industry is an important component of the Namibian economy, and many of the diamonds are literally on the surface waiting to be picked up! Where there are diamonds you will also usually find **garnets**, a dark maroon semi-precious stone. Along the Skeleton Coast the fine garnet sand can be sometimes seen on the dunes forming dark patterns.

If you set your sights on something a little less valuable then you may well stumble across a few small samples to take back home. The area around the northern town of Tsumeb has long been a popular mining region. Here you will find a wide variety of copper ores. One of the most beautiful semi-precious stones is **amethyst**, the deeper the violet in colour, the better the gem quality. This is a versatile stone which can be turned into rings, necklaces and broaches with great effect. Many stones are found around Omaruru and Otjiwarongo as well as the tiny town of Uis close to the Brandberg mountain. Further south is the small town of Usakos, where you may come across **tourmalin**, both blue and green varieties; elsewhere it occurs in red, pink, yellow and black. The uranium mine at Rössing had found **aquamarine** and elsewhere in the desert, just inland from Swakopmund, you are bound to come across outcrops of **rose quartz**, as well as some ancient rock formations which date back to the time when Africa and the Americas were one.

Where there is a town museum you are likely to come across a small display of locally found rocks and minerals. If you wish to collect pieces for your own collection, ask around until you find who the local specialist is – there is always someone. Check with the local police station about access to the land, and once in the bush don't forget about the other more popular attraction – wild animals. Leopards tend to live in rocky regions. In Windhoek you can buy a geological map of the country which shows farm boundaries and mines as well as the major rock types. One final point to note is that in order to remove or possess **meteorites** or **fossils** a permit is needed from the government. Semi-precious stones can be picked off the land as long as you are not trespassing and have a good eye for small glinting stones.

Wildlife

The Big Nine

» *See African wildlife colour section in the middle of the guide.*

It is a reasonable assumption that anyone interested enough in wildlife to be travelling on safari in Africa is also able to identify the better-known and more spectacular African animals. For example an **elephant** (*Loxodonta africana*) or a **lion** (*Panthera leo*) can hardly be confused with anything else, so they are not described in great detail here. It is indeed fortunate that many of the large animals are also on the whole fairly common, so you will have a very good chance of seeing them on even a fairly short safari. They are often known as the Big Five. Unfortunately, no one agrees on quite which species constitute the Big Five! The term was originally coined by hunters who wanted to take home trophies of their safari. Thus it was that, in hunting parlance, the Big Five were elephant, black rhino, buffalo, lion and leopard. Nowadays the hippopotamus (*Hippopotamus amphibius*) is usually considered one of the Big Five for those who shoot with their cameras, whereas the buffalo is far less of a 'trophy'. Equally photogenic and worthy to be included are the zebra, giraffe and cheetah.

But whether they are the Big Five or the Big Nine these are the animals that most people come to Namibia to see. With the possible exception of the leopard, and the white rhino, you have an excellent chance of seeing all of these animals in Etosha National Park or in the parks along the Caprivi Strip. Namibia also has a number of privately owned guest farms and game ranches which offer good game-viewing opportunities, but perhaps not the variety of wildlife that you will find in the larger national parks. Some of the private concessions represent the luxury top end of the game-viewing safari market; it is worth bearing in mind that when you pay top dollar there is far greater pressure on the operator to guarantee his guests see the Big Five or Big Nine. This takes something out of the thrill of game viewing when you know you are just as likely to see a rhino or a leopard as you are a family of impala. Yes you have the pleasure of seeing all these magnificent animals, but a lot of the thrill in looking for them at dawn or dusk has gone.

Of the better-known animals the only two that could possibly be confused are the leopard and the cheetah. The **leopard** (*Panthera pardus*) is less likely to be seen as it is more nocturnal and secretive in its habits than the cheetah. It frequently rests during the heat of the day on the lower branches of trees. A good place for viewing leopard is **Tsaobis Leopard Nature Park** close to Otjimbingwe.

The **cheetah** (*Acinonyx jubatus*) is well known for its running speed. In short bursts it has been recorded at over 90 kph. But it is not as successful at hunting as you might expect with such a speed advantage. The cheetah has a very specialized build which is long and thin with a deep chest, long legs and a small head. But the forelimbs are restricted to a forward and backward motion which makes it very difficult for the cheetah to turn suddenly when in hot pursuit of a small antelope. They are often seen in family groups walking across the plains or resting in the shade. The black 'tear' mark on the face is usually obvious through binoculars. Any visit to a private game farm in Namibia should be rewarded with a sighting of cheetah as Namibia has the largest population of these animals in southern Africa not contained within national parks. The excellent **Okonjima Guest Farm,** 50 km from Otjiwarongo, is home to the **Africat Foundation**; here guests are guaranteed to see cheetah and leopard in natural and artificial surroundings.

Elephants are awe-inspiring by their very size and it is wonderful to watch a herd at a waterhole. Although they have suffered terribly from the activities of war and poachers in recent decades they are still readily seen in many of the game areas, and you will not be disappointed by the sight of them. Everyone has their elephant tale. But it is the rhinoceros which has suffered the most from poaching. Both species are on the verge of extinction, and indeed if there had been no moves to save them during the last 20 years they probably would have gone from the wild by now. The **white rhino** (*Ceratotherium simum*) and the **black rhino** (*Diceros bicornis*) occurred naturally in Namibia. Although today you will find that in many of the reserves where you find them they have in fact been reintroduced. Their names have no bearing on the colour of the animals as they are both a rather non-descript dark grey. The name white rhino is derived from the Dutch word 'weit' which means wide and refers to the shape of the animal's mouth. The white rhino has a large square muzzle and this reflects the fact that it is a grazer and feeds by cropping grass. The black rhino, on the other hand, is a browser, usually feeding on shrubs and bushes. It achieves this by using its long, prehensile upper lip which is well adapted to the purpose.

The horn of the rhino is not a true horn, but is made of a material called keratin, which is essentially the same as hair. If you are fortunate enough to see rhino with their young you will notice that the white rhino tends to herd its young in front of it, whereas the black rhino usually leads its young from the front. The white rhino is a more sociable animal, and they are likely to be seen in family groups of five or more. Their preferred habitat is grasslands and open savanna with mixed scrub vegetation. The black rhino lives in drier bush country and usually alone. They will browse on twigs, leaves and tree bark. Visitors to Etosha National Park have a good chance of seeing rhino with their young at one of the three floodlit waterholes in the evening. It is worth staying up late one night to see these magnificent ancient creatures.

The **buffalo** (*Syncerus caffer*) was once revered by the hunter as the greatest challenge for a trophy. But more hunters have lost their lives to this animal than to any other. This is an immensely strong animal with particularly acute senses. Left alone as a herd they pose no more of a threat than a herd of domestic cattle. The danger lies in the unpredictable behaviour of the lone bull. These animals, cut off from the herd, become bad-tempered and easily provoked. While you are more likely to see them on open plains they are equally at home in dense forest. To see a large herd peacefully grazing is a great privilege and one to remember as you continue your safari. Not found in Namibia south of the so-called Red Line separating the communal grazing lands to the north from the commercial lands to the south, Mahango Game Park in the Caprivi Strip has a good record for sightings of herds of buffalo.

The most conspicuous animal of inland waters is the **hippopotamus** (*Hippopotamus amphibius*). A large beast with short stubby legs, but nevertheless quite agile on land. They can weigh up to four tonnes. During the day it rests in the water, rising every few minutes to snort and blow at the surface. At night they leave the water to graze. A single adult animal needs up to 60 kg of grass every day, and to manage this obviously has to forage far. They do not eat aquatic vegetation. The nearby banks of the waterhole with a resident hippo population will be very bare and denuded of grass. Should you meet a hippo on land by day or night keep well away. If you get between it and its escape route to the water, it may well attack. They are restricted to water not only because its skin would dry up if not kept damp but because the body temperature is regulated closely to 96.8°F. It is essentially an aquatic animal and needs to live in a medium where the temperature changes relatively slowly. Mudumu, Mamili and Mahango game parks all have family groups of hippo, if you are lucky you may also see them in the vicinity of Popa Falls Rest Camp.

The **giraffe** (*Giraffa camelopardalis*) may not be as magnificent as a full grown lion, nor as awe-inspiring as an elephant, but its elegance is unsurpassed. To see a small party of giraffe strolling across the plains is seeing Africa as it has been for millenia. You should note that both male and female animals have horns, though in the female they may be smaller. A mature male can be over 5 m high to the top of its head. The lolloping gait of the giraffe is very distinctive and it produces this effect by the way it moves its legs at the gallop. A horse will move its diagonally opposite legs together when galloping, but the giraffe moves both hind legs together and both forelegs together. It achieves this by swinging both hind legs forward and outside the forelegs. They have excellent sight and acute hearing. They are browsers, and can eat the leaves and twigs of a large variety of tall trees, thorns presenting no problem. Their only natural threat are lions who will attack young animals when they are drinking. Giraffe can be spotted both inside the game parks and in the communal lands of Damaraland and Kaokoveld.

The zebra is the last of the easily recognized animals. There are two common types in Namibia, **Burchell's zebra** (*Equus burchelli*) and **Hartmann's mountain zebra** (*Equus zebra hartmannae*). Burchell's zebra will often be seen in large herds, sometimes with antelope. You are most likely to see them in Etosha National Park. They stand 145-150 cm at the shoulder whereas Hartmann's mountain zebra are larger, standing 160 cm at the shoulder. Generally the latter only occur in mountainous areas close to the Namib Desert. They are found in three isolated pockets: in Kaokoland and as far south as the Brandberg, along the escarpment to the south of the Swakop River and in the Huns Mountains close to the Fish River Canyon. As the name suggests they live on hills and stony mountains. They are good climbers and can tolerate arid conditions, going without water for up to three days. During the heat of the day they seek shade and keep very still, making spotting them more difficult. They are closely related to the Cape mountain zebra, but stand about 25 cm taller than the southern sub-species.

The larger antelope

The first animals that you will see on safari will almost certainly be antelope. These occur on the open plains. Although there are many different species, it is not difficult to distinguish between them. For presentation purposes they have been divided into the larger antelopes, which stand about 120 cm or more at the shoulder, and the smaller ones, about 90 cm or less. They are all ruminant plains animals, herbivores like giraffe and the zebra, but they have keratin covered horns which makes them members of the family *Bovidae*. They vary greatly in appearance, from the small dik-diks to the large eland, and once you have learnt to recognize the different sets of horns, identification of species should not be too difficult.

The largest of all the antelopes is the **eland** (*Taurotragus oryx*) which stands 175-183 cm at the shoulder. It is cow-like in appearance, with a noticeable dewlap and shortish spiral horns present in both sexes. The general colour varies from greyish to fawn, sometimes with a rufous tinge, with narrow white stripes on the sides of the body. It occurs in herds of up to 30 in a wide variety of grassy and mountainous habitats. Even during the driest periods of the year the animals appear in excellent condition. Research has shown that they travel large distances in search of food and that they will eat all sorts of tough woody bushes and thorny plants.

Not quite as big, but still reaching 140-153 cm at the shoulder, is the **greater kudu** (*Tragelaphus strepsiceros*) which prefers fairly thick bush, sometimes in quite dry areas. You are most likely to see them in the northern areas of Etosha National Park and in the much smaller Mahango Game Park, although you have just as much chance of seeing one at dusk by the side of the road in central or northern Namibia. Although nearly as tall as the eland it is a much more slender and elegant animal altogether. Its general colour also varies from greyish to fawn and it has several white stripes running down the sides of the body. Only the male carries horns, which are very long and spreading, with only two or three twists along the length of the horn. A noticeable and distinctive feature is a thick fringe of hair which runs from the chin down the neck. Greater kudu usually live in family groups of not more than half a dozen individuals, but occasionally larger herds up to about 30 can be seen.

The **roan antelope** (*Hippoptragus equinus*) and **sable antelope** (*Hippotragus niger*) are similar in general shape, though the roan is somewhat bigger, being 140-145 cm at the shoulder, compared to the 127-137 cm of the sable. In both species, both sexes carry ringed horns which curve backwards, and these are particularly long in the sable. There is a horse-like mane present in both animals. The sable is usually glossy black with white markings on the face and a white belly. The female is often a reddish brown in colour. The roan can vary from dark rufous to a reddish fawn and also has white markings on the face. The black males of the sable are easily identified, but the brownish individuals can be mistaken for the roan. Look for the tufts of hair at the tips of the rather long ears of the roan (absent in the sable). The Roan generally is found in open grassland. Both the roan and the sable live in herds. Khaudum Game Reserve is home to the largest roan population in Namibia. There are also small herds in Etosha which were originally transported from Khaudum. Sable can be seen in the Waterberg Plateau Park as well as Khaudum and the Caprivi Region; attempts to introduce them to Etosha have failed.

Another antelope with a black and white face is the **gemsbok** (*Oryx gazella*), which stands 122 cm at the shoulder. They are large creatures with a striking black line down the spine and a black stripe between the coloured body and the white underparts. The head is white with further black markings. This is not an animal you would confuse with another. Their horns are long, straight and sweep back behind their ears – from face-on they look V-shaped. The female also has horns but overall the animal is of a slightly lighter build. One of the lasting images of Namibia is a picture of a single gemsbok with the sand dunes of Sossusvlei as a backdrop. Visitors to Etosha will see large herds close to the waterholes, you will also see gemsbok in the Namib-Naukluft desert, western Damaraland and the Unaib Delta in the Skeleton Coast National Park.

The **wildebeest** or **gnu** (*Connochaetes taurinus*) is a large animal about 132 cm high at the shoulder, looking rather like an American bison in the distance. The impression is strengthened by its buffalo-like horns (in both sexes) and humped appearance. The general colour is blue grey with a few darker stripes down the side. It has a noticeable beard and long mane. They are often found grazing with herds of zebra. Blue wildebeest migrate into Etosha during the summer months in search of fresh grasslands, their numbers have been greatly reduced by the construction of game fences and attacks from predators around artificial water points.

The **common waterbuck** (*Kobus ellipsiprymnus*) stands at about 122-137 cm at the shoulder, it has a shaggy grey-brown skin which is very distinctive. The males have long, gently curving horns which are heavily ringed. There are two species which can be distinguished by the white mark on their buttocks. On the common waterbuck there is a clear half ring on the rump and round the tail. In the other species, the Defassa waterbuck, the ring is a filled-in white patch on the rump. Although they no longer occur in Mudumu National Park, due to hunting, herds of waterbuck can be seen in the remote marshlands and flood plains of Mamili National Park.

There are three other species of antelope that you can expect to see in the wetlands of Caprivi: red lechwe, sitatunga and puku. The **red lechwe** (*Kobus leche leche*) is a medium-sized antelope standing at about 100 cm at the shoulder. It is bright chestnut in colour, with black markings on the legs. Only the males have horns. The horns are relatively thin, rising upwards before curving outwards and backwards forming a double curve. Only the sitatunga is known to favour the aquatic environment more than the lechwe. In the past, herds of over 1000 were recorded, but hunting and the destruction of habitat has seen their numbers fall to less than a tenth of the numbers 50 years ago. In Namibia you can still be sure of seeing lechwe along the Kavango or Kwando rivers in the Caprivi Region. They tend to feed on grass and water plants, favouring water meadows. As the river levels rise and fall so the herds migrate to the greenest pastures. All of the large cats as well as wild dog and hyaena prey upon the lechwe. They are unable to move fast on dry land, so when they feel threatened they will take refuge in shallow pools – if needs be, they are very good swimmers.

Puku (*Kobus adenota vardoni*) favour a similar habitat to the red lechwe, but you are only likely to see them in small numbers in Mamili National Park. They have a coat of golden yellow long hair and stand at about 100 cm at the shoulder. Their underparts are white and there are no black markings on the legs. The horns are thick and short with heavy rings, only the males have horns. They usually live in small groups of five to 10 animals, but during the mating season the males gather in groups and will strongly defend their respective territories.

The chances of spotting the **sitatunga** (*Tragelaphus sekei*) are rare since this species of antelope favours swampy areas where there are thick reed beds to hide in. It is the largest of the aquatic antelope standing at 115 cm at the shoulder. If you only catch a glimpse of the animal you can be sure it was a sitatunga if the hindquarters were higher than the forequarters. Their coat is long and shaggy with a grey brown colour, they have thin white stripes similar to those of the bushbuck. The horns are long, twisted and swept back. They have long hooves which are highly adapted to soft, marshy soils. When frightened they will enter the water and submerge entirely, with just their snout breaking the surface. This is a very shy antelope which few visitors will see, but if you spend some time at a quiet location by the river you may be rewarded with a sighting as they quietly move through the reedbeds. Mamili and Mahango are the best locations for viewing the sitatunga.

The **red hartebeest** (*Alcephalus caama*) stands about 127-132 cm at the shoulder. It has an overall rufous appearance with a conspicuous broad light patch on the lower rump. The back of their neck, chin, and limbs have traces of black. Small herds can be seen at Hardap Dam, Khaudum and Etosha National Park. The hartebeest has the habit of posting sentinels, which are solitary animals who stand on the top of termite mounds keeping a watch out for predators. If you see an animal on its 'knees' digging the earth with its horns then it is marking its territory – they are very territorial in behaviour. Their slightly odd appearance is caused by its sloping withers and a very long face. They have short horns which differ from any other animal, they are situated on a bony pedicel, a backward extension of the skull which forms a base.

Finally, you have a good chance of seeing the nyala on your travels. The **nyala** (*Tragelaphus angasi*) stands about 110 cm at the shoulder. Although large in appearance it is slenderly built and has a narrow frame. This is disguised, in part, by a long shaggy coat, dark brown in colour with a mauve tinge. The lower legs are a completely different colour, light sandy brown. When fully grown the horns have a single open curve sweeping backwards. Look out for a conspicuous white streak of hair along the back. Another feature which helps identification is a white chevron between the eyes and a couple of white spots on the cheek. The female is very different, firstly she is significantly smaller and does not have horns. Her coat is more orange than brown in colour and the white stripes on the body are very clear.

Their numbers have been threatened in the past and their status has been one of endangered. You should consider yourself fortunate if you enjoy a clear sighting on safari. They like to live in dense bush and the 'savanna veld'. You will always find them close to water, which makes the task of finding them a little easier once you have located the waterholes. They are known to gather in herds of up to 30, but a small family group is more likely. One interesting aspect of their life is that they are almost exclusively browsers. Research has shown their diet to consist of wild fruits, pods, twigs and leaves. They will eat fresh young tender grass shoots after the first rains.

The smaller antelopes

The best known of the antelope species in Namibia is the **springbuck** (*Antidorcas marsupialis*), or springbok, as it is called in Afrikaans. It stands 76-84 cm to the shoulder. It is the only gazelle found south of the Zambezi River. The upper part of the body is fawn and is separated from the white underparts by a dark brown lateral stripe. A distinguishing feature is a reddish-brown stripe which runs between the base of the horns and the mouth, passing through the eye. When startled they start to 'pronk'. The head is lowered almost to the feet, the legs are fully extended with hoofs bunched together. Then the animal takes off, shooting straight up into the air for some 2-3 m, before dropping down and shooting up again as though it were on coiled springs.

The remaining common antelopes are a good deal smaller than those described above. The largest and most frequently seen of these is the **impala** (*Aepyceros melampus*) which stands 92-107 cm at the shoulder and is bright rufous in colour with a white abdomen. Only the male carries the long lyre-shaped horns. Just above the heels of the hind legs is a tuft of thick black bristles, which are surprisingly easy to see as the animal runs. This is unique to the impala. Also easy to see is the black mark on the side of the abdomen in front of the back leg. The impala are noted for their graceful leaps which they make as they are running after being startled. You are most likely to see them in herds in the grasslands but they also live in light woodlands. They are the most numerous of the smaller antelope and no matter what the state of the veld they always appear to be in immaculate condition. During the breeding season the males fight to protect, or gather, their own harem. It is great fun to come across such a herd and pause to watch the male trying to keep an eye on all the animals in the group. Young males may be seen in small groups until they are able to form their own harem. In parts of Etosha National Park you will see a distinct sub-species, the **black-faced impala**, which, as its name implies, has a black streak on the face (otherwise it is identical in appearance to the common impala).

The **Bohor reedbuck** (*Redunca redunca*), which is often seen in the Caprivi game parks, stands 68-89 cm at the shoulder. The horns are sharply hooked forwards at the tip. Its general colour is described as reddish fawn, it has white underparts and a short bushy tail. It lives in pairs or small family groups and, during the hottest time of day, will seek out shelter in reed beds or long grasses, never far from water.

Another tiny antelope is the **oribi** (*Ourebia ourebi*), which stands around 61 cm at the shoulder. Like the reedbuck it has a patch of bare skin just below each ear, but that's where the similarities end. The oribi is slender and delicate looking. Its colour tends to be sandy to brownish fawn, its ears are oval-shaped and its horns are short and straight with a few rings at the base. The oribi live in small groups or as a pair. As the day-time temperatures rise, so it seeks out its 'hide' in long grass or the bush. Like the reedbuck it never likes to venture far from water. Mudumu National Park has a few family groups.

The last two of the common smaller antelopes are the bushbuck and the dik-dik. The **bushbuck** (*Tragelaphus scriptus*) is about 76-92 cm at the shoulder. The coat has a shaggy appearance and a variable pattern of white spots and stripes on the side and back. There are in addition two white crescent-shaped marks on the front of the neck. The horns, present in the male only, are short, almost straight and slightly spiral. The animal has a curious high rump which gives it a characteristic crouching appearance. The white underside of the tail is noticeable when it is running. The Bushbuck tends to occur in areas of thick bush especially near water. It lies up during the day in thickets, but is often seen bounding away when disturbed. Bushbuck are usually seen either in pairs or singly.

The **Damara dik-dik** (*Rhynchotragus kirki*) is so small it can hardly be mistaken for any other antelope; it only stands 36-41 cm high and weighs only 5 kg. In colour it is a greyish brown, often washed with rufous. The legs are noticeably thin and stick-like, giving the animal a very fragile appearance. The muzzle is slightly elongated which it wriggles from side to side, it has a conspicuous tuft of hair on the top of its head. Only the male carries the very small straight horns. The Damara dik-dik is considered to be the same species as Kirk's dik-dik which occurs in East Africa. What is so unusual is that there are no recorded sightings in between these two regions.

Other mammals

Although the antelope are undoubtedly the most numerous animals to be seen on the plains, there are others worth keeping an eye open for. Some of these are scavengers which thrive on the kills of other animals. They include the dog-like jackals, two species of which you are likely to come across in Etosha National Park (both are about 41-46 cm at the shoulder). The **side-striped jackal** (*Canis adustus*) is greyish fawn and it has a rather variable and sometimes ill-defined stripe along the side. The **black-backed jackal** (*Canis mesomelas*) is more common and will often be seen near a lion kill. It is a rather foxy reddish fawn in colour with a noticeable black area on its back. This black part is sprinkled with a silvery white which can make the back look silver in some lights. They are timid creatures which can be seen by day or night.

The other well-known plains scavenger is the **spotted hyaena** (*Crocuta crocuta*), a fairly large animal about 69-91 cm at the shoulder. Its high shoulders and low back give it a characteristic appearance. Brownish, with dark spots and a large head, it sually occurs singly or in pairs, but occasionally in small packs. Few people talk of the hyaena in complimentary terms. This is as much to do with their gait as their scavenging habits. But they play an important role in keeping the countryside clean. When hungry they are aggressive creatures, they have been known to attack live animals and will occasionally try to steal a kill from lions. They always look dirty because of their habit of lying in muddy pools which may be to keep cool or alleviate the irritation of parasites. Both jackal and hyaena are occasionally spotted along the coast of the Skeleton Coast National Park, where they scavenge for carrion, and they are common enough in Etosha and the other game parks.

Another aggressive scavenger is the **African wild dog** or **hunting dog** (*Lycaon pictus*). These creatures are easy to identify since they have all the features of a large mongrel dog. They have a large head and a slender body. Their coat is a mixed pattern of dark shapes and white and yellow patches, no two dogs are quite alike. The question is not what they look like, but whether you will be fortunate enough to see one as they are seriously threatened by extinction. In many areas of Namibia they have already been wiped out. The problem it seems is a conflict between the farmer and conservation. The dogs live and hunt in packs. They are particularly vicious when hunting their prey and will chase an animal until it is exhausted, then start taking bites out of it while it is still alive. Their favourites are reedbuck and impala. Unfortunately, these days the only chance you have of seeing wild dogs is in Kaudom – one of the least accessible areas for the average visitor.

A favourite and common plains animal is the comical **warthog** (*Phacochoerus aethiopicus*). It is unmistakable, being almost hairless and grey in general colour with a very large head, tusks and wart-like growths on the face. These are thought to protect the eyes as it makes sweeps sideways into the earth with its tusks, digging up roots and tubers. Warthogs often kneel on their forelegs when eating. They frequently occur in family parties. When startled the adults will run at speed with their tails held straight up in the air followed by their young. Look out for them around the edges of waterholes as they love to cake themselves in the thick mud. This helps to keep them both cool and free of ticks and flies.

In rocky areas, such as the Waterberg Plateau, look out for an animal that looks a bit like a large grey-brown guinea pig. This is the **dassie** or **rock hyrax** (*Heterohyrax brucei*), an engaging and fairly common animal. During the morning and afternoon you will see them sunning themselves on the rocks. They have the habit of always defecating in the same place, and where the urine runs down the rock face the latter can have a glazed appearance. Perhaps their strangest characteristic is their place in the evolution of mammals. Ancestors of the hyraxes have been found in the deposits of Upper Egypt of about 50 million years ago. The structure of the ear is similar to that found in whales, their molar teeth look like those of a rhinoceros. Two pouches in the stomach resemble a condition found in birds, and the arrangement of the bones of the forelimb are like those of the elephant. In spite of all these features it is regarded as being allied to the elephant!

You are likely to see two types of monkey on your travels, the vervet monkey and the Chacma baboon. Both are widespread and you are just as likely to see them outside a game reserve than in one. The **vervet monkey** (*Cercopithecus pygerythrus*) is of slim build and light in colour. Its feet are conspicuously black, so too is the tip of the tail. It lives in savanna and woodlands but has proved to be highly adaptable. On your first visit you might think the vervet monkey cute. It is not, it is vermin and in many places treated as such. It can do widespread damage to orchards and other crops. On no account encourage these creatures, which can make off with your whole picnic, including the beers, in a matter of seconds.

The adult male **Chacma baboon** (*Papio ursinus*) is slender and can weigh up to 40 kg. Its general colour is a dark olive green, with lighter undersides. It never roams far from a safe refuge, usually a tree, but rocks can provide sufficient protection from predators. The Chacma baboons occur in large family groups, known as troops, and have a reputation for being aggressive where they have become used to man's presence.

Birds

Over 630 of the 887 bird species listed in southern Africa are present in Namibia. Of these 500 breed locally whilst the others are migrants. There are several birds endemic to Namibia including the Herero chat, rockrunner, Monterio's hornbill and Damara tern. Regularly seen throughout the country are the extraordinary nests of the sociable weaver that hang in trees or off telephone poles. Some of these enormous nests are home to several hundred birds and have been in continual use for over 100 years.

Footnotes

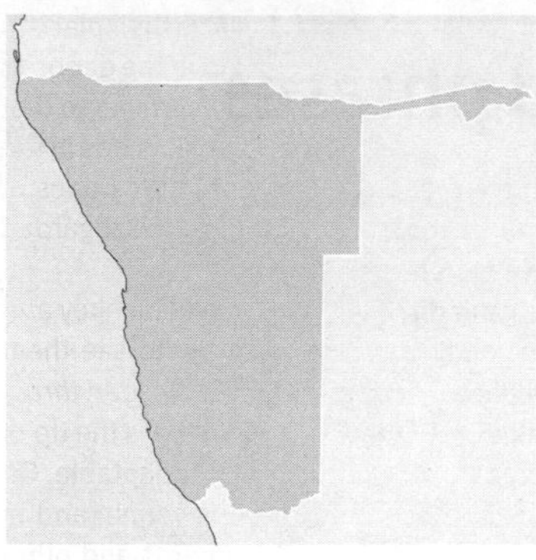

Useful words and phrases

Afrikaans

Good morning!	Goeie more!
How's it going?	Hoe gaan dit?
Very well	Baie goed
Please	Asseblief
Thank you	Dankie
Goodbye	Totsies

Batswana

Hello	Dumela
How are you?	O kae?
Thank you	Ke a leboga
Goodbye	Sala sentle

Caprivi

I greet you!	Ma lumele sha!
Thank you	Ni itumezi
Please	Na lapela
Goodbye	Mu siale hande

Herero/Ovahimba

Are you well?	Perivi?
Yes, well.	Nawa
Thank you	Okuhepa
Goodbye	Kara nawa

Kavango

Hello!	Morokeni!
Thank you	Na pandura

Nama/Damara

How are you?	Matisa?
Thank you	Ayo
Good morning	Moro
Goodbye	Gaiseha

Owambo

Did you sleep well?	Wa lelepo nawa?
Yes!	Eee!
Well!	Nawa!
Thank you	Iyaloo
Good bye	Kalapo Nawa

San

How are you?	Am thai?
I am thirsty	Mem ari gu
I am hungry	Mem tlabe

Index

F

G

H

I

J

K

L

Map index

Advertisers' index

Credits

Footprint credits
Editor: Felicity Laughton
Editorial assistant: Emma Bryers
Map editor: Sarah Sorensen
Picture editor: Kevin Feeney
Proofreader: Stephanie Lambe

Publisher: Patrick Dawson
Editorial: Alan Murphy, Sophie Blacksell, Sarah Thorowgood, Claire Boobbyer, Nicola Jones
Cartography: Robert Lunn, Claire Benison, Kevin Feeney
Series development: Rachel Fielding
Design: Mytton Williams and Rosemary Dawson (brand)
Sales and marketing: Andy Riddle
Advertising: Debbie Wylde
Finance and administration: Sharon Hughes, Elizabeth Taylor

Photography credits
Front cover:
Images of Africa (Sand dune)
Back cover:
Superstock (Quiver tree)
Front colour section:
Images of Africa, Images of Africa Photobank, Lisa Young, Superstock
Wildlife colour section: NATUREPL (Karl Ammann, Ingo Arndt, Peter Blackwell, Nigel Bean, John Cancalosi, Philippe Clement, Richard Du Toit, Laurent Geslin, Tony Heald, Eliot Lyons, Pete Oxford, Andrew Parkinson, Constantinos Petrinos, T J Rich, Jose B Ruiz, Francois Savigny, Anup Shah, Mike Wilkes)

Print
Manufactured in India by Nutech Photolithographers, Delhi. Pulp from sustainable forests

Footprint feedback
We try as hard as we can to make each Footprint guide as up to date as possible but, of course, things always change. If you want to let us know about your experiences – good, bad or ugly – then don't delay, go to **www.footprintbooks.com** and send in your comments.

Publishing information
Footprint Namibia
4th edition

April 2006

ISBN 1 904777 54 6
CIP DATA: A catalogue record for this book is available from the British Library

Published by Footprint
6 Riverside Court
Lower Bristol Road
Bath BA2 3DZ, UK
T +44 (0)1225 469141
F +44 (0)1225 469461
discover@footprintbooks.com
www.footprintbooks.com

Distributed in the USA by
Publishers Group West

Neither the black and white nor coloured maps are intended to have any political significance.

Every effort has been made to ensure that the facts in this guidebook are accurate. However, travellers should still obtain advice from consulates, airlines etc about travel and visa requirements before travelling. The authors and publishers cannot accept responsibility for any loss, injury or inconvenience however caused.

Acknowledgements

Lizzie would like to thank the following people for their help and kind assistance during the research for the update of this book; Cordula and the staff at the **Namibia Tourism** office in Cape Town; the staff at **Air Namibia** also in Cape Town; Jackie and Bossie from **Chameleon Backpackers and Safaris** in Windhoek; Liz at the tourist office in Lüderitz; Kenchen from the information office in Otjiwarongo; the staff at the Keetmanshoop tourist office; Almuth at **Namib-i,** Beth from **Alter Action,** Dave from **Outback Orange** and Craig and Simon from **Ground Rush Adventures,** all in Swakopmund; and Piet from **Klien-Aus Vista.** Thanks to **Camping Car Hire** for the wheels, the staff at Footprint for their back-up and Felicity Laughton for making it all make sense. Also thanks to the readers who found time to write in with suggestions including Karin de Vries, Hilary Emberton, Martin Boll, Marjorie Nielsen, Wayne Eliuk and Mattias Rose. Thanks must also go to Nick Santcross, Gordon Baker and Sebastian Ballard, for all their work on previous editions of *Footprint Namibia*. Finally, thanks to Professor Larry Goodyer, Head of the **Leicester School of Pharmacy** and director of **Nomad Medical,** for providing the Health section.

Complete title listing

Footprint publishes travel guides to over 150 destinations worldwide. Each guide is packed with practical, concise and colourful information for everybody from first-time travellers to travel aficionados. The list is growing fast and current titles are noted below. Available from all good bookshops and online www.footprintbooks.com

(P) denotes pocket guide

Latin America & Caribbean

Antigua & Leeward Islands (P)
Argentina
Barbados (P)
Belize, Guatemala & Southern Mexico
Bolivia
Brazil
Caribbean Islands
Central America & Mexico
Chile
Colombia
Costa Rica
Cuba
Cusco & the Inca Trail
Dominican Republic (P)
Ecuador & Galapagos
European City Breaks
Havana (P)
Mexico
Nicaragua
Patagonia
Peru
Peru, Bolivia & Ecuador
Rio de Janeiro (P)
St Lucia (P)
South American Handbook
Venezuela

North America

New York (P)
Vancouver (P)
Western Canada

Africa

Cape Town (P)
Egypt
Kenya
Libya
Marrakech (P)
Morocco
Namibia
South Africa
Tanzania
Tunisia
Uganda

Middle East

Dubai (P)
Jordan
Syria & Lebanon

Australasia

Australia
East Coast Australia
New Zealand
Sydney (P)
West Coast Australia

Asia

Bali
Bangkok & the Beaches
Bhutan
Cambodia
Goa
Hong Kong (P)
India
Indian Himalaya
Indonesia
Laos
Malaysia & Singapore
Nepal
Northern Pakistan
Rajasthan
South India
Sri Lanka
Sumatra
Thailand
Tibet
Vietnam
Vietnam, Cambodia & Laos

Europe

Andalucía
Barcelona (P)
Belfast & the north of Ireland (P)
Berlin (P)
Bilbao (P)
Bologna (P)
Britain
Cardiff (P)
Copenhagen (P)
Costa de la Luz (P)
Croatia
Dublin (P)
Edinburgh (P)
England
Glasgow (P)
Ireland
Lisbon (P)
London
London (P)
Madrid (P)
Naples & the Amalfi Coast (P)
Northern Spain
Paris (P)
Reykjavík (P)
Scotland
Scotland Highlands & Islands
Seville (P)
Siena & the heart of Tuscany (P)
Singapore
Spain
Tallinn (P)
Turin (P)
Turkey
Valencia (P)
Verona (P)
Wales

Lifestyle guides

European City Breaks
Surfing Britain
Surfing Europe

Also available

Traveller's Handbook (WEXAS)
Traveller's Healthbook (WEXAS)
Traveller's Internet Guide (WEXAS)

What the papers say...

"I carried the South American Handbook from Cape Horn to Cartagena and consulted it every night for two and a half months. I wouldn't do that for anything else except my hip flask."
Michael Palin, BBC Full Circle

"My favourite series is the Handbook series published by Footprint and I especially recommend the Mexico, Central and South America Handbooks."
Boston Globe

"If 'the essence of real travel' is what you have been secretly yearning for all these years, then Footprint are the guides for you."
Under 26 magazine

"Who should pack Footprint – readers who want to escape the crowd."
The Observer

"Footprint can be depended on for accurate travel information and for imparting a deep sense of respect for the lands and people they cover."
World News

"The guides for intelligent, independently minded souls of any age or budget."
Indie Traveller

Map symbols

Administration

- Capital city
- Other city/town

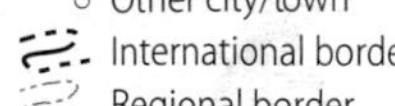

- International border
- Regional border
- Disputed border

Roads and travel

- Motorway
- Main road (National highway)
- Minor road
- Track
- Footpath
- Railway with station
- Airport
- Bus station
- Metro station
- Cable car
- Funicular
- Ferry

Water features

- River, canal
- Lake, ocean
- Seasonal marshland
- Beach, sandbank
- Waterfall

Topographical features

- Contours (approx)
- Mountain
- Volcano
- Mountain pass
- Escarpment
- Gorge
- Glacier
- Salt flat
- Rocks

Cities and towns

- Main through route
- Main street
- Minor street
- Pedestrianized street
- Tunnel
- One way-street
- Steps
- Bridge
- Fortified wall
- Park, garden, stadium
- Sleeping
- Eating
- Bars & clubs
- Building
- Sight
- Cathedral, church
- Chinese temple
- Hindu temple
- Meru
- Mosque
- Stupa
- Synagogue
- Tourist office
- Museum
- Post office
- Police
- Bank
- Internet
- Telephone
- Market
- Medical services
- Parking
- Petrol
- Golf
- A Detail map
- A Related map

Other symbols

- Archaeological site
- National park, wildlife reserve
- Viewing point
- Campsite
- Refuge
- Castle
- Diving
- Deciduous/coniferous/palm trees
- Hide
- Vineyard
- Distillery
- Shipwreck
- Historic battlefield

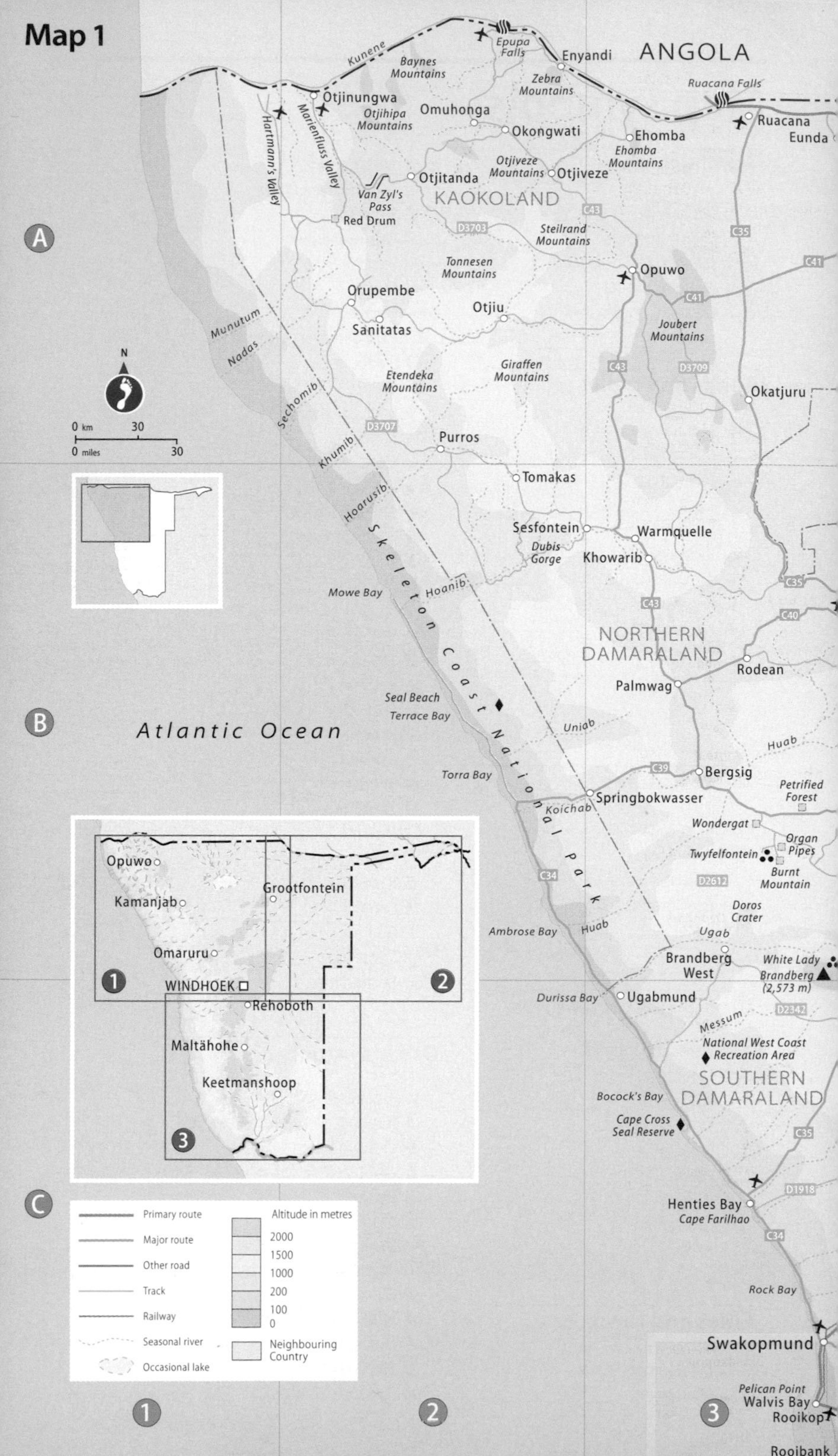
Map 1
ANGOLA
Kunene
Epupa Falls
Enyandi
Baynes Mountains
Zebra Mountains
Ruacana Falls
Ruacana
Eunda
Otjinungwa
Otjihipa Mountains
Omuhonga
Okongwati
Ehomba
Ehomba Mountains
Hartmann's Valley
Marienfluss Valley
Otjitanda
Van Zyl's Pass
Otjiveze Mountains
Otjiveze
KAOKOLAND
Red Drum
C43
D3703
C35
Steilrand Mountains
Tonnesen Mountains
Opuwo
C41
Orupembe
Otjiu
Sanitatas
Munutum
Nadas
Joubert Mountains
D3709
Giraffen Mountains
Etendeka Mountains
Okatjuru
Sechomib
D3707
Purros
Khumib
Tomakas
Hoarusib
Sesfontein
Warmquelle
Dubis Gorge
Khowarib
Mowe Bay
Hoanib
Skeleton Coast National Park
C40
NORTHERN DAMARALAND
Rodean
Palmwag
Seal Beach
Terrace Bay
Atlantic Ocean
Uniab
Huab
C39
Bergsig
Torra Bay
Springbokwasser
Petrified Forest
Koichab
Wondergat
Organ Pipes
Twyfelfontein
Burnt Mountain
D2612
C34
Doros Crater
Ambrose Bay
Ugab
Brandberg West
White Lady
Brandberg (2,573 m)
Durissa Bay
Ugabmund
D2342
Messum
National West Coast Recreation Area
SOUTHERN DAMARALAND
Bocock's Bay
Cape Cross Seal Reserve
D1918
Henties Bay
Cape Farilhao
Rock Bay
Swakopmund
Pelican Point
Walvis Bay
Rooikop
Rooibank
N
0 km 30
0 miles 30
A
B
C
1
2
3
Opuwo
Kamanjab
Grootfontein
Omaruru
WINDHOEK
Rehoboth
Maltähohe
Keetmanshoop
Primary route
Major route
Other road
Track
Railway
Seasonal river
Occasional lake
Altitude in metres
2000
1500
1000
200
100
0
Neighbouring Country

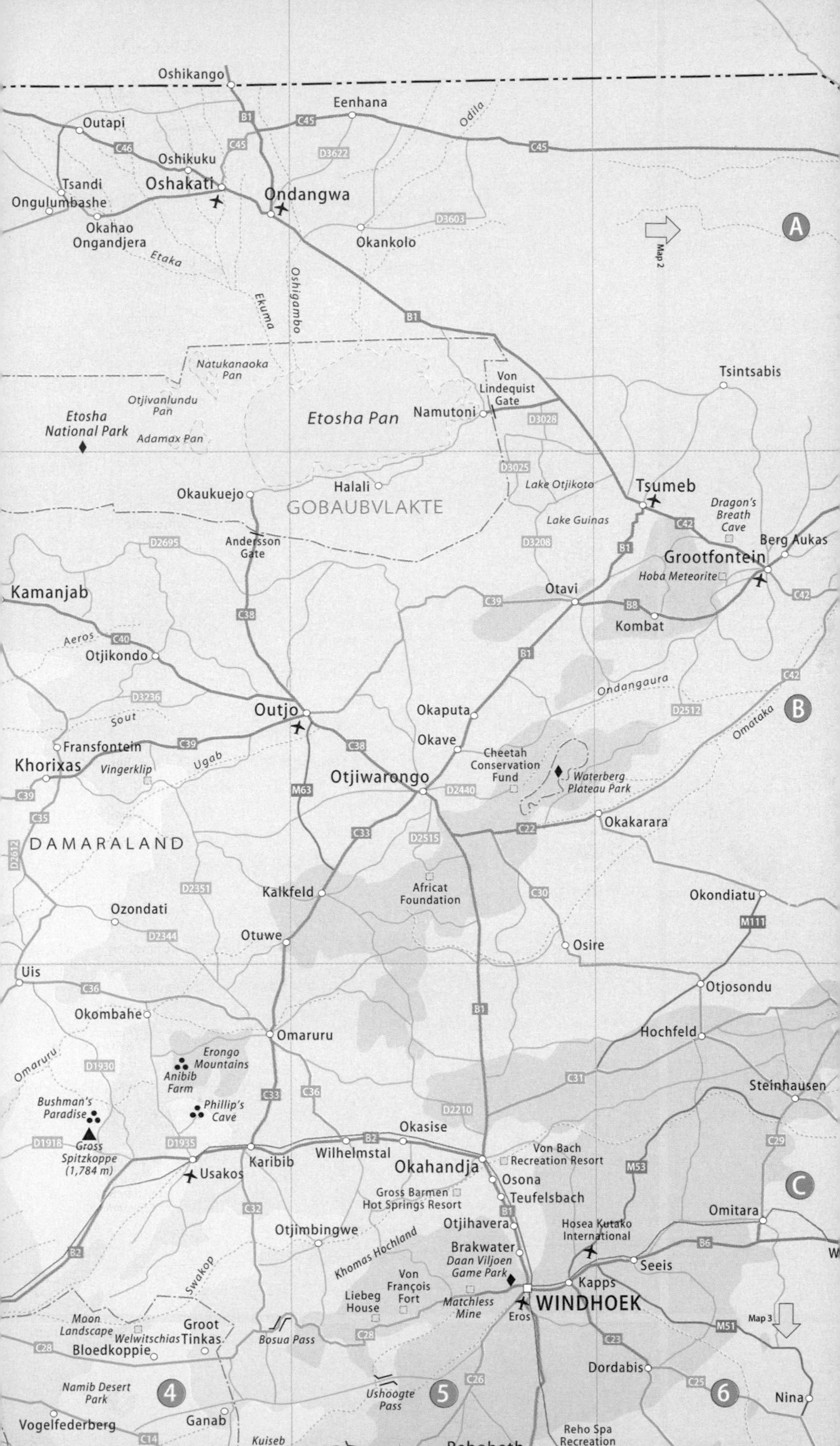

Oshikango
Eenhana
Odila
Outapi
Oshikuku
Tsandi
Oshakati
Ondangwa
Ongulumbashe
Okahao
Ongandjera
Okankolo
Etaka
Ekuma
Oshigambo
Map 2
A
Natukanaoka Pan
Otjivanlundu Pan
Etosha National Park
Adamax Pan
Etosha Pan
Von Lindequist Gate
Namutoni
Tsintsabis
Okaukuejo
Halali
GOBAUBVLAKTE
Lake Otjikoto
Lake Guinas
Tsumeb
Dragon's Breath Cave
Andersson Gate
Berg Aukas
Grootfontein
Hoba Meteorite
Kamanjab
Otavi
Kombat
Aeros
Otjikondo
Ondangaura
Outjo
Okaputa
B
Omataka
Sout
Fransfontein
Okave
Khorixas
Vingerklip
Ugab
Cheetah Conservation Fund
Otjiwarongo
Waterberg Plateau Park
Okakarara
DAMARALAND
Africat Foundation
Kalkfeld
Okondiatu
Ozondati
Otuwe
Osire
Uis
Otjosondu
Okombahe
Hochfeld
Omaruru
Erongo Mountains
Anibib Farm
Omaruru
Steinhausen
Bushman's Paradise
Phillip's Cave
Okasise
Gross Spitzkoppe (1,784 m)
Karibib
Wilhelmstal
Von Bach Recreation Resort
Usakos
Okahandja
Osona
C
Teufelsbach
Gross Barmen Hot Springs Resort
Omitara
Otjimbingwe
Otjihavera
Hosea Kutako International
Khomas Hochland
Brakwater
Daan Viljoen Game Park
Seeis
Swakop
Von François Fort
Kapps
Liebeg House
Matchless Mine
Eros
WINDHOEK
Map 3
Moon Landscape
Welwitschias
Groot Tinkas
Bosua Pass
Bloedkoppie
Dordabis
Namib Desert Park
4
Ushoogte Pass
5
6
Nina
Vogelfederberg
Ganab
Reho Spa Recreation Resort
Kuiseb Canyon
Rehoboth

Map 2

Okavango
Cuito
Calai
Rundu
B8
Shighuru
Okavango
Katere
Mukwe
WEST
CAPRIVI
D4800
A
KAVANGO
Khaudum
Game
Park
Map 1
Tsintsabis
Maroelaboom
Dragon's
Breath
Cave
C42
D2844
C44
D3303
Hoba
Meteorite
Berg Aukas
Grootfontein
Tsumkwe
C42
Okatjoruu
Nyae
Nyae
Pan
Nyae Nyae
Conservancy
Nama
Pan
B8
C42
BUSHMANLAND
Ondangaura
B
Omataka
Okondiatu
M111
Otijinene
C29
M131
Otjosondu
Summerdown
Springvale
Hochfeld
C22
Epukiro
Steinhausen
M119
C30
C29
C
Drimiopsis
Trans Kalahari Hwy
Omitara
B6
Mamuno
Buitepos
B6
Witvlei
Gobabis
C20
Map 3
M51
Arnhem
Cave
C25
Nina
1
2
3
Gr Ums
C22
M40

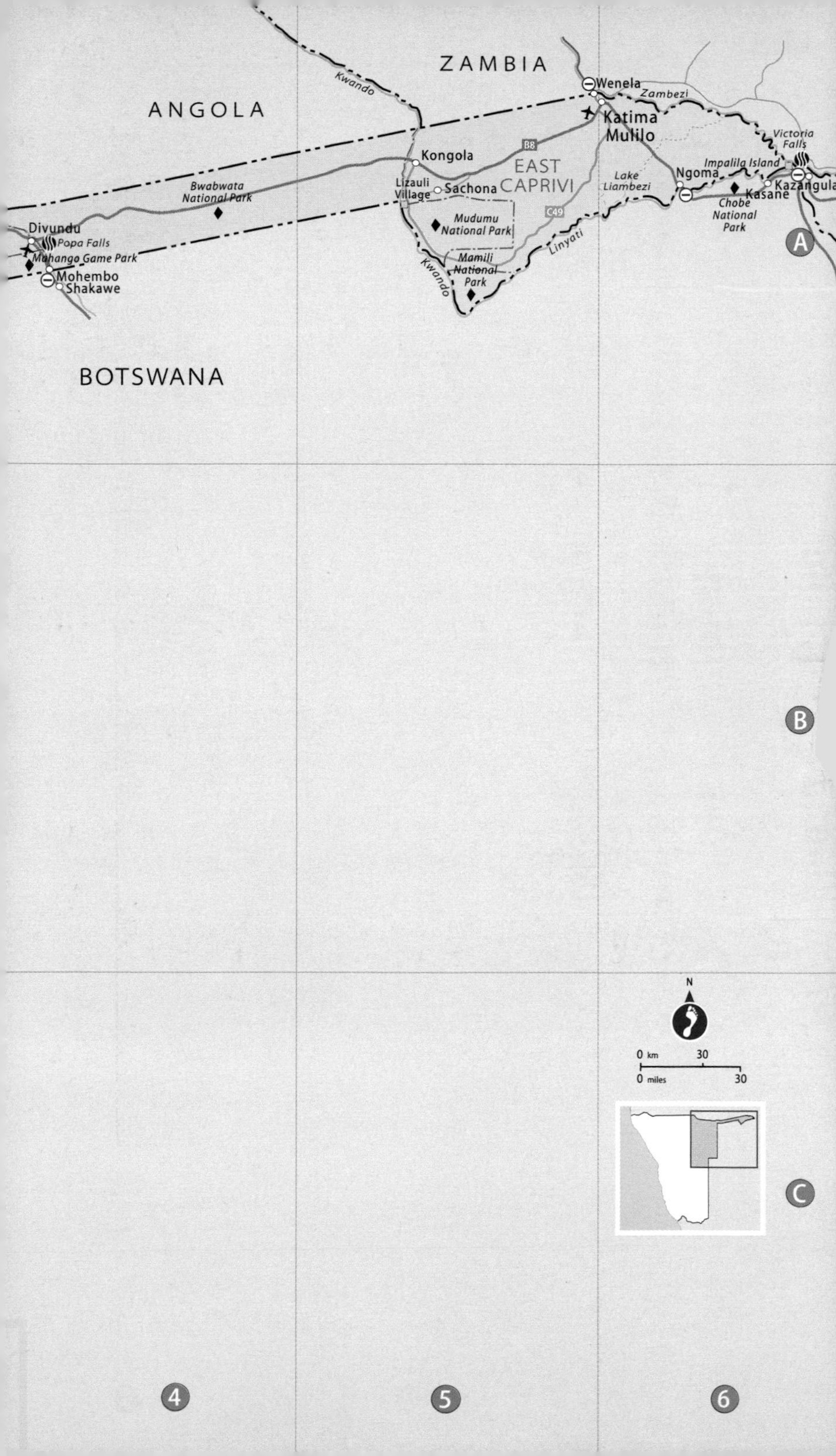
ZAMBIA
ANGOLA
BOTSWANA
Kwando
Wenela
Zambezi
Katima Mulilo
Victoria Falls
B8
Kongola
EAST CAPRIVI
Impalila Island
Ngoma
Kazangula
Lake Liambezi
Kasane
Lizauli Village
Sachona
Bwabwata National Park
Chobe National Park
C49
Mudumu National Park
Divundu
Popa Falls
Mahango Game Park
Mohembo
Shakawe
Linyati
Kwando
Mamili National Park
A
B
C
N
0 km 30
0 miles 30
4
5
6

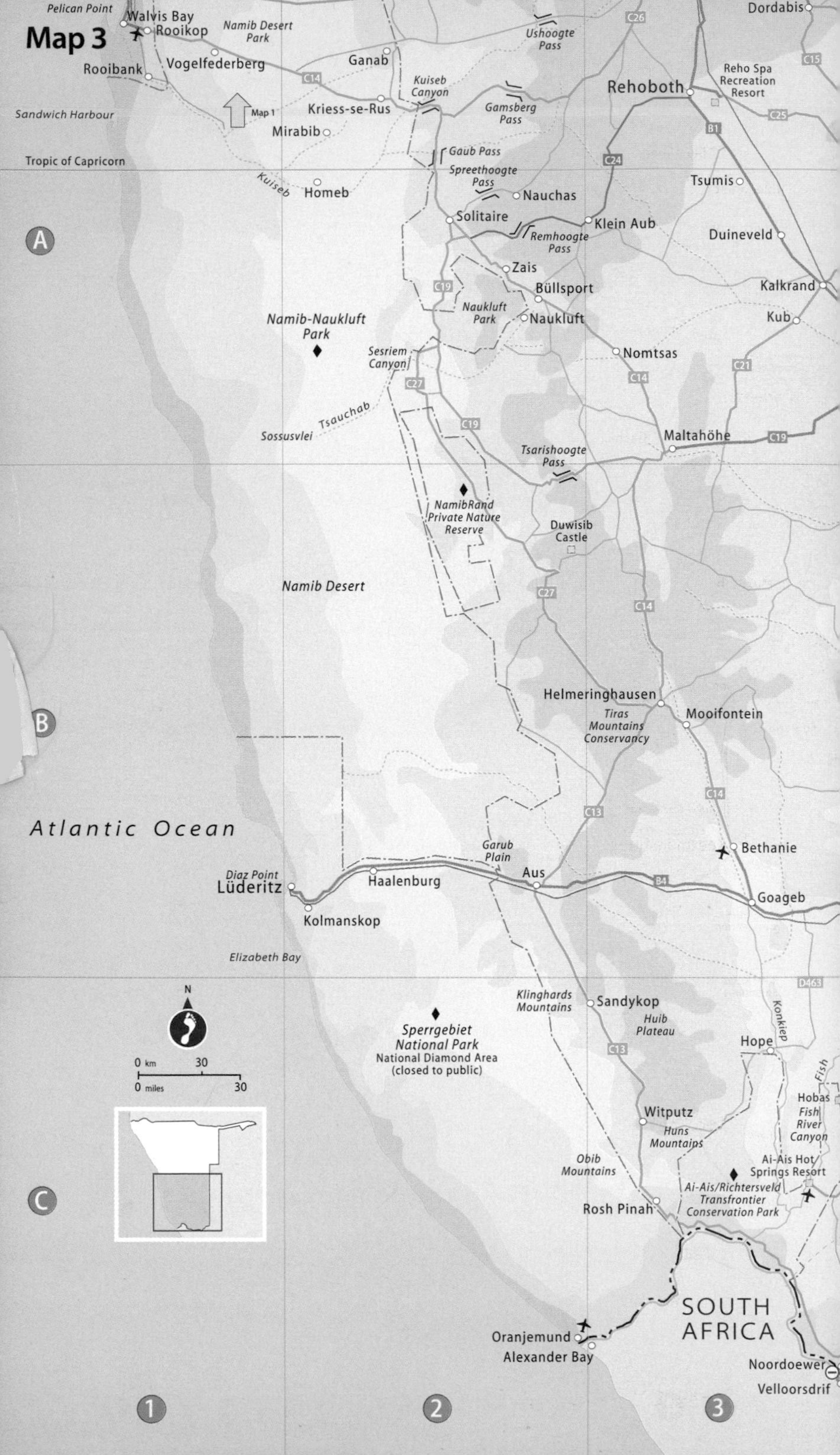

Map 3
Pelican Point
Walvis Bay
Rooikop
Namib Desert Park
Rooibank
Vogelfederberg
Ganab
Ushoogte Pass
Dordabis
C26
C15
C14
Kuiseb Canyon
Kriess-se-Rus
Gamsberg Pass
Rehoboth
Reho Spa Recreation Resort
C25
Sandwich Harbour
Map 1
Mirabib
B1
Gaub Pass
C24
Tropic of Capricorn
Spreethoogte Pass
Tsumis
Kuiseb
Homeb
Nauchas
Solitaire
Klein Aub
Remhoogte Pass
Duineveld
A
Zais
Büllsport
Kalkrand
C19
Naukluft Park
Naukluft
Kub
Namib-Naukluft Park
Sesriem Canyon
Nomtsas
C21
C27
C14
Tsauchab
C19
Maltahöhe
C19
Sossusvlei
Tsarishoogte Pass
NamibRand Private Nature Reserve
Duwisib Castle
Namib Desert
C27
C14
Helmeringhausen
Tiras Mountains Conservancy
Mooifontein
B
C14
C13
Atlantic Ocean
Garub Plain
Bethanie
Diaz Point
Lüderitz
Haalenburg
Aus
B4
Goageb
Kolmanskop
Elizabeth Bay
D463
N
Klinghards Mountains
Sandykop
Konkiep
Sperrgebiet National Park
National Diamond Area (closed to public)
Huib Plateau
C13
Hope
0 km 30
0 miles 30
Fish
Hobas
Fish River Canyon
Witputz
Huns Mountains
Obib Mountains
Ai-Ais Hot Springs Resort
C
Ai-Ais/Richtersveld Transfrontier Conservation Park
Rosh Pinah
SOUTH AFRICA
Oranjemund
Alexander Bay
Noordoewer
Velloorsdrif
1
2
3